HOMOSEXUALITIES

Worlds of Desire: The Chicago Series on Sexuality, Gender, and Culture
A series edited by Gilbert Herdt

Also in the series:

Stephen O. Murray

HOMOSEXUALITIES

The University of Chicago Press

Chicago and London

Stephen O. Murray is a comparative sociologist living in San Francisco.
He is the author of *American Gay* and a dozen other books.

The University of Chicago Press, Chicago 60637
The University of Chicago Press, Ltd., London

© 2000 by The University of Chicago
All rights reserved. Published 2000
Printed in the United States of America

09 08 07 06 05 04 03 02 01 00   1 2 3 4 5

ISBN: 0-226-55194-6 (cloth)

Library of Congress Cataloging-in-Publication Data

Murray, Stephen O.
  Homosexualities / Stephen O. Murray.
    p. cm. — (Worlds of desire)
  Includes bibliographical references and index.
  ISBN 0-226-55194-6 (cloth : alk. paper)
    1. Homosexuality, Male—Cross-cultural studies.   2. Lesbianism—
Cross-cultural studies.   I. Title.   II. Series.

HQ76.25 .M89 2000
306.76′62—dc21   99-087502

For

    Louis Crompton
    Wayne R. Dynes
    David F. Greenberg

in gratitude for many years of discussions in which they have shared their immense erudition and keen insights, and (most important of all) for their steady encouragement.

Contents

Part Three: Egalitarian Homosexualities   357

10 Conclusions   420

Illustrations

Tables

Introduction: Types of Homosexuality

Some same-sex sexual contact probably occurs everywhere. The modern, northern European and American notion that everyone who repeatedly engages in homosexual behavior is "a homosexual," a distinct "species" with unique features, is far from being universally credited. Indeed, the concept of "the homosexual" does not very well explain much of behavior, life, or categorization even in the society that popularized the model. First, not all of those involved in homosexual behavior consider themselves or are considered by others as *homosexual* (Reiss 1961, Humphreys 1975, Weinberg 1978), even in a city such as contemporary San Francisco in which *gay* is clearly recognized as a category of persons, some of who are involved in formal lesbigay organizations. Second, no single type *homosexual* with a unique set of characteristics exists (Hooker 1957, Bell and Weinberg 1978, Roscoe 1988). In the compact (seven-mile by seven-mile) city in which I live, there is an enormous range of homosexual behaviors, typifications, self-identifications, and meanings; just as there are ranges of Latino or Chinese or Italian, working-class or upper-class behaviors, typifications, self-identifications, and meanings.

Avoiding the Scylla of labeling everyone anywhere who engages in homosexual behavior a "homosexual" or a "gay person" (as Boswell [1980] followed psychoanalysts in doing) exposes one to an opposite danger, the Charybdis of arguing that homosexuality[1] exists only in modern, (north)western societies.[2] To be sure, **there is diversity, but there are only a few recurring patterns.** Relatively few of the imaginable structurings of same-sex sex recur in the panorama of known societies, despite the tradition of anthropologists and other travelers of stressing "exotic" differences and the tendency not to bother mentioning what is familiar.[3]

1. Specification of what I mean by "homosexuality" is deferred to pp. 13–15.
2. E.g., Faderman 1978 (1991:37–61), Halperin 1990, 1998. Lexicalization (a word for a category), role (an abstraction for which there may not be a word in use in a society), recurrent behavior (*lifeway* is a good descriptor for this), and *institutionalization* (while I think I know what "gay institutions" are, I do not claim to know what "institutionalized homosexuality" or claims of its absence mean) have not been clearly distinguished in either anti-essentialist or anti-anti-essentialist history, anthropology, and sociology.
3. This is a (genre) convention going back to Herodotus, "the father of anthropology," and characteristic of nonwestern writers about alien-to-them cultures. On the European tradition, see Hodgen 1964, Murray 1981, Roscoe 1995, 1998:168–87, Bleys 1995, Murray and Roscoe 1998:9–18.

There are not hundreds or even dozens of different social organizations of same-sex sexual relations in human societies (Murray 1984:19–21). As for other cultural domains, only a few categorization systems recur across space and time.[4] Barry Adam (1979, 1986) proposed a fourfold typology of social structurings of homosexuality: (1) age structured, (2) gender defined, (3) profession defined, and (4) egalitarian/"gay" relations.[5] While

4. Ethnosemanticists have studied the domain of color more extensively than any other, since for color there is an organization of data (the spectrum with its equal interval calibration of wavelengths) other than that provided by one language with which to contrast the seeming immense diversity of color lexicons in different languages (Lennenberg 1953, Kay and McDaniel 1978). Berlin and Kay (1969, 1991) demonstrated that there is a great deal of order in this seeming diversity, indeed, that the elaboration of color lexicon occurs in a nearly invariant order. If there is a third category (after light/dark), it is red. After red, the order of elaboration is yellow-green-blue, or green-yellow-blue, and so on. All categorization systems overlook and ignore some perceived differences (Goodenough 1990:598–99), and cultural novices (mostly children) learn categories from instructors pointing out prototypical examples, not from exhaustive labeling of all possible shades. For instance, instead of trying to define "red" in terms of a set of wavelengths that is a segment of the spectrum of light, or a checklist of essential/"defining" features of "redness," good examples of "red" are labeled, often in a "not orange, but red" form. Also see Berlin (1992) on universals in ordering of categories for plants and animals. Kay (1978) applied the method of analyzing categories to such contentious social categories as "race" and "class" in Tahiti. Regularities in both synchronic and developmental orders of categorization schema for "nature" and for "culture" exist cross-culturally.

On the extreme selectivity of nominalism in work on "the social creation of homosexuality," see Murray 1983, 1984:18–21, and Dynes 1990b:226–33. Readers of creationist discourse are "left with the impression that other diachronic [and cross-cultural] abstractions are accurate as commonly applied, while this one alone is singularly inaccurate" (Boswell 1990:139; also see 142–44).

Typologists, not least myself, have slid back and forth between contrasting local (emic) categorization schemata and examining patterns that may be locally lexicalized, recognized but not lexicalized ("covert categories" in the usual sense—see Berlin, Raven and Breedlove 1968, and Arboleda and Murray 1985) or locally unrecognized but still patterned. Local "native" models are not always accurate, and absence of a label cannot be taken as proof that a phenomenon does not exist. Study of classifications is interesting and important, but is not the sole or even the primary focus of this book; comparison of status of "partners" in same-sex sexual relations is.

5. Trumbach (1977) demarcated the age/gender distinction, but Adam told me that he was unaware of Trumbach's paper in 1979. Similarly, Trumbach told me that he was unaware of Geoffrey Gorer's earlier age/gender dichotomy, which, in turn, seems to me to derive from the implicit distinction in Richard Burton's "Terminal Essay" to his translation of *The Thousand and One Nights* (first printed privately in 1886). Herdt (1987a) labeled the second type "gender reversed" and the third "role specialized" (religious or social role). Roscoe (1995) identified spiritual archetypes for the main three types: two-spirit for gender, initiation for age, and mirroring twins for egalitarian.

relationships structured by age, gender, profession, and comradeship may coexist in a society, one of them tends to be more visible "on the ground," both among those who are native to the society and in explanation to aliens who ask about same-sex sexual relations.[6] For instance, age-graded male homosexuality was the legitimate form across ancient Greece. Gender-defined and comradely homosexuality also occurred, and at least the former was labeled—with a term for such a kind of person, *kinaidos*.[7] Similarly, many indigenous North American peoples had terms for a gender-variant role labeled "berdache"[8] by alien observers, while there were no labels for males who were masculine by their culture's standards, did male work, and had sexual relationships with other males, or for females who were feminine by their culture's standards and had sexual relationships with other females.

There is **always** intracultural diversity,[9] and even one person may understand the same behavior differently on different occasions with different partners, or even with the same partner. As Adam (1986:20) explained:

> Of course, any single set of cultural institutions never completely contains the full range of human experience and innovation. Social coding practices may be uneven, incomplete, or in transition. Even if sexuality has a culturally specific and internally coherent complex of meanings, and even if culture (in the

6. Throughout this book, by "native" I mean someone born in a society, with no implication of primitiveness.

7. Winkler 1990:45–54. Halperin (1998) accepted that *kinaidos* was a kind of person, a personnage, if not the same kind as "the modern homosexual" (though the first "modern homosexual" was a similarly craven, effeminate receptor). On comradely relations see Halperin 1990:47, 76–87, 225.

8. This originally Arabic or Persian term, this has been rejected by some as "European," and attempts have been made to enforce "two-spirited" (two words from European languages in a binary contrast with "one-spirited") not only as a label for persons in the present but on past discourse. On whether the roles across the seventeenth to the twentieth century and across two continents are part of a gender binary or trinary is hotly contested, see below (p. 353n. 83).

9. Hart (1954) showed diversity even within a single family of aboriginal Australians (peoples recurrently chosen—e.g., by Durkheim—as prototypical "primitives"). I do not understand how any moderately careful reader of *Islamic Homosexualities* (Murray and Roscoe 1997) could interpret the authors as representing a single "Islamic homosexuality," yet some reviewers did (although they did not agree on which was the single type!). I hope that the non-areal organization of this book (as of the 1992 Oceanic one) will make obvious—even to those who have failed to note that I produced a series of areally based books—that I do not think there is, for instance, a single African or a single Muslim homosexuality.

singular) could be shown to channel desires, there remains a larger universe of experience, maladjustment, and emigrations from prescribed interpretive frameworks. Moreover, the dominant sexual codes of one place take on subterranean aspects elsewhere as a "little tradition."

Even a role category may be variously interpreted and lived by individuals within a society. Over time, shared new meanings may move even the cultural categories. Also, traditions that are overshadowed (by dominant discourses) may nonetheless persist, as, for instance, age-stratified and gender-stratified homosexualities do in current-day Amsterdam and San Francisco. Whether the typology applies to female homosexuality has been relatively little discussed.[10] Those interested in "social construction" of sexualities cannot (consistently with their theory, or with the distinct constraints on women's movement and associations in various societies) take a similarity between male homosexuality and female homosexuality as pre-given and "natural." Yet, there has been a marked reluctance to deconstruct this particular equation (of male-male and female-female sexual relations), even though it is this linkage that seems to be what is most unique to the modern, "western" (northwestern European and North American) conception of homosexuality (Dynes 1990b:229, Halperin 1990:24). An equation of male and female homosexuality is very alien to those men involved in recurrent homosexuality in the societies I have observed directly (Mexico, Guatemala, Peru, Taiwan, and Thailand).

The lack of any equivalent of a bachelorhood period between puberty and marriage for females in the gerontocratic or polygynous societies that have age-structured male homosexual relations is a structural im-

10. Blackwood (1985:6) advocated "breaking the mirror," the mirror being the assumption that female-female relationships are mirror images of male-male ones, and demanded "a separate analysis of lesbian behavior." Oblivious to the large number of female ethnographers (and to recognizing that, as Lévi-Strauss notoriously put it, ethnography is "women's work" in the view of male theorists like himself) she blamed the lack of representations of female homosexuality in anthropology on the claim that "anthropological fieldwork was done predominantly by males" (8). She did not entertain the possibility that fewer women than men are involved in same-sex sexual relations in various societies, and/or are less committed to such female homosexual roles as do exist than males are to male homosexual roles. She would not have had to look far to come up with these hypotheses, since they characterize her own society. Nor did she consider the existence of female biases, as well as of male ones (9). Blackwood (1985, 1996) stressed (sexual) agency, thereby posing an important challenge to the widespread feminist view that sex is something that is done to women.

pediment to age-structured female homosexuality (Adam 1986:21, 24). However, there is evidence of at least rudimentary age-stratified female-female relationships in some places. Clearly, the body of women's writings celebrating the charms of budding girls is very slender in comparison to that by men on the charms of budding boys. The extent to which this is an epiphenomenon of the lack of female representations of female desire is hard to gauge. What has survived of Sappho is extremely fragmentary, and there have been very few women whose writings (or paintings, etc.) have survived at all. Although the representations of it outside North America and northwestern Europe are mostly males', female gender-stratified homosexuality occurs. It seems less likely to be exclusive and lifelong than does male gender-stratified homosexuality, and to be less frequent. Similarly, involvement in egalitarian female-female sexuality seems to be more episodic and less enduringly self-defining than men's engagement with egalitarian male-male sexuality typically is (Whisman 1995b).

Below, I shall argue that most instances of "profession-defined" homosexuality are kinds of "gender-stratified" homosexuality, especially those in which the bodies of males are penetrated by spirits of both sexes and by the appendages of male bodies. Whether the insertee takes a nonsexual role (especially a religious one) that commands some respect in the society distinguishes subtypes of gender-defined homosexuality. Some of the occupations (especially entertainers) require young and pretty males, that is, they fall within the category of age-stratified homosexuality. I shall differentiate "age-stratified" homosexuality in which the younger partner is being socialized to masculine roles (generally the role of a warrior) from those in which he is used for his elder's sexual pleasure without concern about the junior partner's masculine development, and from the few instances in which the younger penetrates the elder. With this fine-tuning, the typology seems to encompass the observed empirical variance in social patterns of male-male sexual relations and, insofar as any exist, of female-female sexual relations, as well.

This book summarizes examples of these types as systematically as extant data permit. In that sexual behavior is generally not observed by others,[11] in contrast to readily observed markers of gender,[12] descriptions

---

11. Friedl (1994) and Murray (1998a) suggest different reasons for this regularity.

12. The inference that "he who disowns his manhood by the light of day will surely be shown to play the woman at night" (Clement, *Paidagōgos* 3.20.3, quoted in Gleason 1990:405), i.e., that the more masculine will penetrate the less masculine, seems obvious in many times and places, though it runs contrary to the reported experiences of transvestite

tend to rely more often on suppositions than on self-reports of the sexual component of roles. Norms heavily influence both.

This volume is organized typologically rather than chronologically or geographically. Simultaneous organizations in the same place appear in different sections. A thesis implicit in the ordering of descriptions is that the three main types are noticeable in societies differing in scale and in elaboration of technology. This contrasts with the overtones of quasi-evolutionary ordering of types in the deployment of types by other scholars such as Adam and Greenberg.[13] As in biological evolution, different species (types) occupy different niches more often than they become extinct.[14]

Some Cautions about Overly Deterministic Culturalist Readings

It is important to remember that expressed norms are very inadequate descriptions of behavior. In particular, the only acts that laws bother to forbid are those that some people would like to perform—such as stealing a neighbor's wife, "lying with a man as with a woman," eating pork, or smoking crack. Those concerned about their society's image may deny that proscribed acts occur, or, if they admit that such acts do occur, may attribute them to foreign influences, whether cocaine from Colombia or pederasty from "infidels" (e.g., Arabs or Turks), or "heretics" (e.g., Bulgarians) or some other antagonist (e.g., "the French vice" in the view of the English—and Florentine in the view of the French and Germans). One should be careful about accepting claims that behavior stigmatized in the questioner's society is unknown or alien to the society observed. One should be even more wary about assuming that no one anywhere at any time was aware of same-sex sexual preferences or sexual behavior just because a language seems to lack a term for *homosexual* (Arboleda and Murray 1985, Murray 1988:471, Roscoe 1988:25, Dynes 1990b:225). As I have already cautioned, rather a lot of the homosexual

---

prostitutes and effeminate men in contemporary societies (e.g., Braiterman 1992, Kulick 1998a, Pettiway 1996, Prieur 1998).

13. Although not obvious from his title, *The Construction of Homosexuality* (which more informatively could have continued "by Its Enemies and Would-Be Exterminators," Greenberg's great (in several senses) 1988 book is primarily about the repression of homosexuality, for which there is more plausibly a linear evolution (with a singular rather than plural object). My focus, in contrast, is primarily on how people have lived homosexualities in various societies rather than on how social institutions have attempted to suppress or extirpate homosexuality.

14. And in "social evolution," mutations are not random.

behavior in Anglo North America, and even more of it in Latin America, involves at least one person who does not consider himself to be a *homosexual* (or some similar indigenous label). Much homosexual behavior occurs outside the often-simplistic roles recognized (with labels) in a society. This is true even where, as in contemporary urban North America, there are multiple labels used in self-reference in the public sphere, and where many of those who self-label as gay or lesbian in contemporary urban North American workplaces do not fit the standard of lifelong exclusive homosexuality.

In that social theory grew out of a comparison of laws and means of governance and that anthropology until very recently was focused on jural rules and categories, the "literature" on gender and sexuality outside the "post-modern West" is overly normative, far too little concerned with intracultural variation in behaviors or in meanings. In all societies, not just in our own, individuals adapt and manipulate what Simon and Gagnon (1986) call "cultural scripts" for generating interactional and intrapsychic sexual meaning.[15] While normative models may **channel** perception of others and conception of self, they do not **determine** these. Observers should not assume that everyone in a society shares the same normative models—even unconsciously, or inarticulately. During the 1950s, Anthony F. C. Wallace (1952a, b) demonstrated that even small tribal societies are not homogeneous, and went on to suggest that "culture" should be conceived as "the organization of diversity," rather than as a replication of normative uniformity, so that even small, low-technology, ethnically homogeneous societies are "plural societies." Individuals not only may fail to share cultural understandings, but they may not seek to explain what their own patterns of sexual behavior mean. As Eric Wolf (1990:592–93) recalled Wallace's breakthrough, "he pointed out that participants in social action do not need to understand what meanings lie behind the behavior of their partners in interchange. All they have to know is how to respond appropriately to the cues signaled by others. Issues of meaning need not ever rise into consciousness.

15. They believe that only in "post-modern" societies, "the content and significance of the intrapsychic is limited, at best accounting for minor variations in performance [of culturally scripted roles]" (Simon and Gagnon 1986:99). Elvin (1985) and Spiro (1993) marshalled evidence for conceptions of "self" (*personnage*) in the purportedly "modern" sense across time and space against Mauss (1979 [1938]). Their critiques bear directly on the Durkheimian schema of the evolution of "the self" elaborated by Simon and Gagnon and picked up by Herdt: given his documentation of variable desire among the Sambia, I do not understand how Herdt (1997:13) could write that "individual desires are largely a matter of western history and culture."

This is often the concern only of certain specialists, whose specific job or interest it is to explore the plenitude of possible meanings: people such as shamans, *tohunga,* or academics."

"Culture," like "homosexuality" is an abstraction. Anthropologists (particularly those in the Durkheimian tradition) tend to confuse their systematizing of what they see, infer, and are told as a culture. Too often they proceed to imbue their abstraction of a culture with agency, including the power to create beliefs and even desires. Anthropologists' deity Culture is a reification of human creations, and anthropologists' models of culture easily attain false consistency as well as imaginary power. Those living their lives in the culture of which the analyst is trying to make sense may never reflect upon what seems inconsistent or anomalous to an analyst. For everyday, practical purposes, people can and do operate quite well with fuzzily bounded categories, even if some analysts cannot. Adjudicating border disputes among arcane combinations of features that normally do not occur together is not how people usually use their (language's) categories. Those living with and using a category rarely or never reflect upon the anomalies that arise from fixing classification schemata into writing. The systematizing of inscription may even generate culturally nonsensical problems.[16]

Categories—both folk ones and those of universalistic science—necessarily ignore differences to focus on similarities. In the current intellectual climate of postmodernist nihilism, stressing diversity within categories is less important than stressing that there **are** patternings, many of them recognized by those living within a society, and that emulation of what are thought to be requirements of roles (including homosexual ones) occurs. Individuals are more than "carriers" of a modeled culture, but their acts are not random. It is not only in the modern West that some persons have noticed same-sex sexual desires, either their own or that of others. I consider it incredibly arrogant—specifically chronocentric and ethnocentric—to proclaim that no one recognized homosexual desires before late-nineteenth-century forensic psychiatrists wrote about it.[17] As examples throughout this book will make abundantly clear, there have been both non-Western and premodern patterns of homosexual

16. See Murray 1983, 1994b:466–69, 1987b, building on Goody 1977:52–73; see also Nachman 1984.

17. It is one thing not "to conclude that sexuality a basic and irreducible element in, or central feature of human life" (Halperin 1990:242). It is quite another to assume that no one before 1869 or non-"Western" has noticed and been interested in who has sex with what kinds of persons.

behavior. Not only has such conduct been noticed, but many languages have labels for kinds of persons known to engage in it recurrently.

There are, alas, still only very few societies in which data are available on the interactional negotiation—let alone the meanings to individuals involved!—of homosexual behavior. Most ethnographies (e.g., 114 of the 190 societies surveyed by Ford and Beach [1951]) fail even to mention what is the normative societal view of homosexuality.[18] We know something about how pederasty and gender nonconformity were represented (often by hostile nonparticipants) in a few societies, but practically nothing about how homosexual desire or behavior is or was experienced or represented by/to those actually involved in it. Interpretation of representations is always necessary, but especially necessary for the records of homosexuality across space and time.[19]

The texts reviewed in this volume that touch upon indigenous conceptions of sex and gender and/or homosexual behavior in various societies are fragmentary.[20] They generally fail to answer the questions our current theories pose, especially those about intracultural diversity, individual meaning, the individual or shared salience of categories, the frequency of behaviors and of occupancy of named roles, and what (if any!) the relationship is between what people do and what they say. As

18. Anthropologists—including lesbian and gay ones—have often failed to make any inquiries about that which should not be named among Christians or mentioned in polite company, assuming that other peoples must also stigmatize it and feel uncomfortable discussing it (see Murray 1997c). The history of specious denials of homosexuality and suppression of records considered unsavory (as, for instance, Burton's widow's destruction of his papers) justifies taking the position that in the absence of inquiry on the topic, absence of evidence about sex between persons of the same sex should not be taken as evidence of its absence. Caution also needs to be exercised in extrapolations. Absence of evidence is not evidence of presence, either.

19. The section entitled "A More Technical and Personal Discussion of Methods," at the end of this chapter, elaborates on the extant materials and problems of interpreting them.

20. Few members of my generation (or of later ones) think that a holistic ethnography of a discrete culture is possible, and many reject it as even an aspiration. Fragmentation is currently very chic in anthropology, as well as in other "postmodernist discourses." Although I do not aim to produce an authorless text, I have sought to produce a polyvocal one, quoting earlier observers and (wherever possible) native informants verbatim and at length, rather than abstracting the sources or coding their contents. (I follow the prescriptions of Kluckhohn 1943:268; see Murray 1986:261–64.) Given the lack of materials for systematic comparison of larger sexual cultures, as well as my skepticism about such an entity in the singular, most of what is discussed in this volume is (homo)sexuality in culture rather than "sexual culture" in the sense of Herdt (1997).

Winkler (1990:69) cautioned in regards to one fragmentary corpus of data, "Behind sentences that begin 'The Greeks believed ___' there lies a fairly small set of elite canonized texts. Many of them are what I would broadly call legislative rather than descriptive." The "native views" about gender crossing and homosexuality recorded by explorers, missionaries, travelers, and allegedly "objective" anthropologists similarly tend to mistake elite prescriptions and rationalizations for descriptions of usual behavior. Official accounts, especially for outsiders, may have little do with statistical behavioral regularities, let alone with showing the range of behaviors or the range of roles that individuals play in a society.[21] What the "natives" think the alien wants to hear and what they think the alien approves of (based in part on what they know about the observer's society) shape even unofficial accounts and explanations. Repeatedly, throughout the missionary, travel, and ethnography literatures, "the object of many of these reports seems to have been to stress the moral abomination so that little or no space was left to describe the reprehensible conduct itself" (Bleibtreu-Ehrenberg 1990:14; see also Murray 1997c). Alleged social scientists have often provided little or no more detailed or accurate documentation than their "prescientific" predecessors.

Descriptions and analyses of lived experience should follow surveys of prescriptive norms and distributions of behavior. Unfortunately, we are unlikely ever to learn what homosexual behavior meant in most of the cultures of the world before the massive incursions and disruptions of European colonialism and neocolonialism. We can continue to ask questions of documents from early periods of contact,[22] but salvage anthropology of sexuality in memory cultures was late on the scene, and even salvage anthropology is no longer possible for many of the world's cultures.

Of course, rapidly changing contemporary cultures, not just "traditional forms," deserve study—preferably both more intensive than most sociological work and more systematic than the casual sampling, unexplained data selection, and overgeneralizing that anthropologists have repatriated as they have been driven increasingly out of the rest of the world. Even if the diversity of organizations of homosexuality (and of other phenomena) has been reduced in what is still very far from being a culturally homogeneous world, very little is known about the meaning

21. Overhasty assumptions of preference from behavior, of identity from role, and of exclusivity from recurrence occur even in insider descriptions.

22. See Murray 1994b. Roscoe (1991a,1998) surprised me by showing that new questions can be asked even of the often-examined literature on native North America.

of homosexuality for those involved or for those not involved in it now, even in U.S. cities. We know too little about what was, but we also know far too little about what is.

Changes in Organization

For most societies, data on homosexual behavior and societal reaction to it are so rare, recent, and incomplete that little can be said about patterns of change over time. Even for much-written-about Western Europe, controversy rages about whether there were significant changes in conception (self or societal) of homosexuality and reactions to it in the millennium and a half between the fall of Rome and the rise of England as a world power, or, later, with the coining of the word *homosexuality* and medical discoursing about it. The repressive weight of triumphant sex-negative Christianity is widely believed to have crushed the somewhat effeminized pederastic silver age of imperial Rome, heir to the masculinist golden age of pederasty in Greek city-states.[23]

In the pop-Foucault view, only with the supposed epistemic break of the Enlightenment and with the later replacement of clerical with medical "knowledge" did an intersexed homosexual "species" come into existence.[24] Within this view or (more appropriately) behind these theoretical blinders, between the time of Justinian and that of Magnus Hirschfeld (i.e., between the middle of the sixth and end of the nineteenth century), there were homosexual acts but no homosexual roles for homosexual selves to enact (as, similarly, there were crimes but no criminals, and deranged behavior without madmen and madwomen). However, at the end of the medieval period, traces of a pederastic subculture were still somewhat visible.[25] Before the recent emergence of gay people rejecting gender- and age-differentiated roles, a subculture

23. Boswell (1980), unlike social creationists who did not look beyond the late nineteenth century before proclaiming it the point of origin of homosexual categorization and identity, dissented from this view. I think that he went too far to the opposite extreme. On the *sodomite* as a cultural category beyond "random" acts of sodomy, see Murray 1988 and pp. 141–43 below. On the effeminization of sexually receptive "boys" during the Roman Empire, see pp. 126–28 below.

24. David Halperin (1998) has recently sought to obfuscate the fact that Foucault was making a historical claim by arguing that Foucault did not intend to produce a "theory" of sexuality (which is true but irrelevant). Halperin slipped "sodomite" into the opposition Foucault made (in French, not just in translation into English) between "sodomy" (an act) and "the homosexual" (a kind of person).

25. See Goodich 1979, Murray and Gerard 1983, and the tantalizing document discussed by Dynes and Johansson (1984) from twelfth-century London.

organized by cross-gender assumptions, flourished with varying degrees of covertness.[26]

Thus, Western European societies exemplify a succession in prominence of age, gender, and gay subcultures, with a gap of some years in the late seventeenth century between the predominantly age-stratified and the predominantly gender-stratified eras, and a rapid shift during the 1970s of gender distinctions or "variance" from being normative to being regarded as archaic.

The transformation from gender to gay is usually treated as a revolution, while no one seems to realize that an earlier transformation from age to gender occurred—in Europe, in Japan, and possibly also in China and the Roman Empire. During the period commonly glossed as "the Renaissance" in Europe, there was a homosexual role, "the sodomite," which did not entail crossing gender patterns for dress and demeanor in public, or sexual receptivity in private.[27] Most everyone took for granted that the older and richer would sexually use the younger and poorer. Ancient Greeks and Romans made the same assumption. In medieval and early modern Europe, the "catamite" or his family received gifts or sponsorship in exchange for his complaisance to the sodomite patron's pleasures. We do not know how those playing either the sodomite or the catamite role felt about the sex they had together, or what kind or degree of variance from the ideal-type "cultural script" those performing those roles ad-libbed or rewrote, or how much egalitarian homosexuality occurred outside the pederastic script.

Given that pederastic relationships continue to exist even today in cities with generally recognized gay neighborhoods and institutions, caution is in order in assuming that the rates of behavior changed as attention (and the dominant cultural representation) shifted to the "mollies" in England and to analogous gender-crossing men elsewhere. Perhaps the dominant culture's equation of homosexuality and visible effeminacy camouflaged persisting and clandestine egalitarian and age-graded homosexuality. Trumbach (1977:17–18) noted, "Descriptions of the [molly] subculture which were intended for the general public always emphasized its effeminacy." This public appearance certainly does not prove that in late-seventeenth-century London everyone involved in

26. See Leznoff 1954, Norton 1992, Chauncey 1994.

27. Sexual receptivity to one's social inferiors seems to have been a serious affront to the social order, and violations of taboos against such unbecoming behavior seem to have occasioned the disgrace of the Earl of Castlehaven in 1631, the most discussed case of an English Renaissance sodomy conviction. Also see Perry (1980:143) on the 1597 burning of Alonso Telles Girón in Seville.

homosexuality, or even most of those who were, enacted the "molly" role. Journalists' sensationalist focus on "mollies" may have kept other non-gender-stratified homosexualities invisible, and may even have been manipulated by those whose conduct was so camouflaged.

After the supposedly swift and total shift (at least in England) in emphasis from age-graded to gender-defined homosexuality during the seventeenth century, the conventional wisdom of medical taxonomizing in the late nineteenth century provided spurious causal explanations for expected gender deviation. Chauncey (1982, 1985, 1994; also see Bérubé 1990) convincingly showed that medical experts codified popular prejudices rather than inventing a view that trickled down to the masses. It would be ludicrous to suppose that medical discourse created the "mollies" of seventeenth-century England, given the low prestige of medicine in that time and place and physicians' lack of interest in theorizing about homosexuality. Whether the Society for the Reformation of Manners discovered or crystallized a "molly" role is a more interesting question for labeling dialecticians to consider. No one has yet suggested that medical discourse "constructed" *wakashū* of Tokugawa-era and earlier Japan (see Leupp 1996), or caused an increasing feminization of the role during the seventeenth century, or the seemingly simultaneous feminization of "the love of the cut sleeve" in Qing China (see Xiao 1984, 1997:157–240).

A More Technical and Personal Discussion of Methods

The Difficulty of Measuring "Homosexuality"

By *homosexuality* in reference to males, I mean contact between the penis of one male and the body of another person who was born male and/or the desire by someone born male for contact with the penis, thighs, or orifices of someone else born male. Lesbian scholars have rejected a parallel behavioral definition of *lesbianism*. The eminent lesbian historian Lillian Faderman (1981:17–18) is well known for her statement that: "'Lesbian' describes a relationship in which two women's strongest emotions and affections are directed toward each other. Sexual contact may be a part of the relationship to a greater or lesser degree, or it may be entirely absent." The "lesbian continuum" proposed by Adrienne Rich (1980) seems to me overinclusive, and she herself suggested a less-permeable category of those who live a "lesbian existence," that is, females who organize their primary intimate relationships around females. Not easily observed, let alone measured, living (for at least some time) a "lesbian existence" is still an irremediably contestable category. But, as Rich rightly argued, so is "heterosexuality" of women: there "exist, of course, qualitative differences of experience, but the absence of choice remains the great unacknowledged reality" about female sexuality (across time and space).[28] If females have no choice but to marry men and bear children, even giving birth, a seemingly concrete marker for having had sex with a man, does not establish heterosexual desire. In the majority of times and places in which families arrange marriages, romantic love and desire are neither required nor expected between those breeding new extensions of the family.[29] Such behavior does not establish females' desire for intercourse with males as a class, or even for a particular male sexual partner.[30] "Heterosexual desire" is an assumption even for those with the tangible proof of having engaged in heterosexual intercourse.

As for the males, some male must have ejaculated inside the female who later bore a child, but before DNA testing became available in the late 1990s, there was little proof of which **particular** male had impregnated a female. Except in rare instances of observation by others, there is no evidence of male heterosexuality even in terms of behavior.[31] Correlation of heterosexual desire and behavior is widely assumed, but it is mostly unproven and unattested except for by the self-reports of a few.

For males, erection establishes desire—not an exclusive desire, not necessarily a conscious or willed desire, but erection is a sufficient proof

28. There seems to be a modern Western assumption (and unconscious generalization) that marriage is the primary sexual and emotional relationship, and a conflation in Rich (and others) of "marriage" with "sexuality," so that compulsory marriage establishes the necessary primacy of heterosexuality for those pressed to marry, especially for females. Keeping wives and daughters away from males not of the family tends to keep them with females. Given the incomprehension of the possibility of female sexual agency, males in various societies and some alien observers believe that seclusion from males constitutes control of female sexuality. Even in the contemporary United States, many people do not consider that there can be "sex" without penile penetration (see Murray 1999b, Sanders and Reinisch 1999).

29. Denis de Rougemont (1955) claimed that romantic love was a late-medieval invention, though I find it hard to deny that it applies to male-male couples in ancient Greece.

30. Given how frequently same-sex contact is dismissed as "situational homosexuality," it is remarkable that a parallel notion of "situational heterosexuality" is not deployed. Surely arranged marriages and female prostitution are "situations" in which many females have undesired sexual contact with males.

31. Inferring desire from behavior is more plausible for illicit sex than for socially approved and even mandated intercourse.

of desire's existence.[32] Sufficient but not necessary: there is no question that there is desire without erection—for males as well as for females. A few males ejaculate as a result of being penetrated. Others become erect and manipulate their organ or have it manipulated by another person, but there are also males who desire to be penetrated who do not ejaculate while being penetrated, do not become erect, and do not manipulate their penis or allow it to be manipulated by others. Thus, while erection is evidence of desire, absence of erection is not evidence of lack of desire, so that this surface marker is underinclusive. In that coercion may be subtle, one cannot be sure that sexual contact is chosen and, therefore, is an indication of desire. Imputations by others of desire are data, but my primary focus throughout is on same-sex sexual behavior rather than on inferring a homosexual orientation or on being "a homosexual." I use "homosexuality" to refer to recurrent same-sex sexual relations, but unless I have slipped, I never write of someone as being "a homosexual."

Materials Used

It is obvious to me, but apparently not to everyone, that comparative sociology (/ethnology) necessarily rests on texts, in the broad sense of "text" that includes any inscription, including published ethnography, completed questionnaires, diaries, literature (including fiction, poetry, and play scripts), and visual representations from which something about the people creating them can be inferred. Serious scholarship involves "triangulating" available evidence, trying to tease out an understanding of often contradictory sources. Being explicit about what is at variance with one's interpretation allows readers to reach their own assessments.

Alas, references about same-sex sex in many places and times are few, brief, and/or suspect. Insofar as these can be gauged, the motives and sophistication about sexual possibilities of those purportedly describing behavior or generalizing about cultural norms are relevant, as are what can be inferred about pressures to censor and dissemble. Yes, there is an infinite regress of interpretations with no bedrock of certainty in trying to figure out what happened. For instance, Cataline's political aspirations are as much in need of interpretive effort to extract from hostile texts as are his sexual habits.

Prosecutors' speeches (like Cicero's against Cataline or Timarkhos's against Askhines) and accusations in judicial archives (the primary source used for reconstructing patterns of same-sex sexual conduct in

32. Erection is a prerequisite for anal and vaginal penetration, but not for oral.

early modern Europe) are not notably more objective than the most difficult literary evidence—satires.[33] Both are biased. Both exaggerate. Both ignore most of what is everyday life for most people in a society. Neither is a valid basis for inferring rates of behavior in a society. The minimal claim for literary materials, including satires, is that they contain imaginable doings. If not precise attestation of behavior and social statuses that occurred in history, exaggerations are still cultural products based on imaginable events and extrapolation of existing tendencies. Even science fiction imagines alternate worlds based on authors' experiences of human life on earth.

An advantage of native representations (particularly from earlier times) is that they are uncontaminated with the expectations formed by our theories (about "sexual orientation" in particular). "Poems, plays, and fiction speak from the inside," as Elizabethan literary historian Bruce Smith (1991:25) wrote. Literature written for native audiences provides a "noetic expression of a social and cultural milieu . . . [that] provide[s] readers with a codification of the world that is cognitively and aesthetically credible" apart from its aesthetic accomplishments, according to anthropologist Herbert Phillips (1987:3–4). Although literary works "are refractions and distillations, rather than reflections or replicas," they provide "an unimpeachable source of indigenous meanings, assumptions, and purposes," he added (27, 61). Or, as Prince Genji explains in the twenty-fifth book of *Genji Monogatari,* as translated by I. Morris (1985:316):

> The fact is that works of fiction set down things that have happened in this world ever since the days of the gods. Writings like the *Chronicles of Japan* really give only one side of the picture, whereas these romances must be full of just the right sort of details. The authors certainly do not write about specific people, recording all the actual circumstances of their lives. Rather it is a matter of their being so moved by things, both good and bad, which they have heard and seen happening to men and women that they cannot keep it all to themselves but wants to commit it to writing and make it known to other people—even to those of later generations. This, I feel sure, is the origin of fiction. . . . In every case the things they write about will belong to this actual world of ours.[34]

33. Gauging how much is mimetic in satire is especially difficult in the absence of reliable descriptive detail from the society from which a particular satire arose.

34. I have altered the masculine singular pronouns to gender-unmarked plurals in this passage written by a woman in the eleventh century, a time in which women writers

And not just things, but attitudes, values, and desires: "The mode of discourse that gives us most intimate access to scripts of sexual desire is not moral, legal, or medical, but literary. . . . Moral, legal, and medical discourse are concerned with sexual acts; only poetic discourse can address homosexual desire" (B. Smith 1991:16–17) is only a slight overstatement. "Rather than dictating or being dictated to, poetic discourse more often mediates between the official ideal and the quotidian real" (23).

I am not "hostile to text-based research" as some have supposed.[35] I have elicited some personal narratives about homoerotic meanings (e.g., Kamau 1998, B. Khan 1997, and Murray 1996a:199–201, 1997b: 42, 1998a). Although, ideally, I would like reports from random samples of those living in a particular place and time about what they did and what it meant to them, I have to settle for sifting through fragments, many from biased observers. Worse still, the purportedly scientific observers and records have often passed over homosexuality, so that, far too often, the only indications of it are from those hostile to what they view as "degeneracy," "vice," and so forth.

The Impersonal Vocation of Scholarship

Something that has puzzled some readers of earlier (interim) presentations of my long-running project of looking through writings about homosexualities in various times and places is that I often both take information from and criticize interpretations by an author. This is not puzzling to anyone who understands that all scholarship is provisional and that readers inevitably have to read through representations to try to understand what is represented.[36] It is not just in fiction that "unreliable narrators" report patterned behavior they do not understand but that readers may grasp. Chroniclers of current or recent events have often had to couch their representations in ways that they can publish

---

predominated (Morris 1985:28). Morris's book from which this quotation is taken is itself a superb exemplar of using works of fiction to reconstruct aspects of a particular past social structure. Another is Friedrich 1966. For comparative history, Brown and Gilman 1960 was my first model of systematically examining data from literary texts. The pattern they found was increasing egalitarianism.

35. I am very skeptical of what I call "discourse creationism," particularly that late-nineteenth-century medical texts invented rather than reflected homosexual conduct. I think that even prescriptive texts (say the Bible, *The Book of Mormon*, or the *Qur'an*) reflect (albeit in distorting mirrors) the societies in which they were written. This is not to mistake prescriptions for descriptions, but only to insist that a particular prescription arise from a particular sociocultural situation.

36. This applies to representations of anything, not just of sexuality.

without endangering themselves, sometimes writing in code understood by those in the know, sometimes surrounding their reportage with conventional rhetoric of religious outrage that the authors may have simulated sharing. Reports have also been distorted by a priori theories and the like.[37] The representations herein, as well as those on which they are based, are resources requiring interpretation. As with the case studies in my other major line of analysis,[38] I have endeavored to lay out sufficient detail so that those with interests or interpretations other than my own can read them with some profit, just as I have interpreted various data differently from the way those who supplied them did.

I have been surprised to learn that not just undergraduates (who are supposed to be naive about the vocation of scholarship) but some tenured professors have so little notion of scholarship as a multiperson endeavor, the aim of which is better to understand what is and what has been, that they are shocked that I have (on many occasions) not only used work, but acknowledged helpful comments and encouragement from some of the living scholars whose work I have critically engaged. I have cited and quoted with approval what I think is right in work by some people I personally detest and have criticized aspects of work by other people whom I personally like very much. True scholars—of whom there are many in gay/lesbian studies—prefer being argued with to being mindlessly praised for orthodoxy to current fashions. I know from direct personal observation in a seminar course and during a tête-à-tête that Michel Foucault was a true scholar, even if some of his epigoni are not.[39]

This book and this line of research are my efforts to sort through and make some sense of patternings in representations of some sexual behavior in various societies. It is not a search for my roots, nor for legitimation of how I live my life. I am not looking for gay identities elsewhere. Indeed, even living in one of the symbolic gay capitals, I recognize and have on numerous occasions stated (e.g., in Murray 1984:45, 1992a:xiii–xiv) that not everyone who engages in same-sex sex in late-twentieth-century San Francisco considers himself or is considered by

37. Murray and Roscoe (1998:9–18) discussed reading through less-than-transparent lenses, especially reading late-nineteenth-/early-twentieth-century European observations of their colonies. Also see Bleys 1995, Proschan 1998. Murray (1997c) vents some of my frustration at the thinness of the ethnographic record. Still, if it were blank—not just thin—there would be nothing to write about for many cultures.

38. I.e., social history of "theory groups" in social science; see Murray 1994b.

39. See Murray 1985. I would extend my stand (in Murray 1996c) against disseminating lies that some believe to be useful to representing homosexualities.

his partners "gay." Some of the individuals and roles glimpsed in the descriptions in this book may strike some readers—those identifying as bisexual, transvestite, or transgendered as well as those identifying as gay or lesbian—as historical or spiritual kindred. I have no interest in denying such feelings to anyone or in adjudicating the legitimacy of such genealogies.

It is neither "gay identity" nor "gay people" elsewhere that I have been looking for. I believe that homosexual behavior is a transcultural (etic) phenomenon. "Gender stratified," "age stratified," and "not status stratified" are also labels for cross-cultural comparison, though there often are local labels for particular roles that index these extralocal comparative categories. Although (emic) native cultural modelings of same-sex sex interest me (considerably!), they are simplistic at best and obfuscatory at worst, as will be shown in a number of particular instances in this book. My primary focus is etic. I would love to compare systematic data about the subjectivities of those engaged in same-sex sex, but these data are nearly nonexistent, so an ethnology or a comparative history of homosexual relations with any sweep has to rely on what those—insiders to the society as well as alien observers—not engaging in same-sex sex wrote about the doings of others, not on the carefully contextualized and fine-grained data about individual meanings and desires that I can only wish were available for comparison.

Although there are aspects of their lived experience that are similar to mine, I do not feel "natural" solidarity with everyone born male who engages in sex with other males in the United States today. While I believe that I belong to a community that is based on respecting the choices people make about how to deploy their bodies, I am neither transgendered nor inclined to pederasty. I feel only some abstract alliance with transgendered people and pederasts who live on the same hill in San Francisco as I do. A Spartan *eromenos* or *erastes* 2,500 years ago or a Chukchi transformed shaman a century ago is interesting to me, but not in the sense of being my roots, not as fellow "gays." Their status in their society is no guarantee of mine. I do not wish to recreate ancient Spartan or nineteenth-century Chukchi society and doubt that I would fit very well in either. What such cases (of which there are many in this volume) provide are exemplifications that societies have understood, ordered, and evaluated sex between those born male differently than my own society does.

I have argued (with no claim to originality) that conceiving that social change is possible is the crucial first step to mobilizing to foment change. The certainty that things must be the way they are is eroded by knowledge of alternative ways, even if none of the documented ways strikes one (reader or author) as perfect or as a plausible or a attractive blueprint. Those totally satisfied with a status quo rarely have any interest in comparing social organizations.[40] Some seekers return with a taste of ashes in their mouths, having failed to find what they sought.[41] This is a danger for those looking at attested patterns of homosexuality, as at any other kind of social patterning. Rather than warning such readers off, I would invite them to review what has been without taking precedent as entirely determinative of what might be. One need not have a very deep time perspective to realize that change is possible. Much that was inconceivable to me two decades ago (e.g., peaceful transfers of power from the apartheid regime in South Africa and from the communist parties of the Soviet empire) has occurred, and to those seeking to change the world, the past must be prologue to a scenario that has yet to be written.

Mechanics

A page number cited in the text contains an implicit "ibid.," that is, the name and publication date are the same as those in the previous citation.

I have endeavored to use current romanizations of words from a range of languages,[42] but often quote passages with earlier (I hope, recognizable) alternates. Pluralizing of loanwords in English is inconsistent. In instances where the literature uses plural forms from other languages, I have followed established usage. In other instances I have incorporated some nouns into English with an *s* suffix, though my preference is to treat role labels in the singular as mass nouns, particularly for languages that use prefixes to indicate number.[43]

I have endeavored to be more systematic about verb tense. Any report I can read must have been written in the past. Conventionally, the contents of literary texts are described in the present tense. Thus, Lady Murasaki wrote the *Tales of Genjii,* but Prince Genjii does things (seduces

40. Nor are they motivated to imagine patterns that they consider better than any in existence (Mannheim 1936).

41. The prototype is Claude Lévi-Strauss (1974 [1955]).

42. I am confident that there is no one who commands all of them and certain that, even beyond the vagaries of different writers' romanizations, I have mistyped some.

43. That I have made them mass nouns in English should not be taken as claiming that they are mass nouns in the language from which they have been snatched. Moreover, I almost certainly have nominalized one or another verb, something easily done in English (e.g., "two-spirit" according to Tafoya 1992:256).

people and composes poems). The ethnographic present used in quoted materials spills over into my text to avoid jarring shifts back and forth, particularly when I am unsure about whether what was described by an ethnographer years or decades ago continues to characterize patterns today.

I fail to find any sense in "common era." It is at least as widely supposed to mean Christian (rather than Common) Era as A.D. is thought to mean "After Death" (rather than "Anno Domini"), and the closest approximation to a common era was the easternmost penetration of Alexander the Great. Changing abbreviations does not make the dating any less Christcentric! I have retained the conventional and shorter B.C. and A.D.

Similarly, I have retained the classical feminist distinction of (natal/ biological) sex from gender (roles and attributes understood to be masculine or feminine in particular societies). To me, "same-gender" means masculine-masculine or feminine-feminine (butch-butch or femme-femme); either might be female-female or male-male. Much same-sex sex is heterogender (butch/femme role-demarcated) and euphemizing "sex" in favor of distending the analytical category "gender" makes it impossible to distinguish homogender from heterogender homosexuality.

In the tradition of the Chicago school of sociology, I use "conduct" to mean a recurrent pattern of acts, in contrast to "behavior." "Behavior" is used for those acts for which there is not enough information or the occurrences of which are too scattered to be called "conduct." Rather than being synonyms, "behavior" and "conduct" contrast herein.

Sadly, this already bulky book would be bulkier still if I explained who everyone cited is or was, or where every place mentioned is. I cite sources, including some of my own work, where more detail is available.

Part One
AGE-STRUCTURED HOMOSEXUALITIES

Part I of this book considers three subtypes of age-stratified male homosexuality and concludes with a look at some instances of female age-stratified homosexuality.

The first subtype is one in which a boy's erotic relations with an older male are viewed (within a culture) as enhancing the boy's masculinity, thereby preparing him to be a masculine adult warrior. Although aboriginal Australian and Papuan societies have been seen as prototypes of "primitive" technology (albeit with extremely complex "techniques of the sacred" and cosmologies), the age-stratified homosexuality in urbanized Middle Eastern empires and medieval Japan should caution against a view of age-stratified homosexuality as a part of the "lowest stage" of social evolution. Moreover, the Papuan peoples with boy-inseminating beliefs and practices engaged in agriculture, albeit subsistence agriculture. Ancient Greece and Korea, and medieval Egypt, Turkey, and Japan were distinctly stratified societies extracting agricultural surpluses. Within these societies homosexuality was age-graded and celebrated among the dominant military castes.

"Love between men is a recurring feature of military societies, in which men tend to be shut in upon themselves. The exclusion—the utter absence—of women inevitably means an increase in masculine love," French historian Henri Marrou wrote. In warrior societies "with the glorification of an ideal made up of masculine virtues like strength and valour and loyalty, with the cultivation of a distinctively masculine pride, there goes a tendency to depreciate the normal love of a man for a woman" (1982:27). Plausible as this sounds, as the first chapter in this section shows, there has been considerable variability in the openness of male-male love and the degree of aestheticizing of the beloved among societies with standing armies—along with variability in the prestige of the warriors defending or expanding the boundaries of polities (see Knox 1979). A drift over time away from valuing the masculinity of the youth seems related to the lessening value of warriors during extended times of peace in these societies.

The second subtype is one in which the boy is neither masculinized nor **permanently** feminized in the local cultural conception of age-discrepant male-male sexual relations. These societies were not notably pacific nor higher on any evolutionary scale than the societies in which   23 the first subtype existed. The African cases involved boys doing "women's work" in addition to submitting to penetration of their thighs or anuses by their husbands. Nevertheless, when they became adults, these wives became husbands (and penetrators of younger males and younger females). Youthful sexual receptivity to men did not preclude later marriage to a woman for the Asian "objects" of pederasty, either. Not all "graduated" from being insertees to become insertors, but their adolescent status was not a bar to their later penetrating females or boys, if they were inclined to do so. (The low social status of entertainers affected prospects for marriages with girls of good families, however.)

In the Asian instances, boy entertainers' effeminacy was fostered and rewarded. These are among the roles that led Adam to suggest a type of "profession-defined homosexuality." As I concluded from examples from Asia and Oceania in my 1992 book, selective recruitment rather than professional socialization into homosexuality accounts for the high rate of homosexuality in these roles.[1]

A third subtype involves boys who take the insertive role in sex with their elders, often for hire (or for other rewards beyond any sexual pleasure they experience). Although claims have been made that such encounters and relationships are masculinizing (again, within a local cultural cosmology), I am unconvinced by such claims (for reasons elaborated upon in Part II, pp. 269–70). Ancient Rome provides examples, but the most extensively documented instances are twentieth-century Anglo-American. There is at least a suspicion that any homosexuality is unmasculine in these societies, but I also do not see that the objectification and service to others' desires is generally experienced as effeminizing by either the youths or by the adults who rent the young males' penises.

The final section of Part I considers another scantily documented phenomenon: age-stratified female homosexuality. These fragmentary accounts come from many of the same societies with age-stratified male homosexuality discussed in the earlier sections.[2]

1. Some involuntary recruitment occurred in China, just as some of the selling sons into slavery or castrating them for service in Muslim states occurred with the first subtype of pederasty.

2. I had intended to include something on pedagogical relations in orders of Roman Catholic nuns, but was convinced that emotional and erotic relations between peers are more common. See the personal narratives in Curb and Manahan 1985. Similarly, I could not find a solid basis for classifying the altar boys (and others) who have had sexual relations with priests as "boy tops" or as "not permanently feminized," though my impression is that they belong in the former category.

I

The Reproduction of Warriors

Australia and Melanesia

Mentions of the institution(s) of pederasty among Australian aborigines at the end of the nineteenth century are numerous, but detail is mostly lacking. More recent descriptions of Melanesian boy-inseminating rites are considerably thicker. The cultures in which these cults of masculinity occur are also marked by intense antagonism between the (two) sexes (see Murphy 1959, Herdt and Poole 1982), fears of semen depletion (only, or mostly, from coitus with women), ideologies that minimize female involvement in reproduction (see Meigs 1976), and considerable fascination with male beauty.

Aboriginal Australia

Herdt (1984) noted many explicit reference to boy-wives in early anthropological writings about Australian Aborigines, especially tribes of the Kimberley Plateau in the extreme northwest and of the Central Desert. The prolific early ethnographer R. H. Mathews (1900b:636) went so far as to state: "Among all the aboriginal tribes with which I am acquainted, masturbation and sodomy are practiced on certain occasions. It is more general in the Kimberley district and Northern Territory than elsewhere reached by my inquiries, but I have traced them in the inaugural rites and ceremonial corrobories of the natives in all the Australian colonies." (Emphasis added.)

Intriguing early Western Australian accounts indicate that, until girls pledged as brides attained marriage age, their brothers served as their surrogates. Mathews (1900a:125) wrote that among tribes of Western Australia, after a young man has recovered from circumcision (plus subincision in some tribes) "he is allotted a boy who has not yet been operated upon. This youth is a brother of the woman whom the man is entitled to claim as his wife. The boy is used for purposes of masturbation and sodomy, and constantly accompanies the man."

In the Kimberley District, Hardman (1889:73–74) found boy-wives. Incest prohibitions applied: "The young boy, known colonially as a 'crawler,' is called 'Yadup' till he is five years of age. He then becomes a 'Chookadoo,' and usually is given as a boy-wife to one of the young men. At about ten years of age the initiatory rites commence. . . . [After a   25 series of stages of initiation] in the event of a wife not being obtainable, the youth is presented with a boy-wife, known as *Chookadoo*. In this case also the [elaborate] rules of the marriage sects are observed."

Also in the Kimberley District, Purcell (1893:287) wrote that "every useless member of the tribe gets a boy, not a gin, about 5 or 7 years olds. They are called Mullawongahs, and are used as follows. The man tickles the boy's penis into an erection, then lapping his mutilated one round the boy's, has an emission." One must guess whether "useless" was the native view or Purcell's, but his use of the highly pejorative "gin" (an Australianism for aboriginal females made sexually available by getting them drunk on gin) suggests that it is Purcell's. In that he mentioned customs of genital mutilation (including splitting the glans), it is possible that by "useless" he meant unable to penetrate.[1] The erection of the boy is certainly an interesting aspect of this difficult-to-interpret passage (paralleling Klaatsch 1908:581–82). Purcell (1893:288) also reported that in the third-stage initiation, boys are strengthened by drinking semen collected from six to eight men.

Strehlow (1913:98) reported pederasty as a "recognized custom" among the (central Australian) Aranda, again with choice of boy partners constrained by the same rules as those that operated for wife selection: "Commonly a man, who is fully initiated but not yet married, takes a boy ten or twelve years old, who lives with him as a wife for several years, until the older man marries. The boy is neither circumcised nor subincized, though he may have ceased to be regarded as a boy and is considered a young man. The boy must belong to the proper marriage class from which the man might take a wife" (translated and quoted by Ford and Beach 1951:123). Later, more detailed descriptions by Géza Róheim of Nambutji (western Warlpiri) and Aranda exogamous homosexuality parallel this testimony. For instance, "The future father-in-law goes about with his son-in-law after initiation and regularly has intercourse with him. They call the younger man the 'boy-wife' of the elder one. As a sort of compensation for this [anal] intercourse, in which he is made to accept the passive role, he then receives the daughter of his 'husband' as his wife" (Róheim 1932:251; also see 1950:104,

---

1. I was only able to make some sense of this passage after discussion with Gilbert Herdt and Barry Baker. I gratefully acknowledge their interpretive help. The Gays and Lesbians Aboriginal Alliance (1994:31–33) discussed early reports of subincision intercourse (i.e., a not-yet-subincised boy placing his erect penis in the gap in the erect penis of the older, subincised man) by Helms (1896:291–2), Klaatsch (1908:581–82), and Purcell (1893:287).

1974:243). Spencer and Gillen (1927:470) also noted of the Arunta (Aranda):

> It frequently happens that the woman whose daughter is allotted to him may have a son and no daughter born, and in this case, without waiting on the chance of a girl being born, the man may agree to take the boy as what is called his *Unjipinna.* This establishes a relationship between the boy and the man, as a result of which the former has, until he becomes *Atua-kurka*—that is, circumcised—to give his hair to the man, who, on his part, has, in a certain way, to look after the boy.[2] . . . Whilst accepting the *Unjipinna,* and so waiving his right to the girl, the man still retains his right to the *hari* of the *Tualcha mura* woman.

Pilling (1992) reported evidence from his 1950s fieldwork of young Tiwi men pairing off with their sisters' future or present husbands, and inferred that earlier, when women were monopolized by polygamous elders, homosexual coupling was a major (and public) social phenomenon.[3]

Hiatt (1971:88) provided a sensible (if astringent to the native male perspective) attempt to explain the functions of male initiation in aboriginal Australia: "Aboriginal men assert a pre-eminent role in human reproduction by ritually magnifying male sexuality; and they transform boys into men by imitating female reproductivity . . . to extend male mastery into areas where women have natural advantages. The success of the manoeuvres depends on the ability of men to delude themselves and, through secrecy, to mystify and intimidate the women . . . Women, it seems, are not always impressed."

In addition to glimpses of Tully River (in northern Queensland) husbands having "bestial rights over her younger brother during the absence of his wife," W. Roth (1906:7) made an intriguing (but unfortunately unelaborated) mention of a word for an insertor role: *chi-ngu* as "a word applied to a sodomist" or a man who "habitually consorts."

2. The hair was for weaving waist girdles. Promised female brides also had to give their hair to their future husband (Spencer and Gillen 1927:469).

3. Pilling's (1992) and Read's (1992) memoirs provide insight into the paucity of documentation of homosexual behavior, let alone of native views about homosexuality, in the anthropological "literature." Even those fieldworkers with a personal interest in homosexuality were reluctant to investigate the topic, and excluded what little information they happened upon from the ethnographies they published. Pilling provided evidence that the natives screened what they thought white outsiders abhorred. Read suggested that it was his own inhibitions that kept him from asking about homosexuality, not any native strictures or unease.

Having been a "wife" for a time does not seem to have fixated aboriginal Australian males as receptors. With age, they left the role. There is some evidence of boys' believing they were being strengthened by the semen they collected, and of ideologies of male reproduction. I have not read of any male having been permanently feminized by having been a "wife."

Melanesia

Although Róheim (1926:70, 324–37) argued that the Australian data mirrored the Melanesian, homosexual intercourse was **prescribed,** not just condoned, in some traditional Melanesian initiation rites. Neither all Melanesian nor all Australian Aboriginal groups included boy insemination as part of their rituals.[4] Rather than being part of a ceremonial complex such as initiation, in some groups homosexual relations provided a sexual outlet for young men in the long period before they had any hope of marrying.[5]

Another significant difference between Aboriginal Australian and Melanesian homosexual relations is that the male cult and its practices are supposed to be unknown to Melanesian women. Women clearly knew of couplings of males in the Aboriginal Australian tribes for which documentation exists.[6] Although Melanesian men likely overestimate the ignorance of women (or know that this ignorance is to some degree a social fiction),[7] it is difficult to picture women freely discussing man-boy sexual relationships in Highland New Guinea cultures, let alone revealing who is linked to whom. Nevertheless, in both areas, homosexuality is clearly age differentiated. It is not just that the insertees are younger, but that the insertors are young men in transit to marriage (marriage being a hallmark of adult status).[8] Furthermore, the suitability of homosexual partners is

4. Though not reported as part of initiation rites, the roles (husband or wife) that boys took in earlier accounts of Australian societies were determined by stage of initiation. This does not mean that the sort of homosexual play among young boys that Pilling (1992) observed among the missionized Tiwi during the 1950s was not also present.

5. Male ideology about the dangers of pollution and semen loss from heterosexual intercourse is extensively discussed in ethnographies of Melanesia (notably Herdt's). Descriptions of Australian sexual ideology is much thinner.

6. E.g., "Homosexuality amongst the men did exist. The youths of seventeen or eighteen who were still unmarried would take boys of ten or eleven as lovers. The women had no hesitation in discussing the matter with me, did not regard it as shameful, gave the names of different boys, and seemed to regard the practice as a temporary substitute for marriage (Kaberry 1939:257).

7. Read (1952:7) provided an early recognition of this.

8. Bleibtreu-Ehrenberg (1990:19) put the inseminators on the other side of the mari-

constrained not only by age, but by kinship. In Melanesian initiation, as in Australia, incestuous relations were tabooed. For instance, among the Baruya, "Although all married men were excluded from these homosexual relations, not all unmarried men were permitted to give their sperm to a young initiate.[9] The initiate's direct maternal and paternal kin could under no circumstances become his partners. The exchange of sperm, of the vital substance, between men was thus permissible only beyond the perimeter of relations established by the exchange of women . . . outside the world of women and against them" (Godelier 1986:54).

Kinship taboos constrained age-graded homosexual relations among the Kimam of Frederik Hendrik Island, and among the Jaquai (who live up the Mappi River in Irian Jaya). Among the Kiman, "a boy was placed under the charge of an older youth who 'adopted' him as his 'mentor.' They regularly practiced homosexual anal intercourse. This 'mentor' is usually a classificatory elder brother from the same pabura (village sector). . . . Mentors were often mother's younger brother or cross-cousins, too (biological brothers were excluded)" (Serpenti 1965:162–63). Serpenti (1984:305) noted that the age-graded sexual relationships sometimes lead to lifelong emotional relationships. Among the Jaquai, "A father can order his son to go and sleep during the night with a certain man who will commit pederasty with him. The father will receive compensation for this. If this happens regularly between a man and the same boy, a stable relationship arises, comparable to that between a father and son . . . or anus father and . . . anus son. . . . Such a boy is allowed to consider that man's daughter as his sister and she will be 'awarded' to

---

tal divide, perhaps overgeneralizing from the Marind Anim. Schiefenhövel (1990) attempted to explain Highland New Guinea age-graded homosexuality by unequal sex ratios stemming from female infanticide. As Watts (1992:181) argued against a similar "explanation" of Polynesian gender-defined homosexuality, it is hard to understand why female infanticide would be practiced if a shortage of women was felt to be a problem requiring solution in a society. Cultural obstacles to sexual access to women are more important than the absolute or relative number of women, particularly in gerontocratic societies. In Melanesia, there are also frequent and long stretches of time in which a wife is not sexually available to her husband (see Kelly 1976, 1977). If this is a "shortage," it is a social-cultural, not a biological one.

9. "For the Baruya, it would be the worst possible humiliation, the worst form of aggression, to give seed from a penis that has penetrated a woman to the young boy to drink so shortly after his forcible removal from the world of women. It would be tantamount to treating the boy's mouth like a vagina, and communicating to his mouth all the pollution that comes from women's genitalia. Consequently, only the unmarried young men, the *tchouwanie* and the *kalave*, the eldest among all these virgin boys, could and should give their sperm to the new initiates" (Godelier 1986:53).

him as his exchange sister for his future marriage" (Boelaars 1981:84, quoted by Herdt 1984:29).

A number of Melanesian tribes "share the belief that boys do not become physically mature men as a result of natural processes. Growth and attainment of physiological maturation is contingent on the cultural process of initiation, and this entails insemination because it is semen which ensures growth and development" (Kelly 1977:16). In the native views, "Semen does not occur naturally in boys and must be 'planted' in them. If one does not plant sweet potato [a diet staple throughout the area] then no sweet potatoes will come up in the garden, and likewise semen must be planted in youths if they are to possess it as men" (16). Another "motive for pederastic practices during initiation is the nearly universal belief in these regions that boys before their initiation belong exclusively to their mothers. . . . At first, logically, the new initiates are treated by their initiators as if they were women. It is even believed that pederastic contacts with them could result in pregnancy. . . . Sperm nourishes the still 'female' body of the boy which now must be transformed into the body of an adult warrior" (Bleibtreu-Ehrenberg 1990:16–17; see, especially, Herdt 1981). Since boys lack semen, and men, who have all gone through the initiation process, can produce it, the native theory is verified anew with regularity (see Rappaport 1979:97–144).

The means of insemination vary: oral for the Etero studied by Kelly (1976, 1977) and the Sambia studied by Herdt (1981), anal for the Kaluli studied by Schieffelin (1976), and by masturbation and the smearing of semen over the bodies of the initiates among the Onabasulu (Ernst 1991:5). Despite the shared belief in the necessity of inseminating boys if they are to grow into men, and the whole complex of beliefs about pollution by females and the life-threatening loss of semen to them, the differences in the means of insemination used are ethnic markers, according to Kelly (1977:16).[10] The patterning of intertribal differences is described and analyzed in Herdt's (1984 and 1992a) indispensable introductions. Since these works are readily available, there is no need to summarize here the monumental ethnographic and comparative Melanesian work, which provides many examples of age-defined organization of homosexuality, except to note the abandonment of the term "ritualized homosexuality."[11] As Ernst (1991:2) stressed, "male homo-

10. Ernst (1991:5–6) challenged "the strict separation of tribal groups by insemination practices."

11. Herdt (1991, 1992a) rejected the rationale for using "ritual homosexuality" in Herdt (1984:6). Also see Knauft (1990). Against the retreat from "ritual," I would marshal

sexuality in these groups was never confined to ritual contexts." In the case of the Onabasulu whom he studied, male insemination continued after the abandonment of initiation rites. "Male homosexual activity always exceeded the limits of ritual and continued in the absence of ritual" (4). In another Melanesian culture, Schiefenhövel (1990) noted age-graded homosexual relations unrelated to initiation alongside "ritualized homosexuality" among the Eipo of the eastern highlands of Irian Jaya. Herdt (1991) had become unsatisfied with "ritualized" and "institutionalized" to account for homoeroticism, and emphasized homosexuality outside initiation rites more than in earlier work.[12]

One problem with the notion of "ritualized homosexuality"—a problem of which Herdt was keenly aware even when he was using that label—is the tendency in anthropological discourse to drain any erotic aspects from what tends to be treated as some entirely external-to-the-self duty. As I heard him say nearly two decades ago, ritual requirements do not suffice to produce erections. The inseminator has to be excited; wishing to be dutiful does not suffice.

Herdt has repeatedly stressed that "cultural conventions cannot be studied apart from the individuals who experience them" (1987b:xiii, 1999). Herdt and Stoller (1990; also see Herdt 1992b, 1999) detailed departure from the ideal type—both the folk ideal type of adult males and the formalizations of such norms by anthropologists—with a case study of Kawulto, someone reluctant to "graduate" from the homosexuality appropriate to adolescents to the heterosexuality appropriate to adults.[13] Nevertheless, the man does not cross the line that would constitute perversion in the Sambian view. In the Sambian belief system, someone who can produce semen has no reason to receive it from others, but marriage does not preclude inseminating prepubescent boys who still need it. Kawulto readily achieved the first "graduation" from insertee to insertor. The later shift from inseminating boys to marriage is generally gradual, but for this individual it was unusually difficult.

Bakhtin's (1986:154) aphorism: "Human life is always shaped and this shaping is always ritualistic"—hardly anywhere more so than in initiations.

12. Along with "ritualized," he abandoned "homosexuality," while continuing to eschew "pederasty" as a comparative category.

13. Herdt (1990a:225) rated Sambians on a Kinsey-like scale. He coded adults as 1s (other sex only) for sexual behavior, and Sambian adolescents as 7s (same sex only), but also suggested aspects other than sexual behavior (emotional preferences, social preference, and self-identification) that would be rated 6 to 7. For sexual fantasies and sexual attraction, he rated Sambian adolescents 6 and Sambian adults 2. These numbers refer to the norms, the modal personality.

In an ethnography published after Herdt's (1984) comparative analysis, Knauft (1985:32) noted that among the Gebusi in the foothills of
the Great Papuan Plateau, near Herdt's Sambia, "homosexual partners
should be unrelated or only distantly related to each other. Thus, for example, male affines and matrikin are barred from pursuing sexual relations with each other." Not being part of a ceremonial complex, homosexual trysts there are "matters of personal excitement and hyperbolic
joking." Knauft (1987:172–3) further emphasized that where homosexuality does not have a part in the ritual manufacture of Gebusi men,
"rather than being based on subordination or domination, these [age differentiated homosexual] relations tend to be coquettishly initiated by
the young adolescents themselves. The ideological reason for insemination is to 'grow' the boys into men, but homosexuality appears for all
practical intents and purposes to be grounded in personal affection
rather than obligation."

Denying that jealousy arises ("such liaisons shifting easily among
adolescents and young men"), Knauft (1985:32–33) represented homosexuality as enhancing male solidarity. Although not a "ritual secret" as
among the Sambia, "serious discussion of these relations is avoided, particularly in public or if women are present." He saw homosexual experiences as an alternate base (to kinship) of solidarity: "All men in the
settlement have a strong sense of relaxed friendship and communal
camaraderie. Their network of past or present homosexual relations
reflects [produces?] this spirit of diffuse affections, encompassing men
who cannot trace specific kinship ties to one another" (32).

Knauft (1985:266, 299) distinguished ubiquitous homosexual joking (the province of men) from homosexual behavior (the province of
youths), although treating joking as also enhancing male camaraderie.
Knauft (1986:268) discussed a pair of young men in their mid-twenties
maintaining an "unsanctioned," apparently exclusive and sexually reciprocal relationship beyond the age at which they should have married
women.

Like Knauft, Ernst (1991:6–7) stressed the mutuality of desire among
the Onabasulu, where initiation rites ceased in 1964, but the belief in the
necessity of inseminating boys if they are to grow continued: "Homosexual partners among the Onabasulu court each other. The young man
will act coquettishly and the older man will also flirt. They will exchange
small gifts such as woven leg bands, seek each other's company and engage in much casual body contact as preliminary to the full development
of the relationship. Thus, the relationships are entered into in the way
that most men would like to enter into marriage relationships."

Incest taboos and lineage preferences, like those discussed above, in Australia and other Melanesian cultures also typified the Onabasulu:

> The same regulatory rules which apply to heterosexual marriages apply to the homosexual relationships. This is interesting in that the homosexual relationships are not spoken of as marriages explicitly . . . There is no **explicit** injunction to inseminate wife's brother as is found among the Etoro (Kelly 1976:52, n.6). . . . Affinity is a factor, however. A young man very likely will be from a lineage into which the older man has married. Also it may help chances of achieving a desired marriage to a second wife if a prior homosexual relationship is established with her "actual" or close patrilateral classificatory brother. . . . In many cases of homosexual activity, a special and long term relationship develops between an older man and a youth. . . . The relationship may last until the youth's marriage, when he will inseminate someone else. (6)

Although the sexual relationship "usually" ends by the time the younger male marries, "the friendships that are established in the relationship are usually permanent, even when not formalized in another context, e.g., by the two being brothers in law" (7).[14]

Melanesian examples contradict the American folk view that once a youth is involved in homosexuality ("corrupted"), he can have no interest in heterosexual relations.[15] As Herdt (1984:39) explained, Melanesian homosexuality is masculinizing for both participants: "The boy believes that this act will make him grow and strengthen. He is demonstrating his desire to be masculine, to act in accord with ritual ways, to be unfeminine. On the other hand, his counterpart, the postpubescent inseminator, demonstrates his superordinate maleness [and recently achieved sexual maturity] by the homosexual act of masculinizing the boy" (cf. Hage 1981). Moreover, both (along with their elders) participate in a cult of masculinity, affirming its superiority to femininity. Initiation helps both inseminators and inseminated to achieve and celebrate warrior masculinity.[16]

14. I cannot take Schneebaum's 1987 rapturous account of his homosexual experiences and observations of widespread homoeroticism among a lowland Melanesian people as credible without independent verification, given the invalidity of his earlier writings about a sojourn in the upper Amazon (see Murray 1995a:274–77).

15. One need not look so far away as Melanesia to learn that: see Tindall (1978), Rind et al. (1998).

16. And to assert independence from women, who not only produce babies but raise staple crops (sweet potatoes and taro). Even Melanesian societies without homosexuality

Pederasty in Ancient Greece

Sir Kenneth Dover (1978) presented the ancient Greeks as a proto-typical case of an age-defined social organization of homosexuality. In a military culture based on permanent warfare, in which masculinity was highly valued and women were derogated and secluded, there was nothing effeminate about either partner. Love between males was idealized, particularly that in the Theban Band and that between Patroklos and Akhilles in Homer's *Iliad*.[17] Throughout the Greek world, the ideal pair was a mature lover (*erastes*) and a beardless adolescent beloved (*eromenos*) in a pedagogical relationship that included seminal emission by the elder partner.

Boys were loved by at least elite males throughout the Greek-speaking world. Percy (1996) has provided a survey of the extant records, region by region. Before discussing the sexual pleasure of the *eromenos* in fifth-century B.C. Athens (the usual basis for general assertions about "ancient Greece," because it is the polis about which surviving ancient records are most extensive), I shall discuss three sites in ancient Greece with more martial organizations of boy-love: Crete, Sparta, and Thebes.

Cretan Pederasty

The ancient Greeks variously credited Zeus, Poseidon, Apollo, Orpheus, King Minos, and King Laius as the first boy lover.[18] Percy (1996: 61) listed various ancient accounts that treat Crete as the first site of the

in initiation rites seem (to have been) preoccupied with minimizing female importance in the production and (even more) in the (subsequent) growing of boys. There is a profusion of Melanesian myths about non-uterine origins of new lives.

17. See Plutarch, *Pelopidas:* 18, Crompton 1994, Dover 1988:90–98, Halperin 1990: 76–87. Their sexuality (or even relative age) is not explicit in Homer, but the intense love relationship between Patroklos and Akhilles was understood as sexual at least by Athenians in classical times (notably Aiskhilos (Aeschylus) in *Myrmidons,* and Sophokles in *Akhilleōs erastai* (The Lovers of Akhilles), both lost plays. The classical Greek illustrations (see those in King 1991) support Pausanias's contention (in Plato, *Symposium* 180a) that Akhilles was the *eromenos.* Only long after it stopped being a criterial feature did he begin to be represented as bearded.

18. See Sergent 1986:262–65. Orpheus turned to boys after his descent to Hades and failure to bring Eurydice back with him. See Dynes 1987. Laius attempted to avoid paternity to avoid the prophecy that a son would slay him. While on a visit to King Pelops's, court Laius kidnapped and raped Pelops's beautiful young son Chrysippus. In some versions it was Pelops's curse that Laius's son (Oedipus) would slay him, in which case forswearing sex with females **followed** the passion for Chrysippus; the passion did not arise as a result of deprivation.

institutionalization of pederasty and a number of legendary couplings from Crete.[19] In his *Politics* (1272a) Aristotle attributed a conscious purpose—holding down the birthrate—to "the Cretan lawgiver."

Cretan male children were abducted,[20] not courted like (later) Athenian boys:

> The lover tells the friends of the boy three or four days beforehand that he is going to make the abduction; but for the friends to conceal the boy, or not to let him go forth by the appointed road, is indeed a most disgraceful thing, a confession, as it were, that the boy is unworthy to obtain such a lover; and when they meet, if the abductor is the boy's equal or superior in rank or other respects, the friends pursue him and lay hold of him, though only in a very gentle way, thus satisfying the custom; and after that they cheerfully turn the boy over to him to lead away; if however, the abductor is unworthy, they take the boy away from him. The pursuit does not end until the boy is taken to the Andreium to which his abductor belongs. They regard as a worthy object of love, not the boy who is exceptionally handsome, but the boy who is exceptionally manly and decorous. After giving the boy presents, the abductor takes him away to any place in the country he wishes; and those who were present at the abduction follow after them, and after feasting and hunting with them for two months (for it is not permitted to detain the boy for a longer time), they return to the city. . . . It is disgraceful for those who are handsome in appearance or descendants of illustrious ancestors to fail to obtain lovers, the presumption being that their character is responsible for such a fate. But the *parastrathentes* [comrades, in practice, shield-bearers] (for thus they call those who have been abducted) receive honours; for in both the dances and the races they have the position of highest honour, and are allowed to dress in better clothes than the rest, that is, in the habit given them by their lovers; and not then only, but even after they have grown to manhood, they wear a distinctive dress, a stole given by the lover, which is intended to make known the fact that each wearer has become *kleinos*, ["renowned"], for they call the loved one *kleinos* and the lover *philetor*. (Strabo, *Geography* 10.21, 4)

19. The summary of Ephorus's lost history in Strabo's *Geography* (10.4, 17) is the strongest evidence, followed by the reference to an assertion by Timaeus of Taormina quoted by Athenaeus (*Deipnosophists* 23.602f), and pseudo-Plato (*Minos* 318c–d).

20. The Athenian in Plato's *Laws* (636) says that the Cretans concocted the story of Zeus abducting Ganymede to match their practices.

This passage is the most detailed account of Cretan institutionalized pederasty. It bears stressing that it is the friends of the boy to be "abducted," not his family, who were forewarned and who decided whether the match was suitable. It seems obvious that not all boys were carried off like this. Some were honored (became *kleinos*); others were not. The assertion that the adult male was attracted to virtue rather than beautiful appearance runs through all the ancient idealizations (most famously Plato's *Phaedrus* and *Symposium*) of loving boys.

Male children (*apodromoi*) became youths (*ebioi*) at age twelve. They belonged to a "herd" (*agele*), probably living together in barracks. At some time during their twenties, they became adults (*dromeis*)[21] Neither marriage nor the later moving in with the wife marked off additional named age grades. Aristotle suggested that Cretan lawgivers segregated the sexes (at least until the birth of a first child) and approved pederasty as ways to hold down the birthrate (*Politics* 2).

The removal of the young boy from his natal family for a period of hunting and sleeping with an older man has struck some European classicists (most notably Bernard Sergent) as an instance of a "primitive" people's initiation that must have derived from proto-Indo-European rites. Scholars writing in English have noted the lack of traces of such rites in the earlier (Homeric) Greek texts and the anomaly of what appears to be a path of diffusion from Crete, while the parts of the Greek-speaking world closest to the putative Indo-European pathway (i.e., the northern reaches) seem to have lacked any institutionalization of pederasty. Moreover, Dover (1988) suggested that some of the apparent similarities between the accounts of ancient Greek initiation and recent Melanesian initiation have resulted from filling in the blanks of the Greek records with extrapolations from Melanesian ethnographies.

There are ancient claims that Cretans carried parts of their pederastic customs to Sparta and Athens (by Thaletas and Epimenides, respectively; each was called upon to rid the polis of plague). Homosociality, not least in athletic contests, was already common. I find it hard to believe that same-sex banqueting (symposia), athletic competition, or male-male sexual attraction was constructed by one Cretan lawgiver or exported to other Greek city-states by one Cretan and institutionalized by a single lawgiver in other places (such as Solon in Athens). Soldiers

---

21. This label derives from *dromos*, a running track. It is a puzzling label for an age grade, in that aristocrats began exercising (nude) there at an earlier age. The vagueness of surviving accounts has led to various interpretations of the boundaries of the age grades (see Percy 1996:64, 67, 202n. 22), though there is agreement about their order.

(especially on campaigns) generally eat and sleep together. What strikes me as the momentous social change from Homeric to classical Greece is segregation by sex (particularly, all-male messes that included the men who had sired children and moved out of all-male barracks in which males ranging in age from twelve to their late twenties lived). While Crete was intensely masculinist, the Spartan state went further: to permanent military mobilization.

Spartan Pederasty

At the height of its power between the seventh and fourth centuries B.C., Sparta was an extremely secretive, xenophobic, hypermilitaristic state. As Cartledge (1981a:24) noted, "Even in the seventh century B.C. the Spartans were far from being a Naturvölk or 'primitive' people; and Sparta was not technically a 'small-scale' or 'pre-state' society."[22] What was written (mostly later) about Spartan pederasty was not written by participants or even by direct observers. The Spartan state was idealized by Xenophon (and later by Plutarch) and severely criticized by Aristotle in the second book of his *Politics*,[23] while Spartans' predilection for anal intercourse was regularly smirked at in Attic comedy.[24]

Xenophon (*Lakedaimoniōn Politeia*) claimed that originally (i.e., as instituted by the semi-legendary regent Lykourgos) Spartan *paidikoi erotes* (boy-love) was chaste companionship and mentoring (2), though Spartans of Xenophon's day no longer obeyed Lykourgos's strictures (14).[25]

22. Moreover, "We do not know whether the ancestors of the Classical Spartans had anything approaching an initiatory-cum-educational cycle of age-sets and rites de passage when they first settled permanently in the south-east Peloponnese, probably in the tenth century B.C." (Cartledge 1981a:25).

23. Aristotle did not suggest that pederasty was part of anti-natalist policy in Sparta, as he did in reference to Crete. Sparta had a very pro-natalist policy, especially in its ready acceptance of what elsewhere would be considered "extramarital sex."

24. Henderson (1975:218n. 37) lists instances. Athenians derided Spartan men as being dominated by their wives and Spartan women as shockingly extravagant and licentious (e.g., Aristotle, *Politics* 2.9.6–7). This seems mostly ethnic antagonism (with a considerable admixture if gynophobia). Aristotle added analysis of the unanticipated consequences of specific Spartan arrangements of commensalism, inheritance, and taxation, but did not criticize Spartan educational institutions. Indeed, he suggested (2.9.7) that open approval of same-sex eros (as exemplified by the Celts) was a way that a military state could avoid what he considered the horrors of domination by wives.

25. Percy (1996:75) plausibly suggested that Plutarch's "biography," which was written many centuries after Percy thinks the "tradition" of Spartan pedagogy was invented, "described conditions which probably took their final form just after the Second Messenian War [615 B.C. in his dating] and may actually have reflected what were then bold new

Drawing on Xenophon and sources lost since the first century A.D., in his "biography" (more a hagiography) of Lykourgos (16–18), Plutarch included the most detailed surviving account of raising Spartan boys. Plutarch rhapsodized about the training of Spartan youth in frugality, physical toughness, and obedience to their elders.

Sparta (/Lykourgos) viewed children as belonging to the state, not to their parents. The breeding of soldiers and mothers of soldiers needed to be superintended at least as closely as that of dogs and horses. Once born, the spawn of eugenic mating were inspected. Puny or misshapen infants were culled and discarded. Those permitted to grow up were not swaddled:

> The children grew up free and unconstrained in limb and form. . . . [After their seventh birthday] they were enrolled in companies, where they all lived under the same order and discipline, doing their exercises and playing together. . . . The chief care was to make them good subjects, and to teach them to endure pain and conquer in battle. To this end, as they grew in years, their discipline was proportionately increased; their heads were close-clipped, they were accustomed to go barefoot, and for the most part to play naked.
>
> After they were twelve years old, they were no longer allowed to wear any undergarments, they had one coat to serve them a year. . . . They lodged together in little bands upon beds made of the rushes which grew by the banks of the river Eurotas. (Plutarch, *Lyk.* §16)

Herodotus and Strabo recorded the names for age grades of zero to seven, eight to eleven, twelve to thirteen, fourteen to seventeen, eighteen to nineteen, twenty to twenty-nine, thirty to fifty-nine, and sixty plus.[26] By the time boys had reached the age of twelve, Plutarch contin-

---

innovations that only purported to restore the putative Lycurgan system." A Cretan musician named Thaletas supposedly "imported the 'Dance of the Naked Youths' from Crete to quell a plague that followed the end of the Second Messenian War" (79). Percy sees the cult of nudity as central to pedagogic pederasty, and reducing the birthrate of citizens as the conscious motive of leaders instituting it (not just as its unconscious social function). Lowering birthrates seems to me an unlikely concern during—or immediately after—a plague.

26. The two texts are reproduced in Tazelaar (1967:132) and discussed in detail by him. Cartledge (1981a:27) suggested fourteen as the typical age for the onset of puberty in ancient Sparta. Active military service lasted from the young man's twentieth through his thirtieth year, though he remained liable for military service until his sixtieth birthday (with those aged eighteen to nineteen constituting the main reserve force). The pronatalist policies of exempting the father of three sons from military services and the father

ued, "there was not any of the more hopeful boys who had not a lover to bear him company. The old men, too, had an eye upon them, coming often to the grounds to hear and see them contend either in wit or strength with one another, and this as seriously and with as much concern as if they were their fathers, their tutors, or their magistrates" (§17, 63). In Plutarch's idealized Sparta, boys'

> lovers and favourers had a share in the young boy's honour or disgrace; and there goes a story that one of them was fined by the magistrate, because the lad whom he loved cried out effeminately as he was fighting. And though this sort of love was so approved among them that the most virtuous matrons would make professions of it to young girls, yet rivalry did not exist, and if several men's fancies met in one person, it was rather the beginning of an intimate friendship, whilst they all jointly conspired to render the object of their affection as accomplished as possible. (§18, 64)

When it came time to marry and to sire children (around age twenty-five), males continued to sleep, as usual, with their male age mates, slipping into their wives' bedchamber only long enough to perform their conjugal duty in the dark. "In this manner they lived a long time, insomuch that they sometimes had children by their wives before ever they saw their faces by daylight" (§15, 61). I find it telling about cultural expectations of desire that "she who superintended the wedding comes and clips the hair of the bride close round her head, dresses her up in man's clothes, and leaves her upon a mattress in the dark" (§15, 60). As on Crete, single-sex commensalism (with fifteen or so men in messes, called *pheditia*) continued even for adult males over the age of thirty who slept with their wives.

  According to Plutarch, any man who refused to do his reproductive duty to the state was cut off from access to the young: "Those who continued bachelors were in a degree disenfranchised by law; for they were excluded from the sight of those public processions in which the young men and maidens danced naked, and, in winter-time, the officers compelled them to march naked themselves round the marketplace, singing as they went a certain song to their disgrace, and that they justly suffered this punishment for disobeying the laws" (§14, 60). Although Plutarch may have retrojected later, Roman conceptions of nudity as "disgraceful," this passage is not at all conducive to the view that pederasty was

---

of four from any taxation led to excessive fragmentation of property that weakened Sparta, according to Aristotle (*Politics* 2.9.18–19).

part of an anti-natalist policy in Sparta. Exclusive pederasty was negatively sanctioned, but pederasty was expected. Lykourgos's social engi-
neering of interchangeable human products allegedly also extended to
punishing any fit (*kaloskathos*) Spartan male who failed to be an *erastes*
to some boy of similarly fine character (*kalos pephukotes*), according to
Aelian's *Varia Historia* (3.10, 12), written somewhat later than Plutarch's
Lives.

Cartledge points out that although the *paidika* was prototypically below the age of military service, Plutarch mentioned that males under the
age of thirty "absolutely never went to market, but had the transactions
necessary for the management of their households carried out for them
by their kinsmen and erastai" (*Lyk.* 25). Whether or not he kept the same
erastes he'd had since his early teens, "a Spartan, in other words, might
still be an *eromenos* after becoming a fully adult warrior and member of
a common mess at the age of twenty, when he would grow his hair long
and a beard" (1981:22). Even as adults, former male couples seem to
have remained both physically and emotionally close.[27]

There is no evidence that pairs of lovers went into battle together like
the Theban Band (see the next section of this chapter). Cartledge (1981)
portrayed Spartan pederasty as a secular institution, though noting that
"the second-century B.C. Sosikrates (*Fragmenta Historicorum Graecorum*
416F7) reports that the Spartans sacrificed to Eros before battle in the
belief that victory and safe return depended on *philia* (mutual affection)
in the ranks" (34n. 59; also Athenaeus, *Deipnosophistae* 13.561f).

Dover (1978:194) cautions about inferring about what Spartans
"must have done" based on hostile Athenian accounts or of idealizations
such as those of Xenophon and Plutarch. Based on what we know about
those authors erasing (or spiritualizing) better-documented instances of
same-sex sexual relationships, it seems to me reasonable to suppose they
desexualized their portrait of Sparta and that Lykourgos (and/or those
claiming to renew his arrangements) was less than completely successful in banishing male jealousy, competitiveness, and sexual contact.
Even if—as seems exceedingly unlikely—there was not physical sexual
contact between Spartan *erastes* and *eromenos* and the adult was attracted
only to the (naked) boy's character, that there was an erotic bond between them is clear. "Inspiring" (*eispnein*) a receptor of inspiration (*aítas*)
may not be a metaphor, euphemism, or rationalization for insemination

---

27. Though, unlike the Theban Band, apparently not always in battle ranks (Plato,
Symposium 8.35).

and for receiving physical seeds, but Athenians and subsequent scholars have found the metaphor highly suggestive.

The Sacred Band of Thebes

The *hieros lochos,* the Theban regiment of 150 pairs of lovers who lived, fought, died, and were buried together, are indisputably historical. A large marble lion still marks their grave,[28] which is, in effect, the grave of Greek liberty, for they were the bulwark against the Macedonian conquest of Greece led by Philip II (382–36 B.C.). In the decades before their final battle at Chaeronea (a village twenty miles west of Thebes) in 338 they had been widely hailed as the liberators of (northern) Greece from the Spartan hegemony that followed Sparta's defeat of Athens in the Peloponnesian War in 404.

Boeotians (Thebes was the capital of Boeotia) had a reputation for enduring pairings in which men and boys lived in publicly valued marriages.[29] Plutarch, who was born and lived in Chaeronea, rejected the legendary origin of Theban pederasty in Laius's abduction of Chrysippus, and attributed it to conscious policy by wise Theban lawgivers seeking to channel the natural ferocity of adolescent males to socially useful purposes. While Gorgidas distributed the Sacred Band throughout the front ranks of the Theban infantry, Pelopidas, a subsequent commander of the Sacred Band, thought it better to harness the troop together as a vanguard. Plutarch explained: "For as horses ran brisker in a chariot than singly . . . because being matched one against the other emulation kindles and inflames their courage; thus he thought brave men, provoking one another to noble actions, would prove more serviceable and most resolute where all were united together" (*Pelopidas* 19.2).

From Plutarch's biography of Pelopidas, the primary ancient source on the Sacred Band, it is not clear that the rebels who seized the citadel at Thebes were members of the Sacred Band, or even that the patrol led by Pelopidas that defeated more numerous Spartan troops was the

28. It was restored in 1902 (see the photographs in Crompton 1994:28). Cemented to the statue's base were spears and shields, some with still-legible names of male couples who fought (and fell) together. Graves with remains of 254 men in seven rows have been excavated (see plate 208 in Green 1973).

29. Xenophon contrasted this with the transitory couplings at Elis (*Sparta* 2.12). Pausanias asserted in Plato's *Symposium* that "in Elis and Boeotia, and where people are not clever speakers, it is simply laid down that it is right to gratify lovers, and no one young or old would call it wrong, as, I think, they wish not to take the trouble to convince the young" (182c).

Sacred Band (a corps Plutarch introduced midway through the biography). Pelopidas was supported in resisting the Spartans by Epaminondas, who, though more interested in learning than in bodily exercise, was sufficiently brave and able a soldier to have saved the life of his fallen comrade Pelopidas in an earlier battle (when the Thebans were allied with the Spartans against the Arcadians in 376). There is no indication that they were lovers, but they were close friends and political allies (unusually unrivalrous ones with no recorded fallings out). Between Epaminondas's strategy and Pelopidas's and the Sacred Band's valor, Sparta was defeated in the battle at Leuctra in 371. As co-commanders, they liberated Elis, Argos, and all Arcadia and invaded Laconia (the Spartan homeland). After Pelopidas's death in typically rash combat in 364, Epaminondas engineered another rout of the Spartans at Mantinea in 362. Both he and his (second) *eromenos* Caphisodorus died in that battle and were buried together.

Ironically, Philip of Macedon used what he had learned as a hostage prince in Thebes for three years (starting in 367 when he was fifteen years old) to defeat Thebes, where he was said to have been the *eromenos* of Pelopidas.[30]

It was Pammenes's "pleasant saying" that Homer's Nestor's organization of the Greek army by tribe "so that kinsmen might kinsmen aid" was inferior to an army of lovers and their beloveds,

> for men of the same tribe or family little value one another when dangers press; but a band cemented by friendship grounded upon love is never broken, and is invincible; since lovers, ashamed to be base in sight of their beloved, and the beloved before their lovers, willingly rush into danger for the relief of one another. . . . According to tradition, Iolaüs, who assisted Hercules in his labours and fought at his side, was beloved of him and Aristotle observed that, even in his time, lovers plighted their faith at Iolaüs's tomb [in Thebes]. It is likely, therefore, that this band was called sacred on this account; as Plato calls a lover a divine friend. (*Pelopidas* 18.2–4, trans. Clough)

Philip's adaptation of Theban methods showed that the Sacred Band was not invincible, but it perished unbroken. At Chaeronea all of its members stood their ground and perished together in 338.[31] Philip

---

30. Dio Chrysostom (49.5). This seems too schematic a connection to have existed. According to Plutarch (*Pelopidas* 26.5), Philip lived in the house of Pammenes, the general who assumed command of the Theban army after Epaminondas's death.

31. According to Plutarch, when the triumphant Philip came upon their corpses (some

mopped up the rest of Greece, and his son Alexander (356–23), after succeeding him in 336, conquered the known world.[32]

The Mamlūks of Medieval Egypt

The mamlūk military elite, purchased anew in each generation from the steppes of Eurasia, ruled Egypt and Syria from 1249,[33] when they defeated an invading army of Crusaders led by Saint Louis, until they were defeated by the mass army of Napoleon in 1799. Their unusual social system suggests an intercorrelation among absence of inherited wealth and position, relatively high status of women, and widespread pederasty, although amid the details of battles and palace intrigues in histories of the period, there is practically nothing about the everyday life of even the rulers.

Neither the wealth nor the status of mamlūks was heritable. Upon the death of a warrior, his property, house, goods, wife, and slaves were sold for the benefit of the Treasury.[34] Thus, the common motivation in most social systems of passing on wealth and position to one's children was blocked for the mamlūks. Their children (*awlād al-nās:* children of [the best] people) bore Muslim names distinct from the Turkic names of the mamlūks, and spoke Arabic rather than the Turkic languages of their fathers. The children, along with all others who were born and raised

---

those of men whom he had known three decades earlier), he shed tears and said, "Perish miserably any man who suspects that these men either did or suffered anything that was base" (*Pelopidas* 18.5).

32. Seeing himself as a new Akhilles, Alexander cast his closest comrade, Hephaistion, as Patroklos. Like Akhilles, Alexander was unhinged by the death of his Patroklos and did not long outlive him. As with the Homeric pair, the relative ages and which of the Macedonian pair was the erastes and which the eromenos are uncertain.

33. Ayalon (1980:325) dated the beginnings of the institution much earlier: "As early as the first half of the ninth century A.D., in the reign of Caliph al-Mu'tasim, the first large-scale recruitment of Mamlūks in the service of the 'Abbāsids takes place." The word mamlūk means "owned thing," but "its practical meaning is 'white slave'" (Ayalon 1980:324).

34. By the eighteenth century, mamlūks could transfer property to their wives, who were not sold as slaves (Hatem 1986:260), and to their sons (Ayalon 1960:158, 288–90). Whether mamlūks remained slaves after successfully completing their training, when they took on responsibilities as warriors and tax collectors, is a controversial question. Volney (1787) consistently wrote of mamlūks as freedmen (*affranchis*). Irwin (1986:9) stated that manumission was the rule in Egypt; Papoulia (1963:4–10) extended this to throughout the Ottoman world; Ménage (1966), Repp (1968), and Glubb (1973) argued that mamlūks remained slaves. Ayalon (1987b:206, 1988a:327, 1988b:248, and elsewhere) considered that most, but not all, were manumitted. Because mamlūks' children were raised Muslim, they could not be sold as slaves (Ayalon 1986:4–6, 1988a:329).

Muslim, were proscribed from becoming soldiers, riding horses, or even from dressing like their mamlūk fathers; the elite of the next generation was always recruited afresh from Eurasia and removed far from natal families (Poliak 1939, Mayer 1952). "Like all slaves, they were genealogical isolates. . . . Deracination was the very essence" of the institution, and the caliphs who imported mamlūks believed that "natally alienated persons, having no basis of existence in their new societies except their masters, were likely to be totally loyal to him" (Patterson 1982:309). However, the hopes for loyalty were structurally unsound: "Behind the trust and loyalty between the ruler and these slaves lies a complex, adversary relationship; the more he trusts them, the more power they acquire; the greater their independent power grows, the less loyal they become" (Pipes 1978:35; quoted by Patterson 1982:314). Nonetheless, status hang-ups (about "honor") and the degree of family aggrandizing expected from the local populace made aliens a preferable source of servants and officials (Ayalon 1975a:49; Patterson 1982:310–11). At least the mamlūk was

> cut off from all his former ties: his environment, his religion, his race, his tribe, and—what is particularly important—his family. . . . He got a new family instead of that which he had lost. This was a family which was not based on blood relations, but on the relations of slavery and patronship. The patron who had bought the Mamlūk became his father; and his comrades in servitude in the school, whom he—in most cases—never knew before, and who quite often belonged to other races and other tribes, became his [family]. (Ayalon 1980:327–28)

Separation from relatives removed temptations of nepotism and dangers of divided loyalties. Transplantation decisively removed the mamlūks far from their natal families, both geographically and culturally (especially in religion).[35] The rigorously meritocratic mamlūk system was also designed to cut them off from their descendants (Ayalon 1980:328).

35. Such removal occurred less frequently during the rule of Circassian mamlūk sultans, i.e., after 1382. "The immigration of relatives reached particularly large proportions from the middle of the fifteenth century onward" (Ayalon 1949:144) and training became more perfunctory: "The period of study was considerably curtailed as compared with the early Mamlūk period, and a large proportion of adults—relatives of the Circassian amīrs—were admitted to the Mamlūk corps without passing through the school at all. This practice was completely at variance with the principles underlying the system of military servitude" (145). Without significant external enemies, the mamlūks of the Circassian era relaxed the rigors of the whole system, not just of training but of impersonally meritocratic standards for promotion. The Kepchak mamlūk era before that was much closer to the

Eunuchs (*khasi*), who were also taken from outside Dar al-Islam, were more decisively blocked from accumulating wealth or honor for their children. Even more than mamlūks, eunuchs in Islamic societies are the ideal type of a one-generation nobility (Ayalon 1980:338, 1979b). In buying boys from the peripheries—both those who had been or were slated for castration and those who were going to be trained to be cavalrymen—amirs and sultans were ensuring that the natal family of the eunuch and mamlūks would not be around to accumulate wealth and exercise influence. Whatever goods (including land) the eunuchs and mamlūks accumulated could not be passed on to their sons (the eunuchs not having any). Castration was not viewed as conducive to military prowess, so it was unsuitable (indeed, probably, unthinkable) for those chosen for military service. Among the many duties of eunuchs "was the supervision and education of the young Mamlūks in the military schools. . . . They formed a barrier between those youngsters and adult Mamlūks," sometimes being penetrated in their stead—at least that is how I interpret the footnote to this passage: "The eunuchs themselves were a constant object of pederasty" (Ayalon 1979a:72n. 9).

The sultan's mamlūk novices (*kuttābī*) were not herded together into a single one of the twelve barracks in the Cairo citadel, although each barracks seems to have had a special section for novices. Novices of lesser officials also were housed with the mamlūk garrison. Developing an identification with a unit (*bayū;* house) seems to have been judged more important than protecting the cadets from penetration by their elders.

Within the units, nonetheless, there existed some identification with and special feeling for one's cohort (*khushdāshiyya*) as well as for one's patron (*ustādh*). Kinship idioms were used: the patron was called "father" (*wālid*), the mamlūk "sons" (*awlād*) called each other "brothers" (*ikhwan*), sometimes distinguishing "older brothers" (*aghawat;* singular *agha*) from "younger brothers" (*iniyyāt;* singular *ini*) and *tāʿifa* was used in the sense of "family" (as well as of "faction") for mamlūks. Even other mamlūks were regarded as outsiders (*gharīb*) who could not become part of such families (Ayalon 1990:318, 1980:328, 1987b:207).

---

ideal type of genealogical isolates (as was the Ottoman system through the reign of Suleiman the Magnificent, as discussed in the next section). Mamlūk intrigues increased after the incorporation of Egypt as a province of the Ottoman Empire. After 1671, local mamlūk houses (*buyūt;* singular *bayt,* which included mamlūk sons) usurped the power and retained the revenues of the ostensible Ottoman "governors," who, de facto, were more ambassadors to the mamlūks than their governors (see Ayalon 1960, 1987a; P. Holt 1961).

Recurrently, attempts were made to pass on the sultanate itself through primogeniture, but time after time the throne was usurped by the strongest amīr. See Glubb (1973), Ayalon (1987b:210), and P. Holt (1990:323–24). Lesser mamlūks more successfully attempted to guarantee a place for descendants by endowing a pious foundation (*waqf*, generally mosques, libraries, or schools) to be administered by heirs, who could not directly receive any patrimony.

The mamlūks were a caste apart with no motivation to mix with the Arab populations they were bought to protect. Their appearance was distinctive. In addition to their light skin, one 1792 visitor observed that "the Mamlūks suffer not the beard to grow till they be emancipated, and hold some office, as Cashef, &c" and described their dress (W. Browne 1806:54–55).

For the most part, the mamlūks attained puberty in their homelands. This was the point at which steppe fathers gave their sons a bow and arrows and expelled them to fend for themselves, or sold them (Ayalon 1986:2–4). As Ayalon (1988b:248) noted, large-scale traffic could not have occurred without willing cooperation in the slaves' places of origin, including that of the parents of those sold to become mamlūks. The youth were illiterate, mostly despised the Arab language that they did not encounter until they were adolescents,[36] and continued to speak their native (Turkic) languages. They also lived apart from the existing cities in their own colonies (including the Cairo citadel with its barracks for the Royal Mamlūks, *al-mamālik al-sultāniyya*) and only rarely intermarried with local notables' daughters.[37] Besides being the result of an obvious wish to keep troops from forming social relationships with the governed, residential segregation may have been partly an attempt to preserve expensive investments from other dangers. As Ayalon noted, "The toughness which the Mamlūk acquired in his country of origin helped him very much in carrying out his military tasks. However, it did not make him in any way immune to diseases and epidemics in many of the Muslim lands to which he had been transferred, certainly not in

36. However, "If they have a disposition for learning they are taught the use of letters; and some of them are excellent scribes; but the greater part can neither write nor read, a striking example of which deficiency is observable in Murad Bey himself" (W. Browne 1806:54).

37. Mamlūks' wives and concubines were mostly slaves from the same natal region (i.e., the steppes of southwestern central Asia) and, after the depopulation resulting from extensive removal of the fittest of the Kipchak young (male and female), Georgian (*al-Jurjī*) and Circassian (*al-Jarkasī*).

Egypt and Syria. He was much more vulnerable to them than the local inhabitants. Epidemics would kill off very high proportions of the Mamlūks, especially the newcomers among them" (1980:338–39).[38]

Along with many special prerogatives (notably their own courts of law), the mamlūks were distinguished from the rest of the population by being forbidden divorce. Still more astonishing, their wives received fixed salaries of their own from the state, just as did the warriors themselves. These two customs greatly enhanced the autonomy of women among the mamlūks (Ayalon 1968), although they may, perhaps, also have discouraged some women from marrying.[39]

The mode of homosexuality to which the mamlūks purportedly were "addicted" was pederasty, with the boys recruited from the wilderness and undergoing military training (*furūsīya*), not with boys raised in civilized Egypt (Glubb 1973). Although Ayalon (1956:66) noted that the main function of a corps of eunuchs was "keeping Mamlūk adults away from Mamlūk boys at the military schools," it does not seem to have occurred to any of the military historians who have written about the mamlūks that sexual attraction might have played some part in selecting which boys to buy. At least one British traveler to Mesopotamia (Iraq) early in the nineteenth century remarked that most of the upwards of fifty Georgian and Circassian mamlūk bodyguards of the pasha of Mousul were "extremely handsome, and all of them young and superbly dressed" (Buckingham 1827:21, cf. 167). Similarly, an earlier (pre-Napoleonic) traveler, W. G. Browne, remarked that the mamlūks "are in general distinguished by the grace and beauty of their persons" (1806:54).

38. The most devastating epidemic, the bubonic plague of 1348–49, was followed by severe epidemics at the rate of one every seven years during the last century of the mamlūk sultanate (Ayalon 1946:68); see also W. Browne 1806:76, P. Holt 1990:324. Nonmamlūks (albeit not so large a proportion of the cadet *kuttābiyya*) were also struck down, so less wealth was produced, and the tax revenue needed to purchase replacement mamlūks also diminished.

39. Ca. 1394 in Damascus, Ibn Sasrā wrote of mamlūks spending all their money on drink and prostitutes, even selling their horses and arms, and quoted Ahmad ibn Hanbal's despairing counsel: "If you feel no shame, do as you wish" (1963:212). In general, the "mamlūk birthrate was extremely low" (Ayalon 1960:157). Writing of his observations in Egypt before Napoleon invaded, W. Browne noted that mamlūks "seldom marry till they acquire some office. . . . It is worthy of remark that though the Mamlūks in general be strong and personable men, yet **the few who marry** very seldom have children. As the son even of a Bey is not honoured with any particular consideration, the women perhaps procure abortions. However this be, of eighteen Beys, whose history I particularly knew, only two had any children living [in 1792]" (1806:56, emphasis added).

In addition to the general pederasty with mamlūk cadets, several amirs and sultans showed marked favoritism for some of their courtiers.[40] The most interesting case is that of the young Sultan al-Nāsir Mohammed born Qalāūn, who scandalized his society in 1497–98 by the "unnatural" interest he showed in the [black] Sudanese slaves ('abīd) who bore firearms, and for their leader, Farajallah, in particular. This sultan attempted to raise the status of the modern weapons that only a few years later would be turned on the traditional sword-wielding mamlūk cavalry with devastating results by the Ottomans. This attempt to modernize the technology of warfare at the expense of the traditional skills of archery, horsemanship, and swordsmanship was motivated in part by the malik's taste for the black men whose proficiency with firearms confirmed in mamlūk minds the unworthiness of such weaponry. Mamlūk cavalrymen literally looked down from their horses on foot soldiers and successfully resisted the raising of mass armies of infantrymen. Mamlūks were somewhat more willing to accept artillery, because

> artillery is the province of specialized technicians, whose numbers form only a small part of the fighting force, requiring little change in the structure of the army. The arquebus, on the other hand, is a personal and mass weapon and its introduction affects a large number of troops. Hence its large-scale adoption was bound to involve far-reaching changes in the organisation and methods of warfare. To equip a solider with an arquebus meant taking away his bow, and, what was to the Mamlūk more distasteful, depriving him of his horse, thereby reducing him to the humiliating status of a foot soldier. . . . [whereas] horsemanship and all it stood for were the pivot around which the whole way of life of the Mamlūk upper class revolved and from which it derived its courtly pride and feeling of superiority. (Ayalon 1956:61)[41]

40. Christian boys were also sold by their parents and transported by Christian merchants to Egypt to serve as prostitutes, horrifying William of Adam, among others. See N. Daniel (1975:224) on it being more politic in Christendom in the eleventh and twelfth centuries to criticize the trade in boys than to fault other kinds of trading with the enemy (of the Crusades). Boys raised Christian (and to a lesser extent, those raised Jewish) were taught to be antagonistic to Islam, so nonmonotheists were preferred as mamlūk candidates (Ayalon 1986:4–6). Most of these were transported to Egypt by Frankish vessels, even when the mamlūks were fighting European crusaders (Ayalon 1988b:254).

41. Also see Ayalon (1975b:37–39). In addition to a distaste for firearms, the increasing reluctance of any of the Royal Mamlūks to be garrisoned outside Cairo reduced their effectiveness in securing the borders of the sultanate or in quelling rebellions within it

Homophobic historians (beginning with al-Makrīzī) have faced the dilemma that the sultan who tried to modernize the army—in precisely the way they recognize was necessary for continued military success— was a youth of "unstable character" much given to "debauchery" with black men, and that his "debauchery" was inextricably tied together with his motivation for the modernization that might have maintained mamlūk military superiority. "Less than twenty years before their own overthrow by firearms, nobody except a lightminded youth could seriously envisage the adoption of firearms as the chief weapons of the [Mamlūk] Sultanate," is how Ayalon (1975b:36) put it, perhaps overhastily accepting the horsemen's view of Nāsir as "frivolous" and "foolish."

When the white slaves revolted and slew Farajallah and about fifty other black slaves, the mamlūks told Nāsir, "We disapprove of these acts [of favor for the black firearm users]. If you wish to persist in these tastes, you had better ride by night and go away with your black slaves to far-off places!" (B. Lewis 1971:75–76; Ayalon 1956:69–70) includes two slightly variant accounts). The sultan agreed to desist. Thus, when the mamlūks began the sixteenth century with one of their traditional thirteenth-century cavalry charges against the Ottoman infantry of Selim I, they met their first defeat, scandalized that Muslims would shoot other Muslims. The mamlūks regarded the Ottoman army of Selim I who defeated them as unchivalrous, immoral, and far inferior in the traditional arts of war.[42]

Concerned more with the external Safavid threat from Persia than with internal rebellion, and short of personnel to defend and administer the vast territories he had conquered, Selim largely left mamlūks in charge of Egypt and Syria. Immediately upon his death, the mamlūks in Syria rebelled and were crushed once and for all. The Egyptian mamlūks did not join the Syrian ones, and Selim's son Suleiman continued to use them. The cavalry charge remained the main (only?) mamlūk tactic— whether against Mongols, Ottomans, or the French armies of Saint Louis and Napoleon. The last charge resulted in mamlūks being mowed down by fusillades from Napoleon's army. The 1798 rifles proved even more deadly than the 1517 models that had first revealed the obsolescence of the mamlūk cavalry. The French triumph and ensuing occupation "undermined the basis of Mamlūk legitimacy and the raison d'être for the

(Ayalon 1990:319). Since Royal Mamlūks refused to be stationed in Syria, *halka* regiments (in which the children of mamlūks served) were much more important there (Ayalon 1979b, 1987).

42. See Ayalon (1956:86–97) for a précis of Ibn Zunbul's history of the Ottoman occupation of Egypt, *Fath Misr*.

continued importation of Mamlūk slaves, for Mamlūks had failed to defend Islam against a Christian rival power. More importantly, determined French pursuit of the Mamlūks drained their forces and paved the way for their final liquidation by Muhammed 'Ali who assumed power in 1805" (Hatem 1986:264).

Lest it be supposed that the fall of the mamlūks had anything to do with homosexuality, it should be emphasized that the victors were no less pederastic than the mamlūks (as will be seen in the following section).

The mamlūks exemplify a social system not built on family aggrandizement and patrimony. Without inheritance, with a very slim likelihood of living to a peaceful old age, and with wives paid directly by the state, the usual motivations for building families were lacking.[43] If, as Hocquenghem (1978:136) wrote, "The great fear of homosexuality is that the succession of generations on which civilization is based may stop," the mamlūk case shows that a (highly aestheticized) military tradition can be transmitted from generation to generation without shared blood. Rampant pederasty was no obstacle to the dominance by this warrior elite who, for centuries, guarded Arab civilization against barbarians. With all the ardor of converts, they were fierce (and successful) defenders of Islam against both Christian Crusaders from the northwest and Mongols from the northeast, the very regions from which they derived. Moreover, each new, unrelated generation of recruits to the elite was noted for its appreciation and patronage of the arts. Although they were recruited from their rude surroundings not for their refined tastes but for their horsemanship and prowess with sword and bow, the mamlūks built the mosques, palaces, and tombs that are the glory of Cairo, and "delighted in the delicate refinement which art could afford their home life, were lavish in their endowment of pious foundations, magnificent in their mosques and palaces and fastidious in the smallest details of dress, furniture and court etiquette" (Lane-Poole 1898:97; Wiet 1964, 1966).

In Ayalon's (1980:322–23) summary,

> Mamlūkdom lasted in Islam about 1000 years, although as a decisive power it existed for a considerably shorter period. . . . The acquisition of slaves for the purpose of using them as soldiers is not, indeed, limited to Islam alone; but nowhere outside Muslim civilization was there ever created a military slave institution

---

43. See Ayalon (1987b) on why mamlūks kept other mamlūks from passing on what they accumulated to their sons.

which had been planned so methodically; which had been created for such a grand purpose; which succeeded in accumulating such an immense power, and in registering such astounding achievements; and which enjoyed such a long span of life, as in Islam.

Pages and Janissaries in the Ottoman Empire

Othman/Osman, for whom the dynasty was named, acceded to the throne of a small state around Sögüt in northwestern Anatolia around 1281 and ruled until about 1326.[44] The dynasty was overthrown by "the young Turks" led by Mustapha Kemal (Atatürk), founder and first president of the Turkish Republic, who abolished the caliphate in 1924. In the long durée of the Ottoman Empire, with fast and vast expansion in size at first and later slow contraction, the apogee was the reign of Suleiman the Magnificent between 1520 and 1566. The particular focus of this chapter, the institution of a foreign elite troop without local ties, began devolving almost immediately thereafter. The Ottomans increasingly focused on firearms and on the recruitment of Turkish soldiers as *kulkardasi*, "brothers of the slaves" (Inalcick 1973:48, Parry 1976:122), and increasingly included sons of slaves (Ménage 1966:66). This was a major difference from practices in Egypt and Syria, where during the mamlūk era "every Royal Mamluk, on finishing his early training at military school and becoming a fully trained soldier, legally had the same right to become Sultan as any other Royal Mamluk. . . . the Ottoman Sultan was a free and hereditary ruler" (Ayalon 1956:99). With elite units of archers, not just cavalry like the mamlūks, bordering Europeans who used firearms, the Ottomans incorporated firearms relatively easily in contrast to the mamlūks, who unstintingly resisted such degradingly mass weapons.

In the Ottoman Empire, as in the mamlūk regimes eventually subdued by and incorporated within it, the ruling elite consisted of "slaves" (*kullar;* singular *kul*)[45] who had been born outside *Dar al-Islam* (i.e., in *Dar al-Harb*), acquired mostly at ages of ten to twelve, and then trained to defend and administer the empire. Like the mamlūks, *ajemi-oghlan*

---

44. On the preceding flux in the region, see Vryonis (1971).

45. Papoulia (1963:4–10) has argued that graduation from training schools was a sort of manumission, so that thereafter those who served the sultan were clients (*mawla*) rather than slaves. Ayalon (1956:99) asserted that "the Ottoman slave was never manumitted until his very death," in contrast to mamlūks. On their distinctive legal status, see Mumcu 1963. Ménage (1966:66) discussed the status of a sultan's *kul* being higher than that of other subjects of the Ottoman sultans.

(foreign-born youths) were separated early from parents, homeland, and the faith. The exclusion of those born Muslims, including the sons of the ruling elite, was consciously designed to prevent the concentration of inherited fortunes and the concomitant feudal growth in power of rich families.

Free of family obligations, carefully selected foreign-born slaves were bound only to the sultan (or vizier or bey) who raised them. Originally, boys were captured as spoils of war, or purchased. As the empire grew, beginning on a large-scale basis with sultan Murād II around 1438,[46] a head tax (*devshirme*) of one in forty boys for sultans' military and other uses was imposed on Christian provinces. Reports of frequency of collection vary from once every five years to annually. It seems likely that the collection became more frequent over time between the end of the fourteenth and the beginning of the seventeenth century, or that scheduling it was ad hoc. Before lapsing, *devshirme* was extended from European to Asian provinces during the sixteenth century. Reports of age vary from as low as eight to as high as twenty, though the basis for the calculations was one from every forty of those still living who had been baptized fourteen to eighteen years before.[47]

Boys were selected for their "bodily perfection, muscular strength, and intellectual ability, so far as it could be judged without long testing" (Lybyer 1913:74; relying on Ricaut 1971 [1668]: 11–12, 46; and Postel 1560). The very choicest—"all handsome boys, physically perfect, and of marked intellectual promise" (Lybyer 1913:74)—were taken into the palaces of the sultans as *iç oghlanlari* (pages):

> Upon their arrival in Constantinople the tribute children, who had been collected by the palace gatekeepers, were brought before a board of expert examiners presided over by the chief white eunuch in his capacity as director-in-chief of the system of palace education, a procedure that was applied also to pur-

46. This is the most widely accepted—but still-controversial—dating: see Babinger 1978:6, 85, 438; Cahen 1970; Papoulia 1963; Parry 1976:159. The earliest certain attestation is an outraged (Christian) sermon by Isidore Glabas in 1395 (Vyronis 1956). Vryonis (1964:150) suggested that what is known about the Seljuk slave institution in pre-Ottoman Anatolia indicates "(a) That the Ottoman system was directly inspired by that of the Seljuks of Rum. (b) There is great probability that the levying of Christian children from amongst the subject populations of the Muslim rulers was practiced in Anatolia between the eleventh and thirteenth centuries."

47. Ménage (1960) discusses the difficulties of dating the origins, end, and ages of those subject to *devshirme*.

chased slaves and prisoners of war. By a kind of test which in its shrewdness seems curiously to anticipate the modern intelligence test, and by an examination of physical points similar to those applied at a horse, dog, or cattle show, the youths were separated into two classes. The *sine qua non* of the sultan's service being physical beauty and bodily perfection, the most promising in every respect were set aside for palace service. . . . The remainder, who were distinguished chiefly by reason of their physical strength and dexterity, were assigned to the Janizary corps. The comeliest and cleverest, "those, in whom, besides the accomplishment of the Body, they discover also a noble Genius, fit for a high Education, and such as may render them capable of Serving their Prince, sometime or other," were designated as student pages (*ich-oghlanlar*). The remainder, who were classified as novices or apprentices (*ajemi-oghlanlar*), were put through a stiff course in manual training. . . . From a group set apart for student pages, the cream was for a third time skimmed for the Palace School of the Grand Seraglio. (Barnette Miller 1941:81–82, quoting Baudier 1624:110)

According to Postel (1560:17), when presented before the Sultan, the pages wore silk and cloth of gold and silver thread.[48] As the Hapsburg ambassador to Suleiman the Magnificent between 1554 and 1562, Ogier Busbecq (1968:262) noted that "Turks rejoice greatly when they find an exceptional man, as though they had acquired a precious object, and they spare no labor or effort in cultivating him." Lybyer (1913), in the major "Western" recommendation of the system, did not consider that criteria such as bodily perfection might have an attraction sexual as well as aesthetic or functional in the Ottoman empire, where, he was forced to acknowledge, "the vice which takes its name from Sodom was very prevalent among the Ottomans, especially among those in high positions" (74). He also recognized that intellectual ability could not be so readily assessed as bodily perfections, and noticed that the imperial harem was a parallel institution to the school of pages, writing that "the harem might be considered a training-school of slave wives" (79). Nonetheless, Lybyer (1913:71) pressed a view of the Ottoman empire as entirely meritocratic, even as improving upon Plato's scheme for *The Republic*. A Harvard scholar of the Progressive Era (see Hofstader 1956) was

---

48. Ricaut (1971 [1668]:49), Lybyer's most trusted source, reported that clothing and diet of *iç-oglans* were simple, but there is no contradiction in accepting his reports of quotidian simplicity and Postel's of splendor of couture when in the sultan's presence.

likely to stress meritocracy and not wish to think about homosexual favoritism in a system he was invidiously comparing to the corruption rife
in the United States.[49]

J. Drake (1966), Hidden (1916), Barnette Miller (1941:78–79), and
others have stressed that parents groomed sons for sexual service to the
rulers and, when successful, sold them. Davey (1897:247n) noted that
the Muslim Georgians and, especially, Muslim Kurds sent male slaves
despite the religious ban on enslaving Muslims: "The Georgians and Circassians, whose physical types were especially admired by the Turks,
found the slave trade with Constantinople so profitable that they maintained slave farms to meet the demand. They not only regularly captured
children for the purpose of selling them in the Turkish slave markets, but
even reared their own children with this end in view" (Barnette Miller
1941:78).

Upon the Ottoman conquest of Bosnia and mass conversion to Islam
in 1463, the Bosnians "requested that their children should nevertheless
be eligible for the devshirme" (Ménage 1966:211). Most of the Bosnian
slave boys (called *Potur oghullari*—"boys who are circumcised, but not
Turkish-speaking") appear to have gone into Palace service rather than
through military training. Ayalon (1986:6) explained that "the Ottomans
recruited their slave army mainly from amongst the Christians of their
realm, and in glaring violation of the sharī'a, because of the Islamization
of the south Russian steppe in their neighborhood and because they
wanted to eliminate one of the main drawbacks of the Mamlūk system:
dependence on a source of supply on which they had no control."

Although, besides conscription and purchase, many thousands of
youths (Christian and Muslim) were stolen each year, slaveries do not
necessarily depend on "naked violence."[50] Many of those on the peripheries are eager to move to the imperial metropolises.

From Beauty to Sexuality

Because a sultan could not enjoy "association on terms of intimate
friendship with those who are high officials of state," he was "practically
forced by combination of principles and circumstances to spend his
leisure hours with boys, eunuchs and women" (Lybyer 1913:122).

---

49. Lybyer's praise was continued by Barnette Miller (1941:42), who, however, noted
(based on Angiolello) that Muhammad the Conqueror, the founder of the Palace School
(*Enderun*) scandalized his own son (Bayazid II) by commissioning lascivious pictures.

50. I borrow this locution from Patterson (1982:309), who underestimated the importance of parental consent, indeed initiatives, in supplying mamlūks, janissaries, and
eunuchs.

Moreover, "the visible court and retinue of the monarch was wholly un-graced by the presence of the fair sex; all great ceremonies and caval-cades were participated in by men alone. . . . Before the middle of the [1520–66] reign of Suleiman, no woman resided in the entire vast palace where the sultan spent most of his time" (121).

The fact that the boys, organized in groups of ten, "were watched carefully by eunuchs, both day and night" (Lybyer 1913: 33) "to see or overhear if there be any wanton or lewd behavior or discourse amongst them" (Ricaut 1971 [1668]:27)—another parallel to the harem—indi-cates that homosexuality **among** *iç oghlans* was a concern, whether to promote/ensure bureaucratic rationality, as Greenberg (1988:439) con-tended, or to secure a monopoly for the master (whether he was the sul-tan or one of his pashas). According to the early European observer Paul Ricaut (1971 [1668]:31) pages "studied Persian Novellaries [that] endues them with a kind of Platonick love to each other." Since "the restraint and strictures of Discipline makes them strangers to women; for want of converse with them, they burn in lust one towards another." They were also desired by others:

> This passion is not only among the young men to each other, but persons of eminent degree in the seraglio become involved, watching out for their favorites, courting them with presents and services. . . . They call it a passion very laudable and vir-tuous, and a step to that perfect love of God, whereof mankind is only capable, proceeding by way of love and admiration of his image estamped on the [young, male] creature. This is the colour of virtue they paint over the deformity of their depraved inclinations; but in reality, this love of theirs is nothing but li-bidinous flames each to other, with which they burn so vio-lently, that banishment and death have not been examples sufficient to deter them from demonstrations of such like ad-dresses [to the sultan's pages]. (Ricaut 1971 [1668]:33)[51]

Two Status Hierarchies and Attenuated Bureaucratic Impersonality

Greenberg and Bystryn (1982:518) plausibly argued that "a juvenile male can be dominated by older men in a patriarchal society without incurring a stigma, because the subordination of the young is a 'natural' (and, for any individual, temporary) feature of a patriarchal social struc-ture." To have so served a sultan might not be in itself stigmatizing. How-ever, it is a past that a high-placed Ottoman official was not eager to

---

51. Some of this seems a derogation of Sufi mysticism. For a less extreme—but still skeptical—view of boy-love metaphors in Turkish (and Persian) poetry, see Murray 1997d.

publicize, because it too easily armed the already resentful and subordinated faithful with taunts (similar to those reminding Julius Caesar of his youth under the royal weight of Nicomedes of Bythinia). Being sodomized might have improved one's position within the Ottoman hierarchy, but not one's prestige among the faithful. Exactly because they lacked the honor of those born to Islam, they could be in intimate service (sexual and other kinds) to a sultan (see Patterson 1982:310–11). Generally, they were paid salaries rather than granted land. This was another means to keep them from becoming independent feudal powers (Parry 1976:104).

There are many reports that sodomy was rife in the Ottoman Empire.[52] None that I have encountered, however, suggest that being inseminated increased one's masculinity.[53] Youthful homosexual receptivity clearly did not debar one from the responsibilities and fruits of high office. Although the services of some pages to their masters were exclusively sexual, Ibrāhīm, the constant companion of Suleiman the Magnificent, was raised to the office of *sadr-i azam* (grand vizier) in quite unbureaucratic fashion, enjoyed favor, power, and, apparently, also Suleiman, for decades beyond his adolescent blossom.[54] He was not unique: "Favorite boys grew up to marry their masters' daughters, to take over management of businesses, properties, etc. The Sultan's favorite boys often grew up to be generals, governors, and high court

52. Lybyer (1913:304–22) assessed the reliability of various travelers (also see Inalcik 1973:74–75). The Genoese Jacopo de Promontorio (ca. 1475; quoted by Babinger 1978:450) attributed the low birthrate of native Turks (specifically in Anatolia and Rūmelia) to the "infinite lechery of various slaves and young boys to whom they give themselves." Having more than one son was rare, he wrote.

53. J. Drake (1966:24–25) concluded that "Turkish evidence suggests that the boys loved most tenderly grew into the most virile men, those used most brutally became effeminates," quoting a "classical" Turkish saying: "Fear makes a boy into a woman, love makes him into a man." Even this suspiciously enthusiastic claim does not provide any basis for interpreting boy insemination (in itself) as masculinizing the one inseminated.

54. He was promoted from grand falconer and master of the pages to first officer of the royal bedchamber, governor of a province, vizier, and grand vizier, the highest position in the structure of offices. "They ate their meals together, went boating, and in times of war shared a tent—or even the same bed. . . . When each August the Sultan moved his court (and harem) to the more bracing climate of Adrianopole [now Edirne], he and Ibrahim spent days together engaged in falconry . . . and in their splendid tents each evening Ibrahim was always ready with his music, or at hand if the Sultan felt the urge to write a poem . . . At times the two men even wore each other's clothes. . . . The Ottoman court was scandalised. To them it was totally unsuitable for the world's greatest emperor to show such a favour to a slave. (Barber 1973:36–37, 47; Ibrāhīm was strangled in 1536).

officials" (J. Drake 1966:19) and also major slaveowners (Papoulia 1963:7).[55] At the time of his death, Rüstem (a Croatia-born page of Suleiman's), for instance, owned 1,700 slaves (Babinger 1978:87).

Like court officials, the janissaries enjoyed more tangible consolations beyond the realm of honor—in which they were all equal, that is, nonentities.[56]

Francis Osborne (1656:253) is one Northern savant and comparativist historian who recognized distinct advantages in deploying over vast spaces an army of unmarried men, noting that for the janissaries, "quite unshackled from the magnetical force of an affection to wife and children, by use made natural (which chains Christians like fond Apes to their own doors), every place is fancied their proper sphere. . . . Neither doth the want of Wives raise such cries made by the Relicts and Children of slain souldiers."[57] That is, not only could they be dispatched anywhere, but there was no one to mourn them after they were slain, or to press their commanders not to put them in harm's way.

The Initial Success but Gradual Erosion of a System to Avoid Accumulation of Official Advantages

By short-circuiting the succession of generation and the accumulation of riches, prerogatives, and honors by powerful slaves (or by former slaves), the Ottoman system effectively blocked transgenerational accumulation of official positions (and of the riches accumulated by those

55. At least three such boys became grand viziers: Rüstem and Ibrāhīm during Suleiman I's reign and Kara Mustafa during that of Mahomet IV a century later (Barber 1973:103). Still, despite the amassing of riches and high offices by some slaves, in the Turkish stratification of honor, even the richest and most powerful slave was "socially dead." For instance, Ibrāhīm, "the second most powerful man in the most powerful empire of the time" could not testify in a trial (Patterson 1982:313, following Repp 1968:138–39).

56. "Janissaries" was the usual Western designation for the Ottoman army. It is derived from *yenicheri*, which meant "new troops," i.e., the sultan's six infidel-born mounted regiments, which consisted of about fifty thousand men and constituted about a quarter of the army. Janissaries were also known as Sipahis of the Porte. Two of the six regiments included "men born Muslim, but born outside the confines of the Ottoman empire," hence also lacking local relatives, "the other four regiments being composed of recruits drawn in general from the palace schools" (Parry 1976:104, 158). Although there are claims that *yenicheri* existed earlier, the argument of Ménage (1966:72–76; also see J. Palmer 1953) that they were "new" some time between 1361 and 1365, early in the reign of Murād I, seems compelling.

57. I interpret "made natural" to indicate that Osborn did not believe domesticity is natural for men, but that they may become habituated to it. He did not get into the question of what is "natural" sexual conduct for those not "chained to their own doors."

occupying those positions). The Ottoman system of taking youths from the peripheries of the empire was more effective in keeping its administrators from enriching their natal families than was the Chinese bureaucratic system, in which officials were dispatched (at the start of their careers, at least) far from their place of origin, but eventually tended to return to the capital. Employing eunuchs in high office, as both Chinese emperors and Ottoman sultans did (see Ayalon 1979a), totally blocked enrichment of descendants. But unless considerable distance was put between the eunuch and his natal family, eunuchs promoted family interests.[58] Even more in the case of foreign-born eunuchs than in that of foreign-born but reproductively intact *kullar,* the native population could invidiously compare its honor to the lack of honor of the unmanned. Along with their monopoly on honor, "to the Muslim-born subjects of the sultan was reserved exclusive control of the Muslim religious, legal and educational institutions of the empire" (Parry 1976:103).

For a time, the system of staffing administration and army with aliens was successful in preventing hereditary power accumulating outside the control of the sultanate.[59] However, as among the mamlūks, the one-generation elite system did not prevent collective action against the sultans on behalf of group interests. The janissaries intrigued, meddled in successions, refused to go too far afield (thus saving Persia and Vienna from conquest), rioted, and increasingly extorted sultans in the same way the mamlūks did (Lybyer 1913:91–97), especially in the revolt of 1703 (see Barber 1973:125–35). Moreover, "in spite of the attempt by the sultan to keep his professional army apart from the local population, in course of time they began to mingle. By the end of the seventeenth century janissaries were pursuing crafts and trades, and membership of the corps became a kind of property, conferring a right to privileges and pensions, which could be handed to sons, or be bought by members of the civil population" (Hourani 1991:237).

This process proceeded at different rates and to different extents in different provinces, with troops in Tunis notably autonomous already by the late sixteenth century, in contrast to Algiers, where control from

58. The same has been true of "princes" of the Catholic church. Church property was guarded from individual expropriation for the benefit of heirs by forbidding the clergy to marry (i.e., enforcing celibacy with or without chastity), but church officials throughout history have advanced the political and economic interests of their natal families, especially those of their siblings' children.

59. Especially insofar as they did not marry/procreate. Dervish (Bektashi) asceticism as well as pederastic preferences may have been involved in this (in my view not clearly established) demographic phenomenon.

Constantinople remained more effective (Hourani 1991:229–30). Although I have absolutely no evidence for it, I would hypothesize (postdict) that over time the masculinity of those conscripted in the Ottoman *devshirme* declined in importance and that the ratio of soldiers to sex toys among the Christian boys decreased.[60] The latter part of this surmise, at least, seems testable through the use of Turkish archives, although it is complicated by the variety of attributes sought among those not selected for military service.[61]

The Ottoman case probably provides an example of the gradual effeminization of age-stratified homosexuality. More obviously, it demonstrates the difficulty of building and maintaining a body of functionaries who will rule impersonally. The isolation of mamlūks and janissaries from their natal families and from the general population in the empires they governed and defended fostered same-sex emotional and sexual relation. Removal from their natal families and neighbors did not suffice to make the relationship of the foreign-born mamlūk or *yenicheri* to his owner the only social and emotional tie. Both the mamlūk and *yenicheri* cases show that, even when elites are genealogically isolated, they still can manage to disrupt bureaucratic rationality (and other kinds of authority) by advancing their favorites (friends as well as sexual partners) and by acting collectively. That is, the family is not the only impediment to impersonal order.[62] Moreover, the history of increasing loosening of

60. This is based less on hostile European discourse about janissary degeneracy than on what seems to me a tendency for the beauty of the boys involved in age-stratified homosexuality to be increasingly valued over military attributes as a rising mercantile bourgeoisie shares with the military elite in the cultivation and consumption of pretty boys, e.g., in feudal Japan (see pp. 77–86).

61. "The Palace school produced artists and scholars as well as soldiers and administrators, and craftsmen working for the sultan created some of the finest and most original works of Ottoman civilization. The Palace was the principal creative source in Ottoman culture. The great architect Sinan (1490?–1588), for example, came originally as a *devshirme* boys from Kayseri" (Inalcik 1973:88).

62. I agree with David Greenberg (1988:439) that "advancement was generally based on seniority and merit rather than birth," and that this is a significant step away from "feudalism." Yet, I do not believe that the advancement of a sultan's (past or present) sexual favorite posed no "organizational problem." Nepotism is not the only kind of departure from universalism, common though it has been across space and time. Precisely **within the state structure**, homosexual favoritism could stimulate resentment among those passed over. That, "with the exception of state functionaries, the Turkish population was not bureaucratized and not trained for future employment in the bureaucracy" (Greenberg 1988:439; see Mumcu 1963:71) is true, but irrelevant. It is within precisely the realm of the exception—"in the state structure" among "state functionaries," not just in the training academies—that there was a bureaucratic/patrimonial tension. The difficulty was greatest

the principle of recruiting the governing elite anew also suggests that a social system without any accumulation of official status (and riches concomitant to high office) is very difficult to maintain. Men find ways to ensure the prosperity of their sons (or, in their absence of sons, other kinds of favorites), even when and where their own positions cannot be inherited.

Albania

In 1853 Johann von Hahn (1811–69) wrote that in Albania "young men between 16 and 24 love boys from 12 to 17. A Geg [Albanian Muslim] marries at the age of 24 or 25, and then he usually, but not always gives up boy love" (von Hahn 1853:166–68). He quoted a native saying:

> The sight of a beautiful youth awakens astonishment in the lover, and opens the door of his heart to the delight which the contemplation of this loveliness affords. Love takes possession of him so completely that all his thought and feeling goes out in it. If he finds himself in the presence of the beloved, he rests absorbed in gazing on him. Absent, he thinks of nought but him. If the beloved unexpectedly appears, he falls into confusion, changes color, turns alternately pale and red. His heart beats faster and impedes his breathing. He has eyes and ears only for the beloved. (Crompton 1985:134–35)

Early in the twentieth century, an unnamed German linguist familiar with Albania (whom I would guess to be the distinguished Balkanologist Gustav Ludwig Weigand) wrote sexologist Paul Näcke that among the Tosks (South Albanian Greek Orthodox):

> male love is deeply inracinated, as everyone knows from Hahn. I have made inquiries among persons familiar with the country, Germans, Russians, and likewise natives, and all confirmed Hahn's statements point for point. For handsome boys and youths these Shqipëtars cherish a truly enthusiastic love. The passion and mutual jealousy are so intense that even today they kill one another for the sake of a boy. Many instances of this kind were reported to me. In particular this love is supposed to flourish among the Moslems . . . [and] even the Christians pay homage to this *amor masculus*. It is further true that pacts of

---

within military-training academies, but such tension existed throughout the Ottoman system of government by officials far away from their families (often enough, from any wives and children, as well as from parents and siblings).

brotherhood, when they occur among Christians, are blessed by the *papas* in church, both partners receiving the eucharist. Otherwise with the Turks. My innkeeper in Ohrid had concluded a pact of blood brotherhood with an Albanian Moslem (Geg). Each pricked the other in the finger and sucked out a drop of blood. Now each has to protect the other to the death, and that for the Christian host is an important guarantee. (Näcke 1965 [1908]:40)

After noting that oral intercourse was in vogue with the Turks, Näcke's correspondent explained that the Albanians practiced intercrural intercourse. Although sexual practices were "enveloped in profound silence," Näcke and his correspondent did not think that this meant that male-male love and pacts of older-younger brotherhood in Albania were "platonic." Bremmer(1980:289) culled from Krauss's (1911) Albanian sexual lexicon *büthar*, literally "butt fucker," and *madzüpi* for the practice of pederasty. Weigand assured Erich Bethe (1907: 475), who sought to argue that pederasty had originally diffused from the area, that the relationships were "really sexual, although tempered by idealism" and that "while most prevalent among the Moslems, they are also found among the Christians, and receive the blessing of the priest in church" (quoted by Crompton 1985:135).

François Poucqueville (1770–1838), Napoleon's unhappy consul to Ali Pasha's court in Yanina, agreed that the notion of "sin" was absent: "far from seeing it discredited, he finds it rewarded by the chief to whom he is subjected." The major difference between his report and others is that Poucqueville related acceptance of pederasty to the freedom rather than to the seclusion/subjugation of women, writing that "The wandering lives led by these people, their days passed chiefly amid camps, perhaps encourage this revolting passion. It is general among all classes. The women are not shut up under lock and bars, but in the mountains may be seen walking about perfectly free and unveiled (Poucqueville 1813:405, quoted by Crompton 1985:134–35).

The chief to whom Poucqueville referred was Ali Pasha (1741–1822), the Ottoman vizier of Albania and father of Veli, the vizier of most of Greece. Although possessing a harem of five or six hundred women, another French observer, the Baron de Vaudoncourt (1772–1845), wrote that Ali "is almost exclusively given up to the Socratic pleasures, and for this purpose keeps a seraglio of youths, from whom he selects his confidants, and even his principal officers" (quoted by Plomer 1936: 79; Crompton 1985:135). Ali's son Veli, vizier of Morea (southwestern

Greece) emulated his father's appetite for money and for boys (see Plomer 1936:162).

Anthropologist Ian Whitaker (1981:149) noted the persistence in Albania of a traditional

> permissive attitude to [age-structured] male homosexuality, particularly when shepherds were away from feminine company in the hills," and found among my informants a common expectation that young married men would engage in such relationships, having, as one informant put it, "just learned what his penis is for." The subject of homosexual unions does not arouse among the Albanian mountaineers feelings of either shame or amusement in the same way that they do among other ethnic groups. There is instead a pragmatic assumption that the male is entitled to frequent orgasms, however these might be procured.

Ldab Ldob: A Tibetan Monastic Role

The Japanese monk Ekai Kawaguchi, who spent the last years of the nineteenth century in Tibet, wrote of warrior priests (romanized as Thab-to) in the Sera college in Lhasa who paid for their Buddhist studies by gathering yak dung, carrying wood, and serving in various ways (not least as bodyguards) the scholar priests. Kawaguichi found them to be not only daring but very quarrelsome: "They scarcely ever fight for a pecuniary matter, but the beauty of young boys presents an exciting cause, and the theft of a boy will often lead to a duel" (1909:292). Lest there should be any doubt of the warrior priests' appreciation of the beauty of boys, Kawaguichi noted, "they really seem to be the descendants of the men of Sodom" (470).

Both the Moravian missionary Walter Asboe, who ran a dispensary/hospital at Leh (in eastern Kashmir) and Nono Tse-P'hün, ethnographer Prince Petros's main informant and interpreter, told the prince that homosexuality was prevalent in the Buddhist monasteries of central Tibet. Nono Tse-P'hün contrasted Kashmiri proscription with Tibetan acceptance: "He felt sure that no one indulged in it, not even in the monasteries [in Ladakh]. In Tibet, it was another matter, he added, and it was known that it was practiced in the large monasteries of Central Tibet, as any monk returning from Lhasa or Shigatse where he had gone for his studies could tell" (Petros:1963:386). Heinrich Harrer, the Austrian mountaineer, who was one of very few Westerners in Tibet in the last years before the Red Army conquered it, wrote that monks "live in strict celibacy and are forbidden to have anything to do with women. Unfortunately, homosexuality is very common. It is even condoned as giving proof that women play no part in the life of those monks" (1996 [1953]:217).

Based on interviews with Tibetan refugees, including a relative by marriage who had been one, Goldstein (1964) produced a functionalist analysis of a role called *Ldab ldob*.[63] This accepted role allowed Tibetan Buddhist monasteries to harness the energies of young monks not ready for disciplined lives of contemplation and study. The ethnographic present of his analysis (and of my discussion of it) is the 1920s through 1940s (see Goldstein 1989). The extent to which the role continues in such monasteries as the brutally repressive Chinese colonial regime has allowed to operate (as a lure for tourists' hard currency) is not clear.

Before the PRC invasion, most monks were in their mid-teens when they entered the monasteries. Many lacked any personal sense of monastic vocation. That is, parents placed many of them in monasteries. Some would leave, but most "get over their sadness and remain," Tibetans told Goldstein (1964:125).

Some aggressive young monks, as much as 10 percent of the population in the larger monasteries, become *Ldab ldob*. These seeming anti-monks take monastic vows, live in a monastery, and wear monkish dress, albeit in some distinctive ways; they are also recognizable because they do not shave their heads completely (retaining a lock of hair behind each ear that is wrapped around the ear), visibly carry weapons, and wear eye shadow to appear more ferocious (127; also noted by Kawaguchi 1909:469). Harrer (1996 [1953]:146) added that they wear red armbands, stick a huge (often knife-sharp) key in their belts, blacken their faces with soot, walk with a "provocative" gait, and "are quick to strike." Traditionally, *Ldab ldob* fighting was between monasteries (some in athletic contests), but they put up armed resistance to the Red Army in 1950.

Ldab ldob are especially interested in sports contests, but also do the "grunt work" in the monasteries. Their work and their eagerness for combat are useful (or, at least were, before the communist Chinese conquest and supervision) for protecting and maintaining the "system" of a monastery.

According to Goldstein('s informants) homosexuality "carries an extremely derogative stigma and is almost unknown" in the lay population of Tibet. *Ldab ldob*, however, have a general reputation for sexual relationships with boys. As with the ancient Greeks, the only permissible

---

63. On "role" in contrast to "status" and "self," with particular focus on homosexual roles, see Murray 1996a:143–66.

intercourse is intracrural: "Although a monk who practices homosexuality is at the least committing the two sins of "sexual desire" (*'Dod chags*) and "perverse view" (*Log lta*), he will often rationalize that he is not breaking the [monastic] prohibition to derive pleasure from the three doors (anus, mouth, and vagina) since, in Tibet, homosexuality is practiced only between the legs from behind. Any other practice is considered unthinkable."

As for the ancient Greeks, one might wonder how descriptive this prescription is. There is also a certain air of legend, particularly what is used to frighten children in Goldstein's account of *Ldab ldob* kidnapping:

> Kidnapping might begin with a *Ldab ldob* striking up a conversation with a young girlish-looking boy (either monk or lay). If the boy is not receptive to his advances, the *Ldab ldob* may forcibly lead the boy away. Unless the *Ldab ldob* has an arrangement with friends to use their house, he will have to take the boy back to the monastery in order to have privacy. If this is the case, the boy will be forced to spend the night there because of the distance between the monastery and Lhasa (using Lhasa and the three large monasteries as an example). *Ldab ldob* are not reluctant about taking a boy from the aristocracy against his will, and some *Ldab ldob* are even famed for taking nobles' sons. There are also instances where *Ldab ldob*s took adults, and even aristocrats who were government officials.
>
> The *Ldab ldob*s are able to continue this behavior because their "victims" fear retaliation by the *Ldab ldob*s, but more because of their shame at having been a homosexual partner (*Mgron po*). In Tibet, the main stigma goes to the victim, or to the voluntary partner, and not to the doer, the *Ldab ldob*. (Goldstein 1964:135)

On the same page, Goldstein reported schoolchildren vigorously resisting kidnapping, sometimes even killing would-be abductors with their penknives. As for the *hijra*s south of the Himalayas (see pp. 306–11 below), the reputation for kidnapping unwilling youths is probably exaggerated.[64]

64. Cabezón (1993:93) called attention to Goldstein's sample size (five persons whose background Goldstein detailed) and asserted that "although the fact of homosexual activity among the *Ldab ldob* can hardly be denied, the details, especially concerning the abduction of youths, have been challenged." He did not specify who (let alone how many) his sources are, in reporting, "My own sources, who would not deny that homosexual activity existed, not only among the *Ldab ldob* but among other monks as well, stated that they were unaware of the abduction scenarios described by Goldstein and his informants"

Homosexual relations of the *Ldab ldob* are (mostly) age stratified. Although not an age grade, *Ldab ldob* is at least an age-delimited role: "*Ldab ldob*s are a phenomenon of youth. By the age of forty they 'outgrow' this role and assume new ones in the monastic system" (137). Some former *Ldab ldob* even became abbots.

Goldstein explained the role as more than a safety valve for youthful energy: "The *Ldab ldob*s are a channel by which the monastic institution absorbs deviants[65] and gives them a useful role within the institution and a place both in monastic society and Tibetan society in general. By this device, the monastic order is able to change potentially hostile members into productive members; potentially anti-monastic elements into completely pro-monastic elements" (140). Indeed, the *Ldab ldob*s provide the strong backs to perform needed labor and guard the monasteries. They say that they are the "outer wall" to the "inner treasure" of the contemplative monks (136).

The literature in English about this topic does not discuss any effects on the *Ldab ldob*'s sexual partners, nor does it deal with what is expected of these partners, other than that they resist the penetration of the two "doors" that males have.

The Hwarang of Ancient Korea

The origins and early development of the Three Kingdoms of Korea (Koguryo [also romanized as Korai] in the northwest, Paekche in the southwest, and Silla in the east of the peninsula) and their social institutions in the first century B.C. were already rather dim in 1145 when Kim Pusik completed his *Samguk-sagi,* which purports to contain their complete history from the beginning. Prior to the introduction of Buddhism, elite youth called *hwarang* (flower of male youth) seem to have been involved in shamanistic practices.[66] The *Samguk-sagi* and also the

---

(99n. 50). Prince Petros (1963:385–86) acknowledged that he had been mistaken earlier about the absence of homosexuality in (Western) Tibetan monasteries.

65. In his use of the word "deviants," Goldstein was referring to the fact that the The *Ldab ldob* is conventionally masculine (or hypermasculine) in a monastic society not valuing masculine aggressiveness (especially sexual conquests).

66. Rutt rejected the view of hwarang as cadres for the propagation of Buddhism, emphasizing continuities with shamanism that Peter Lee also has emphasized, while considering hwarang "knights." The last two recorded hwarang (late in the ninth century A.D.) both danced to subdue demons. See Rutt (1961:43–44). Mishina Shoei (1943) (also see Rutt 1961:22) discussed suggestions that hwarang wore women's clothing. Documentation is insufficient to sort out changes in the role over time. My guess (extrapolated from roles elsewhere) is that, over time, beauty supplanted military prowess as the prime desideratum.

Samguk-yusa (compiled by the monk Iryon a century later) recount that, some time between the twelfth year of his reign (551 A.D.) and its final year (576), King Sok Pobun (posthumously known as Chinhung) disbanded a group of pretty girls (either dancers or Buddhist nuns, depending on the source) after one girl drowned another out of jealousy for her beauty. He then chartered a grouping of beautiful boys "arrayed in cosmetics and fine clothes called hwarang" (*Samguk-sagi;* translated by Rutt 1961:16). "They gathered followers in large numbers. They encouraged one another morally, and delighted one another with singing and music, playing among the hills and streams—there was nowhere they did not go." Kim Pusik appended a quotation from the lost *Silla-kukki* (Account of the Country of Silla) by the Tang-dynasty (Chinese) official Ch'eng Ling-Hu that said: "They selected handsome sons of the elite and adorned them with powder and rouge. They call them *hwarang.* The people all revere and serve them. Good generals and brave soldiers are produced by reason of it."[67]

Initially, Buddhism in the Korean kingdoms was a cult patronized almost exclusively by court circles. Not until after the fifth century (simultaneous with Silla dominance of the whole of Korea) did it become genuinely popular even in Koguryo, where it first was introduced (Gardiner 1969:49). The barrier of the central mountains insulated Silla (at least relatively more than the other two kingdoms) from Chinese cultural influences. Chinhung instituted major (sinicizing) changes. If he did not invent the hwarang role/institution, at the very least, the hwarang code began to change from social and religious concerns to political and military programs during the sixth century: pride in being a soldier, bravery, and loyalty to the Silla kingdom were the virtues of the new code (Choy 1971:29).

The hwarang were recruited in the early teens. Fidelity in friendship was one of their five commandments.[68] The earliest-dated hwarang for whom a biographical account has survived (in the *Samguk Yusi*) is Sada-

---

67. Quoted by Henthorn (1971:44–45), who added, "The hwarang are reminiscent of the elite Ottoman Janissaries." Rutt (1961:17) did not include the last sentence of the passage, which P. Lee (1969:68) translated as "This was a way to facilitate the king's government."

68. The other four were loyalty to the king, filial piety, never fleeing a battlefield, and not killing unnecessarily. (Rutt 1961:63 reproduced the Chinese set; on page 24 he asserted that they were pre-Buddhist). They were formulated by Won'-Gwang (556?–640), mentor of some hwarang who died in battle against Paekche in 602 (P. Lee 1969:79–80, 13–14).

ham, who distinguished himself in the conquest of Kaya in 562. The *Samguk Sagi* praises him as "a youth of sixteen from an aristocratic and distinguished family, handsome and elegant, square[-faced] and upright. He was regarded as being all the more admirable for having declined a number of rewards from the grateful king" (P. Lee 1959:139). "When Sadaham was seventeen, his friend Mugwan, with whom he had sworn friendship to death, died of sickness. Sadaham mourned him for seven days, and then died himself" (Rutt 1961:32).

The *Haedong kosung chon* (Lives of Eminent Korean Monks) compiled by the Buddhist abbot Kakhun in 1215, credited King Sok Pobun with seeking to develop a meritocracy. Lee suggested that the institution derived from ancient initiation rites, as some French classicists have suggested ancient Greek age-graded homosexuality did:

> The origin of the Hwarang is obscure. Since the idea of considering them the nucleus of society cannot have grown spontaneously, we must take it to be the crystallization of historical and cultural traditions. There is an opinion that this institution might have risen from primitive *Knabenweihen*—like the ritual celebrating the assumption of adulthood—where youths of the same age gathered together and performed certain religious ordeals. It is further speculated by students of ethnography that the Koreans had in early days customs similar to *Knabenweihen*. It is understandable that in the Silla society, which was based on a consanguineous class system, the members of the Hwarang had to be chosen from noble families or from those who were strongly recommended by the society. (1959:140)

Kakhun's 1215 account continued, "They instructed one another in the [Buddhist] Way and in righteousness, entertained each other with songs and music, or went sightseeing to famous mountains and rivers, no matter how far away. From all this a man's moral character can be discerned, and the good were recommended to the court" (P. Lee 1969:67). Their number exceeded two hundred, according to early eighth-century Silla historian Kim Taemum's *Hwarang segi* (Annals of the Hwarang; quoted by Kakhun; P. Lee 1969:67). The sons of the Silla elite were given austere military training involving archery and horsemanship. Each hwarang led a group of subordinates, as many as one thousand men in the case of Sadaham. During the wars of unification (subordination to Silla), the hwarang fought fiercely in the vanguard. The most famed of these was Kim Yu-Sin [594–673], who became a hwarang at age fifteen. He later became the most famous general in the wars of unification, and served as prime minister (Rutt 1961:36). "Other examples recorded in histories indicate that they were most serviceable in times of war, famine, and other national crises. The Hwarang was a chivalrous institution whose function was to serve the country in times of emergency and to foster a sacrificial spirit for the sake of the country. Thus they were called 'the pillars of the State,' 'the paragon of youth,' and 'leaders of society'" (P. Lee 1959:139).

Military arts were not the only ones the hwarang cultivated:

> They were not only gallant soldiers. In times of peace and prosperity, they visited famous mountains and beauty spots to appreciate and to contemplate the beauty of Nature. Among their favorite spots were the Diamond Mountains with 30,000 peaks facing the Japanese Sea. Here spiritual cultivation was emphasized, and they learned on these occasions how to adhere to their principles, how to enlighten and correct one another, and how to become champions of public enlightenment . . . Learning meant not only the reading of classics, but also discussion and exchange of views and observations of the deeds of other members. In this manner, they would discuss poetry and philosophy as they walked up and down the paths, not of a Lyceum, but of the Diamond Mountains, or along the Eastern Sea. Many of them excelled in poetry and music, and many impromptu verses were attributed to them. The poet Siro, who was a member of the Hwarang, praises his Master Taemara, in one of the fourteen Silla poems that are extant. The Prince Wolmyong was asked by King Kyongdok (742–65) to write a poem for him: he is said also to have excelled in the flute. It is no wonder that the Hwarang were praised as "national paragons" or "national geniuses" and not only as "the paragon of youth." (P. Lee 1959:139)

P. Lee (1959:106–8) discussed the poem to a master who had to have been over sixty at the time it was written ("wrinkles lance your once handsome face") in Rutt's 1961 (49) translation. It begins with seeming transience ("The whole world weeps sadly for departing spring") and then contrasts the cyclical nature of the seasons (with spring recurring) and the noncyclical nature of human life (Taemara's own "spring" being long past). The last two lines, "Fair lord, what hope for my burning heart? / How can I sleep?"] "achieve the culmination of his intense admiration for his master: until he sees him again, even for a moment, he cannot enjoy peace of mind. His anxiety will torment him 'even in the mugwort-covered swamps,' meaning he will not forget him under whatever hardships or in whatever predicament" (P. Lee 1959:107). Unending male-male devotion is also indicated by the king having said that he would not forget his friend "even though the oak would wither" (107).

This praise song for the hwarang Kilbo attributed to the monk Ch'ungdam also strikes me as a love poem:

> The face of the hwarang Kilbo
> Was reflected in the pale green water.
> Here among the pebbles of the stream
> I seek the bounds of the heart he bore.
>
> Ah, ah! Hwarang hero,
> Noble pine that fears no frost!
> (Trans. Rutt 1961:51)

The ardent youths did not have to rely entirely on each other for philosophical guidance, for prominent Buddhist monks

> not only counseled the members of the hwarang as to conduct in light of the "Five Commandments," but served them as chaplains in their liberal education and perhaps even on the battlefield. Scattered references in historical sources suggest that some members of the hwarang were believed to be reincarnations of [the bodhisattva] Maitreya; and Kim Yu-sin, a leader of the hwarang, and his group were called the *Yonghwa hyangdo,* a "band of the Dragon Flower tree," the bodhi tree of Maitreya when he comes to earth to save the living beings. What sustained the hwarang was this belief in Maitreya, a patron saint of the institution, and belief that its members were no less than reincarnated Maitreyas. Indeed, Buddhism provided a formidable ideology for the unification and protection of the country. (P. Lee 1969:14)

—and for the avoidance of polluting contact with female bodies.

After the peninsula was unified in 676, the members of the hwarang were rewarded with land and slaves. Some of them became retainers of the king in the central government, and many were distributed around the country as local officials (Choy 1971:29).

Although the Korean state, first unified by the Silla army and legitimated by Mahayana Buddhism, survived for nearly a millennium, little regarding court life has been translated into European languages.[69] Claims that "the Hwarang bands lost their fighting prowess and degenerated into groups of effeminate dilettantes" (Fairbanks and Reischauer

69. The Silla dynasty was overthrown by Wang Kien of Koguryo in 935. Later, Yi monarchs heavily repressed Buddhism in Korea (Kroeber 1947:327).

1960:415) seem based more on Western assumptions about how empires decline and on horrors of male ornamentation than on any credible Korean evidence. They also ignore the fact that in the mid-sixth century, precisely when they were involved in the expansion of Silla
dominance over the entire Korean Peninsula, hwarang were already ex-
quisitely powdered, rouged, and dressed dancing boys as much as warriors—and, also from the recorded start, were deeply devoted to their
comrades.

Acolytes and Pages in Japan
Monastic relations

Boy-love among Japanese Buddhist monks seems to have been more
prominent than in Chinese Buddhisms, although legend credits the
Buddhist monk Kūkai (A.D. 774–835; usually referred to posthumously
as Kōbō Daishi) with importing boy-love to Japan from China in A.D. 806
as part of Shingon (True Word) Buddhism.[70] The intimacy of master and
adept provides fertile grounds for sexual relationships, even without
Tantric-derived doctrines about mystical sexual essences. Younger monks
in monasteries certainly became objects of aesthetic and spiritual appreciation in the great Shingon center at Mount Kōya, and the founder of
the order was annexed as the founder of monastic boy-love as well as—
or as part of—Shingon (Watanabe 1989:32–36, Ackerley 1961).[71]

By the end of the sixteenth century, "Kōbō Daishi" was a byword for
male love. The 1598 text presented as *Kōbō Daishi's Book* provides instruction in the "mysteries of loving boys," mysteries implying a connection with the esoteric mysteries of Shingon Buddhism (Schalow
1992:217). It consists of three parts. The first decodes hand signals
young acolytes use to communicate their feelings to priests. The second
is a kind of field guide, containing advice on how to recognize boys who
are ready to be penetrated and how to prepare those who are not. The
readiest candidates exhibit *nasake*, an empathetic sensitivity to love, but
"no matter how lacking in sensitivity to the mysteries of love an acolyte

---

70. Buddhism in China was at its apogee of influence and prestige in the early ninth
century, just prior to "the great suppression of Buddhism between 842 and 845, which
brought empire-wide destruction of temples and shrines, confiscation of Buddhist lands,
and secularization of the clergy" (Wright 1959:83). It is possible (as Gary Leupp suggested
to me) that documents on sexual relations between Chinese Buddhist priests and acolytes
were lost in this wave of repression. Kūkai spent time in Fujian, widely considered the part
of China in which male-male sexual relationships have been best accepted. See pp. 181–85.

71. Similarly, the Yellow Emperor, the great culture hero of Chinese legend, is credited
with showing his people the possibilities of boy-love.

may be, he can be made yours if you approach him right" (translated by Schalow 1992:218). To take acolytes insensitive to love, *Kōbō Daishi's Book* recommends: "stroke his penis, massage his chest, and then gradually move your hand to the area of his ass. By then he'll be ready for you to strip off his robe and seduce him without a word," just as cedars bend to the wind (218). The third part describes methods of anal penetration in the idiom of Tantric meditation postures.

Tendai, the dominant Buddhist grouping a millennium ago in Heian Japan was another, exceptionally syncretic Buddhist tradition, named for Heavenly Terrace Mountain in Zhejiang, China. Its founder, Saichō (Dengyō Daishi), was seven years Kūkai's elder, and returned to Japan from China (specifically from Zhejiang) a year earlier than Kūkai. His revelation of the divinity of young boys is supposed to have occurred on Mount Hiei. In 785 (i.e., **before** going to China, and nine years before the imperial capital of Kyoto was established below the southwestern slope of the mountain), the then-hermit Saichō is supposed to have encountered a beautiful boy on Mount Hiei who identified himself as "the divine child who rules the world: the god Dosei" (Watanabe 1989:36). Along with the appearance of another beautiful boy who calmed a storm during Saichō's return from China, the vision of Dosei was used as a warrant for Tendai warrior monks to regard young boys (*chigo*) as incarnations of the divine children Saichō encountered: "During the following centuries, it was the custom of aristocrats to enter their sons temporarily in the monasteries . . . and it was natural that these well-brought-up young boys, called *chigo*, should be the object of sexual love. At the same time, 'because they are gods incarnate', these *chigo* were also the object of worship and spiritual admiration" (Watanabe 1989:38). By the end of the ninth century, Mount Hiei was the major center of Japanese Buddhism—and of man-boy love.

The attribution of boy-love to the founders of both Tendai and Shingon Buddhisms occurred generations later (Leupp 1995:32). The later traditions probably tell us little about what the historical personages Kūkai or Saichō did,[72] although the work on creation of "traditions" that anthropologists such as Richard Handler (1984) and Jocelyn Linnekin (1983) have done should prepare us to understand the "authenticity" of traditions as something other than historical literalism. "The record of

---

72. Saichō himself is not represented in the accounts as having a sexual relationship with Dosei. Guth (1987) discussed a number of "divine child" representations—without considering even the possibility that any erotic motivation or response might have been involved for Japanese artists and connoisseurs.

the past exists to be exploited, rephrased, abridged, or ignored. What is not in the record can be invented," as Robert Smith (1983:9) wrote. "The Japanese are not particularly unusual in the way they manipulate the record of their past, but are unusually adept at it." In the present instance, the prestige of China in Japan a millennium ago, not literal documentation, is probably the basis for the alleged diffusion of boy-love from China to Japan. While it is beyond doubt that the Shingon and Tendai monasteries were locales in which a cult of prepubescent boys developed, and to which Japanese boy lovers were increasingly drawn in later centuries, it is absurd to accept the idea that homosexuality diffused from China in 806. For one thing, there is no recorded parallel to the public adoration of boys in various Japanese Buddhisms in Chinese Buddhism of any era.[73] For another, despite the scantiness of records of everyday life in pre-Tokugawa Japan, and the lack of historical records of any sort prior to the eighth century (A.D.), there are earlier references to what seem to be male-male sexual relations in the oldest (i.e., eighth-century) Japanese chronicles. Iwata (excerpted in Watanabe 1989:32) pointed to references to Prince Funado's relations with a child servant in 757 in the *Shoku Nihongi*,[74] and found an account of a pair of *unruwashiki-tomo* (beautiful/intimate friends) named Shinu no Hafuri and Ama no Hafuri in the *Nihongi*. When the former died, the grief of the latter was so great that he reportedly killed himself beside his friend's corpse, and they were buried in the same grave.[75]

73. Although there is little material available in European languages on Korean Buddhism of that time, Wayne Dynes (1990 personal communication; also see Stevens 1990:139–40) suggested that Korea may be a better place than China to look for a prototype of Buddhist pederasty. The Tang (618–907 A.D.) emperors, nearly as much as the Han emperors a millennium earlier, were noted for homosexual love, and male prostitution was widespread and open through the Song dynasty (960–1280 A.D.). Song emperors also had male favorites, but since a bureaucracy based on examinations open to all largely eliminated an emperor's ability to provide his favorites with high offices, the sexual conduct of emperors had considerably less impact on Chinese society than in Han times. Whether monasticism is "un-Chinese" or only contrary to the neo-Confucian standards of filial piety that became ascendant after the Ming dynasty supplanted the Mongol Yuan dynasty in 1368, monastic Buddhism was never prominent in China (see Wright 1959:58, 75, 90, 95, 104; Bullough 1976:294–309; Xiao 1984:104–47), and, in particular, acquired neither the land nor the political power Tendai and Shingon Buddhism had in Heian Japan (I. Morris 1985:117).

74. Leupp (1995:23) translated Negishi Kennosuke's *Kodaijin no sei seikatsu* (*Sex Lives of the Ancients;* Tokyo 1983:66) as saying, "Even before the official mourning period for the ex-emperor was finished, and even before the grass upon his tomb had dried up, (Funado) secretly had sexual relations with boy attendants [*jido*]."

75. The term *azunai*, on which Iwata's case rests, is marked as "unclear: the burial of

Attestations of earlier homosexual devotion does not mean that there was a subculture of male-male love in Heian or Kamakura Japan. Whatever homosexual behavior occurred earlier or in other strata of Japanese society, **public rationalization** of boy-love was a monastic Buddhist innovation (albeit almost certainly one later than the time of Kūkai and Saichō). Buddhist monks were forbidden to have sexual intercourse with women but were not prohibited from engaging in other forms of sexual activity. Schalow (1981:6) and Leupp (1995:35–38) reviewed some seventeenth-century apologias. Leupp stressed the greater isolation of monasteries after the 794 move of the capital from Nara to Kyoto. In discussing the genre of stories about *chigo*, Childs (1980:127) noted "no trace in the tales themselves that homosexuality per se met with disapproval. It was, at least, no more immoral for a priest than heterosexual relations, and certainly not a moral issue for a layman."

According to one early, long-time Western observer, eleven of the twelve leading sects of Japan prohibited carnal connections with women." Although the priests are not allowed to have any communion with women," François Caron wrote (ca. 1631), "they keep catamites; and this they do openly, without being considered wrong. . . . Being forbidden the use of women, [priests] have recourse to unnatural practices" (translated in Pinkerton 1811:630). A late-seventeenth-century Japanese apologia explained that "the Buddha preached that Mount Impose [the home of love for women] was a place to be avoided [by those seeking enlightenment] and the priests of the law entered the Way of [Loving] Youth (wakashudō) as an outlet for their feelings, since their hearts were, after all, made of neither stone nor wood. . . . This love has surpassed in depth the love between women and men."[76]

Although the proper Buddhist aspiration is to transcend desires of **any** sort, it is important to remember that religious careers were (and are) pursued for reasons other than spiritual callings (see Collcutt 1981: 292) and that strictures on monks differed from those that were expected to govern the conduct of laymen. In a properly Buddhist understanding,

---

two close male friends in one spot, or possibly, male homosexuality" in the authoritative *Iwanami Kogo Jiten (Iwanami Dictionary of Ancient Language;* Tokyo 1974:37), with Iwata as the source of the latter interpretation. In addition to providing this translation of the dictionary entry, Leupp (17 July 1990 letter) called my attention to Aston's (1972:238) translation of the passage in which *azunai no tsumi* was rendered "the calamity of there being no sun" and suggested the possibility that a taboo against two priests being buried together may have been the primary native concern.

76. Kitamura Kirin, preface to *Iwatsutsuji* (Wild Azaleas), 1676, translation from Schalow (1993:1).

the fleetingness of youth is an exemplar of evanescence, and loving a boy can demonstrate the fragility of attachments in this world.

A boy is like another favorite Japanese motif, the beautiful cherry blossom, which is doomed to fading quickly. Indeed, "cherry blossoms forever bloom the same, but people change with every passing year. This is especially true of a boy in the bloom of youth. . . . His blossom of youth falls cruelly to the ground. All told, loving a boy can be likened to a dream that we are not given time to have" (Ihara in Schalow 1990a:69). *Mujokan,* the sense of impermanence, and *aware,* "the pathos inherent in the beauty of the outer world, a beauty that is inexorably fated to disappear together with the observer," form a leitmotif of Japanese literature, as well as an essential conclusion of Japanese Buddhisms (see Keene 1988:18–21, 86). Direct emotional experience is crucial, not any intellectualization of the pathos of evanescent beauty (I. Morris 1985:208, 121–27).

A male child of the noble classes who was as young or five or six would be entrusted to a monk whom he would address as older brother (*anibun*) and who would address him as "younger brother" (*otōtobun*).[77] The "older brothers" sometimes dressed these young boys as girls, and shaved their eyebrows (Lowe, 1972:37–38). In addition to powdered faces, Zen Buddhist *kasshiki* (postulants aged five to eight) sported shoulder-length hair, in marked contrast to the monks and to the older novices who were termed *shami.* Also,

> in contrast to the somber black robes of the *shami* and precepted monks, *kasshiki* were dressed in finely-wrought silken robes and vividly-colored, variegated under-robes. . . . Rivalries in conspicuous consumption indulged in by wealthy *bushi* [warrior- samurai] families were carried on within the Zen cloister by their sons. . . . Gorgeously arrayed youths became the center of admiration in lavish monastic ceremonies that were far in spirit from the simple, direct search for self advocated by the early Ch'an

77. Some lower-class boys as young as eight years old were indentured for a decade of training to become pleasing prostitute actors (Leupp 1995:134). The brotherhood bond (*kyōdai musubi*) between boys and monks constituted a parallel institution for upper-class boys. The lower-class boys frequently were prostituted by their mentors, while the upper-class boys tended not to be shared by theirs. See the discussion of kabuki below. Arranged marriage of ten-year olds was not at all uncommon in Heian Japan. Similarity in class of sexual partners, whether of the same or of different sex, was far more important than closeness in age (I. Morris 1985:229–30). Given "the fantastic lack of specificity in Heian writing" (289), the preference for allusion rather than direct statement, and the failure to identify individual names, it is often difficult to know who was doing what to whom in ancient Japanese texts.

masters. Poems were written by *gozan* [Five Mountain, i.e., Rinzai Zen] monks to attractive *kasshiki* or *shami*. (Collcutt 1981:
246–47; based on R. Takahashi 1935:38–43)

Young boys were cultivated and memorialized in verse throughout
the feudal period in various Buddhist traditions. Indeed, the purported
Tendai motto *Ichi chigo ni sannō*—"*Chigo* first, the [Hiei mountain] god
second" (Childs 1980:127, Watanabe 1989:38, Leupp 1995:38) suggests
that the boys were the priests' highest priority.[78] Childs (1980) and Watanabe (1989:39–44) translated and discussed several *chigo* narratives.
Any doubts that this cult celebrated anal penetration should be dispelled
by the 1321 story and illustrations of a *chigo* in the abbey of Ninna-ji
(in Watanabe 1989:41–43, Leupp 1995:40–45, and Rawson 1968:
294). This is an important difference between Japanese and Athenian
age-graded homosexuality, anal penetration having been proscribed in
the latter (Dover 1978:98). A kinship idiom (*kyōdia musubi*—sworn
brotherhood) for Japanese age-graded relationships developed, with fraternal obligations running both ways. Over time, these increasingly were
formalized with written oaths (Leupp 1995:41–42).

Many of the great early Japanese literary works that depict homosexuality were written by monks (M. Cooper 1965:47). Ichiko (1955:
137) interpreted their motivation for writing to be a need to rationalize
their preoccupation with *chigo*. Against Ichiko and Araki Yoshio, Childs
(1980) argued that the majority of *chigo monogatari* (tales about *chigo*) are
didactic religious works showing the tragic transience of this-worldly attachments.[79] She cautioned against interpreting the impermanence of
relationships as indicating that it is the homosexuality that accounts (in
the Japanese view) for relations being doomed: "Frustrated love was a
popular theme in medieval [and later!] Japanese literature, and heterosexual love affairs also typically ended in separation or death" (128).

---

78. Some caution about whether this was a Tendai motto or an anti-Tendai slur may
be in order. Buddhist texts and the practices of Buddhists both in the past and the present
diverge as much as the practices of Christians diverge from theologian's versions of what
"Christianity" is. In regards to the followers of religious orders in both traditions, vow-
ing to eschew marriage (celibacy) needs to be distinguished from abstaining from sex
(chastity). "Lack of religious discipline was a common and persistent problem in temples
and nunneries and, because of their hypocritical ways of life, priests and nuns were often
the target of satirical literary attacks" (Childs 1980:128). This could as easily be said of medieval Christian Europe as of Buddhist Japan.

79. The metaphors of boy-love—with considerable concern about the transience of
boyhood—has been extensively used by Muslim poets, especially Sufi ones: see Schimmel
1975, 1982; Murray 1997d.

The poems (*kwaka*) written by monks of the Heian era (794–1184) and Zen poems and prose from the Muromachi period (1336–1573) often refer to the joys of love with boys (DeVos 1973:269, Katō 1979:283). Ihara Saikaku (1964 [1682]:147–49) included a vignette of the beginning of a passionately devoted relationship between a priest named Keisu who had been pining for a kabuki actor named Sansaburo, who later has "Kei" tattooed on his arm as proof of his devotion, and a chief priest who "amused himself by dressing Ito Kodayu in stage costume and a female wig so the boy looked exactly like a lovely girl" (Schalow 1990a:220).

Not all the early Japanese writing about same-sex relations were Buddhist parables of the transience of youthful beauty, however. There are isolated references to homosexuality prior to the thirteenth century, including the already mentioned account of the relations of Prince Funado and his servant, and the night in Lady Murasaki's great novel *Genji Monogatari* (Tale of Genji) in which Genji, missing his beloved, sleeps with her younger brother.

Over time, the age of the beloved increased. From the twelfth century, the last quarter of the Heian era, the cult of the *chigo* diffused from monasteries to the imperial court. The ex-emperor Shirakawa-In (1053–29), who ruled Japan for forty-three years after leaving the throne, was particularly dedicated to homosexual pleasure, and the next ex-emperor, the highly cultivated (and devout Buddhist) Toba-no-In (1103–56), was also an admirer of youthful male beauty, and, especially, of *chigo* dancing. Being attentive to the fashions of the court, powdering oneself, painting false eyebrows, using perfume, and dressing very elegantly seem to have become popular among the men of high society (Watanabe 1989:74), as in China during the Western Han dynasty (206 B.C. to 1 A.D.). Caron asserted (ca. 1631) that, "all the priests and some of the nobility are strongly attached to unnatural lusts; they do not make any sin of their propensity, and neither feel shame nor remorse on account of it" (Pinkerton 1811:631)—as he and other Christian visitors, notably St. Francis Xavier, felt they should (see Watanabe 1989:19–26).[80]

Although he regards the isolation from women as the basis for the cult of somewhat effeminized male youths, Leupp (1995:46), stressed the distinctions between *chigo* and females: "Although the boys looked rather like girls, they were not trained to imitate female behavior. Their

---

80. There is sufficient Japanese documentation of monastic pederasty that the horrified accounts of Catholic missionaries need not be interpreted to attest it. Watanabe (1989: 19–26) reviews these. Also see M. Cooper (1965); Schurhammer (1921, 1922).

speech was quite different from that of young women, and they cultivated arts (such as flute playing) that were regarded as exclusively masculine pursuits [McCullough 1966:242]. The acolytes exuded a unique, androgynous attraction that some men may have found more fascinating than feminine charms"—as was (and still is) the case for patrons of males who played (or play) female roles on stage (discussed on pp. 171–75).[81]

Samurai Boy-Love

As Leupp (1995:51) noted, the samurai, the warrior caste, "respected the Buddhist clergy and embraced many of their values," including misogyny. Samurai incorporated elements of the monastic tradition of sexual relations with the boys they trained. In Leupp's view, "the sexual relationship between males in the martial and samurai class unquestionably came to be modeled in part on the traditions of monks and courtiers" (the latter itself influenced or even modeled on the former). More generally, "military, like monastic, society is by its very nature conducive to the formation of male-male sexual relationships . . . [and] military emphasis on physical cultivation [recurrently] has led to glorification of the muscular male physique" (47). This last factor probably accounts for the samurai preference for "somewhat older partners— boys in their mid-teens—but they preserved the tradition of age-structured, contractual and exclusive relationships" (241n. 165). During the centuries of warlord civil war before the pax Tokugawa (i.e., before the seventeenth century), samurai beloveds were dressed elegantly, but not in feminine styles (57).

Age-graded homosexuality was prevalent and accepted at least by the upper classes in Japan's feudal hierarchy prior to the Meiji "restoration" in 1868. However,

> the cultural tradition of homosexuality underwent a remarkable transformation in the world of the samurai: the term which designated the object of pederastic love changed from *chigo* (literally, young child) to *waskashū* (literally, young man). This corresponds to a change in the age suitable to be loved: the *chigo* would have been from about ten or eleven to sixteen or seventeen years old; the *waskashū* was now from about thirteen or

81. Leupp cautioned against the view of "situational homosexuality," noting that "some individuals may have taken holy orders in part because they preferred an all-male environment and its [particular] sexual opportunities" (1995:56).

fourteen to eighteen or nineteen, sometimes even more than twenty years old.[82] There appeared a homosexuality of a military type comparable to that of the Spartans. This kind of pederasty was called *shudo*. (Watanabe 1989:47)

Shudō is a shortened form of *wakashū-dō*, i.e., "the way" (*dō;* the Japanese word for the Chinese *tao*) of young (*waka*) men (*shu*), analogous to "the way of the gods" (*Shin-to*), or "the way of Buddha" (*Butsu-dō*), "the way of the warrior" (*bushidō*), and so forth. Despite the increase in age of the beloved, the *-dō* construction demonstrates that the love of the adolescent *wakashū* remained a spiritual endeavor, just as the cult of the *chigo* in Tendai and Shingon monasteries was conceived to be. The morality and spirituality were already stressed in the text in which the word *shūdō* is found for the first time, Ijiri Chusuke's 1482 *Essence of the Jakudō*, quoted by Watanabe (1989:109). He was already bemoaning the corruption of the spirit of the way. Later writings continued to stress spirituality: "It is the 'soul' which is the foundation of *shudo*. Insisting in this way on the morality and spirituality of *shudo* sometimes leads to the doctrine that the features and external appearance of the *waskashū* are only of secondary importance. The author of the *Danshoku ni rin no sho* (Book of the two moralities of homosexuality, 1665) says, for example, 'We call *waskashū* with pure souls "excellent *waskashū*." The goodness or badness of a *waskashū* reside not in his appearance but in his soul'" (Iwata in Watanabe 1989:113).

The explicitly Buddhist rationale in the 1643 "Record of Heartfelt Friends" (Noma 1976) treated "the boy's ability to respond to a man as evidence of *nasake*, [compassionate/]responsive love]. . . . Together, the man's lust and boy's relief of it serve as a form of Buddhist spiritual experience of mutability (*mujō*)," (Schalow 1990b:2). For a beautiful boy not to give himself to those lusting for him was to be like a flower with

82. In the *Shudō Monogatari* of 1661 (the 1643 *Shin'yūki* retitled) youth was trichotomized: childlike boys aged twelve to fourteen, beauty's peak between the ages of fifteen and seventeen, and the mature love with training in manly conduct of those aged eighteen to twenty. At twenty, the way of boy-love (*shūdō*) ended within this schema (Schalow 1990b:8–9). The *Wakashū no haru* (Springtime of Youths) calls those aged eleven to fourteen "blossoming flowers," those fifteen to eighteen "flourishing flowers," and those nineteen to twenty-one (poignantly) "falling flowers" (Leupp 1995:124). Japanese (like Chinese) are one year old at birth, so by Western reckoning a year needs to be subtracted from each of these ages. Leupp (1995:148) suggested that "pederastic interests seem to have been frowned upon even in men approaching thirty." This may have been so, but I find his evidence for this age break for ceasing to be a connosieur of boys unconvincing.

Figure 1. Clove oil lubricant being applied to an acolyte. From *Chico no sōshi* (Acolyte scroll), 1321.

no fragrance. Not to give himself to a suitable male lover was shameful and carried the risk of physical deformity in the next incarnation (Ihara 1990 [1687]:76, 119), while "no stigma was attached to the performance of the insertee role" (Leupp 1995:172).

In the ethos portrayed and legitimated by Ihara in *Nanshoku Okagami,* "there was a mutual emotional exchange between man and youth which embodies *ikiji,* or 'shared masculine pride.' . . . A youth was deemed worthy of male love if he possessed *nasake,* a form of empathy or love involving emotional sensitivity to the suffering of a potential lover and a desire to alleviate that suffering" (Schalow 1989a:122).

Leupp (1995:128) noted that "literature also commonly portrays *nanshoku* as an emotionally rewarding experience for the boys pursued. For example, they may be deeply touched by love letters from male admirers. They frequently take the initiative in offering themselves to men who attract them." In "Manners of the Wakashu," the poet Sōgi (1421–1502) wrote that "to have been loved provides happy memories for one's old age" (quoted in Watanabe 1989:110).

As for the ancient Greeks, the older warrior had a pedagogical duty: "To reward the wakashu for his giri [embracing his obligations], the nenja is duty-bound to see to his education" (Watanabe 1989:113, based on the 1687 *Nanshoku jussun no kagami*). In addition to the Buddhist duty to alleviate the suffering of others' longings, the youth was supposed to feel honored to submit to tutelage that included serving as the sheath (receptacle) for his mentor's sword (phallus):

> As in marriage, sex was only one element of the man-boy rela-
> tionship. The adult male lover (called a *nenja*) was supposed to
> provide social backing, emotional support, and a model of man-
> liness for the boy. In exchange, the boy was expected to be wor-
> thy of his lover by being a good student of samurai manhood.
> Together, they vowed to uphold the manly virtues of the samu-
> rai class: to be loyal, steadfast, and honorable in their actions.
> Not infrequently, the sincerity of the vow was proved by self-
> mutilation such as cutting the flesh on the arms or legs or sev-
> ering parts of fingers. (Schalow 1990a:26)

Yamamoto Jōchō (1649–1719) cautioned that "what is really important is to practice the martial arts. It is only in this way that the shudo be-comes bushido" (quoted in Watanabe 1989:116).

Besides the spiritually tinged term *shūdō*, relationships were also re-ferred to with a brotherly term: *kyōdai keiyaku* (fraternal troth). Schalow (1990a:28) noted the use of *kyōdai-keiyaku* in two *nanshoku* stories "to designate a form of male love unknown in townsman society in which an adult male samurai and his *wakashū* lover were separated in age by only a few years. The term suggests the fictive kinship roles played by each in the relationship, one taking the role of elder brother (*ani-bun*) and the other taking the role of younger brother (*otōto-bun*)."

The *wakashū's* eager subordination was more important than his ac-tual age. In sociological terms, one might say that the rights and obliga-tions of the role outweighed the expected characteristics—**even the generally supposed prerequisite**—for incumbency in the roles. *Nan-shoku* was "legitimate whether or not a real man and real boy were in-volved, so long as one partner took the role of 'man' and the other the role of 'boy' in the relationship" (Schalow 1990a:29). Ihara's first and last samurai stories in *Nanshoku Okagami* (Great Mirror of Boy-Love, 1687) have boys of the same age playing the complementary roles, and the penultimate one has "two old cherry trees still in bloom," with a sixty-six-year old still loving a sixty-three-year old as a boy, "though his hair was thinning and had turned completely white" (Ihara 1990:181). Leupp (1989:139, 149–50) quoted a 1709 haiku in which a page forever

Figure 2. "Younger brother" (with forelocks) and "older brother" in bed. From *Iro monogatari*, ca. 1625.

remains "the lord's goods" and the lord forever remains the lord,[83] and discusses *Kikika no chigiri* ("The chrysanthemum vow"), a tale of devotion between adult men that is joyfully approved by the mother of one of them from Ueda Akinari's 1768 *Ugetsu Monogatari* (Zolbrod 1977:109–20). The latter collection of ghost stories also shows sons inheriting male bedmates of their dead fathers.

As already mentioned above, the boy following *wakashū-dō* was supposed to submit without thought of how attractive his *nenja* was. In the etiquette prescribed by Sogi in the late fifteenth century, "When one is courted, even if the admirer is not very pleasing, one may not fail to respond to his passion" (quoted in Watanabe 1989:110; see Schalow 1990b). In Ihara's story "Within the Fence," a fifteen-year old setting off to take up a position as a page worries about how terrible it would be to be viewed as a "heartless youth" (64). At least in fiction, boys were eager to be loved. In another story, "Love Vowed to the Dead," a boy gives himself to an old man who had once been an admirer of his lover. Although "such a love was very repulsive to Muranosuke, he had sworn at Gorokitji's deathbed to love the creature in his friend's place and he was bound by the honour of a samurai to fulfill his promise" (1972:8). The attractiveness of the *nenja* was normatively irrelevant to the *wakashū*, although if the youth was unattractive there would be no lust to extinguish, and, therefore, no chance to accumulate merit by selfless submission to men's passions.[84]

In Ihara's stories, and in many collected in the 1930s by Jun'ichi Iwata (see Watanabe 1989:52–73, 111), the *wakashū*'s obligation to be faithful to his master conflicted with his obligation to submit to the passion of other adult males when they were seen to be pining for the *wakashū* (Schalow 1990a:34). Discovery often led to death, but suicide was (and remains) a very popular ending for Japanese love stories. In other stories, the boy was not found out, or the *nenja* realized that the *wakashū* was motivated by compassion (*jihi*) for the suffering of some other man

83. One should not assume that continued loyalty and veneration necessarily implied continued sexual relations. Yamamoto Jōchō laid down the rule that, for samurai, homosexual pleasure must not be pursued at the same time as pleasure with women (1979 [1716]:59); an alternate interpretation of "one should not divide one's way into two" is that only after ceasing to be a *wakashū* can one follow the way of the samurai, *bushido*, rather than contrasting *nanshoku* and *joshuko*; see Leupp (1995:252n. 11). Yamamoto Jōchō himself fulfilled the Confucian obligation of marrying and siring descendants. Many, though not all, samurai "moved on" to marry women after their wakashū formally came of age (*genpuku*).

84. See Ihara (1990:118). Cf. I. Morris (1985:207) on the Heian era.

hopelessly in love with the *wakashū*,[85] whatever their rank (e.g., Ihara 1990 [1687]:71, 153; Watanabe 1989:52–65). Although Ihara deflated the pretensions of others, especially Buddhist priests, he **never** attributed the "infidelity" of a *wakashū* to the *wakashū's* lust. In the idealized picture of *wakashū-dō* he presented, the *wakashū* was motivated by duty to alleviate suffering, sacrificing his own interests, even breaking his vows, in order to share his body with those burning with desire for it. The *wakashū* Shume in "He Fell in Love When the Mountain Rose was in Bloom" exemplifies noble candor in telling his daimyo (lord): "A certain man has fallen in love with me. If I refuse him, I betray my honor as a follower of the way of boy-love. If I act freely, it means breaking my lord's laws and is tantamount to rejecting your longstanding benevolence toward me. Please kill me so that I may escape this quandary" (Ihara 1990:156). This request was not granted, and in other stories ("Love Letter sent in a Sea Bass," "Within the Fence") forbearance and/or an understanding of the honorable motivations of the *wakashū* also preserved the "unfaithful" *wakashū* from death.[86]

The other pressing contradiction of the way of boy-love was between the pledges of eternal love and the finiteness of youth. As already noted, at least in Ihara's fiction, there were *wakashū* older than twenty. In "At Last Rewarded for His Constancy" Inosuke encountered a man he knew desired him in his youth and told him "'It grieves me much that I was unable to return your love at that time; but my Lord loved me. Now I am free to love you; but I am no longer the pretty page I was when you cared for me so deeply. I am now a faded flower. But why regret the past? I have become a samurai, and am no longer a page; but I have the same heart for you. Love me, if you can feel the same ardency as before. I shall be happy to be loved by you.' And Inosuke put on his old page's dress

85. Schalow (1990a:34) remarked that karma providing "a Buddhist excuse for Confucian failings is common in Ihara's tales," but in addition to this convenient exculpation, compassion provides a worthier Buddhist motivation. It should be noted that in some of his other stories (e.g., "Grudge Provoked by a Sedge Hat" and "The Sickbed No Medicine Could Cure") the *wakashū* spurns advances from men smitten by his beauty other than the lover to whom he has pledged eternal fidelity.

86. In "Within the Fence" the *wakashū* was ordered to undergo an early coming-of-age ceremony. A relationship after the coming-of-age ceremony seems to be implicated for the illicit but rewarded pair in "A Sword Is His Only Memento." Schalow (25 May 1990 letter) interpreted the sexual relationship between the two who are now "true brothers" as put in the past by the coming-of-age ceremony. In "Within the Fence" and also in "He Fell in Love When the Mountain Rose was in Bloom" the illicit pair were separated after the lovemaking forborne by their lord.

with long sleeves, although it was not suitable for a grown man" (1972: 80). Elsewhere in the canon of samurai boy-love stories told by Ihara, Katsuya apparently continued to play the *wakashū* role after his coming-of-age ceremony in "A Sword Is His Only Memento" (Ihara 1990:96). Mondo in "Two Old Cherry Trees Still in Bloom" is the aforementioned sixty-three-year old *wakashū*, albeit one who retained the hairstyle of a boy (Ihara 1990:182). Watanabe (1989:121) also mentioned a *noh* play "Mastumushi" in which both members of the pair are grown men.[87]

As Buruma (1984:128) put it, "At the height of samurai power during the Kamakura period [1185–1333] women were despised as inferior creatures, 'holes to be borrowed' for producing children. Only manly love was considered worthy of a true warrior." The example of an ardent cult of boys' beauty, and of enduring patronage relationships for sexual favorites, came from the top in succeeding centuries. The third shogun, Ashikaga Yoshimitsu (1358–1408), the patron of the *noh* theater, was a bridge from monastic *chigo* to *sarugaku* troupes. His sons, notably the fourth shogun Yoshimoki (1368–1427) and the sixth shogun Yoshinori (1394–1441) were also smitten by admiration for lower-class actors, but promoted upper-class youth favorites, as well. Liaisons between lords and pages were entangled in the clashes between the Akamatsu clan, the Yamana clan, and the Ashikaga shoguns in the fifteenth century, including the civil war of 1467–68 (see Watanabe 1989:49–50).

The shogun most focused on male favorites was Tokugawa Tsuna-yoshi (1646–1709), whose

> reputation suffered from the excessive manner in which he indulged his sexual proclivities and the air of scandal that emanated from his affairs with handsome boys as well as women. Homosexuality was still common, perhaps even customary, among military aristocrats in the seventeenth century, and it could not have been considered remarkable that the shogun preferred boys to women. His father Iemitsu had a similar preference.[88] His great-grandfather Ieyasu [the first Tokugawa shogun], though he produced eleven sons and six daughters by this thirteen wives and concubines, and had six additional acknowledged concubines as well, had more than his share of boys. What

87. Although one can hardly expect representative samples of behavior or relationships in works of fiction, it seems to me that representations of variations from the norms are especially likely to reflect existing patterns.

88. See Caron (1671:24) on Ieyasu having "no lawful wife and being much given to Sodomy." Leupp (1995: 143–44) noted that Iemitsu, the third Tokugawa shogun, had played the "younger brother" (insertee) role with two older pages.

was unusual was the degree of Tsunayoshi's indulgence; he appointed a large number of youths of all classes to posts as attendants, and he promoted eleven or more of them to daimyo. (Shively 1970:97–98) [89]

According to the *Sanno gaiki* (Unofficial History of the Three Rulers), Tsunayoshi was passionately interested in males "no matter how humble [their origins], if they were handsome, he appointed them attendants." It listed nineteen daimyo who "were all selected because of sex. There were only a few who were not appointed attendant because of sex [three names listed]. Both Yanagisawa Yoshiyasu and Kuroda Naoshige pleased him with love from the time they were young pages, and finally they were promoted to daimyo. Others who please with sexual love and received stipend and rank are too numerous to count" (quoted by Shively 1970:98). Yanagisawa's estate increased a thousandfold, and he became not just a daimyo, but grand chamberlain. Shively (1970:98) remarked, "He was evidently clever in anticipating and pandering to Tsunayoshi's whims. He does, however, seem to have been in addition intelligent, well-educated and an able administrator," who was the most powerful minister during the last two decades of Tsunayoshi's rule. [90]

Tsunayoshi's example was imitated (99). In addition to shoguns, many of the great daimyos and samurai kept male lovers to provide emotional support as well as entertainment and sensual pleasure. In return for such services, the beloved youth was often given a secure official position in the hierarchy. It was esteemed an honor, although not a secure one, to serve the shogun or a high-ranking samurai as a lover. Shively, (1970:98), drawing on the official chronicle, the *Tokugawa jikki,* noted of Tsunayoshi's favorites, "Some youths who later displeased him, including some who had been made daimyo, were stripped of their ranks and sent into exile or put into the custody of daimyo. There were several youths who caught his eye but who, fearful of the risks that went with an appointment, declined the offer. They too were exiled."

Still, as Mathers wrote, "The sons of samurai families were urged to form homosexual alliances while youth lasted, and often these loves

89. In this he resembles the Han Emperor Ai, who promoted his favorites to important posts. Impersonal examinations for official posts was one T'ang social institution that was not borrowed in Japan (I. Morris 1985:84, 186; see note 73 above).

90. Ibrāhīm, the one-time catamite and later grand vizier of the Ottoman ruler Suleiman (1494–1566) seems an apt analog to Yanagasiwa Yoshiyasu, though Tsunayoshi's accomplishments in the realm of statecraft do not bear comparison with Suleiman's. Those who achieve high rank through sexual favoritism are not necessarily incompetent administrators (nor are all who do well on civil service exams necessarily competent ones).

matured into lifelong companionship. . . . The homosexual loves of the samurai ranged from those of high platonic ideals to sensual pederasty. The general attitude toward women was similar to that of classic Greece, specifically that women were for breeding but boys were for pleasure. Women in both cultures were thought to make men cowardly, effeminate and weak" (1972:xi–xii).

Bisexuality?

In addition to the two types of patronized insertees (younger samurai warriors and kabuki actors) Ihara's *Nanshoku Okagami* portrays two types of patron-insertors: connoisseurs of boys (*shojin-zuki*) and woman-haters (*onna-girai*). "*Shojin-zuki* had a nonexclusive interest in boys, which means that they generally were married, maintained households, and continued to have sexual relations with women. *Onna-girai*, on the other hand, did not marry and they completely rejected women as sexual partners" (Schalow 1990a:4).[91] *Nanshoku Okagami* has practically no representations of *shojin-zuki* heterosexual behavior or interest.

From this unsubstantiated distinction of behavior, Schalow leapt to making inferences about identities: "Since both groups could engage in man-boy sexual relations without stigma, their appreciation for boys did not serve as a distinguishing feature. As a result, sexual identity for men with an exclusive preference for boys was constructed from their sexual antipathy for women, and they thus got the name 'woman-haters'" (4; also see Schalow 1987:43, 1989a:120, 1989b:53). A term used by others increases the possibility of an identity crystallizing, but evidence that persons identify themselves by such a name or criterion is necessary. The existence of a label does not prove salience, let alone any self-application. Although there are characters with pronounced aversion to contact with women in three of the nineteen samurai boy-love stories, and in three of twenty kabuki stories, there is only one self-reference as "woman hater" in each half of *Nanshoku Okagami* (Ihara 1990:139, 310).[92]

91. An *onna-girai* in Ejima Kiseki's *Seken Musuoko Katagi* (Characters of Worldly Young Men) of 1715 was supplied a wife by his parents, but he refused to enter her room and did not want even to see women (Hibbett 1975:145–51). In *San no asa*, the onna-girai Hiraga Gennai categorically stated that "those who like female prostitutes dislike youths; those who like youths revile female prostitutes" (trans. Leupp 1995:101–2).

92. Statler (1961:161) retold a satire of a travel diary about Kamakuni, "a famous sodomite," and his servant, Kakuhei, who shares his master's tastes. Their journey is an epic of frustration. Typical is the night they stop at an inn in Samegai. Kamakuni's heart is set on a massage, but when he hunts for a masseur, he can find only a "thickly painted

As for bisexuality, it bears noting that, in the nineteen samurai stories, there is only one mention of intercourse with women by someone who has sexual relations with boys as well. Nagayoshi in "Drowned by Love" quite clearly loved women, even if he eventually is bored with them and finds a boy "a perfectly satisfactory replacement" for women, since "he found it impossible to abstain completely from sex" (Ihara 1990:165), which I read as ceasing sexual relations with women. There may have been a cultural "assumption that the interests of men depicted were directed at both women and boys," as Schalow 1987:44) wrote, but the text (as he translated it) is not a convincing basis for showing such an assumption, and still less for demonstrating a "more-or-less balanced interest in both women and boys" (45).[93]

In the kabuki stories, only one male (a boy-actor, not one of the patrons of boys) has sex with a woman, and in that case the dying girl is misrepresented as a dying boy when Shizuma agrees to the encounter in "He Pleaded for His Life." Although he is "sincerely devoted to the way of male love" (Ihara 1990:200), Shizuma continues from this deed of charity for a suffering creature directly to the monkhood. That is, even this rare instance of heterosexual behavior within *Nanshoku Okagami* is not part of a recurrent pattern of bisexual behavior. The boy-beloved considers himself polluted by sexual contact with a woman and rushes off for purification.

Unlike libertines in Restoration England, who were represented as having a boy on one arm and a woman on the other, the lovers of boys

---

woman, coquettishly revealing her red silk undergarment, while smoking a silvered pipe and spitting all the time." As Kamakuni's two greatest aversions are women and tobacco, he is "sick at heart," and that night, massage-less, he sleeps very badly. He is overjoyed "when he reaches Seikenji. Swept along exuberantly from one shop to another, Kamakuni and Kakuhei sample the wares in each. . . . When they finally stagger from the town, they are so burdened with salve [having bought from so many] that Kakuhei has to carry a huge bundle of it."

93. That "the boys were so skilled in lovemaking, it was like being with a woman" (Ihara 1990 [1687]:400) does not seem to me to warrant Halperin's (1991:400) interpretation that women were the standard against which to measure the beauty and erotic aptitude of boys. This may have some application to the kabuki boy-actors (in the second half of *Nanshoku Okagami*. As Danly (1990:941) noted, "Frequently enough, the youth's appeal is his masculinity, sufficient to draw women as well as men." In other instances it was ambiguity, not womanliness, that was the draw. Skill differs from both beauty and aptitude and would not be expected in samurai boys (although it could be expected of actor-prostitutes). The standard of beauty was not muscular/masculine, but more direct evidence than the equation of a boy-actor to Hakata courtesans (Ihara 1990 [1687]:400) is needed to establish that medieval Japanese who had sexual relations with boys saw young male beauty as feminine.

in *Nanshoku Okagami*, are not shown maintaining relationships with women.[94] For instance, in "Tears in a Paper Shop," Juroemon "stopped seeking other forms of sexual pleasure" (Ihara 1990:194). Those who shared the bed of Heihachi "lost interest in their wives" (242) and after a night with the actor Han'ya—even without sexual relations—the man from Tosa "was utterly bored with even the shapeliest of courtesans" (260) and died of love for Han'ya on the voyage home. The norm—at least the statistical norm in *Nanshoku Okagami*—is for the man who loved a boy to become a monk once the boy ceases to exist (either dying or metamorphosing by coming of age), not to return to women or to a bisexual savoring of women and boys. Nor do the boy-actors in this canonical collection "grow up" to love women, or even to engage in heterosexual behavior (203, 236, 266, 282).[95]

Similarly, in the kabuki play *The Scarlet Princess of Edo*,[96] the priest Seigen, who (seventeen years earlier) failed to join Shiragiku (his "younger brother" acolyte) in committing suicide,[97] does not succeed in seducing the beautiful woman, the Princess Sagakura, who—in any case, as he comes to realize—is the reincarnation of his earlier love. It is the acolyte Shiragiku that Seigen sees and loves in Sakura.[98] Even if this does not make the woman "really a man," the priest does not have sex with her/him, and (in some sense) she causes him to die, so the play does not instantiate bisexuality, let alone unproblematic bisexuality, as Leupp (1995:99) wanted to take it as doing. Nor does the tale of an Osaka boy lover who agrees to visit the female prostitute quarter but does not actually get there (advanced as an example of "even characters particularly attracted to other males are often open to heterosexual adventures" by Leupp 1995:96). I also question Leupp's (1995:98) interpretation of why an acolyte in Ihara's *Kōshuoku gonin onna* should not commit suicide

94. The nobleman who mistakes Kichiya for a woman in "A Secret Visit Leads to the Wrong Bed," and exclaims "All the better!" when he learns that Kichiya is not a woman, "and proceeded to give Kichiya the full measure of his affection" ((Ihara 1990 [1687]:241) may prefer boys and also pursue women, but within the story he does not have sexual relations with any women. The nobleman indicates lust for what he thinks is a woman, but "All the better!" does not suggest a preference for women.

95. Women yearned for a number of the actors in Ihara's stories, but compassion for such suffering led to only one liaison (on the part of the aforementioned Shizuma).

96. Translated in Brandon (1975:245–349). The play was first performed in 1817, but the theme of Seigen's love for Sakura had been popular since at least 1674 (242).

97. Shiragiku was the last of several "white chrysanthemums" Seigen had loved (Brandon 1975:283–84).

98. After failing to consummate his eternal passion with the incarnation of Sakura, Seigen tries to kill her, then asks her to kill him (Brandon 1975:328–89).

while his "older brother" is away: "The implication is that the 'older brother' will forgive his partner's heterosexual affair." While the "older brother" might indeed do so, I think that what is more salient is that the decision about what to do is the "older brother's" and should not be arrogated by the errant "younger brother." In Leupp's next example, Chikamatsu's *Mannengusa shinjū* (Stonecrop Temple Love Suicide, 1708) the Mount Koyā monk Yūben regards his nineteen-year-old "younger brother" Kumenosuke's affair with a girl as a disgrace (to Yūben) and breaks all ties, although he tells the ashamed boy that he will take him back "if only you break with the woman" (Kume so swears, and probably breaks his oath again before killing the woman and himself that night).[99] And it would hardly be necessary for the advocate of *joshuku* in *Denbu Monogatari* (an anonymous dialog from some time between 1636 and 1643, which Leupp (1995:205–17) translated as "A Boor's Tale") to feel sorry for parents who "have taken the trouble to finally arrange a good marriage for a son, only to be told 'I only like youths,'" or when the son "marries in order to please his parents but then greets his bride with 'I'm a boy lover'" (323). Still, the stigmatization of failure to sire sons was much greater in China, where ancestor worship, the obligations of filial piety, and Confucian dogma were stronger, and Buddhist rationales less readily accepted.

At least in the world of *Nanshoku Okagami*, outgrowing boy-love to become a lover of women, or a connoisseur of both boys and women, was not represented. Those who left *shūdō* behind renounced the world altogether, by becoming monks. This cannot be counted on as removal from the world of boy-love—and still less as "graduating" to heterosexual relations.

In Ihara's other work, boys are one savory dish rather than a *do*. Yonosuke, the libertine in his first great popular success *Koshoku Ichidai Otoko* (The Life of an Amorous Man 1964 [1682]), recorded 725 male and 3,742 female conquests in his diary, and Gengobei in *Koshoku Gonin Onna* (Ihara 1956 [1686]) moves from boys to girls, but such a transition is not visible in *Nanshoku Okagami*. If its readership[100] assumed that the samurai youths or the actors who provided sex to patrons settled down to marrying women and raising families, the evidence is extrinsic to the text. The text, especially the first and last story, present an ideology of

99. In Keene 1961:140–41.

100. Drake (1991:516–17, 519) argued—on the basis of literary style, printing format, and by contrast to other works—that Ihara aimed for the readers of his earlier books, not for a male-love connoisseur audience. Drake also called attention to Hiragi Gennai as a more direct proponent of male love than Ihara.

the superiority of boy-love.[101] The superiority of this way of life is assumed by most of the characters in the book.[102] The mercenary focus of
sexual transactions in the Genroku era is a leitmotif in *Nanshoku Okagami*,
with frequent invidious contrasts to an earlier, purportedly nobler and
less materialistic age (and a hoped-for future in which the cult will again
have more adherents). Nonetheless, therein Ihara consistently celebrated
devotion to one's patron and charity to one's admirers regardless of their
station; just as consistently he decried the commercial world of his day.[103]

Literary accounts of acolytes who developed passionate relationships
with girls or women do not establish the universality or even the gener-
ality of bisexuality. The Tokugawa story (translated in Levy 1973:196)
about "one who liked boys" but is persuaded by a friend to accompany
him to a house of female prostitution (advanced by Leupp 1995:96) is
particularly weak evidence for polymorphous libertinage in that the boy-
lover changes his mind and returns to the male quarter before getting to
the female quarters, let alone having intercourse with a woman.

Schalow (1989a:507n. 7) asserted that "the evidence for the bisexual
norm is convincing," but did not marshal any more evidence than the
example of Ihara's first popular hero, Yonosuke.[104] It may well be that
the general view was that "those who pursued sexual relations exclusively with women or exclusively with youths were in a minority and
were considered mildly eccentric for limiting their pleasurable options"
(Schalow 1989a:120). Even if the normativeness of bisexual behavior in
Tokugawa society were established, this would not, however, show that
those involved in *wakashū-do*—as *wakashū* or as *nenja*—were bisexual

101. Although these chapters are exaggerated for comic effect, it is hard to be sure
across time and space what would have seemed exaggerated to boy lovers of the time—or
to other Japanese then.

102. Two exceptions occur. A boy is no more than "a perfectly satisfactory replacement" for one man who is so "utterly bored with women" that he makes a beautiful young
lady "a widow with a living husband" (Ihara 1990 [1687]:165), and in "Loved by a Man in
a Box," the narrator, who can remember the names of a thousand boys from his "twenty-
seven years as a devotee of male love" is a discordant voice in the general celebration of
loving boys, in that he recalls "shar[ing] a sense of honor and masculine pride" with only
a few.

103. This is especially true in "Loved by a Man in a Box" and "The Koyama Barrier
Keeper," in which renting out one's body is de-romanticized. Distinguishing Ihara's own
"real" views from what those he had to espouse in order to be published is a hopeless endeavor, but insofar as he spoke in the voice of public morality, it was against the ruinous
cost of renting boys.

104. Some of the anonymous ribald seventeenth-century anecdotes Schalow (1996)
later translated (viz., 17, 18, 23) show men appreciating the orifices of both females and
males.

in behavior or identity. Moreover, the claim that either the ideal or statistical norms of those following *wakashū-do* (in contrast to those renting bodies) was bisexual needs a review—not just an assertion—of evidence.

Wakashū Masculinity

At least while the warrior caste predominated, which is to say prior to the unification of Japan in 1590 and the establishment of the Tokugawa Shogunate in 1603, boys who were sexual favorites of adults were not thereby rendered effeminate. Aristocratic boys were educated, and, at least officially, the masculine honor of their souls was the paramount consideration. In one of many invidious contrasts of the Genroku era (the late seventeenth century) and "the good old days" of a more sincere, more masculine, and less mercenary homosexuality, Ihara recalled, "In the old days, boy-love was something rough and brawny. Men swaggered when they spoke. They preferred big, husky boys, and bore cuts on their bodies as a sign of male love. This spirit reached even to boy actors, all of whom brandished swords" (Ihara 1990:307). Leupp (1995:52) quoted an 1813 historical explanation that "during the time the country was at war [ca. 1467–1600], nanshoku became prevalent, and many strong and courageous warriors emerged from among the [warrior's] male sex-partners." Good examples include Ishida Mutsunari, who became a page to Hideyoshi, fought beside him in major battles, and was designated by him to lead the invasion of Korea; and Bansaku, who died with his master following failure in resisting Hideyoshi's dominance of the country (Iwata 1989:52). In the debate about loving women or loving boys in *Denbu monogatari* (ca. 1640), the advocate of the latter points out that "most of those who storm onto the battlefield, warding off the enemy and accompanying their lords to the end, are the lords' male sex-partners [*gomotsu*]" (translation from Leupp 1995:214).

As among the ancient Greeks or early-twentieth-century Azande (see pp. 161–63), once they graduated from the role, most *wakashū* married, and they became the leading warriors of the next generation. Not all "outgrew" exclusive male homosexuality. Some did not even "outgrow" the boy role.

It is important to note that beloved boys did **not** do women's work. Prowess with a sword was expected of even the youngest *wakashū*.[105]

---

105. In the corpus of the *Nanshoku Okagami*, Rammaru in "Grudge Provoked by a Sedge Hat" slays a man who insults him. Katsuya in "A Sword Is His Only Memento" avenges his father's death. Jiinnosuke in "Love Letter Sent in a Sea Bass" cuts down two antagonists in a nocturnal battle. Even the "thoughtful, gentle-hearted" actor Hatsudayu

Figure 3. Man anally penetrating and masturbating a male prostitute (the chrysanthemum pattern on the quilt symbolizes the anus).

However, as in ancient Greece, over time, and with the decline of a warrior ethic (specifically, during the peace that followed the 1600 battle of Sekigahara), the ideal for the boy became increasingly effeminate.

In the woodblocks showing adult males penetrating *wakashū* there is nothing akin to the depiction of developed musculature in Greek sculpture and vase paintings (for the adult male, let alone for the boy).[106]

---

in "Tears in a Paper Shop" does not lack masculine pride and stands guard, ready to do battle on behalf of a patron. Hayanojo, who is monogamous to a fellow actor, exceeds even the samurai conception of honor in killing himself (Ihara 1990:266). "Boys in those days were real boys, concerned with love and honor, not just money" is something of a formula in *Nanshoku Okagami* (190). Ihara also repeatedly celebrated contemporary (to 1687) examples of selfless, compassionate service by actors giving themselves to impecunious and/or unattractive men out of loyalty to the ideals of love (1990 [1687]:199, 205, 224, 231, 245, 255, 263, 275, 300, 304).

106. E.g., those reproduced in Bowie 1970, Watanabe 1989, Schalow 1990a, Leupp 1995.

Indeed, nudity was avoided: robes were "often partially, strategically, but never entirely removed" (Bornoff 1991:180; "never" is—albeit only slightly—too categorical). As Bowie (1970:175) remarked,

> Whatever philosophy of beauty may have been evolved by Japanese estheticians, it is certain that it is not based on the harmonious proportions of the human body. What is most carefully represented is the costume, **not the body,** which seems to have served as something on which to hang costumes, and not the faces, which are not individuated. Indeed, the coiffures seem more expressive and are more carefully rendered than stylized, entirely expressionless mouths and eyes. Unclothed and/or partially-clothed bodies are vaguely drawn, [albeit] sometimes with very detailed drawings of gargantuan sexual organs.[107]

I want to conclude by dwelling on three comparativist points. The first is a significant **difference** between boy "wives" and ancient and feudal Japanese boy beloveds. Either as subtypes or as a continuum within the type, there are differences in the masculinization involved in age-graded homosexuality, which seems irrelevant for Zande boy wives, even though they grew up to become warriors, and central to the ancient Athenians, whose masculine honor could be affected by their behavior as an adolescent. In the Japanese case, the boy was not referred to as a "wife." As in Ming-era Fujian and contemporary Taiwan, "younger brother" was used sometimes, although the kinship idiom seems to have been relatively rare in Tokugawa-era pederastic relationships. Residues of earlier initiation rites have not been posited for the *wakashū,* as for the Korean *hwarang* and the Greek *eromenos.* Rather than being in training as a warrior, as in other cultures with age-graded homosexuality, it seems to me that the samurai youth's ability to fight with a sword was supposed to be inherent. The samurai were a **hereditary** military caste, and the caste's highly developed sense of honor was regarded as "natural," not as a product of indoctrination. Sexual receptivity to worthy elders was not viewed as detrimental to the masculine development of young samurai. It was both a duty and a pleasure—concevied as **physical** pleasure, not just the pleasure of serving a status superior. Taking pleasure in being

107. As Marguerite Yourcenar (1980:7) noted in explaining the effect of Guido Reni's painting of Saint Sebastian on the narrator of Mishima's *Kamen no Kokuhaku* (*Confessions of a Mask*), "Japanese art, even in its erotic engravings, never indulged, as did Western art, in the glorification of the nude. . . . The heroes of ancient Japan love and die within their shells of silk and steel." Also see I. Morris (1985:214), Buckley (1991:167).

anally penetrated was not stigmatized,[108] and there are Togukawa-era attestations of the view that "anal sex with an admirable older partner conferred the latter's virtues on the receptive one" (Leupp 25 Jan. 1996 letter, retracting 1995:128).

Leupp (1995:179) opined that it "seems to have been widely understood" in Togukawa Japan that "some men enjoyed anal penetration on purely physical, rather than emotional grounds."[109] It is difficult to distinguish pleasure from pain in facial expressions (when any were drawn). In Leupp's (1995) illustrations 5, 24, and 25, as well as in 11 and 29 (in both of which the youth is simultaneously penetrating a female), the *wakashū* also has an erection (visible non-erect *wakashū* penises are shown in illustrations 10, 15, 17, and 26; in illustrations 18 and 20 the man handles the erect penis of a boy he is not penetrating). Leupp (1995:180) refers to some woodblock prints that "show the passive partner ejaculating during anal intercourse" and relates several stories of adult males eager to be anally penetrated. Levy's (1973:194–95) story in which a matchmaker takes the wife's place for a night and the husband, grasping the matchmaker's penis, exclaims "No wonder it felt so good! I've come out all the way through the front" only makes sense if the matchmaker's penis was erect (an arousal which also seems consistent with his willingness to take the place of a woman who told him her husband always sodomized her).[110]

On a continuum of anxiety about masculinity within homoerotic relations, the African boy-wives would be at the low end, with the Japanese *wakashū* and the Cretan and Spartan *eromenoi* only slightly higher, Melanesian initiates markedly higher, the Athenian *eromenoi* (who were sons of citizens) higher still, and contemporary Anglo North America highest.[111] Not doing "women's work" differentiates the *wakashū* (along

108. Supposed (or fantasized) physiological consequences—hemorrhoids and becoming bowlegged (e.g., in the dialog translated in Leupp 1995:209)—suggest that there was, however, some ambivalence by the eighteenth century. There is nothing in Tokugawa (or earlier Japanese) literature at all like Aristophanes's satirical/scatological derogation of the distended anuses of males who permitted themselves to be penetrated, or like Roman invective against pathics.

109. I do not claim to understand how he can measure this distinction with available evidence, however.

110. See the similar Chinese story of a Buddhist priest and his disciple's ejaculation, p. 184.

111. In early modern Europe, the "catamite" role was not as public as the *wakashū* role was in medieval Japan, but there does not seem to have been anxiety about the boys being warped by sexual involvement with older boys or with adult men. Both life expectancy and marriage age were considerably lower than they are at present, and there are senses

with the Hawaiian *aikane*) from an African boy-wife, but women could know about his sexual behavior, which differentiates the *wakashū* from Melanesian (at least Sambian) initiates.[112]

I argue on pp. 95–105 that the Athenian ideology that the *eromenos* felt no sexual pleasure is belied by conventional representation of courting boys in Greek vase paintings in which the (sometimes seated) man reaches for the (invariably standing) boy's penis. I see more similarity between ancient Greece and pre-modern Japan pederasties than other comparativists have, and want to conclude by suggesting a diachronic regularity in the effeminization of the boy-beloyeds. The European scholars who see Greek pederasty as a residue of a trans-Indo-European male initiation rite have noted that the masculine ideals continued to erode over the period of Greek ascendancy for which there are historical records. The usual monk-samurai-kabuki order of discussing homosexuality in Japanese history obscures the fact that gender differences became increasingly salient during the seventeenth century in the domains of **both** kabuki and demobilized samurai. A parallel transformation of the dominant social organization of homosexuality from age-stratified to gender-stratified occurred somewhat later, around the beginning of the eighteenth century, in a Great Britain similarly recently unified after civil war (and subsequent naval warfare with the Dutch), and with similarly ascendant prosperous merchants and a similarly destabilized aristocracy (see Murray 1984:43, 1988). That is—despite the widespread equation of effeminacy and aristocracy (reviewed by Dynes 1985:14–15, 1990:74)—in both Japan and Great Britain **it was a rising, mercantile bourgeoisie in which effeminate homosexuality**

---

in which the cultural categories "childhood" and "sexuality" did not then exist (see Ariès 1962 Halperin 1990). Palpable anxiety about the effect of early sexual involvement exists in the United States of the present. There is unexamined application of the label "abuse," with a priori conclusions about "consent," along with cultural presumptions indicate that the older partner must have been the instigator, and that what might appear as seductiveness in a younger partner is illusory (children being "naturally" innocent and devoid of sexual drives, even after puberty in the view of some). Quite clearly, these presuppositions were inoperative in the seventeenth century, either in Japan or in Europe. "Consent" was not viewed as problematic; children did not have "rights," and, at least in Japan, were represented as seeking out relationships with admired elders (of varying age disparities; as noted, some were only nominal). In comparative perspective, one of the most interesting aspects of Ihara's samurai tales of male-male love is that he often wrote of the boy's viewpoint, whereas ancient Greek representations ignored the subjectivity of the boys involved in age-graded homosexuality.

112. I'm not sure what women were supposed to know about pederastic relations in ancient Greece.

became prominent. The popularity of boys on stage preceded the mid-seventeenth-century closing of theaters in (Puritan revolutionary) England, whereas it increased after the mid-seventeenth-century elite attempts to close Japanese theaters. With the Qing dynasty replacing the Ming in mid-seventeenth-century China, a parallel eclipse of pederastic patronage and comradely homosexual relations by gender-crossing actor-prostitutes occurred (see pp. 185–88).

2
Neither Masculinizing nor Feminizing Relations

The Hawaiian *Aikāne*

In Hawai'i at the time of European contact in the late eighteenthth century, the retinues of leading chiefs (*ali'i*) included young nobles, called *aikāne*. "All the chiefs had them," according to Lt. James King (Beaglehole 1967:624; also see Gunson 1964:58). An American sailor, John Ledyard (1963:133) averred that "sodomy is very prevalent if not universal among the chiefs, and we believe peculiar to them, as we never saw any appearance of it among the commonality."[1] Ledyard (1963: 132) stressed that the *al'i* bestowed "all those affections upon them [*aikāne*] that were intended for the other sex."[2] He further elaborated that "the cohabitation is between the chiefs and the most beautiful males they can procure about seventeen years old. . . . These youths follow them wherever they go, and are as narrowly looked after as the women in those countries where jealousy is so predominant a passion; they are extremely fond of them, and by a shocking inversion of the laws of nature, they bestow all those affections upon them that were intended for the other sex" (132). The institution was official, not in the least covert. According to Captain Cook's second in command, Charles Clerke, these youths were kept "for the amusement of his [the *ali'i*'s] leisure hours: "they talk of this infernal practice with all the indifference in the world, nor do I suppose they imagine any degree of infamy in it. . . . They are profligate to a most shameful degree in the indulgence of their lusts and passions" (Beaglehole 1967:596). The expedition's surgeon, David Samwell, mentioned *aikāne* whose "business is to commit the Sin of Onan upon the old King. This, however strange it may appear, is fact, as we learnt from frequent Enquiries about this curious Custom, and it is an office that is esteemed honourable among them & they have frequently asked us on seeing a handsome young fellow if he was not an

---

1. Whether he or anyone else looked for such an appearance is not mentioned. Robert Morris (1990) took proposals to enlist members of the British expedition into the *aikāne* role as evidence that commoners might undertake it, but the status of these alien beings was not that of commoners within the existing, highly stratified society.

2. Morris (1990) stressed that the word *aikāne* in old Hawaiian was explicitly sexual, suggesting "man-fucking" as a direct translation. There was more to the *aikāne* role than sex, but sex was a defining part.

Ikany [*aikāne*] to some of us" (1172). Exactly what sexual act Samwell was euphemizing is unclear,[3] but that a sexual relation was part of the *aikāne* role, and that this was considered natural by the Hawaiians, is quite clear from this and other passages, and from the word itself (see Robert Morris 1990). The Hawaiians, certain that the British must have a similar role, sought to learn which sailors were *aikāne* to which officers (1172), and tried to make competitive bids for the more desirable British sailors. For instance, Samwell recorded that as the ships were about to leave the island of Kaua'i, a chief sought to pay six hogs as brideprice for leaving behind temporarily "a handsome young fellow whose appearance he liked much" (1226). The future commander, Lt. King, also recounted that a chief asked Captain Cook "very seriously to leave me behind; I had had proposals by our friends to elope, & they promised to hide me in the hills till the Ships were gone & to make me a great man" (518–19). Hawaiian chiefs obviously thought such an offer was an honor, not the unthinkable dishonor Englishmen saw in sexual service to another man (and a "heathen" to boot). It bears stressing that had they agreed to serve as an *aikāne*, they would have been great **men**, not great women, or womanly men. Despite the distaste for such abominations recorded in officers' journals, they did not challenge the institution or the individuals involved in it, who often were the intermediaries between the chiefs and foreigners. For instance, no one demanded that the *aikāne* of Kamehameha I (the Great, ca. 1758–1819) be barred from spending the night on board ship. Samwell reported, "He with many of his attendants took up his quarters on board the ship for the Night: among them is a Young Man of whom he seems very fond, which does not in the least surprise us as we have had opportunities before of being acquainted with a detestable part of his Character which he is not in the least anxious to conceal" (Beaglehole 1967:1190). When younger, not unlike Julius Caesar and also his adopted son Octavius/Augustus, Kamehameha was supposed to have served as an *aikāne* himself, competing with another noble youth for the affections of Kalaniopu'u (512–13). There was certainly nothing effeminate about Kamehameha, who united Hawai'i and Maui by force of arms, nor about the *aikāne* Palea who represented Kalaniopu'u in his absence when the British first sought to confer with the chief of Hawai'i (509). The *aikāne* "was a male sexual companion who in every other manner fulfilled the typical male roles within

---

3. Morris (1990) interpreted this as a reference to fellatio, but a non-insertive form of sexual congress seems more likely to me.

the society, often having one or more wives and children" (Gutmanis 1985:38). The British explorers were too shocked by sodomy to inquire about whether the young nobles were being formally trained to rule, or were only participant observers of governance.[4] Robert Morris (1992, 1995) and Kame'eleihiwa (1992) show that the *ali'i/aikāne* relationship was official as well as personal both in the canon of Hawaiian legend and in what can be reconstructed of pre-contact Hawaiian history: *aikāne* "had mana, participated in sacred rites, and were desirable members of the community" (Robert Morris 1992:91). Despite differences in status and a tendency for there to be differences in age, Morris's work considered such relationships relatively egalitarian same-sex love. Indeed, he asserted a lack of

> clearcut class, status, or age differentiations in the *aikāne* relationships. *Aikāne* seems to apply to both partners and sexes equally, and there are stories where the ages and ranks are the same, others where they are radically different, and still others where they are not even stated. Also, once the two men or women become the *aikāne* of each other, any distinctions tend to disappear. The language reveals this in formulae such as "Ua noho pu iho la laua" (the two of them lived on together, both *pu* and *laua* giving the flavor of equality). The best example of this concept is the Lono and Kapa-ihi relationship in Fornander IV(2). (Robert Morris 1990 personal communication; see Robert Morris 1992:82–83)

Ancient Athenian Pederasty: Eros, Idealization, and Normative Constraints

What most people mean by "ancient Greece" is Athens. There, in contrast to in Sparta, Thebes, and Crete (each discussed above as instances of the first subtype), the representations of pederasty are somewhat ambivalent and, in Plato's case, decorporealized. The ideal for comportment of an *eromenos* (the beardless adolescent beloved) included "refusal of payment, obdurate postponement of any bodily contact until the potential partner had proved his worth, abstention from any sensual enjoyment of such contact, insistence on an upright position, avoidance of meeting the partner's eye during consummation, denial of true penetration" (Dover 1978:107). In his magisterial account in *Greek*

---

4. They piously deplored the low status of Polynesian women, as if their own women were treated as equals and were included in every aspect of the lives of their husbands— who were half way around the world from their female companions.

Homosexuality, Dover pressed this ideal as a **description** of all real behavior,[5] even though his evidence does not support his view of exclusively intercrural intercourse (*diamerion*) without eye contact. After describing vase paintings in which man and youth face each other, he noted that anal copulation was represented between unbearded males and between satyrs,[6] and that "in Greek comedy it [anal copulation] is assumed, save in *Birds* 706, to be the only model: and when Hellenistic poetry makes sufficiently unambiguous reference to what actually happens on the bodily plane, we encounter only anal, never intercrural, copulation" (99).[7] To take one example, in Theokritos's fifth idyll (from the early Hellenistic period) the shepherd Komatas reminds his former protégé Lakon: "Once when I buggered your bum and you said that it hurt. . . . Don't you remember the time I was up you, and you with a grimace wiggled your bottom deliciously, holding on tight to that oak tree?" (116–17, trans. Daryl Hine; Lakon then reminds Komatas that Komatas was fucked against the same tree by Eumarus).

5. Cf. D. Cohen's (1991) much more sophisticated analysis of the interpretation and manipulation of norms and of collusion in not confronting contradictions between what occurs and what is said to occur.

6. Shapiro (1981) called attention to the relatively brief florescence of man-boy courtship scenes on Athenian vases (550–500 B.C.). He also noted that "by the late sixth century the erastes is often a beardless youth himself, and his eromenos also appears younger [than in earlier representations], sometimes barely pubescent" (135). He cautioned that artistic conventions cannot easily be distinguished from social conventions, although the vogue in homoerotic pottery coincides with the vogue of Anakreon's homoerotic poetry in the Athens of Peisistratos and his sons (who were ardent pederasts).

7. According to Henderson (1991:212) "A small phallus and a large rear-end, like some of the athletic youths we see displayed on vase-paintings, meant manliness and anal integrity [citing Aristophanes, *Clouds* 1014, 1018, *Eubulus* 11.2]. A large phallus and a small rear end (much worn by buggery rather than well-muscled by exercise) meant idleness and pathic depravity [citing *Clouds* 1014, 1018, *Frogs* 1070]." The British Museum has a vase (ARV 1154, fig. R954 in Dover 1978, fig. 263 in Keuls 1993, fig. 12 in Percy 1996) in which a smaller, naked boy with what seems to be an erect penis is climbing onto the lap of a larger (but unbearded) nude male with an unmistakably erect penis. A cup in Boston (see fig. B598 in Dover, fig. 253 in Keuls) shows a youth first stroking the beard of the elder who fondles his genitals and then pulling himself up ("not a gesture of supplication," as Dover (1978:96) drily puts it; I would say that it represents a youth's enthusiastic participation), and a cup in Toledo, Ohio (see fig. 51 in Keuls) shows a beardless but seemingly full-grown young man looking quite happy at being about to be penetrated from behind by a bearded man (whose staff symbolically goes all the way through him at an only slightly different angle from that of his penis). DeVries (forthcoming, 30) discussed bearded eromenai on black vases, especially those done by the artist known as Affecter, and the lack of comedy about intercrural intercourse: "The one mention of *diamerion* intercourse in a homosexual context comes in the *Birds* [706] and is neutral, if not downright favorable."

Evidence such as his quotation (on page 52) of the view expressed in Xenophon's *Symposium* (8, 21) that "the boy does not share in the man's pleasure in intercourse, as a woman does; cold sober, he looks upon the other drunk with sexual desire" shows that the *eromenos* was not **supposed**—at least by one of the sternest upholders of heterosexual marriage—to enjoy sexual activity; it does not constitute evidence that none did. If the eromenos role was all love (*philia*) and no eros, as Dover (1978:53, 103) maintained, it is puzzling that in the vase paintings, the erastes's conventional approach is made by reaching for the boy's penis (e.g., fig. 4). Boys frequently grasp an arm of the man—often not the one reaching for the boy's penis (rather than one reaching for the chin chuck; some of the boys are also shown reaching for the man's chin). Even those instances in which the boy holds the arm reaching for his genitals, he is as likely to be pulling the arm toward him as he is to be pushing it away.[8] Any doubt that the men are reaching for the penis and not for the thighs is dispelled by Dover's illustration R651. It seems to me that the penises of at least two of the three boys in R196a, as well as that of the one in R295, may also be erect: they are pointed out, whereas, despite their small size and the large size of their testicles, boys' penises generally point downward in representations of homosexual courtship in Greek vase paintings.[9] But even if neither of these boys' penises were intended by the painters nor read by ancient Greek viewers as erect, why would the penis of someone with no sensual part to play be fondled? If the aim was not to arouse the boy, then the man doing the fondling must have had some erotic interest in the boy's penis,[10] though the norms

8. DeVries (1993) compared depictions of male-female pairs in which "the standard iconographical interpretation is strongly at variance with that of the parallel homosexual scenes" (3) and argued that both the chin chucks and the graspings of the other's arm indicate closeness and warm feelings, not domination, resistance, or restraint (4).

9. Moreover, "in scenes of the most approved male intercourse—in which the erastes put his penis between the eromenos' thighs—the junior partners are indeed aroused. Of the four times in which an eromenos' penis is shown in these scenes, it is enlarged three times" (DeVries 1993:5).

10. Similarly, the gibe in Aristophanes's *Wasps* (568) at Philokleon attending the *dokimasia* (presentation and interrogation) of young men seeking to join the ranks of adult citizens in order to see their genitals and the report of the need for boys to brush the sand where they have sat to efface the imprint of their young appendages in *Clouds* (972–73) is inexplicable within the normative culture envisioned by Dover (1978), though earlier, Dover (1972:114) noted Right's considerable interest in boys' genitals in *Clouds*. In an addendum almost as startling as that in Halperin (1990), Dover (1978:204) added "the assumption that the erastes handles the penis of the eromenos during anal copulation" and that "this helps to explain why the erastes touches the penis of the eromenos in courtship (94–96)"! Albeit much later, Strato's collection of pederastic poems (*Mousa Paidiké*,

described by Dover provide no room for the boy's penis to be involved in Greek homosexuality. "What does the eromenos get out of submission to his erastes? The conventional Greek answer is no bodily pleasure," Dover (1978:52) explained. "What the erastes hopes to engender in the eromenos is not eros but love.[11] . . . Love inspired by admiration and gratitude towards the erastes, coupled with compassion, induces the eromenos to grant the 'favours' and perform the 'services' which the erastes so obviously and passionately desires; in that case, there is indeed love on both sides but eros on one side only" (53).

I cannot imagine very many people quarreling with Halperin's formulation: "Neither boys nor women were **thought to** possess the sort of desires that would impel them to become autonomous sexual actors . . . scanning the erotic horizon for attractive candidates uniquely adapted to their personal requirements" (1990:35; emphasis added). However, "ought not" does not establish "does not," and I would hesitate to conclude from the proscription of erotic experience that no Athenian boys or women chose their sexual partners or sexual acts, or that they were always "sexually inert," never experiencing any pleasure from wherever the male lovers whom they sought to please happened to thrust their erect penises. The boy was supposed initially to refuse, resist, even flee until he was certain the man was worthy. Coquetry was also wrong.[12] Boys could be too reluctant or too hasty.

Theognis recurrently warned boys (especially Kyrnos) who resisted his wooing about the transitory nature of young male beauty and the power the beloved had over the yearning adult lover, e.g., "Knowing in your heart that boyhood's bloom, for all its loveliness, is quicker than a spring around the track, seeing this, undo these bonds [i.e., those of Theognis's unsatisfied desire]. You may be bound someday, wild boy, when you get to the harder parts of love, like me now with you. So be

---

ca. 125 A.D.) included representations of men masturbating the boys while anally penetrating them, e.g., 12.22 from the *Palatine Anthology* and this one:

> Boy's cocks, Diodore, have three phases, or so those in the know say.
> Leave 'em alone and they babble, let 'em swell and they wail,
> but when a hand yanks 'em, those pricks talk.
> That's all you need to know.
> (PA 12.3; trans. Thomas Meyer in Jay 1981:270–71)

11. In Plato's *Symposium* (182c), Pausanias speaks of Aristogeiton's *eros* building Harmodius's *philia* (not a reciprocal eros or *anteros*, a returned eros). (The two were celebrated for their attempt to overthrow the tyrant Hippias in 514 B.C.)

12. In Aristotle's view (*Nicomachean Ethics* 1128b.16–20), the young ought to be bashful and inhibited by fear of doing anything shameful.

Figure 4. Young *erastoi* fondling or reaching for the penises of *eromenoi.* From Red-figure cup.

careful, or you could be undone by a bad boy" (Second Book 1305–10; trans. Bing and Cohen 1991:98–99).

He continues: "I beg, respect me, boy. Give pleasure. if you're ever to have the gift of Kypris with her wreath of violets, when it's you who's wanting and approaching another. May the goddess grant that you get exactly the same response [as you now make to me]." (Second Book 1330–34; trans. Bing and Cohen 1991:100) Similarly, Plato's Sokrates complains of overindulged beauties behaving like despots (*Meno* 76b), and his Pausanias complains of men eagerly seeking an extremity of enslavement that no slave would tolerate (*Symposium* 183a; also see *Critobulus* at 4.14), while some of the poems in the Palatine Anthology (PA) of Greek poems rejoice that age (in the form of hair) has ambushed formerly arrogant boys, for example,

> Nicander, ooh, your leg's got hairs!
> Watch they don't creep up into your arse,
> Because, darling, if they do, you'll soon know
> How the lovers flee you and the years go.
> (Alkaois of Messene, PA 12.30; trans. Tony Harrison in Jay
> 1981:121)

Or: "Beard and shaggy thigh-hairs, how quickly Time changes all things. Is this, Connichus, what you have come to? Did I not tell you, 'Seek not to be so harsh and rude in all ways; even beauty has its Nemesis?" Proud fellow, you have come within the fold [of those not sought as beauties]. That you want it now, we know; you might have had as much sense in those days" (Automedon 10; quoted by Tarán 1985:92, PA 11.326).

The preceding two extracts represent one kind of non-normative desire (the *eromenos*'s wish to continue). The following two represent another (an *erastes*'s willingness to tarry with an overripe *eromenos*):

> Your love won't last much longer, Pamphilus.
> Already there's hair on your thing,
> down on your cheeks and another lust ahead.
> But a little of the old spark's still there,
> so don't be stingy—opportunity is love's friend.
> (Phanias, 12.31; trans. Thomas Meyer in Jay 1981:157)

And: "Even though the invading down and the delicate auburn curls of thy temple have leapt upon thee, that does not make me shun my beloved, but this beauty is mine, even if there be a beard and hairs" (Strato, ca. 125 A.D., PA 12.178; quoted by Tarán 1985:104).

The following suggests that another youth (Arhestratus) had been accustomed to spurning admirers and, after puberty had reduced his desirability, now sought them: Philip of Thessalonika complained, "Now that you are darkening with loathsome hair, you drag me to be your friend; you give me the straw, having given the harvest to others" (59; quoted from Tarán 1985:94, PA 11.36). Still, the poet seems to be going along, not avenging earlier slights by refusing the boy who, during his prime, had spurned him.

Winkler (1990) stressed that ancient Greek women (like modern Mediterranean women) exercised choices—erotic and other—behind the facade of respectability and passivity they had to keep up.[13] Evidence that boys, too, exercised some choices and departed from the prescriptive norms seeps through what Plato and Xenophon wrote about some of those who wanted Sokrates to be their *erastes*.[14] Halperin (1986: 64n.10) maintained that when Plato's character Aristophanes in the *Symposium* (191–92) speaks of "a willing boy [who] 'enjoys' and 'welcomes' his lover's physical attentions," one must distinguish "welcoming" his lover's physical attentions from "desiring them sexually [which] is quite another" phenomenon. This is a difficult distinction to maintain

---

13. Maintaining appearances obviously constrains autonomy, but not totally.

14. In Plato's *Symposium* (192b), *philerastes* is a kind of person, one who seeks and loves an *erastes*.

intellectually. I would hazard the guess that it is even more difficult to maintain while naked and in physical contact.[15]

Enjoyment of sex was similarly proscribed for Victorian women. Indeed, refusal of payment, obdurate postponement of any bodily contact until the potential partner had proved his worth, and abstention from any sensual enjoyment of such contact, were also attributed to Victorian "ladies" in Great Britain and the United States, as well as to the objects of male desires in any number of cultures throughout history. One notable example is the boy loved by Japanese samurai, who were also normatively motivated by compassion to relieve the sufferings of those who desired them.

Proper *eromenai* who conformed exactly to the highest ideal standards may well have regarded others who enjoyed sex as ("no better than") prostitutes, just as proper Victorian ladies did. Scholars, however, should reserve "prostitution" for use as a technical term defined by monetary exchange, rather than follow popular moralisms (past or present) that lump all sensuality together as "prostitution." Dover did just that in the course of his argument, ignoring his own methodological cautions against "the readiness with which people extend an originally precise term for a specific type of sexual behavior to all sexual behavior of which they disapprove and even to non-sexual behavior, which is for any reason unwelcome to them. *Porneia*, for example, means 'prostitution' in classical Greek [from 'to sell'] but in later Greek (e.g., I Corinthians 5:1) is applied to any sexual behavior towards which the writer is hostile" (Dover 1978:17).

While Dover (1975, 1978) rightly considered persuasive orations as a better guide to general cultural assumptions than philosophical discourses were, such evidence must be used carefully. Aiskhines's indictment of Timarkhos was not intended to—and does not—provide a description of Athens, ca. 346 B.C.. Timarkhos sought to have Aiskhines

---

15. See Murray (1995:264–73) on a relatively recent parallel denial about what young Amazonian males were "really doing" when they were fondling each other's penises to ejaculation. Halperin (1990:160n. 31) re-drew the distinction as "between wanting to coöperate and wanting to submit," a slightly clearer distinction, so long as the *erastes* did not seek to penetrate the *eromenos*. In a startling one-page afterword to his book (225), Halperin accepted that there are hitherto neglected vase paintings both of "a reversal of conventional erotic roles between man and boy" and "of reciprocal erotic contacts between adult males." (If he used "reciprocal" here as elsewhere in the text, this means that a pair of men penetrate each other in sequence.) I saw a black-on-red pot on display in the National Archaeology Museum in Athens in October 1996 (bearing no catalog number and of which photographing was forbidden) that shows two bearded men embracing.

disenfranchised to block Demosthenes' party (of which Timarkhos was a prominent advocate) from prosecuting him (for selling out Athens as one of its ambassadors who arranged the peace treaty with Philip II of Macedon). As Hoffman noted, "In such politically motivated trials it was the standard procedure to attack the opponent with a law that was both vague and destructive to the reputation. The possible truth of the accusation was irrelevant, for the purpose of the prosecution was to damage the credibility of the opponent. . . . The classic example of such a political trial is that of Sokrates, who had broken no laws at all" (1980:419).[16]

Even keeping its sensational political purposes in mind, interpreting Aiskhines's oration is difficult. As it is the only surviving example of a *dokimasia rhētorōn* (a challenge to the fitness of a citizen to participate in public life), we have no way of knowing what were its genre conventions. (For comparison, imagine the American culture that would be reconstructed from one prosecutor's closing statement to a jury.) As Winkler explicitly recognized, "Behind sentences that begin 'The Greeks believe ___' there lies a fairly small set of elite canonized texts [and] many of them are what I would call legislative rather than descriptive" (1990:69),[17] plus this one oration. A lawyerly political harangue—particularly in the fractious atmosphere of Athens as it was losing its dom-

---

16. Dover too readily accepted conviction as proof that Aiskhines's charges were true, as do those late-twentieth-century scholars who have in effect retried those convicted of sodomy in early modern Europe and America (see p. 140 below). Aiskhines presented no direct evidence, such as the lists of prostitutes compiled for taxation (Hoffman 1980:420).

17. Like Winkler, Halperin (1990) sometimes understands that ideal norms are mystifications for public consumption that people—especially non-elite Mediterranean men and women—may ignore or subvert in quotidian practice. For instance, "avoidance of anal intercourse in paederastic relations is the normative ideal [in fifth-century Athens], not the reality" (55), and "the general requirements of Greek morality radically underdetermine the definition of proper conduct for an individual in any particular situation" (68). Halperin's goal was "to recover the terms in which the experiences of individuals belonging to past societies were actually constituted" (29), but, before completing even a single page, treated sexual behavior in classical Athens "as an action performed by one person upon another." Despite "hasten[ing] to emphasize that this formulation does not purport to describe positively what the experience of sex was 'really' like for all members of Athenian society, but to indicate how sex was represented" (30), a paragraph later Halperin shifted to claiming this as "experience" ("deeply polarizing experience," to be exact). He has written about "sexual protocols," not about what the *eromenoi* (or slaves or wives) experienced. Like Weeks and others, Halperin asserted that "their [classical Athenians'] very desires had already been shaped by the shared cultural definition of sex" (32). This is an affirmation of faith, not anything Halperin (or Foucault or Weeks) has demonstrated. (And, even if more evidence were extant, they could not demonstrate it without exploring what he calls "erotic phenomenology" of particular individuals and eschews.)

inance—should not be taken as an evenhanded and transparent account of Athenian law, or of the offensiveness of what someone was accused of doing. Unfortunately, Dover's facile equation of sexual enjoyment and prostitution led to a dubious interpretation of the trial of Timarkhos, the data he most extensively discussed.

As David Cohen (1991:222) noted, Aiskhines (1.7–8) in his successful prosecution, listed "an imposing array of offenses . . . exclusively concerned to protect minors and to exclude from public life those who had accepted a sexual role unworthy of an Athenian citizen. Athenian law left males of all ages free to dispose of their bodies as they saw fit," though some conduct disqualified them from political participation. Hoffman (1980:420) explained the law forbidding citizens to participate in public life after having prostituted themselves as follows:

> The Athenians, like the Romans, treated their citizenship extremely seriously, and also like the Romans, they enacted laws to discourage citizens from engaging in occupations considered so indecorous that the majesty of citizenship was threatened. Prostitution was one of these professions for two reasons. On the one hand, most prostitutes were of the lowest social order. . . . On the other hand, the very nature of prostitution was repugnant to the concept of the free citizen, viz., the selling of one's body to another as if one were a slave.

Aiskhines's (29–32) explanation of the rationale of the law debarring from addressing the assembly anyone who had prostituted himself was "because the legislator considered that one who had been a vendor of his own body for others to treat as they pleased would have no hesitation in selling the interests of the community as a whole" (Dover 1978:20). This pragmatic judgment about prostitution was entirely distinct from religious proscription of sex between males, or denial of full citizenship to someone known to have been an *eromenos* or an *erastes,* or both. Indeed, in prosecuting Timarkhos, Aiskhines stated that he had been and continued to be a boy lover who wrote the boy-love poems attributed to him (§136; translated in Dover 1978:42). Even had the Greeks not valued and institutionalized such relationships, "the Greeks neither inherited nor developed a belief that a divine power had revealed to mankind a code of laws for the regulation of sexual behaviour; they had no religious institution possessed of the authority to enforce sexual prohibitions" (203; also see D. Cohen 1991:222–23). Indeed, far from condemning male-male eros, their religion attributed involvement in and enjoyment of it to their gods, as their poets and playwrights did to legendary and

historical heroes. Greek writers (particularly in the poems Strato collected in Book 12 of the *Palatine Anthology*) recurrently "avow with fer-
vor their preference for boys and proclaim the love of boys to be far more
enthralling than that of women" (Richlin 1983:35), not least because a
boy has an appendage with which to fill the man's wandering hand
while the boy is being anally penetrated. This is far from the undifferentiated "perfect nonchalance" about the sex of the object that Halperin
(1990:33) claimed. Not only did ancients notice that many, such as
Sophokles, "prefer liaisons with males to those with females," but the
Greeks believed that pederasty "is zealously pursued in those cities
throughout Hellas which, as compared with others, are ruled by good
laws," (Athenaeus, *Deipnosophistae* 13.601e), and "tyrants, to whom such
friendships are inimical, tried to abolish entirely relations between males.
Some even went so far as to set fire to the wrestling schools, regarding
them as counter-walls to their own citadels, and so demolished them;
this was done by Polycrates, the tyrant of Samos" (13.602c).

As in ancient Rome, what one did with slaves did not matter, any
more than what the slaves felt or thought mattered.[18] Moreover, there
is every reason to suppose behavior did not invariably conform to the
ideal of age-differentiated lovers with the beloved chastely submitting,
while never enjoying his submission. Even the hyperschematic Michel
Foucault (1986:194) was careful to distinguish the ideal norm from the
range of behavior, warning against imagining that only age-stratified
male-male sexual relations occurred: "One finds many references to
male love relationships that did not conform to this schema and did not
include this "age differential." We would be just as mistaken to suppose
that, though practiced, these other forms of relations were frowned
upon and regarded as unseemly. Relations between young boys were
deemed completely natural and in keeping with their condition. On the
other hand, people could mention as a special case—without censure—
an abiding love relationship between two men who were well past adolescence."[19] To deduce from prescription to description is the normative

18. A ready availability of slaves ("at every corner," according to D. Cohen 1991:194)
was not constant across classical Greece, or even throughout Athenian history, however.

19. Also see D. Cohen (1991:221–40); Aristophanes in the *Symposium;* and (David
Greenberg added), the heads of the Platonic Academy. The example Foucault (1986:
194n) gave of adults was Euripides continuing to love Agathon. (Euripides explained that
"in the beautiful, even the autumn is beautiful" (quoted in Plutarch, *Erotikos* 770). Of
course, a particular person remains younger that another, i.e., even when the former
ceases to be "young" he remains "younger." Foucault's example of boys eyeing each other
(Plato, *Charmides* 154c) indicates desire, but is not evidence of a relationship. As Foucault

fallacy. It seems to me that Dover (1978) committed it in concluding that (1) there were no same-age-group couples, (2) there was only inter-crural intercourse, and (3) the "passive" partner never enjoyed himself. In each case, he ignored evidence to the contrary. Such reasoning, as Hoffman (1980:421) suggested, is tantamount to concluding from Pro-hibition Era rhetoric that North Americans stopped drinking alcohol. Alas, such reasoning is not uncommon in inferences about homosexual behavior based on "Oh, no we don't do that" rhetoric elicited by ethno-graphers or happened upon by historians.

The case of ancient Greece demonstrates that adolescent "submission" to sexual relations with one's elders does not necessarily foster lifelong ef-feminacy, nor does it prevent one from later siring children. Indeed, un-due ardor for women or for a particular woman was what was regarded as effeminizing in Ancient Greece.[20]

Some European classicists interpret ancient Greek pedagogical ped-erasty as a residue of an earlier proto-Indo-European male initiation complex, and, therefore, as masculinizing in the same way that Melane-sian ritualized boy-insemination does.[21] British and American classicists

---

(1986:199) noted, some Greeks criticized men who frequented over-age boys, and scoffed at the Stoics for keeping their beloveds too long, up to age twenty-eight to twenty-nine, before moving from *eros* to *philia*. Around thirty was the proper age to marry as far back as Hesiod (ca. 800 B.C.) (*Work & Days* 696) and through Plato, while Aristotle (in *Politics* 7.14.6) recommended thirty-seven or a little earlier for men (and eighteen for women). By the end of the third century A.D., Charicles, the advocate of loving women in pseudo-Lucan's *Erotes*, expresses wonder that a twenty-year-old male could still have any appeal (§26). In reply, Callicratidas maintains a noncorporeal (Platonic) love that properly con-tinues beyond youth (§48–49).

20. King (1991) shows the that both the classical and later Greeks regarded enthusi-astic **hetero**sexuality as effeminizing a man. Traditions of Akhilles as an ardent hetero-sexual suitor have him (like Herakles) undertaking women's work and even cross dressing. While love with Patroklos was masculinizing for the young warrior, falling in love with Deidameia "is not merely the result of assumed effeminacy that allows him to move freely among beautiful maidens but is the cause of that effeminacy" (King 1991:182). By the time of the Hellenistic dialog of the pseudo-Lucan, the advocate for the love of woman, Charicles, a young man from Corinth, is described by the narrator as "not only handsome but shows some evidence in skillful use of cosmetics, because, I imagine, he wants to at-tract the women" (*Erotes* 9). Reliance on artificial beauty aids is a recurrent reason ad-vanced to scorn women, not least in the diatribe in the response of Callicratidas, Charicles's opponent (§38–44).

21. E.g., Dumézil 1969, 1986; Sergent 1986; Bremmer 1980; and Patzer 1982, resur-recting Bethe 1907. Their favorite text (e.g., see Sergent 1986:9–13) is Strabo (10,483), which describes a Cretan custom of abducting a noble youth, as quoted above (see pp. 35–

who are critical of linking fifth-century B.C. pederasty to male initiation do not consider the boys whose compassion (never, in their view, desire) motivated them to permit men access to the inside of their thighs to have been masculinized by such behavior, even if their masculinity was enhanced by their relationships with older mentors.[22] In the view of Anglo scholars, although temporarily in an inferior position of submission, so long as the freeborn youth avoided penetration, payment, and any public indications of sexual desire to be penetrated, and ceased passive intercrural intercourse when he reached maturity (made generally visible by the growth of a beard), he remained distinct from the socially inferior, penetrable categories of women and slaves. In this view, although playing the *eromenos* (beloved) role did not masculinize the boys,[23] neither did it stigmatize or effeminize them.[24] In his turn, an *eromenos* was

---

36). Halperin (1996:722) rightly distinguished classical Athenian pederasty from pederastic rites of passage by noting that the former "proceeded by means of elective pair bonding, not by compulsory induction of entire age classes" and that "pederastic sex was not a prerequisite for admission to any rank or group membership in Athenian society." Elective pair bonding characterized even Cretan custom: although all Cretan boys went through compulsory training, only some of the aristocratic ones were taken away by one of their elders.

22. Dover (1988:115–34) argued that the didactic relationship between man and boy was superimposed on the erotic. He criticized Sergent's method of recognizing the oldest version of myths as consisting of nothing more than choosing whichever one best fits his theory of initiation, and he also accused Sergent, Bremmer, and others of retrojecting materials from twentieth-century New Guinea ethnography back to provide some content and motivation for supposed proto-Indo-European initiations.

23. In 1999 comments on an earlier draft of this chapter, David Greenberg argued that pederasty imparted to the *eromenos* courage in battle and philosophical wisdom, both of which were considered masculine. I am not convinced that courage in battle was an outcome in the Athenian view (in contrast to Theban and Spartan ones). At least for Plato, the second is plausible.

24. Even far into Hellenistic times, in Achilles Tatius's decidedly heterosexual romance *Clitophon and Leucippe* (variously dated from the second to the start of the fourth century A.D.), in which virginity is not only highly valued but is long preserved (with considerable difficulty) by the title characters, no stigma attaches to the boy lovers, or to their devoted boys (only to the main villain, Thersander, whose calculatingness and undue enjoyment of being many men's *pathicus* are recalled in a trial in *Ephesus* 8.9). The two boy lovers are not the main characters, but they are brave and loyal as none of Clitophon's woman-loving supposed "friends" are. There is nothing effeminate about their beloveds, either. Both die while engaging in masculine pursuits (trying to break a horse, and standing before the charge of a wild boar) before they could be polluted by women and marriage. And, although Clitophon argues for loving women, he does not condemn those who love boys. He not only gladly associates with them, but seeks advice about love from Clinias, who he recognizes was "initiated before me into the mysteries of the god [Eros] and [is] better acquainted with the course required to become an adept" (1.9).

expected to join the ranks of the phallic insertors. Most eventually married and sired children,[25] although doing so did not preclude continuing to play the *erastes* role to new cohorts of youth.[26]

Latin America

The dominant idiom for homosexuality across Latin American is gendered (see pp. 267–75 below). Patron-client relations are ubiquitous in Latin American societies. In homosexual contexts, one of the scarce resources the patron may be able to supply is access to a place in which to have sex without being interrupted. Some Peruvian *pasivos* told me that they preferred older men both because they knew what to do and because they were more likely than younger men to have some place to go (to have sex) (1985 fieldnotes from Lima). The ability to exchange sexual favors for help with careers (or gifts or cash) is a factor in many male-male sexual relationships. Higher class and more advanced age are intertwined. The younger males in these relationships are not expected to cook and clean, or to dress or act like traditional Peruvian women.

The stray representations of (homo)sexual patron-client relationships involve the older and more affluent partner penetrating the junior, poorer one, though I heard reports of men in Mexico and Peru who are

---

25. However, by Hellenistic times, there were conceptions of some males who avoided any sexual involvement with females. In Firmicus Maternus's *Matheseos,* the final (ca. 334 A.D.) and most complete compendium of ancient Greek astrological theory, conjunctions of the planets Mercury and Mars on the ascendant at the time a male was born determine that he will be a lover of boys, and a particular angle makes lovers of boys who never wish for intercourse with women (7.15.1–2; Bram 1975:248–49). And back in late classical times, in the *Nicomachean Ethics* Aristotle distinguished males born with an exclusive preference for sex with males from those habituated to it, while treating both as natural. Both are among the dispositions or patterns of conduct the pleasure of which "are in some cases, due to nature, but which for others is the result of habit, as, for example, for those who were first sexually abused (*hubrizein*) when they were children. No one would describe as 'lacking in self-control' those for whom nature is the cause, any more than (one would so describe) women because they do mount but are mounted sexually" (1148b; translated and discussed as referring to adult male pathics by Dover 1978:168–69).

26. DeVries (1990) marshals evidence against the view that playing the *erastes* role was a circumscribed transitional phase (between being an *eromenos* and being a husband), showing that "the treatment of heterosexuality in Attic vase painting from the sixth to the fourth centuries strikingly parallels that of homosexuality throughout. . . . Shifts in homosexual representations and the cessation of particular types cannot be explained by changes in political attitudes toward homosexuality, since the depictions of heterosexuality underwent a closely similar development" (18,20). He also shows that there were *erestai* and would-be *erestai* in all classes, even among slaves (contrary to the recurrent view of homosexuality being an "aristocratic vice").

more interested in their protégés' front appendages than in rear entry-
way. Several stories in Damata (1983) represent age-stratified homosexuality—with a strong class basis in paying to use younger, poorer
men. The noncommissioned officers in the Brazilian novella *The Volunteer* unequivocally represent this pattern, labeling themselves (in Lacey's
translation) as "boy-lovers," and accept that their "nature" is to prefer
boys to women (217–19; also see the monologue in Abreu 1990:81–82).
Moreover, they pay the younger enlisted men they penetrate, departing
from the schema of queens paying studs for sexual services rendered.
And the "nature" of the boys (at least Ivo, the central object of desire in
The Volunteer) is to grow up and escape to women and marriage. There
are also representations of Mexican boys seeking sex with the narrator
in Ceballos (1969), and the variegated career of Adonis García, the narrator of Zapata (1979). For Argentina, there is N. Miller's (1992:201) discussion of the economic bases for age-differentiated lesbian and gay relationships, and earlier reflections on the situation there in the expatriate
Polish novelist Witold Gombrowicz's diaries from the early 1950s.

Love of *Pueri Delicati* in Republican and Early Imperial Rome

According to its traditions, the city of Rome was founded in 753 B.C.
Remains of settlements from as early as the middle of the second millennium B.C. have been excavated there, but the earliest written records
are from about 500 B.C. Around that time, several hamlets were beginning to coalesce at the strategic location where the main north-south
road crossed the Tiber River by means of an island. Linguistically and
culturally connected with their Latin and Italic (i.e., Indo-European)
neighbors to the east and south, the nascent city-state of Rome was
nonetheless initially under Etruscan domination. According to Athenaeus, "It is no disgrace for Etruscans to be seen doing anything in the
open, or even having anything done to them, for that is the custom of
the country. . . . They consort very eagerly with women, but find more
pleasure with boys and young men, who are very beautiful, since they
take the greatest care of their bodies and remove any repulsive hair that
sprouts on their bodies with pitch plasters or by shaving [rather than by
singeing, as Greeks did]" (*Deipnosophistae* 12.517d,518a–b). The influence of Etruscan customs was tenacious, and may still have been active in Rome as late as the first century A.D. Nonetheless, the Romans did
supplant their Etruscan tutors, overcome the Carthaginian threat, and
eventually impose their rule on the entire Mediterranean. Unlike the
Persians, Germans, or Egyptians, the Romans were not a large popula-

Table 1. Life Dates of Writers Mentioned, and of Selected Emperors

Writers	Emperors
Plautus 254–184 B.C.	
Terence 185–159 B.C.	
Lucilius 180–102 B.C.	
Catullus 84–54 B.C.	Julius Caesar 100–44 B.C.
Horace 65–8 B.C.	
Virgil 70–19 B.C.	Augustus 63 B.C.–14 A.D.
Tibullus 55–19 B.C.	
Ovid 43 B.C.–17 A.D.	Tiberius 42 B.C.–37 A.D.
Seneca the Elder 4 B.C.–65 A.D.	Claudius 10 B.C.–54 A.D.
Pliny the Elder 23–79	
Lucan 39–65	Nero 37–68
Martial 40–103	
Plutarch 46–119+	
Epicetus 55–135	
Juvenal 60–121	Hadrian 76–138
Tertullian 155–220+	Elagabalus 204–222
John Chrysostom 347–407	Constantine 306–337
Prudentius, b. 348	Julian 331–363
Jerome 374–419	
Augustine 396–430	

tion able to control much territory by force of numbers. Rather, they were a small group that managed to impose itself as a *Herrenschicht,* a thin layer of domination.

Greek Influences

As their dominions grew, the proportion of the population that could claim to be Roman through ancestral connection with the city of Rome inevitably declined. If "Roman" is confined to genealogical bases, some of the emperors were not Roman. For the Romans themselves, as the Empire grew, the basis for the appellation "Roman" came to be not blood but citizenship. The heterogeneity of those contained in the category provides a start to understanding the diverse evaluations of sexual behavior in a culture that spread across centuries and stretched across vast spaces.

Romans confronted peoples not only more numerous than they were, but possessed of venerable cultural traditions that those peoples strove to retain and foster even under foreign domination. Culturally pre-eminent among the older peoples on whom the Romans imposed their rule were, as is well known, the Greeks. To paraphrase Horace, politically prostrate Greece nonetheless triumphed culturally over her conqueror, and Rome became the first exemplar of a post-Hellenic civilization.[27] Not only Roman statuary, but a host of literary work such as Ovid's *Metamorphoses* and Virgil's *Aeneid* show how pervasive the Greek contribution to the masterworks of Roman culture was. Sometimes philological analysis permits examining more than one stage in the process of appropriation, as in the case of the common noun *catamitus*. This word is an early derivative of the name Ganymede, the beautiful boy snatched by the king of the gods (Roman Jupiter, Greek Zeus) in the guise of an eagle. *Catamitus* eventually came to be the label for any sexually receptive male prostitute.[28]

Borrowings from the Greeks were accompanied by a hounding sense of inferiority to Greek culture (see MacMullen 1982:486–88). In reaction, some Romans withdrew into a kind of anti-intellectualism that abandoned such fripperies as literature and the arts to the decadent Greeklings. Such an attitude is exemplified by Anchises in the sixth book of the *Aeneid*: Virgil portrays him as recommending that the Romans specialize in governing, leaving the arts to others. Since the late eighteenth century, this notion of Roman cultural inferiority has been revived by Philhellenes following Johann Winckelmann's lead. Often, it is assumed that the Romans did not merely fail to replicate the Greek

27. "Graecia capta ferum victorem cepit" (*Epistulae* 2.1.156).

28. *Pathicus* and *cinædus* also derived from Greek (see p. 255 below). C. Williams (1995:521–22) argued that Greek loanwords were so widespread that this should not be taken as evidence of the diffusion of the phenomenon from the Greeks. According to Boswell (1980:79), insertive male prostitutes were commonly called *exoleti*, but also *drauci*, *paedicatores*, and *glabri*. Since the last means "without hair" and generally refers to young pages and depilated (i.e., effeminate) men, prostitutes characterized as *glabri* can be presumed to have been sexually receptive. *Paedicator* did not apply only to prostitutes, but to penetrative customers of male prostitutes, slave owners, and lovers of freeborn Roman boys. *Drauci* were a kind of bodybuilder, who, like more than a few twentieth-century ones, could be rented. It was more of an occupational role within circuses than one defined by prostitution, even though entertainers' sexual availability has been a cliché across space and time. Although Laberius (70) marked receptivity by using *exoletus patiens*, there are many instances in which being the insertive partner in sex is an impossible reading of unmodified *exoleti*, notably Caligula turning his sisters into *exoleti* (Suetonius, *Caligula* 24; also see his *Julius* 49, *Tiberius* 43, and *Titus* 7). That Suetonius characterized Galba as preferring *praeduros* (hardbodied) *exoleti*, means that he liked post-adolescent males, not that they penetrated him (*Galba* 22). If Galba had been rumored to like being penetrated, Suetonius surely would have included that (more serious) charge. The connotation of *exolescere* was growing old and being worn out, not being hard and mature. Cf. the Greek contrast between *hōra* (prime-aged, i.e., downy-cheeked) and *exōros* (past the prime) (Dover 1978: 172). That, from early on, there were male prostitutes penetrating citizens is obvious from the indigenously Italian *fabula Atellana*, especially Pomponius's *Prosibulum* (frag. 75–76, 125–26, 148–50, 151, 153–54; the genre is discussed by Richlin 1983:41–44).

achievement, but that they caricatured and debased it—that the conquerors' bad taste and low morals combined to produce a pitiful mockery of "the Greek miracle." These perceived failings included substituting sensual anal penetration for (the lofty pedagogical ideology of) Greek pederasty confined to intercrural intercourse of boys indifferent to any pleasure.[29]

Another response to perceived inferiority that can be found in extant sources emphasized the primordial simplicity and purity of Rome before its people were corrupted by alien luxury. According to the patriotic fables of Livy and others, the early Romans exemplified guileless virtue. Toiling in the fields kept them too busy to plot intrigues against their neighbors, and, in any event, there were few worldly goods to incite envy. This idealized picture of the Republican past served as a foil for castigating later ubiquitous luxury, corruption, and coveting of goods (including sex objects). The image of early Roman purity exemplifies what Lovejoy and Boas (1935) labeled "hard primitivism." Wide acceptance of such myths of a vanished golden age of virtue legitimated attacking contemporaries for "un-Roman" behavior, especially sexual indulgence. In fact, as Veyne (1985:28–29) wrote, "Rome did not have to wait for hellenisation to allow various forms of love between males. One of the earliest relics of Latin literature, the plays of Plautus [died 184 B.C.], which pre-date the craze for things Greek, are full of homosexual allusions of a very native character. A much-repeated way of teasing a slave is to remind him of what his master expects of him, i.e., to get down on all fours."[30] As C. Williams elaborated, "Plautus makes references to the realities of sexual experience between males in so comfortable a manner as to suggest that those realities were a fact of life quite familiar to his audience, as familiarly Roman as the references to food, topography, military and political themes, and indeed heterosexual behaviour that are found throughout his plays. Rather than poking fun at bizarre foreign practices, Plautus's [homo]sexual jokes invite knowing chuckles" (1995:

29. "Not only are there no known examples of intercrural copulation in these Roman representations of male-to-male intercourse, the Roman artists infused images of anal intercourse between males with the same tender intimacy that pervades the images of male-female lovemaking on the Arretine ware and the House of Meander cups. The artists went to great pains to make the partner who is in the receptive position [but often on top of the penetrator] as dignified and attractive as the insertive partners. . . . These Roman depictions make both males as attractive as possible and show them mutually attracted to each other" (Clarke 1998:78), often gazing into each other's eyes.

30. In one unusual instance (Plautus's *Asinaria* 699ff.) a master appears to take the receptive role. The comic point of this is "his utter dependence on his slaves, who have money in their possession" (Lilja 1982:32n. 79).

519; see also Verstraete 1980:232; Cantarella 1992:99–100). Still, the invidious contrast between present corruption and past simplicity increased in popularity during the last century or so of the Roman Republic (146–27 B.C.), a period marked by brilliant military success abroad and political disaster at home. Rome's modest institutions were not designed to cope with the sudden influx of booty—luxury goods, art objects, and, especially, slaves—from foreign conquests. Shifts among many citizens from straitened circumstances to great wealth stimulated a vulgar opportunistic tone that grated on those loyal to the old ways—families whose relative status was declining. Despite Augustus's earnest strivings to reform imperial Roman society, the ostentatious nouveau-riche style persisted for several generations, into the second century A.D.

The Importance of Slaves

This great lurch forward was accompanied by a massive influx of slaves: Hopkins (1978:9, 102) estimated that by 31 B.C. there were at least two million slaves in Italy, out of a total population of six million. Although, like most ancient societies, the Romans probably had always countenanced slavery, the slaves of the peasant community of the early Republic were, of necessity, few. However, success in a series of wars yielded enormous infusions—as many as 25,000 captives in a single day. According to Finley (1980), by the end of the Roman Republic, slaves comprised 30 to 35 percent of the population of Roman Italy, a figure comparable to that for the antebellum American South. The cheapness and abundance of this form of property clearly invited arbitrariness and maltreatment. Slaves were routinely beaten for "sport" and to relieve masters' frustrations. Until the time of Hadrian, Roman law permitted summary execution of slaves by their owners.

Besides serving as targets for sadism, slaves, particularly those called *pueri delicati* ("a special type of handsome young voluptuaries . . . on intimate terms with their masters," according to Prescott's [1920:261] explanation) were also objects of lust. As the elder Seneca remarked, "Unchastity (*impudicitia*) is a crime in the freeborn, a duty (*officium*) for the freedman to his former masters (*patroni*), and a necessity (*necessitas*) for the slave" (*Controversies* 4, pref. 10). Attractive slaves in the great houses of the rich were expected not only to cater to their master's lust, but also to be sexually available for guests (see Horace's *Satires,* 1.2.116–119). Their plenitude made the role of slavery within Roman same-sex relations far more salient than it was in Greece, where, though it was not absent, it was much smaller and was counterbalanced by the concept of pederasty as an instrument of state building.

For all its importance, we know tantalizingly little about the sexual aspect of the Roman trade in slaves. The paucity of information reflects not only the prudery of modern scholars, but also blaséness about the activity in ancient times: slaves were an omnipresent part of the taken-for-granted background of life. We do know that many slaves were sold by free but indigent parents. Others were foundlings. Thus, there was an abundance of succulent young male and female flesh with which slave markets supplied the numerous brothels. Slaves would be set upon a slowly rotating platform, while the auctioneer lifted their garments so as to display not only the musculature and general physical condition of the specimen, but also the genitalia.

Contempt for Sexual Receptivity

Although Roman women had somewhat more power and influence than those of ancient Athens, there is no denying that the society was overwhelmingly male dominated. Accordingly, the Mediterranean normative model of dominating penetrator and subordinate penetratee was valid, so no disgrace fell to the insertor, although the insertee, if an adult citizen, could suffer opprobrium and even legal sanctions. The master/slave dichotomy intensified an agent/pathic distinction. The implication that the man who "takes it" enslaves himself to his penetrator is distinctively Roman. The compounding of degradations lent itself to particularly vicious exploitation in Roman politicking, as in Cicero's attacks (discussed below) on Marc Antony, whom he accused of enjoying being penetrated when he was an eager adolescent prostitute.[31]

The notion of self-abasement through accepting the role of **adult**

31. Marc Antony's defeater, Octavius (later Caesar Augustus) was rumored to have prostituted himself to Aulus Hirtius, governor-general of Spain, for three thousand gold pieces, to have been mounted by Julius Caesar as part of the price for being adopted by him, and to have singed his leg hairs to soften them for his older admirers (Suetonius *Augustus* 68; see Cicero's explaining away Octavius's youthful penetrations by Julius Caesar and by others in *Pro Caelio* 3.6). Some popular military commanders of the next generation, Sejanus and Otho (the latter of whom was briefly emperor) began their rises to power as catamites, according to Tacitus (*Annals* 4.1; *History* 1.30), and Suetonius's biography added that Otho attempted to keep his beard from growing (*Otho* 12). Otho's successor, Vitellius, gained favor by satisfying Tiberius (Suetonius, *Vitellius* 3, where he is represented as one of the *spintria*). Licinius Mucianus was able to presume a great deal on the emperor Vespasian for shared past sexual escapades (Suetonius, *Vespasian,* 13), and the future emperor Domitian was known to have offered (in writing) his body for hire as a youth and

pathic seems to have struck an especially sensitive nerve.[32] Perhaps it was being so vastly outnumbered in their empire that led Roman citizens to regard one member of the collective yielding himself to sexual "degradation" as a lessening of the strength of the community. Official concern that sexual inviolability (*pudicitia*) "should be kept safe for the Roman bloodline" was quite explicit (e.g., Valerius Maximus 6.1.9). Restrictions on coerced homosexual behavior in the army aimed to maintain group solidarity. At least de jure, soldiers were not allowed to marry women, but they were not obligated to be sexually complaisant even to well-connected commanders.[33]

Evidence from poetry and belles lettres is more abundant than is that from theatrical representations.[34] Catullus wrote some of his most plaintively eloquent lyrics on the joys and sorrows of being in love with the boy Juventius, who was outgrowing his role.[35] In his poem 61, he tells the bridegroom Manlius that he will have to cease his inordinate devotion to beautiful young slave boys and tells his *concubinus* that, once shorn of his locks, he will have to stop despising female love (121–50).[36]

---

was thought to have been enjoyed ("corruptum") by his eventual successor, Nerva (Suetonius, *Domitian* 1).

32. At the age of nineteen, Julius Caesar was very old to have been penetrated by Nicomedes, King of Bithynia. Gaius Memmius accused him of acting as a cup bearer with the rest of the prostitutes ("cum reqliquis exoletis"). His troops in Gaul, and both senators opposing his elevation, alluded contemptuously to the Bythinia interlude (Suetonius, *Julius* 49 includes these and more instances).

33. E.g., Plotius's successful defense of killing the tribune Lusius in 104 B.C., recounted in Valerius Maximus's history (6.1.12) and Plutarch's *Life of Marius* (13.4–8).

34. There are also visual artefacts, including some made of clay for a less affluent stratum than could own cameos, or even silver goblets. J. Clarke (1998) presented a plethora of possible interpretations of how representations of male-male anal intercourse might have been read by people he claims "were not at all like us in their sexuality" (3).

35. And, at least in poem 24, Catullus chastises Juventius for having permitted a particularly unworthy man entry to his *flosculus* ("'little flower' is a direct translation of the Greek word that represents the anus as a rosebud" [Greenberg 1995: 247n. 18] and the form of address to Juventius in the first phrase of the poem).

36. Manlius "is in exactly the same predicament as Victor, the husband-to-be in Martial 11.78: heterosexual intercourse is *ignortum opus* [unfamiliar work] to him (specifically, to his *mentula* [penis] as Martial has it)" (Thomsen 1992:68). He only knows male love (line 140). Whether Attis's self-castration is motivated by an inability to make a transition from the receptive role with men to an insertive role with women in Catullus's poem 63 is a subject of controversy (cf. Quinn 1972: 249–51; Lilja 1982: 59–60), as is the autobiographical content of Catullus's Juventius cycle. A classical Greek example of a recently married man whose desires were not re-chanelled by the rite of passage of marriage is the speech by Kritoboulus in praise of his *eromenos*, Kleinias, in Xenophon's *Symposium* (4.12–16).

Catullus appears to have been obsessed with forcible oral sex: being supine to daily irrumation by Memmius in 28.9–10, fantasizing, threatening, or attributing such degradation to his rivals in others (e.g., 16, 21, 28.12–13, 74, 80, 97, 113; see Richlin 1981:42–44, 1983:149–51).[37]

Beloveds

Catullus' pederastic love poetry is echoed in more muted fashion by his contemporary Tibullus's elegies 4, 8, and 9 celebrating a beautiful but fickle boy called Marathus. Horace wrote of his love for the beautiful, long-haired boy Lyciscus (*Epode* 11, 23–28). Noting his earlier love for Inachia, he wrote that in the future he was as likely to find another boy as another girl to enjoy (27). He recommended taking whatever was available (*Satire* 1.2.119), with the analogy "Do you need gold cups when thirst burns your throat?" (1.2.127; trans. Richlin 1983: 175). In the last collection of his odes (ca. 13 B.C.), he declares a new love, for another charming, long-haired boy, Ligurinis (1.4; also see *Epode* 2.11).

Virgil's famous second eclogue, centered on Corydon's love for Alexis, is interesting as an object case of the Greco-Roman duality, for the poem's principal source is a heterosexual idyll of Theokritus (see p. 100 above). It bears noting that this portrait was of bucolic, not urban passion, and that Corydon knows he "will find another" male to love in the countryside. At the end, he does not think about moving to a city, but recalls his vines and trees in need of pruning. The immense popularity of this eclogue is evidence that rural same-sex passion was plausible. The *Aeneid* includes several pairs of devoted male lovers, including the Italians Cydon and the last of his boy-beloveds, Clytius (10, 324–27); the devoted Trojan couple of Nisus; and the exceptionally beautiful, slightly younger, not-yet-bearded Euryalus.[38] The ninth book of the *Aeneid* celebrates at considerable length their love and valiant deaths.

---

37. In addition to being throat rammed, Catullus warns rivals of anal penetration (e.g., 37,40,112,116), including being split open with horseradish (in 15) or sneers at their penchant for it (e.g., *culo voraciore* of Vibennius's son in 33.4) or for performing analingus (97,98). Threats against those who would seduce Juventius never blame him or treat him as sluttishly available. Richlin (1983:152) stressed this. I do not see malice for the *pueri* even in the two poems where she does: 56, in which the poet mounts a boy whom he finds fucking a girl, and 106, in which he infers from seeing an attractive boy with an auctioneer that they have had sex.

38. Virgil introduces Euryalus to the reader as a *puer* (9.181), but he is later addressed as *vir* (9.252). They are lovers more on the model of the Theban band, fighting and dying together (see Makowski 1989).

The normative age difference was not hard and fast:

> Exact age in the puer delicatus is hard to pin down and is seldom
> specified. Meleager (A.P. 12.125) mentions an eighteen year old
> boy, but later for Sythinus (A.P. 12.22) sixteen is the fatal age,
> while Strato (A.P. 12.4) considers that a boy's attractions in-
> crease from the twelfth to the seventeenth year. . . . Technically,
> 'puer' was used about someone up to the age of fourteen or
> fifteen (Varo *Cens. cap.* 14, Ibid. *Orig.* 11.2.4) while 'juvenis' was
> applied to someone as young as sixteen (Horace *Ars Poet.*
> 161). . . . Rather than a pedantic reckoning of years, the poets
> were more concerned with the absence of hair on the face and
> elsewhere on the body as a sign of youth. (Murgatroyd 1977:
> 105, 111, 105)

There was an *eromenos* type—and some committed *erastes* types, too,
with a preference for boys, whether or not they were pressed into marriage (like the inexperienced and reluctant bridegrooms in Catullus 61
and Martial 11.78). Virgil, Horace, Catullus, and Tibullus, the Roman poets who wrote on pederastic themes, all remained unmarried, whereas
"Ovid, who considered bisexuality as natural, but showed a certain restraint as to homosexuality, married" (Lilja 1982:86). While it is difficult
to infer how much is autobiographical in Roman literature in which boy-
love was represented, what is certain is that audiences were familiar with
the idea (L. Wilkinson 1978:29), and that the poets and their audience
conceived that some Romans had a predilection for boys (including some
whose boyishness was artificially maintained, discussed on pp. 258–63),
not the undifferentiated "perfect nonchalance" about penetrating male
or female orifices that Halperin (1990:33) claims for ancient Greece and
Rome.

Satire is the distinctly Roman literary form. Although the satirist
claimed to be acting from the high motive of purging the body politic of
hypocrisy and corruption, often he was actuated by personal spite and
love of gossip. Juvenal's criticism of Roman same-sex customs in the first
century A.D. revolved around the familiar contrast between the artless
simplicity of the revered past and the luxury of the perverted present.
For him, a symptom of this degeneration was the violation of class bar-
riers in the obsessions of Roman aristocrats with their low-born favorites
(some even "plowing" their patrons, as in the ninth satire). In his second
satire, Juvenal showed a scion of a particularly distinguished ancient Roman family (a Gracchus) offering himself in marriage, replete with Oriental rites, to a favorite with a "dowry" sufficient to raise the status of

his new "husband" to knightly rank. As in analogous cases recorded by Martial (e.g., 12.42, 1.24) and Dio (68.4), they sought to dignify their male-male unions by assimilating them to religious rites whereby the initiate "weds" the god (Colin 1965:56). Stripping away Juvenal's veneer of moral indignation, we can see these weddings as strivings to regularize a type of male-male relationship that was at odds with the official structure of patriarchal Roman ideology and institutions.[39]

Very different is Petronius's *Satyricon,* a vast picaresque novel of which only about a tenth has survived. These fragments, called by Gilbert Highet "one of the least improving books ever written," recount the picaresque adventures of two sexually versatile friends who are rivals for a particularly fickle pretty boy, Giton (who is allowed to choose which will be his *frater* ("brother"),[40] although Encolpius thought his relationship with Giton was of sufficient duration for them to become blood brothers.[41] While upholding very definite opinions about literature and art, Petronius was as nonjudgmental about sexual behavior as any Roman could be.

Martial, too, has been considered not only unedifying but too obscene for classicists to translate, and has often been accused of having a tabloid mentality and of purveying scurrilous gossip for mere titillation. Yet, there can be no doubt that he operated within certain cultural restraints, for example, believing it better to fuck than to be fucked,[42] better to have the means to invite others to dine with one than to cadge invitations, and, best of all, to be open about one's tastes rather than hypocritical. His writings are a valuable source for Roman customs relating to sex, for example, the cutting of the hair of slave boys to signal the end of their availability as sexual utensils (11.80). For all his invective about

39. That Callistratas, the bride in Martial 12.42, was bearded is especially remarkable, not least given Martial's recurrent gibes at depilation as an indication of sexual receptivity (e.g., 2.62,6.56,9.27). The same Graccchus whose donning the bridal veil outraged Juvenal was also accused (by Juvenal 2.143–48) of displaying himself to the masses half naked as a net-casting gladiator—conduct disgraceful for the high born, but hardly effete or cowardly.

40. This is the recurrent term for such a relationship in the *Satyricon.* See Richardson (1984).

41. "Vetustissimam consuetuinem putabam in sanguinis pignus transisse" (80). In a later adventure, they tie themselves together when they think they will drown (114). Matters get really tangled when Truphaena takes the part of an *erastes* in seducing Giton. She was already Encolpius's mistress, and, in that her husband recognized Encolpius's penis, it seems that Encolpius also penetrated him (113.7,109.3), leaving out only one conjunction of the four characters.

42. He showed a particularly notable aversion to oral sex, whether involving males or females (see Sullivan 1979:294). Earlier, Tranio, the main character in Plautus's *Mostellaria,* regards having to perform fellatio as the most onerous aspect of his slavery (782).

adult pathics, epigram 12.75 unequivocally states a preference for five
boys, even over a woman with a large dowry.[43]

As Richlin (1983:136) put it, for Martial, "extravagant pederasty in
another can be a source of amusement, while the poet takes his own love
affairs more seriously, with no sign of embarrassment—chagrin, yes;
shame no." Martial scorned adult men who were sexually receptive,
especially those who tried to hide their desires (2.54, 2.62, 3.71, 4.48,
9.57, 11.88, 12.33). He mocked effeminate male adults (e.g., 6.37, 7.58,
10.65), but hypocritical departures from both approved age-stratified
homosexuality and contemptuously viewed gender-stratified homosexuality elicited furious satire:

> Martial reserves his strongest invective in this area for men who
> pretend to be especially old-fashioned and severe but are actu-
> ally pathics. Usually this severity takes the form of a pretense of
> being a Stoic philosopher. The hypocrisy of such a sham excites
> both Martial and Juvenal to orgies of disgusted and hilarious ex-
> posure, as if the thought that an especially virile-looking man
> might be eager for anal penetration was particularly fascinating
> to both them and their audience. . . . Again, in *Satire* 2, it is
> deceitfulness that Juvenal claims he hates most in his victims,
> who are pathic homosexuals pretending to be puritanical Stoic
> philosophers; it is their hypocrisy that galls him most, and he
> claims not to mind a blatant effeminate nearly as much. (lines
> 15–35) (Richlin 1983:138, 201)

Juvenal's satire 9 (130–33) consoles the hustler Naevolus that he can
easily find another pathic in Rome to employ him; his pathic patron
Virro ("Manly," i.e., in Juvenal's view what Roman manliness had degenerated into) is far from being the only one.

Legal Status

As for law, the *Lex Scantinia,* purportedly dating from the third century B.C., casts a long and fuzzy shadow.[44] Judging from incidents re-

---

43. "Secundus, the only one with a Roman name, has *pastas glande natis,* literally 'a
butt fed on acorn,' *glande* being slang for the glans penis" (Richlin 1983:42). This is a rare
metaphor of penetration being good for the penetrated boy, not just pleasant for the penetrating man. Martial wanted *pueri* to be preserved as long as possible, and in 11.22 warned
against hastening their sexual maturity (*praecipitantque virum*) by fondling their penises,
though an interest in the size of such ornaments is recurrently indicated in his epigrams
about boy lovers (e.g., 1.96), once even in self-reference (11.63; see Richlin 1983:42–43),
and the contrast to his own chaste and small ("proba et pusilla") *mentula* (7.65).

44. No text has survived. Lilja (1982:112–21) discussed allusions to it in texts that
have survived. Also see Christ 1727 and Richlin 1993:569–71.

ported by Valerius Maximus, and alluded to more briefly by other authors, the law seems to have provided sanctions against some kind(s) of homosexual behavior among freeborn men.[45] To interpret this evidence as indicating that the Romans were anti-homosexual because "they had a law against it" is to commit a grave error of anachronistic retrojection. As is so often the case, superimposing the modern comprehensive notion of homosexuality onto an earlier era that had no such overall concept is a source of mischievous confusion. As a counterbalance, it is useful to recall the Latin term *stuprum*, which covered penetration of widows, maidens, boys, or other men's slaves (*Digest* 1.18.21, 48.5.35). It was the status of the person used, **not** the particular acts themselves, that were proscribed. The same act might or might not be *stuprum* according to the participants. To copulate with a freeborn teenage girl was *stuprum*, but not with a teenage prostitute—whether slave or free (C. Williams 1994, 1995:532–33). It seems likely that the boundaries of what was *stuprum* expanded and contracted over time, but the late imperial codifications, extending from Ulpian to Tribonian, resulted in earlier legislation not being preserved (Fantham 1991; C. Williams 1994).

Any restrictions on same-sex behavior that may have been in the *Lex Scantinia* do not seem to have been enlarged, nor even reaffirmed at any later stage of lawmaking, although there were complaints from some moralists that the statute had fallen into disuse. (A contemporary analog would be laws against adultery.) And, as Lilja (1982:96) convincingly argued, Cicero, who threw every calumny against those he attacked in the Senate or in trial court, certainly "would have availed himself of the opportunity if there had existed a law forbidding homosexual relationships between Roman citizens, but nowhere in his forensic speeches is there the slightest hint of such a law." Rather, in defending Cnaeus Plancius, he flatly stated that taking a male off for sex is not a basis for prosecution.[46] Similarly, if there had been a law forbidding those who had prostituted themselves from later public life, like that in Athens that Aiskhines used against Timarkhos, Cicero surely would have used it against Antony in his *Philippics*.[47] Moreover, as Boswell (1980:70) noted,

45. Most probably involuntary penetration of an adult male citizen (i.e., male-male rape), possibly including voluntary receptivity by a citizen. It may also have involved protection of soldiers from sexual importuning by their commanders.

46. "Quod non crimen est" (*Plancio* 30). Lilja (1982:96) explained that "*crimen* is here used in the sense 'charge,' which was the usual one in Cicero's times, not 'crime.'

47. Lilja (1982:125). Addressing Antony in the second Philippic, Cicero contemptuously recalled, "You took on a man's toga and at once turned it into a whore's. At first, you were a common prostitute, with a fixed and not low price. Once you met Curio, he drew

"Homosexual acts could hardly have been illegal in Augustan Rome, where the government not only taxed homosexual prostitution but accorded boy prostitutes a legal holiday" (the *Fasti Praenestini,* twenty-fifth day of the fourth month on the Roman calendar; Veyne 1985:29). Back in Republican times, male prostitutes were already well established. Cato famously complained that they were more highly valued than good Italian farmland (Polybius 31.25). He did not complain that what they were doing was illegal, however (Boswell 1980:68).

The *Lex Julia de maritandis ordinibus* and the *Lex Julia de adulteriis* of 19 B.C., together constituted an Augustan codification of what moralists of that day thought should have been "traditional family values." The slightly later *Lex Papia Poppaea* attempted to restrict divorce and discourage adultery in the interests of increasing the birthrate of Roman citizens. Interestingly, this series of pro-natalist legislative initiatives was entirely devoted to curbing men's activities with prohibited women, completely disregarding any dalliances with boys. Indeed, legitimacy seems to have been an even greater concern than the birthrate in that (lacking effective technology to prevent pregnancy) adultery increases the latter.[48]

In contrast to Cicero's denunciations of political enemies for having enjoyed (and/or been paid for) sexual receptivity in their youths, Lu-

---

you away from that meretricious pursuit and, as if he had given you a matron's robe, you became his wife [more literally, "were established in enduring and stable matrimony"]. No boy bought for libidinous use ever was as much in his master's power as you were in Curio's" (2.44–45). Obviously, this is not a neutral account, but it is hard to interpret it as not focusing on youthful sexual receptivity. Cicero mentioned no other aspect of gender variance herein. Earlier, he had railed against Verres and Gabinus for continuing sexual receptivity as an adult (in 70 B.C. and 57 B.C., respectively) and engaged in what can justly be labeled "fagbashing" of Cataline (*In Catilinam* 1.13,2.4,8,22–25). Lilja (1982:88–97), Gonfroy (1978), and Richlin (1992:86–104) discussed the homosexual content of these orations in detail. Establishing the facts of a particular alleged criminal act was often subordinate to reviewing the character, family, and whole life of the accused, and Cicero, in particular, endeavored to use trials to destroy political rivals. Like many politicians in many times and places he equated what was good for himself with what was good for the community.

48. Augustan family laws focused on trying to prop up patriarchal control (*patria potestas*) over wives and over children of both sexes, particularly guarding their *pudicitia*. See C. Williams (1994, 1995:532–35) on the primacy of adultery as *impudicitia/struprum,* and Nisbet (1970) on the social changes that led to attempts to legislate "traditional [i.e., Republican] family values" in the early Empire, and thereby constituted state interference in families (the *Leges Juilae* in 18 B.C. were "the first official limitations in Roman history of the historic authority of the patria potestas" 213).

cretius was indifferent, nowhere condemning same-sex relations, writing that a man might love either a boy or a woman (*De rerum natura* 4.1048–54). Beauty, regardless of the sex of the beautiful person, stimulates the production of the seed and the wish to plant it in the beautiful person.[49]

It is often alleged that at least the later Stoics opposed same-sex pleasure, and indeed all sexual indulgence outside marriage, and bequeathed this view to Christian rigorism. On the whole, evidence fails to support so austere a view, and many of their contemporaries regarded the Stoics as especially fond of boy-love.[50] The Stoics did stress the advantages of moderation and indifference to passion. One could be a moderate pederast, instead of a frenzied one, however. Only Musonius Rufus seemingly followed the track of Plato in *The Laws* in rejecting same-sex copulation as "against nature" and specifically sought to discourage homosexuality.[51] In the sphere of sexual morality, the early church fathers' debt to the Stoics was slight (Spanneut 1957). Dio (61.10.3–6) reported that the Stoic moralist Seneca himself was passionately involved with post-pubescent boys (and taught "this vice" to Nero). The Loeb translator recalled this in relation to Seneca's seemingly self-revealing formulation, "secret acts which press upon the conscience and which every man denies that he has done" (quae secreta quoque conscientiam premunt quaeque sibi quisque fecisse se negat) in a denunciation in *Naturales Quaestiones* (1.16.4) of Hostius Quadra for watching in magnifying mirrors the penises which penetrated his mouth and anus.

To sum up the evidence gleaned from Roman thinkers, a few denounced or discouraged homosexuality in part or as a whole, but most did not comment on the subject—and in the general setting of Mediterranean social life, it can reasonably be concluded that silence was tacit consent.

49. Since Lucretius (among many others) equated desire with the production of semen, those without it (females and prepubescent males) cannot desire. In the following lines (1058–1191) he warned of the dangers of love (of males or of females). As in Buddhism, it is the attachment and desire that is problematic, not the sexual anatomy of the beloved.

50. In *Deipnosophistae* (13.563), Athenaeus quotes invective from the *Iambics* of Hermeras of Curuin: "Oglers of boys you are, emulating the founder of your philosophy, Zeno the Phoenician, who never resorted to a woman, but always to boy favorites, as Antigonus of Arystus records in his biography." 13.453c quotes Amphyis's sarcastic query from *Dithryambus:* "Do you expect to convince me that there is any lover who loving a handsome boy, is a lover of his character without regard to his looks?"

51. Shorn of its original, lost context, a citation of Seneca offered by St. Jerome is of dubious validity.

As has been mentioned, unlike in classical Greece, pederasty played no role in the training and toughening of young men for duty to the Roman state. Attractive *pueri* were "never viewed as potential adults who will become freedman, carry on business and government, have children, or grow old. The *pueri* . . . are 'sex objects' in the starkest sense—lovely, desirable, romantic *things*" (Richlin 1983:34, emphasis in original). Relatedly, the Romans permitted nudity only in the baths, a milieu of selfish and hedonistic indulgence, in marked contrast to the Greek consolidation of the link between pederasty and male character formation through public nude athletics. As Verstraete (1980:235) put it, the Romans "never utilized the homoerotic bond between men to build and sustain their culture but treated homosexuality solely as a source of sexual gratification."

Having mentioned the lurid sexual careers of Roman emperors recounted by Suetonius (and Lampridius), it seems necessary to conclude with some reflections upon the purported link between homosexuality and the fall of the Roman Empire. Modern historians have assembled a bewildering variety of contradictory explanations for the Empire's decline, including external pressures versus internal decay; failure of leadership at the top versus festering anger welling up from below; a shortage of manpower versus maldistribution of resources; and physical causes such as plagues versus collective psychic exhaustion signified by the fading of Roman's ancient religion and civic spirit before cults from the East, such as Christianity (cf. Chambers 1963; Mazzarino 1966).

The modern stereotype of Roman decadence draws in part on the harsh judgments of the Roman satirists and historians, but was mainly shaped by nineteenth-century French writers and painters, who were uncomfortably aware of parallels between the decline of their own cultural hegemony and that of their Latin forebearers. The lurid image that emerged was picked up by popular culture (especially in representations of Caligula). The interesting thing about all this moralistic sleaze is its complete irrelevance to the fall of Rome, for most of it is firmly set in the first century A.D., when the Empire had not yet reached its zenith and the happy age of the Five Good Emperors was still in the future. In order to consider this material causally related to Rome's fall, we would have to assume a "latency period" of six to eight generations. To conflate Caligula and the fall of Rome is like finding in Sir Walter Raleigh's behavior the cause of the American Civil War. No more was Caligula contemporary with the fall than was Raleigh with Lincoln. If there is any connection between "the rise and fall of the Roman Empire" and male-male eros, it is with the rise of the Roman Empire, not with its fall!

What were the views of the Romans themselves? As already mentioned, there was much rhetoric castigating abandonment of the sturdy virtues of the early Republic. Such conduct was seen as individually and collectively shameful without being as such threatening to the foundations of the Empire, however. For Rome had been given *imperium sine fine,* dominion without limit. Even during the dark days of the third century, orators regularly summoned up the image of *Roma aeterna.* Only later was the idea expressed that indulgence, sexual or otherwise, caused Rome's collapse. The first instance of what was later to become a commonplace reproach is in *De gubernatione Dei,* a moralistic diatribe composed by the early church father Salvian about A.D. 450. In discussing Carthage (the contemporary Roman city, not the old Semitic realm) Salvian contrasted the former degenerate effeminacy of the city, its ostentatious queens on parade, with the severe, highly moral regime instituted by the Germans after their successful siege. Thus, in Salvian's view, the material and intellectual losses caused by the barbarian incursions were compensated for by elimination of sexual freedom.

In sum, Rome shared with both classical Greece (and other Mediterranean cultures) the fundamental agent/patient distinction in sexual transactions. Along with a common Indo-European heritage, Rome was subject to a massive and continuing influx of Hellenistic culture, with Greek models adapted to and merging with native tendencies. Nevertheless, there were significant differences, both structural and ideological, which make the appellation Greco-Roman civilization questionable:

1) Roman life was much more centered on the family than on the polis. The prototypical adult Greek male was a citizen first, a husband and father second. The prototypical adult Roman male was head of the household first, a citizen second.

2) Rome generally lacked the Greek concept of pederasty as contributing to the collective (civic) good beyond pleasure afforded the agent.[52]

---

52. Romans "did not make love to freeborn boys, as the Greeks did. They loved young slaves. This fact by itself is enough to show very clearly that homosexuality was not imported from Greece. For a Greek, loving a slave would be meaningless. The educational and cultural functions of pederasty required, by definition, that the beloved boy should be free: the lover had to make a good citizen of him, and the slave, as a lesser being, did not belong" in the political realm, as Cantarella (1992:99) argues. "In Greece, as we know, anyone who loved a boy had to court him, flatter him, prove his love for him, persuade him of the seriousness of his intentions. For a Roman, all of this would show a lack of virility. As his psychology was that of a conqueror (and in the sexual field, that of a rapist), ped-

3) Roman education involved classes taught by instructors with little or no emotional contact with their many pupils, rather than the intense emotional relationship between Greek mentors and their special protégés.[53]
4) Public nudity in the socially sanctioned pedagogical setting of the gymnasium was lacking in Rome.
5) With hordes of slaves, imperial Rome differed from the Greek city-states, and the master-slave relationship was the paradigm of sexual pleasure in Rome, but not earlier in Greece.
6) In the nouveau-riche atmosphere of the late Republic and early Empire, the role of a *puer delicatus* with respect to his patron paralleled those of the more respectable clients to their patrons.

As Churchill (1967:142) noted, "The Roman adaptation of Greek paederastia, like most of its other adaptations from Greek culture, did not represent the original very faithfully. . . . More often than not the[ir] relationships] involved sheer voluptuousness, particularly during the imperial period." Greek idealism about sex improving the mind of the sexually receptive contrasts sharply with the thoroughly materialistic Roman using his property—whether owned or rented—for sexual gratification.

Accommodations to Pederasty across the Abode of Islam

The pioneer historian of sexualities Vern Bullough (1976:205) argued that the Arabic tradition regarded sex as good,[54] and that Mohammed did not alter that basic valuation. Although there is some basis for such a characterization, positive valuation of (male) sexuality in Muslim societies seems to be accompanied by frequently acute anxiety, and more-than-sporadic puritanism.[55] Moreover, as Sabbah (1984:110) remarked, "You have to be a man and a man with a special political con-

---

erasty for him, with all that it involved was in effect something quite inconceivable" (98) only slightly overstates the contrast.

53. See Marrou (1982:31–33). The Roman father was held responsible for his son's actions. In contrast, the Spartan *erastes* was held responsible for his *eromenos*'s (Plutarch, *Lykourgos* 18). Also, the focus of Roman education was much more practical than Athenian philosophizing. When sexual submission ("simillimi feminis mares") was involved in initiation, as Livy (39.10.8) asserted it was.

54. Bouhdiba (1985) enthusiastically seconded this claim. Also see Pellat (1977:776).

55. Although there are uniformities across the vast spaces and considerable times considered in this section (even more than within a singular "ancient Rome"), there are multiple societies in which most people are Muslim. Away from the Sunni/Sh'ia border, Muslims often have believed that there is a single Islam in which Muslims everywhere understand the Qur'an the same way. I.e., the local variations on which post-Orientalist

ception of woman and her place in society, to decode the Koranic message as a positive one regarding sex."

Even for men, loving (*'ishq*) without touching—let alone penetrating—is what has been valorized (Giffen 1971:99–115; Mauzalaoui 1979:43–44). Aim-inhibited martyrs to a love kept pure from any physical contact (let alone from consummation) have been considered noble. What some viewed as permitted gazes tended to lead to "tasting forbidden pleasures" and, even when they did not lead there, invariably distracted men from focusing on God and what he said to his Prophet. Therefore, even looking and yearning at (male or female) objects of desire was condemned by religious leaders skeptical of most men's capacity for self-control (Giffen 1971:10–11, 118–20; Bell 1979:127–44; Mauzalaoui 1979). Those who came to be called "orthodox" "cautiously tried to minimize the risks to the social and moral fabric of the community. "Profoundly distrusting the self-possession and self-discipline of the average Muslim, they wished, by hedging against every possible slip due to weak human nature, to insure that there was no danger of transgressing the precepts of Holy Law. They were sure that sin would almost necessarily result from the activity of the wandering eye and the temptations of face-to-face encounters" (Giffen 1971:123). How much (if any) effect on actual practice puritanical rigorists had is open to question. There are scholars, such as Norman Roth (1991:159) and Franz Rosenthal (in Marsot 1979:37), who judge that there was no effect. Rather than "sex-positive" or "sex-negative," the Arab conception of Mohammed's day that is inscribed in the *Qur'an* can better be described as a restrictive, though not generally ascetic, sexual morality (Greenberg 1988:173). Naim (1979:120) provided a native Muslim (though not Arab) view that Islam is neither "sex-positive" nor "sex-negative":

> [Most Western analyses] tend to oppose the negative valuation of homosexuality in the West with what they see as a positive one in the East, particularly in the Islamic societies. It would be more correct, however, to posit for the latter an in-between state of indifference which can, given sufficient impetus of one kind or another, turn into either sagaciousness or harsh disapproval. In other words, if the European response to homosexual love has been totally antagonistic, the Islamic East has neither celebrated in an unequivocal fashion nor looked at it with total impassivity. [Samuel] Klausner's phrase, "tolerant jocularity"

---

scholars dote are often not recognized by the locals as local. On various homosexualities within Muslim societies, see Murray and Roscoe 1997.

comes closest to describing the latter's response, but only at one end of the scale; at the other end, religious condemnation always remains a viable threat.

Irresistible male sexual urges that require release of accumulated semen have been and continue to be taken for granted in Islamic societies (Wikan 1977:315, 1982:181; Crapanzano 1980: 108–9).[56] Moreover, as Schmitt (1985:54) put it, "for North Africans and Southwest Asians it is self-evident that men like to sodomize all kinds of objects [and] it is understandable that men prefer boys over women." Boys are much more available, and their sexual use less serious than the expropriation of the bodies of women to which some other man has the rights or the responsibility of conserving (especially preserving the virginity of unmarried females and clear paternity for all children).

In Mohammed's homeland, Arabia, male-male sexual relations apparently were ridiculed, but not formally sanctioned. Poetry celebrated heterosexuality, while proverbs and ritual insults stigmatized men "acting like women" by being sexually receptive to other men.[57] "Mohammed shared the contempt of his countrymen towards homosexuality," according to French historian Marc Daniel (1977:3; also see Rowson 1991a). However, despite his familiarity with the Talmudic tradition, its influence on him (*Qur'an* LVI,17ff.; LII,24; LXXVI,19), and his view that sodomy ran contrary to God's will (*fasiq*), Mohammed did not include it among the "abominations" offensive to Allah for which he related specific punishments (Bullough 1976: 222). Moreover, in the *Qur'an*, male sexual pleasure is "good-in-itself" not merely as a means to procreation, but as prefiguring paradise, which is staffed with beautiful serving boys (*al-fatā,*) as well as girls (the term *houri* includes both).[58] In marked contrast to the many later stories of the Prophet (*hadith*) in which male-male sex is condemned, there is a famous tale in which Mohammed saw God in the form of a beautiful youth (Schimmel 1982: 67–68; Ritter 1955:445–46), the belief that the Prophet loved a man

56. In the major Hanbalite treatise on love, *Rawdat al-muhibbīn*, Ibn Qayyim al-Jawzi'ya (1292–1350) contended that men can survive without sexual intercourse, but not without food (Bell 1979:132).

57. See Dundes, Leach, and Özkök 1972, and Glazer 1976 for examples from relatively recent times.

58. The *houri* are generally believed to be reserved for those who forbore forbidden pleasures in their terrestrial life: "no man being allowed both the pleasures of forbidden women or boys in this world and the delights of the houris in the next" (Bell 1979:136). The *Qur'an* does not explicitly indicate that *houri* provide sexual service. See Bouhdiba (1985:75) and Wendel (1974) on the tradition of assuming so.

(Arberry 1956:53n. 24), and the ease with which early companions of the Prophet discussed details of sexuality recalled by Al-Jāhiz (ca.776 to ca. 868) in introducing his *Kitab Mufakharat al-jawari wa-al-ghulman*—A Book of the Debate Comparing the Advantages of [Sex with] Women and Young Men (AbuKhalil 1993:33).

After the death of the Prophet, the rapid Arab conquest of an ethnically diverse empire spread the faith to areas where previous civilizations had exalted pederastic love and also had sacralized some gender variance (see Roscoe 1996, 1997). Without anything like the papacy's centralization of authority over definition of God's will and sacred book, various interpretations co-existed. Most Islamic religious leaders have been married, not segregated into monasteries of celibate, religious specialists. Although not lacking in ascetics, the Islamic tradition has generally not regarded altogether refraining from sex as a necessary part of holiness— although refraining from unlawful intercourse with a beautiful beloved was praised (Giffen 1971:99–115).

The possible exception to the pattern was Persia (now Iran), where the procreative sexual ethic of Zoroastrianism included sometimes virulent condemnations of homosexuality.[59] Even there, however, Herodotus (*Histories* 1:135) reported that homosexuality was far from unknown a century before Zoroaster/Zarathustra is generally supposed to have lived (i.e., ca. 629–551 B.C.). Around 200 A.D., the Greek physician Sextus Empiricus wrote that male-male intercourse was a "habit" of the Persians.[60] Indeed, a durable Arab conception is that pederasty came from northeastern Persia (Khorasan) with the ʿAbbāsid army in the mid-eighth century.[61] In *The Schoolmaster*, Al-Jāhiz attributed this to the ʿAbbāsid general Abu Muslim forbidding his soldiers having anything to

59. See Duchesne-Guillemin (1966:149ff.), Darmesteter (1880:101–2), Surieu (1967: 16). Zaehner (1961:27,171) questions any real application. Zoroastrianism was a sect, albeit an increasingly influential one, before Arab conquest of Persia. Zoroastrianism was not a state religion, except briefly. Greenberg (1988:188–89) suggested that an abhorrence of pederasty may have served as an ethnic marker for Parsis (contemporary Zoroastrians) in contrast to Muslims, as it did earlier for Parthians in contrast to their Macedonian conquerors. Some scholars (viz., Wikander 1938; Widengren 1969:52) have argued that there were earlier Persian pederastic initiation rites.

60. *Pryyhoniæ Hypotyposes* 1:152, quoted by Greenberg 1988:188.

61. Although there is not a clean revolutionary break (with an epistemic rupture à la Foucault), between the Umayyad patrimonial state to the administration by relatively permanent officials of the ʿAbbāsid dynasty, major changes in finance and administration occurred in the eighth century (beginning before the ʿAbbāsid triumph). Practices changed, and a literati arose in intimate connection with ʿAbbāsid administrative practices (Grunebaum 1952:338, 1954:155–57; Hourani 1991:34–35).

do with women (Mez 1937:358n. 2; also see Ritter 1955:351).[62] It also
bears noting that the *Gathas*, the early texts that might be attributable to
Zoroaster, contain no references to homosexuality. Condemnations of
homosexuality appear to have developed after Zoroaster's death.

In Persia, as elsewhere, mystic writers, especially Jalal al-Din al-Rūmī
(1207–73), produced a rhetoric of sexual union between two males as a
metaphor, or as training for, or as a foretaste of, or as (in itself) ecstatic
union with God.[63] While, as early as the middle of the eighth century,
with the rise of the ʿAbbāsid caliphate, as Marc Daniel (1977:10) pointed
out, "Moslem mystics adopted the vocabulary of boy-love poetry in order to signify the love of God, . . . they never succeeded in integrating it
into their conception of the relationship between man and God." Perhaps there was more integration than has been seen by outsiders, because the focus of Orientalist research has been on written texts rather
than on the homoerotic relationship between spiritual masters and their
disciples. As Trix (1993:147) observed, "Previous Islamic studies have
preserved the poetry of *murshids* and certain biographical details but
have tended to take for granted the process of teaching."[64] Naim (1979:
123) explained, "A Sufi seeker [*talib*] should first direct all his love toward his mentor (*murshid*), who is always a male; only later, through the
help of the mentor, can he reach his true love, God, who is again always
referred to in the masculine."[65]

Perhaps the real gulf is between legalists and antinomian mystics.
While rigorists (Hanbalites, in particular) sought to proscribe even
glances at beautiful boys (and at any women outside the household),
some Sufis considered beauty as a manifestation of God, and love of
beauty as love of God. "The mystic who claimed to see all things in the

62. The belief that "our people" (whatever people that is) didn't use to engage in homosexuality, but learned it from "x" (where x is another people regarded with contempt)
is very common, as is the view that if people learn of the possibility, they will find it irresistible. I do not mean to suggest that pederasty really diffused from Persia to the Arabs, although some Greek ideas about it probably did.

63. See Chittick 1983, Schimmel 1975, 1982, M. Daniel 1977, Bouhdiba 1985:119,
Murray 1997d, Wafer 1997. Although there is a considerable tradition of what one might
label aim-inhibited boy gazing, there is also plenty of ardent celebration of union. As the
sixteenth-century Turkish poet Pir Sultan Abdul wrote (with no specification of the sex of
the beloved) "Didar muhabbet'le doyulmaz / Mahabetten kaçan insan sayilmaz," (quoted
and translated in Trix 1993:153 as: "Love is not fulfilled with glances / Who flees from love
is not a man.")

64. An exception she explicitly notes is Lings (1971).

65. At least metaphorically, this makes the adult male the object of love and the boy
the agent, i.e., the lover, though he imbibes the *murshid's* essence (spiritual wisdom) both
actively and passively.

moment of ecstatic union only as God sees them—as divine acts and therefore good—could justify any [conventionally] unlawful deed." That is, "The distinction between good and evil is an illusion and does not exist for the mystic who sees the world from God's perspective." From there, it is a short step to inferring that "if God's love is identical with his will, then if it is granted that he wills all that occurs, it must likewise by admitted that he loves all that occurs" (Bell 1979:203). Both the legalists and the mystics considered themselves to be good Muslims, even as they reached quite contrary interpretations of the *Qur'an* and selected hadīths.[66]

As in ancient Greece and Rome, what a free adult did to slaves did not count (Lombard 1975:146). In Islamic societies, the structural contrast was between believers and nonbelievers rather than between citizens and noncitizens. Some (such as Abū-Nūwās and jurists of the Maliki school) rationalized making nonbelievers submit to penetration by believers as means of glorifying the superiority of Islam: that is, as a duty for Muslims rather than as a sin.[67] I know of no claims that being anally penetrated by a Muslim sacralized the penetrated male—or that it converted anyone to the True Religion. Nor was being inseminated thought to make men out of boys.

Unlike in ancient Greece, in the Abode of Islam, boys' suitors did not claim to be motivated by the opportunity to educate the boys in masculine endeavors. Lacking any rationales of pedagogical masculinization for men's sexual relations with boys, homoeroticism in medieval Islamic societies was more like that in ancient Rome than like that in ancient Greece (or recent Melanesia).[68] None of the suitors in any of these societies expressed any interest in providing pleasure to anyone but to themselves by having sexual relations with beautiful boys.

---

66. Alternately, one could say that (some) Sufis considered proscriptions as good for the masses, but not applicable to spiritual virtuosi such as themselves, i.e., "they held the religious law to be merely an exoteric science intended for the common people, while they reserved esoteric knowledge to themselves" (Bell 1979:43), believing that God chose only a few saints to understand the deepest mysteries.

67. This view continues, e.g., Edi: "If the Arabs would have had war with the Israelis using cocks, we would have defeated them easily. The Israeli are a bunch of feminine males who want and should be fucked by the Arabs" (1970 interview quoted by Sofer 1992c: 109). Schmitt (1992b:125) generalized that "fucking Westerners, whether male or female, is seen as a well deserved revenge . . . and as an expression of physical and moral superiority over a decaying West."

68. Romanticizing the beloved was un-Roman. It was more akin to Hellenistic literature than to ancient Roman or Greek literature, and, seemingly, it was an impetus to European courtly poetry aimed at female love objects.

The beloved (i.e., the one penetrated) was not always idealized, either. As in ancient Greece and Rome, some yearning suitors derided handsome boys-beloveds as overly knowing, manipulative, and fickle. According to Lacey (1988:20), the "*ghulam,* or male slave, kept for sexual purposes was a Persian institution that became naturalized among the Arabs around the time of Harun al-Rashid" in the late eighth century. For more than a millennium thereafter, the choicest specimens were often pale Christian boys, generally sold by their parents (but occasionally stolen), and often also transported by Christian merchants to Egypt, Syria, or Turkey.[69] A part of William of Adam's late-thirteenth-century scandalized criticism of trading with the enemy in *De modo Saracenas extirpandi* (2:523–25) was that Muslim merchants "take suitable boys, and fatten them up, and wash them often in all kinds of baths, and dress them in soft garments so that they are 'plumper and pinker and more delightful,' and so sell them as male prostitutes on a market where a man and an effeminate may live as man and wife." (quoted in N. Daniel 1975:224). The slave trade "placed at the disposal of the rich conquerors throngs of beautiful boys" (M. Daniel 1977:4), not a few of whom were sold into slavery by their fathers.[70]

Some Muslim fathers also have often been unconcerned about their sons' sexual receptivity, or abetted display of their availability. About the Damascus of 1395, the moralistic Ibn-Sasrā wrote that:

> each of them [the beardless youths] would like to be loved and promenades in the market, past the immoral people. Boys are more bashful than girls, matters are reversed and customs changed, what was hidden is revealed, until they have become like brides in finery and in dress. They commit immorality openly, and no one expresses disapproval; for most of the people have dressed in garments of shame and have boasted of sins, yet no one is indignant at his child's conduct. They have exchanged their honor for the passion of their desires. (1963:217)

69. Sons of Christian merchants resident in Muslim cities also were prime objects of desire (e.g., see Mez 1937:360–61).

70. Not all fathers were delighted to have their sons sodomized by those with wealth and power. Herbert (1971 [1626]:99) recounted the Persian "king" (presumably Shah Abbas) allowing a poor father to punish (i.e., cut off) the parts of a duke that had offended the patriline by sodomizing the man's son "against the Boyes will, his parents knowledge and the Law of Nature." Surieu (1967:171–72) related a similar case of an officer in the service of Shah Safi "fain to ravish any handsome boy whom he encountered," who was also castrated by a boy's father with royal consent. Rape and rights to the property of the boy's body seem to have been more salient than the boys' feelings of outrage in both these cases.

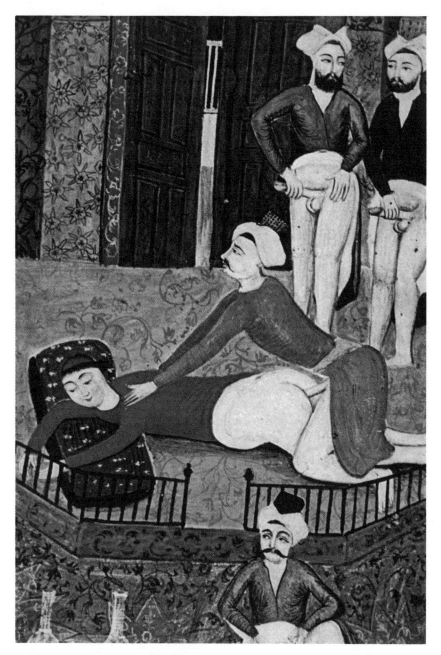

Figure 5. From *Sawaqub al-Manaqib*.

Generally, once a boy is known to have been fucked, whatever his own reactions to the experience, he is fair game for others. The Dutch psychologist Andreas Eppink reported from his fieldwork in contemporary Morocco that:

> boys look for younger boys (seven to thirteen years old) who are 'fit' for this. Persuasion is effected by nice words, money or force. From my conversations it is clear that tips are exchanged about boys/young men/men who could be/are 'fit.' Usually one cannot claim somebody for oneself. . . . This 'informing' has as a consequence that some boys get the reputation of *zamel* (someone submitting to anal intercourse). If a boy has this image it will be most difficult for him to submit [i.e., mount] another from his own circle; he will be forced to fulfill the passive role until he goes outside his circle or gets married.

He also quoted Tony Duvert:

> A penetrated anus attracts the bachelors of the community like a pot of honey draws flies. One is known to be available (coupable) and talked about. Everyone goes to him to relieve their need, sometimes by force. It would be shocking if he refused once he had been breached. . . . A proper boy keeps his asshole sealed tight. The one whose is open[ed] becomes the whore of the other boys and thereby helps save theirs. It is like an educational game: one will be the bottom for all. The first who relaxes (his guard) is fucked [*pédé*]. (1976:77–78)[71]

In some sense, one's honor can only be lost once (even though males do not have a hymen that is either intact or not). These Moroccan observations suggest that it is less that the *pédé* becomes addicted than that he lacks choice once others know that he has been (and therefore can be) penetrated—at least until he becomes a hairy adolescent and, therefore, no longer attractive. Without indicating the extent of the sample on which it is based, Schmitt (1992a:3) made the interesting observation: "I never met a first-born [Arab] youth willing to take the submissive position of being penetrated, whereas many younger brothers viewed it as inevitable." According to De Martino (1983:26), the cultural expectation is that those who have been used anally will outgrow being desirable and stop getting fucked (despite the dangers of addiction to it): "By the age of fifteen or sixteen a *zamel* loses his admirers or he starts refusing advances: [he] becomes a 'man,' i.e., he fucks boys and courts girls."

71. I have retranslated the French text that was quoted and very systematically mistranslated (avoiding nominalizations of kinds of persons) in Eppink (1977:40).

For a beloved to "become a man" may be more a gradual process than a clean break. Fictional representation of Turkish man-boy relations by Istrati (1926:155, 168) and Kazantzakis (1953:299, etc.) show that before being ready to let go of their boy toys, patrons were willing to arrange for the boys to have sexual relations with women. Similarly, Pierre Loti's Turkish boatman/ravisher aided him in his quest for a woman.[72] Ibn Hazm (ca. 1025:267) mentioned an Andalusian boy lover who allowed "his harem to be violated, and exposed his family to dishonour, all for the sake of gratifying his amorous whim for a boy." And Walters (1991:46) alluded to a sixteen-year-old Yemeni neighbor who was reputed to be the passive partner of other young adult males, and who refused to wear pants to school as other adolescent males did, making advances to a foreign woman (Walters' lover).

Some boys who have been regularly used for sex are fated (or traumatized or addicted, or choose) to continue seeking to be penetrated,[73] and may, therefore, also seek to preserve an androgynous appeal. In Morocco those who depilate and otherwise emulate female appearance are called *hassas*, in Turkey *köçek*, in Oman *khanith*, in Pakistan *khusra*, and so forth. I have been unable to find any data on the relative proportion of sexually used boys in any Islamic society who grow up as proper men or as gender variant.[74]

Whatever the behavioral frequencies, the cultural conception seems to be that a boy who gets fucked is more likely to grow into a man who gets fucked, and who also will dress in a way that advertises his sexual availability, although he **should** outgrow it. If he does, no one, not even

72. See Blanch (1983:110–11). A photograph of the male couple appears facing page 128.

73. "He wanted it" is not always a rationalization of force. Ahmad al-Tīfāshī (or his Syrian translator into French) recounted a teenage boy of well-to-do family complaining that "when he was a child he had never found anybody to break him in and train him suitably, to help him breach his dam and widen its narrow opening" (Lacey 1988:197). A more complex quest for transgression (specifically against his father) motivated the young Algerian protagonist to accept a sexual proposition from a man in Ghanem's (1986:109–10) autobiographical novel, *The Seven-Headed Serpent*. Blackmail is yet another motivation: see, e.g., Bouhdiba 1985:200–01; B. Khan 1997b:290; Mutjaba 1997:271.

74. I know of no estimates of rates of mobility from the role of the fucked to that of the fucker in any Islamic society. There are only statements like Crapanzano's (1973:52n. 17) that "adolescent boys who play the passive role are teased and are expected when they are older to assume the active role." American research (e.g., Tindall 1978) about the lack of long-term effects on boys who had been involved sexually with adults cannot just be extrapolated, not only because of differences in cultural expectations, but also because the American boys were not necessarily the insertees, and because they were in relationships, not open to all comers.

those who remember it from personal experience, will mention in his presence (or, probably, at all) his pre-adult sexual behavior. His male honor depends on his conduct as an adult. In contemporary Oman, this extends even to those who openly practiced transvestite homosexual prostitution as adults (Wikan 1977:308–9, 312). The sarcastic maxim of the Persian wit 'Obeyd-e Zakani (ca. 1300 to ca. 1370), "Do not withhold your posterior favors from friends and foes when young, so that in old age you can attain the status of a sheik, a preacher or a man of fame and dignity" (1985 [1350]:65), surely is an exaggeration, but one does not exaggerate what does not exist, nor satirize what has no relation to what the audience recognizes as reality (see Javadi 1988).

'Obeyd's anecdote—"Sultan Mahmud [reigned from Ghazna, 988–1030], accompanied by Talhak, the jester, attended the sermon of a certain preacher. When they arrived the preacher was saying that whoever had made love to a young boy, on the day of judgment would be made to carry him across the narrow bridge of Sirat, which leads to heaven. Sultan Mahmud was terrified and began to weep, Talhak told him: "O Sultan, do not weep, be happy that on that day you will not be left on foot either" (1985:78)—superficially seems to provide a counterexample of youthful receptivity not being brought up, but it actually illustrates the general non-noticing and public forgetting of adolescent sexual receptivity. The court jester has a special license to say what is generally unsaid, extending to remembering what has been obliterated from social memory. Another of 'Obeyd's Persian anecdotes even more directly contrasts clerical castigation of male sexual receptivity with its ubiquity in the society: "A preacher was saying in Kashan that on the day of Resurrection the custody of the holy well of Kothar [in Paradise] will be with Imam 'Ali (the cousin of the prophet), and he will give its water to the man of anal integrity. A man from the audience got up and said, 'Your reverence, if this is the case, he will have to put it back in the pitcher and drink it all himself'" (82).

Across vast reaches of time and space, the predominant idiom for same-sex relations in Islamic societies has been age-stratified, where the older penetrates the younger male, who ceases being penetrated soon after reaching puberty and then may penetrate younger boys in turn, although in many times and places there have also been gender-variant roles in which the unmasculine males are sexually receptive to masculine ("regular") men.

Bullough (1976:238) saw widespread homoeroticism as a "natural outgrowth of a sex-positive, sex-segregating religion in which women had little status or value." Similarly, Dickemann (1993:62) asserted that man-boy love "is predictable from a few variables: social stratification with a controlling patrilineal elite and a large poverty class, seclusion of women, [a] decentralized political system involving individual political networks, absence of formal education." Patrilineal inheritance, rather than open political competition, is the determinative variable in her account, resulting "in intense paternity concern, with the seclusion and devaluation of women as household workers and childbearers, dangerous to men." Polygamy further alienates the sexes. Wikan (1977:314) saw the acceptance of homosexual prostitution as state recognition of the utility of a "safety valve" for the men's pressing need for sexual release in a social system in which access to women is rigorously restricted. The availability of boys' and effeminate men's anuses thus protects and makes more possible the virtue of women.[75]

Although, clearly, waves of puritanism rose and fell before contemporary "fundamentalism," traditional and modern Arab states (and non-Arab Islamic ones, with the exception of contemporary Iran and Afghanistan) have not attempted to extirpate homosexual behavior or its recurrent practitioners from society.[76] However, what some see as "tolerance" depends on not making any claims for acceptance of a homosexual way of life or of ongoing same-sex sexual relationships (see B. Khan 1997a, 1997b; Murray 1997b).

"Sodomites" in Early Modern Europe

In a foundational article on the history of homosexuality, Randolph Trumbach (1977) argued that there was a continuous series of networks and shifting trysting places in Europe.[77] Guido Ruggiero (1985:135–43, 150–51) vacillated between considering that there was an increasing official awareness of a subculture of same-sex sexual liaisons in Venice and that such a subculture developed in the fifteenth century (diffusing to some extent from Florence, which was regarded across Europe as the modern Sodom).

Most work done on the history of homosexuality in medieval and

---

75. As detailed below (see pp. 275–80), the local type Wikan studied, Sohari women's circles, seem to accept the *khanith*. The far-from-libertarian masculinist state also does not interfere with them.

76. For a review of current legislation, see Sofer (1992a).

77. See also Dynes and Johansson 1984; Murray and Gerard 1983, arguing that there were recognized types literally in touch with one another. Whether some clusters formed a "subculture" depends on how distinct from the dominant culture "subculture" is defined as being.

early modern Europe has drawn data from forensic records. This may account for the popularity of neo-Durkheimian views about exemplary punishment and boundary maintenance. Generalizing about "real sexual patterns" from unsystematic (indeed, often seemingly accidental) prosecutions should be suspect. Surviving records were produced (and preserved) by fortuitous circumstances, so the historian must "resist the temptation to make too much of the previous or subsequent silence of such sources."[78] Flurries of cases, most notably the Dutch "pogrom" of 1730, can be traced to a single informant whose arrest was followed by naming names of former sexual partners. Thus, attempts to date the formation of a homosexual subculture on the basis of variations in the frequency of recorded sodomy trials risk inculcating "an illusion created by especially vivid evidence."[79] Certainly, the fluctuations in rates of prosecutions can **not** be taken as indicating changes in rates of homosexual behavior.[80] Before the late seventeenth century, there does not seem to have been any Northern European police force attempting systematically to monitor sodomy.[81] Having reviewed post-Carolingian documents, Payer (1982:10–11) concluded that prior to 1048—the date of the Leo IX's election and of Peter Damian's *Book of Gomorrah,* the only continuous medieval discourse focused on homosexual offenses (which was insightfully analyzed by Jordan 1997:45–66)—"the church [had already] displayed a consistent and uninterrupted pastoral concern with homosexuality. . . . Both the penitentials and the sections dealing with sins and confession in the collection of canon law provide overwhelming evidence that homosexuality was included in the catalogues of sins worthy of frequent mention." As Bullough (1976:385), Crompton (1978) and others have noted, Christian institutions were willing—indeed eager—to persecute sodomites, but they lacked the twentieth-century technology for mass murder.[82]

78. Trumbach 1977:9, reiterated in Trumbach 1985:110 and elsewhere; Murray 1988:465–67.

79. Trumbach (1977:11), challenging McIntosh (1968:188) on the lack of any homosexual role (in England) before the end of the seventeenth century.

80. Rocke (1996) provided many examples of invalid extrapolations from forensic records to sexual conduct, e.g., number of lifetime partners (and roles) on pages 126 and 173. Abundant as they are, the records of the Ufficiali di notte (Officers of the Night) should not be taken as "fairly representative" (113), least of all on the self-conceptions of those engaged in pederastic liaisons.

81. As will be discussed below, there were organized attempts to prosecute homosexuality in Florence and Venice, but this did not involve going out and observing trysts or entrapping men cruising, but relied on denunciations and confessions.

82. "The Church turned over those found guilty of sodomy and heresy to the state for

"Sodomites" and Cruising Grounds in Early Modern Italy

While during the High Middle Ages "sodomy has been regarded as a French vice, the Italians were increasingly identified with the freer sexual mores that were to characterize the Renaissance," Michael Goodich (1979:13) wrote. In Rome in 1578, a group of Spanish and Portuguese men were allegedly married to one another in a church (Labalme 1984: 254). At the very least, such an allegation shows a conception of same-sex preference quite beyond the occurrence of disconnected acts of sodomy.

Dall'Orto (1988) reviewed other evidence that same-sex preference was defended (as *amor socraticus*), especially in the 1469 *Commentary on Plato's Symposium* by Marsilio Ficino. In 1584, Giordano Bruno in *Spaccio della bestia triunfante* went even further, writing of the physical love of boys as a natural inclination (*la sua natural inclinatione al sporco amor di gargioni*). Ficino and his neoplatonist followers conceived innate male-male love, noting that some men "naturally love men more than women and those nearly adults rather than children." One of the "natural" forces noted was birth during the conjunction of Venus and Saturn.[83] The author of this explanation certainly conceived of—indeed embodied—the type of love he theorized. He did so without the revelations of late-nineteenth-century medical discourse that some have alleged first constructed the notion of an ongoing orientation. Ficino was himself inflamed by desire for an idealized youth, but sought to defend (his own) boy-loving nature by distinguishing spiritual from carnal love. The Florentine intellectuals Giovanni Pico della Mirandola and Girolamo Benivieni, who were buried in the same tomb (Saslow 1989:97), presumably also noticed that they had some intense bond, whatever they may have called it.

Dall'Orto (1988) showed that for Renaissance Italians, records of Socrates's and other ancients' behavior and philosophy legitimated same-sex love in which carnal union could not easily be kept distinct from its transcendence—"a very strange place and time are the bed and the night to admire boys' pure beauty," as one of Castiglione's characters remarked (46). By the late sixteenth century, Socrates had been debased to exemplifying a sodomitical and misogynist pedant. Even so, his love for boys was called a natural inclination, and certainly was not conceived to have

---

executing. This pious hypocrisy . . . kept the Church officially from shedding blood" (Bullough 1976:391).

83. This was already established in Hellenistic astrology. See p. 111n. 25 above.

been random acts with no meaning from within undifferentiated sexual potentiality.

Even though the platonic rhetoric was increasingly distrusted by the pious, it was used to legitimate pederastic desire by Michelangelo Buonarrati (1475–1564) and Benedetti Varchi (1503–65). The palpable homoeroticism visible in Michelangelo's (visual) art was not unknown to the artist: the artist consciously (if cautiously) celebrated his pederastic inclination. (See Saslow 1986:17–62). When the fifty-seven-year-old Michelangelo met the exceptionally beautiful twenty-three-year-old Roman nobleman Tommaso Cavalieri, Michelangelo's heart was completely captivated, becoming "un prigion d'un cavalier armato" (a pun on "armed knight" and his inamorata's name).[84] As Saslow (1986:28) wrote, "the swooning ecstasy of the *Ganymede* [a drawing that Michelangelo gave Cavalieri] and the fevered, often torturous language of his writings are the outpourings of a passionate man who feels he has at last satisfied a deep longing for earthly love that foreshadows the divine."

More down to earth, the satires of Pietro Aretino (1492–1556) show a popular conception of committed sodomites in the center of Christendom. He wrote of himself having been "born, a sodomite" (quoted by Saslow 1986:72).[85] Aretino was regarded as an archetypal boy lover by Ludovico Ariosto (1474–1533) and others, especially in England.[86] From early on, his frank erotic expressions explicitly rejected neoplatonist idealizations as hypocritical (71). In "The Tale of Porcellio," Matteo Bandello, a contemporary of Aretino who also was patronized by the hedonistic Gonzaga court at Mantua,[87] portrays a confessor (summoned by a wife who knows of her husband's pederasty) repeatedly inviting the poet Porcellio to confess to sinning against nature. Porcellio denies any such

84. See Frommel 1979. Michelangelo never returned to Florence. Cavalieri was at Michelangelo's deathbed thirty-two years later and later took on completing several of Michelangelo's projects.

85. Although writing of his "conversion, "Aretino must "not altogether have given up homosexual affairs, since he was forced to flee Venice briefly in the spring of 1538 to escape charges of sodomy" (72). Luzio (1888:23–24) discussed poems by Aretino written in the first person by a sodomite (possibly a character rather than the poet's own confessions); Fusco (1953:34–39) skeptically discussed accusations that Aretino was a sodomite.

86. Nicholl (1995:54). Aretino was characterized as a devilish disciple of Lucian, defending "execrable and horrible sins of forbidden and unlawful fleshliness" by E. K. (in commentary on Edmund Spenser, quoted by Bredbeck 1991:203).

87. Baldassare Castiglione (1478–1529) set *Il libro del cortegiano* (The Book of the Courtier, first published in 1528) in Urbino, from which he fled to Mantua in 1516. He was a courtier in Mantua until 1524. Urbane about appreciating the beauty of young males, the characters in his book are contemptuous of effeminate males.

thing. When the exasperated priest finally tells him that he knows Porcellio is a thousandfold more attracted to boys than goats are to salt, Porcellio tells him that "to divert myself with boys is more natural to me than eating and drinking to man, and you asked me if I sinned against nature!" (quoted by Saslow 1986:74). That is, Porcellio considered his own nature to include pederasty.

While Italian records likely contain an abundant lode of thus far unmined information about sodomy and sodomites, much interesting information has already been unearthed. During the Renaissance epoch, Italian municipal authorities seem to have taken the initiative in ferreting out sodomites. In his 1221 manual for confessors, Paul of Hungary, a law professor in the university town of Bologna, attacked "a homosexual culture which does not consider the act a sin." In some regions, he reported, men "call those with whom they sin 'favoured ones' (*gratiosos*)" (207b; quoted by Payer 1991:135). Two priests were burned to death in Bologna during the fifteenth century, and in the small city of Ferrara between 1440 and 1550 there were eight cases, accounting for 4 percent of all capital punishments there (Goodich 1979:13; Gundesheimer 1972:114).

Firenze

Hectored by San Bernardino's sermons, the city of Florence established a special anti-sodomy magistracy, the Ufficiali di notte, (Officicers of the Night) in 1432. Additional legislation against sodomy was enacted in the 1490s during the zenith of Savonarola's influence.[88] As Rocke (1988) showed, analyzing the corpus of sermons and the extensive surviving official archives, sodomy continued to be a focus of concern in Florence through the sixteenth century. He estimated that one in twelve Florentine youths between the ages of twelve and twenty-five was denounced to the Officers of the Night between 1478 and 1483. Those younger male (*fanciulli*) invariably took the passive role. Being the *paziente* in sodomy, according to Rocke (1996:91–94; supported with some specific instances), included being fellated as well as being anally penetrated. Although a startling departure from the usual view of penetration defining Mediterranean (homo)sexual dichotomization, and aberrant to the greater castigation in ancient Rome for taking a penis in the mouth than for taking one in the rectum, Rocke found the older party using his mouth to sodomize the younger in 12 percent of the case

---

88. Bruckner (1971:201–6); Greenberg and Bystryn (1982:541). Bernardino lived from 1380 to 1444, Savonarola from 1452 to 1498.

records (which I would not extrapolate as an estimate of how often it oc-curred in male-male sexual congress in Renaissance Florence, but which is nevertheless remarkable).[89]

Thirty-five of 36 of those older than twenty (*giovani*) took the active role; only two (of 38) younger than sixteen did (27). In the 1,232 cases specifying age in the Ufficiali di Notte records from 1478–1502 that Rocke (1996:243) examined, 90 percent of those accused of passive sodomy were younger than nineteen, and 82.5 percent of those accused of active sodomy were nineteen or older. In alleged relations between two minors, the active partner was the same age or older in 122 of 133 instances. In alleged relations involving a passive partner aged nineteen or older, 8 of the active partners were younger, 29 the same age or older (244; Rocke did not present the data in such a way as to distinguish those the same age from those older or to examine how much older those in discrepant roles were).

"In this small city of around only 40,000 inhabitants,"[90] Rocke (1996:4) wrote, "every year during roughly the last four decades of the fifteenth century an average of some 400 people were implicated and 55 to 60 condemned for homosexual relations." He estimated that between 1432 and 1502 "17,000 individuals were incriminated at least once for sodomy, with close to 3,000 convicted."

Dante's contemporary Fra Giordano exclaimed (early in the four-teenth century), "Oh, how many sodomites are among the citizens [of Florence]! Or, rather, all of them indulge in this vice!" (quoted by Saslow 1986:214n. 73). The major artists, beginning with Donatello, were no-torious for having beautiful apprentices.[91] Among those accused of sod-

89. Rocke (1996:110) went on to claim that undertaking the "active role as anal in-sertor or even fellator failed to compromise his masculinity and in some circumstances might even have enhanced it." He failed to specify what circumstances or to marshal even an anecdote to support the claim that such enhancement occurred. It seems to be an ex-trapolation from twentieth-century *pasivo* fantasies elsewhere (see pp. 268–70 below).

90. The last serious outbreak of bubonic plague in Florence occurred in 1430. "The Black Death of 1348 swept away as many as 80,000 Florentines, two-thirds of the esti-mated population of 120,000 in the 1330s. . . . Only after 1460 did population growth show signs of renewed vigor" (Rocke 1996:28). Across four decades of population regeneration, considerably more than 40,000 total persons inhabited Florence.

91. In "a collection of *Facetiae* printed in Florence in 1548 but compiled in the late 1470's by an author intimately connected with the Medici household . . . artists are not of-ten mentioned, except for Donatello, the only one who appears more than once. Seven stories are told about him, and three of these hint at his emotional involvement with ap-prentices" (Janson 1963:85). Number 85 had him sighing that the prettier boy will stay with him a shorter time, number 322 reported that he tinted (*tingeva*; the means of this

omy were the twenty-four-year-old Leonardo da Vinci (accused of sodomizing a seventeen-year-old model) in 1476, the forty-seven-year-old Alessandro Botticelli in 1502,[92] and Benvenuto Cellini (1500–71) in 1523 (when he was fined) and in 1557 (when his patron, Duke Cosimo de Medici, reduced his prison sentence of four years to house arrest).[93] In 1490, the thirty-eight-year-old Leonardo took in a beautiful but dissolute ten-year-old Gian Giacomo de Caprotti (called "Salai," i.e., "devil") who lived with and robbed him for the next twenty-six years and whose image is grafted onto Leonardo's in the Allegory of Pleasure and Pain, a drawing from the early 1490s.[94] Three decades after Leonardo's death, he was represented in a dialogue with the ancient Greek sculptor Phidias not merely as admitting to sodomizing Salai, but as defending "Greek love":

> *Leonardo:* . . . Salai, whom in life I loved more than all the others, who were several.
> *Phidias:* Did you perhaps play with him the game in the behind that Florentines love so much?
> *L:* And how many times! Bear in mind that he was a most beautiful youth, especially when he was around fifteen years old.
> *P:* You aren't ashamed to say this?
> *L:* Why ashamed? There is no matter of more praise than this among the best men [*virtuosi*]. . . . Masculine love is solely

---

tinting is unclear, with interpretations running from painting to branding) his assistants, so others would not be attracted to them, and number 231 recounted him setting off in a murderous rage at a boy who had left him, but being reconciled when they met.

92. Bullough 1976:417; Mesnil 1938:98, 204. Neither Leonardo nor Botticelli married. After his imprisonment, Leonardo seems to have feared sex, while Botticelli was an outspoken misogynist horrified by the thought of marriage. See Saslow 1986:89–90, 231n. 50; Wittkower and Wittkower 1963:152–53. Earlier, Donatello (ca. 1386–1466) and Filippo Brunelleschi (ca. 1377–1446), both "free of family worries" (Vasari's characterization) moved from Florence to examine Roman antiquities together. Donatello was notorious for his ardent relations with young assistants. In contrast, Sodoma married and sired a son and a daughter (Stephens 1906:25).

93. Saslow: 1986:150; Greci 1930. Records of the first trial are lost. In the second, Cellini was convicted of sodomizing a young man named Ferdinando di Giovanni, probably a shop assistant, five years earlier (i.e., when Cellini was fifty-two). "Eleven separate criminal accusations against Cellini are documented, ranging in date from 1516 to 1557 and in venue from Rome to Florence, Siena, and Paris, including charges for sodomy, murder and assault" (Saslow 1986:235n. 1). It was while under house arrest in Florence that Cellini wrote his autobiography, which could not very well revel in the "crime" for which he had been convicted, though some of his ardor for beautiful young men slips through.

94. It and a drawing of Gian Giacomo with the same profile are reproduced opposite page 176 in Wittkower and Wittkower (1963).

the product of merit [*virtù*] which joins together men of diverse feelings of friendship so that they may, from a tender age, be brought up to manhood. . . . All Tuscany, and especially the wisest Florentines, value this [embellishment of life, i.e., pederasty]. By fleeing the volubility of women, many rare spirits in the arts emerged. [Later,] Neapolitans have also adopted the practice.[95]

More notorious still was one of the most celebrated of the Sienese painters, Giovani Antonio Bazzi (1477–1549). He "also worked with great success in Milan, Florence, and Rome, where he was honoured in 1519 by Pope Leo X with the title of Cavaliere, although by then he had been known everywhere as 'Sodoma' for at least five years" (Wittkower and Wittkower 1963:173).[96] Just after Bazzi's death, Giorgio Vasari described him as an outrageous, self-indulgent queen: "a merry and licentious man who kept others diverted and amused by leading a life of scant chastity, in consequence of which—and because he always surrounded himself with boys and beardless youths whom be loved beyond measure—he acquired the nickname of Sodoma. This not only failed to trouble or anger him, but he took pride in it, making stanzas and satirical poems on it which he sang very prettily to his lute" (quoted by Wittkower and Wittkower 1969:173–74). When his horse won a race in Siena, Bazzi insisted on the winner being announced as "Il Sodoma—"arguably the first 'coming-out' statement in Western history,"[97] one hard to imagine being made anywhere except in Florence or Siena.

Venezia

Venice, powerful center of a maritime commercial empire and the second-largest city in Europe, rivaled Florence in its notoriety, being viewed as a "flourishing center of pederasty, transvestism, lesbianism, and prostitution" (Goodich 1979:13; also see Labalme 1984; Ruggiero 1985). Records of Venetian sodomy prosecutions have survived from 1342, 1354, 1357, 1365, and 1368—with a total of seven executions of those convicted.[98] Ruggiero (1974: 22–23; 1985:129–31, 137–40) pre-

95. Giovan Paolo Lomazzo, *Gli Sogni* (manuscript ca. 1560 in the British Museum), partly translated in Eissler (1961:141–42).

96. Earlier, he had been called *Il Mattacio* —the arch fool, carried into English as *mattachine* (Stephens 1906:24).

97. Saslow (1989:100), based on one of Vasari's anecdotes.

98. Ruggiero (1974, 1985); Chojnacki (1972). Ruggiero (1985:115) mentioned a particularly poignant case in which two boatmen who had been together for some years and shared a business each lied trying to protect the other.

Figure 6. "Sodoma."

sented evidence indicative of an extensive sodomitical subculture in
Venice during the early fifteenth century, although one seldom noticed
by nonparticipants prior to the beginning of that century:

> In 1406–1407, however, a large group of homosexuals, includ-
> ing a considerable number of young nobles and clergymen, was

discovered by the Signori di Notte. Because the crime was such a serious one and the penalty was burning, the Council of Ten stepped in, ostensibly because state security was involved in the burning of sixteen or seventeen Venetians of the highest family, but more realistically to suppress the evidence and reduce the number of those executed to a minimum." [99] Nevertheless, at least forty-one prominent Venetian homosexuals were exposed before the scandal could be contained, and Clario Contarini, a member of the family that had served most often on the Council of Ten during the preceding fifteen years, was executed when his claims to benefit of clergy were shown to be groundless (Labalme 1984:223).

Venice remained notorious throughout the fifteenth century as a center for homosexual activity, despite efforts such as those described by Goodich (1979:14), Dall'Orto (1983), Labalme (1984), and Ruggiero (1985):

The situation was apparently regarded as so grave by 1445 that two nobles were to be appointed for a year to find out where pederasts loitered and committed their illicit acts. . . . In 1455 the Consiglio dei Dieci decreed that a certain number of places (e.g., the *bastie*) were to be put under police surveillance, since they were gathering-places for sodomites. For the same reason, in 1488, the porch of the Santa Maria Mater Domini church was closed with wooden planks. . . . In 1460, the council described the existence of a sodomites' union [*scola sodomitii*]; and in the following year, the physicians and barbers of Venice were ordered to report to the captains of the council within three days after treating any man or woman whose anus had been damaged by sodomy. . . . [100] In 1468, the widespread existence of women and boys who engaged in acts of sodomy for profit was noted. . . . In 1500 . . . [records] refer to specific spots in the city that were notorious as homosexual trysting places. In 1496, it was reported that the bordellos were a site of homosexual activ-

99. Ruggiero (1985) showed beyond any reasonable doubt that "once the Council of Ten began to take responsibility for the crime, they pursued the matter more vigorously with a resultant increase in the number of prosecutions and in the number of important Venetians tried and sentenced" (127). There was a widespread concern (and considerable evidence) "that the Signori were not capable of resisting the pressures applied by major clans to protect their own. Only the Ten had the standing and power to push through such cases" (133).

100. See Ruggiero (1978, 1985) and R. Palmer (1979) on the use of physicians in maintaining the Venetian moral order; Ruggiero (1985:117) glossed the category as "broken in the rear part."

ity and that the red-light districts of the Carampana quarter was a well-known gathering-place for sodomites. Other reported meeting places included the field beside the Cruciferian monastery, the dark corners of the palaces of the dukes of Modena and Ferrara, and the city's gondolas and barbershops. The records also cite classes most prone to "unnatural vice": the clergy, foreigners . . . and the nobility. . . . The homosexual prostitutes themselves often came from the large Greek contingent in the city. (Dall'Orto 1983: 230)

Schools of music and song, dance, and gymnastics were particularly suspect, and the Ten imposed curfews on them in 1444, adding schools of abacus and fencing in 1477 (Ruggiero 1985:138). In 1445, fencing schools that had sprung up in various parts of the city became suspect, and the Council of Ten ordered that all such schools be located in the vicinity of San Marco or the Rialto, the most patrolled and otherwise trafficked areas of Venice (Labalme 1984:227; Ruggiero 1985:138). In 1477, the Ten forbade schools to have private or secret rooms for individual instruction. They required that all teaching be done in public halls with groups.

The Ten clearly felt that homosexual activity with young boys was often initiated in these settings and that these schools were dangerous headquarters for sodomy—literally schools of sodomy.

Another danger area that this [1477] *parte* referred to was apothecary shops throughout the city, often run by barber-surgeons. Such shops were also forbidden to keep any private rooms for games or exercises for the young. Prosecution reveals a strong relationship between barbers and homosexual [sodomy], suggesting that they may have provided important links to the subculture. In an occupational breakdown they lead by far the list of those prosecuted. Moreover, many cases were associated with their workplaces. (Ruggiero 1985:138)

The Ten also attempted to restrict dining and gambling parties in private homes (140) and, in 1420, complaining that there was so much homosexuality on Venetian ships "that it is surprising that divine justice has not sunk them," they initiated a campaign to restrict the "vice of sodomy" in the fleet (134).[101]

All in all, the records bequeathed by those attempting to suppress

---

101. Before then, when Venetian ships were outside Venetian territory, it had been claimed that they were outside the authority of Venetian law. The Ten ordered it to be pro-

sodomy in Venice (as well as Antonio Rocco's 1652 paean to sodomy, *Alcibiade fanciullo a scola,* discussed in Dall'Orto 1983) make it difficult to credit the Foucaultian notion of acts without actors, specifically, spontaneous same-sex couplings without any recognition of recurrent needs or tastes for same-sex coupling. Whether those recurrently involved accepted the label of "sodomite" except under the persuasive force of torture is unknown,[102] but this quite overt classification was sought out and located by the guardians of Venice's morals. Can it be that those most involved neither recognized their own patterns nor considered the possible fit of their conduct to the patterns noted by the city's council?

The recognition of patterns of conduct both by those desiring it and those attempting to extirpate it does not mean that those who cruised in fifteenth century Venice are indistinguishable from those involved in twentieth-century gay subcultures.[103] If a twentieth-century analogy is needed, it would seem that cruising playgrounds after school lets out for

---

claimed publicly that anyone committing sodomy on a Venetian ship would be punished as if he had committed the crime in Venice (134–35).

102. The acceptance of "Sodoma" mentioned above is a counterinstance. Another is the French poet Saint-Pavin's accepting the title "le roi de Sodom."

103. Rocke (1996:301n. 4) faulted Murray and Gerard (1983) for "do[ing] little to promote a better understanding of what constituted a 'subculture.'" This was not our aim, but is one of his (149). One could substitute "San Francisco" or "Manhattan" for "Florence" in his conclusion that "homosexual interactions in Florence occurred in a wide range of contexts and probably carried a variety of individual and group meanings, all of which are hard to subsume within a single distinctive subculture" (151) or "Sodomy in Florence was not limited to any particular social group or to a distinctive and permanent 'homosexual' minority" (146). Rocke is another of those so intoxicated by fumes from Foucault and so eager to deny that any conscious organization of homosexuality existed among earlier (than late-nineteenth-century) people that his (never-explicit) criteria exclude "the modern homosexual" as well. Similarly, in that homosexuality is only one (albeit a prominent one) of the targets of the current Christian Right in America, an argument parallel to Rocke's (150) could be made that there is not a "neat, illicit subculture" in any U.S. city now. Rocke did not provide for comparison even one example of a neatly bounded subculture at any time or place in the history of the world. The evidence he and others present of sites known to authorities as places where males went to find male sexual partners; abundant documentation of the organization of male prostitution; sources including chronicles, sermons, and burlesque poetry in which "sodomites were occasionally portrayed as constituting an *arte* (corporation) or even 'sects'" suffices to convince me that there were more than partially overlapping networks. The question in our title "Renaissance Sodomite Subcultures?" is open elsewhere in early modern Europe (see the "ramble" in Murray and Gerard 1983), but if "subcultures" exist, there was a pederastic subculture in Renaissance Florence. I would be more cautious about claiming "a collective social identity" (as Rocke 1996:185 did), given the far sketchier data about self-conceptions of those involved.

the day would be a closer one. Although only 78 of the 246 sodomy cases examined by Ruggiero (1985:128) that did not involve females specified involvement of boys under fourteen years of age, information on those involved was very uneven. That is, this is a minimum estimate. The cases that he discussed and the focus of official concern and surveillance were pederastic and ephebophilic, not androphilic:[104] although "boys were occasionally prosecuted for playing the active part and older men were at times convicted as passive participants . . . partners described as passive were usually labeled boys or adolescent . . . frequently referred to as a boy (*puer*), an adolescent (*adolescens*) or an individual under legal age. According to Venetian custom, male children under the age of legal responsibility were not culpable and thus not to be prosecuted for their crimes" (Ruggiero 1985:123, 118, 121).[105] In 1424, Venetian lawmakers lowered the age of culpability from fourteen to ten, although lesser penalties continued to be meted out to sodomized youths (123). At least into the early sixteenth century in Venice, the sodomite was the masculine penetrator, from whom pretty boy *patientes* were protected (Labalme 1984:225–27, 236). Before 1500, the *patiens* was perceived as a victim, and was not punished. By 1516, it was recognized that there were adult *patientes* as well as the more commonly conceived users of beautiful boys (251; Ruggiero 1985:121–25). Venetian fathers allegedly prostituted their sons (Pavan 1980:285).

Surely some activity must have occurred in specific locales to bring a reputation for forming liaisons to the attention of the Ten. Among those they were aware of were apothecary shops (private rooms for games and exercises were forbidden), under the portico of the drapers near the Rialto (ordered better lighted), in the entryways of the Church of San

104. The same person might engage in more than one, e.g., the Venetian priest mentioned by Saslow (1989:93) who seduced both a noble whom he served as chaplain, and the noble's son.

105. I fail to see the basis for Trumbach's (1988b:508) contention that "Ruggiero [1985] shows most prosecutions were for an assault by a man on a boy, many made on a noble boy by a man of lower social status." Ruggiero (1985:125–26) wrote that "homosexual rape occasionally went up the social scale," but rape was not usually the charge. Bray (in Gerard 1988:500–501) also free associated about "homosexual" and then egregiously misrepresented what Ruggiero wrote by claiming that official concern with sodomy was a by-product of concern with general libertinage. Ruggiero (1985) took considerable pains to show that official concern with sodomy was greater than it was with other conduct, and that a concern that God's wrath would be visited on Venice as it had been on Sodom was very frequently expressed. In the representations of Sodom in early modern Europe, nearly all of the residents of Sodom were viewed as sexually interested in males, not happening into isolated, undefining acts.

Martino (ordered chained shut at night) and the portico of the Church of Santa Maria Mater Domini (ordered closed off after the twenty-third hour each night) (138–39). If the authorities knew that males there engaged in illicit acts, it is hard to imagine that those who repeatedly went there failed to conceive any patterns of desires and satisfactions of them!

Male Homoeros in Tudor England

Compared to that for the major Italian city-states, documentation of sodomy in the British isles is paltry, later, and lacking evidence of particular cruising grounds (i.e., any incipient subculture).[106] Sodomy was not criminalized in civil law in Great Britain until the Henrician statute of 1533, but the law seems to have been little used throughout the Tudor era (1485–1603).[107] During the reign of Henry VIII, only one executions for sodomy has been discovered, that of Lord Hungerford in 1540.[108] Since Lord Hungerford was also charged with many other (more political) crimes—including dabbling in sorcery to determine the date of the king's death and employing a priest sympathetic to the revolt caused by Henry's closure of monasteries—it is clear that the sodomy charge was thrown into a barrage of accusations to bring down a political opponent of the king. The advice Henry VIII gave his nephew, James V of Scotland, to emulate his uncle in investigating "abominations" as a cover for seiz-

106. Richard of Devizes's *Chronicle of the Times of King Richard,* ca. 1192, included among the types of denizens of the London underworld *molles* (effeminates), *mascularii* (man lovers), *pusiones* (catamites, with the implication that they were prostitutes), *glabriones* (catamites, with less of a connotation that they were prostitutes, but also than that they were sexually receptive), and *asinarii* (ambiguous, seemingly sexual pursuers) (Dynes and Johansson 1984). Whether these terms were used in self-reference or whether those so labeled formed networks cannot be inferred from their inclusion in this list.

107. Unlike Germans, who saw Florence as the seedbed of homosexuality, Britons blamed the Catholic Church. Part of the Tudor rationalization for seizing monastic lands was clerical sodomy. Later, Bernard de Mandeville (1724:7–8) blamed the ban on female prostitutes by Pope Sixtus V for driving the Italians to boys. Earlier, Italian merchants were blamed (Hyde 1970:36).

108. In 1641 (i.e., post-Tudor, pre-Puritan Revolution) Bishop John Atherton and his proctor, John Childe, were hanged. The woodcut in Bray (1982:15) shows both as bearded adults. See Bray (71–77) and B. Smith (1991:48–49) on the rarity of cases involving male-male sodomy, although Bruce Smith (41) characterizes Tudor England as one of the four periods most intolerant of same-sex love in all of European history (the third[?!], thirteenth, and early nineteenth centuries are the other three in this Anglocentric view; surely the sixteenth to seventeenth centuries in southern Europe were more severely repressive than the third or the early nineteenth century, the latter being when the Code Napoleon was extended across much of Europe).

ing monastic lands further illuminates the use to rulers of sodomy accusations.[109] Rooting out monastic sodomy may inadvertently have
fostered urban migration of homosexually inclined young men. Initially,
the seizure of monastic lands made land available to the would-be gentry. The number of families who could consider themselves part of the
gentry increased. Primogeniture blocked many younger brothers from
inheriting land. "Since the Reformation, there were no longer available
monasteries to absorb surplus children. . . . Most made their way to
London" with its burgeoning underworlds, including the theatrical one
with its young male actors and young aristocratic audience (Griswold
1983:674).

In 1569, during the reign of Elizabeth I, Roland Dyer of Margate was
executed for sodomizing the five-year-old Barnaby Wright. This was the
only conviction in the Home Counties (Essex, Hertfordshire, Sussex,
Surrey, and Kent) during the reigns of Elizabeth I and James I, and 1 of
only 4 indictments (out of a total of 12,725). The other recorded ages of
the sodomized were eight and ten (no age was recorded for the fourth
one) (B. Smith 1995:430). Although the statute was broader, in Tudor practice indictments involved adult males raping underaged boys:
"Sir Edward Coke, in part three of his *Institutes* (1644) consistently uses
the term *puer* to specify the victim of an act of sodomy, he insists on
proof of anal penetration, and in the sample case that he cited both in
the *Institutes* and in *A Book of Entries* (1614) he implies that use of force
has to be demonstrated" (B. Smith 1995:429).

Predominantly pederastic male-male eros seems to underlie a great deal
of the work of the two great English playwrights of Tudor times. How
much of the frustrated desires Tudor audiences grasped or resonated
with is far from clear. Whether Shakespeare was conscious of his plays'
recurrent psychodynamics is uncertain. Christopher Marlowe wrote that
"Love is a naked boy, his years sans stain / And hath no clothes, but open
doth remain" (elegy 10.15–16). Into Piers Gaveston's mouth he put a reference to a boy "hid[ing] those parts which men delight to see" (*Edward II*
1.1.65), and in the uncompleted poem "Hero and Leander," Marlowe
provided an extended instance of a god smitten by a long-tressed, naked
young male. First Triton and then Neptune mistake Leander for Ganymede (2.157–95), and Marlowe lavished praise for Leander's incom-
parable beauty (1.51–86, with specific comparison to Ganymede in

109. See the documents quoted in Knowles (1959:204–5).

1.148 and the conclusion that "in his looks were all that men desire" in
1.84).[110] "Ganymede" was the widely used label for "catamite" at the
time, unequivocally defined in Blount's 1670 dictionary as "any Boy
loved for carnal abuse, or hired to be used contrary to Nature to commit
the detestable sin of Sodomy" with *catamite* and *ingle* listed as synonyms
(defined, respectively as "a boy kept for Sodomy. See *Ganymede*" and "a
boy hired to be abused contrary to nature, a *Ganymede*"). For no plot-
related reason, Marlowe began *Dido, Queen of Carthage* with Jupiter's lust
for (and Juno's jealousy of) Ganymede.[111] Whether Marlowe really ut-
tered the equation of the Beloved Disciple as Christ's Alexis (i.e., catamite) or not,[112] someone at the time was able to think of that, and Marlowe's choice of Kings Henri III and Edward II to put on stage strongly
suggests an agenda of showing martyrs of same-sex eros—who were not
in league with the Devil, however unsettling their preference for their
favorites was to those nobles who were passed over.

As in classical discourse, loving another male does not effeminize
a man in Marlowe's and Shakespeare's plays. If anything, it was loving
females too much and desiring to spend time in female company
that made men effeminate. This is part of Iago's view of Cassio and of
Othello's preoccupation with Desdemona rather than with seemly male
pursuits, Mercutio's jibes at Romeo's love and phallus,[113] the Greek view

110. Woods (1992:76–77) noted that in Marlowe's play *Doctor Faustus*, Faustus says
nothing about the body of Helen, ostensibly the most beautiful woman in history. She
would have been played by a boy, and a boy does not lack a face or lips (Re: "Was this the
face that launched ten thousand ships" and "heaven is in those lips," 5.2.99, 104).

111. A more relevant reference is Queen Isabella's bitter comment about her husband
early in *Edward II:* "For never doted Jove on Ganymede / So much as he on cursed Gaveston" (1.4.180–1).

In a marked instance of intra-Marlowe intertextuality, Gaveston likens his ardor to
crossing a body of water to reach his love (i.e., King Edward) to Leander's (1.1.8).

112. Nicholl (1995:45) argued that this was part of a posthumous cover-up of Marlowe's murder by members of the Essex faction (Marlowe having been a spy in the Walter
Raleigh faction and earlier in Walsingham's secret service).

113. Porter (1989:135) characterized Mercutio as "Shakespeare's most phallic character," but as one who "very readily grants the phallus to others, notably including his friend
Romeo." For elaboration of this analysis of homoeroticism and of the argument that Mercutio is a sort of figure of Christopher Marlowe (mixed with Virgil's Mercury warning
against dangerous entanglements with women), see Porter 1988:158–63. Also see Snow
(1985) on Romeo's irresolution, narcissism, and submissiveness (in contrast to Juliet's ardor and resolution) and Wheeler (1985:196–98) on Bassanio's irresolution, narcissism,
and submissiveness (in contrast to Portia in *The Merchant of Venice,* and quite like the fair
friend of the *Sonnets*). More generally, see Fiedler 1972, Kahn 1985, Levin 1985, and Adelman 1985 on unenthusiastic (and/or anxious) male heterosexuality, marriage as a means

of Trojans in *Troilus and Cressida,* and a general Roman view of Marc Antony preferring to keep company with Cleopatra rather than to subordinate such personal pleasures to Roman imperial adventures and military life, and so forth. Shakespeare repeatedly represented a comrade hurt and enraged at what he regards as desertion from the male world by an age mate or (somewhat junior) playmate who has taken up wooing or loving a female (i.e., going beyond taking pleasure from one, which was "normal").[114] As Bruce Smith wrote,

> Plutarch['s *Lives*] supplied Shakespeare not only with the biographical facts he needed . . . but with a dramatic universe in which the male protagonists find their identities, not in romantic love or in philosophical ideals, but in their relationships with each other. . . . This, too, is the world of Shakespeare's [English] history plays. However different they may be as individuals, Richard II, Henry IV, Henry V, Henry VI, and Richard III play out their varied careers in the same imaginative universe, an aggressively masculine, staunchly patriarchal society in which women have only a peripheral place. (1991:57)

Other males rendered melancholy by what they feel is the abandonment by their friends turn to "the inferior sex." These include Valentine in *The Two Gentlemen of Verona,* Antonio in *The Merchant of Venice,* Antonio in *Twelfth Night,* Polixenes and Leontes in *The Winter's Tale,* Arcite in *The Two Noble Kinsmen,* Don Pedro in *Much Ado About Nothing,* and Musidorus in Sir Philip Sidney's *Arcadia.* (See B. Smith 1991:139–43; Levin 1985:24–25, 38, 46, 91–94, 102–4, 142–43; Adelman 1985.) Mercutio is slain before Romeo fully abandons the male pack: Mercutio "manages to spare himself the pain of someone else's happy ending by dying before his beloved friend is quite Juliet's," as Fiedler (1972:90) put it.[115] Worried that love for Juliet has made him soft and effeminate and caused his friend's death (3.1.115–17), Romeo quickly strikes out and avenges him.

"All of Shakespeare's comedies and tragicomedies end with male

---

of obtaining filthy lucre, and the regret for the weakening of ardent male-male bonds across Shakespeare's oeuvre.

114. The classic statement of the point of view is that in which Protogenes recalls that Aristippus did not think his wine or his fish liked him, although he enjoyed both, and was no more interested in the feelings of those he used sexually than he was in those of what he ate and drank. This occurs in Plutarch's dialogue on whether love for males or for females is truer (*Erotikos* 750).

115. "How bitter a thing it is to look into happiness through another man's eyes!" as Orlando says when his brother is betrothed in *As You Like It* (5.2.43–44).

friendship yielding place to heterosexual love. What varies are the feelings that attend this inevitable event," B. Smith (1995:72) observed.[116]
Pity for the abandoned male is a recurrent theme, one that has been
quite variously interpreted in conjectures about Shakespeare the man
and what his emotions must have been. While the comedies end on the
verge of marriage—often multiple marriages—heterosexual bonds appear to lead directly to catastrophes in *Romeo and Juliet, Antony and Cleopatra, Hamlet, Macbeth,* and *Othello.* These include the death within these
plays of every one of their title characters.[117]

Bruce Smith (1991:76) argued against the widespread (and sometimes simplistic) view that homosexuality was age stratified in Renaissance (and later) England and Europe, contending that "age-graded
homosexuality, gender-marked homosexuality, egalitarian homosexuality: all three were possible ways of enacting male bonds among Shakespeare and his contemporaries" ("enacted" here means imagined and
performed on stage). In that his subject is decoding desire from coded
poetic and theatrical texts rather than representations of conduct offstage, this does not bear on social history. I and the other scholars who
have popularized the age/gender/egalitarian typology have stressed that
the (positing of) a dominant type does not preclude the simultaneous

116. Although there is controversy about the genre of *Troilus and Cressida,* it seems to
me a counterexample in that Achilles's love for Patroclus leads to his breaking the peace in
which his heterosexual dalliance with the Trojan princess Polyxena had been complicit.
Achilles orders the slaughter of her brother Hector, who had slain Patroclus, labeled his
"masculine whore." (This is the jester Thersites's definition of *varlet* at V.i.17, although the
term is applied to others in the play with no such sense and may not even indicate Shakespeare's view about who was the *eromenos.*)

117. In the case of Hamlet, it is his mother's marriage that is salient; Ophelia does
not come between Hamlet and Horatio as Lady Macbeth does between Macbeth and Duncan and between Macbeth and Banquo. Adelman (1985:95) saw overwhelming, sexual
mothers (the kind of mother seen by American neo-Freudians as frightening sons away
from heterosexual development) as the monsters haunting the mature Shakespeare's
imagination: "*Hamlet, King Lear, Macbeth, Coriolanus, Cymbeline,* and even *The Tempest* imagine the rupture of male bonds in the context of the catastrophic mother." In the comedies,
she argued, mothers are "banished" (not portrayed), and their banishment "allows Shakespeare both to imagine marriage as a comic solution and to evade the full consequence of
marriage for male bonding by imagining his women at least partly as men. When this fantasy solution fails, as it does after *Twelfth Night,* marriage itself becomes frightening and we
are squarely in the domain of tragedy" (96). The comedies end on the verge of marriage.
None (even *The Merchant of Venice,* the one in which the wedding occurs inside the play)
show male-female couples living happily together, let alone happily ever after. In contrast,
moreover, there is an established male-male couple (Salerio and Solanio, friends of Antonio and Bassanio) in that play.

existence of behavior (and desire) not following the dominant type, or even the coexistence of traditions other than whatever is the dominant one.[118] The existence of some counterexamples does not falsify claims that are statistical rather than categorical. In that at least three and arguably five of the six models B. Smith proposed are age stratified (and the gender-confusion ones were set in Italy, as B. Smith [1991:138] noted), it seems to me that even in the literary imagination of late-sixteenth-century England, age was the predominant organizing principal of male-male eros.[119] As B. Smith (1991) showed, *boy* was a term for someone of lower status, not someone who was necessarily very young.[120] However, relative youth, relative effeminacy, and lower status coincided in many of the males loved by their social superiors in literary representations. There were more terms for the penetrated (including

118. I did not just mention this as an abstract possibility: before this book, I argued in print for the simultaneous occurrence of all three organizations in contemporary North America, Tokugawa Japan, and ancient Greece.

119. On the same page in which he called attention to the plurality of types, B. Smith (1991:76) contended that the Myth of Combatants and Comrades is the basic, "broadest, most inclusive" one, one that "remained current throughout the period. In social terms, it represents a licit public way of acting on homoerotic desire." In that the aggrieved masculinists seem to me a bit older than those they regret are becoming "pussy-whipped," I am not convinced that this underlying myth is not also age graded. (Clearly, the age disparities are not a whole generation.) At any rate, the masculinist comrades (Mercutio, Coriolanus, Patroclus, Hector, Achilles, and "the noted pathick of the time" the title character in Ben Jonson's *Sejanus*) die, often hacked up by bands of hostile males (B. Smith 1992:136, 1995). Smith's fourth model is gender defined, the first and last arguably egalitarian. (He rightly stressed status ["class"] differences overlapping age differences and that there was more than one type of same-sex desire in Elizabethan England.)

120. Or in the case of the historical model for Gaveston, not a mindless pretty youth: the two historical passages quoted by B. Smith (1991:213–14) show that Gaveston was "no Ganymede. The son of a Gascon knight he was born in the same year as the king (1284) and the two were raised together. In Edward and Gaveston we have, not a man and a boy, but two men." Drayton's, Holinshed's, and Marlowe's Edwards seek to raise Gaveston as close to equality as a subject can be to his king (which to me is trying to lessen, not to "eroticize" status differences). As it did in the cases of Lord Chancellor Francis Bacon (1561–1626; see Bray 1982:49), his elder brother Anthony (an ambassador and spy who was charged with sodomy in France in 1586 for buggering a favorite page; see Maurier 1975:50–52) and the Earl of Castlehaven (hanged in 1631; see Herrup 1996), preferring the company of social "inferiors" and "squandering" resources on them seem to have bothered contemporaries more than whatever sexual acts they supposed occurred. In Marlowe's play, Gaveston and Edward's courtiers make much of Gaveston's rise in status, but Gaveston's class origins do not seem to me to be of particular interest, let alone erotic appeal, to Edward, in what Marlowe has him say either to Gaveston or to others. The same could be said for Drayton's Gaveston (also published in 1594).

catamite, ingle, ganimede, and *bardache*) than for the penetrators, but there was a term, *sodomite,* in direct contrast to *catamite.*[121] And, by the eighteenth century, *bougre* (buggerer) was used as the role complement for the buggered *bardache.*[122]

The increasingly shrill Puritan polemics against immorality in and around theaters contended that playing at and playing with gender on stage led to imitation offstage. In 1583 Phillip Stubbes claimed that the "pageants being done, every mate sorts to his mate, every one bringes another homeward **of their way** verye freendly, and in their secret conclaves (covertly) they play the *Sodomits,* or worse. And these be the fruits of Playes and Enterluds" (Lb^v, quoted by B. Smith 1991:155, my emphasis).[123] John Rainolds's 1599 polemic for *Th' Overthrow of Stage-Playes* asserted that boy actors' long hair and female dress are abominations sparking lust and kindling "uncleane affections, as Nero shewed in Sporus, Heliogabalus in himselfe" (11).[124] He regarded boys dancing like women as even more certain to inflame lust than women dancing, taking as axiomatic that, once tried, boys would be preferred to women (see Orgel 1989:16). Laura Levine (1986:134) noted that "this theme reaches a crisis in Prynne's *Histrio-Mastix* (1633:329). Citing long lists of precedents for the notion that sodomites titillate themselves by dressing their boys in women's clothing, Prynne claims that theater is always a pretext for male homosexuality." Playhouses were tarred as haunts of the sodomite "who is at every play and every night sups with his *Ingles,*" according to Edward Guilpin (*Skialetheia* B1v). Nonetheless, in marked

121. The distinction was less frequent in the seventeenth century, and *sodomite* became an even more generic term. (It had always covered penetrating animals as well as penetrating boys, and intermittently included both bodies involved in "sodomy.") In asserting that there was no "cant term" or "piece of slang," perhaps B. Smith (1991:186,196) considered *sodomite* a technical forensic term, but it is also attested in other discourses.

122. Senelick (1990:49). In note 33 on the same page, he distinguished *bardache* in use by the mid-fifteenth century from *berdache,* which he asserted was not borrowed into English until 1724.

123. Both Bruce Smith and Louis Crompton (in 1996 personal communications) agreed that the syntax here is strange, though they interpret "of their way" as relating backward to home (meaning literally "on the route, on the path to home") rather than forward to being of the same (sodomite) kind.

124. Not just for spectators: "For the apparell of wemen is a great provocation of men to lust and leacherie: because a woman's garment being put on a man doeth vehemently touch and moue him with the remembrance and imagination of a woman; and the imagination of thing desirable doth stir up the desire (Rainolds 1599:34; quoting a bishop of Paris). On the epistolary debate between Rainolds and Alberico Gentili (centering on an interpretation of Deuteronomy 22:5) that was partly published in *Th' Overthrow of Stage-Playes,* see Binns 1974. On the Roman prototypes, see pp. 259–64.

contrast to China, Japan, and Indonesia (as discussed elsewhere in this volume), there are no reports of specific English boy actors engaging in homosexuality or transvestism offstage. As B. Smith (1992:129) cautioned,

> Whatever Phillip Stubbes and other Puritan detractors may have said, a spectator's "desire" for characters onstage is an act of imagination, not an act of body. Only the desire of spectators for the actors onstage, or for people outside the theatre who might resemble characters inside the theatre, involves actual people with actual bodies capable of satisfying actual desires. About spectators' desire for people outside the theatre we are in a position to say nothing. About spectators' desire for actors onstage the evidence is radically contradictory. Puritan divines and academic snobs may have chafed in print to the very pitch of passion, yet all the unpolemical witnesses we have from the seventeenth century—John Manningham, Henry Jackson, Simon Forman, Abraham Wright—register no erotic interest whatsoever in the characters they saw onstage, much less a specifically homoerotic interest in the boy actors they watched.[125]

Trumbach (1977:9, 11) suggested that there was a continuous subculture since at least the twelfth century, although the only evidence he cited for England prior to the eighteenth century was a reference to transvestite boys in Elizabethan theatrical circles. He has since then written repeatedly about what he calls a "gender revolution" during the eighteenth century.[126] Bray adopted the Foucault/Weeks position that there were only acts of sodomy, not sodomites, prior to the mysterious appearance of molly-culls in the late seventeenth century. This claim, which seems to have enchanted many historians and sociologists, is vulnerable to the very evidence Bray reviewed in the first half of his 1982 book, specifically, that there were categories such as *sodomite* and *bugger* with role complements: their *catamite/ingle/ganimede* sexual partners,[127]

---

125. Also see Traub (1992:156; cf. Stallybrass 1992) on recurrent—even fetishistic—undressing by female characters who were being played by boy actors in Elizabethan tragedies.

126. This begs the question of why Pryne, Rainolds, and Stubbes were so concerned about contagious effeminacy more than a century earlier. Having renounced his earlier position, Trumbach seem to posit a cleaner break than what marks other kinds of revolutions. Political, social, and scientific ones are marked by substantial continuities from pre- to post-revolution.

127. Eventually, Bray (1993:192) acknowledged that Foucault's acts without actors dogma is indefensible (without mentioning his earlier allegiance to it or his role in popu-

and that "masculine love" in the sense of a same-sex erotic preference and of "masculine conversation" in the sense of same-sex sexual congress was recognized.[128] It was a type of person, not just the act of sodomy, which was invoked whenever acts of sodomy came to judicial attention. That is, the perpetrator was regarded as kind of person, a kind for which there was a label: *sodomite*.[129]

Those who found themselves cast by religious or judicial authority in this role did not rush to embrace the diabolical definition of their "kind," at least not prior to torture, and, even under torture, De Molnay and the other leaders of the Knights Templar never admitted to sodomy.[130] The "social construction" of "the sodomite" does not appear to have led to the "leagues with the devil" posited by the experts of that day; at least subsequent historians wrote of outbreaks of witch-hunters rather than

---

larizing it), writing that "there have been times when it has been understood as a role with a hard-edged outline of its own, not the same role as today, but something more than a mere act nonetheless." Like many words, *sodomy* was sometimes extended from its canonical (prototypical) meaning of anal penetration. None of Foucault's voluminous publications evidence any research on the usage of *sodomy* in early modern Europe (even in one country), so his assertion that *sodomy* was an "utterly confused category" (1980:101) seems more a wish than a conclusion based on any sort of historical research. Some saw it as the culmination of the slippery slope of debaucheries (see Bray 1982:14–16 for examples), some saw it as penetration of human anuses or nonhuman vaginas, and some saw it as penetration of and emission into male rectums. These are different boundaries around the same center, not a random congery of anything under the sun that some Christian might condemn. Although he was at the time maintaining the "acts anyone might commit" view of Foucault and Weeks, Bray (1982:26) already realized that for the jurists who wrote of "crimes against nature" "there was nothing vague or imprecise" in such locutions. Also see Rousseau (1985:136).

128. Cady (1992) and Forker (1996) discussed unambiguous attestations of these.

129. For Foucault (1983 personal communication), the lexical recognition of persons' homosexual patterns was irrelevant, since such categorization was not the basis for the practices of repression (this from the man who popularized the notion that "power" is everywhere!). Penetration and emission were more the foci of juridical decisions than the personality of an accused sodomite, but juridical interests were much broader (as Herrup 1996 showed was the case in the 1631 hanging of the Earl of Castlehaven). Although Foucault did not believe there is sufficient evidence to support the notion of a subculture, he readily acknowledged that folk (in contrast to juridical) characterizations existed of types of persons (i.e., actors) based on homosexual tastes (and distaste for heterosexual liaisons). Presuming the Parisian police are within the realm of "juridical attention" for a French theorist of social control who emphasized surveillance, the category *sodomite*, which was superseded by (relexified to) *pédéraste* in the 1730s, is of interest (Rey 1985:188). Also see Senelick (1990:37) on recognition of "woman-haters" in England around 1700.

130. "In fact, only three of the thousands who were examined over the seven-year period confessed to engaging in any kind of sexual act" (Bullough 1976:397).

crediting the past's own views of contagions of witches as constituting genuine epidemics.[131]

Boy-Wives in the Sudan

In a number of Sudanese tribes with "widespread homosexuality," anthropologist Siegfried Nadel (1947:300) reported a fear of heterosexual intercourse sapping virility accompanying a common reluctance to abandon the pleasures of all-male camp life for the fetters of permanent mixed-sex settlement. He noted that he knew "men of forty and fifty who spent most of their nights with the young folk in the cattle camps instead of at home in the village." In these pervasively homosocial societies, the boys who were wives were left at home with the women, that is, were not in the all-male camps, so their role was not part of their socialization as (future) warriors.

In traditional Azande culture, before the pacification occurred that made it safe for ethnographers like Nadel and E. E. Evans-Pritchard to work in the Sudan, "men used to have sexual relations with boys as they did with wives. A man paid compensation to another if he had relations with his boy. People asked for the hand of a boy with a spear, just as they asked for the hand of a maiden of her parents. All those young warriors who were at court, all had boys" (Kuagbiaru; quoted by Evans-Pritchard 1970:1430). Evans-Pritchard also wrote:

> Homosexuality is indigenous. Azande do not regard it as at all improper, indeed as very sensible for a man to sleep with boys when women are not available or are taboo. . . . In the past this was a regular practice at court. Some princes may even have preferred boys to women, when both were available. This is not a question I can enter into further here beyond saying I was told that some princes sleep with boys before consulting poison oracles, women being then taboo, and also that they sometimes do so on other occasions, just because they like them. (1971:183)

Kuagbiaru told Evans-Pritchard that when a prince considered a boy (between the ages of twelve and twenty) appealing, the prince would summon the boy as a page. Later, the prince "provided bridewealth for his pages when they grew up," although "when a prince dies they do not let his pages escape; they kill them after the prince is dead, for they have eaten the prince's oil" (185). In addition to princes having pages at their disposal,

131. On the growth of the diabolical role as an explanation, see Langton 1977: chap. 7; Bullough and Brundage 1982.

Many of the young warriors married boys, and a commander might have more than one boy-wife. When a warrior married a boy he paid spears [brideprice], though only a few, to the boy's parents, as he would have done had he married their daughter. The warrior in other ways acted towards the parents as though he had married their daughter. . . . He addressed the parents as *gbiore* and *negbiore*, "my father-in-law" and "my mother-in-law." He gave the boy himself pretty ornaments; and he and the boy addressed one another as *badiare*, "my love" and "my lover."[132] The boy fetched water for his husband, collected firewood and kindled his fire, bore his shield when traveling. . . . The two slept together at nights, the husband satisfying his desires between the boy's thighs. When the boy grew up he joined the company and took a boy-wife in his turn. It was the duty of the husband to give his boy-wife a spear and a shield when he became a warrior. He then took a new boy-wife. Thus, Kuagbiaru, a member and later a commander of one of Prince Gangura's companies, married three boys in succession. (Evans-Pritchard 1971: 199–200)

The boys did boys' work, not women's work. In particular, they did not cook porridge for their husbands. Rather, they fetched it from their natal household (Evans-Pritchard 1970:1430). Generally, the boys were with their husbands only at night.

Another commander, Ganga, told Evans-Pritchard (1970:1431) that "there were some men who although they had female wives, still married boys. When a war broke out, they took their boys with them," although they were left in camp, as befitted their wifely status, not their future status as fellow warriors. "The warrior paid bridewealth (some five spears or more) to the parents of the boys and performed services for them as he would have done had he married their daughter. . . . Also, if another man had relations with his boy, he could, I was told, sue him at court for adultery" (1429).

Evans-Pritchard believed that "it was on account of the difficulties of getting satisfaction in heterosexual relationships that boy marriage was recognized," because with easier (and earlier) marriage between men and women, "boy-marriage has in post-European times entirely disap-

132. Evans-Pritchard (1971:1430) wrote that the boy addressed his husband as *kumbami* (my husband) and was addressed as *diare* (my wife). I have no idea why these contradictory reports of address terms were published a year apart, four decades after his fieldwork. The two publications include different long quotations about the custom from Kuagbiaru.

peared" along with the cultural contexts. That is, the military companies and the royal court also disappeared. Even after the custom and much else of the culture had been disrupted, "I have never heard anyone speak of sleeping with a boy with distaste," he noted (1429). Another colonial-era observer, De Graer (1929:362), did not consider any homosexual preferences, instead attributing unnatural vices among young men to the monopoly of women by the rich and powerful.

Similarly, French colonial administrator Adolphe Cureau (1904:644–45) attributed warrior pederasty among the Sandeh (Zande) to the monopolization of women in the vast harems (*bodimoh*) of Sandeh royalty. Vassals, soldiers, and servants had to make do with what the rulers left. Boy *servants d'armes* took the place of women. Wearing their hair artfully parted, with arms and necks loaded with decorations, a woolen skirt around the hips, and their bodies oiled and glistening, the boys were at the disposals of soldiers. These *ndongo-techi-la* followed the soldiers on their marches, carrying their husbands' rifle, hammock, and a little bag with pipe, firestick, and some millet. In the camps, they cooked and managed household finance (i.e., away from home they undertook "women's work"). Mossi *soronés* (pages) were chosen from among the most beautiful boys aged seven to fifteen, were dressed and had the other attributes (including *le rôle*) of women in relation to chiefs, for whom sexual intercourse with women was denied on Fridays. I do not read Tauxier's (1912:569–70) report as indicating the sexual unavailability of the boys during the rest of the week. He did stress that only the chiefs were forbidden women on Fridays and that the *soronés* who proved their discretion were entrusted with state secrets.

While serving as a *soroné*, a boy underwent annual tests (of some unspecified sort) to make sure that he had not been sexually intimate with any woman. After the boy reached maturity, the chief gave him a wife. The first child born to such couples belonged to the chief. A boy would be taken into service as a *soroné*, as his father had; a girl would be given in marriage by the chief, as her mother had.

Wives of South African Mines and Prisons

The 1890s were a time of violent dislocation of black South Africans. One notable group of rebels/bandits south of Johannesburg, called *Umkhosi Wezintaba*, the Regiment of the Hills, by its Zulu refugee *Inkoos Nkulu* (King), 'Nongoloza' Mathebula, emulated the armies of the great Zulu conquer Shaka (on whom see D. Morris 1965). The Zulu leader who took the name Jan Note and was called by whites the "King of

Nineveh" ordered his (mostly non-Zulu) troops to abstain from all physical contact with females: "Instead, the older men of marriageable status within the regiment—the *ikhela*—were to take younger male initiates in the gang—the *abafana*—and keep them as *izinkotshane*, 'boy wives'" (van Onselen 1984:15). In 1900, Nongoloza was captured, but his organization extended from townships to diamond-mining camps to prisons. The sex ratio was very skewed in all of these, and there was great concern about contracting venereal disease from such few women as there were. The homosexual relations were not, however, a result of the prison environment. Nongoloza testified that the practice [*hlabonga*] "has always existed. Even when we were free on the hills south of Johannesburg some of us had women and others had young men for sexual purposes" (Director of Prisons Report; quoted by Achmat 1993:99). South African activist Zackie Achmat—who as a political prisoner in 1978 had personal experience of the enduring Ninevite allocation of young prisoners for sex with Ninevite leaders who then undertook their protection [133]—has castigated social historians (van Onselen in particular) for eliding local understandings (this self-report by the leader of the Ninevites in particular). Achmat stressed that "Nongoloza did not apologise for the fact that some of the Ninevites 'had young boys for sexual purposes.' He did not try to justify its existence by referring to venereal disease or tradition. Instead, he justified it in terms of sexual desire" (100).

The Swiss Presbyterian missionary Henri Junod (1927: 492–93, 294) vacillated between attributing elaborately organized homosexuality among Tsonga migrant laborers in South African mines to the unavailability of women in labor camps or to a pre-existing, indigenous homosexual preference. The *nkhonsthana*,—the boy-wife,[134] "used to satisfy the lust" of the *nima* (husband)—received a wedding feast, and his elder brother received brideprice. Junod mentioned that some of the "boys" were older than twenty, and also described a transvestitic dance, *tinkhonsthana*, in which the *nkhontshana* donned wooden or cloth breasts, which they would only remove when paid to do so by their *nima*.

133. Achmat was allocated to the de facto cell boss for the one night he spent in a group cell. The sex was variegated: "We had sex for hours; he fucked me, kissed me, masturbated me. I wanked him and showed him what a sixty-nine was" (1993:94). That is, the dominant male did not ignore the penis of the subordinate one.

134. Junod (1927:492) glossed the term as "girlfriend." It "apparently corresponds to the Xhosa *intombi*, used for the junior partner in love affairs, whether biologically female, at home or in town, or male, on the mines" (Moodie 1988:237). *Nkhonsthana* is distinct from *nsati*, wife, although this latter term is also sometimes used for the boy-wife.

An aged Tsonga ex-miner named Philemon recalled that wives of the mine (*tinkonkana*) were expected to perform domestic chores for their "husbands": "Each of these *xibonda* [room representatives] would propose a boy for himself, not only for the sake of washing his dishes, because in the evening the boy would have to go and join the *xibonda* on his bed. In that way he had become a wife. The husband . . . would make love with him. The husband would penetrate his manhood between the boy's thighs" (Sibuyi 1993:53).

The grateful husbands bought presents for these wives, including clothes, blankets, and even bicycles. Moodie et al. (1988:231) explained that intercrural intercourse "is typical of a form of sexual play amongst adolescent Nguni boys and girls called *metsha* among Xhosa-speakers and *hlobongo* by the Zulu. These young 'boys' of the miners are not merely sexual partners, but are also 'wives' in other ways, providing domestic services for their 'husbands' in exchange for substantial remuneration." He added that these homosexual dyads occurred "almost exclusively between senior men (men with power in the mine structure) and young boys. There is in fact an entire set of rules, an *mteto*, governing these types of relationships, whose parameters are well-known and enforced by black mine authorities." Fidelity was expected, and jealousy on occasion led to violence.[135] Philemon was very explicit that "some men enjoyed 'penetrating the thighs' more than they did the real thing [i.e, penetrating vaginas]" (54). Moreover, agency was not always a monopoly of the established elder, since Philemon mentioned the consequences "when a boy decided to fall in love with a man" (54) and that male couples "would quarrel just as husbands and wives do. Some quarrels would also lead to divorce" (58). When Sibuyi asked Philemon whether the boys wished to become someone's wife, he replied, "Yes: for the sake of security, for the acquisition of property and for the fun itself" (62).

The Taberer Report in 1907 noted that

> it appears to have become a well-recognized custom among the mine natives recruited from the East Coast to select from the youths and younger men what are termed *amankotshane* or *izinkotshane*. An *inkotshane* may be described as a fag and is utilised for satisfying the passions. Any objections on the part of

---

135. From the German colony of South-West Africa, (now Namibia) Bleys (1990:222) read Falk (1925) as portraying Ovambo "boys from ten to twelve years, who were not only employed as kitchen assistants near the mines, but also served as catamites . . . sent out by the miners' wives to guarantee their husbands' fidelity while away from home" (Falk contrasted the effeminate *ovashengi* to his virile adult sex partner).

the youth to becoming an *inkotshane* are apparently without very much difficulty overcome by lavishing money and presents upon him. . . . An *inkotshane*'s duty appears to be to fetch water, cook food and do any odd work or run messages for his master and at night time to be available as bedfellow. In return for these services the *inkotshane* is well fed and paid; presents and luxuries are lavished upon him. (2; quoted by Moodie et al. 1988:234)

An old Mpondo added that *tinkonkana* "were boys who looked like women—fat and attractive" (232).

Cross dressing does not appear to have been a requisite of the wife role, although there are archival reports of parties in which some boy-wives donned artificial breasts and impersonated women.[136] Proper wifely behavior did not include ejaculation by the youth, or any kind of sexual reciprocity:

The boys would never make the mistake of "breathing out" [ejaculating] into the hubby. It was taboo. Only the hubby could "breathe out" into the boy's legs. . . . [Another] thing that a *nkonkana* had to do was either to cover his beard with cloth, or cut it completely off. He was now so-and-so's wife. How would it sound if a couple looked identical? There had to be differences, and for a nkonkana to stay clean-shaven was one of them. Once the nkonkana became a "grown-up," he could then keep his beard to indicate his maturity, which would be demonstrated by him acquiring a boy. . . . When the boy thought he was old enough he would tell the husband that he also wished to get himself a wife, and that would be the end. Therefore the husband would have to get himself another boy. (Philemon, in Sibuyi 1993:58, 57, 55)

As elsewhere in the world, the sprouting of a beard indicated that a boy had become a man and was no longer a sex object for other men, but was now a competitor for boys.

Too preoccupied with economic aspects of relationships, and unwilling to take seriously statements such as "We loved our boys better [than our wives]," Moodie et al. (1988) interpreted the institution of mine marriages only as resistance to the proletarianization of those laboring in the mines but committed to traditional life back home, for example, a

---

136. Bryk (1939:150) reported this for Nandi, Badama, and/or Baganda *hanisi* (the language of the term is not specified; it appears to me to be an Arabic loanword), whose penises had died, he was told.

young man who in 1940 consented to be a *tinkonkana*, because he wanted to accumulate money to buy cattle for brideprice. Thus, in some cases "men became 'wives' on the mines in order to become husbands and therefore full 'men' more rapidly at home" (240). Those playing the wife role could accumulate money (bridewealth and gifts)—while the husbands not only received domestic and sexual service, but spent less than they would have in dance halls with women prostitutes.

"Although these relationships for the Mpondo seldom extended beyond one contract and were never brought home, and although men preferred to conceal these liaisons from their home fellows, everyone knew that such affairs existed and joked with each other about them," Moodie et al. (1988:233) wrote. "According to Philemon, among the Tsonga 'mine marriages' were accepted, indeed taken for granted by women (including wives) and elders at home and relationships might extend beyond a single contract." Philemon mentioned that when one partner finished his contract before the other the husband might go to their boy-wives' homes, or boy-wives might go to their husbands' homes. They would be "warmly welcomed" (57), everyone knowing "that once a man was on the mines, he had a boy or was turned into a wife himself" (56).

At least some of the older men who continued to return to the mines may have preferred young male "wives" to female ones, though Moodie et al.(1988) did not consider this.[137] In recent years, the institution has declined, if not disappeared. Migrant labor has become less common. With the breakdown of rural society, wives accompany or follow their husbands and live as squatters near the work sites. "It is precisely because mine marriages were isomorphic with marriages at home that they are breaking down as the home system collapses" Moodie et al. (1988:255) concluded: "The old arrangements represented accommodations to migration and at the same time resistance to proletarianisation. . . . The contemporary turn to 'town women' and squatter families represents accommodation to the exigencies of stable wage-earning" (255).

137. Gevisser (1995:71–72) summarized South African critiques of assuming exclusively economic motivations for continuing in the mines, for assuming that every husband found boy-wives only an inferior substitute for "the real thing," and for confusing normative restriction to intercrural intercourse with reality (specifically, anal intercourse). Junod (1927) at least considered black agency as a part of the phenomenon (on Junod, see Harries 1990, 1993, and Achmat 1993. On traditional male-male sexual relations at the time of colonial expansion in southeastern Africa, also see Epprecht 1998a, 1998b.

Although the "wife of the mine" role developed under conditions of migration to capitalist enterprises owned and operated by white Europeans, there is no evidence of it being imposed or suggested by white Europeans.[138] As an adaptation to the conditions of prolonged sex segregation, it drew on conceptions of what a Tsonga (etc.) wife should be and on behavior (viz. intercrural intercourse) within the existing repertoire of adolescents in the rural society. Sources do not discuss whether the same asymmetry of roles occurred among boys involved in sex play with each other in the home villages, or whether certain individuals specialized in sexual receptivity and were regarded as effeminate. Shangaan workers from Mozambique were reputed to be the most frequent and enthusiastic participants in *bukhontxana* (Harries 1990:327).[139]

The elderly Pondo ex-miner Themba, whom Ndatshe interviewed in 1982, told her that "most of the miners agreed to be 'girls of the mines.'"[140] Ndatshe continued, "Some wanted to pay *lobola* [bridperice] once they had returned to their homes. . . . He also mentioned that boys always said, 'Why should we worry since we can't get pregnant'" (Ndatshe 1993:51) and stressed the domestic duties of cooking, washing, and cleaning that went with the role.

Early-Twentieth-Century Korean Pretty Boys

The Korean "lower orders" appear to have had no horror of either age- or gender-defined homosexuality. Father Rutt wrote that

> it is certain that homosexuality was well known in rural society during the Yi dynasty [1392–1910]. I have heard of it from older men in the villages of South Kyonggido, and Bishop Cooper has spoken of its occurrence in the same area at the beginning of this century. There is a vaguely unsavoury reputation sometimes

138. Bastian (1872:173n. 1) provided some basis for suspecting that, before the mines developed, at least among the "Basuto" (Sesotho) there were men who did women's work and adopted all female manners and expression.

139. Shangaans lived in the Transvaal as well as in the then-Portuguese colony of Mozambique. And in the mine compounds, "each tribe lives separately to others, and so compounds housed only Pondos, Xhosas, etc. People only mixed at work," although "boss boys" had greater mobility, according to the Pondo former "boss boy" Daniel interviewed in 1982 (published in Ndatshe 1993:46; confirmed by Themba in Ndatshe 1993:49).

140. He reported eluding "a boss boy [who] was after him because he was young and fat" (Ndatshe 1993:49). He also recalled seeing "men dressed like women, and miners proposed love to them. Most of those people were clerks, but I don't know which tribe they belonged to" (51).

connected with the *chiban yangban* or provincial gentleman, but I heard in the villages more of the practices of the lower classes, among whom, for instance paederasty seems to have formed a recognized outlet for a young widower, and caused very little stigma to be attached to his favourite who on growing older could turn to normal sexuality in marriage. I was told that the presents, especially of clothing, given to the boy would make his status public knowledge in the village. (1961:58)

Rutt (1964:112) added, "The boy would receive nice clothes and would be fairly conspicuous. But his position would involve no ostracism and would not impair his chances of marriage."

Transvestites are a part of a very acrobatic kind of theater called *Nam-sadang*,[141] which, "up until the 1920s, was the voice of the common people" in Korea (Kim Young Ja 1981:9, 16). As was shown in the brief historical account in this volume (see pp. 65–70), Buddhism in Korea was conducive to the development of a homosexual cadre that later disappeared under the influence of Confucianism imposed from above. For the *Namsadang*, too, homosexuality and popular Buddhism went together: "The *Namsadang* troupe appears to have been a homosexual community. It was composed of forty to fifty single homeless males, including about fourteen senior performers and a number of novices. According to Sim Woo-song in *Namsadanp'ae*, they were divided into groups of *Sutdongmo* ('butch') and *Yodongmo* ('queen'); all newcomers belonged to *Yodongmo*" (10). Newcomers (*Ppiri*) being trained were youngsters who left their homes when the Namsadang moved on. Some appear to have been seduced sexually, others were seduced more metaphorically by the magic of performing on stage. The *Ppiri* were

> supposed to put on women's dress during the performances and play the female part in their community, whereas the senior members played the male role. The number of *Ppiri* was often less than half of all the members. The competition among the *Namsadang* groups for handsome *Ppiri* was noticeable. According to Kim Keun-bae, a former *Namsadang* performer, some senior performers made extra income by letting their male lovers sleep with the servants in the villages where the troupe was performing. . . . Their homosexuality does not seem to have concerned their audience, the common people. (10)

141. According to Leupp (1995:19), "the term *hwarang* came to be applied to itinerant performers often clubbed in 'male temple-troupes' (*namsadang*)."

Earlier, Rutt (1961:59–60) wrote that

> the word *midong* and the reputation for homosexuality were
> particularly attached to the wandering players and musicians. It
> was almost normally assumed that the all-male teams used the
> boys as catamites. They were dressed attractively, often in girl's
> clothes, though not always, and on occasion it seems that they
> were also prostituted. Professor Ch'oe Sangsu tells me that regu-
> lar berdache marriages were sometimes entered into within the
> bands. . . . I know of one case where the village band maintained
> a *midong* chosen for his good looks, who was not expected to
> work, but to dress prettily and entertain the labourers. He had
> reached the age of twenty and still held this position, which was
> beginning to be thought of as undesirable by other people. There
> was no clear imputation of paederasty, but a strong sense of in-
> version setting in. (1961:59–60)

More generally, "among the itinerant players—the dancers and acrobats
and puppet-show people—paederasty, male prostitution, and regular
homosexual marriages, sometimes with transvestitism, were common
and well known" (Rutt 1964:112). With a keen interest in historical continuities with the shamanistic components of the *hwarang*, Rutt (1961:
59) added that the namsadang belonged "to a lower stratum of Korean
life, with possible primitive religious connections" and noted that

> Song Sokha speaks of the *namsadang* as troupes of perform-
> ers whose chief purpose was to earn money as boy prostitutes,
> and says that they were formed on the analogy of the strange
> husband-and-wife teams for traveling prostitution which were a
> feature of rural Korea from the middle of the Yi dynasty on-
> wards.[142] He claims that the male teams were not set in circula-
> tion until the end of the dynasty, but adduces no evidence for
> this statement. He points out that they were often associated
> with buddhist temples and with young monks collecting alms
> for their establishments. It is in such a connection that one may
> come across the word *namch'ang* or boy entertainer.
>   The *namsadang*, however, were also associated with shaman-
> istic practices. Very occasionally one can still meet them per-
> forming kosa and other religious ceremonies in the Korean
> countryside, w[h]ere the boys have a specific role in the danc-
> ing. The connection of shamanism with homosexuality is a com-

142. Based on the same authority, Rutt (1964:113) provided a somewhat different
history: "According to the late Song Sokha, in his *Korean Folklore Studies*, these bands of
players were formed in the late Yi dynasty in direct imitation of highly organized groups of
low-class female prostitute-entertainers such as can still occasionally be met with."

mon and well attested practice for shamans of both sexes, although in the recent periods tranvestitism among Korean adult male shamans does not seem to have been normal. (59)

The masculinity of the youthful favorites (actors as well as non-actors) does not appear to have been valued, and some of those enacting female roles onstage also wore female dress offstage. Nonetheless, even particularly effeminate male actresses were expected to outgrow their sexual receptivity and to undertake male roles (offstage as well as on).

Feminized Boy Actors in Japan

Writers on the history of theatrical traditions in Japan (on whose research this section depends) treat it as an entirely endogenous development. Lacking any specialist competence in Chinese or Japanese theatrical history, I can do no more than remark on the parallels in popularity (and prostitution) of men performing women's roles between performers in "the Peking opera" (see Mackerras 1972) and kabuki traditions, and have no evidence for cultural borrowing(s). The Chinese analog of the second half of *Nanshoku Okagami,* Chen Sen's *Pinhua Baojian* (Precious Mirror of Ranking Flower; see Ruan and Tsai 1987:3) was not published until 1849, more than a century and a half later. As discussed on pp. 169–70, 194–96, homosexuality and female impersonation were also linked in Korean and Javanese stage traditions. The latter clearly derives from South Asia rather than from East Asia or from the Japanese archipelago.

Male actor-dancers were already being bedded by Japanese aristocrats in the mid-twelfth century, and "handsome boys [were] retained for sexual purposes by Emperors Shirakawa (r. 1073–87) and Toba (r. 1107–23) . . . [and] Go-Shirakawa (r. 1156–58)" (Leupp 1995:25–26). An especially consequential admiration of a Japanese monarch for a dancer occurred in 1374, when the young third shogun, Ashikaga Yoshimitsu (1358–1408), deigned to visit a popular entertainment, the *sarugaku* (dance of the monkeys) at the Shinto temple of Imagumano:

> This theatre, hitherto regarded as vulgar, was highly regarded by the shogun. He was particularly taken by the playing of Kan'ami (1333–84) and by the beauty of his son Fujiwaka, who was eleven years old. He very soon brought them to his Court. From then on, the *sarugaku,* later called *sarugaku no no,* or simply *no,* developed under the protection of the shoguns. Kan'ami died ten years later. His successor Fujiwaka, now called Zeami . . . during his long life of eighty years [1363–1444], wrote words and music for forty plays, and left twenty-one books of theory,

always trying to realize the *yugen*, the aesthetic ideal of the *no* theatre. *No* would have remained, like the "dance of the monkeys," merely an entertainment for the lower classes if it had not been for Yoshimitsu's protection of Zeami. The great shogun favoured the young actor not only for his prodigious talent but also for his beauty. (Watanabe 1989:75)

Some of the traditional aristocrats found the shogun's very public affection disturbing,

> not because of its homoerotic implications, but because Zeami seemed to come from among the lowest classes in society. One of them, Go-oshikoji Kintada (1324–83), wrote disdainfully in his diary: "*Sarugaku* like this is the occupation of beggars, and such favor for a *sarugaku* player indicates disorder in the nation. Those who give things to this boy find favor with the shogun, so the *daimyo* [lords] all compete with one another in making him presents, and they spend prodigious amounts." (Hare 1986:16)

Elders concerned about decadence need not have worried. Yoshimitsu proved himself a dynamic leader, reunifying northern and southern courts and opening trade with Ming China, in addition to cultivating and facilitating the development of what has become one of the glories of Japanese culture. And, even in his youth, not all aristocrats were troubled by his attachment to Zeami: Hare (17) quoted a letter from the senior (sixty-year-old) court statesman and *renga* (linked poem) master Nijo Yoshimoto rhapsodizing that when Zeami dances, "swaying in the gentle breeze of the second month, more beautiful than all the flowers of the seven autumn grasses soaked with the evening dew. It's no surprise the shogun is so taken with this boy. . . . I should compare him to a profusion of cherry or pear blossoms in the haze of a spring dawn; this is how he captivates, with the blossoming of his appearance." Yoshimitsu's successors, especially his younger son, the sixth shogun Yoshinori (1394–1441) also cultivated actors (Watanabe 1989:48–49).

With its powerful patronage, Zeami's Kanze theater could afford to keep boy actors' charms subtly erotic and highly aestheticized,[143] but most of the numerous troupes inspired by the vogue for *no* toured the

---

143. Keene (1988:106) explained that (in relation to no particular time): "All roles in professional performances of No are taken by men, though there are skilled women amateurs. When a man performs the role of a woman he in no way seeks to imitate the voice, walk, or gestures of a real woman; that would be contemptuously rejected as *shibai*, or 'theatricals,' by the actors and aficionados."

province and had to provide sexual access, not just theatrical art. They had to rely on the sexual attractiveness and complaisance of their actors more than on their not-highly-developed skill as actors to attract clients. Inspired by the example of companies of traveling players, small companies arose within the provinces, also relying on the erotic attractions of their handsome young men to draw customers, and prostituting these young men, as other kinds of street performers and traveling troupes also did (Watanabe 1989:79; Leupp 1995:65).

The kabuki theater of Japan is also said to have developed as a result of one shogun's preference for male performers (Varley 1973:103), although the conventional account credits an itinerant woman dancer named Okuni in Kyoto in 1603.[144] Kabuki performers were originally women entertainers who were also often prostitutes. Indeed, entertainers of all kinds, both male and female, engaged in prostitution (Shively 1978:8).

Kabuki actors gained a monopoly when women were banned from the kabuki stage (in decrees of 1629, 1630, 1640, 1645, and 1646), but "even before the ban against actresses, at least as early as 1612, there were troupes made up entirely of boys or young men who performed *wakashū kabuki* (youths' kabuki)" (9). Actors playing men were termed *tachiyaku*. Later, this term was confined to the heroes, while villains were called *katakiyaku*. Actors specializing in women's parts were *onnagata*.[145] Those in girl's parts were called *waka-onnagata*. Boys playing the part of boys were *wakashūgata* (shortened to *wakashū)* or *iroko* ("color children" in Leiter's 1979 gloss [142], although sexual desire is the more relevant

---

144. See Shively (1978:5). Jackson (1989:26) derived it from *kabuko* ("to bend forward") in an "obvious and essential[ly] homosexual innuendo." The more usual derivation is from *kabuku* in the sense of "to be inclined" with connotations of "to be eccentric" (Leupp 1995:251n. 105).

145. Keene (1988:118) professes (again, across time): "An onnagata's stage presence alone can create an impression of feminine beauty, and it is really no exaggeration to say that a skillful imitator of women can come closer to the feminine ideal than a real woman." This is a recent endorsement of the classical onnagata dogma codified by Ayame (1673–1729) that the female ideal can only be expressed by male actors (E. Ernst:1974:195; also see Chikamatsu in Keene 1955:388). Keene (1988:118) continues: "But as anyone who has seen a Kabuki performance knows, the great onnagata are not likely to be mistaken for real women. . . . Only an inferior onnagata attempts to persuade the audience that he is actually a woman. The ideal of the onnagata being an abstraction of womanhood, the superior onnagata imitates the onnagata of the past, rather than real women." Without adducing any evidence from any time, Leupp (1995:134) speculated that many onnagata develop a female gender identity.

meaning of *iro*—see Leupp 1995:145). As Leupp (1995:130) put it, "men with a sexual interest in the actors seem to have constituted the bulk of early theater audiences. Thus, the homosexual appeal of the kabuki actor was not the subtle homoeroticism of the noh *chigo* character but a brash provocative sensuality that drove male (and female) spectators wild with desire."

Plays about male-male love filled the repertoire during the time female impersonation was banned (1651–54), and continued after the ban was replaced by a 1654 regulation of permissible actors' hairstyle (Shively 1968:237). The long forelocks (*mae-gami*) were the glory of the boys' appearance, and the shearing of the *wakashū* was a shocking mortification to actors and a source of mourning for their patrons. Ihara wrote that shaving the *mae-gami* was "like seeing unopened blossoms being torn from the branch." (1990 [1687]:214). As Iwata explained, "A *wakashu* without his *mae-gami* was no longer a *wakashu*. He was, as they said at the time, no more than a peasant. Finding that their beautiful *wakashu* were no longer *wakashu*, their admirers, it is said, wept tears of blood" (in Watanabe 1989:84). However, enterprising actors

> did not give up in the face of this attack. They covered their foreheads with a violet kerchief, and thus found a way to make themselves as erotic as before and to remain the objects of homosexual love. This little violet cap was called *yaro*. . . . The transformation of *wakashu kabuki* to *yaro kabuki* had unexpected effects on its development. The working life of the actors became longer. [They were] no longer relying on the charm of the *mae-gami,* whereas the actors of the *wakashu kabuki* were generally at the height of their popularity at fifteen or sixteen years of age. (84)

This provides a splendid example of the unanticipated consequences of legal edicts. As Ihara noted, in 1687,

> It used to be that no matter how splendid the boy, it was impossible for him to keep his forelocks and take on patrons beyond the age of twenty. Now, since everyone wore the hairstyle of adult men, it was still possible at age thirty-four or thirty-five for youthful-looking actors to get under a man's robes. . . . These actors hid their years from others . . . [but] the more observant theatergoers realized to their great shock that actors whose stage debuts had come at the same time were now playing villains and old hags opposite them. If skill is what the audience is looking for, there should be no problem in having a seventy-year-old

perform as a youth in long-sleeved robes [another distinctive marker of boys]. (1990:215)

Thus, "when being entertained by a kabuki boy actor, one must be careful never to ask his age" (267). The actors Ihara wrote about in the second (kabuki) half of *Nanshoku Okagami* (Great Mirror of Male Love) were almost all historical people whose existence and characteristics can be verified from independent sources (Schalow 1990a:38), including Tamamura Kichiya in the story (Bamboo Clappers Strike the Hateful Number) he introduced with the warning about asking *wakashū* their ages. (In it an unnamed *wakashū* is unwillingly revealed to be thirty-eight.) "The most extreme example was that of a *kaegema* called Hagino Yaegiri.[146] By reason of his profound love for a man, he never wished to know a woman, and even after the age of sixty he never changed his *wakashū* dress. Nor did his partner forget this *kaegema*, and he always slept with him until they were very old." This rather excessive example is to be found in a book entitled *Fumoto no iro* (Colour at the Foot of a Mountain) which appeared in 1769 (Iwata in Watanabe 1989:104).

Effeminization and Commercialization of Male Beloveds in Demilitarized Tokugawa Japan

As noted above (see pp. 83–84), some of the casting into age roles involved only nominal differences. In the seventeenth century, especially after the assault on the *mae-gami* of the *wakashū* in 1654, some actors remained permanently effeminate. The extension of *wakashū* careers by replacing *mae-gami* with costuming and acting has already been mentioned. Another unanticipated consequence of the prohibition of *mae-gami* was the development of the specialist in women's roles, the *oyama*. The greatest *oyama*, Yoshizawa Ayame (1673–1729), told his patron (Gorosaemon) that he had to live as a women to be effective: "One cannot become an excellent *oyama* without living as a woman in everyday life. In fact, his masculinity betrays itself easily in him who makes an effort of will to become a woman [only] on the stage" (quoted by Watanabe 1989:86).

This principle of constantly performing as a woman, offstage as well as on, became *oyama* dogma, even into the twentieth century. (See Scott 1955:157–98; Mishima 1966:140–46.) Actors who were serious about playing women's part onstage dressed as girls or women, used the distinctive features of women's speech, emulated women's coiffure, posture,

---

146. The literal meaning of *kaegema* is shade room. It became the generic term for male prostitute (Iwata in Watanabe 1989:97).

and intonation, squatted to urinate, and even entered the women's side of public bathhouses without anyone objecting" (Shively 1978:41)."The make-believe of his daily life supported the make-believe of his stage performance," as Mishima (1966:145) wrote in "Onnagata," a story based on his close friendship with the *onnagata* Utaemon (Stokes 1974:139), and stuffed with quotations from the *Ayamegusa*. There, in a much-quoted passage, Yoshizawa wrote: "The *onnagata* should never forget he is an *onnagata* even when in the green [dressing] room. When he takes lunch, he should turn away so that people cannot see him. If he eats heartily with the *tachiyaku* and then has to play a love scene on stage with the same man, he will not succeed. It will be difficult for him to portray tender feeling, for the *tachiyaku*'s heart will not in reality be ready to fall in love" (trans. Scott 1955:174).[147]

Youths had previously graduated to playing male roles as their beauty faded (or, earlier, when their forelocks were cut off as part of coming of age at nineteen or twenty), but Yoshizawa condemned this, and most *oyama* remained *oyama* for life, representing "the ideal models of traditional Japanese femininity" (Inawara and Kawatake 1981:189). When he was told that he was "acting in the style of courtesans five years ago," he opined that being old-fashioned was preferable: "only a teahouse girl or bathhouse attendant are up-to-date." Similarly unconcerned about timeliness, Ayame told his disciples that an artful *onnagata* should be called young even if he is over forty (Scott 1955:174).

The increasingly rich and dominant class of merchants (townsmen; *chonin*) became patrons of theater and of impecunious youth,[148] and the ideal in boys onstage and off became decidedly more effeminate. By the late seventeenth century, male houses of prostitution with effeminate boys existed alongside female houses, especially in the larger cities. There were at least fourteen wards (*machi*) in Edo (the city which is now

147. The logic of this realism would seem to lead to offstage romantic liaisons between *onnagata* and *tachiyaku*, although this has not been recorded in the literature with which I am familiar. Perhaps a mere actor could not compete with rich admirers of the *onnagata*. Cf. the discussion of offstage relationships of Korean and Indonesian men playing women's parts (see pp. 169–71, 194–96.)

148. Kabuki "gave the audience, many of whom were non-noble, a sense of participation in upper-class aristocratic affairs" (Lewis 1974:78), just as in the "flowering" of Northern European feudalism, "burghers could also welcome the courtly ideal and share it" (A. Lewis 1974:69). Representations of intrigues and romantic love replaced representations of military triumphs in the literatures of both increasingly prosperous feudal societies. However, in Europe, pederasty was more an ancient and Renaissance than a feudal-era flower.

Tokyo) with *kagema-jaya* (catamite teahouses) during the 1760s (Leupp (1989:55–56). Three of these were in theater quarters. The rest were adjacent to shrines.[149] And there were many of these teahouses, especially in the Yoshichō District. Kansei (1934:264) drew on a 1766 list of eighty-five in the Miyagawa-cho District in Kyoto and forty-seven in the Dotōnbori District in Osaka. The houses particularly catered to the merchant middle class (Childs 1977:41–45). In fact, it has been noted that in the late eighteenth century, one house employed as many as one hundred boys for sexual purposes (Levy 1971:10)[150]

In the episodic 1682 novel *Koshuko Ichidai Otoko,* Ihara's young (fourteen-year-old) hero, Yonosuke, encounters/rents a former kabuki actor (ten years his senior) in a rural inn (1964:37–39). Later, he briefly turns a hermitage (to which he has retreated from his life of libertinage with female courtesans) into an inn where the sexual services of three "good-looking womanish lads" provide him "a convenient means of eking out a living" (56), although living off prostitutes' earnings was considered "ignoble" (58). These attractive youths were "peddlers of dainty goods." Before setting up his own male brothel, Yonosuke was told that the itinerant perfume sellers who will tarry for awhile in his employ "were masqueraders: womanish youths who called at rich widowers' estates or made the rounds of poor sections where country samurai lived. . . . Their trade was a screen to hide their true identities from the unknowing. They followed a set pattern of conduct and a line of talk easily recognizable to men acquainted with their secrets: men who felt no attraction to real women" (56). Some itinerant male prostitutes were nominally kabuki trainees. Euphemisms included "traveling boys" (*tobiko*) and "jumping boys" (*tabiko*) (Sargent 1959:215n. 26, 218n. 7).

There were sedentary as well as itinerant ones. In the 1690s, the Dutch visitor Englebert Kaempfer wrote of stopping at a town in Suruga Province on the road between Edo and Kyoto:

> At Seikenji, they make a famous plaister, the principal ingredient of which is the rosin of the firs growing on the mountain

149. Shively (1978:38). Such location, and a philippic from a 1660 booklet on actors that he quoted (39), suggested patronage of priests to Shively, but it seems to me that the patrons of the shrines were likely to visit the teahouses and extend their patronage there, in effect competing with the priests, some of whom undoubtedly also patronized pretty boys.

150. Shiveley's biography of Tokugawa Tsunayoshi notes records of at least one hundred and thirty pages selected for sex, but not all at one time. "The favorites were jealously guarded from the possibility of other liaisons by being confined in the women's quarters" (Shively 1970:99).

[above it]. . . . I cannot forbear taking notice, before proceeding
any further, that on the chief street of this town, through which
we passed, were built nine or ten neat houses, or booths, before
each of which sat one, two, or three young boys, of ten or twelve
years of age, well dressed, with their faces painted, and feminine gestures, kept by their lewd and cruel masters for the secret pleasure and entertainment of rich travelers, the Japanese
being very much addicted to this vice. However, to save the
outward appearances, and lest the virtuous should be scandalized, or the ignorant and poor presume to engage with them,
they sit there, as it were, to sell the abovesaid plaister to travelers. Our bugio, or commander in chief of our train, whose
affected gravity never permitted him to quit his palanquin till
we came to our inns, could not forebear to step out at this place,
and to spend half an hour in company with these boys. (Statler
1961:158)

In introducing a 1707 sales pitch, Statler (1961:159) noted, "all medicine shops had their boys, many of whom, as they grew older, took to
the road as traveling salesmen. Then they forsook the feminine kimonos
they had worn in the shops, and dressed in the foppish style of an ex-
quisite young dandy. They were frequently found at the fairs which were
held monthly in the compound of every Shinto shrine and Buddhist
temple. There they energetically peddled their salve, and discreetly offered themselves." At least in the nostalgic view of traditionalists such
as Ihara,

by the late seventeenth century, the developing money economy had removed much of the romance and reduced the charm
of sex with kabuki youths. . . . Although the pleasure quarters
allowed men of all classes more opportunities for homosexual
sex, with more attractive partners, than ever before, such *nanshoku* was a radically different experience from the idealized relationships between monks and their acolytes or between samurai and their pages. . . . Commoner men did not typically
reproduce the "brotherhood bonds" characteristic of the samurai. *Nanshoku* for them tended to mean the patronage of male
prostitutes or the informal exploitation of vulnerable young
males to whom the older partner owed no long-term commitment. By the early seventeenth century, chōnin entrepreneurs
(including derogated samurai) were establishing some of the
most extensive and elegant urban pleasure districts ever known.
(Leupp 1995:74, 65)

Late Imperial China (with Keelung Hong)

The ideals of the unselfish love of the Western Han emperor Ai for his beloved Lord Dong Xian and the poetic expression of devotion between high officials of the Tang and Song dynasties were remembered and celebrated in later eras.[151] The legions of male favorites (*chong*) of various emperors were also remembered, though they were generally uncelebrated, by imperial historians.[152] The doings and lovings of less-grand figures was little recorded until the later years of the Ming dynasty (1368–1644) and the (Manchu) Qing dynasty (1644–1911) that supplanted it, when increasing literacy was served (and fostered) by more efficient and larger-scale publishing technologies. A number of representations of devoted age-stratified pairs will be discussed in the first part of this section; that discussion will be followed by a discussion of actors and their patrons.

Li Yu, a particularly popular and gifted writer, provided several representations of male youths who were devoted to their older lovers. In the "Tower of Collected Elegance" ("Cuiya lou"), one of the *Twelve Towers* (*Shier lou,* ca. 1660), two young businessmen, Jin and Liu, share a youth named Quan from southern China.[153] The three run adjoining book, antique, and flower shops. Jin and Liu both marry women, but take turns spending the night "guarding the shop" and "enjoying the flowers of the rear courtyard" of Quan. When a predatory court official, Yan Shifan, hears of Quan's beauty, he goes to see for himself. Jin and Liu tell Yan that Quan is not a prostitute (*menzi*) to be used by officials,

151. On these, see Xiao (1984:39–119, 1997:51–134). Terms, dynasties, and titles are rendered in the pinyin romanization even in quotations from scholars who used other romanizations.

Whether the Tang poets' love for each other had physical (sexual) expression is not recoverable from the restrained record of their letters. One famous pair who clearly did have sexual relations in the third century A.D. was discussed by Liu Yiqing (402–44) in the nineteenth chapter of *Shihshuo xinyu* (New Tales of Many Generations). The passage was translated by Van Gulik (1961:92–93) and by Hinsch (1990:64).

152. Favorites included eunuchs, adolescents, and beautiful young married men. Dong Xian, the beloved for whom the Western Han emperor Ai (who ruled from 6 B.C. to 1 A.D.) cut off the sleeve of his own robe rather than awaken (the basis for calling male-male love *duan xiu,* the "love of the cut sleeve"), was married and had children. Since Dong Xian did not take the leaves of absence the emperor granted him, Ai moved Dong Xian's wife and children into the palace (and ordered Dong Xian to sleep with her sometimes; see Xiao 1984:55; 1997:68).

153. Hinsch (1990:123) labels the relationship "trans-generational," but the difference in age is not that great.

and Quan refuses Yan's offer of employment. Yan locks Quan up for three nights, but Quan adamantly refuses Yan's importunings. In revenge, Yan arranges for a powerful eunuch, Sha, to drug and castrate Quan. After Sha dies, Quan enters imperial service. When he tells the Wanli emperor his story, the emperor orders Yan beheaded. (Quan tells Yan's skull, which he uses as a urinal, that the high [Yan's head] was exchanged for the low [Quan's genitals].)

This tale represents both a loving relationship in which the youth is a shopkeeper like his lovers by day (i.e., does "men's work") and is sexually receptive by night.[154] When offered the plush life as an official's male concubine, he insists on remaining faithful to his lovers of humbler status. It could be argued that serving no one sexually is not one of Quan's options. Nonetheless, he is represented as being very devoted to the men who can do less for him than the one he rejects.

Especially if Li Yu is the author of *Rou pu tuan* (Prayer Mat of Flesh),[155] he had something of an obsession with castration. In his *Nan Mengmu jiaohe sanquian* (A Male Mother Mencius Moves Three Times), Li Yu wrote of an exceptionally beautiful young scholar, Jifang, who "as a boy had been a catamite of extraordinary gifts, and many older friends gathered about him, dallying with him all day, vying for his favour. . . . The sight of him also made women boiling hot, but the sight of them turned him to ice" (Li 1990:102–3). He fulfilled his duty by producing a son, whose mother—conveniently for Jifang, who had no feelings for her—died, leaving him free to seek what he really wants, a devoted and beautiful boy-wife. He finds a beautiful pubescent poor boy (thirteen years of age, twelve by Western reckoning) and pays an unprecedentedly high brideprice (amounting to half of his total assets). The two are fervently devoted to each other. Jifang expresses concern that Ruilang

---

154. Similarly, in Lü Tiancheng's *Xiutu yeshi* (Hidden History of the Embroidered Sleeping Mat, ca. 1600) the Master of the Eastern Gate has a student. "During the day they were brothers and at night they were like husband and wife" (1.4; Vitiello 1994:35), though the master also has a female wife. He later passes on his wife to his student, extolling the student's sexual equipment, and seeks to watch them have sex (Xiao 1997: 402–03).

155. The protagonist, the Before Midnight Scholar, initially "scorns the hard bast prayer mat and prefers a soft one made of [human, mostly female] flesh" (R. Martin 1963:1). Mao and Liu (1977:90–95) presented the case for attribution to Li Yu of this novel of numerous earthly amours and eventual Buddhist transcendence of desire (the Before Midnight Scholar eventually castrates himself after earlier enlarging his penis surgically) that was first published in 1633. Xiao (1997:399) argued against this attribution of authorship.

might become interested in sex with women as he develops, and that excessive masturbation might also spoil his looks.[156] Ruilang resolves to end this worry: "Better to cut it off and put an end to all the trouble it's going to cause me. . . . My [dead] parents can hardly blame me if I decide to sacrifice the chance of having children in order to repay his generosity" (120).

Other connoisseurs of boys are jealous of Jifang's exclusive enjoyment of Ruilang and report the outrage of an unauthorized castration to the local prefect. He orders Jifang flogged. Ruilang testifies that he castrated himself out of loyalty (*pao*), so the magistrate shifts the penalty to him. Jifang insists on taking it, and dies from it. On his deathbed, as Ruilang cries blood, Jifang tells him, "The reason those people provoked this catastrophe was, firstly, that they coveted you, and, secondly, that they were jealous of me. After my death, each of them will hatch his evil plots and you must move far away from here and hide, if you are going to preserve your chastity for my sake," and asks him to ensure that his son is educated (127). Left with the three-year-old Chengxin, Ruilang, now sixteen, passes as a woman and devotes himself to raising Jifang's son (moving three times to avoid male suitors). Once Chengxin has passed the imperial exams and become an official, Ruilang is honored as an exemplar of widowhood, like Mencius's mother was venerated for sacrificing her life to her son's education.[157]

A youthful Li Yu also offered a less melodramatic representation of appropriately orderly sexual use of a devoted young male servant by his bisexual master in the sixth chapter of the aforementioned *Rou putuan*. The rake called the Before Midnight Scholar has two attractive male servants, aged sixteen and eighteen; "With their smooth fresh cheeks they might have been taken for girls if their big feet had not betrayed their sex" (R. Martin 1963:106). The older one fails to understand the hints

156. At the time of his marriage, "the organ in his loins was the size of a little finger. When he slept with Jifang it was passive and unobtrusive, like a woman's. But after a year it suddenly became quite impressive, leaving Ruilang in a fever of desire that became harder and harder to control. In addition there were those five meddling fingers to rub and knead it" (117).

157. Only at age twenty-five does Chengxian learn that his stepmother had been born male. The story ends with a conventionally moralistic postscript: "If all the world's catamites were as chaste as You Ruilang, the Southern Mode would be worth enjoying. And if all the world's lovers were as fond as Xu Jifang, young Ruilang would be worth emulating. But I fear that there are no others like Ruilang and Jifang. Men waste their [yang] essence and ruin their conduct to no purpose whatsoever, which is why I consider the practice deplorable" despite its prevalence and celebration, especially in Fujian (134).

and innuendoes of his master. The foxy younger one (called Book Cabinet) misses little, certainly not how to provide pleasure to his master. He knows how to take hints and has learned to raise his "rear chamber" for ease of penetration. While being fucked, he moans with pleasure like a woman. In serving his master's desire, he hopes later on to have the maids of some of the ladies his master will be fucking with his about-to-be-enhanced penis. The Before Midnight Scholar promises to arrange for that, and the servant "redoubled his efforts to make the farewell reception as warm and pleasant as possible for his master's ambassador" (108).

The elder partners in Li Yu's representation have wives and sire children. Even the misogynist Jifang produced a son. Two of the younger (and otherwise subordinate) partners do not grow up to penetrate women. The sexual service to the Before Midnight Scholar is more casual. The servant seems to enjoy being penetrated—there is no indication that this is an unpleasant duty for him—but he also eagerly anticipates heterosexual copulations.[158] The servant is expecting pleasures from those copulations, too; he is not just doing his duty to produce sons to worship his own ancestors.

As far back as the Han Imperial Annals, it was recognized that some males, that is, Emperor Ai, did not care for women (11:8b). By late Ming times a label is attested for males who liked to be sexually receptive to males: *hao nanfeng de* (e.g., the beautiful seventeen-year-old Zhang Yang in *Huanxi yuanjia* (Happy Together) 1.3, and the very eager youth in the first novella in *Yichun xang zhi;* see Vitiello 1994:37, 137). That a masculine penetratee feels pleasure (as well as devotion) is clear in a seventeenth-century story from *Bian er chai* (Hairpins Beneath His Cap) of a soldier who is penetrated while in a drunken stupor and becomes passionately devoted to his ravisher.[159]

The fierce loyalty of the beloveds Quan and Riuji, and the importunities of a villain, recur in the third story from *Bian er chai*.[160] In it, the

158. Another servant eager to be sexually complaisant who also desires to penetrate women is Shutong, a beautiful and pleasingly scented youth from Suzhou, who flavors his kisses with cinnamon tablets (in the Ming novel *Jin Ping Mei cihua,* translated as *The Golden Lotus,* the name of the leading female character in it). He expresses his willingness to do whatever his master, Ximen Quing, wants on page 97 of the second volume of Egerton's translation.

159. *Qingxia ji* (Chronicle of Chivalric Love). Epitomized by McMahon (1988:75–76); Vitiello (1994:99–110).

160. *Qinglie ji* (Chronicle of Self-Sacrificing Love), epitomized by McMahon (1988: 76–77) and Vitiello (1994:110–19).

boy Wen Yun kills himself out of loyalty to his lover rather than submit to the sexual demands of his kidnapper. (His spirit then aids in revenge, and the lover and beloved are rejoined in the afterlife.) In the fourth story, Li Youxian is so loyal to the man who buys him from a male brothel (at age sixteen) that, when his lover is killed, he rescues and raises (in a nunnery!) his son. Like the "male mother" Li Yu wrote about, he was venerated for this sacrificing any life of his own to focus on raising the son of his dead lover. All four stories in the book are variations on the theme that love finds complete fulfillment only in the sexual relationship between two men. Each extols the "mystical union that corresponds to but is better than that between man and woman" (McMahon 1988:74). The scholar in the first story (*Qingzhen ji* [Chronicle of Faithful Love]),[161] tells his young beloved, "Those who are bound by the difference between man and woman or life and death have not lived love to the fullest. I have often said, 'The sea may become dry, the mountains may erode, but Love alone cannot surrender to Reason'" (74:11b–12a). Under the scholar('s tutelage), the boy discovers "a nest of pleasure"(*le chao*) inside his rear (75:3a).

Set in the southeastern province of Fujian (a major source of diaspora to Taiwan and elsewhere), *Nan Mengmu* provides not only a representation of homosexual devotion, but, in a prologue, some explications of "the southern custom" (*nanfeng; nan* meaning "southern" differs by only one tone from *nan* meaning "male," so "southern custom" sounds like "male practice"). No one, not even those who practice it, know when or how the "southern custom" began. According to Li Yu's (100) view of yin and yang, women need a penis to fill their emptiness, and heterosexual intercourse is necessary to produce sons. Rather than "repairing" the female's "lack" of a penis, "the southern custom" produces mutual delight—particularly for the poor, to whom few other pleasures are available. Such relations are "natural," and not just to humans. Li even adduces the existence of a "southern custom tree" (*nanfeng shu;* banyan) in which one trunk embraces another and they become inextricably entwined (101).

Hinsch (1990:133) quoted from a story titled "Tuer shen" (Leveret Spirit): "According to the customs of Fujian province, it is acceptable for a man and boy to form a bond [*qi*] and to speak to each other as if to brothers."[162] Fujian was famed for male-male marriages and sworn

161. Epitomized by Vitiello (1994:120–36) and McMahon (1998:74–75).
162. That the spirit of an enamored man convinces villagers to build a temple does not seem to me to warrant "organized homosexual cultic activity." It seems to me a matter of

brotherhood (*guanhe; qiyou* in Mandarin).[163] The idiom of older and younger brother (*hia* and *di* in Holo/Fujianhua; *xiong* and *di* in Mandarin/Beijinghua) were used in both relationships. In *Bizhou zhai yutan* (Gossip from My Humble House), Shen Defu (1578–1642) reported the passionate devotion of Fujianese male-male lovers: "The Fujianese men are extremely fond of male beauty. No matter if rich or poor, handsome or ugly, they all find a companion of their own status. . . . They love each other and at the age of thirty they are still together, sleeping in the same bed like husband and wife. . . . Such passion can be so deep that it is not uncommon that two lovers, finding it impossible to continue their relationship, tie themselves up together and drown themselves" (trans. Vitiello 1992:363). He also passed on the belief that pirate captains began the custom of having harems of boys. (To have women on board ship was unthinkable courting of disaster.) He contrasted such transgenerational relations with the romantic relationships of those near each other in age—father:son rather than older brother:younger brother.

Generally, the boy partners did the work of subordinate males rather than what was "woman's work" in Ming and Qing China. While their pleasure in being penetrated was represented as being less than the pleasures of penetration, for most of them it was still a pleasure, not only a duty. Moreover, the pleasures of the penetrated partner included erection and ejaculation, as in the instance of a priest who "seduced the young disciple and sweet feelings arose, but the young disciple's penis got larger and [semen] oozed out. The priest grasped it from the rear with his hands and sighed, 'Oh, Amida Buddha, it's pierced through'" (i.e., the priest thinks his own penis has gone all the way through the boy) (H. Levy 1974:233).

In some cases devotion to the "older brother" was extreme, even fatal, while the acquiescence of others comes across as pragmatic. (The same could be said for sex within heterosexual marriages, particularly arranged ones, which often include somewhat older male patrons and compliant younger female dependents.) We do not see any greater status differences in the representations of acquiescence than in the cases of extreme devotion, although it bears stressing that in addition to differing

---

assuaging the demand of a ghost who might otherwise inflict harm, rather than any cult to homoeroticism.

163. A ceremony after which the sworn brothers repair to bed and talk about sex with women occurs in the third chapter of *Rou putuan* (R. Martin 1963:52–60). The talk is more pragmatic than erotic and does not seem an instance of males getting so aroused talking about sex with women that they have sex with each other. (The Before Midnight Scholar is the younger brother seeking advice.)

in age, the partners are generally from different strata, that the deference of a younger to an older brothers was expected in Chinese culture, and that the rights to deference in client-patron relationships are accompanied by the patron's obligations to protect and enhance the well-being of the client.

We have not failed to notice that several of the beloveds are castrated over the course of narratives, and/or live as widows. However, it was as youthful males that they were loved, not as eunuchs (who were also notoriously abundant in imperial China). As in some Japanese representations, often neither partner wanted the beloved to outgrow the beauties and charms of boyhood. Nevertheless, the more intense devotions are represented as lasting not only lifelong, but beyond death.

Actor Prostitutes

During the Ming dynasty, and especially in the last half of the Qing dynasty (i.e., the mid-eighteenth to the early twentieth century) young male actors sold by their parents from southern China were popular courtesans and concubines in the capital.[164] Pretty boys were particularly favored (see Mackerras 1972:149–53). Often referred to as "rabbits" (*tu*), they were sometimes euphemized as "officials" (*xiao guan*).

Real officials were forbidden to visit the red-light district or to hire "singsong girls" (female prostitutes), "although they could hire actors. In order, therefore, to keep within the law, officials and scholars often invited actors to their feasts, enjoying their singing, dancing, and conversation. Once famous scholars had written in praise of this the thing became fashionable, growing more and more popular. At the beginning of the Qing dynasty this craze died down a little, to be revived later in a more licentious form" (Lu 1976:320).

The canonical representation of the milieu, Chen Sen's *Pinhua baojian* (A Mirror of Theatrical Life), first printed in 1849,

> deals with Beijing actors . . . and a number of passages in it are obscene. The author apparently believed that some actors were

164. "It was often said that Fujian and Guangdong were the centers of such sexual practices; actually, however, homosexuality was commonplace in Jiangnan as well. Southern officials—claimed Xie [Zhaozhi, *Wu za zu* {1618} 8:4–5a]—had brought their habits with them to Beijing, where the wine shops were filled with young male prostitutes (*xiaochang*) who worked as waiters and singing boys for the literati. Most prostitutes originally came from the Ningpo/Shaoxing region in Zhejiang, but there were also professional catamites from Linqing in Shandong, so that people frequently distinguished between 'northern' and 'southern' *xiaochang*" (Wakeman 1985, 1:95).

respectable, some disreputable, just as their patrons might be cultured or vulgar. . . The finest characters in this book, idealized figures like Mei Tzu-yu and Tu Chin-yen still belong to the school of "talented scholars and beauties," the actors being the beauties and their patrons the scholars. The whole novel is filled with tender and romantic sentiments, the only difference [from heterosexual romances] being that the "beauties" are young men . . . Most of the characters in *A Mirror of Theatrical Life* were based on real persons, and can be identified from their names and idiosyncrasies. (Lu 1976:320, 322)

The intense, mutual love between Mei and Tu, the archetypal couple, is countenanced by Mei's wife.

In liaisons between scholar-officials and actors, there is at least some indication that both parties became aroused (Chen Yinguan; quoted by Mackerras 1972:100), and there is a famous instance of fidelity between an actor wife (Wei San [Li Guiguan?]) and the mandarin He Shen in the late eighteenth century,[165] which inspired Chen Sen's 1849 novel based in part on his own experience of male courtesans, *Pinhua baojian* (Precious Mirror of Ranked Flowers). "The popular *xiaochang* (little singers) worked hard, sometimes performing at more than one banquet in a day. . . . They received handsome payment for their services, but usually had to hand it over to their teacher. . . . The children themselves possessed virtually nothing of their own. One character in the *Pinhua baojian* [3, 19a] complains that even the clothes he wears belongs to his teacher. The comfortable life a master gave his [most prized] apprentices was a lever to force them to do his will" (Mackerras 1972:150).

Although many of their patrons were officials, the actors were socially disabled, even when not indentured to their teachers. Among the more staid members of the elite not enamored with a particular boy actor, "even the magic of money could not overcome the social stigma attached to them or their lack of family connections with influential people," and not only the sons but the grandsons of actors were forbidden to sit for imperial examinations (by edicts of 1652 and 1770) (219). Moreover, "because their appeal as actors depended to some extent on physical attraction, the *xiaochang* enjoyed but short careers. Most of them left the *dang zi* [young boy parts] when they lost their appeal, at about the age of twenty" (152).

---

165. In that Wei had a grandson, he was probably not exclusively homosexual (Mackerras 1972:97)—only "probably" because adoption was common, especially in southeastern China.

In some unusual instances, the actor was wealthier and pursued a husband.[166] The short careers on stage and the brief period during which they were in favor with those who rented male flesh was, surely, generally less glamorous than were the lives of the few "stars" who became lifetime concubines for rich or high-status men, but it is not at all obvious that the former were worse off than they had been as extra sons in poor southern rural families that were only too happy to sell them into de facto slavery (de jure, there were contracts for years of repaying their teachers for training in how to act on stage and with clients).

Most of the boys sold in China (whether to opera troupes or to brothels) had to be available sexually and were trained in being anally penetrated. Some anuses were stretched with pegs or dildoes of increasing size. In "Qingqi ji," the final novella in *Bian er chai* (discussed on pp. xx–xx; see Vitiello 1994:110–19), the sixteen-year-old Fujianese student Li Youxian, who sells himself to keep his father from being imprisoned, is tied up and raped until he feels pleasure instead of pain. He is the hero of the novella, and is presented as a heroic example of filial piety. Late imperial China provides the closest approximation of institutionalized forced socialization into homosexuality (rather than the occupation associated with homosexuality being chosen). Obviously, it was boys of poor families who were sold into quasi-slavery, so I would categorize it as a class-based more than a profession-defined type or subtype (of age-stratified homosexuality).

In late imperial China, as in other cultures in which adolescent male beauty was especially celebrated by older lovers, those aged sixteen to seventeen were considered the choicest flowers. Their natural beauty (which was preferable to artificial female beauty) was thought to wilt by age twenty. As in Japan and Rome, those who sought to maintain their youthful looks by artificial means were derided as effeminate. Ambiguity was more highly prized than femininity (Vitiello 1994:72–74). Nonetheless, the number of ersatz youth appears to have increased in late Qing times (as in Togukawa Japan).

Taoist beliefs about depleting *qi* (life spirit, i.e., vitality) in ejaculation do not seem to have been accompanied by any ideas of gains (either in masculinity or longevity) for boys who were inseminated.[167] At least

---

166. Mackerras 1972:141; also see the instance in Waley 1970:27.

167. See Vitiello 1992:250–53 and the sources cited there on the non-loss or even gain of yang for the penetrator. Sex with males is neither condemned as sinful nor regarded as sickness in Chinese traditional medicine/religion.

some of the lovers of boys had been boy-beloveds at an earlier age.[168] There is a body of Ming and Qing literature about intensely devoted male-male loves analogous to *Nanshoku Okagami* (discussed on pp. 79– 84).[169] As in the Japanese collection, there are more than a few supreme sacrifices in this literature. Romantic excesses sometimes conflict with familial obligations (the prime one of which is to sire sons), but in other instances, including several discussed above, the relationships involve exemplary self-sacrifice to preserve the life of the partner or of his son (which is to say, the elder partner's lineage).

Finally, it may bear noting that the subordinate partners, the pene- trated youth, were supplied either by poor families or by those that sud- denly became downwardly mobile. That is, the lovers differed from the beloved in wealth and status as well as in age and sexual role. The multi- fold hierarchies of Chinese society were not "transgressed"; there was no equivalent to the Roman *exoletus* penetrating his clients,[170] or of age over- riding other status considerations in taking the penetrated role, as oc- curred even in the Japanese imperial families (see p. 84n. 88).

Effeminized Boy Entertainers/Prostitutes in Some Islamic Societies

A number of nineteenth- and early-twentieth-century European and American travelers wrote about boy entertainers/prostitutes in Islamic societies. However redolent of Orientalism these travelers were, no one has suggested that they imagined or invented the occupations. To take particularly well-known examples from major literary figures, in 1810, Byron and John Hobhouse saw transvestite boys dancing at coffeehouses in Galata, a Constantinople suburb (Crompton 1985:143–44). Ali Pasha,

168. E.g., Jifang in *Nan Mengmu* and Master Zhong in the first story of Yichung, *Xing zhi* (Fragrant Stuff for the Spring Palace) (1:16a; see Vitiello 1994:138–39).

169. See Vitiello 1992, 1994 on the main collections of "fragments of the Chinese love discourse" involving two males.

170. Vitiello (1992:361) stressed this. There is an example of violation of hierarchies in the first story from *Yichung xing zhi* of an eleven-year-old Suzhou student obsessed with males who is penetrated by a servant (i.e., a social inferior) and then by all eighteen of his classmates (i.e., social peers). His voracious receptive sexuality does not prevent him from finding true love and receiving the approval of the Earth God (see Vitiello 1994:136–46): he is avenged as a hero, cremated as a great man, and reincarnated as the son of his lover. Although probably the most ardent bottom in Chinese literature, Sun Yi spends all the money he has accumulated on a female courtesan whom he impregnates, showing again that being sexually receptive to males, even eagerly so, does not preclude desiring and pen- etrating females and continuing the penetrated male's (ancestors') lineage.

the Ottoman despot who ruled Albania and Greece in the early nineteenth century (and who found Byron very attractive), staged a dance of a circle of more than forty "ganymedes" for the ardently philhellenic fifth Earl of Guilford. Although it was "limited in its variety of movement, nevertheless was full of tantalizing turns and postures, calculated to exhibit the contours of the body to the best advantage."[171]

Nineteenth-Century Egypt

Flaubert's 1849–50 letters from Egypt included a vivid description of cross-dressing dancing boys, and documented sodomy in the baths, as well.[172] A bit later, Klunzinger (1878:190–91) reported from Egypt: "The performance of the *chauel* [*khawal*] or male dancer is not much of an improvement on that of the female dancer. Clothed and tricked out like a dancing girl, he goes through the same kind of motions on another evening to the delight of the spectators. Sometimes he also plays on some instrument, and sings as well. . . . This class of hermaphrodites, the product of the luxurious East, also resembles the dancing-girls in their abandoned morals." A few decades later still, Edward Lane (1908:389) wrote:

> Many of the people of Cairo, affecting, or persuading themselves, to consider that there is nothing improper in the dancing of the Ghawázee but the fact of its being performed by females, who ought not thus to expose themselves, employ men to dance in the same manner; but the number of these male performers, who are mostly young men, and who are called "Khäwals," is very small. They are Muslims and natives of Egypt. As they personate women, their dances are exactly of the same description as those of the Ghawázee; and are, in like manner, accompanied by the sound of castanets: but, as if to prevent their being thought to be really females, their dress is suited to their unnatural profession; being partly male, and partly female: it chiefly consists of a tight vest, a girdle, and a kind of petticoat. This general appearance, however is more feminine than masculine: they suffer the hair of the head to grow long, and generally braid it, in the manner of the women; the hair on the face, when it

171. Cristowe (1941:327). On Christian as well as Muslim involvement in pederasty (into this century) in Albania see Crompton 1985; Murray 1997e; Näcke 1907.

172. See Flaubert 1973:567–74 on Egypt; see also Flaubert 1973:638, 669 on Constantinople. Byron referred to the Turkish baths as "marble palaces of sherbet and sodomy" in 1819 (quoted by Crompton 1985:142) and in an 1810 letter wrote that "in England the vices in fashion are whoring & drinking, in Turkey, Sodomy & smoking. We prefer a girl and a bottle, they a pipe and a pathic" (143).

begins to grow, they pluck out; and they imitate the women also in applying kohl and henna to their eyes and hands. In the streets, when not engaged in dancing, they often even veil their faces; not from shame, but merely to affect the manners of women. They are often employed, in preference to the Ghawázee, to dance before a house, or in its court, on the occasion of a marriage-fête, or the birth of a child, or a circumcision; and frequently perform at public festivals.

There is, in Cairo, another class of male dancers, young men and boys, whose performances, dress, and general appearance are almost exactly similar to those of the Khäwals; but who are distinguished by a different appellation, which is "Gink;" a term that is Turkish, and has a vulgar signification which aptly describes their character. They are generally Jews, Armenians, Greeks, and Turks.

I take this to mean that the body of the "Gink" was more explicitly available for rent than was that of the *khawal*. Note that these dancers mixed gendered dress rather than trying to pass as women.

Nineteenth-Century Iraq

Journeying from the ruins of ancient Nineveh along the Tigris River toward Baghdad in the summer of 1817, James Silk Buckingham stopped at Hebheb, where the appearance of the people, their town, and the Arabic spoken, reminded him of Egypt. Buckingham wrote about the duty to indicate even "unspeakable" lifeways of the debauched Orient. Beyond the standard litany of "indescribable" and "infamous," the following passage is interesting because it shows that such attitudes were being reflected back by some "natives" who were aware of the Christian European denigration of Islamic societies' acceptance of "depravity," and therefore denied that anything sexual was going on.

This was the first place . . . I had ever seen boys publicly exhibited and set apart for purposes of depravity not to be named. I had, indeed, heard of public establishments for such infamous practices at Constantinople, but I had always doubted the fact. I saw here, however, with my own eyes one of these youths avowedly devoted to purposes not to be described, and from the very thought of which the mind revolts with horror. This youth was by no means remarkable for beauty of person, and was even dirtily and meanly dressed. His costume was that of an Arab, with a peculiar kind of silk handkerchief, called *keffeah*, hanging down about the neck, and thrown over the head. He wore, however, all the silver ornaments peculiar to females; and from his traveling *khoordj* he exhibited to the persons in the coffeehouse a much richer dress of muslin and gold stuffs, in which he arrayed himself on certain occasions. The boys was about ten years of age, impudent, forward, and revoltingly fond and fawning in his demeanour. . . . This youth was under the care of an elder and a younger man, who traveled with him, and shared the profits of his exhibition and his use. (Buckingham 1827: 166–68)

Note, again, the mixing of gendered dress that ensured that customers knew that this was a boy.

More recently, Thesiger (1964:123–24) also noted male prostitutes and transvestite dancers and discreet peer homosexual relations in southern Iraq towns.

Uzbeki *Bacabozlik*

Eugene Schuyler—who was U.S. consul in Moscow and then in St. Petersburg beforehe traveled in central Asia in 1867—presented an extended account of effeminized boy dancers/prostitutes in Uzbekistan:

In Central Asia Mohammedan prudery prohibits the public dancing of women; but as the desire of being amused and of witnessing a graceful spectacle is the same all the world over, here boys and youths specially trained take the place of the dancing-girls of other countries. The moral tone of the society of Central Asia is scarcely improved by the change.

These *batchas,* or dancing-boys, are a recognized institution throughout the whole of the settled portions of Central Asia, though they are most in vogue in Bukhara, and the neighboring Samarkand. Batchas are as much respected as the greatest singers and *artistes* are with us. Every movement they make is followed and applauded, and I have never seen such breathless interest as they excite, for the whole crowd seems to devour them with their eyes, while their hands beat time to every step. If a batcha condescends to offer a man a bowl of tea, the recipient rises to take it with a profound obeisance, and returns the empty bowl in the same way, addressing him only as *"Taxi,"* "your Majesty," or *"kulluk,"* "I am your slave." Even when a batcha passes through the bazaar all who know him rise to salute him with hands upon their hearts, and the exclamation of "Kulluk!" and should he deign to stop and rest in any shop it is thought a great honor.

Figure 7. *Batcha* and admirers.

In all large towns batchas are very numerous, for it is as much
the custom for a Bokhariot gentleman to keep one as it was in
the Middle Ages for each knight to have his squire. In fact no establishment of a man of rank or position would be complete
without one; and men of small means club together to keep one
among them, to amuse them in their hours of rest and recre-
ation. They usually set him up in a tea-shop, and if the boys is
pretty his stall will be full of customers all day long. Those
batchas, however, who dance in public are fewer in number, and
are now to some extent under [Russian] police restrictions. In
Kitab there were only about a dozen, in other towns even less,
and the same dancers sometimes go from place to place. They
live either with their parents or with the entrepreneur, who
takes care of them and always accompanies them. He dresses
them for the different dances, wraps them up when they have
finished, and looks after them as well as any duenna.

. . . The natives seem most pleased with those dances where
the batcha is dressed as a girl, with long braids of false hair and
tinkling anklets and bracelets. Usually but one or two in a troop
can dance the women's dance, and the female attire once donned
is retained for the remainder of the feast, and the batcha is much
besought to sit here and there among the spectators to receive
their caresses. . . . [The dances] were by no means indecent,
though they were often very lascivious. One of the most frequent gestures was that of seizing the breast in the hand and

then pretending to throw it to the spectators, similar to our way of throwing kisses. In some dances the batcha goes about with a bowl of tea, and choosing one of the spectators, offers the tea to him with entreating gestures, sinks to the floor, singing constantly a stanza of praise and compliment. The favored man hands back the bowl with thanks, but the boy slips from his proffered embrace, or shyly submits to be kissed, and is off to another. If the spectator is generous he will drop some silver coins into the empty bowl, and if he is a great lover of this amusement he will take a golden *tilla* in his lips, and the batcha will put up his lips to receive it, when a kiss may perhaps be snatched.

The songs sung during the dances are always about love and are frequently responsive between the batcha and the musicians. . . . [E.g.,]

"Tchuyandy, my soul! why didst thou delay, if thou were sad?" "Nightingale! I am sad! As passionately as thou lovest the rose, so loudly sing, that my loved one may awake. Let me die in the embrace of my dear one, for I envy no one. I know that thou hast many lovers; but what affair of mine is that? The rose would not wither if the nightingale did not win it; and man would not perish did not death come."[173]

The batchas practice their profession from a very early age until sometimes so late as twenty or twenty-five, or at all events until it is impossible to conceal their beards. The life which they have led hardly fits them for independent existence thereafter. So long as they are young and pretty they have their own way in everything; every command is obeyed by their adorers, every purse is at their disposition, and they fall into a life of caprice, extravagance, and dissipation. Rarely do they lay up any money, and more rarely still are they able to profit by it afterwards. Frequently a batcha is set up as a keeper of a tea-house by his admirers, where he will always have a good *clientèle*, and sometimes he is started as a small merchant. Occasionally one succeeds, and becomes a prosperous man, though the remembrance of his past life will frequently place the then odious affix, batcha, to his name. I have known one or two men, now rich and respected citizens, who began life in this way. In the old days it was much easier, for a handsome dancer might easily become *Kushbegi*, or Grand Vizier. More often a batcha takes to smoking opium or drinking *kukhnar*, [a liqueur made from poppies from which the seeds have been removed] and soon dies of dissipation. (1876 I:132–35)

---

173. The nightingale and the rose are recurrent metaphors for wooer and wooed, although the rose is usually a female beloved (in contrast to the candle drawing a moth).

Again, everyone knew the desired *batcha* was biologically male. Baldauf (1988) discussed Soviet suppression of Uzbeki dancing boys and the continuation of the role among Uzbekis in Afghanistan at least through the 1980s.

Moroccan Boy Sex Slaves

Harvard anthropologist Carleton Coon (1931:110–11) wrote more specifically of boy sex slaves in northwestern Morocco in the 1920s:

> In the Jebala, markets were formerly held in which boys stolen from their families were sold. They were and still are kept by their purchasers for the purpose of sodomy, and other uses [i.e., apprenticeship] are made secondary to it. When they have grown to an age at which they cease to interest their purchasers sexually, they are released and allowed to earn their own living. The market el Had Ikauen of Ktama was a famous boy market and was not closed until the advent of the Spanish forces of occupation [1910] who have been trying to prevent such sales, although it is difficult to stamp out private transactions. Boy markets are found in the Western Arabaphone Senhaja, Ghomara, and Ktama [tribes], also, of course, in the rest of the so-called Jebala and centered at Sheshawen and in the tribes of Beni Zerwal.[174]

Boy Actresses in Indonesia

Near the opposite end of the Islamic world, across Indonesia, traveling troupes of entertainers provide an occupational niche for concentrations of men attracted to men and for men who act women's roles. Among the Makassarese of southern Sulawesi,[175] at least through the 1940s, there were *masri* dancers aged nine to twelve, who dressed somewhat like women. They covered part of their face with a long white shawl, like a veil. The main purpose of the dance they performed before audiences consisting mostly of married men, according to Chabot (1950: 156), was "sexual incitement, emanating from the combination of verse,

---

174. Coon (1931:111) claimed that "the whole Jebalan area is permeated with this type of sexual depravity, which is practiced without mutual shame or any attempt at concealment." Also see Maxwell 1983:286–89.

175. Traditional Makassarese society included a prestigious gender-mixing shamanistic role (*bisu*). Largely dependent on a court disrupted by Dutch conquest, the role had declined by the 1920s. "Homosexuals called *kawe* . . . have remained, seeking to satisfy their needs and plying their profession in markets and busy city quarters" (Van der Kroef 1954:261; see Nootenboom 1948:245–55).

rhythm and the young boys half-dressed as women." The men in the audiences showed their approval by slipping often large amounts of money under the the young boys' collars. In 1928, when Chabot observed it, the dance enjoyed great popularity, which continued after World War II (van der Kroef 1954:263).

On the island of Java, which had been Islamicized for much longer, Wilken (1893:118) mentioned boys taking girls' roles in some dance troupes in the late nineteenth century: "Sometimes the *bedaja* and *serimpi* are replaced by boys, who then are dressed as girls and also belong to the nobility. It has been rumored that they serve as concubines of prominent men, and, therefore, other boys of this kind who do not serve as dancing girls are also called *bedaja*. So little evil is seen in pederasty that no secret is made of it" (Human Relations Area File translation). Nearly a century later, in 1972–73 fieldwork, Weiss (1977:529–30) observed that "a form of institutionalized homosexuality occurs in the Ponorogo area. . . . The practice of keeping young boys (on the part of either individuals or service organizations) was once and still is a prestigious pattern. Formerly, men who kept boys could often get married, not because they preferred sexual relations with women, but apparently because they felt compelled to realize the Javanese ideal of marriage and procreation. Some even continued to keep boys after they were married."

In contemporary rural Java, performing troupes continue to need a pretty young boy for *rayag* performances. The parents of Javanese *gemblakan* (singular *gemblak*) trade their sons for gifts and money from the dance troupe in which their son performs women's roles (for a year or two). Offstage, a group of unmarried young men pass the boy around for intercrural intercourse. W. Williams (1990) added that the *gemblak* may on occasion be fellated, that they generally marry women later, and that members of the troupe do not have sexual relations with other members except for the *gemblak*. Displaying the resources to keep a *gemblak* and to dress him expensively is still today a source of prestige for men. Despite the increasing commercialization of the *gemblak* role, parents are both honored and enriched by having a son spend several years as a *gemblak*. As with other effeminate performers in the Philippines and Tahiti, traditional Aleutian male concubines, or eunuchs and catamites in the Roman or Ottoman Empires, some are socialized into the role by parents seeing a chance to profit from attractive sons. Moreover, a successful *rayag* troupe brings prestige to the village, and no *rayag* can be successful without a star *gemblak*, so maintaining the status of the village as well as the prosperity of the family motivate treating the *gemblak* well.

The boy outgrows his stage role, and also his desirability as a sexual partner. If he marries and bears children, like the Omani *khanith* or Moroccan boys who cease being sexually receptive, the former *gemblak* is treated like other male villagers. He is not reminded of the glory or of the sexual aspects of his earlier vocation.

In the northeastern edge of the Islamicized world (Indonesia and the Philippines), gender-mixed homosexual roles are more obvious than pederasty (see Peacock 1968), but those who take on these roles in Indonesian and Filipino cultures often start young.

Across the Abode of Islam (in time and in space) conventionally masculine men prefer boys who are both young and pretty; these men enjoy the boys on stage and off. It is difficult not to infer that there was homosexuality with effeminate youths on these islands before Islam reached them, although effeminate boy entertainers have long been appreciated and courted by adult male Muslims in Egypt and across the southern, Islamic parts of mainland Asia. Those in organized troupes are able to take on other less prominent jobs within the company once their allure has faded. Some reject sexual receptivity as adults; such men are less likely to continue in the entertainment business, with its uncertain income and low social status. Those who want to continue to be sexually receptive (and also those who want to take the insertive role with young males) are more likely to stay in it.

3

Boy "Tops"

Thus far, the age-stratified homosexuality I have discussed has involved the (at least nominally) older male penetrating the younger one. In ancient Rome, there was a kind of prostitute, the *exoletus*, who penetrated his affluent elders. In this chapter, several other instances in which the younger participant is the penetrator will be noted.

Africa

Among two Sudanese peoples, Siegfried Nadel (1947:242) mentioned marriages of Korongo *londo* and Mesakin *tubele* to males for the bride-price of one goat (1947:285).[1] The generally young husband in these marriages might also obtain women wives. He did not specify whether *londo* and *tubele* were older than their husbands, although marking the latter as "young" implies this.

Among the Bantu-speaking Pangwe peoples (Bene, Bulu, Fang, Jaunde, Mokuk, Mwele, Ntum) north of the Congo River, homosexual intercourse was *bian nku'ma*, a medicine for enhancing wealth. The good luck was transmitted from bottom to top in anal intercourse, according to Tessman (1904:23, 1921), who also mentioned that "it is frequently 'heard of' that young people carry on homosexual relations with each other and even of older people who take boys, who as is well known 'have neither understanding nor shame' and readily console them by saying '*biabo pfia'nga* (we are having fun, playing a game).' . . . Adults are excused with the corresponding assertion: '*a bele nem e bango* = he has the heart (that is, the aspirations) of boys.' Such men were said to have a heart for boys: *bian nku'ma*"(1904:131; HRAF translation).

Even more remarkable than Pangwe belief in the medical benefits the penetrator enjoys as a result of anal intercourse is Hulstaert's (1938: 86–87) report that among the Nkundó, the younger partner penetrated the older one, a pattern quite contrary to the usual pattern of age-graded homosexuality. His conventional Christian rhetoric of unnatural vice (and benighted savages) makes it unlikely that Hultsaert had any personal sympathy for homosexuality; for example, he wrote that "the game of *gembankango* in which boys, imitating monkeys chase each other

---

1. He glossed the two terms as (male) "homosexual."

through the trees and creepers can—and does—result in reprehensible scenes" (73).

Although urban male prostitutes in contemporary East and West Africa are mostly effeminate and penetrated (see Davidson 1988:167–72, Kamau 1998, Kleis and Abdullahi 1983), there are also conventionally masculine-appearing men who pay (directly or indirectly) to be penetrated (Kamau 1998).

Seville

Seville in the sixteenth century was one of the half-dozen largest cities in Europe, and was the port through which flowed into Spain the riches of its New World conquests. A special inquest to determine the extent of sodomy in 1606 set off a panic among Seville's sodomites. Contrary to The Foucault-Weeks claims that there were only chance acts of sodomy without self-aware actors (sodomites) before the late nineteenth century, the fact that some men fled rather than facing interrogation shows that some of them recognized a connection between the objects of the inquest and their conduct. Several dozen less fleet or less insightful men were arrested, and twelve convicted of sodomy were publicly burned to death (Lea 1907:362).

Perry (1980), drawing on a 1619 manuscript compendium of the experience of Padre Pedro de Léon while attending 309 persons prior to their execution in Seville, showed that nearly 90 percent of the capital convictions for sexual offenses were for sodomy (fifty-two cases, in contrast to two for bestiality, two for adultery, and one for rape). While "many accounts do not mention any profession or occupation other than the crime for which they were prosecuted," there was mention of six clerics, two schoolmasters, one nobleman, and "an old street vendor [who was] fat, deaf, and blind" who were executed for sodomy (Perry 1980:72).

Léon's compendium showed clerics and other sodomites taking poor youths home, giving them presents, dressing them up (sometimes effeminately) and sexually "using" them. A sheriff kept a gambling house with boys to sodomize. Departing from this pattern, one Negro (case 308) reported being paid to take the active role, and Perry (1980, 1988) suggested that a group of fifteen men burned together in 1600 (but not reported on by de Léon) and a group of eight men burned in 1585 were all a part of an effeminate subculture (like the later mollies of London), rather than traditionally masculine sodomites. Whether a shift in cases represented a changing organization of homosexuality, or whether class- and age-graded sodomy continued apart from a growing effeminate subculture, cannot be determined, at least from the evidence Perry presented.

Two of the most sensational Spanish cases in the early 1570s involved grandees and a younger male prostitute who took the insertive role with his customers. Martín de Castro "informed his judges that he 'never rode on poor men, only on lords who gave him lots of money' and boasted to an Inquisitor that he had made more money with his penis than the Inquisitor had with his church bells" (Monter 1990:134).

Nevertheless, young male prostitutes seem generally to have been sexual receptors. The twenty-year-old Nicolas Gonzales, arrested in 1624 in Orihuela and tried in Valencia, confessed to having taken the *paciente* role with the eight men who accused him (and who went on to accuse more than sixty others). The tribunal added that Gonzales furnished boys for sex, renting them to off-duty slaves and freemen. Despite his claim to be under the age of legal majority when he performed all his homosexual acts, Gonzales was executed. He and the men to whom he provided male sex partners, renting them either his own body or that of another, did not just happen to commit an act of sodomy now and again. As in other cases of garrulous defendants, his showed a **network** of men and boys seeking commercial same-sex sex. There were enough males sufficiently aware of such recurrent and predictable desires to support commerce catering to them. Almost none of the cases involved two consenting adults:[2] "the nearly invariable pattern of relationships was between older men and adolescents, between dominator and dominated 'whose sine qua non condition was the absolute submission of the dependent and paid subject to the will of his overlord.'. . . Nearly half of all sodomy defendants tried by the Inquisition were under the legal age of majority, and thus could not be executed regardless of their degree of guilt" (Monter 1990;290).

American Hustlers

In "The social integration of queers and peers" an ethnographic study of Nashville, Tennessee, sociologist Albert Reiss (1961) described masculine, young *peers*,[3] whose insertive behavior maintained their sense of being properly masculine. In their view, only insertees were *queer*. Peers'

---

2. "The only clear example of a couple of consenting adults occurred in rural Aragon, when a French weaver, aged thirty-five, and an Aragonese fieldhand, aged thirty-four, were surprised in a false closet they had built for privacy" (Monter 1990:290n. 31). Aliens, especially Italians, were frequently involved in cases of sodomy in Spain between 1580 and 1630.

3. Surely the rhyme is Reiss's, and the vernacular term was *trade*.

participation did not challenge their masculine status, so long as they gave nothing more than their penises (and possibly an occasional beating), that is, so long as they "never took it," maintaining anal impenetrability. What they might take that was consistent with the role was queers' money or possessions. Taking these things without the consent of the queer was a tribute to the ingenuity and/or masculine prowess of the peer. No one regarded direct payment for sexual service as masculinizing, but, apparently, the insertors evaded the label of *prostitute*, along with that of *queer*.[4]

Such a system could persist only with the collusion of those willing to enact the role of the queer, specifically, by not challenging the valuation and self-image of those who lent or rented their penises to queers. So long as both parties credited this system's script for the "natural" submission of the queer to the ostentatiously masculine youth, "deviant" acts validated both peers' masculinity (/heterosexuality) and the deprecation—specifically, as necessarily feminizing—of homosexuality. Kneeling to worship the symbol of trade's masculinity, and to ingest its tangible product, queers protected fantasies shared by both peers and queers about the unhomosexual masculinity of the peer.

Beyond the financial rewards, sexual release, and reassurances about their marketably exciting masculinity, peers saw the dangers of succumbing to any temptations toward passivity. Most presumably "learned" they weren't *queer*—and didn't have to be to get off with men. Reiss's study did not assess the degree of "role distance," versus the degree of self-hatred, of those enacting the queer role, but to whatever extent those playing the queer role credited the truth (and justice) of the evaluation of insertors as superior to insertees, their "deviant" conduct reinforced the moral order in general, and the superiority of heterosexual males in particular.[5]

If sexual behavior then was really so rigidly dichotomized, it has become less so. Now, there are males who rent their mouths and anuses,

---

4. Wescott (1990 [1937]:9) remarked on the "commercialization of one's sex [being] more respectable than the free gift of it," after mentioning a sailor who, having "manifested some enthusiasm, begged Jack not to tell any of his colleagues, who would not respect him if they knew." On "trade" neutralization of homosexual conduct, see John Rechy (1961; and in Leyland 1978:260); and Gore Vidal (in Leyland 1978:291, 273, 275).

5. Reiss was concerned (à la Durkheim) with functions for the society, not with cost and benefits for individual's egos. On role distance from homosexual involvements see Murray 1996a:149–50. On the apparent acceptance of inferior status (more generally) see Adam 1978a:113–14.

and there are many male sex workers who are gay identified.[6] Nonetheless, there is still sexual behavior that a sex worker withholds from his customers.[7] Kissing, condomless anal sex, and specializing in one role for hire while enacting another in "private life" are conduct that recur.[8] Many gay-identified sex workers reserve what they regard as more intimate connections for partners they choose, though they are paid for enacting particular sexual roles in the customer's fantasy scenarios.[9] As one major patron (of up-scale sex workers) noted, "Even though boys seldom reject clients, they reject acts. Frequently. They don't have to do anything they don't feel like doing, and they're all trained how to decline gracefully" (R. Brown 1996:79). He also found that one can buy a wide array of sexual "services," but not "love," and, because sex workers "are selling what most people will not—access to their private parts and intimate services—it is important to them to be clear about what they will never sell but will preserve for a merger with a self-chosen other person, a true love" (250).[10]

6. In interviews with past, present, or prospective clients (aged sixteen to twenty-five, most of whom were between the ages of eighteen and twenty) for Streetwise Youth, conducted in West London in 1988, West and Villiers (1993:86) found that four of twenty-three punters who said that they were heterosexual reported being anally penetrated by some customers. Seven denied engaging in anal sex, either receptive or insertive. This seems to leave eleven who engaged in anal sex only as insertors and four versatile straight-identified punters. All eighteen of those who identified as homosexual engaged in anal sex, half only as insertors. Of the nine who identified as bisexual, two had been anally penetrated by clients, and one had not engaged at all in anal sex.

7. Val, a semi-retired call boy (with earlier experience as an independent) told me: "If someone wants to kiss and it gets you a tip or the possibility of a repeat session, you do it. Usually the client has to initiate the behavior or ask for it, though. . . . Some hustlers, especially those at the lower end economically, may well (if they are willing to be fucked at all) get fucked without a rubber (I suppose they try to size up the client for risk) because they really need the money or figure they're already exposed or may even know they are positive. Some hustlers still stipulate exclusions though: when I worked for escort services I specifically stated that I didn't like getting fucked and didn't want to do that. I was hired anyway, but it did cut down on my clientele a little" (28 Mar. 1998 E-mail).

8. Prostitutes who use condoms for penetrative sex with customers but not with non-customers (one-time chosen partners as well as live-in lovers and legal spouses) have been reported from every continent, making for a "risk factor" of "love" (Henriksson 1995).

9. These range from very general to very specific and from totally clichéd to extremely idiosyncratic. According to Val, "a lot of clients really want their dicks sucked, so a lot of gay prostitution (like straight prostitution) is giving blow jobs." He added that "offered enough money or experiencing enough need, most people will do anything."

10. Even a sex worker willing to do anything for the right price and willing to be bribed to simulate love cannot be forced to feel what he (or she) is enacting, though I think that not all have "a sense of inner self [let alone one] that is not for sale" (R. Brown

Sex workers (of both sexes) are sometimes cast against chronological differences in age (e.g., playing "daddies" to their elders), just as cross-dressed male sex workers (especially black "she-males") are regularly called upon to penetrate their masculine-appearing customers.[11] Despite these vagaries of sexual demand, the sex worker/client relationship in the modern West, as in ancient Rome, is (usually) age differentiated.[12] What the customer wants may be to be penetrated rather than to penetrate, but the flesh he rents tends to be young.

In contemporary North America, there are some male sex workers who are successful beyond the age of twenty-five or even thirty, but a youthful appearance seems to be even more important for male sex workers than for their female counterparts, perhaps because so many modern Western male customers of male sex workers are seeking to be penetrated. This is the case even though dependable and sustainable erectile potency is not an invariable correlate of youth for males. It is widely supposed, not least by those renting it, that customers could not gain access to the kind of young flesh they want without paying for it. A reason for at least some of the structuring of these relations by age is that most of those with the money to pay for sexual services are older. That is, the supply and demand of money (for sexual services) is involved, not just the supply and demand for sex. In ongoing relationships, the "power of the least interest" is not invariably the sex worker's. Similarly, contempt may run both ways in an encounter or series of encounters. Not all consumers are as romantic as Roger Brown (and a long line of

---

1996:250) and that role distance is frequently difficult to maintain. There are some obviously desperate street hustlers lacking even the feasibility or the psychological or financial security necessary to establish any sense of an inviolable core. "The money is not for the necessities of life. It is for the little extras, small luxuries" (78) is not true for many, and it is those lacking a sense of self-efficacy who are most likely to feel that they have to engage in unprotected intercourse. Which is not to say that all sex workers feel soiled by what is for some a lucrative occupation (even if it is also a dangerous and undependable source of income involving long stretches of waiting) or that all find the sex repellent or are desperate for money or eager to retire to conventional respectability.

11. Pettiway 1996. Afro-Brazilian and Mexican transgendered prostitutes also have gleefully or sadly reported this. See Braiterman 1992, Kulick 1998, Prieur 1997. Although the Brazilian *travestis* are generally younger than their customers, it is clear that there are gender-structured roles for some sex workers who were born male, in addition to the age-structured masculine-appearing "hustler" role that exists in Latin as well as in Anglo cultures.

12. This is less of a concern in the specialty trades—S&M, bondage, etc. or where skill, or equipment or visible musculature, is a factor. Val pointed out that "'young' is also creeping up a bit" with the aging of baby boomers.

literary and celluloid lovers of glamorous prostitutes), and some sex work-ers are looking for love, even though the finite commitment of a pay-ment for service may be the preference of both parties. Whether it is "ob-jectification" or "deification," being desired can be very confusing—and such confusions may be used by self-assured consumers (see the ac-counts discussed in Murray 1998b).

4

Age-Stratified Female Homosexualities

Female-Female Eros on Lesbos and Elsewhere in Ancient Greece

Although practically no evidence of female-female eros has survived from ancient Greece, what has remained suggests that it was predominantly age stratified, as male-male eros was. One indication, that Keith DeVries (1990:24) noted, is the differing heights of the female partners in six or seven of twelve lesbian scenes on surviving ancient Greek vases.

A fragment from the Academic philosopher Hagnon suggests that there was Spartan initiation by female elders of female youths: "Among the Spartans, it was customary [viz. for adult women] to have intercourse with girls before their marriage, as one did with boys" (13.602D; quoted by Bremmer 1980:292). Page (1951:66–67) interpreted this as a result of the close association between women and girls in gymnasia and in the choral dancing that was central to Spartan religious rites; Calame (1977, 1:433–36) contended that such associations had a pedagogical function.

Plutarch's biography of the semi-legendary law promulgator Lykourgos (18.9) also recalled that "women of good repute were in love with girls" (quoted by Dover 1978:173; he regarded this as a female equivalent of the *erastes/eromenos* relationship). Just as young Spartan males exercised, danced, and processed in the nude, so did Spartan females. Lykourgos mostly proscribed contact between males and females, even between those who were joined to produce children (which were taken from the mother at age seven) until the male attained the age of thirty. Spartans spent most of their time in single-sex environments,[1] and girls were enrolled in public education in Sparta (as in no other Greek state) (Cartledge 1981b:91). "Spartan law, in sharp contrast to that of Athens and many other Greek cities, allowed them to inherit property in their own right," and by around 400 B.C. women owned 40 percent of Spartan land.[2]

---

1. Aristotle (*Politics*, book 2) found the Spartan polis considerably less ideal than had Xenophon and would Plutarch, regarding it with distaste as ruled by women (*gynaikokratoumenoi*).

2. Talbert 1988:47. Wives managed the affairs of (often) absent husbands and were encouraged to undertake extramarital procreative relations (a pro-natalist policy).

204

Although there are only fragments of her work, Sappho, the famous poet from Lesbos (born sometime around 612 B.C.), indubitably addressed women in the language used by male *erastai* in speaking to their *eromenoi*. Her *thiasoi* had at least two rivals on Lesbos, those led by Gorgo and Andromeda. Cantarella (1992:79) glosses *thiasoi* as "communities of women . . . with their own divinities and ceremonies, where girls, before marriage, went through a global experience of life which was in some way analogous to the experience of life that men had in corresponding masculine groups. And the girls received an education within this group." They were taught singing, dancing, and other arts, and, more generally, the grace (*charis*) that made them more desirable.[3] In *Tristia* (2.365) the Roman poet Ovid recalled Sappho teaching girls to love, or through woman-girl love ("Quid Lesbia docuit Sappho, nisi amare puellas"), and a surviving fragment of biography refers to her as *gunaikerastria*, that is, a female *erastes* of women.[4] The "I" in Sappho's surviving work repeatedly calls upon Aphrodite—not on a panoply of gods, but only on Aphrodite—for aid in her loves and their losses when her students married.[5]

The approximately 5 percent of Sappho's writing that survived several Christian attempts to destroy all copies of it,[6] represent the physical effects of being in love, not physical acts, though the papyrus known as fragment 99 contains reference to a leather phallus.[7] Sappho had a daughter, so she must have had sex with at least one man.

There is also fragment 1 from Sappho's Spartan male contemporary, Alkman.[8] Written for a chorus of girls to sing, it may be an instance of female celebration of other females' beauty, but its meaning is far from clear.

In pre-classical Greece, male homosexuality was less organized by age

3. Valuation of the female body was part of this. See Friedrich 1978:106, 109.

4. Dover 1978:174. Sappho, the character of the poems, expresses desires. Not only does she express erotic subjectivity, she can be said to have invented representation of it.

5. According to Friedrich (1978:110), the "main function" of such groups was "to prepare girls for wedding and marriage, but the cultural, human, and often very personal bonds formed between the members and their leaders could be expected to continue and grow in later life." I do not see evidence in Sappho's oeuvre on which to base this expectation; it seems to be an assumption about pan- and proto-Indo-Europeans (or about human nature?).

6. And the burning of the Alexandria library in the fourth century: see Friedrich 1978:126; Barnstone 1965:xxi–xxii.

7. And joyful proclamation of "randy madness," in Davenport's (1965:111) translation, quoted by Friedrich (1978:114).

8. See Page 1951. Whether Alkman was born in Sparta is contested, but it is where he worked (Grant 1987:95).

than it was in classical times. This seems also to have been the case with
female lovers. Some of the passionate female-female relationships involved teacher and students, but others appear to have involved girls of
the same age.[9] Some myths that suggest goddesses playing an *erastes* role
to female human *eromenoi* include Athena to Pallas (closely paralleling Athena's brother Apollo's accidental killing of Hyacinthus),[10] and
Artemis with her nymphs (who were pledged to remain unsullied by
males), and even the over-intense love of Demeter for her daughter
Persephone. The strongest hint of sexuality in these relationships is
the initial responsiveness to kisses and embraces of the most beautiful
of the nymphs, Callisto, to Zeus when he disguised himself as Artemis
(Hyginus, *Poetic Astronomy* 2.11 Apollodorus 3.8.2; Callimachus, *Hymn to
Artemis.*) When Artemis noticed Callisto's pregnancy, she turned her into
a bear, and girls initiated at the Artemis temple at Brauron were known
as "bears of Artemis."[11] Whether they were told about sex or physically
initiated into it is a question that cannot be answered from the surviving
records. Maidenly toys and garments and also garments of women who
died in childbirth were sacrificed to Artemis, who can be presumed to
have mourned the loss of girls with whom she had played before they
were taken by men, as her nymphs were. As Dowling (1989:197–98)
noted, the nymphs "were dedicated to stay virgins, to stay true to their
virginal goddess; but almost every myth about such a nymph described
her as being pursued and raped by a god (or dying in the attempt to escape his pursuit). The commitment of women to women is represented
as intolerable to men; that it might be represented [by men] as succeeding—even in myth—is therefore impermissible."

Female-female sex is unmentioned in Attic comedy, and only once in
all of classical Attic literature: in Plato's *Symposium* (191e) the character
Aristophanes derives *hetairistriai,* a word nowhere else attested, from a
legendary double-female being naturally seeking to be reunited.[12] In

9. Cantarella (1992:83–84), interpreting Alkman. She argued that between women
no submission is necessary (in contrast to the older male "inspiring" his youthful partner
by anal (or intercrural) penetration, and rejected the idea that sexual relations between
women were a necessary part of girls' "initiation."

10. Athena then added her dead friend's name to her own, becoming Pallas Athena.
In her bellicose guise as Athena Parthenos, she might be considered unfeminine, but ravishing women was not part of her warrior role.

11. Brauron is thought to be the burial-place of Iphigenia, a virgin and priestess of
Artemis whom Artemis rescued from the flames of being sacrificed by Agamemnon, Iphigenia's father.

12. Presumably, the two halves do not differ in age.

contrast, in the late Hellenistic dialogue written in the manner of Lucian about the relative merits of loving boys and loving women, women loving women seems so ludicrous to Charicles that he uses it in a reductio ad absurdem argument against pederasty (pseudo-Lucan, *Erotes* 28, ca. 300 A.D.).

What women did among themselves at home was of little interest to those whose writings survived. David Greenberg (1995:246n. 12) noted that "it is conceivable that [married women's] affairs with slaves could have taken place without the knowledge of their husbands." Greek literature showed no interest in what went on in the domestic sphere to which women had been confined by classical times.[13]

Upper Egypt

A recognition of age-stratified female-female carnality in the eastern Roman Empire occurs in *De vita monachorum* by Shenute of Atripe, who presided over the White Monastery (on the western bank of the Nile near Panopolis) beginning in 383 A.D. In castigating the ways in which monks and nuns violated vows of celibacy, he wrote: "Cursed is she, namely a woman among us, who will pursue young girls and anoint them and who is filled with a passion or who ___ them with a lustful passion" (trans. Michael Foat; quoted by Brooten 1996:349).[14]

Scattered Indications of Female Age-Stratified Homosexualities on Pacific Islands
Melanesia

The only relatively clearly documented instance of "institutionalized" lesbianism in Melanesia comes from Malekula Island in the New Hebrides. The best and brightest of the Cambridge School ethnographers, A. Bernard Deacon (1934:171) was able to learn that, among the Big

13. The classical view, expressed by Aristotle, was that "the woman must be controlled not only by her husband [or, before marriage, by her father] but by the state. . . . Equipped with diminished and imperfect reasoning powers, incapable of controlling her lustful feelings, she is in fact highly dangerous if left to herself" (*Politics* 1254b). As Grant (1987:30) summarized, "Females generally, never possessed citizenship in their city-states, never held office and took no overt part in political activities at all. Disallowed charge of their own affairs, they were, as a matter of law, under the care of a male, and they had no legal right to own or dispose of property." Cohen (1991:149–54) argued that exclusion from political activity has been mistakenly extrapolated to viewing women as secluded, and amassed a considerable amount of evidence that Athenian women were not confined to the home.

14. As Brooten (1996:73–113) shows, Upper Egypt was somewhat notorious by the second century for female-female unions that were sexual, not just economic.

Nambas of the northern part of the island, "between women, homosexuality is common, many women being generally known as lesbians, or in the native term *nimomogh iap nimomogh* ("woman has intercourse with woman").[15] It is regarded as a form of play, but, at the same time, it is clearly recognized as a definite type of sexual desire, and that women do it because it gives them pleasure" (170).[16]

Harrison (in Deacon 1934:410) also made passing mention that among the Big Nambas "women have developed a parallel pleasure system of their own, less elaborate than the male," which leaves the reader to guess whether this "system" had ritual importance, or even to be sure that it was age structured. Beatrice Blackwood (1935:255ff.) suggested (to me at least) something close to ritualized lesbian behavior, that is, homosexual play during the coming-of-age (menstruation) celebration in the Solomon Islands.

Polynesia

Suggs (1966:84) asserted there was lesbian activity among girls and women in Polynesia, but mentioned no particular data. Suggs (1966:65–66) noted homosexual stimulation in Marquesan females' sex education/demonstration at the time of puberty. Handy (1923:103) had earlier suggested that the number of lesbians in the Marquesas was few.

From fieldwork in the easternmost outpost of Polynesia, the Easter Islands, Métraux (1940:108) asserted, "Abnormal sex relationships between women is tolerated and accepted. Such relationships are between middle-aged women who are unattractive to men, and young women whom they have seduced." This is far from being "thick description," but it does indicate age-stratified female homosexual relations.

15. Among the Big Nambas, as in North Raga, "homosexual practices between men are very highly developed. Every chief has a number of boy-lovers, and it is said that some men are so completely homosexual in their affections, that they seldom have intercourse with their wives, preferring to go with boys" (Deacon 1934:261). Deacon stressed that "in the choice of his *mugh vel* a man is restricted by certain rules. He need not necessarily select a boy from another clan than his own, but he must be careful that no genealogical relationship can be traced between them. To have intercourse with a boy of one's own clan to whom one is allied by known kinship bonds is to be guilty of incest" (261–62). I would guess that the same was the case for female-female sexual relationships, though there is no indication of the age or other status of female partners in Deacon's posthumously published book.

16. That desire and play are antithetical is not commonly supposed for heterosexual motivation, and I see no reason that homosexual motivations must be one or the other, but not both.

Japan

In *The Life of an Amorous Man,* first published in 1682, Ihara Saikaku described female dancer-prostitutes in Kyoto who were "trained as dancers from early childhood and learn to imitate the deportment and behavior of men," who catered to female customers: "From age eleven or twelve to age fourteen or fifteen, they are engaged by women as drinking companions, then their forelocks are shaved, and they are trained to imitate men's voices," as well as "don[ning] male clothing, sporting swords and adopting a samurai-like swagger" (Leupp 1998:11).

Leupp (1998:11) includes a nineteenth-century illustration of a nurse discussing sex and fondling a teenage girl's genitals. It seems to me that in figure 11, on page 405, the woman adjusting a large dildo is going to insert it into a smiling younger women. The older woman's other hand may be stimulating the younger woman's genitalia. It is not clear how the smaller dildo lying in the foreground of the illustration was used. My guess is that it was used first, and the couple are graduating to a (much) larger one.

Pflugfelder (1990) discussed age-graded female-female relationships, called "S" (for "sister") and involving schoolgirls in early twentieth-century Japan.[17] The normative age difference was two school grades, so that "transgenerational" is inappropriate, as, indeed, it is for many instance of medieval Japanese male-male relationships, as was discussed in chapter 2 (pp. 80, 83–84).

Eastern and Southern Africa

In central Tanzania, some Kaguru men mentioned to anthropologist Thomas Beidelman (1973:266) that "some Kaguru women practice lesbian activities during female initiation, women taking both the roles of men and of women in demonstrating sexual congress to initiates. Women were unwilling to discuss this in detail with me, but conceded that women did demonstrate with one another how to have proper sexual congress."

Further south, Kidd (1904:209) was not specific about what "indecencies," "degradations," and "obscenities" Bantu female initiation involved that, he claimed, demoralized their womanhood forever. Falk (1925:209–10) noted that homosexuality was common, especially

---

17. J. Robertson (1992b:175) suggested that "'S' stands for sex, sister, or shojo, or all three combined." She glossed *shojo* as "a not-quite female female" (173), normatively during the years between puberty and marriage to a man.

among Hottentot (Nama) young married women. And to the east, Schapera (1938:278) reported that among the Tswana—in addition to homosexuality among the men laboring in the mines together— back home, "lesbian practices are apparently fairly common among the older girls and young women, without being regarded in any way reprehensible."

Judith Gay (1985) described what she considered a relatively new (i.e., 1950s onward)[18] institutionalized friendship relationship among women left behind in Lesotho by migrant men working in South Africa:[19] "Young girls in the modern schools develop close relationships, called 'mummy-baby' with slightly older girls. Sexual intimacy is an important part of these relationships. Mummy-baby relationships not only provide emotional support prior to marriage, but also a network of support for married and unmarried women in new towns or schools, either replac- ing or accompanying heterosexual bonds" (97).

"Relationships are always initiated voluntarily by one girl who takes a liking to another and simply asks her to be her mummy or her baby, depending on their relative age," Gay reported. "The most frequently given reason for initiating a particular relationship was that one girl felt attracted to the other by her looks, her clothes, or her actions" (102).

Although eager to deny that these relations are in any way marriage- like, Gay also wanted to interpret them as preparations for "the dynam- ics of heterosexual relations"—even as "explicit opportunities for initia- tion into heterosexual relations" (109)—or as substitutes for relations in the absence of men who are working in South African mines. She also provided some hints about marriage resistance (or at least delay) and contrasted the autonomy of "mummies" with the constraints on Sesotho wives. Moreover, "in many cases the relations established with other girls are transformed, but do not cease altogether" (107, 109, 110).

A "mummy" may have more than one "baby," but Gay claimed that the "baby" can only have one "mummy," although one female may be a

18. She considered use of the English terms ("mummy" and "baby") in Sesotho or En- glish sentences evidence of recency (100). She did not consider that the terms may have changed rather than the phenomenon being entirely new.

19. The patrilineal, patrilocal Lovedu of Lesotho were unusual in being ruled by queens who had wives (indeed, a harem; see Krige and Krige 1943:165–75). The Lovedu queens were assisted in their judicial role by "the mothers of the kingdom." The neigh- boring Khaha, Mamaila, Letswalo (Narene) and Mahlo peoples were also ruled by female monarchs (310–11). An interesting western hemisphere analog is M. G. Smith's (1962) re- port that in the Afro-Caribbean nation of Grenada, older married women form bonds pro- viding economic and emotional assistance to younger, generally unmarried women, using money remitted by husbands from their wages working elsewhere.

"baby" to one female and a "mummy" to another (108). However, all three of the women who provided her "case studies" had, over time, had more than one "mummy" (one had nine, one six, and one two).

Although "Sesotho initiation for girls is no longer practiced in most lowland villages, where about half the nation's population lives" (99), girls continue to lengthen their own or each other's labia minora. They believe that having done this or having had it done will later enhance sexual pleasure: "The process of lengthening is done alone or in small groups, but is not directly tied to initiation [now]. The process is said to heighten *mocheso* (heat) and appears to provide opportunities for auto-eroticims and mutual stimulation between girls" (101). Without alluding to any evidence (or any kind of inquiry), Gay (1985:112) asserted that "the contacts which may be involved in lengthening the labia minora are apparently not regarded as emotionally significant, whereas falling in love with a girl and simply caressing her is" (112).

Mueller (1977) also described similar relationships in two Lesotho villages. Blacking (1959) reported fictive kinship relationships among Venda schoolgirls of the Transvaal earlier, and Zulu schoolgirls in 1978. I consider this strong evidence that "age-stratified" is a type of female, not just of male, homosexuality in southern Africa. Age differences need not be great, even though the idiom is transgenerational. In the eleven instances in which Gay (1985:114–15) specified the age of both, the mean age differences was 4.8 years, the median age difference was 5 years (the range was from 1 to 12; those playing the "baby" role ranged in age from 8 to 24, those playing the "mummy" from 15 to 35).

Part Two

GENDER-STRATIFIED ORGANIZATION OF HOMOSEXUALITY

Unlike the age-stratified organizations in which the warriors regard homosexual receptivity on the part of young males as masculinizing, and, in some cultures, even as necessary to the development of masculinity, the natives of cultures with gender-stratified organizations of homosexuality expect the insertive partner to be hypermasculine. They also expect the sexually receptive partner to enact some other aspects of the feminine gender role: usually, to behave and/or sound and/or dress in ways "loose" women do in that society and/or to do what is "women's work" there. Roscoe (1988:28) wisely cautioned that those engaged in what he typifies as nonmasculine "socio-sexual specialization" may mimic female **stereotypes.** These may have little to do with how most women in a society usually behave. Similarly, "butch" females outswagger the most stereotypically virile males (and, more than occasionally, fight with biological males).

Recurrently, a bodily (i.e., biological) basis for desiring penetration by males is presumed, whether it is lack of male genitalia (eunuchs, hermaphrodites, and those said to have small penises), procreative inadequacy (men who are impotent with women, men or women who are unable to please the other sex and/or lack interest in having sex with the other sex), or internal imbalances (of yin/yang, or hot/cold humors, or masculine/feminine "seed" in ancient Greco-Roman physiognomic theory; various prenatal forces and experiences in others). The relative importance of sexuality, sexual organs, dress, and occupation to the natives of the cultures is often unclear in accounts by missionaries, anthropologists, and other kinds of travelers—and, often, even in those from natives. While alien observers generally do not observe actual sexual behavior, they are especially likely to notice a man wearing clothing distinctively different from that worn by most men, or one who does what is regarded there as "women's work," or women dressing and acting in what are locally marked as masculine ways. It is not clear whether those born female who are "manlike" in one or another sense are less numerous, as numerous but less visible, or just less problematic (because aspirations for upward mobility are readily understood) and thereby less remarkable than those born male who are "womanlike."

The prototypical gender-defined male homosexual role is the *pasivo* role widespread in the Mediterranean and Latin American culture areas. 213

The "active" male in homosexual copulation is an unmarked male, not officially regarded (and especially not by himself) as "homosexual." One of the pleasures that must be forborne by adult males in such cultures is sexual receptivity. Winkler (1990:67ff.) showed that the ancient Greeks conceived such pleasure, while Leupp (1995:179–82) showed that the pleasures of anal receptivity were celebrated in Tokugawa Japan.[1] Exactly the fear of coming to enjoy being penetrated recurs in Muslim societies as a reason not to try the behavior (Schmitt 1985:54–55, Murray 1997b:18). Similarly, in Mesoamerica I have also heard *activos* say that if they got fucked they might want it all the time, so that the safest course to ensure their continued masculinity is to avoid trying it. Thus, although the penetrator may have little concern about whether the penetrated person has a pleasant time, he conceives the possibility that someone biologically male **may** enjoy being penetrated.

Those born male who wear what is locally considered "women's dress" and/or engage in what is locally considered "women's work" generally retain some male prerogatives (see Roscoe 1998), and often are said to be better at "women's work" than mere women are.[2] Because their dress and work often mixes what is typically male with what is typically female or is not typical of either, some Anglo North American theorists have suggested (with little established basis in native enumeration of sex or of genders) that various cultures have three genders (male, female, berdache) rather than two.[3] Mesoamericans I have asked insist that a *maricón* is "a kind of a man," definitely not "a kind of woman." Badruddin Khan (1993 personal communication quoted below, p. 310) insisted that the South Asians conceive of *gandu* and even of *hijra* as kinds of "man" (albeit inadequate specimens), not as a third gender or third sex (cf. Nanda 1990). Similarly, Vinson Sutlive (1990 personal communication) unequivocally stated that the northern Borneo Iban regard their gender-crossing shamans as men, not as a third kind of person. Dickemann (1997) showed that "sworn virgins" in the Balkans were socially male, not any intermediate or distinctively third gender.

1. The folk beliefs that hemorrhoids and bowleggedness were consequences suggests that there was some ambivalence, even if there was no legal prescription for social condemnation.

2. For a long time I thought this was just male ideology, i.e., whatever men do they must do better. Although I remain unconvinced that blind evaluation of men's and women's work would be unequivocal, I now believe that men doing women's work frequently command the best raw materials. They also can concentrate on their crafts with less interruption from children than craftswomen typically can.

3. On the looseness of standards for claiming a "third gender" in some (emic) cultural conceptions, see Murray 1994a, 1996a:161–66.

In my own work, I think that I have been not just careful, but insistent that drag queens, *pasivos*, *hijra*s, and the like are conceived of as kinds of males, albeit inferior ones, and that their "femininity," which is often partial, is especially likely to involve exaggerated sexual availability and the flamboyance of "star" entertainers rather than is that of everyday housewives. I do not (and have not) thought that a gendered idiom of same-sex relations means that the nonmasculine male is considered a female, and have repeatedly stressed that the male prerogative of being able to go out from the home (geographical mobility in "public") is generally maintained by such males, whether their costume is conventionally male, conventionally female, some combination of the two, or unique. Drag queen performers seek to act and look like drag queens, not to be mistaken for women, and even many of those pretending to be women are seeking male sexual partners without wanting to be transformed into women.[4] Similarly, many butch women are seeking female partners without wanting to be surgically reconstructed as a male.

Latin Americans generally stigmatize *pasivos*. As is discussed in detail below, Afro-Brazilian cults, however, provide a niche in which some *pasivo* males exercise spiritual powers and claim the attendant prestige. Important powers also attached to transvestite shamans along both sides of the North Pacific, and even down into Borneo and Indochina. Those playing the role commanded awe—an admittedly ambivalent emotion. In Latin cultures, the Catholic priesthood is also a niche in which boys who do not seem "normally" masculine can wear colorful robes and avoid marriage.[5]

In Mediterranean and Mediterranean-influenced societies, people take for granted (regard as "natural") that some men won't attain masculinity. Attempts to extirpate homosexuality are not traditional, though violence—extortion, beatings, rape and murder—is the "fate" of effeminate men (cross-dressed or not) in cultures (including those of Latin America and the Philippines) influenced during colonial domination by the Iberian code of male honor and Catholicism. This is also the case in the prototype of "acceptance of homosexuality": contemporary Thailand. Although Latino family members may give up on their children

4. Kulick (1998a), Pettiway (1996), and Prieur (1998) have documented transvestite male prostitutes' unwillingness to have their male genitalia permanently removed and these prostitutes' reports of using their penises with some regularity, both professionally and privately.

5. For many Latin American men, priests' manhood is suspect. Respect for them is generally slight; jokes about their "dresses" and lack of *cojones* (testicles properly bursting with semen that must burst out in a normal man) are common.

marrying and producing more children, they often make major efforts to discourage overt gender nonconformity of children and siblings. In that unmarried children continue to live in the natal home indefinitely, families often demand ongoing decorum even from those whose gender and sexual "abnormality" they have ceased trying to alter.

As clear as are the cultural norms of role distinctions, in Latin America, even before the diffusion of *gay* models, behavior was far less clearly dichotomized than the simple *activo/pasivo* contrast would suggest. Over time (in an individual's sexual "career"), or with different partners, one's behavioral repertoire often diverges from the ideally clear dichotomy. The clarity and simplicity of cultural schemata is not matched by uniform, entirely predictable behavior.

"Occupation-defined" Organization of Homosexuality

I have been dubious about whether it makes any heuristic sense to distinguish an occupation-defined organization of homosexuality (Murray 1992a:257–72). The major question about occupations monopolized or disproportionately staffed by gender-variant and/or homosexually engaged persons is whether there is self-selection by those seeking a niche for homosexual desire and/or gender deviance,[6] or whether there is sexual resocialization of "heterosexuals" in roles such as shamans, dancing boys, transvestite singers, and prostitutes.

Concern about the cultural primacy of gender, sexuality, and occupation is bootless, according to Roscoe (1988), who proposed including these (along with self-identity, social role, and spirituality) as dimensions of "sociosexual specialization." His essay is an interesting attempt to delineate an object of study, but it begs the question of the relative importance and empirical intercorrelation of the dimensions. In the cases reviewed here, desire for same-sex copulation was secondary, though highly correlated for those called to service by spirits. A predisposition for gender-crossing is far from invariable, and resistance to the call is conventional in African, Afro-Brazilian, Siberian, and West Pacific cultures in which spirit possession is valued highly. In the prototypical case, among the Siberian Chukchi studied by Vladimir Bogoraz (1904:418), men especially resisted calls from the spirits that included demands for sexual transformation.

Evidence of seeking a call from the spirits is missing from the historical literature, and the question is unasked in such more-or-less contem-

6. Alfred Kroeber (1940) and his student George Devereux (1937) suggested that this was the case among California Native Peoples. For industrialized societies, see Ashworth and Walker (1972), Fry (1995), and Whitam and Mathy (1986).

porary anthropological literature as exists on gender-variant spirit medi-ums.[7] Cultures in which spirit possession is positively valued do not consider possession a choice made (even unconsciously) by the person possessed.[8] Spirit mediums routinely deny learning and training (see Bogoraz 1904; Murray 1992a:296). Agnostic questions about predispo-sitions, psychopathology, training, and rewards that might be sought by those whom the gods/spirits have chosen to borrow are not just rude, but blasphemous to believers. Generally, those living in a cosmology that includes beliefs in the reality of spirit possession (1) do not view their ideas as arbitrary, conventional, or dependent upon local consensus, or as dependent on the imagination, desire, or will of individuals, (2) be-lieve that their reality-posits express significant insights into reality and explain real experiences, (3) remain convinced that their reality-posits constitute knowledge about the world, even after alien observers "ex-plain" that the beliefs are individual or collective delusions, wishful think-ing, false consciousness, and so forth, and, (4) within presuppositions alien to atheistic ones, reason rationally.[9]

Predispositions for gender variance are more common, albeit far from being universally apparent, in the case of some other occupations that are "notoriously homosexual" and involve public display (e.g., actors, es-pecially those who play women's roles; male dancers; and, in North America, males who perform on keyboard instruments, especially or-gans) or are widely considered to involve doing "women's work" (e.g., nurses, librarians, secretaries, hairdressers, and interior decorators in industrialized countries). Some "pretty boys," especially those who per-form on stages, may be pressed into male prostitution, but in all these occupations believed to include higher concentrations of "homosexuals" than in the general population, there are enough males with unswerv-ing preferences for females to make it implausible that undertaking one of these occupations **causes** a redirection of sexual interest from fe-males to males. That is, rather than resocialization, selective recruitment accounts for concentrations in some occupations. Moreover, I believe that these concentrations are less than is widely supposed.[10] Employer

7. E.g., Fry 1987; Matory 1994; Wafer 1991; Sutlive 1976. Arctic shamans seek to mas-ter spirits even though their initial possessions are normatively unsought.

8. This contrasts with cultures, such as North American Plains ones, in which some in-dividuals seek visions (but not possession).

9. This list derives from a generalization from orthodox Hindu conceptions of karma and reincarnation to witchcraft by Shweder (1991:58).

10. Neuringer (1989) argues that contemporary American actors are no more likely than are other men to be "homosexuals." Some boys from rural China sold into stage

discrimination against gender-variant individuals varies by sectors. It is generally easier for males to "come out" in occupations that are predominantly female,[11] so that some of the seemingly heightened rates of "homosexuals" in these compared to other occupations are differences in openness about homosexuality rather than differences in sexual behavior patterns. Moreover, "in any field, there is routine insider trading of information about job vacancies and even secrecy about them. Therefore any concentration (of any category of employees) is likely to be reinforced over time" (Murray 1995a:74–75), so concentrations may not even evidence a preference for a particular line of work.

The descriptions of various gender-stratified male homosexualities that follow are split between those in which the gender crosser has a sacralized occupation and those in which gender crossing is wholly secular. The actual sex with the cross-gendered person is not sacralized in either kind of gender-stratified homosexuality, however. There is no religious meaning attached to having sex with such persons: no merit or magical substance or honor or blessing derives from it, only sexual pleasure—for both insertors and insertees. Sexual relations *per se* are not ritualized and are not thought to convey supernatural benefits on those having sex with the religious functionary. I do not see evidence that the transvestite healers, dancers, or priests were sacred because they were available for penetration by males. They were available for penetration by males because they were "like women" in appearance and were not siring sons, two departures from masculinity so extreme as to inspire awe in some, especially any who believe that the transgendered male had renounced masculinity out of religious devotion (rather than "giving up" what had no interest for him). In that they derive income from sacred offices (taking office very loosely, to include *hijra*s dancing at weddings, and celebrations of the birth of male children), effemininate/transvestite/homosexual men may be "good matches" for poor or lazy spouses.

Sacred roles for masculine women are largely lacking. Gender-crossing/mixing female roles have been represented across wide expanses of space and time, though information about their sexualities is rare. In that modern Western women have especially dramatized heterogender

---

apprenticeships that required prostitution provide an example of forcible socialization into sexual complaisance.

    11. It does not seem easier for females in stereotypically male occupations to "come out."

homosexual relations, I begin with them, however, and discuss other gender-stratified female-female patterns before turning to "purely sexual" and then to allegedly "sacralized" transgendered male roles.

One way in which the female and male literature mirror each other is in the absence of attention to the gender-conforming partners. The female femmes and male butches have been all but ignored, while the gender nonconforming have received almost all the attention.[12] This is as true of current queer discourse about gender performativity and transgressiveness as it is of earlier ethnographic work.

12. Prieur (1998) is an exception. For Anglo-American lesbians, there is some published material on femme subjectivity (e.g., Nestle 1987, 1992) along with that on butch subjectivity (e.g., R. Hall, 1928, Feinberg 1993).

5

Gender-Stratified Female Homosexualities

North American Butch/Femme

American butches of the 1950s sought to achieve a working-class masculine look, which later segued into the "hoodlum look" (white t-shirt, tight jeans, black leather jacket, slicked-back hair) of such surly and rebellious 1950s icons as the young Elvis Presley and the Marlon Brando of "The Wild One." They also emulated stereotypical masculine behavior.[1] In particular, butches fought other butches over perceived attempts to poach their partners, and fought males for territory and respect. As one 50s butch recalled, "you walk down the street and they knew you were gay, and there'd be two or three guys standing on the street corner, and they'd come up to you and say, 'You want to be a man, let's see if you can fight like a man.' Now, being a man was the last thing on my mind, but man, they'd take a poke at you and you had to learn to fight" (quoted in Kennedy and Davis 1993:180–81). She added: "When you go out, you better wear clothes that you could really scramble in if you had to."

Relations with femmes also needed to be managed. In the expected sexual scenario, the butch "took" the femme, as a man "takes" a woman—only, in their view, better (i.e., applying greater knowledge about the pleasure of the one "taken"). A major difference—at least at the level of cultural norms—is that the (prototypically Italian) male stud penetrates to "get off" (to provide pleasant friction to his penis) and to impregnate a woman, while the butch is primarily giving pleasure—even while experiencing the secondary pleasures of controlling and satisfying the femme. If sex involved "going down" on the partner, the butch woman was in the position of the "faggot": often on her knees "servicing" a partner who lay or leaned back, accepted, and enjoyed the service. In my view, the recipient of oral sex is "passive," and the "active" one is the one whose tongue and mouth are doing the work. In that working-class men, especially those from Mediterranean backgrounds, were notably reluctant to perform cunnilingus,[2] doing it cannot have been obviously or unproblematically "masculine" in the 1940s and 50s.

---

1. More 1950s Lee Marvin and Jack Palance than Brando or Presley.

2. Kinsey et al. (1948:369) reported that 18.4 percent of white American men with some college education had performed cunnilingus before marriage, in contrast to 8.5 per-

The iconic butch was the "stone butch," that is, one who was unpenetrated. How "untouchable" and stone the butch was (/is) varies—from not undressing while stimulating her femme partner, to having the femme "suck my cock" (i.e., clitoral stimulation by the femme's tongue or fellatio performed on a strapped-on dildo). Standing stonily back while bringing the femme to orgasm(s), the butch is, normatively, always in control, while driving her partners to surrender to the pleasure she delivers. (This is not to say the stone butch has no pleasure. "Surrender" to penetration is not the only kind of pleasure; giving pleasure to a partner is another one, not unique to stone butches.)

A paradox of butch-femme relationships is that despite the lower pay for doing what is regarded in the culture as "women's work" and the butch self-image of taking the initiative, in "the olden days" of the 1950s and 60s, few butches were "breadwinners." The femmes often supported the butches. Those who lived full time as butches sought to do (what was regarded as) "men's work." They were, however, unwilling "to take any shit" from male employers and coworkers, and often had trouble getting and holding jobs (except during the labor shortage during World War II)[3], while conventionally gendered femmes got and held jobs doing (not-well-paid) "women's work." "Working fems gave many tough lesbians the freedom to live the way they wanted" as Kennedy and Davis (1993: 291) noted (also see Faderman 1991:171). One Buffalo butch recalled that femmes supported butches who "couldn't work or didn't want to, because they looked so butch and all of this, so the [conventionally gendered] woman supported them" (Kennedy and Davis 1993:291). The 50s masculine breadwinner defined by a job that paid for the services of a feminine housewife was not part of "classical" lesbian butch/femme relationships. Some butches aspired to this aspect of masculinity, but "very few [of the women they interviewed], no matter the decade, were ever in a relationship where the butch worked and not the fem" (292).[4]

---

cent of those with less than nine years of formal education. Inside marriage, the disparity was even greater: 45.3 percent compared to 4.1 percent. (I am taking education as an indicator of class. Admittedly, it is imperfect one.)

3. In the recollections of women-loving women who were adults during World War II in Buffalo, New York, "jobs for lesbians were not a result of the war. They and their friends had been working since their teens. . . . In their minds the important effect of the war was to give more independence to all women, thereby making lesbians more like other women and less easy to identify" (Kennedy and Davis 1993:38, cf. Faderman 1991:122).

4. In that the command of greater resources generally leads to a greater share of decision making within couples of all sorts, including decisions about when and how to have

A similar pattern of unemployable butches and femmes working as secretaries and so forth recurs in Indonesia, Thailand, and elsewhere (see Thongthiraj 1994). In my view, the femme supporting an idle masculine partner also recurs in relationships between males who work as transvestites and their un- or underemployed lovers. (In such male couples it is the gender-crossing partner earning a living; in female couples it is the gender-conventional one). Just as many of the masculine-appearing males in sexual relationships with other males are penetrated by their more feminine-appearing partners, the phenomenon of women who are "butch in the street, femme in the sheets" is no secret, though it may be a source of embarrassment for particular butches who have been "flipped."[5]

To me, the variances I have been discussing from the prescriptive norms for (Anglo-American) husbands and wives show that those "playing gendered roles" were not merely copying heterosexual roles. Just as drag queens are trying to be like established drag queens, butch dykes try to "imitate dykes, not men" (Grahn 1984:30).[6] Emulating (working-class) masculine dress and demeanor made butches visible to each other and to those women who were attracted to the image. Lillian Faderman concluded that, around midcentury, acting out butch and femme roles "created a sense of membership in a special group, with its own norms and values and even uniforms" (1991:174). To some extent, butches and femmes created lesbian gender forms, but these forms drew very heavily on the heterogender roles of heterosexual men and women. Against

---

sex (Blumstein and Schwartz 1983, Carrington 1999), the degree of "stoniness" of the butch can be understood as financed and propped up, in part, by the desires of the femme for a sexually aggressive and impenetrable partner, just as the queen/*maricón* manufactures and supports a "real [i.e., impenetrable] man" (see Murray 1995a:59). What butches experience as obligations to live up to such a role is not easily disentangled from some "pure" or innate desire to be such a person. However, if a desire must be devoid of any social influence to be "authentic," no adult's sexual desires are fully authentic.

5. See Rosenzweig and Lebow 1992; Kennedy and Davis 1993:177–78, 212–13, 287; Weston 1997. Even in the days of hyper-reified gendering, some gay women played with and took the pleasures of transgression with the sex roles and dress codes prescribed by their usual gender presentation. "Ki-ki," "pancake," and "bluff" (combining Butch with fLUFF) were labels for a woman who was not predictably butch or femme (Faderman 1991:168, 170).

6. "Passing women" are another matter, and the women who were unsatisfied with being "female" varied (and vary) in the extent to which they wanted to be[come] men. Wanting to have the status and opportunities of men and wanting to have a wife may co-occur with contempt for (biological) men, just as some drag queens have contempt for (biological) women.

the romanticizing of gender outlaws that Judith Butler and many others have done, as Sally Munt (1998:427) puts it, one may be "sympathetic to claims that butch/femme constitute new gender configurations which must be understood in their own terms, [but] they are not intrinsically radical forms springing perfect from the homosexual body. Nor are they naïve forms in the sense that they express a naturally good, pure, and primitive desire."

Not all women who were sexually interested in women were comfortable with the roles when role dichotomization seemed the only way to be a lesbian. Poet Audre Lorde (1982:224), who thought that she "wasn't cute or passive enough to be a 'femme'" or "mean or tough enough to be a 'butch'" recalled being frightened by the heavy role dichotomization she saw among the few black women in gay bars during the 1950s. It is incontestable that some reveled in the frisson between exaggerated masculinity and exaggerated femininity, as many women discuss in Nestle 1987, Kennedy and Davis 1993, and Weston 1997— even if role playing was muted and even stigmatized in middle- and upper-class lesbian circles and resisted by some in working-class milieux (see Faderman 1991:175–87; Kennedy and Davis 1993:31–45).

Just as there were gay women uncomfortable with "pre-liberation" butch-femme role dichotomizing, there were lesbians during the heyday of lesbian feminism who did not want to be "liberated" from enacting their highly eroticized scenarios of differences and ravishings. Many found "sisterhood" incompatible with sexual arousal (feeling it as incestuous). Some women resisted the dominant scenario, both the gendered one of the 1950s and the egalitarian one of the 1970s. A resurgence of butch/femme role playing and identities was part of the generational rebellion against lesbian-feminist orthodoxy (discussed by Faderman 1992; Weston 1997). Now, as during the 1950s, femmes are often suspected of being less than fully committed to loving women.[7] And "lipstick lesbians" are regarded with horror by some as engaging in not only

---

7. Indeed, the frisson of difference may more often come from exogamy between a woman committed to being a lesbian and one less committed—"primary" in contrast to "elective" lesbians, to use Ponse's (1978) labels. (Also see Vance and Green 1984, distinguishing "exclusive lesbians" from "bisexual women" and, on more recent times, Stein 1997:161–64). Butches have generally been thought to be (and presented themselves as being) more committed to being lesbians, and have worried about femmes "turning straight," but gender-mixed or gender-crossing appearance does not always signify the strongest commitment to being lesbian (or to being the "lover" rather than the "beloved object"). There are butches who are not committed to being "lesbians," some preferring to think of themselves and/or reconfigure hormones (and more of their bodies) as men.

the objectification but the commodification of women (Deb Amory 23 May 1998 E-mail).

Ancient Athens

In classical Athens, men viewed women as constitutionally subrational, devious, and dangerous to them. The "female sphere" rarely extended outside the household. In addition to the Thesmophoria, a three-day woman-only festival, there was also a one-day festival called Skira during which

> the women left their homes and organized an *ecclesia,* a political assembly or parliament. Much of our information about this ritual comes from Aristophanes' play *The Parliament of Women,* because for once this playwright did not invent a "fantastic idea" but used one that was ready-made in the customs of the city. . . . In Aristophanes' comedy the women go to the assembly disguised as men, in long cloaks and coarse shoes; they have tanned their faces and glued on artificial beards, and they carry walking sticks. These details are probably authentic. A number of vase paintings depict women attired as men. (Keuls 1993:357)

Although in Greek myth there were the women of Lemnos who slaughtered the men on the island to form a gynocracy, the rebellious daughters of Danaus killing the husbands forced upon them, and the Amazons governing themselves, I have not found any indication that gender-role polarity was imagined among these groups of women choosing to live without men (not just to play at it for a day). The Amazons were represented as having queens, but I also find no consideration of age- or other status-differentiated female-female sexual roles. Rather than "one must play the man's role," these whole groups were imagined as playing men's roles—including governing and killing men. Male "Greeks thought of marriage as the taming of wild, ungovernable, basically irrational womanhood" and "in most Greek city-states a woman had, in law, no standing in any question" (Grant 1987:31). Only in the irrational realm of religion (i.e., in dealing with the unpredictable, savage deities the Greeks conceived) did women have public roles.

Ancient Rome

Although the sexual behavior of female Romans was more closely monitored than was that of female Greeks, Roman mothers raised sons; they didn't just bear them. Also, their control lasted longer: male children became adults at fourteen—twice the age at which Spartans were when removed from their mothers (Cantarella 1992:217–18). Over time, the autonomy and status of upper-class Roman females increased.

There are a few scattered Roman references to sex or love between women. All were written by men. Most involve heterogender role-splitting (including some that would now be classified as "transsexual"). In both Plautus's *Persa* (227) and his *Truculentus* (262f), the maid seems to be a regular penetrator (*subigitatrix*) of her mistresses. Horace's labeling Folia *masculae libidinis* (in ode 1.41) may be an indication that she was sexually insertive, though Lilja (1982:72n. 89) doubts this.

For a married woman to have sex with anyone not her husband was "adultery" in the view of the Elder Seneca (*Controversiae* 1.2.23). He argued that if a husband caught his wife *in flagrante delicto* with a woman, he had the same right to kill her partner as he had to kill a male partner caught with his wife. This is

> the earliest extant appearance in Latin literature of the word *tribas* itself, and as *tribas* is the only noun employed by Roman authors to designate women who engage in same-sex love, we might note that the word and its usage have several things in common with literary representations of tribadism. For one, *tribas* is a purely Greek formation, from *tribein* "to rub," "to wear down." Unlike other Latin nouns derived from this Greek verb, *tribas* retains its Greek nominative ending. It is also associated with women who appropriate masculine behavior by seeking physical gratification not merely by rubbing, but by penetrating, as one would with a male organ, the orifices of other females. (Hallett 1989:183)

Martial, forty-four years Seneca's junior, addressed the woman Bassa as a masculine penetrator (*fututor*), but found it hard to conceive that there could be adultery without a man.[8] He also portrayed another woman, Philaenis, who could outdrink and outeat any man, compete successfully at male sports (including wrestling and jumping with weights), and who "pounds" eleven girls a night.[9] Martial represented both Philaenis and Bassa as individuals with whom he was personally

8. 1.90. The riddle more perplexing than that of the Sphinx is "hic ubi vir non est, ut sit adulterium," which Seneca had answered in the affirmative.

9. 7.67, 7.70. He also claims that Philaenis penetrates the anuses of young boys (*pueri*) as a man does. Martial derides her for substituting her tongue for a penis (*mentula*) with the females she penetrates. He does not specify with what she penetrated boys. David Greenberg suggested that elongated clitorises are one possibility, as for other phallocentric writers across history (e.g., Luisi Sinistrari [1622–1701; *Peccatum mutum* I,6]).

acquainted, and as alive and functioning in the urban scene of his day (the late first century A.D.).[10]

The fifth of Lucian of Samosata's *Dialogi meretricii* (Dialogues of the Courtesans; written in Greek) includes a woman from Lesbos (where, she reports, there are many woman-loving women) who has seduced Leana, who appears to be living with a woman named Megilla and Megilla's wife, a woman from Corinth. Although Leana is reticent, Clonarium eagerly seeks details. Megilla, who shaves her head, boasts that she is "a man in every way," saying that she was born a woman, but that her mind (*gnōmé*), desires (*epithumia*), and all the rest (*talla panta*) are those of a man. Leana does not detail the (*aischra*—shameful) details of how Megilla demonstrated the truth of her claims to her (5.3). Megilla is a representation of a transgendered being, whatever she did to Leana, or what "the rest" included.

In Juvenal's second satire (47–53) a Roman named Laronia denies that females engage in reciprocal oral sex. She asserts that they confine their masculine activities to wrestling and special meat eating that builds up muscles (the same endeavors that Martial attributed to Philaenis—apparently stereotypical markers). As Hallett (1989:188) noted, Laronia does not deny female-female eroticism, only licking (*lambit*) each other. Through Laronia, Juvenal excoriated male effeminacy, and the degredation of receptive oral sex, while not criticizing *tribades*. He did minimize their number as *paucae* (few).

Writing before any of the other Roman writers so far mentioned here, Ovid, in *Metamorphosis* 9, told the story of a young pious Greek woman Iphis who was changed (by Isis, in response to Iphis's lament) into a man on the day she wedded Ianthe. Hallett warned that

> Iphis's revulsion at female homoerotic passion must not be confused with a view of Ovid himself. Indeed, Ovid's narrative displays immense sympathy with Iphis's plight, a sympathy contrasting with Iphis's own self-condemnation and negative view of female homoeroticism. As a matter of fact, the transformation of Iphis from human female to human male stands out conspicuously among the changes undergone by characters in the Metamorphoses. Here Ovid does not resolve a painful human dilemma in his typical fashion, by turning this particular person into a vegetable, mineral or subspecies of animal. Rather, Ovid

10. Hallett (1989:186); also see Martial (1.90, 7.35) and Juvenal's satire (6.246–64, 425–33) on women undertaking masculine tasks, such as spear-throwing.

accords Iphis's story an unusually happy ending—inasmuch as Iphis, unlike many others in the Metamorphoses, need not relinquish her living human identity, and even improves upon the one the gods have created for her. (1989:187)

In telling about the miraculous growth of a penis on Galatea's and Lamprus's daughter, who had been raised as a boy named Leucippus in the seventeenth of his *Metamorphoses*, Antonius Liberalis mentioned another instance of a woman becoming a man, Hypermestra.[11] The elder Pliny (*Natural History* 7.23) included four such cases of women who became men, including one he himself met who had become male on the day she wed a female. That is, the greatest of Roman natural scientists (who was born before Martial and Juvenal, though after Ovid's death) considered such a metamorphosis as a verified empirical phenomenon (albeit a rare one), not just as legendary occurrences from Greek antiquity. If we retroject current distinctions, these are instances of females becoming male (transsexual, not just heterogender), rather than of homosexual relations.

Though most representations involve a masculine partner, not all of them grew a penis. Caelius Aurelianus,[12] a fifth-century physician, wrote of *tribades* "more eager to lie with women than with men; in fact, they pursue women with almost masculine jealousy" and, like effeminate male pathics (*molles*) "are victims of an affliction of the mind" (*De morbis chronicis* 4.9; trans. Drabkin 1950:901–3).[13] Also, Clement of Alexandria wrote of women who "play the man against nature" (*Paidag* III:3, 21, 3) rather than changing their genital morphology.

11. He also mentioned the transformation back and forth of Tiresias, and a Cretan man who was punished by being turned into a woman for happening upon Diana bathing.

12. Since the Greek treatise of Soranos (from the time of Trajan) is not extant, it is impossible to distinguish with certainty Caelius Aurelianus's translation from his own additions. I suspected that he added the comparison of *tribades* to Soranos's discussion of *molles/malthakoi*, but am cowed by the authority of Schrijvers (1985:7–8) and Brooten (1996:148), who regard the analogy between penetrating women and penetrated men as deriving from Soranos.

13. *Tribades* were purportedly "worn out by their two-fold sexuality" (Brooten 1996: 150; translation of "iuvamini humilitate duplici sexu confectam [or confectae]" from 4.9§132). Brooten (1996:151) glossed *duplex sexus* as meaning "'having within oneself the characteristics of both sexes,' since *sexus* refers to the specific qualities associated with being female or male." That is, *tribades* had sex with males (though they preferred sex with females) rather than being sexually versatile with females—although "the text does not explicitly describe the tribades in remission as being sexually healthy, that is, passive, and therefore feminine" (151–52).

Early Modern Europe

Historian Judith Brown (1986) excavated and discussed records of early-seventeenth-century investigations of Benedetta Carlini, abbess of the Theatine nuns in Pescia, Italy, whom Brown calls a "lesbian nun." Sister Benedetta was a visionary with a popular following beyond her abbey (easily interpreted as a threat to male ecclesiastical authority). She had stigmata and spoke in the voice of Christ. His voice, among other things, exhorted nuns to follow Benedetta. Sister Bartholomea told investigators that for two and a half years Sister Benedetta forced her to have sex for hours at a time, several times a week. Benedetta told Bartholomea that Bartholomea's body was inhabited by an angel, Splenditello, and Bartholomea testified that she believed the angel wanted her to do as he said. As Pamela Walker (1986:10) wrote,

> It is clear that they were no lesbians in the modern sense of the word yet they clearly chose each other to engage in activities that had both spiritual and personal significance. . . . However, it is difficult to know what meaning Benedetta and Bartholomea attached to their relationship because the documents available contain only what each woman chose to tell the investigators. With the threat of burning ever present, they would not be likely to speak freely, even if they had the language to express themselves. Yet not naming certainly does not equal not conceiving. (1986:10)

Had the authorities decided that the nuns had committed sodomy, they could have burned them at the stake. This they clearly did not do. As for Bartolomea, there is no mention of imprisonment, and she seems to have lived out her life in the general convent routines.[14]

Women **could** be sodomites in the medieval Christian view:

> Lesbianism was singled out as a sin in some early penitentials, notably that of Theodore of Tarsus, Archbishop of Canterbury, which dates from about 680 A.D., and of the Venerable Bede, compiled before 734 A.D. Two works that were to become definitive guides to Christian moral theology also set lesbianism morally on a par with male sodomy. Gratian's *Decretum* of 1140 remained a standard work of canon law until 1917. It incorporated a passage from the *Contra Jovinianam* ascribed to Augustine: "Acts contrary to nature are in truth always illicit, and

---

14. J. Brown (1986:132–34).

without doubt more shameful and foul, which use the Holy Apostle [i.e., Paul in Romans 1:27] has condemned both in women and in men, meaning them to be understood as more damnable than if they sinned through the natural use by adultery or fornication." . . . Aquinas set his seal on the received interpretation of Paul and placed lesbianism unequivocally in the same moral category ["sins against nature"] as male relations. (Crompton 1980:14–15)

In general practice, if not in legal theory, however, "lesbian impunity" existed—at least impunity from capital punishment, and a general unconcern about premarital female-female eros. I would generalize what Traub (1992:159) wrote specifically about some characters on the Elizabethan English stage: "homoerotic desires of these female characters existed comfortably within the patriarchy until the onset of marriage; it is only with the cementing of male bonds through the exchange of women, or, in Titania's case [in *Midsummer Night's Dream*], the usurpation of the right to formalize bonds through the bodies of others, that the independent desires of female bodies become a focus of male anxiety and heterosexual retribution"; female-female desire "becomes significant only when the time comes for the patriarchal imperative of reproduction to be enforced" (163).

As with males, the penetrator (here the *tribade*) was judged more harshly as the one committing sins on the passive other. "Henri Estienne [1879:178] mentions a woman from Fontaines who disguised herself as a man, married another woman, and was burned alive in about 1535 after the discovery of the 'wickedness which she used to counterfeit the office of a husband,'" and two Spanish nuns were burned in the sixteenth century for using "material instruments" (Crompton 1980:15). Crompton also mentioned the drowning "for lesbian love" of a girl in Speier in 1477 (17). The "wife" of the couple Montaigne heard about in Vitry-le-François, a small town on the Marne in southern France, was not executed along with her partner in 1580. The "husband," Marie, who worked as a weaver, was said to prefer hanging to being forced to endure living as a female, which may indicate that she might have evaded a death sentence if she had repented her ongoing gender transgression (Montaigne 1948:869–70; see Greenblatt 1988:66–67). In a German case in 1721, only the woman passing as a man was executed (Eriksson 1980), while in Leiden (in the Netherlands) in the only two seventeenth-century cases Noordam (1983) could find, the guilty parties were banished. Seizing male prerogatives by passing as a male in the streets or in bed was capitally punished when it was discovered. Female-female embraces or fondling (or, as far as I can tell, even cunnilingus) were not. As Traub (1992:164) explained, "In the psychic landscape of the time, 'femmes' would be assumed available to give birth; tribades and sodomites would not. The 'femme' involved with a tribade was seen as 'abused', the not altogether innocent victim of another woman's lust; her crime was correspondingly more minor, her punishment less severe."

Crompton (1996) discussed two early-seventeenth-century French texts exculpating lesbian sex (while condemning male-male sex). The abbé Brantôme, who used the term *lesbienne* as well as the traditional term, *tribade,* contended that a wife did not cuckold her husband if she had sex with a woman, and wrote with approval of lesbians' courage (1955:135, 129). In the second of the dialogues written by Nicolas Chorier, but attributed to Luisa Sigea of Toledo, Tullia seduces Octavia, citing classical precedents. Tullia claims that Octavia's mother seduced her, which must count as a representation of age-stratified female homosexuality. The rare cases that went to trial involved one woman passing as a man in society and/or using a "counterfeit phallus," often on a feminine partner who purported not to know that her " husband" was not a male.

Despite the inclusion of female acts in sodomy laws, medieval and early modern Europeans "long found it difficult to accept that women could actually be attracted to other women. Their view of human sexuality was phallocentric—women might be attracted to men and men might be attracted to men [and boys], but there was nothing in a woman that could sustain the sexual desire of another woman. Thus, for instance, Dante sees male sodomites in the *Inferno,* but not female analogs" (J. Brown 1986:6).

In the last decade of the sixteenth century in England, there are representations of females attracted to females passing as males. For example Olivia is attracted to Viola in the guise of Cesario in Shakespeare's *Twelfth Night,* and Phebe for Rosalind in the guise of Ganymede in *As You Like It.* And (more unusually) in Sir Philip Sidney's *Arcadia* the princess falls in love with her wooer Zelmane in the guise of an "Amazon." Once disguises are dropped, in all these cases a "proper" male-female couple emerges from the earlier gender confusions.

Earlier in the century, in canto 25 of the *Orlando furioso* of Ludovico Ariosto (1474–1533), Fiordispina, a Spanish princess, falls in love with the Amazon knight Bradamante, whose head was shaved to treat a head wound. Although Bradamante clearly states her sex, and this is recognized by gifts of female attire, the princess's "wild desires" continue unabated. These desires are not shared by Bradamante, who, after one night of sharing a bed with a sighing and weeping bed mate, sends her twin brother Richardet to take her place. This does not immediately make everything conventionally right (as, for instance, substituting Rosalind's twin Sebastian for her in *Twelfth Night* does). Instead of claiming a bride as a male, Fiordispina supplies Richardet with female attire. The rest of the court does not learn that he is not female for several months.[15]

Except for this last instance (which after one night of unconsummated longing becomes heterosexual), Renaissance European literary imaginings of desire for those passing as another sex are mostly heterogender.[16] Whether the desires were what Freud called " aim-inhibited" or could not be unable to be expressed in print, female homosexual behavior is not represented in these works.[17] However, in English Renaissance literature, neither is heterosexual behavior: couples at the end of Shakespeare's comedies and romances have remained chaste. They may be about to wed (or in the *Merchant of Venice* to consummate a marriage interrupted by attending the case of Shylock versus Antonio), but do not do so before the plays end. Thus, one could argue that **heterosexual behavior** is not represented in these works, either. There are pairings, but not explicit copulations.

Pacific Societies
Oceania

In passing, Niko Besnier noted that

> in contemporary Polynesian contexts, one does find women
> who dress like men, perform certain tasks for which men are

---

15. When her father and his followers learn that a male has been sleeping with the princess, they are amused and nearly kill Richardet, who in telling his tale continues to believe that pursuing one's pleasure is always right. He says that Fiordispina craved what he had. The twenty-eighth canto of *Orlando Furioso* elaborates on women's insatiable appetite for infidelity, which could be read as female desire.

16. The "Pasquil Courtizan" (Courtier's Libel) included in Pierre de l'Estoile's *Mémoires-Journaux* for November 1581 (during the reign of Henri III) mentions males marrying each other and women marrying each other with no indication of differentiated roles ("Ce son mariages tels . . . un homme à l'autre se marie et la femme à la autre s'allie" (quoted in Cady 1996:148n. 11). My suspicion is that "marriage" implied a husband and a wife, so that lack of mention of roles is not evident that even this (scurrilous) representation is one of egalitarian relations between same-sex partners.

17. Partner (1996) called attention to the ongoing reading out of sex (whether under the cover of "gender" or "eros") in analyses of mystics. In passing, she mentioned that *The Vision of the Monk of Eynsham* (ca. 1194, chaps. 25 and 26) included recognition that women as well as men were involved in the sin of sodomy (305).

traditionally responsible, are sexually aggressive with women and are given labels that mirror terms referring to liminal men (e.g., Tongan *fakatangata* and Samoan *fa'atama*, "in the fashion of a man"). Liminal women are considerably fewer and less noticeable than liminal men . . . [and] there is anecdotal evidence that female liminality may be of relatively recent origin, in contrast to historically well-established male liminality. (1994:288)

Carol Robertson (1989:314) noted that in contemporary Hawai'i the category *māhū* includes women who dress and work as men and "women and men who might, in English, call themselves 'gay.'" Explaining that transvestitism is but one aspect of the māhū phenomenon, she reported having met several women who were raised as boys by their parents or grandparents. She did not report any female-female sexual behavior, but cited Pukui et al.'s (1972, 2:113) documentation that "girls were raised as boys to keep them free of sexual liaisons with men. In earlier days, these girls would have been considered kapu (taboo)." [18]

Deborah MacFarlane (1984:307) elicited accounts "of elderly Maori women, whom they [her informants] had known when children, who lived and dressed as men," but did not mention whether they were sexually involved with women. Te Awekotuku (1991) and Hinewirangi (1993) unequivocally affirmed a continuity between honored and revered roles among ancient/tribal Aotearo and contemporary Maori lesbians.

On the Micronesian island, Pohnpei (Ponape, in the east Caroline islands), Martha Ward recorded the case of a young woman who was socially reclassified as a man:

A young girl named Maria began exhibiting the habits of a boy as she grew into her teens. She began to go walking about at night looking for girls. The activity itself was acceptable, but a girl doing it causes consternation. Family and neighbors held a meeting to discuss the problem. Then they held a feast where they publicly declared her a boy. Her hair was cut and she was presented with male clothing. Henceforth, they accounted, Maria would be Mario. I heard that Mario became a responsible citizen with a wife and children. (1989:42)

Ward did not specify whether Mario was the biological or just the social father of the children. If the former, sex reassignment was a correction

18. She noted that in the hula revival, female māhū presenting themselves as men are the only māhū who are not actively involved (315).

of sex, if the latter, it was one of gender. Neither evidences any acceptance of female-female sexuality in the society.

In Aboriginal Australian Societies a century ago, Strehlow (1913:98) wrote that "the unnatural vice of the women, *woiatakerama* (carried out using a little stick bound with string, called *iminita*, by two women, one of whom performs the role of the man), is practiced by the eastern and western Aranda. It also occurs among the western Loritja, the Yumu and Waiangara in the west, and among the Katitja, Ilpara, Warramunga, etc., who live north of the McDonnell Ranges" (trans. Jim Wafer in Gays 1994:41).

Turn-taking (in the penetrative role) has been reported for other aboriginal Australian groups, and perhaps "one performs the role of the man" should not be read as an ongoing gender-role dichotomization.

Indonesian Societies

Scattered, inconclusive reports from the Indonesian archipelago exist (e.g., Westermarck 1906; Mead 1961 [1448]; see Murray 1992a:397–405), but nothing has been found to parallel the established occupational roles for transvestite male homosexuality there. Adriani and Kruyt (1950:243) noted that "women [who] behaved like men occurred only rarely" among the Toradja of Sulawesi. They told of a pregnant woman who, disgusted by the cowardice of her husband, went on a head-hunting expedition, gave birth, stowed the baby in a tree, and went into battle. They also mentioned "girls irritated by the touch of man" (264), but did not indicate any occupational niches for such women.

Chabot (1960:154–55) mentioned Taklar, a woman who "wore her hair like a woman, but her sarong like a man. She preferred to work in the fields with the hoe (typical male work)." Although this passage was coded by HRAF as "838, homosexuality," Chabot made no mention of her sexual behavior.

Mead (1949:93) wrote that on Bali "where female homosexuality occurred—as it did in the palaces of the old rajahs—mock phalluses were part of the game," without indicating whether there was division into recurrent roles or reciprocity.

The French admiral Augustin de Beaulieu, who visited Aceh in 1620–21, wrote that its sultan had three thousand women palace guards (1705, 1:744). The English traveler Peter Mundy saw Aceh women guards armed with bow and arrows in 1637 (Temple 1936, 3:131). Rijklov van Goens (1956:259–60), who visited Matarm in the mid-seventeenth century, reported that the corps there consisted of about one hundred and fifty young women. Thirty accompanied the sultan when he gave audiences, ten as porters, twenty as guards. They were trained in singing and dancing and playing musical instruments as well as in using weapons. In the late eighteenth century, the Sultan of Jogjakarta also had female guards (Ricklefs 1974:304). In 1821 the Surakarta court (*kraton*) of Solo (central Java) included a group of 150 female bodyguards, called prajurit Keparah Estri. Their official dress was the male Javanese fighting costume (*prajuritan*). "Some of the amazones were armed with shields, bows and arrows, pikes and muskets, while others bore the ruler's impediments." Like the male soldiers, they were trained in singing, dancing, and playing musical instruments, as well as in fighting. Dances like the still-current Retna Tnadhing depict fighting movements (Carey and Houben 1987:18). Kumar (1980:5–6) includes foreigners' reports that the *prajurit estri* were better at wielding weapons than were the males. Javanese female commanders fought the Dutch during the 1820s (at least one, Radèn Ayu Yudakusuma, a sultan's daughter, shaved her head like male commanders in the holy war against the infidels). Again, females joined military struggles against Japanese and Dutch colonialisms during the 1940s (Carey and Houben 1987:20–21). In the Surakarta court during the early 1820s, one of the ruler's concubines "acted the male role" with "frustrated royal concubines" (20; based on Winter 1902:39), so more than "gender variance" was involved, but for how many, or how often, the historical record is silent.

In a much more recent essay on her sexual relationship with a Minangkabau woman during her 1989–90 dissertation fieldwork in western Sumatra, Evelyn Blackwood reported herself to have been stunned by strong butch/femme role dichotomization.[19] She explains that

> alternatively gendered females are called *supik-jantan* (a Minangkabau word meaning girl-boy) or *tom-boi* (a more recent term from the English for a male-like woman). These terms are now used alternately with *lesbi* and *gay*, due to the close connection of gender with homosexuality in West Sumatra and Indonesia. Alternatively gendered individuals find partners among same-sex individuals who appear straight-looking and are usually bisexual. The masculine (*jantan* or *tomboi*) partner in a les-

19. I find this odd in that I know that she knows American lesbian anthropologists with views of gender quite similar to those of Dayan's (Blackwood 1995:67). Dayan took the "male role" in sex, and did not want to be touched herself: "Acts that emphasized her female body made her uncomfortable; she perceived them as corporal negation of her maleness" (68).

bian couple is also called *cowok,* an Indonesian slang term for a young man meaning "guy", or *laki-laki* (man) while her feminine partner is called *cewek,* Indonesian slang for a young woman. . . . *Cowok* are not attracted to other *cowok.* (1995:62, 66)

She added that both gender variance and homosexuality are ignored as long as family duties (i.e., procreation) are fulfilled. This is an instance of the limited "tolerance" in Muslim societies that I call "the will not to know" (Murray 1997b).

Saskia Wieringa (1996) also reported that in Jakarta "butches tried to teach me to be one of them, and the femmes made clear what they expected from me by way of chivalry and lovemaking" (5), and interpreted butch/femme sexuality as "the expression of autonomous sexual desire of women for each other" (10). For some women, butch dress and demeanor was more important than other concerns, even financial safety, so that some are financially supported by their gender-conforming femme lovers. Femmes control the scene—that is, the butches are "sex objects" servicing the femmes (just as I have suggested is the case for "husbands" and other "real men" fashioned by and in male queen's fantasies). Her friends were astonished by reports of reciprocal sex among Europeans: "'How is that possible?' they asked. 'Isn't that confusing, for in that case, you would have to play two roles at the same time'" (Wieringa 1987:16; trans. Wieringa 1996:17).

B. J. D. Gayatri (1993:14) reported some tacit acceptance of some Javanese daughters' relations with other females, so long as they were discreet enough to permit plausible deniability, as well as some married women who give their bodies to their husbands, but their hearts to women.[20] She reported that "butch lesbians" were sometimes referred to as *banci* (a term commonly used in reference to male transvestites; as she noted, Javanese do not distinguish "homosexual" from "transvestite"). *Lesbi* is known by some, and a term that "used to be used exclusively among lesbians" is *lines* (9). Srikandhi, the name of a woman in the Javanese wayang versions of the *Mahabharata* who prefers masculine activities (notably archery), has a very close relationship with one of her co-wives, commands troops, and heroically slays Resi Bisma, is used for females rejecting their gender role, with some connotation of a sexual

---

20. She included segments of interviews of a devout young lawyer who considers herself a "good lesbian," while maintaining her virginity until marriage, and of a divorced woman who identifies herself as a lesbian, but does not consider physical sex as necessary, though she has had sex with some of her lovers.

component.[21] Gayatri distinguished women she called "female transvestites" (who consider themselves men trapped in women's bodies) from women involved in butch-femme (*kantil-sentul*) roles.

In her fieldwork in Jakarta, Alison Murray (1995) found such lesbian subculture as exists to be highly fragmented with little basis for coalition with gay men. She found some urban working-class butch-femme role playing. Similarly, Oetomo wrote:

> Lesbian couples exist in many parts of Indonesia. There are certain hang-outs (pubs, restaurants) frequented by lesbians, but such contacts are necessarily limited, given the limitations on going out alone or even in groups, especially at night, that women face in Indonesian society. There have been reports that some lesbians hang out at prostitution complexes and buy sex there, and that a small number of female sex workers are predominantly homosexual. . . . Since the pressure to get married and set up a family is even stronger on women [than on men], most lesbians are, have been, or will be married. (1991:125)

On Cebu, a southern island in the Philippine archipelago, Donn Hart described females who cross dressed and engaged in male occupations. These females were sometimes referred to with the term for male cross dressers (*bayot*), sometimes with their own (*lakin-on*) and sometimes passed as men away from their natal village (1968:223–26).

North Pacific Societies

In the classic work on transformed shamans among the Chukchi of the farthest northeastern part of Siberia, Vladimir Bogoraz described one female transformed into a male, complete with a wife to penetrate:[22]

> The case of *qa'cikIcheca,* that is, of a woman transformed into a man, is still more remarkable than that of the "soft man." I obtained detailed information of only two or three instances. One was of a widow of middle age, who had three half-grown children of her own. She received at first an "inspiration" of a more usual kind, but, later, the "spirits" wanted to change her to a man. Then she cut her hair, donned the dress of a male, adopted

---

21. Although in some versions she is born with a bow in her hand, usually Srikkandhi learns archery from Arjuna to defend her country from the ire of the husband her parents have arranged for her to marry, Jungkungmardea. In some versions, she slays him. She bears no children as a woman, but marries a woman (Durniti) and fathers a child (with a borrowed penis). See Pausacker 1991:271, 279, 286.

22. The reports in this section—and their reporters—are contextualized and quoted at much greater length in Murray 1992a:293–352.

the pronunciation of men, and even learned in a very short time to handle the spear and to shoot with a rifle. At last she wanted to marry, and easily found a quite young girl who consented to become her wife.

The transformed one provided herself with a gastrocnemius from the leg of a reindeer, fastened to a broad leather belt, and used it in the way of masculine private parts. I have said before that the gastrocnemius of a reindeer is used by Chukchee women for the well-known unnatural vice. After some time, the transformed husband, desiring to have children by her young wife, entered into a bond of mutual marriage with a young neighbor, and in three years two sons were really born in her family. According to the Chukchee interpretation of mutual marriage, they were considered her own lawful children. Thus, this person could have had in her youth children of her own body, and in later life, other children from a wedded wife of her own. Another case was that of a young girl who likewise assumed man's clothing, carried a spear, and even wanted to take part in a wrestling contest between young men. While tending the herd, she tried to persuade one of the young herdswomen to take her for a husband. On closer acquaintance, she tried to introduce the same implement made of reindeer gastrocnemius tied to a belt, but then was rejected by the would-be bride. This happened only a few years ago; the transformed woman is said to have found another bride with whom she lives now in her country on the headwaters of the Chaun River. (1904; adumbrated in 1900:29)

On Kodiak Island, east of the Alaska Peninsula, Father Gideon noted in 1804 that parents who had wanted a boy, but had produced a girl, might give her a masculine name and raise her as a son (Valaam Monastery 1978 [1894]:121). He did not record what the sexual expectations were in such cases.[23]

A special efficacy in sexual transformation remained a part of North Pacific belief systems beyond the time of "transformed shamans." Thus, for instance, Jane Murphy reported a kind of ritual for

"changing everything and making everything right." The customary prescription for a girl would be that she cut her hair like a boy's, start smoking a pipe, wear boy's clothing, and associate with male groups. For a boy, it would be to don girl's clothing and feminine demeanor. . . . Despite the decline in shamanism,

---

23. He also failed to report on the sexuality of boys raised as girls in the same locale.

a number of villagers had experienced this kind of therapy in their early years and then had gradually resumed their normal sex roles. Presumably, if shamanistic belief were still orthodox and intact, some of these people would have maintained the sexual metamorphosis and might possibly therefore have been recruited to the ranks of the shamans who practiced trans-vestism and homosexuality. During the 1954–55 field trip, one ten-year-old girl was undergoing the change-of-name-and-sex therapy and for several years had dressed and behaved like a boy.(1964:63)

She reported that the tradition of transvestism and homosexuality either separately or as part of shamanizing has not been entirely extinguished on St. Lawrence Island,[24] attesting *anasik* as the term for "soft man" or "womanly man" and *uktasik* as the counterpart for women.

Asian Societies
China
Chinese Wives Sharing Concubines with Their Husbands

Dui shi (literally, eating facing each other) as a label for a relationship suggests that mutual oral sex was the practice of women in ancient Han courts. Ying Shao (ca. 140–206) wrote that "When place women attach themselves as husband and wife it is called *tui shih*. They are intensely jealous of each other" (quoted by Wilbur 1943:431n. 10). In a chronicle (reproduced by Wilbur 1943:424) of the Han emperor Cheng, who ruled from 32 B.C. to 7 B.C. (the predecessor of Ai of cut-sleeve and shared-peach fame, and one who also had male favorites), his wife and a Kung, a female student clerk who taught her poetry, had a *dui shi* relationship. The emperor also favored Kung by deigning to impregnate her, so that de facto she was a concubine to the emperor as well as to the empress.

A well-known example of a female's love for another female is the focus of the 1645 play *Lian xiangban* (Loving/Pitying the Fragrant Companion) by Li Yu. In it, Cui Jian-Yun, a masculine young married woman (who is sure that she will be reborn male) loves a young, talented fifteen-year-old girl, Cao Yu-Hua. To ensure that they will be together, Cui

---

24. "Homosexuality was severely disapproved even though the transvestite shamans who sometimes practiced homosexuality were thought to be the most powerful" among St. Lawrence Eskimos (at some time in the past), according to Murphy (1964:64). There were resident Chukchi and Chukchi visitors to St. Lawrence Island as early as the mid-nineteenth century.

arranges for Yu-Hua to become her husband's concubine, and the three live happily, without jealousy.[25] The autobiography of Shen Fu (1763–1808) *Fusheng liuji* (translated in 1960 as *Six Chapters of a Floating Life*) recalls his wife wanting to install as Shen's concubine a singing girl whom she loved. (He was more than willing, although his family blocked the liaison, and the girl was forced to marry another man.)

Ancient warrant for having two women rub together to warm each other up (i.e., tribadism as a prelude to heterosexual penetration) was provided by the legendary founder of many aspects of Chinese culture (including pederasty), the Yellow Emperor:

> Lady Precious Yin and Mistress White Jade lay on top of each other, their legs entwined so that their jade gates (genitalias) pressed together. They then moved in a rubbing and jerking fashion against each other like fishes gobbling flies or water plants from the surface. As they became more excited, the "mouths widen and choosing his position carefully, Great Lord Yang thrusts between them with his jade root (penis). They moved in unison until all three shared the ultimate simultaneously. The triple flow of essence will strengthen bones and sinews as well as the breathing. It will also assist the Great Lord Yang to avoid the Five Overstrainings and the Seven Sex-injuries.[26]

In these instances, the wives are (at least presumptively) older than the female subordinates who are expected to acquiesce to what their mistresses and masters want them to do. Some less-compliant females from the lower orders have been documented in southeastern China.

One of the two most famous Chinese novels, *Honglou meng jiaohuan dale fu* (The Dream of the Red Chamber; also known as Story of the Stone, ca. 1750) includes a poignant scene in which a woman who specialized in playing male parts, Nénuphar, burns spirit money for the dead Pivoine, who always played the principal female parts opposite Nénuphar. Parfumée (who herself sometimes wears male dress), scoffs at this excessive display, explaining, "They became so accustomed to acting the part of lovers on the stage that gradually it came to seem real to

25. Xiao 1984, 1997:324. The date is from Mao and Liu 1977:14.

26. Lieh-Mak et al. 1983:22–23. They interpret this as the male conserving his sexual energy (22). It seems to me that in this passage, while the two women get each other excited, Lord Yang still expends some of his male essence (*yang*) and receives female essence (*yin*) from Lady Yin and from Mistress White Jade, who also exchange some with each other and receive some yang from Lord Yang.

them" and tells the young master Baoyu that Nénuphar is similarly involved with Pivoine's successor as the female lead. However, he resonates with admiration and sympathy once Parfumée tells him of Nénuphar's devotion to her dead "wife" (Cao and Gao 1987:132–33).

The final novella in *Yichung xing zhi* (Fragrant Stuff for the Spring Palace, ca. 1700) is an erotic variation on the most famous of all Chinese novels, *Xi you ji* (Journey to the West). Its hero, Niu Jun, a homely (male) student who is granted his wish to become beautiful, is entrusted by The Master Instructor and Inspirer of Love in the Three Worlds (Sanjie Tiqing Jiaozhu) to his Second Heir Apparent, Master Instructor of Love for Men (Naquing Hiaozhu). After becoming the consort of the King of the Kingdom of All-Sons (Yinanguo), half of whom live in female dress (but do not bind their feet), and being attacked by a gang sent by the queen he supplanted and nearly raped to death by the creature that rescues him, Niu Jun arrives in the *Kingdom of Holy Yin* (Shenyinguo),

> a place inhabited only by women who form couples and reproduce by making love to each other, through magical dildoes but still joining their bodies. When Queen Niu—who, we remember is dressed like a woman—reveals his sexual identity to the King, her reaction is one of amusement and of curiosity. The King is a woman with the sexuality of an active man: she quickly dismisses her wife and takes the newly arrived delicacy to the bedroom, much as the King of All-Sons had done earlier. She says she had always wanted to try men, without ever having had the chance, and, when Queen Niu shows no signs of arousal, she readily resolves to sodomize him with a dildo. . . . She is a libertine with hundreds of women lovers, who has the luck to try [penetrating] a man as well. (Vitiello 1994:170)

This phantasmagorical novella is not a representation of the empirical world and is almost certainly a male product. Perhaps the deployment of dildoes reflects a male view of the necessity of a phallus, but such implements existed in imperial China.

Both imagined same-sex worlds include gender roles, and, despite the female king's curiosity about a male body, the women of Shenyinguo do not want males around: "When baby boys are born, the ministers of the Kingdom of Holy Yin are far from happy. They see the arrival of men as a plague, a sort of bad omen proving the unworthiness of their King" (170). It is also of interest that both the all-male and the all-female realms are part of the empire of the Master Instructor of Love for Men, although the all-female realm seems to be the equal of the all-male one.

At least one writer could imagine women who were sufficient unto themselves.

Cocoons of Marriage Resistance in Pre-Revolutionary Guandong

In silk-raising rural areas of the Pearl River Delta from the mid-nineteenth to the early twentieth century, some women organized themselves into sisterhoods (*jimui*) and either refused to marry (*tzu-shu nü,* "women who dress their own hair") or refused to have marriages consummated or to live with their husbands (*pu lo-chia,* "women who do not go to live with the[ir husband's] family").[27]

The area was a stronghold of the semi-secret, messianic, millenialist, and anti-natalist Hsien-t'ien Ta-tao (Great Way of Former Heaven) religion. Vegetarian residential halls disguised their allegiances as Buddhist, to escape official (first Ching, then Guomingdong) persecution. Members were often sworn sisters (*suang chieh-pai*). Topley (1975:76) noted that "several features of the local ecology encouraged the formation of such sisterhoods: teamwork in various phases of silk production; residence in girls' houses; membership in the same sectarian 'family'; and the ties between girls who were bonded to the same deity because of their 'bad' (often nonmarrying) fates and who worshipped the deity together on ceremonial occasions."

In addition to the view that some of these women were not fated to marry, there was a view that two souls might be fated to marry over and over in different incarnations. If both happened to be incarnated as females at the same time—well, they were still made for each other. Some sworn sisters had sexual relations with each other. The popular name for tribadism was (and is) grinding bean curd (*mo tou-fu*). Dildoes made of silk thread and filled with bean curd or expandable raw silk were also attested.

In contrast to women elsewhere in "traditional" China, women in the Guandong silk areas learned to read, worked outside the home, lived with other women (away from fathers and husbands), and traveled freely, visiting other vegetarian halls, temples, and theaters. In contrast

27. Based on her 1930 inquiries, Smedley (1945:87–88) was told that female spinners were "notorious throughout China as Lesbians. They refused to marry, and if their families forced them, they merely bribed their husbands with part of their wages and induced them to take concubines. The most such a married girl would do was bear one son; then she would return to the factory, refusing to live with her husband any longer. . . . Now and then two or three girls would commit suicide together because their families were forcing them to marry." Secret "Sister Societies" had "even dared strike for shorter hours and higher wages" (88).

to most women in the rest of China, these women could support themselves.[28] In that some of their income was remitted to natal families that
also did not have to pay any dowry for daughters, "early signs of an aversion to marriage or of marked intelligence might be interpreted as indications of a 'nonmarrying fate.' If a horoscope-reader confirmed this
view, the daughter's future was set" (81–82).

Before moving out of the natal home, a daughter's hair had to be specially dressed. For weddings, others dressed it. The nonmarrying women
were called *tzu-shu nü*, in reference to the fact that they dressed their hair
themselves.[29] Like the bride, the *tzu-shu nü* received gifts (money in red
envelopes), and a banquet was held.[30]

In addition to the vegetarian halls, there were spinsters' houses (*ku-
p'o wu*) and sisters' houses (*tzu-mei wu*) that looked like vegetarian halls
(with altars to Guan Yin, the bodhisattva of mercy), but were less focused on religion, and in which meat could be served. According to
Sankar,

> If the sisterhood remained together thirty to forty years and
> there were enough members (usually five or more) to make it
> financially feasible to retire together, the women generally chose
> a secular lifestyle for old age. . . . Usually sisterhoods had five to
> six members, although they were frequently called seven-sisters
> associations. . . . Sometimes two or three women would form es-
> pecially strong attachments and become sworn sisters. In the
> cities to which the women migrated, several sisterhoods would
> join together to form larger associations of up to forty members.
> (1985:75, 71)

She did not mention what was the warrant for these authoritative-
sounding assertions, or how many of the seven sisterhoods she found
were involved in any particular living arrangement.

My reason for considering the *tzu-shu nü* who engaged in sex with
other *tzu-shu nü* age structured (in the absence of detail about sexual
pairings) is that "if they could save enough, they retired early—around

28. "Elsewhere the only alternatives to marriage were religious orders or occupations
connected with sex and procreation: prostitution, matchmaking, midwifery. A married
woman could sometimes supplement the family income and improve her [or its!] status by
engaging in cottage industry, but it was unlikely that a separated wife could earn enough
to support herself by such means" (Topley 1975:80). Nor could unmarried daughters stay
home: that would bring bad reproductive luck to the natal household.

29. Actually, the *tzu-shu nü* was assisted by an elderly celibate female, while the bride's
hair was arranged by a woman who had produced and raised many sons.

30. Some of them received part of what had been saved for their dowries.

forty—and adopted a *mei-tsai* [younger sister], whom they brought up in their 'faith'" (Topley 1975:83). There is no information on the relative age of even one pair in the published literature.

There were plenty of reasons other than desiring other females for Chinese women not to want to become junior daughters-in-law. Elsewhere in China, even in other silkworm-raising areas, there was less demand for women working outside the home, and nowhere for unmarried women to live. Women in the silkworm-raising part of Guandong could earn cash, and there celibacy had a strong counter-Confucian religious rationale. As Topley (1975:87) noted, none of these features was unique to the resistance area, but their combination was. Even with ideological warrant, once the economic base was weakened by the collapse of the silk market in the international depression of the 1930s (followed by Japanese invasion), the women's institutions were devastated, and their members disproportionately migrated to Singapore and Hong Kong, where, especially after World War II, unmarried women were in demand to work in factories, stores, and offices (85–86). Although it does not specify when she did her fieldwork, Sankar's 1985 article reported discovering that some of the spinsters from earlier times were still alive and that some "sisterhoods remained intact" (71). I interpret the following to mean that she found lesbian relationships (and that this is what "groups" means in the second and third sentences) both in colonial Hong Kong and across the border in communist Guandong:

> Stable lesbian relationships tended to choose the more traditional form of retirement, the spinster house or its Hong Kong equivalent. These groups were by their intimate and private nature not easily located. Of the seven such groups I did contact, only one had decided to join a gaai tong made up primarily of lesbian couples and ménages à trois. Because they feared religious persecution from the Chinese Communists if their location became known, I was unable to continue my work with them. The non-jaai tong affiliated groups which I met often came to my attention because of some serious problem which plagued the relationship. (81n. 2)

She stressed that in China, love has long been viewed as a shaky basis for important relationships that supply physical sustenance during and after life (i.e., ancestor worship), stability during life, or continuity beyond it, and that dyadic relationships could disrupt larger associations (the quasi-family of the sisterhoods): "Although sexual relationships were part of sisterhood life for some of the women, few chose to base their future security on such bonds. Instead, they worked at strengthening and supporting their larger sisterhood networks" (81).

Korea

In passing mentions, Rutt (1964:113) mentioned that "formal tribadistic unions were common among palace women in the capital" of the Yi dynasty (1392–1910) in Korea. Sasama (1989:489) added that lesbian relationships were common in the seraglios of the (Japanese) shoguns and that there were also instances in which relationships occurred among women "who despised liaisons with men." Neither author established whether there were gendered roles in either country, though this seems likely to me.

Japan

The twelfth-century novel *Torikaebaya* (*The Changeling*) focuses on a brother and sister, each born into the "wrong" sex('s body). They crossdress and exchange roles. The sister marries a woman (Leupp 1998:31). From the twelfth through fourteenth centuries, the Kyoto court was enlivened by female dancers called *shirabyōshi* ("white tunic dancers") who dressed in clothes marked as male performing "male dancing" (31).

In Osaka's fashionable Nagamachi ward, a kind of woman called *otoko nikumi bikuni,* (male-hating nuns, with "nun" being a frequent euphemism for itinerant prostitutes) existed, paralleling the better-documented male women-hater type (*onna-girai,* see p. 86 above), according to Leupp (1998:10-11, 17). Leupp called attention to the hiring of female prostitutes for a woman in the 1717 *Seken musume katagi* (Portraits of Young Women in This World) by the popular writer Ejima Kiseki. The woman expresses hatred for having a female form, bemoaning the bad karma to be born female (14).

An early-eighteenth-century woodblock illustration (reproduced in Hibbett 1975:109 and Leupp 1995:191) shows a Japanese woman not merely wearing male clothes, but carrying a sword, being told that the courtesan is ready and waiting for her. A literary representation from a few years earlier was included in Ihara Sakiaku's *Kōshoku ichidai onna* (1686, translated as *The Life of an Amorous Woman*): the heroine Yonosuke recalls a job as a maid that included sleeping in the same bed as the mistress, where "I was bidden to take the woman's part, while my mistress assumed that of a man." Her employer tells Yonosuke that she is confident that she will be reborn (next time) as a man: "Then I shall be free to do what really gives me pleasure" (188). For her, male privilege includes mounting females. Although surprised, the servant acquiesces.

"Later in the same novel the woman is employed as the attendant of a 'graceful young lady, hardly nineteen years of age, who boasted a more elegant demeanor,' and her reaction to this new mistress might suggest a physical attraction . . . : 'Can there really be such fine ladies in this world, I thought enviously, and though she was of my own sex, I gazed on her with fascination' (trans. Leupp 1998:13)." More unequivocally corporeal a representation of female desire for a female body is a maid in Chikamatsu's 1717 play "Gonza the Lancer" exclaiming, "Even a girl's heart get hot, and she wants to embrace her naked body and sleep with her" (about a young woman of a samurai family) (trans. Leupp 1998:16).

Kittredge Cherry reported Japanese female audiences' continued enthusiastic support of male impersonators on stage:

> The romantic fantasies of many Japanese girls focus on love-affairs with dashingly handsome women dressed as men. These "male roles" (*otoko yaku*) are the superstars of the four hundred–member Takarazuka Grand Theater troupe, the twentieth-century female counterpart of the historic Kabuki theater. The Takarazuka actresses stage about seven performances a week at both of their three thousand-seat theaters for almost entirely female audiences. . . . Most adults laugh indulgently at the packs of teenage girls waiting breathlessly at the stage door for the moment when they can see, take photographs of, beg autographs from, given presents to, and maybe even touch their favorite male impersonator. (1987:34–35)

She did not report on the sexual orientation of *otokoi yaku*, or any other aspect of their offstage life, or on those of their admirers. Jennifer Robertson (1992a, 1992b, 1998), stressed that those playing male roles (*otoko yaku*) are not supposed to live their cross-gender role offstage (as Ayame yaku insisted for the classic kabuki *onnagata*). In contrast to the Takarazuka management's attempts to desexualize *otokoyaku*, her

> archival research and interviews suggest that on the contrary, female fans of all ages, classes, and educational levels do not see a man on stage, but rather *acknowledge* a female body performing in a capacity that transgresses the boundaries of received femininity. The *otokoyaku*, in short, is appreciated as an exemplary female who can successfully negotiate both genders and their attendant roles, without being constrained by either. . . . The characterization of their appearance as "androgynous" is necessarily premised on a priori knowledge of the underlying *female*

body—knowledge that nullifies or compromises the "male" gender of the surface. (1992a:433, 435)

Between the world wars, the Takarazuka Revue was seen as at once a symptom and encouragement of *hentai seiyoku* (abnormal sexual desire), but Cherry and Robertson have been too fascinated by gender to deign to address vulgar questions of the offstage sexual behavior of those who take *otokoyaku* roles.[31] Whether they are models for a lesbian subculture in which they do not participate or are involved in more than platonic loves with women is a question they do not ask.

Without lexical recognition of a Way of female-female love (such as the path for men who love boys, *nanshoku,* or application to women who love women of *oshoku,* the term for men who love women), heterogender homosexuality (*ome no kankei*) is common: "Life in the closet usually includes masculine and feminine role playing, except among feminists who strive to overcome gender stereotypes. The Japanese "femme" is called *neko* (cat) or *nenne* (ingenue). The "butch" is *otachi,* from the Kabuki term for leading actor (*tachiyaku*). Japanese lesbians lack a verb for coming out of the closet, though a few, modifying the English phrase, do say *kamu auto suru*" (Cherry 1987:35).

> Takarasiennes and their fans also have used the kinship terms *aniki* [older brother] and *imoto* [younger sister], as well as the stage terms *otokoyaku* and *musumeyaku* [one playing female roles on stage] to denote the parties of a "butch-femme" couple. *Tachi,* written in the *katakana* syllabary with the likely meaning of "one who wields the 'sword,'" is another term for the "butch" woman. The corresponding term for the "femme" woman is *neko,* literally "cat" but also a historical nickname for unlicensed geisha. . . . Tachi may also be an abbreviated reference to tachiyakyu, the theatrical term for "leading man."

> The leading *otokoyaku* and *musumeyaku* of each troupe are paired as a "golden combination" (*goruden konbi*) for the duration of their careers. This dyadic structure alludes to the monogamy and fidelity underlying the idealized heterosexual relations promoted by the state since the Meiji period. In addition, the "butch" has been called *garçon* and *onabe* (literally, a shallow pot), a term coined (probably in the early 1900s) as the "gender" opposite of *okama* (pot), the term for a male homosexual. The

---

31. "For female fans, especially, the Takarazuka otokoyaku represents an exemplary female who can successfully negotiate both genders, and their attendant roles and domains, without (theoretically) being constrained by either" (J. Robertson 1992b:184).

term "lesbian" (*rezubian*), although used since the early 1900s, was not adopted by women to name a politicized female identity—as opposed to sexual practices per se—until the 1970s. (Robertson 1992b:175–76)

The age-differentiated "S" relationships discussed above on p. 210 were strongly gendered as well as having age-differentiated roles,[32] and, as discussed below (see p. 407), "modern lesbian" homosexuality has emerged to some extent in Japan alongside traditional, highly gendered forms.

A Stray Report from Taiwan

Hinsch (1990:177) noted a 1988 news report about a gang of about thirty school-aged girls who wore male clothes and called themselves the "H" (for "homo") gang. Allegedly, the leader coerced sex from other young women.

Thailand

Eric Allyn (1991:229) attested a number of Thai terms for females who desire females: "Though the English word 'Lesbian' is borrowed into the Thai language, Thai Lesbians are offended by the term. Instead, they use *tam-dee*. . . . *Tam* (Tom) is equivalent of the 'butch' or 'masculine' role; *dee* refers to the one who is 'fem.' *Tam* comes from the English word 'Tom-boy' and *dee* from 'Lady.' A vulgar term for Lesbians and for Lesbian sex is *dhee-chìng* (hit cymbals). A formal term is *yïng' rák' rüampēd. Gan lēn pēuan* (playing friends) is often used to refer to Lesbians or Lesbianism."

Thongthiraj (1994:47) reported that the (gender-conforming) *dees* have to come on to the (gender-nonconforming) *tams*, because only the latter are recognizably available. Butches waiting for femmes to take the initiative is not how the system worked in pre-liberation North America, so perhaps this can be considered a modern solution to the invisibility of potential partners. She speculated that female gender nonconformity may be more accepted in rural Thailand than in the capital, where women must wear dresses to hold jobs (48) and decried modern compulsive heterosociality (55–56).

32. J. Robertson (1992b:175–76, 1998:68) and Pfugfelder (1990) wrote about "class S" (*kurasu esu*), still conjuring an age-stratified couple of schoolgirls, and *demae bento* (take-out lunchbox), which seems to me a metaphor for an open secret, that is, everyone assumes they know what is inside the box, but it is not visible. Robertson, however, focuses on distinguishing rice (*gohan*) from "dishes eaten with the rice" (*okazu*) for butches and femmes.

In writing about *Pu-Mias* (men-women), former British consul at Chiang Mai William Wood (1935:112) wrote that

> female *Pu-Mias*, who dress and behave as men, are not so common as the male kind. I have only met one of them. She lived at Lampang, and was a dependent of the hereditary Prince of that province. She invariably wore male costume, and did all sorts of heavy work in the Prince's palace, utterly despising every sort of feminine accomplishment. Like "Colonel" Barker, whose case attracted so much attention in England a few years ago [after World War I], this *Pu-Mia* decided to marry, and asked the Prince for the hand of one of his female servants. The pair were duly wedded, and the "husband" worked hard to support the wife, and was said to be very jealous of any attentions that were paid to her. Finally she out-Barkered Barker by becoming the proud "father" of a fine baby boy. (1935:112)

Rosalind Morris (1994:29) also called attention to glimpses of "Amazon" women dressed as men in late-nineteenth-century Western accounts of Thai kings' courts. In regard to northern Thai opera of the 1920s, Chandruang (1940:87–88) mentioned another possible locale: "All the players were women, and some of the female spectators would fall in love with the women who portrayed the leading man." Whether any did anything about such love he did not mention—and probably did not know, since he was recalling preteen experiences.

Wijeyewardene (1986:159) noted that in contemporary northern Thailand, most female spirit mediums are possessed by male spirits, often of princely or warrior rank. The mediums' "costumes create the impression of an intermediate sexless category, rather than transforming females into males" and added, "As a significant minority of female mediums appear to live without the company of men, the question must arise as to the incidence of lesbianism. There is occasional gossip, but no firm information is available."

Sub-Saharan African Peoples

Although I would not wish to deny that there are women-identified women in "traditional" black Africa, nor that age-stratified relationships may be maternal (as in the mummy-baby idiom Gay reported (discussed above; see pp. 210–11), the major African idiom of homosexuality for both men and women is gender. Where there are age disparities, the younger is generally cast in the feminine role. This is true for "boy-wives" and male "wives of the mine," for Lesotho "babies," and for the wives of women from Benin to Kenya (i.e., from the Atlantic to the Indian Ocean coasts).

Mombasa, Kenya

In arguing against a third sex or gender conception in Oman or Mombasa, Shepherd (1978a:133) wrote that "Lesbians [in Mombasa] are known as *wasaga* (grinders) and that "the dominant partner . . . is not seen as a man." She had earlier claimed, on the basis of an unspecified sample of *wasaga* (134), that "there is almost always a dominant and subordinate economic relationship between them." Shepherd (1978:254) elaborated, "The word in Swahili glossed as 'lesbian' is *msagaji* (plural *wasagaji*)—'a grinder.' The verb *kusaga* (to grind) is commonly used for the grinding of grain between two millstones. . . . The upper and lower millstones are known as *mwana* and *mama* respectively: child and mother" (1987). Perhaps Swahili is unlike English in spatializing hierarchy in terms of top and bottom (cf. Lakoff and Johnson 1980) since the bottom millstone is the predominant role, but there is something of the *mama* and her dependent *mwana* to lesbian relationships in Mombasa, even though these are not distinct lexemes for the roles paralleling *basha/shoga* for male homosexual pairs. Clear status distinctions characterize *msagaji* relationships, with the dominant woman usually being older as well as wealthier. Whether these distinctions affect sexual behavior inside the relationship, Shepherd did not report.

Against any interpretation of a third-gender role, Shepherd (1987: 259–60) argued, "Lesbians dress entirely as women. Their wealth enables them to dress in a rich and feminine way, and though dominant lesbians are more assertive in manner and conversation than most other women, they make no attempt to look like men. When they go out they wear the veil (*buibui*) like all other coastal women . . . Dependent lesbian women are expected to behave like ordinary women. Dominant lesbian women display energetic personalities very similar to those of active, intelligent non-lesbian women." However, she also reported, "Women who are dominant lesbians do not obey strict seclusion rules. As household heads they welcome male visitors to the house and sit with them in the reception room, and they frequently go out of the house" (260). Her analyses of homosexuality among women, as among men, are contradicted by the behavior she reported.[33] *Msagaji* seem to be

33. Strobel (1979:166) was not clear about sexual aspects of the Mombasa Muslim women's dance, *lelemama,* that she discussed. On women using dildoes on other women in Zanzibar, see the translation of Haberlandt (1899) in Murray and Roscoe 1998:63–66.

bidding for some male privilege beyond that of having sex with submissive women. That is, they do not (entirely) conform to Mombasa conceptions of how women should look and act.

As for the *shoga*, Porter (1996:144) stressed gender variance as more salient than sexual behavior for labeling women *misago:* especially women resisting marriage and interested in education and careers are labeled "*misago* regardless of the erotic preferences of the women. They are being condemned for behaving in ways that are inconsistent with being a woman and for challenging the gender/status system." The word *misago* itself is derived from the same verb root as *msagaliwa: kusaga*, a Bantu word meaning "to grind." It refers to the sexual activities of women, rather than to grinding aromatic wood (142). The etymological primacy of sexuality does not prove that sexuality is more important than gender in the use or native understanding of the word, but more systematic data collection than either Shepherd's or Porter's would be necessary to settle the question of primacy of gender or sexuality. The prototype *misago* differs from "normal" women in both gender patterning and sexual partnering.

West Africa

In contrast to gender, which is marked by terms meaning "husband" and "wife," the sexual component of the role is controversial in the literature on female-female marriage in Africa. Carrier and Murray (1998) attempted to sort out this literature, which is too equivocal to consider here.

Gaudio (1996:136n. 17) noted that there are Hausa lesbians (in Kano of the 1990s), some of whom know of and use the terms for male homosexual roles, and that gay Hausa males assert that "lesbians engage in the same types of relationships as they themselves do, i.e., involving the exchange of material gifts and the attribution of [dominant/submissive] roles."

"Amazon" Troops in Nineteenth-Century Dahomey

In his two-volume account of his 1863–64 mission there, Richard Burton devoted a chapter to "the so-called Amazon" troops of King Gelele. In his view, "the origin of the somewhat exceptional organisation" of the women troops that he estimated to number about twenty-five hundred was "the masculine physique of the women, enabling them to compete with men in enduring toil, hardship and privations" (64), although he also offered a historical explanation—the early eighteenth-century king Agaja's depleted ranks of male soldiers (65). Noting that Dahomeyan women "endured all the toil and performed all the hard labour" there was to do, Ellis (1965 [1890]:183) elaborated on the historical evolution of the Amazon institution:

> The female corps, to use the common expression, the Amazons, was raised about the year 1729, when a body of women who had been armed and furnished with banners, merely as a stratagem to make the attacking forces appear larger, behaved with such unexpected gallantry as to lead to a permanent corps of women being embodied [by King Trudo]. . . . [Gezo, who attained power in 1801] . . . directed every head of a family to send his daughters to Agbomi for inspection; the most suitable were enlisted, and the corps thus placed on a new footing. This course was also followed by Gelele, his successor, who had every girl brought to him before marriage, and enrolled those who pleased him. (1864, 2:63–85)

Ellis reported nothing and Burton next to nothing about the sexuality of these "Amazons." They were distinguished from the king's (also numerous) wives (Burton:64). "Two-thirds are said to be maidens" (68). In his "Terminal Essay" to his translation of the *Arabian Nights,* Burton (1930 [1886]:88) wrote "At Agbome, capital of Dahome, I found that a troop of women was kept for the use of the 'Amazons,'" citing page 73 of the second volume of Burton (1864), but there is nothing there about women reserved for the Amazon troops. There is only an expression of his belief that passion for combat excites rather than substitutes for love: "All the passions are sisters. I believe that bloodshed causes these women to remember, not to forget LOVE."

Commander Frederick Forbes's journals (1:23–24) of his 1849–50 missions to King Gezo of Dahomey did not deal with sexual behavior of the "Amazon" troops, but he was even clearer than Burton about hypermasculine gender identification:

> The amazons are not supposed to marry, and, by their own statement, they have changed their sex. "We are men," say they, "not women." All dress alike, diet alike, and male and female emulate each other: what the males do, the amazons will endeavour to surpass. They all take great care of their arms, polish the barrels, and, except when on duty, keep them in covers. There is no duty at the palace except when the king is in public, then a guard of amazons protect the royal person, and, on review, he is guarded by the males. . . . The amazons are in barracks within the palace

Figure 8. Dahomey king.

enclosure, and under the care of eunuchs and the camboodee or treasurer. (1:23–24)[34]

Indeed, in a 13 July 1850 parade, amazon troops sang about the effeminacy of male soldiers they had defeated:

We marched against Attahpahms as against men,
We came and found them women.
What we catch in the bush we never divide.
(2:108)

After a parade of 2,400 amazons pledging to conquer Abeahkeutah (a British ally in Sierra Leone) or to die trying, an amazon chief began her speech by asserting gender transformation: "As the blacksmith takes an iron bar and by fire changes its fashion, so we have changed our nature. We are no longer women, we are men" (2:119). Whether they took women as men did is not recorded.

Central Africa

Gustave Hulstaert (1938:95–96) wrote the following about relationships between Nkundó women (in what was then the Belgian Congo): "Nkundó girls play at 'husband and wife' and even adult married women engage in this vice. According to my informants, the causes are as follows: first, an intense and very intimate love between two women, second and above all, the fact that wives of polygamists find it difficult to satisfy their passions in a natural way. Often they engage in this practice with co-wives of the same man." He further noted that "in establishments where girls are too securely kept away from the opposite sex, there has been an increase" in sexual relationships between girls. The latter often engage in sex with co-wives. A woman who presses against another woman is called *yaikya bonsángo*" (96).

La Fontaine (1959:34, 60–61) mentioned a Gisu (Ugandan) woman living as a man, but did not specify the sex of this person's sexual partners (if there were any).

Southern Africa

Ngonga, Hambly's (1937:426; 1934a:181) main Ovimbundu (an Angolan people) informant, told him, "There are men who want men, and

---

34. Forbes (1:77–79, 2:59–60, 106–21, 123–24, 168, 226–27) described parades of bellicose amazon troops, the parallel ranks in male and female troops, and competition for greater glory between them.

women who want women. . . . A woman has been known to make an artificial penis for use with another woman." Such practices did not meet with approval, but neither did transvestitic homosexuals of either sex desist (cf. Estermann 1976:197).

Colson (1958:139–40) mentioned a possible man-woman and a possible woman-man among the Tsonga of what is now Zimbabwe. From her research on Nyakyusa age-villages, Monica Wilson (1951:88) reported that "lesbian practices are said to exist, but we have no certain evidence of this." She went on to speculate that they were "much more likely to be among the older wives of chiefs and other polygynists than among the girls, who have so much attention from young men." This pattern was her logic; it did not come from a Nyakyusa report. She noted that "a case was also quoted of a doctor in Tukuyu who 'is a woman; she has borne children, now her body has grown the sexual organs of a man and her feelings have changed also; but she keeps it very secret, she is spoken of as a woman'" (197). She did not note to what, if any, use the new male organs were put.

In most of the instances discussed in this chapter, it is not clear whether those born female who did not want to live as women were considered by those around them as masculine women, as failed (because not procreative) women, as men who had been born female, or as a distinct sex. What was most often rejected by those I'll call "butches" was domestic labor. They wanted wives to do that while they did "men's work" or, in some instances, hung out with males in formal and informal male societies. In many instances, including the chapters on Iraqui and Balkan female-born gender rebels in *Islamic Homosexualities* (Dickemann 1997, Westphall-Hellbusch 1997) and on female husbands in Africa (Carrier and Murray 1998), it is unclear whether mounting and penetrating females was one of the male prerogatives of those rejecting female roles. Not having sexual relations with males was central to the Balkan sworn-virgin role, but not to that of all African female husbands. The sexual receptivity of "femmes" extends to penetration by males, while in some instances (wives of African female husbands, Takaruza) it is not clear that it extended to physical intimacy with a natally female partner. In others, including most of those discussed in this chapter (Chukchi transformed shamans; Lucan's Megilla; Benedetta Carlini; and tribades in early modern Europe, lesbians in contemporary Thailand, Indonesia, Europe, and the United States), it did.

6

Male Receptacles for Phallic Discharges

Ancient Greek and Hellenistic Pathics

Ancient Greek males took involvement in pederasty for granted. Winkler (1990:65) wrote that there was also "a certain idea of male sexual deviance was strongly articulated but only very selectively enforced." The *kinaidos* was "a man socially deviant in his entire being, principally observable in behavior that flagrantly violated or contravened the dominant social definition of masculinity," adding that the three components of the accusation of being a *kinaidos* were "promiscuity, payment [prostitution], and passivity to another man's penetration" (45–46).

Diverging from Foucault (and his followers), Winkler clearly stated that the *kinaidos* was a kind of person, not "just an ordinary guy who now and then decided to commit a kinaidic act"; (45) "Aiskhines mentions a group of men who, in contrast to the chaste and honorable [*erastes* and *eromenos* engaged in intercrural intercourse when not engaged in other forms of pedagogy] lovers known to the city at large, are notorious for 'sinning against their own bodies.'" The *kinaidos* was also "one of the "natures" that can be detected in the Aristotelian *Physiognomonics*.[1]

Similarly, Gleason (1990:411) concluded her review of Hellenistic and Roman physiognomy by stressing that "the notion that a person's character, including his sexual temperament, is written all over his face and body is actually an ancient one. Indeed, Foucault's description of the purportedly new nineteenth-century homosexual species fits the *kinaidos* remarkably well."[2]

Multiple terms for a gender-defined homosexual role existed in ancient Greece:

> There is a broad and colourful range of terms used to denote passive homosexuals in Aristophanes. One of the most frequent terms was *europrōktoi*—people whose hinder parts (*prōktoi*) had

---

1. Winkler (1990:63, 67). Halperin (1996:722) also eventually acknowledged that *kinaidos* is not only a kind of person but an ancient "identity."

2. Foucault and his followers (especially Halperin 1998) have obscured that the "modern homosexual" allegedly constructed ex nihilo during the late nineteenth century was a gender-variant "intermediate type," not the late-twentieth-century gay man. Trumbach's "modern homosexual," a century and a half older than Foucault's, was markedly effeminate.

been enlarged through excessive use. . . . As well as words deriving from *prōktos*, there are words from *pygē*, the hindquarters.
First and foremost is *katapygōn*, which is very frequent and often
used to contrast the homosexual with a respectable, reliable and
proper person. . . . To add extra effectiveness to the reference, it
was quite common practice to add a dash of colour. To have a
pallid complexion was considered a sign of effeminacy. And so
the homosexuals became *leukopygoi*, "white arses", obviously in
contrast with the *melanpygoi*, the "black arses"—or with the
dasuprōktoi, "rough arses." (Cantarella 1992:47) [3]

Aristophanes also used the more explicit *chaunoproktos* (glossed by Keuls:
1993:291 as "with gaping asshole"), and *katapygon*—"broad assed," one
whose buttocks had been widened by being penetrated—is preserved in
Attic inscriptions long before Aristophanes deployed it. In *Clouds* (1094–
1104) Wrong forces Right to admit that tragic poets, politicians, and
most of the play's audience are *euryproktos* (wide assed). In contrast,
there does not seem to have been a term for one who regularly (or pref-
erentially) "aphrodited" an adult male.

Winkler (1990), Halperin (1990), and Boswell (1990:154–55) all
contended that adult male sexual receptivity, and male prostitution,
were not negatively sanctioned, so long as one who had been so used did
not attempt to hold public office or participate in citizen assemblies or
enter *gymnasia*.[4] That some men opt out of masculine competitiveness is
a view that recurs in many cultures. To become an honorable man is a
difficult achievement, not at all an automatic consequence of being born
male. Those who won't or can't make it as men are cast down to female
society, where male pretensions are not taken so seriously.

Accepting as inevitable that some will fail to attain masculinity and
honor is not what I would label "tolerance." Instrumental use, contempt,
and violence (sexual and other) are the lot of effeminate men (cross
dressed or not) in cultures influenced by the classic Mediterranean code

3. Henderson (1991:209–20) reviewed the derogatory pathic labels and their application to forty-nine characters in Aristophanes's popular comedies. On stage, "comic effeminates were dressed in an odd combination of male and female clothing," he noted (219),
"carried objects identified with women, wore their hair long and often curled, depilated
their bodies, especially around their anus, shaved, stayed out of the sun, and were believed
to be indiscriminately available to any male" (220).

4. On the banning of *hetaireukotes* (male prostitutes) from gymnasia and temples in
Athens and Beroea (in Macedonia), see Demosthenes *Against Androtion* 30, 73; Cantarella
1992:28–29. Aiskhines's prosecution oration *Against Timarkhos* (12) appeals to regulation
purportedly instituted by Solon (who was the first Athenian of whom we know who
praised pederasty, encouraging, but not compelling it; see Percy 1996:177).

of male honor (including Latin America). "Selective enforcement of manhood rules" only against serious contenders "is not the same as a laissez-faire attitude," as Winkler (1990:66) wisely noted. Especially where sexual behavior by females may discredit the family's honor, fuckable males (a category including slaves as well as prostitutes in ancient Greece and Rome) are useful. They just don't count for anything of value in male calculus.

Winkler (67ff.) showed that pleasure from being anally penetrated was conceived. Indeed, for some males, the pleasures of being sexually penetrated were considered natural. No more did being sexually penetrated constitute evidence of moral weakness (lack of self-control) for a man than it did for a woman, according to Aristotle in the *Nicomachean Ethics* (1148b).[5] The (much later) pseudo-Aristotle of the *Problemata Physica* noticed and attempted to explain (by varying locations of seminal fluid and by postpubescent habituation) "why some men enjoy being penetrated (*aphrodīsiazesthia*), some of whom also (enjoying) penetrating (*aphrodīsiazein*), while others do not" (4.26). The usual reason was "nature," specifically accumulation of seminal fluid in the rectum giving rise to "an urge in a place other than that of procreative ejaculation,"[6] though early habituation also can make the habit "increasingly like nature" (quoted from the translation by Dover:1978:169–70). Another explanation in terms of nature—at the time of conception—was offered by the greatest of the pre-Socratic philosophers, Parmenides (frag. 18) in the late sixth century B.C.[7]

In Hellenistic times, especially in the new cities Alexander and his successors founded in north Africa and Asia, but also back in Greek (especially Ionian) cities, effeminates and eunuchs (including slaves and prostitutes) became popular. The masculinity of future warriors became a less important part of the erotic appeal of the young.[8] This effeminization of the beloved—and recognition that some males found being

5. The passage was quoted above; see p. 111n. 25.

6. The author believed "the liquid [there] is small in volume, does not force its way out, and quickly cools down," so that males with semen in the wrong place are (by nature) "insatiable, like women" (quoted from Dover 1978:70).

7. The cause of gender was the testicle from which the seed came and the side of the uterus to which it went. Some masculine females and feminine males were conceived by the seed crossing to the other side. This explanation was cited with approval by Caelius Aurelianus's fifth-century A.D. Latin translation of the first- or second-century A.D. treatise of Soranos of Ephesus. On Parmenides's model of the origins of gender not matching sex (i.e., genitals), see Tarán (1985:264–66).

8. Despite (or because?) of exposure to eastern neighbors with male prostitutes in or around temples, the classical Greeks "failed to build large-scale temples with permanent

anally penetrated pleasant and even arousing—preceded annexation by Rome.[9]

Both Hellenistic astrology and medicine provided explanations for effeminate, sexually receptive men (*malthacoe* is the Greek term that Caelius Aurelianus used) whose nature was determined at conception. Late Latin translations of systematic Greek etiological treatises are discussed in the next section.

Roman Effeminates

A preoccupation with male sexual receptivity both of effeminate and of apparently masculine men is evident in surviving Roman orations (Cicero's in particular), poetry (especially Juvenal and Martial, with a special obsession about irrumation on the part of Catullus), gossip (Suetonius, *Historia Augusta*), history (Tacitus, Livy, Dio Cassius), the one surviving novel (Petronius's *Satyricon*), and in the non-elite graffiti excavated at Pompeii.[10] At least some Romans clearly noticed gender-variant homosexual characters. Indeed, for ancient Romans and Athenians, character explained everything. Not just recent adult conduct, but earlier conduct as an adolescent, was central to elucidating (or to smearing) adults' public character (Long 1996: 107; on some classic examples see 70–77).

Although the document is late (ca. 334 A.D.), Firmicus Maternus's *Matheseos* is the final and most complete compendium of ancient Greek and Roman astrological theory. In it, particular locations of the planet Venus at the time of birth of make effeminates, hermaphrodites, eunuchs, those impelled to amputate their genitals with their own hands, male prostitutes, and "lovers of boys who pay for this vice with use of their own bodies" (6.30.4–5, 18, 40, 6.31.4–5, 7; Bram 1975:207–9, 210–11, 214).

Similarly, Caelius Aurelianus's fifth-century Latin translation of the

staffs and remained alien to the idea of male temple prostitutes," as Percy (1996:47) noted. When the then-known world was conquered by the Macedonians (and, subsequently, by the Romans), this ethnic marker was smudged, especially in Anatolia (see p. 299 below).

9. The large, apparently erect penis of the male being penetrated (by a similarly beardless male) on a gem from Pergamon (an early ally of Rome on the west coast of Anatolia) that is now in the Royal Coin Cabinet, Leiden (reproduced in J. Clarke 1998:39) is especially striking. The man on the bottom is not only responding, but is turning to meet the gaze of the man atop him.

10. Also the graffiti in what J. Clarke (1991) calls a "gay hotel" at Rome's seaport, Ostia, featuring a central painting of Jupiter chin-chucking Ganymede.

treatise of Soranos (from the time of Trajan or Hadrian) includes a section (chap. 9 of the book on chronic diseases) about male pathics (*molles;* the chapter title Greek *malthakoi*). The text refers to "Parmenides in his work *On Nature* [frag. 18] indicat[ing] that effeminate men [*molles*] or pathics [*subactos homines*] come into being as a result of circumstances at conception" and "many leaders of other sects hold[ing] that the condition is an inherited disease, that is to say, is passed on from generation to generation by way of the seed" (trans. Drabkin 1950:903, 905). In this view, either the mixture of male and female seeds (*germina*) or the content of the impregnating semen produces males who seek penetration (and who cannot be satisfied by it, so that their lusts increase with age and the waning of such virile power as they have).

Thus, there were two bodies of theoretical knowledge about nature that accounted for such destinies and enduring characters of same-sex lust (not just happenstance acts of sodomy). Both attributed the phenomenon to the point of conception, not to any post-natal (or even post-conception) causes. Below, I shall discuss some of the recognized Roman types, that is, some of the social roles occupied by such persons. (Those seized by "sacred frenzy" to sacrifice their genitals to the Great Mother—a particularly un-Roman action regarded by traditionalist Romans as horrifyingly "Oriental"—will be discussed on pp. 298–300.)

Depilati

An urban fashion of male depilation still shocked some rural visitors in the mid-first century A.D., as in Persius's (4.33ff.) account of being denounced by a stranger who happened upon him naked, so that the careful plucking out of hair on and between his buttocks was visible. Male prostitutes plucking out or shaving off body hair became increasingly common in imperial Rome, though it was denounced by Stoics as "effeminacy," (i.e., the elder Seneca 1.10, Epictetus 3.1.28ff, the younger Seneca, *Naturales quaestiones* 7.31.2; *Epistles* 47, 122, Marital 2.62, 39; Juvenal 2.11–13). In Middle Comedy, "effeminate men who pluck or shave themselves in order to do things that are only fit for beardless boys, i.e., in order to retain their sexually passive role" were mentioned (Lilja 1982:36, in specific reference to Alexis frag. 264).

The legendarily profligate emperor Elagabulus[11] was accused of going to the women's public bath and there using their depilatory ointments on

---

11. Originally named Varius Avitus, Elagabulus reigned from 218 to 222 A.D. (when he was fourteen to eighteen years old) under the name Marcus Aurelius Antoninus.

his beard—the same beard he is supposed to have shaved with the razor with which he shaved the pubic regions of pretty boys (*Historia Augusta* 32.7), and of addressing an assemblage of female prostitutes in female dress that did not cover his genitals (36.5). These reports come from the tales of excess that follow his biography (the first eighteen sections, based on the no-longer-extant accounts of Marius Maximus) in which Elagabulus is portrayed as frequenting public male baths (including one he made in the imperial palace) in search of men with large members (*onobeli;* i.e., those "hung like donkeys") who seemed especially virile (8.7).

The allegedly (more) historical part of the *Historia Augusta* also has an entirely depilated Elagabulus playing the part of Venus, dropping his clothing, offering his buttocks to whomever was playing the complementary role of Paris, and generally seeking to raise the libido of the greatest multitude (5.4–5); receiving lust in every orifice (5.2);[12] joining frenzied worship of the Great Mother (*Mater Deum Magna Idaea*) with castrated *galli* (7.2);[13] taking as his husband an athlete from Smyrna named Aurelius Zoticus in a(n immediately consummated) nuptial ceremony (10.2–6); either fellating or rimming the freed-slave Hierocles (5.5),[14] and assembling courtiers who put their hair in nets and boasted of their husbands (11, 7). Oddly, only the last of these accusations was accompanied with a skeptical grain of salt: "Some say that they pretended this so as to gain increased favour with him by imitating his vices" (trans. Birley 1976:299). If there is a "Depraved, Luxury-Loving Queen" archetype (along with that of "Shameless Exhibitionist"), the characterization of Elagabulus in the *Historia Augusta* approximates it, whatever relation there is between it and actual behavior.

The more conventional historical chronicle, by someone who lived through Elagabulus's reign, does not imagine so outlandish a taste for luxuries, but, if anything, portrays an emperor more voracious for large male members than the later author of his biography in the *Historia Augusta*. The somewhat less-tabloid historian Dio Cassius (79.13) attributed Elagabalus's marriages and other sexual liaisons with women to his

12. "Cuncta cava corporis libidinem recipientem."
13. He tied up his genitals when consorting with the *galli,* rather than removing them. Similarly, rather than spilling his own blood (especially from severing his genitals), his initiation was a *taurobolium* in which a bull's blood was poured over the initiate (7.1; Birley 1976:295n. 11).
14. Anus seems more likely than penis in "Inguina oscularetur quod dicum etiam inverecundum est."

wanting to learn to imitate them when playing the receptive role with men. Dio continued,

> He used his body for doing and allowing many unheard of things which no one would endure telling or hearing, but his most conspicuous acts, which it would be impossible to conceal, were the following. He would go by night, wearing a wig of long hair, into the taverns and ply the trade of a female huckster. He frequented the notorious brothels, drove out the prostitutes, and prostituted himself. Finally, he set aside a room in the palace and there committed his indecencies, standing all the time naked at the door of it, as the harlots do, and shaking the curtain, which was fastened with gold rings, the while in a soft and melting voice he solicited the passers-by. Certain persons had been given special orders to let themselves be attracted to his abode. For, as in other matters, so in this business, too, he had numerous detectives through whom he sought out the persons who could please him most by their foulness. . . . He worked in wool [woman's work], sometimes wore a hair-net, painted his eyes, and once shaved his chin and celebrated a festival to mark the event. After that he went with smooth face, because it would help him appear like a woman. (trans. Foster 1906:95–96)

Dio told of a blond, beardless charioteer (slave), Hierocles, whose "nocturnal feats" captivated the emperor to such an extent that Elagabulus took Hierocles as his husband. Dio also mentioned Zoticus, who had a beautiful body and who "surpassed everyone in the size of his private parts. The fact was reported to the emperor by those who were on the lookout for such features and the man was suddenly snatched away from the [gymnastic] games and taken to Rome," where the emperor immediately bathed with his guest, and was able to verify the reports of Zoticus's endowment. Worried that he would be displaced, Hierocles had drugs added to Zoticus's wine that made him impotent. After a night of frustration, Zoticus was banished (98).

Earlier emperors (including the first two) reputedly had been penetrated when young, and Elagabulus did not live beyond his teens. Octavius and Otho attempted to hold back the signs of age (hair on legs and on the chin, respectively), according to Suetonius, and Aelius Lampridius wrote of the Emperor Commodus that "every part of his body, even his mouth, was polluted by intercourse."[15]

---

15. "Omni parte corporis atque ore in sexum utrumque pollutus" (*Comm. Ant.* 5.2–3).

Gleason (1990:405) argued that depilation and other "dainty grooming" derided as effeminate aimed to preserve or simulate the prized
beauty of smooth-chinned and smooth-bodied ephebes into adult life for
diverse appreciative audiences: "Women, boys, and at least some men
found the result attractive." Although there is no first-person testimony
on the experiences or motivations of those who adopted "the smooth
style," it is certain that "some men aspired to the sort of chic that might
attend the successful 'carrying off' of elegant grooming habits that invited accusations of effeminacy" (406). Indeed, trying to please women
(and boys) instead of simply taking them was suspectly effeminate and
un-Roman.[16]

Effeminati and *Cinaedi*

Effeminati were denounced in Republican times by Seneca the Elder
for "taking others' chastity by storm, and being heedless of their own."
He regarded them as "born feeble," but also expressed his repugnance
for men braiding their hair, refining their voices, and competing in bodily softness and fine dress with women. He was particularly disturbed
that these voluptuaries had become a model for fashionable Roman
youths, not just for those born to be effeminate (*Controversiae* 1, preface,
8). He complained that fashionable effeminacy extended from ridiculing
masculinity to removing male genitals (*Naturales Quaestiones* 7.31.3; also
see Martial 9.8, Statius, *Silvae* 2.6.38–41). The younger Seneca described
as "contrary to nature" males who appeared in effeminate dress.[17]

Cinaedus originally meant "dancer" (Kroll 1921; Lilja 1982:26; Richlin 1993:530, 549; Henderson 1975:219–20) and was used in this sense
in Plautus's *Miles gloriosus* (668), *Persa* (804) and *Stichus* (754ff.), but in
reference to effeminate dress in *Menaechmi* (145ff.,511f.) and *Pseudolus*
(1317f.) and to sexual receptivity in *Asinaria* (627f.) and *Aulularia* (422).
Along with *fellator, cinaedus* was a popular slur in Pompeiian graffiti (the

16. See Gleason (1995:65). However, conventionally masculine husbands' contemptuous interpretation of the lack of virility of males overly concerned with grooming may
have made easier the latter's sexual access to women. That is, instead of advertising their
availability to sexual penetration by hirsute men, some were slipping into the company of
women for sexual purposes under the camouflage of deficient virility (as some men in
Africa and Brazil suspect of effeminate men who spend much time in female company).

17. "Non videntur tibi contra naturam vivere qui commutant cum feminis vestem?
Non vivunt contra naturam qui spectant, ut pueritia splendeat tempore alieno?" (Epistle
122, 7: "Do you not think that men are living contrary to nature when they adopt feminine clothes? Do not men live contrary to nature who try to pass for [look like] boys when
they are too old [to be sex objects]?")

main corpus of non-elite representations of sexuality from ancient Rome), more popular than *pathicus* ("passive"), according to Lilja (1982: 98). In the furious invective in his second satire against hypocritical moralists who covertly welcome sexual penetration, Juvenal acknowledges that effeminacy is the fate of some unfortunate men.[18]

In late Republican and early imperial times, there were many other terms for effeminate or sexually receptive males, including *concubinus* (male concubine), *exoletus* (male prostitute; see p. 114n. above), *pullus* ("chick"), *scortum* ("notorious male prostitute"), *spintria* ("sphincter"), *delicatus* ("delicate"), *discintus* ("loose-belted") and even more explicitly condemnatory labels such as *impurus* ("impure"), *impudicus* ("unchaste"), and *morbosus* ("sick").

Clearly, before significant Christian influence, there was a conception of a kind of intact male who was effeminate and sought to be penetrated.[19] There were also males whose testes had been removed. Here I shall discuss those without religious motives/rationales. (See pp. 298–302 for a discussion of the religiosi).

Eunuchs

Lucan called the title character of *The Eunuch*[20] "neither man nor woman" (47.6), while Philostratus referred to Favorinus of Arles (a favorite of the emperor Hadrian) as "two-natured" (8.489) and the biography of Severus Alexander in the *Historia Augusta* (22.7) refers to eunuchs as a third kind of person (*tertium genis hominum eunochos*). Charicles, the antagonist of boy-love in the pseudo-Lucian debate (from about 300 A.D.) about which form of love is best, expressed typically Greek horror at castration: "The daring of some men has advanced so far in tyrannical violence as even to wreak sacrilege upon nature with the knife. By depriving males of their masculinity they have found wider range of pleasure. But those who become wretched and luckless in

18. For example, Peribomius: "hunc ego fatis inputo, qui vultu morbum incessuque fateur; horum simplicitas miserabilis, his furor ipse dat veniam" (2.16–18) translated in the Loeb edition as "I charge Destiny with his failings. Such men excite your pity by their frankness; the very fury of their passions wins them pardon."

19. In *Priapea* (51 and 64) Priapus realizes that some males trespass on his garden in hopes of being caught and anally raped: coming "here to steal, because he wants to feel the punishment he knows applies" and "it seems the treatment rude is what attracts them" (trans. W. H. Parker).

20. The word "eunuch," from Greek *eunen echein*, meaning to have charge of guarding women's sleeping quarters, and thereby ensuring that the paternity of any children conceived was the eunuch's master's.

order to be boys for longer remain male no longer, being a perplexing riddle of dual gender, neither having kept for the functions to which they have been born nor yet having the thing into which they have been changed" (*Erotes* 21, trans. M. D. Macleod). Stevenson (1995) discussed the distinction made in Justinian's *Digest* (the official concerns were with adoption and inheritance of those without seed or those whose testes were pressed [*thilbae*], crushed [*thaladiae*], or severed [*castrati*], the *spandonii*.)[21]

As discussed above (see pp. 127–28), developing latent masculinity in the attractive male youths they used sexually was not a concern of Romans. If they did not "debase" Greek pederasty, the Romans certainly disenchanted it of any pedagogical goals and rationales. A particularly notorious example is that of the ardently Hellenophile emperor Nero,[22] who "caused a youth, Sporus to be castrated, then 'married' him in public and declared the boy to be his 'Empress.' This shows how wide of the mark Nero was from anything resembling the Greek love of boys. While the Greeks were charmed by the masculinity of their favorites and looked upon their passion as an opportunity to better the condition of the beloved, it was necessary for Nero to remove the clearest evidence of masculinity in Sporus, to feminize him and to degrade him rather than to elevate him" (Churchill 1967:143).

In that the economic independence of Roman women was greater and their status concomitantly higher than those of women in classical Greece, "feminizing" involved less status loss for Roman males, although they seem to have treated male sexual receptivity with at least as much contempt as the Greeks had.

Romans were not convinced, however, that eunuchs' sexuality was exclusively receptive homosexuality. Stevenson (1995) discussed the penetration of women by those whose testes were removed after puberty. Martial (6.67) explained that Caelia has only eunuchs for servants so she can get fucked without having to give birth ("volt futui Caelia nec parere"). Martial (3.81) accused a *gallus* of performing cunnilingus, and posing as a eunuch was (at least suspected to be) a means of gaining ac-

21. Ammiamus reported that Constantine (the earlier emperor who had converted to Christianity) gave himself in love to *spadoni* (21, 16, 2).

22. Nero later took a husband named Doryphorus in a public wedding in which the emperor wore the bridal veil (*nubere*—Tacitus, *Annals* 15.37) and, on the wedding night, screamed and moaned like a girl being deflowered, according to Suetonius (*Nero* 29; the Sporus marriage is described in §28). After mentioning both marriages, Dio reported that Nero also simulated the travails of childbirth (58.4–5).

cess to women's quarters.[23] Effeminate men generally were suspected of being oversexed with both sexes.[24]

A Nod at Effeminate Homosexual Roles in Early Modern Europe
Portugal

In seventeenth-century Portugal, there was a named role for effeminate homosexual males, *fanchono*. Like the British mollies of the same time (and the Italian cognate, *finocchio*), *fanchonos* used female nicknames. Francisco Correa, the author of the 1664 letters that Mott and Assunção (1988) uncovered, did not use a woman's name, and, indeed, began the very first letter to Manuel Viegas, a guitarist and maker of musical instruments on whom he lavished gifts, by distinguishing himself from women: "If men sleep with me, it is not to find a pussy. They place the cock between my legs and there they have their way. I do not achieve it" (93). There is no record of whether Francisco Correa considered himself a *fanchono* or a *sodomite* or had no label for his sexual orientation; the vicar who denounced him to the Inquisition termed him a "fatuous whore of a sodomite," although he was the *paciente* (in intercrural intercourse).

England

The molly clubs of London in the years around 1700, and the attempts to suppress them, have been much discussed since McIntosh (1968) retrieved and popularized the account of Iwan Bloch (1938 [1901]:328–34). (See Bray 1982:81–104, Trumbach 1977 et seq., Norton 1992, and many others.) This contemporary description (with its difficult syntax and peculiar spellings) comes from Edward Ward's *Secret History of London Clubs* (1709:28–29):

> There are a particular Gang of Wretches in Town, who call themselves Mollies & are so far degenerated from all Masculine Deportment of Manly exercises that they rather fancy themselves Women, imitating all the little Vanities that Custom has reconcil'd to the Female sex, affecting to speak, walk, tattle, curtsy, cry, scold, & mimick all manner of Effeminacy. At a certain Tavern in the City, whose sign I shall not mention, because

23. Wiseman (1985:203), recalling the counterfeit *gallus* in the *Satyricon*.
24. Richlin (1983:222), citing particularly the Oxford fragment of Juvenal (0.1–34); Martial (3.63, 5.61, 10.40, 12.38).

I am unwilling to fix an Odium on the House, they are met, together, their usual Practice is to mimick a female Gossiping & fall
into all the impertinent Tittle Tattle that a merry Society of good
Wives can be subject to. Not long since they had cushioned up
one of their Brethren, or rather Sisters, according to Female
Dialect, disguising him in a Woman's Night-Gown, Sarsanet
Hood, & Night-rail who when the Company were men, was to
mimick a woman, produced a jointed Baby they had provided,
which wooden Offspring was to be afterwards Christened whilst
one in a High Crown'd Hat, I am old Beldam's Pinner, representing[ed] a Country Midwife & another dizen'd up in a
Huswife's Coif for a Nurse & all the rest of an impertinent *Decorum* of a Christening.

And for the further promotion of their unbecoming mirth,
every one was to talk of their Husbands & Children, one es-
tolling the Virtues of her Husband, another the genius & wit of
their Children; whilst a Third would express himself sorrowfully
under the character of a Widow.

Thus every one in his turn makes scoff of the little Effeminacy & Weaknesses, which Women are subject to, when gossiping o'er their cups on purpose to extinguish that Natural Affection which is due to the Fair Sex & to turn their Juvenile desires
towards preternatural polotions. They continued their practices
till they were happily routed by the conduct of some of the under Agents of the Reforming Society, so that several of them
were brought to open Punishment, which happily put a Period
to their Scandalous Revels.

Activos and *Pasivos:* Simplistic Cultural Norms and Not-So-Simple Homosexual Conduct in Latin America

The former Iberian colonies in the New World provide the most-
often-described example of the gender-defined organization of homosexuality.[25] Across Caribbean, South American, and Mesoamerican cul-

---

25. This section draws heavily on the chapter from Murray (1995a:49–70) challenging the stereotyped conventional wisdom about a frozen ontological contrast between "active" and "passive." For works that have been translated into English, page citations are
from English translations, though the Spanish or Portuguese originals are listed first in the
references. I am using the Spanish forms *activo* and *pasivo* as the generic term for (apparent) penetrator and (apparent) penetratee. The Portuguese cognates are *ativo* and *passivo.*
There are local terms for these two natures (apparently, *mayate* and *joto* have become more
common in Mexico than they were when I did fieldwork there in the late 1970s and early
80s; now they are even used in self-reference). Indeed, there are many terms, especially
for *pasivos* (Dynes 1987, 1995; Murray and Dynes 1987, 1995).

ture areas, and around the Mediterranean Sea, as well, ideal (cultural) norms distinguish masculine insertors (*activos*) who are not considered *homosexuales* from feminine insertees (*pasivos*) who are. The queen, as vividly represented in the work of such writers as Manuel Puig and Reinaldo Arenas, "has accepted and bowed to the macho ethic . . . and become a woman—a 'fallen' one at that" (Lacey 1983:10).

Whether the complementary role is that of a "gay macho" (*bujarrón*) indifferent to what he penetrates is a matter of some controversy among observers—and of disagreement among natives.[26] Some of the confusion in the anthropological literature on Latino homosexualities arises from Parker, Kutsche, Lancaster, and even Prieur confusing the men with the boys. Specifically, homosexual experimentation is more acceptable among the unmarried young,[27] but is increasingly threatening to masculine reputation with age and for those whose status is above working class.

Drawing on the representations by Latin American writers such as Gasparino Damata, Mario Vargas Llosa, and Luis Zapata, Lacey (1983: 10) insisted upon the existence (and native conceptualization) of a masculinist *activo* with homosexual preferences, who "has accepted and bowed to the macho ethic, in a different way from the queen, by completely internalising and assimilating its code of rules, and attempting to live by them." *Joto* and *mayate* or *maricón* and *hombre* (in Spanish), *bicha* and *homem*, or *veado* and *bofe* (in Portuguese) are ideal types—**native** ideal types, not just the model of non-native observers. The typological system is very simple: there are *pasivos* and *activos*, that is, males who want to be penetrated by males and males who want to penetrate— preferably to penetrate females, but willing to use substitutes.

26. On the way to generalizing an essential connection between effeminacy and homosexuality, Fred Whitam eliminated *activos* from the category "homosexual." Constructionists enamored by an "anything goes in private" ethic (e.g., Kutsche 1995 and R. Parker 1991) similarly exclude publicly masculine men from a "homosexual" category. In their view, males who penetrate males are just ordinary men. Usually, the category is linguistically unmarked (*hombre;* man) although Schifter and Madrigal (1992) reported *hombres de verdad* (true men), Lancaster (1992) seemingly coined the reduplicated (hence, highly marked) *hombre-hombre*, and Tierno (1961:74–76) listed *muy hombre* and *mucho hombre* (very man and much man). The masculine partner, then, is at least sometimes referred to with linguistically marked forms and is, thereby, distinguished from men in general. Such men who are invested in conventional masculine self- and public images are far more difficult to interview than are voluble queens (Carrier 1995:198; Prieur 1998:179–223), and what they say seems especially suspect, particularly when it contradicts what one has directly observed (Murray 1996b:239, 242; Prieur 1998:190, 199).

27. I would hazard the hypothesis that the age has been increasing along with the age of marriage.

Behavior, desire, and identity are more complex in messy reality. Certainly there are individuals who impersonate the ideal type of undifferentiated phallic supremacy of the penetrating *hombre/homem*. However, the sexually omnivorous *hombre* who doesn't have any preferences in "object choice"—the man for whom "meat on the hook is meat on the hook, no reason to be choosy; no opportunity should be allowed to slip by and it doesn't matter who or what you fuck as long as you fuck" (Lane 1978:84)—is more a *maricón* fantasy than a plausible empirical observation. As one veteran observer suggested, "The mirage of the *hombre* who doesn't care where his prick goes is a consoling rationalization of the macho-adoring *maricón* [or foreigner]. He probably does care and have preferences. He just can't get into his girlfriend often enough, or at all, and you're there as a temporary substitute or relief" for him (Vladimir Cervantes 1987 personal communication). The Argentine writer Lucio Ginarte (1983 [1960]:19) wrote (specifically of Recife), "The sexual problem of the young men is acute. They're poor, and love is expensive. They don't have enough money to pay for a girl [still less to marry and set up a household], so they turn to homosexuals. But even though they come, and feel pleasure and normalise the functioning of their glands, they want money." Even one who "earns a good salary" (and gives the money back once he's received it) insists on payment: "he must maintain the privileges of virility intact" (Ginarte 1983 [1960]:49). Accepting money for sex does not make them prostitutes, and projection of what I call "the blind phallus fantasy" (Murray 1987a:196) is undoubtedly flattering to young men who are insecure about their masculinity—as to some extent is any Latino male who has not fathered children.[28] They are very unlikely to contradict flattering *pasivo* claims about how masculine they are . . . or to make public either to *pasivos* or to their families and friends that they seek to and like to have sex with other males.

Increasingly, in Latin American cities, men tend to marry a decade or

28. As Gilmore (1990a:41) pointed out, paternity is the key test in the circum-Mediterranean machismo complex: "In those parts of southern Europe where the Don Juan model of sexual assertiveness is highly valued, a man's assigned task is not just to make endless conquests but to spread his seed. Beyond mere promiscuity, the ultimate test is that of competence in reproduction. . . . The Mediterranean emphasis on manliness means results: it means procreating offspring (preferably boys). At the level of community endorsement, it is legitimate reproductive success, more than simply erotic acrobatics." Nineteen is not too young for this ultimate test to be definitive in Mexico or Puerto Rico. Also, in both places "one or more women" might be substituted for "wife" in Gilmore's statement.

more after puberty.[29] With no farm to inherit, marriage in the mid-twenties "if I can accumulate some money" is a hope of many men. The possibilities of vaginal penetration of "good girls," who are the only candidates for future wives, are virtually nil, so "bad girls"—a category that for some includes effeminate men—provide culturally expected, quasi-legitimate sexual outlets for unmarried youths. However, in the dominant cultural calculus, penetrating the *huecos* (holes) of *putos* is not as good or as desirable as is penetrating those of females. Exclusively heterosexual Latinos with whom I have discussed claims that masculinity can be enhanced by fucking a *maricón* vociferously disagree with Lancaster's (1992:242) assertion that fucking men enhances "male honor." They also deny that adult Latinos banter about homosexual exploits or could do so in conventional male circles without inviting aspersions on the genuineness of their masculinity.[30] Lancaster does not appear to have asked direct questions of the residents of the working-class barrio in Managua, Nicaragua, among whom he lived about whether one gains honor from using a *pasivo* (*cochón* in the local lexicon). Nor did he ask (as I think is the case), whether, under certain circumstances that include

29. In terms of gender, relatively few urbanites have physically demanding occupations. Generally, in contemporary cities, there are not many ways to demonstrate "traditional" masculinity. Foreign observers may mistakenly interpret flamboyant verbal sexual posturing (*piropos*) as indicating that Latino men are hypersexual. It is easy to play the role of a *lobo listo* (literally, "ready wolf"; *listo* can also mean "crafty," which in this context also means able to take orifices as prey) when few demands are likely to be made: the Latino male is rarely if ever going to be pressed to demonstrate that he really is ready—not least because there are few places to have sex in private.

30. Still less can they do so in family settings. The only evidence Lancaster adduced that men gain status by boasting about fucking *cochones* is as follows: "I once heard a Nicaraguan youth of nineteen boast to his younger friends: 'I am very sexually experienced. I have had a lot of women . . . . I have **even** done it with *cochones*.'" No one in the group thought this a damning confession, and all present were impressed with their friend's sexual experience and prowess" (241; emphasis added). He did not tell readers how he knew that all present were impressed. Moreover, the "even" suggests that women and *cochones* are not **equally** desirable and empowering to those who "use" them. One may reasonably wonder if the youth could have bragged about fucking *cochones* if he hadn't established that he'd fucked "a lot of women" and preferred women. This anecdote is not very convincing evidence of the irrelevance of the sex of those fucked by the *hombre-hombre*. Lancaster's eager followers, Alonso and Korceck (1988:111), also fail to present even a passing anecdote in support of their fantasy that fucking males enhances male prestige. (Cf. Arboleda 1997; Prieur 1998:197.) Queens like Mema may fantasize about males considering fucking males proof of masculinity (Prieur 1998:263), but *mayates* barely talk to anyone about sex with (biological) males, let alone routinely brag about it.

established heterosexual prowess and preference, the man who thrusts the hard synecdoche of masculinity up the available orifice of the weak, less-than-masculine (and therefore penetrable) man neither loses nor gains any macho reputation, let alone accumulates any honor.

Too-frequent forays into this kind of *Banco de Inversiones* undercuts a macho reputation, as does emotional investment in those a man uses sexually. As one longtime participant observer put it,

> For an *hombre* to boast of fucking men, he must be perceived as having a substantial surplus balance in the *Banco (Hembra) del Macho* before he can publicly invest in this kind of *Banco de Inversiones* [i.e., allow to become known that he has sex with *maricones, jotos, cochones*]. At no time must the two accounts be equal, and he must loudly proclaim that he prefers women. This is not the happy-go-lucky phallic maniac who doesn't care—or even notice!—where he plants his stalk. . . . Further evidence against what you label 'the blind phallus' [a hole is a hole is a hole] assumption is that when money or gifts are exchanged, the flow is from the *hombre* to the girl, but from the *maricón* to the *hombre*. The first pattern may (if rarely) be reversed, but the *hombre* never pays the *maricón*. (V. Cervantes 1987 personal communication; also see Prieur 1998:240)[31]

Payment (which may be indirect—presents or paying for meals and entertainment) is economically important for many, even if for others it is more an ego need than an economic necessity.[32] Beyond "the power of the least interest," the asymmetry seems important in rationalizing that "I'm doing that for profit, not pleasure," even while taking pleasure (as a bonus). Payment is proof that the *homosexual,* not the *hombre,* is the one who wants the sex more—enough to pay for it. The *pasivo* must also take the initiative: leave the band of his friends, approach the *activo* (who hunts alone, or purports not to be hunting at all, but only to have noticed the *pasivo* eyeing him), suggest a place, supply condoms, and offer his orifices to the *activo's* use. Real men (machos) don't initiate sex with males; supposedly only *homosexuale*s are interested in that. In the domi-

31. Transvestite prostitutes are paid and also steal from their customers (see Kulick 1996, 1998a).

32. In longer-term relationships, however, the *activo* may relax: not always require payment, become more passionately involved, and—if the approach is gradual and does not challenge his masculine self-image—allow penetration. Keeping up appearances (for masculine reputations) is more important than what actually happens in the dark or behind closed doors.

nant culture's view, it is the latter who are hungry to have their orifices filled—so eager that it does not matter how roughly or how quickly discharge and withdrawal occur. There is certainly a lot of heterosexual sex in Latin America in which any pleasures the penetrated woman might want are also ignored, but women are understood to be doing a favor in opening their bodies to penetration—and are paid by men, directly or indirectly. In contrast, machos believe that they are doing *homosexuales* a great favor by letting them borrow and take into their bodies the penis of a "real man." The macho should be rewarded, and the homosexual should not expect (and certainly should not demand) affection, any technical excellence, or any consideration of the pleasures beyond having an often quickly ejaculating penis roughly thrust into him.

Any variation (or, more correctly, anything that anyone chooses to **consider** a variation) from (elastic) norms of masculinity risks loss of face, even though direct public criticism is exceedingly rare. As in other Mediterranean-influenced cultures, one's "reputation" is important, but it is difficult to be sure how others regard one (Wikan 1984:646).[33] There are elaborate collusions to avoid questioning appearances that could easily be challenged, and to preclude noticing deviance—in gender, sexual behavior, or other kinds.

Just as males not involved in sex with other males reject the claim that penetrating male orifices enhances "honor," many of those who seek to be penetrated are quite unashamed about getting what they want (which is not "masculine honor," though this is a cult at which some worship and many manipulate). Those who are not competing for regard as machos generally have the sense not to rattle the fragile masculinity of those who present themselves as machos, knowing that the latter are all too likely to lash out at anyone who questions their (sacred and often fragile) masculinity.[34] Just as it takes a slave to be a master, the *pasivo*

33. I am referring to interactions occurring in spaces not marked as homosexual. Gossip **among** *pasivos* is incessant (and *pasivos* hang out together when they are not snaring and bedding the *activos* who travel solo and do not hang out with each other). Aspersions on how masculine and impenetrable another *pasivo*'s partner really is are especially common (see Prieur 1998; Kulick 1998a), though some are surely based entirely on spite rather than on actual experience with the particular male whose masculine credentials are challenged (in his absence).

34. The efforts that consumers of young male phalluses devote to propping up vulnerable male egos are visible in Ceballos Maldonado 1969, Ginarte 1983 [1960], Lane 1978, Penteado 1983. et al. Zapata 1983, Ribondi 1983, and Marchant Lazcano 1983 portray *activo* panics, and Gombrowicz (1988 [1955]:142–46) discussed "panic-stricken fear at the woman in themselves of Argentinean 'manly' men." Lancaster's (1992:248) claim that

invents, persuades, polishes, and maintains his (or his objectified *activo*'s) fantasy of the "real man."

Pasivos are not just unashamed of being penetrated by masculine men, but delighted and eager to recount the details of the experience.[35] Whereas *activos* are skittish about discussing or even admitting to having sex with males,[36] overt *pasivos* are "shameless" in the view of the majority culture and of their *activo* partners—the very ones whose honor Lancaster claims they enhance by opening their legs to. Many of those worshipped as hypermasculine by males they penetrate come across as being ashamed to let it be known that they have sex with males, while their purportedly "dishonored" partners enthusiastically discuss what should (if Lancaster were right) shame them. Abashed insertors and proud receptors is what one sees on the ethnographic ground (where Lancaster did not venture) of males who have sex with males, not the "subject honor, object shame" deducible from the dominant culture's values.

Behavioral Variance (and Its Dangers to Self-Image)

The rigid "I'm a man [hombre]; if I fuck you, you're not a man" logic is familiar and more than a little internalized by Latinos *en de ambiente* (in the homosexual subculture). The (*norteño*) conception that males who have sex with males, regardless of the sexual role taken, are "homosexual" is not unknown and may account for some of the unease and outright denial Prieur (and I) have elicited from *activos*. Aside from and before that, however, was a recognition that some seemingly ultra-masculine men could be "flipped" and penetrated. The phenomenon is

---

such panics are "impossible in Nicaragua" is almost certainly based on lack of inquiry. (Indeed, his whole discussion is based on no observations or interviews of males who have sex with males.) Cf. Arboleda 1997, Mott 1995, Schifter and Madrigal 1992.

35. What is embarrassing is to learn that one's penetrator (especially one whose masculinity one has bragged about) has been penetrated by others. There is a widespread contempt for two *pasivos* going to bed. In that sex is believed to require a phallus (*pasivos* may have penises, but not phalluses . . .), the same "What could they possibly do?" question arises that is asked about two women having sex with each other. *Pasivos* together are like lesbians, who are imagined as only able to rub against each other, not to penetrate. The euphemism is *hacer tortillas* (making tortillas involves kneading). The metaphor "lesbian" is applied in Brazil (Kulick 1998b) and Africa (Gaudio 1998) as well as in Mesoamerica.

36. Insertive sex. Receptive sex is literally unthinkable, which is not to say it doesn't happen. Statements of the "I never get fucked" sort are more about self-image and self-presentation than they are reliable summaries of actual behavior—affirming what a man is expected to be and not to do rather than what he really does. See Murray 1995a:63–64, 1996b:246–48, 255; R. Parker 1999:69.

frequently discussed among male transvestite prostitutes, and the pleasure of "surrender" to penetration is not inconceivable to masculine-appearing males.

Some observers (e.g., Brandes 1981:232–34) have claimed that a fear of enjoying being anally penetrated is a salient concern for Latino males. "If I let him fuck me I'd probably like it and then I'd do it again, and then I'd be queer," a young Guatemalteco told Lane (1978:56). For Hermes (in Abreu 1983a 277) that fear is realized: "I knew that once it had been awakened, it wouldn't sleep again." A *manía* for sex with males can become a "habit," as Jaime, a young Mexican, told Prieur (1998:201). Similarly, Roberto expressed his concern to her: "You don't know how your body might react, or your mind. Morally, you don't know what might follow. And if I am a man, I want to stay like that forever"(Prieur 1998:200).[37] Such a belief seems to have a circum-Mediterranean diffusion and to have been carried to the New World by Iberian *conquistadores*.[38] In Mexico, "there is even a term, *hechizos* [made ones], for former *mayates* [insertors] who have become complete homosexuals over time" (Lumsden 1991:45).

Still, the feared anal penetration does not turn everyone who has experienced it into a *maricón*. Nor does it inevitably compromise masculine deportment or end masculine self-conception, especially if the stigmatized behavior occurs with aliens—including ethnographers whose own sexual adventures may have confused them about what Latinos readily do with each other.[39]

Within the culture (i.e., among natives), the insertee's masculine reputation may be *quemado* (singed) at any time by reports or rumors of receptivity. (Even when obtainable, the luxury of privacy is not as safe with peers as it is with foreigners.) Thus, to say that it doesn't matter what a Latino male does as long as no one finds out (Lacey 1979;

37. Also see Domingos (1983:313). For a nineteenth-century representation of this conception, see Caminha (1979 [1895]:89).

38. A man's anxiety that he may like getting fucked if he tries it parallels the anxiety about one's women (especially one's wife) getting to like sex and slipping from the Madonna to the *puta* (or, at least, *chingada*) role, a nagging concern of those living by the particularly acute double standard of Latin American culture. Only Santa María was able to be both a mother and a virgin.

39. Murray 1991b and 1996b discussed reasons for caution about such extrapolation. In particular, it is safer to experiment with someone who can be counted on to go away, and doing what a potential patron wants is one of many excuses for doing what one may not want to admit to wanting to try. A macho should be able to withstand in silence any pain that weak *maricones* can, so fear of any possible pain of being penetrated is not a motive that can be expressed by a macho.

R. Parker 1991) doesn't say much, because of the necessary caveat that "hardly ever does no one find out." Some things remain hidden (*escondidas*), but guarantees of eternal silence are dubious. Anyone especially concerned about his reputation is not all that safe getting fucked under the sheets or between four silent walls when "no one is watching," or even during Carnival when, supposedly, "anything goes" (R. Parker 1987:163–66, 1991:100).[40] In the words of José, Richard Parker's primary informant, "Sometimes one gives (*dá*) first, or sucks or jacks off the other, and then when it is the turn of the one who received pleasure first, he doesn't want to do it for the other. There are some times when this same first person goes about telling others that the second did this or that with him. . . . The active defames the passive, giving rise to fights and shame, if not blows and serious punishments coming from family members. The game can sometimes get complicated" (1991:128). The walls may not speak, but those cavorting between them tend to do so— sooner or later. The ending of Hecker Filho's 1951 novella *Internato* provides an excellent example (of sooner).[41]

Latinos (and others) can compartmentalize homosexuality—in space or time. According to Goode (1960), compartmentalization of roles is a common response to role strain; by no means is it unique to managing masculine self-presentation while engaged in homosexual behavior in Latin America. In Latin America, as in Anglo North America (despite the high valuation on "genuineness" and "sincerity"), there is "a traditional difference between that which people know and that which they agree to admit that they know, that which they see and that which they speak of," as the Master of portraying maneuvering around liaisons, Henry James, noted.[42] Some people's homosexual involvement is an open secret, that of others is not discussed, and some is genuinely secret.

40. "Tudo: (everything) in "Tudo pode acontecer" (R. Parker 1987:164, 1991:100) is hyperbole, although Parker in his (early) eagerness to overthrow any rigid sexual orthodoxy (especially recurrent sexual roles) took it literally. "Todos" and "nada" in the Spanish formula "Todos hecho, nada dicho" (Everything is done, nothing is said) are similarly hyperbolic.

41. For examples of such "news" trickling out more slowly, but very damagingly, see Abreu 1983b:283, Damata 1983:210, Domingos 1983:313, Donoso 1966:87, Penteado 1979:241, Zapata 1983:97. On the perils of threatening to reveal a married man's homosexual dalliances, see Ribondi 1983:339–40 and the film by Zuleica Porto based on that work. In contrast, see Penteado 1983:243 for at least the fantasy of escaping having one's masculine reputation singed.

42. Quoted by Halperin (1990:58). For an Argentine example, see N. Miller (1992: 209–10). Denial of homosexual behavior is by no means exclusive to Latinos. In the U.S. National Survey of Adolescent Males, more than a third of those who had reported engag-

Despite the reticence about discussing one's own homosexuality or that of one's friends or family members,[43] there is essentializing pressure to bundle sex(uality) and gender.[44]

It seems to me that in labeling boys and men *cochón, joto/a, maricón, veado,* and so forth, gender nonconformity is primary. Those who are perceived as not being able to take care of themselves (a Chicano definition of *maricón* I elicited in the early 80s) will also get taken advantage of: they will get both fucked and fucked over (as another Chicano who was present added).[45] Since the cultural assumption is that gender and sexuality will be consonant, natives do not usually make the (alien) analytical distinction: the less than masculine, by local standards, get fucked (and beaten up, too) and those who are known to get fucked are less than masculine. There are certainly masculine-appearing males who are insertees, and effeminate-appearing males who are mostly or exclusively insertors, but the clear, simple masculine/feminine division is paramount in Latino views of sex/gender. Behavioral variance is irrelevant to this organizing principle, which does not seem to have disappeared in lower-class neighborhoods in Latin America. Below (see pp. 409–12), I shall explore data on "modern" (post-gender-dichotomized) homosexual behavior in Latin America.

The Sohari *Khanith*

During the summer of 1974, halfway through her first fieldwork in the town of Sohar (in Oman on the southeastern coast of the Arabian Peninsula), Norwegian anthropologist Unni Wikan was astonished one day when one of her women friends stopped and talked freely with a

---

ing in male-male sex in 1988 claimed never to have done so when they were queried again in 1991 (Turner et al. 1998:867–68).

43. Indeed, the reticence extends to discussions of masturbation and prostitution, or to speculating about close friends and family members. For instance, I knew a pair of brothers in a Latin American capital city who were both involved in homosexual liaisons. They slept in the same room at home, but for many years neither knew that the other also engaged in homosexual behavior, nor was either willing to speculate about what the other did sexually (even in the general sense of "he's probably an *activo*" or "he's probably a *pasivo*").

44. The nuances of technical distinctions between sex, sexuality, and gender can be illustrated, but are not locally important.

45. Manuel Fernández (27 May 1998 E-mail) added that the assumption is that "true men should be able to take care of others, i.e., having children and women who depend on them." This seems to me to dovetail with the expectation of social as well as biological paternity being part of the male role for Latinos. See Guttman (1996) for a view of machos as more nurturing than they appear in many other representations.

man. Almost as surprising as a woman conversing with a man on the street in Sohar was his costume: a pink tunic. Wikan's friend explained that this gaudily dressed man was a *xanith* (*khanith* is a more conventional romanization of the Arabic term and will be used here except in direct quotations). In the course of a twenty-minute walk through town, the friend pointed out four more. She "explained that all male servants (slaves apart) are *xanith*, that all *xanith* are homosexual prostitutes." She estimated that 2 percent ("about sixty" of three thousand) of adult Sohari men are *khanith*.[46]

Wikan then realized that a man who had earlier startled and puzzled her by entering a bride's seclusion chamber and seeing her unveiled before a wedding, and who later ate with the women at the wedding meal, was also a *khanith*. "Women bare their faces freely" to *khanith* (1977: 307). The *khanith* differs in dress from males and from females:

> [The *khanith*] is not allowed to wear the mask, or other female clothing. His clothes are intermediate between male and female: he wears the ankle-length tunic of the male, but with the tight waist of the female dress. Male clothing is white, females wear patterned cloth in bright colours, and khaniths wear unpatterned coloured clothes. Men cut their hair short, women wear theirs long, the khaniths medium long. Men comb their hair backward away from the face, women comb theirs diagonally forward from a central parting, [*khaniths*] comb theirs diagonally forward from a sideparting, and they oil it heavily in the style of women. Both men and women cover their head, khaniths go bare-headed. Perfume is used by both sexes, especially at festive occasions and during intercourse. The khanith is generally heavily perfumed, and uses much make-up to draw attention to himself. This is also achieved by his affected swaying gait, emphasized by the close-fitting garments. His sweet falsetto voice and facial expressions and movements also closely mimic those of women. If khaniths wore female clothes I doubt that it would in many instances be possible to see that they are, anatomically speaking, male not female. (Wikan 1977:307; I have followed her later practice 1982:172 of substituting "khanith" where the original had "transsexual.")

The *khanith* is also intermediate in mobility: moving freely (like men) during the day, secluded (like women) at night. Moreover, their occupa-

---

46. Wikan (1977:305, 1982:169). Her work did not specify how many were available for sexual rent, or, of those who were, how many had regular patrons, or how many servants identified themselves as *khanith* (or were so labeled by others).

tions (domestic servants and prostitutes) are ones unacceptable for either proper men or proper women.[47] Doing housework is considered "women's work," but Sohari Arab women do not do housework for employers. Neither Wikan nor her critics presented any evidence that "the natives" consider that there are three sexes (man, woman, *khanith*), or three genders (male, female, *khanith*).

Although gender variance most struck Wikan, "homosexual prostitute" is the native characterization Wikan quoted, and, in her original article, she wrote that homosexual relations are "the essence" of Omani *khanith* behavior.[48]

Just across the Arabian Sea, in Pakistan, are *hijra*. As discussed on pp. 306–11 below, the hijra also has been classified by a feminist anthropologist as a "third gender role," though desire for sex with men was consistently specified as the motivation for becoming *hijra* in the statements by *hijra* that Nanda (1990) quoted.[49]

In a 1 Feb. 1994 letter, Wikan emphasized that "prostitute" does not have the ugly connotations in Oman that it has in northern (European and American) Protestant societies. "Several aspects of xanith behaviour and identity converge in people's characterization of it. One prominent one is that xanith sing at weddings.[50] But this is not taken up by my Western colleagues much more interested in prostitution than singing at weddings."

Legally, *khanith* are men. That is, they are able to represent themselves in legal proceedings, whereas, in contrast, "women are jurally minors and must be represented" by an adult male (Wikan 1977:308, 1982:174). The *khanith* are "referred to in the masculine grammatical gender." The first-person plural in Arabic, which they use to refer to

47. Wikan 1977:307, 1982:173. There are female prostitutes, though Wikan (1978b: 670) rejected Feuerstein and al-Marzooq's (1978:666) surmise that they are "foreigners working in the country." On the lack of public challenge to respectability in Arab societies, see Wikan 1984, as well as the example of the female prostitute in Wikan 1977 (312).

48. Wikan 1977:310. In a 1 Feb. 1994 letter, Wikan stressed that she "did not use the word 'essence' in the sense that it has got in current anthropology," and that she did not mean to imply that there are not other essential aspects of the role. She reminded me that the binary logic of alien analysts' categorization is not a native concern. In this particular instance, for Soharis, the khanith need not be z or not-z (with z being various alien categories), but may be both.

49. On longstanding and intensive South Asian influences on Oman see J. Wilkinson (1987:63–66).

50. This accepted role at one of the central celebrations of heterosexuality parallels that of the *hijra*.

themselves, does not specify gender (Wikan 1 Feb. 1994 letter). Wikan wrote that *khaniths* "speak of themselves with emphasis and pride as 'women,'" and also noted that "when in old age a xanith loses his attraction and stops his trade, he is assimilated to the old-man (*agoz*) category" (Wikan 1982:168, 176).

Khanith "are not allowed to dress in women's clothes." Indeed, they are punished by imprisonment and flogging if they cross dress (Wikan 1977:309, 1982:175). And a *khanith* may marry a woman. So long as consummation of the marriage is publicly verified, the groom will be respected as a man (and thereby will lose the prerogative of easy familiarity with women). This seems to me to support the inference that sexuality, not gender, is the most salient part of the *khanith* role, in the Sohari view.

There does not seem to be a lexicalized or a covert role category "ex-*khanith*." Nor are there any indications of a role of connoisseur or frequenter of *khanith*.[51] As in other cultures with an institutionalized transvestitic homosexual role (e.g., the North American berdache, the eastern Siberian shamans, or the Polynesian *māhū*, each of which is discussed below), those who sexually use the *khanith* do not seem to be marked (i.e., differentiated from men in general) (Wikan 1977:314, 1982:182).

Though she has published a more sustained description than most of a non-Western homosexual role, Wikan provided little in the way of description of specific *khanith* (or ex-*khanith*) and none of their own accounts of motivation/causation, concerns, or desires. The only assertion that is explicitly marked as coming directly from a *khanith* challenges the non-*khanith* view that *khanith* cannot attain erection (Wikan 1977: 318n. 8, 1982:177–78n. 6; cf. Roscoe 1991:122). Whether *khanith* identify themselves as women or "derive fetishistic pleasure from female clothing" are the defining features for the distinction of transsexual and transvestite from homosexual that Wikan (1978b:669) insisted upon, but lacked the evidence to resolve.

51. There is also no indication of pederastic role terms, but especially without elicitation, one cannot take absence of evidence as evidence of absence. Wikan represented herself as having stumbled on the *khanith* role. Hanging out with untalkative women is unlikely to lead to stumbling on pederasty. Her fieldwork was not focused on the varieties of homosexual behavior—or even roles—but on the lives of women, so, even had she been inclined to be more inquisitive, she may well not have elicited any data on this. Wikan reported that some *khanith* hire sexual partners: "The young and pretty *xanith* receives substantial gifts and payments from his paramours whereas the old and unattractive *xanith*, according to Sohari, 'will pay the men to do it to them'" (1978a:474).

In her 1982 book, *Behind the Veil in Arabia: Women in Oman,* Wikan added a statement of the native (male) view of *khanith* genesis:

> The folk understanding of why some young boys turn into *khaniths* is deceptively simple. Men say that when young boys at puberty start being curious and exploring sexual matters, they may "come to do that thing" together, and then the boy "who lies underneath" may discover that he likes it. If so, he "comes to want it," and, as the Soharis say, "An egg that is once broken can never be put back together," "Water that has been spilt can not be put back again." Thus the homosexual activity of the *xanith* is seen by others as a compulsion: degrading to the person, but springing from his inner nature. Although it is performed for payment of money, its cause is emphatically not seen as economic. (1982:172–73)

This is the only statement I have found about the *khanith* role in Wikan's various writings that is marked as deriving from a male perspective (although obviously from a non-*khanith* one). She did not say what kind of man or how many men say this is. It is certainly consistent with the very widespread (circum-Mediterranean and beyond) belief that the pleasures of being penetrated are addictive. Fredrik Barth (1983:79) also referred to the adage that once an egg is broken it cannot be put back together and quoted a Sohari man who said that *khanith* are happy being the way they are: "that is what they want." Reinforcement that Wikan's final view is that sexuality is the defining feature of *khanith* is provided in Barth's book on Sohar, published a year later than hers: "In the case of gender, identity is initially ascribed by anatomical criteria, but Wikan (1977, 1978a, 1987b, 1982) shows convincingly that its key expression, and thereby ultimate ascriptive criterion is found in the sexual act rather than sexual organs in Sohar" (Barth 1983:78).

At the risk of overinterpreting Wikan's "Men say," I would suggest that perhaps sexual behavior is more salient a feature of the *khanith* role for men than for women, and that gender markers may be somewhat more salient for women—even though it was a woman who first explained *khanith* as homosexual prostitutes to Wikan (as quoted above), and although both women and men expect a simple relationship between sex, gender, and sexual propriety—insofar as these distinctions are made at all in Sohar. On the last dimension, *khanith* are classified with "fallen women," but instead of taking this as evidence that they are "a kind of woman," it seems more likely that a man or a woman can be virtuous and that a man or a woman can be improper ("fallen from grace"). Pending more direct data from Sohar, we do not know if Soharis consider there to be three genders. From the evidence Wikan presented, my hypothesis is that the answer to "Is a *khanith* a kind of woman?" would be "no," and to "Is a *khanith* a kind of man?" would be "yes"— a less-than-fully realized man, a "failed man," but still a kind of man.

Polynesian Gender-Defined Homosexual Roles
Tahiti

One of the first European visitors to the Society Islands (Tahiti) in the closing decades of the eighteenth century wrote, "They have a set of men called Mahoo. These men are in some respects like the Eunuchs of India but are not castrated. They never cohabit with women but live as they do. They pick their beards out and dress as women, dance and sing with them and are as effeminate in their voice. They are generally excellent hands at making and painting cloth, making mats and every other woman's employment. They are esteemed valuable friends in that way and it is said that they converse with men as familiar[ly] as women do" (James Morison; quoted by R. Levy 1973: 130).

His lieutenant elaborated:

> Mahu are particularly selected when boys and kept with the women solely for the caresses of the men. Here the young man took his Hahow or mantle off which he had about him to show me the connection. He had the appearance of a woman, his yard and testicles being so drawn in under him, having the art from custom of keeping them in this position. Those who are connected with him have their beastly pleasures gratified between his thighs, but are no farther sodomites as they all positively deny the crime. . . . The women treat him as one of their sex and he observed every restriction that they do, and is equally esteemed. (William Bligh 1789; quoted by R. Levy 1973:131)

Another early traveler, John Turnbull (1813), reported oral rather than intercrural copulation, hinting at a belief in masculinization by insemination, though this may have been his fantasy rather than that of the natives: "They put the penis into the unfortunate's mouth and go on to emit the semen which the wretch eagerly swallows down as if it were the vigor and force of the other; thinking no doubt thus to restore himself greater strength" (translated from Latin and quoted by Levy 1973: 131–32).

Lt. Bligh was puzzled: "It is strange that in so prolific a country as this, men should be led into such sensual and beastly acts of gratification, but perhaps no place in the World are they so common or extraordinary as in this island." James Wilson, the captain of the ship transporting the first missionaries to Tahiti, was too appalled to specify sexual acts, even in Latin, but provided some information on nonsexual aspects of the place of the *māhū* in Tahitian society at the end of the eighteenth century:

> The *mahus* choose this vile way of life when young; putting on the dress of a woman, they follow the same employments, are under the same prohibitions with respect to food, etc. and seek the courtship of men the same as women do, nay, are more jealous of the men who cohabit with them, and always refuse to sleep with women. We are obliged here to draw a veil over other practices too horrible to mention. These *mahus*, being only six or eight in number are kept by the principal chiefs. So depraved are these poor heathens, that even their women do not despise those fellows, but form friendships with them. (Wilson 1799; quoted by Oliver 1989:635–36)

A diary entry by someone named Jefferson from 1800 referred to one of a group of women from Oriatteea:

> Among them was a man, not otherwise to be distinguished from the women but by a little coarser features & rougher voice: this man keeps himself for the abominable sin of sodomy. We have lately learnt it is usual for some persons from their youths to set themselves apart for this base purpose. They go among women, observe all their customs, eat & drink & sleep with them & do all the offices of females in making cloth &c. and prostitute their bodies to men for the above sin. They never cohabit with women, but only with men. They are not paid by men, but pay men for sinning with them. Some of them are so effeminated as not to be distinguished by their countenances, voices or manners from the women. They are, when spoken to, called by the same name of endearment that men use to women, & women to women, Pattaa. (quoted by Watts 1987:14)

Ignoring the rhetoric of "abominable sin" in this passage, there are two points worth noting. The first is a repetition of Wilson's assertion that a *māhū* chose the role when young and studied women. The second is the direction of payment, which is incompatible with the view of some earlier observers (Wilson and Turnbull) and of Oliver (1974:373, 1111) that *māhū* invariably were sex toys of chiefs and nobles.

Almost two centuries later, Levy's informants "speak of 'the *māhū*' of a village or district and say that most villages have a *māhū* even if they do not know who it is" (1973:132). There is never more than one, one informant explained, "because when one dies, then another substitutes. God arranged it like that. . . . Only one *māhū* and when that one dies, he is replaced" (132; see also 472).[52] In the countryside "one is a *māhū* or one is not," although "a young man who in his early adolescence dressed from time to time in girls' clothes and was thus a *māhū* in his early twenties rejected (*fa'aur'e;* "cast off") the role. It is assumed in the village that this is the end of it and that he is leading an ordinary masculine life" (133).

Cross-dressing was not an invariable concomitant of the role in the village Levy studied, and he found some disagreement there about whether homosexuality was, either, although younger men in the village in which Levy lived claimed that the village *māhū* serviced most of the young males.[53] "Males describing their relationships with *māhū* tend to stress their passive participation in the relationship and the lack of symmetry . . . [e.g.] 'He ate my penis. He asked me to suck his. I did not suck it'" (Levy 1973:135). The sexual activity of the *māhū* is invariably specified as "*'ote moa'* (literally, 'penis sucking'). Anal sodomy is categorically denied as a *māhū* activity. . . . Intercourse between the thighs [cf. Blighs earlier account] is said not to be done" (135). One of Levy's (1973:137) *māhū* informants opined that anal intercourse (in which he sometimes engaged) was a recent, "not-Tahitian" (specifically French) activity, contrasting with traditional fellatio.

As in other gender-defined systems (e.g., that of Latin America), *māhū* concur "that a male who engages as a partner [even husband—see Oliver 1974 {1145}] with a *māhū* is not at all a *māhū* himself, nor in any way an abnormal man" (138). That some men are "like that" is accepted as natural, both by the *māhū* who reports no shame about his sexual behavior and by non-*māhū*:

> When people are asked to evaluate *māhū*, they usually say in Piri
> [the village Levy studied] that they are "natural," and that there-

52. Oliver (1981:535) encountered one *māhū* in one Tahitian village, but two in another. Watts (1987:45) referred to a Tahitian friend (who regarded himself as a *māhū*) reporting as many as twenty transvestite men in some villages on Bora Bora. Similarly, in rural Samoa in the 1970s, there were one or two *fa'afine* per village (Mageo 1992:443).

53. Of ancient Tahitian society, Oliver (1974:548) wrote, "The term *māhū* referred specifically to transvestites, and only coincidentally to homosexuals" (although his practice in that volume and elsewhere has been to include diverse sexual practices and gender attributes, including having male wives, under the term).

fore moral evaluations don't apply. There is no consensus about how the *māhū* gets to be a *māhū*, since this is not an issue for "natural" things, but the explanations tend to be in terms of something which has not connection with the *māhū*'s will or moral worth [when the anthropologist had them reflect on the question of aetiology]. (Levy 1973: 139)

It is stated that there is nothing abnormal about this as far as the male *taure'are'a* bachelors are concerned. Some adults in the village found the idea of homosexual relations with the *māhū* "disgusting," but they did not seriously stigmatize those males who engaged in them. Sexual contact with the *māhū* tends to be treated in conversation as a standard kind of sexual activity, which is often justified as due to a lack of available women. (1973:134; see also 473)

Levy recorded the view of one Tahitian, Oro, who found being fellated by a *māhū* more pleasurable than heterosexual intercourse:[54]

It's just like doing it with a woman, but his way of doing it is better than with a woman, as you just take it easy while he does it to you—He doesn't let go quickly and it makes you very limp. When you go to a woman, it's not always satisfactory. When you go to the *māhū*, it's more satisfactory. The sexual pleasure is very great. You can't stand it any more, because of that you try to push his head away. . . . You're better off [i.e., get more pleasure out of it] than they do, and they don't have the same thing done to them by other *māhū*. (135)

Another villager presented a "semen gain" explanation: "A common joke among the young men is that the *māhū* swallows the semen after his partner's ejaculation. According to Toni, "They really believe that is first class food for them. Because of that *māhū* are strong and powerful. The seminal fluid goes throughout his body. It's like the doctors say about vitamins. I have seen many *māhū* and I've seen that they are very strong"(134–35).[55]

Samoa

Mead (1928:147–48) noted that in Western Samoa, "native theory and vocabulary recognised the real pervert who was incapable of normal

54. Not that Oro had a great deal of sexual experience with women or *māhū*—he had been with two or three of the former and two of the latter (Levy 1973:73)—or that the reader can separate out cultural ideology from individual excitement.

55. However, Timi, the village *māhū* Levy interviewed, who acknowledged that he occasionally engaged in receptive anal intercourse, denied swallowing ejaculate (137).

heterosexual response." Although she did not list the vocabulary, her statement is clearly an assertion of a type of person, not just of homosexual acts. She also briefly described the local specimen of this gender-mixing or gender-crossing type. Sasi, a boy of twenty who was studying for the ministry

> was slightly but not pronouncedly feminine in appearance, was skilled at women's work and his homosexual drive was strong enough to goad him into making continual advances to other boys. He spent more time casually in the company of girls, maintained a more easy-going friendship with them than any other boy on the island. Sasi had proposed marriage to a girl in a pastor's household in a distant village and been refused, but as there was a rule that divinity students must marry before ordination, this had little significance. I could find no evidence that he had ever had heterosexual relations and the girls' casual attitude towards him was significant. They regarded him as an amusing freak while the men to whom he had made advances looked upon him with mingled annoyance and contempt. (Mead 1928:148) [56]

On the basis of Samoan fieldwork done half a century later, Shore (1981: 209) denied that there was a Samoan word meaning homosexual: "*Fa'afafine* means literally 'like a woman.'" He stressed that a *fa'afafine* "is not a female, but rather a derivative third gender class. *Fa'afafine* is a distinct gender class because it is normally not confused with either Male or Female." Although Shore saw gender rather than sexuality as the defining characteristic of *fa'afafine*—in that he also wrote about men cohabiting with transvestites (210)—it appears that gender and sexuality remain highly correlated in Samoan practice, even if (as has not been established) they distinguish gender from sex.

Poasa (1992) also regarded gender as the defining feature of *fa'afafine*. Eleven of the fourteen *fa'afafine* she interviewed said they desired a sex-change operation. All felt they were females trapped in male bodies, and desired estrogen treatment. Five were initiated between ages six and ten into sex by an adult male. Tina, an elementary-school teacher Poasa interviewed, was the youngest of ten children of a Protestant minister in Western Samoa, wore girls' clothes around the house while growing up, did girls' chores, and played mostly with girls. She wore a boy's uniform but rarely associated with boys in play in elementary school. "If she was

56. This part of her first fieldwork escaped attack by Freeman (1983). It seems to be based, at least in part, on observation, not just on what natives told her. On Mead's heterosexism and inability to conceive male homoerotcism, see Long and Borneman 1990.

put with boys in school or church groups, she always felt out of place. The boys also recognized her as belonging to the girls' group and did not include her in their play" (43).

Her father did not comment on her obvious feminine dress and interests, but he died when she was thirteen. A brother pressed her to "'start acting like a man.' . . . "He didn't actually say *fa'afafine* to me. . . . When he realized I graduated from college and got a job, he never said anything else about it" (46). The sexual history Poasa elicited began very early. When Tina was five, a twenty-year-old friend of her brother "tricked her into participating in sexual acts by playing games that led to fondling and would culminate with him rubbing his penis between her legs from a rear position to the point of ejaculation." This went on for about one year. "She does not report being scared or avoiding the man, but also knows she did not seek him out or enjoy what he did. She feels that, as a good Samoan child, she was obeying the requests of an older person and did not understand what was happening. When she became a teenager and sexually active, she understood that it had been sexual abuse" (45). However, she recalled that when she was eleven or twelve, she was scared of and tried to avoid males in their twenties who often tried to force her to have sex with them. By the age of fifteen or sixteen, she began to be willing to be sexually receptive to "straight" males a few years older than she was. As an adult, she

> always takes the insertee role in anal sex and would never consider reversing it. She states she would like to have a long-term relationship and adopt children, but it is not a high priority. She places success in her career and family before her relationships. . . . [She] said that *fa'afafine*s never engage in sex with each other or take the inserter's role. They feel that these are "gay" behaviors, which is a classification they reject. They consider themselves female and believe that the men who have sex with them also see them as female. They do not feel that their partners are "bisexual" because of this. Tina's definition of "gay" is "when one real man likes another real man, and neither one of them is acting like a female." The adoption of the female gender role is so complete that Tina does not really approve of "gay" behavior and sees no similarities between "gay" behaviors and her own situation. (47)

Poasa added that "subjects firmly believe that their effeminate behavior preexists and attracts the attention of older men, rather than effeminate behavior resulting from being sexually abused by a member of one's own sex" (48–49).

Mageo (1992:443) wrote that *fa'afafine* means "'the way of women,' when that way is taken by someone who is not female." She also asserted that

> Samoans never did, and in some measure still do not, categorize sexual practices as heterosexual or homosexual. . . . A boy who goes to bars in Apia or Pago Pago and finds no willing girl may let a transvestite take him home, but he is not thought "queer" as a result . . . Because Samoans inhabit society as role players, sexual identity is perceived in terms of gender roles. Although personal practices may become the basis for a jocular social identity in *faipona* [lampoons], they do not count as "real" social identity. Only transvestitism—taking the public role of the opposite sex in dress and manner is considered noteworthy. (449–50)

Nonetheless, "common terms for *fa'fafine* are *'ai laolagi* (eat earth), *'ai paneta* (eat planet), and *'ai karoti* (eat carrot), all of which allude to fellatio" (453).

The Marquesas

Even before Mead went to Samoa, Handy (1923:103) had stressed the primacy of gender in the *māhū* role in the Marquesas: "*Mahui* or *mahu* were men who adopted the life of a woman, dressed in woman's garb, allowing their hair to grow long. They devoted themselves to all the activities and relationships of women rather than to those of men. Native informants told me that these men were not deformed physically, but that they merely preferred a woman's life and desired men." [57]

Ralph Linton (1939:174), who had been part of the same Bishop Museum (Honolulu) expedition (as an archaeologist) as had Handy, wrote that male homosexuality "is common enough. Male transvestitism is also known to exist" (1939:218) and, that "there was some homosexuality among males; pederasty [apparently meaning anal intercourse], however, was rare, the usual form being mutual fellation. There were occasional cases of transvestites who assumed the woman's role and sometimes entered the household as subsidiary wives, though they never became head wives and were held in considerable contempt" (Linton 1939:265).

Two generations later, Suggs (1966:45, 55, 83–84, 173) reported

---

57. Earlier, Vincentdon-Dumoulin and Desgraz (1843:221, 231–32, 264) reported that there were cross-dressed men called *hokis* or *koioas* who traveled from village to village performing (music, dance, poetry). They reported nothing about the performers' sexual behavior.

masturbation contests and mutual masturbation among young, unmarried Marquesans, noting that "no stigma attached to casual homosexuality" (103):

> Homosexuality involving married individuals is rare and practiced only under conditions of prolonged enforced abstinence. There is some indication that adult males prefer younger boys for this purpose. The preference is frequently verbalized, the observation being made that young boys have softer bodies, more like those of girls. Such contacts are casual and fleeting, and do not lead to any permanent relationship between the parties involved. Permanent relationships are considered to be characteristic of the deviant *mahu* or male homosexual and are regarded as unnatural. There are relatively few *mahu* in the archipelago. (121)

He also wrote,

> Acts of homosexuality are accepted as a substitute for heterosexual relations in times of scarcity of women, and as especially characteristic of adolescent behavior. On the other hand, habitual homosexuality, in which female company is eschewed almost entirely and male lovers are taken, earns the appellation of *mahu* (deviate). Such conduct in the male is usually associated with transvestitism to varying degrees, assumption of female economic roles and feminine posture, gait, and motions. A transvestite is known as *mahu'o hiva* (homosexual of the ridgepole), referring to his abiding around the house in the performance of female chores. (83)

The existence of a marked term for one kind of *māhū, māhū'o hiva,* might be taken to indicate a native concept of a distinction between gender role (*māhū o'hiva*) and a homosexual role (*māhū*). If most *māhūs* took on the mannerisms, dress, and occupational roles of women, it is difficult to understand why there would be a marked term for a domestic subtype of *māhū*.

In addition to describing one effeminate man termed by fellow villagers as a *māhū* who "indulged in habitual homosexuality," walked and dressed like a woman, but who lived with a woman and reputedly fathered her children, Suggs observed

> two other homosexuals, not transvestites, but very markedly effeminate, [who] were also married; they used their wives to attract males and compromise them for homosexual acts. Other males who showed interest in their wives were propositioned and promised use of the wife if they could indulge in pederasty

[anal intercourse] or fellatio first with the husband. The women involved in these relationships did not appear to be overly concerned about the husbands' deviation. Both of these individuals practiced fellatio as well as pederasty. At least one experienced a very strong orgasm during pederasty. Natives who had consorted with him remarked (with some amazement) that he was "just like a woman—making noise in his orgasm." [58] Fellatio was resorted to for the purpose of exciting a lagging male before pederasty, as well as to produce an orgasm. (1966:122)

Linton (1939:218) had claimed that "the perversion of fellatio and not anal intercourse is the form in which it [male homosexuality] is expressed," which he leapt to interpret as "making good a long-felt craving for dependency" deriving from supposed food anxiety.[59] Suggs (1971) severely criticized Linton (1939), and especially the claimed food anxiety and unbalanced sex ratios. Suggs (1966:83) wrote, "Fellatio is apparently uncommon in 'normal' male homosexual behavior, but is considered characteristic of the behavior of the *māhū* or homosexual deviate." Non-*māhū* Marquesans more commonly practice anal intercourse and mutual masturbation (Suggs 1971:169).

Analysts' Attempts at Explanations

Levy followed Devereux's (1937:520) explanation ("an abscess of fixation localizing the disorder in a small area of the body social") of the berdache role among the Southeastern California Mojave: "It may be that the *māhū* role, with its clear-cut rules, its high visibility, its limited incumbency, and its pre-empting of homosexual behavior, carries essential information—is part of men's minds. It states, 'There, clearly out in the open is the *māhū*, the one man who has taken a female role. I am a non-*māhū*. Whatever feelings I have about men and about being a man are no threat to me and to my eventual role as family head. I can see exactly what is, and I am clear about myself in that I am not he'" (Levy 1973:473).[60]

---

58. Besnier (1994:303) similarly reports Tongan men graphically describing and laughing at the arousal of *fakaleitī* they penetrated (intercrurally or anally). Also see Mageo (1992:453) in regard to Samoa.

59. If reciprocity was the norm, as Linton (1939:174) claimed, it is difficult to derive either dependency or nourishment in an exchange of semen (or nourishment from semen that is not swallowed, as in the case of Timi in Levy 1973:137), although I would not want to underestimate the slipperiness and imperviousness to disconfirming evidence of Freudian explanations.

60. However, Levy (1973:139) recorded a "vague feeling that Tetua was trying to

Such an encapsulation of sexual/gender deviance into a flamboyant negative role model would make more sense if Levy (or anyone else) had demonstrated Tahitian preoccupation with or anxiety about gender deviance. As Gilmore (1990a:208–9) noted, gender differences are relatively unimportant among Tahitians, so Tahiti is an unlikely site for horror at male effeminacy: "There is absolutely no evidence that masculinity is itself a matter of any great concern for the Tahitians. They never actually say anything like, 'We are manly because we are not *māhū*s,' either explicitly or implicitly, and, despite probing, Levy never detected any observable sexual anxiety in his informants. On the contrary, they seem to have little use for a manliness that is separate and opposed to femininity."

Mageo suggested that the *fa'fafine* now performs the social function for girls (as well as for boys) that Levy saw the Tahitian *māhū* performing for boys, that is, being a visible negative role model. The open sexuality and sexual promiscuity of the *fa'fafine* "serves to remind sisters of how they are not supposed to behave . . . [thereby] stabilizing the sister's gender role" (1992:454). She also stressed that part of what makes the *fa'fafine* a negative role model is the lack of a husband (453).

Whatever their societal origins or individual motivations, similar accepted but disvalued female roles probably existed throughout "traditional" Polynesia.[61] Feldman (1981:146) asserted that fellatio (*kai mu'a;*

---

coach the boy into being a *māhū* rather than to tease him out of being one. . . . A series of pushes from the child and pulls from some members of the community may well be involved in the filling of the *māhū* role," so his explanation goes beyond the simplistic functionalism of the *māhū* as a gender anti-schema.

61. R. Pierson (1978) and Shore (1981:209–210) echoed Levy's explanation for Samoa. On Tonga, the other candidate for the Polynesian source culture, Gifford (1929: 203–4) wrote:

> Little could be learned about berdache (*fakafafine,* a word which Baker defines as "a monster"). Only a single informant, a man of Namuka Island, vouchsafed information concerning them. He said that anciently there were many, but in 1920 he knew of but one, a person of Maufonga, Tonga-tabu. The informant knew of no special activities of berdaches, except that they took part in fighting like men. The informant conceived the *fakafafine* as hermaphrodites rather than as real males with feminine tendencies: . . . "men who have the habits of women and do the work of women"

Either Gifford missed transvestitic homosexuality, or there has been a revival since then in the heartland of Polynesia. See Keener 1978; Fineanganofa 1978; Feldman 1981; and Urbanowicz 1977 (90). Besnier (1981:30) attested *fakafafine* as meaning transvestite or effeminate homosexual (literally, "in the fashion of a woman") in Tüvaluan, another Western Polynesian language. Besnier (1994:286) asserted that "Tuvaluans normally use

literally, "eat front") is not popular among Tongan women, but that it is quite popular, however, among the *kau fakaleitī*,[62] a group of extremely flamboyant transvestites, who congregate at the Dateline Hotel and especially at Joe's Hotel in Nuku'alofa.[63] They often proposition European men, particularly those from visiting military vessels, but do not ordinarily have sexual relations with each other.

Arboleda and Murray (1985) argued against accepting claims that homosexuality did not occur among the pre-contact Maori because missionaries did not write about it.[64] Danielsson (1956:181) earlier suggested that missionaries chose not to write about *māhūs* in various parts of Polynesia. The original Maori, like the original Hawaiians, almost certainly derived from the Society Islands (of which Tahiti is the best known) around 800 A.D. (Jennings 1979),[65] and it seems highly unlikely that the last-populated islands of Eastern Polynesia lacked a role similar to the Tahitian *māhū*. [66]

The horror sometimes expressed by early visitors to Tahiti about

---

the Gilbertese borrowing *pinapinaaine*" (more commonly than Tongan *fakafafine*, which is also used, but "more rarely," he reported on page 321) and noted that the various terms (including *māhū*) can function as verbs and adverbs as well as nouns (and, presumably, adjectives). Neither in print nor in response to two queries from me in January 1996 did he explain what the basis is for "normally used," or why *fakafafine* but not *pinapinaaine* was in his 1981 lexicon.

62. Besnier (1994:286) asserted that "the root *leitī* is borrowed from the English 'lady.'"

63. Besnier (1994:297) presented a more domestic picture of Tongan *fakaleitī* keeping to "well-lit domestic settings and to the company of women," rather than roaming about at night as masculine young Tongan men do.

64. No one denies there is current knowledge, not even Gluckman (1967, 1974), who claimed there was no Maori male or female homosexuality before the mid-twentieth century. MacFarlane (1984) asserted that transsexual prostitutes in New Zealand are wildly disproportionately (90 percent) Maori, although they represent only 10 percent of the population of New Zealand, or of Wellington, where she did her study. Watts (1987:45) described a self-identified "gay" Maori who "derives no inspiration from any traditional Maori *māhū* status, but instead believes the acceptance he gets from his community is because Maori are just a lot less uptight than the white people about alternative lifestyles." For an equivocal contact comment from 1770 (quoted and misdated 1789 by Besnier 1994:292) see Salmond 1991 (251–52). Moreover, Rawhiti Searancke found a Maori term for "intimate companion of the same sex": '*Takatapui* (N. Miller 1992:302).

65. Maori, Hawaiian, Marquesan, Rarotongan, Tahitian, and some others are in a single subgroup of Austronesian derived from a Proto-Central-Eastern Polynesian. See Clark (1979) on the family tree of Polynesian languages.

66. The purported absence of "homosexuals" and presence of "berdaches" on the Cook Islands are discussed in Murray 1992a (163–64n. 15).

recurrent patterns of behavior "not spoken of among Christians" was echoed by the explorers and missionaries who seized Hawai'i, Both the word *māhū* and the role associated with it continue to exist in Molokai, according to W. Williams (1985).[67] Now, people who are called and/or call themselves *māhū* have been centrally involved in the Hawaiian culture revival of the late twentieth century. The contemporary Hawaiian category includes

> an astounding variety of individuals. It can designate women who dress and work as men, men who dress and work as women, women or men who dress and act so as to obscure their biological classification, women who will only associate with other women, men who dress festively, men who undergo hormone treatments and/or eventually change their sex surgically, true hermaphrodites, and women and men who might, in English, call themselves "gay." Any of these people may choose to procreate or to raise children through the traditional adoption arrangement known as hanai. In fact, parents sometimes put their children in the care of mahu, for mixed-gender individuals are recognized as special, compassionate, and creative. (C. Robertson 1989:315)

As with Native North American "two spirits," or with "traditional family values," caution is in order when it comes to extrapolating backward from what is presented as "tradition" to what existed in the past.[68] Whether continued (as Besnier 1994:296 supposes), revived (as C. Robertson supposes), or invented recently, the "tradition" of the *māhū*

67. Robert Morris found only a few mentions of *māhū* in traditional Hawaiian folklore,

certainly nothing to compare with the sheer volume and interest of the materials on the *aikane*. The most developed story is about the several "wicked *māhū*" "who controlled a district of Kaua'i and were overcome by a hero, to whom they later became 'friends' (*makamaka,* not *aikane*). I have found no text where *māhū* and *aikane* are synonyms or cognates for each other. . . . Many people want to see the apparent "effeminacy" of the Tahitian *māhū* in every Polynesian homosexual relationship, but the Hawaiian *aikane* stories do not allow such confounding. . . . The *aikane* were in every way masculinized in their persons and roles. . . . They did not live with the women or do women's work as the did the Tahitian *māhū*. All of the Hawaiian *aikane* stories that indicate prized physical characteristics state that "manliness" was the norm. (24 Sept. 1990 letter)

68. Except for the Hawaiian revival Robertson (1989) described (and that Besnier 1994:299 suggested is inspired more by Native North American than by Polynesian mobilizations, the Polynesia *māhū* (etc.) have not been associated in the ethnographic or travel literatures with sacred roles. The lack of a religious role presumably made *māhū* (etc.) less central a target of missionary attack than Native American berdache were.

(et al.) exists now in Polynesia, with homosexuality recurrently regarded as a criterial feature, though not the only one, and the most important one in the view of some.

Besnier (1994:310) concluded that it is "impossible to define a list of necessary and sufficient conditions" for what he calls Polynesian gender liminality, having earlier eliminated participation in homosexual activities as either necessary or sufficient (299), both because Polynesians who are not "gender liminal" engage in homosexual behavior, and because some "gender liminal" individuals do not. It seems to me that a lack of a definitive checklist of necessary and sufficient conditions is endemic to categorization of roles everywhere. It was to move beyond empirically unmeetable standards for neatness in human categorization schemata that prototype semantics was developed as a more realistic alternative to checklist semantics. (See Fillmore 1975, Kay 1978, and, for historical context, Murray 1994b:461–68). Not just homosexual and/or gender-variant categories, but most categories, especially social categories, are fuzzily bounded. In general, there are "prototypical" instances of a category and less-good instances that are still within a fuzzily bounded category, so it is not surprising that not every *māhū* (etc.) is the same in every detail, or that one or another is not always "on," that is, that even a "master status" is not always primary in every interaction. Not just "gender-liminal identity is foregrounded or backgrounded depending on the nature of the social context" (312), but all identities are, especially if Polynesian personhood is less consistent, atomistic, and homogeneous than "Western middle class" personhood, as Besnier follows other Oceanists in contending (see White and Kirkpatrick 1985, and Besnier 1991). Disappointingly, especially from a gay linguistic anthropologist, Besnier seems to me to provide another instance of demanding more exclusivist rigor for homosexual categories than exist or are required for other kinds of human categorization.

Before wandering into his travesty of "prototype" semantics, Besnier (1994:321–26) provided an interesting case study of a less-than-prototypical (physically handicapped rather than effeminate) *pinapinaaine*. He also stressed that, whether the *fakaleitī* or *pinapinaaine* wants to be sexually receptive to men (or a particular man),

> they are always perceived as a possible sexual conquest by men
> in societies like Samoa and Tonga, in the same way that women
> who are not classificatory relatives always are the potential target of a man's sexual advances. . . . He is frequently the target of
> harassment and physical violence, particularly from men in var-

ious states of inebriation. The gender-liminal individual is viewed as potential sexual "fair game" in a broader sense than women are, in that no brother-sister relationship shields him from the all-out sexual advances. (300–01)

This constant threat of sexual violence is very similar to the that faced by lower-class gender-variant men, including Thai *gatuhy* and Filipino *bakla'*, in other places supposed by some Westerners to be havens of "tolerance." (See Manalansan 1991; Mott 1995; Murray 1991b, 1999a).

Conclusion

That transgendered males have sexual relations with males is much more unequivocally documented than that transgendered females have sexual relations with females, though some recent analysts have pressed interpretations of third (and fourth) genders. Existing data does not establish whether gender or sexuality is the more defining feature in the local views. It seems to me that in these instances that I am classifying as "gender-stratified homosexuality," gender variance and sex with the same sex into which a person was born are very highly correlated. Furthermore, no one in the societies in which gender-variant roles arise shares the Western analytical concern with specifying whether gender or sexuality is more important in defining these kinds of people. What visibly sticks out, that is, what is salient to observers, especially alien ones, is gender nonconformity. Rather than gender abnormality causing homosexuality or homosexuality causing gender deviance, the explanatory models from these societies are that something else (position of the planets or other circumstances at the time of conception, ancestral spirits, parental attributes, etc.) causes both. Not that etiology of either component is a pressing local concern!

In societies in which females are paid to be penetrated, effeminate males are often believed to have such a strong desire to be penetrated that they pay conventionally masculine men for the privilege of extracting the latter's ejaculate. What I find especially interesting about this is that these are societies in which females are also thought to have threateningly voracious appetites, so that it is not at all clear that females have less interest in being penetrated than males have in penetrating them.

An Omani *khanith* may leave the role behind, but in contrast to age-stratified receptive roles, the ones discussed in this chapter, including the *khanith* one, are not transient. Those living as such beings are not expected to change, even though they may not be exclusively receptors or exclusively engaged in sex with male partners.

The last two instances (*khanith* and *māhū*) strike me as less stigma-tized than the European and Latin American instances. The following chapter considers other feminized homosexual males with special reli-gious niches—or at least for whom some observers have claimed a spiri-tual status.

7

Purportedly Sacralized Male Homosexual Roles

The Myth of Male "Temple Prostitutes"

Jewish identity was established by differentiation from the sexual and religious conduct of idol-worshipping neighboring peoples.[1] Even against
this background of hostility, and although biblical passages (collated in
Greenberg 1988:94–95) ban *qdeshim* and link them with gods and forms
of worship detested by orthodox followers of Yahweh (whom they
claimed was the one true god), the texts say nothing of the sexual behavior of the *qdeshim*. Although *qdesh* (masculine) and *qdesha* (feminine)
have often been translated from Hebrew as "temple prostitute" (or as
"sodomite" and "harlot," respectively, in the King James Bible), literally
they mean "consecrated person."[2] The most recent serious examination
of evidence found no evidence that either *qdeshim* or their female counterparts practiced "sacred prostitution," despite the common Jewish and
Christian assumption over the last eighteen centuries that they did: References are to "a cultic prostitute whom no one ever saw and whose
functions are described nowhere. . . . There is no hint in the Hebrew
Bible of how it [sacred prostitution] was allegedly practiced."[3] There is
no evidence that their sexual services were sold to men or that having
sex with them had any religious significance.[4]

---

1. This differentiation was ongoing; it was by no means completed once and for all
by Moses. That Josiah, who reigned from 641 to 609 B.C., found it necessary to purge the
Temple (or its environs—II Kings 23:70 is ambiguous) in Jerusalem of *qdeshim* shows that
they were again or still near the center of Judaism within historical times.

2. St. Jerome's influential Latin translation of the Old Testament, done around the end
of the fourth century A.D., renders *qdeshim* in Deuteronomy as *scortes* ("fornicator"), but as
effeminati in Kings.

3. Henshaw 1994:221, 220, where a bibliography of claims is provided; also see his endorsement of Arnaud's (1973:232–33) contention that "sacred prostitution" even in
Mesopotamia is a myth.

4. Greenberg 1988:95. Deuteronomy 23:18 bans male and female *qdeshim*, and I read
Deuteronomy 23:19 as forbidding the earnings from secular male (*kelev*) or female (*zonah*)
prostitution being brought "into the house of Yahweh thy god" for any vow. Whereas the
first verses of Deuteronomy 23 ban castrates, bastards, Ammonites and Moabites (all kinds
of people) from Yahweh's temple, the verses following verse 19 deal with usury. It may be
(as Greenberg suggested to me in a 5 May 1995 E-mail) that ancient readers and hearers
knew that *qdeshim* were temple prostitutes (so that it was not necessary to specify what
they did), but it seems to me that verses 18 and 19 are not parallel. Verse 19 commences

Similarly, the Hittite texts that "document the existence of male transvestite eunuch temple priests do not state clearly that they had sexual relations with worshipers."[5] Touching the head of Babylonian and Assyrian *assinu*—religious functionaries particularly associated with the goddess Ishtar, who danced, played musical instruments, wore masks and female garb, and who were considered effeminate—was believed to have good military and curative results.[6] Debate continues about whether *assinu* were homosexual prostitutes, and, if they were, whether semen they took into their bodies was conceived by anyone as a gift to the goddess they worshipped, or merely as a corollary of their effeminacy. The omen "if a man has intercourse with an *assinu,* trouble will leave him" (Grayson and Redford 1974:148–49; quoted by Greenberg 1988:96; see also Lambert 1992:151–53) rules out the possibility that the *assinu* were chaste. Moreover, according to Greenberg (1988:97), the root of the noun is the same as that of the verb *assinutu,* "to practice anal intercourse."[7] Although providing a strand of evidence for beneficent effects, this omen text falls far short of providing evidence for sacred warrant or for (homo)sexual prostitution being "part of the religion(s)." Like more recent religious functionaries, at least some of these priests had (homo)sex,[8] but the data needed to establish what such sex meant to either the priests or to their sexual partners do not survive.

------

the discussion of ill-got gains; verse 18, in concert with earlier verses, bans a kind of person. Koehler and Baumgartner 1995 (2:476) has "ritual pederast" as one meaning of *kelev* in Ugaritic, Phoenician, and Jewish Armaic, which undercuts my sacred/secular distinction between *qdesh* and *kelev,* but the primary pan-Semitic meaning of "dog" for *kelev* seems to me more consonant with being penetrated from behind than with being the penetrator.

5. Greenberg 1988:96. Frymer-Kensky is another skeptic about cult prostitution.

6. Greenberg 1988:96. Roscoe (1997:66) noted that "in the Erra myth, Ishtar changes the 'masculinity' of the *kurgarrū* and *assinnu* into femininity (4.55–56). Although this has been interpreted as evidence of a physical transformation, namely, castration, it could as easily refer to a *psychological* transformation, the result of divine possession or visitation."

7. *Assinu* joins the signs for dog and woman (Greenberg 1988:95). For *assinu,* as for *kelev* (see note 3 above), I would suggest that the connection to "dog" is being sexually penetrated from behind.

8. Roman Catholic priests now and the African and Afro-Brazilian priests discussed below engage in same-sex sex, but not during rites or as part of their religious duties, though they may gain access to sexual partners from the ranks of catechists and altar boys who feel some duty to do whatever those whom they believe to be closer to the gods ask or demand that they do.

Claims about the Prostitution of Temple Functionaries during the Conquest of Peru

In *Chronicles*, written between 1539 and 1553, the conquistador historian Pedro Cieza de Léon's mentioned that, near Guayaquíl, Popayán men "pride themselves greatly on sodomy." He added (but did not explain what this meant) that they were "religiously inclined to it" (1959: 293). Cieza quoted Father Domingo de Santo Tomás's accounts of punishing male temple prostitutes in Chincha (south of modern Lima near Pisco on the coast) and in Conchucos (near Huánuco in a highland valley) during the years of the conquest:

> It is true that as a general thing among the mountaineers and the Yungas [i.e., Chima] the devil has introduced this vice under a cloak of sanctity, and in each important temple or house of worship they have a man or two, or more, depending on the idol, who go dressed in women's attire from the time they are children, and speak like them, and in manner, dress, and everything else imitate women. With these, almost like a rite and ceremony on feast [days] and holidays, they have carnal, foul intercourse, especially the chiefs and headmen. I know this because I have punished two, one of them of the Indians of the highlands,[9] who was in a temple, which they call *huaca*, for this purpose, in the province of Conchucos, near the city of Huánuco, the other in the province of Chincha. . . . When I spoke to them of the evil they were doing, and upbraided them for the repulsiveness of their sin, they answered me that it was not their fault because from childhood they have been put there by the caciques [chiefs] to serve them in this cursed and abominable vice, and to act as priests and guard the temples of their idols. So what I deduced from this was that the devil held such sway in this land that, not satisfied with making them fall into so great a sin, he made them believe that this vice was a kind of holiness and religion, to hold more power over them. (314)

9. This is notable in that Cieza judged the Inkas and other mountain peoples (serranos), specifically including the Colla (the conquistadors' label for the Aymara others living on the high plateau [*collao*] generally) and Tarma, free of the nefarious sins so common on the coast, especially in what had been the Chimú empire, which was conquered by the Inkas less than a half century before the arrival of the Spaniards (Cieza 1959 [1553]:277). He distinguished groups to which he attributed sodomites from those to which he did not, though it would be very incautious to conclude that same-sex sex occurred only in the former.

While this constitutes an unusually specific claim of "sacred prostitution," it is suspect coming from someone dedicated to extirpating the religion of those conquered in the name of a Christian king. Such horrors were not attributed to all the conquered peoples in the New World,[10] but the rhetoric of benighted Others practicing "sacred prostitution" goes back to the original differentiation of the Chosen People from other peoples practicing pre-Mosaic religions; this differentiation provided a religious rationalization of seizing the land of those following false gods or demons. Reveling in sodomy was also a then-recent rationale for driving Moorish rulers off the Iberian Peninsula.

Galli

The *fanatici galli* and *galli matris magnae* Roman troops encountered during their campaigns in Asia Minor in 190 and 189 B.C. were mostly itinerant devotees, although some were loosely attached to Cybele temples.[11] These "Phrygian missionaries," as Farnell (1896:297, 300) called them, were centrally involved in disseminating the worship of the Anatolian Great Mother best known as Cybele through the Hellenistic world that Philip of Macedon and his son Alexander the Great had conquered.

During the Second Punic War, panicked by Hannibal, Romans heeded an oracle in the Sibylline Books that told that the only way to drive out an invader was to bring the Great Mother to Rome. In 204 B.C., Pergamon's King Attalos I gave Rome a black meteor said to be Cybele from the main Cybele temple at Pessinus (near modern Ankara, on the Gallus River). It was installed in a temple on the Palatine Hill (that was dedicated on 10 April 191 B.C.), and Hannibal was defeated. A "very expurgated version of the Great Mother's worship annual festival," the Megalensia (*ludi Megalenses*), was added to the official annual religious calendar of the Roman Republic, "with stage performances for six days (4–9 April) and chariot-racing or beast-hunts in the Circus on the anniversary of the day itself. The Megalesia were celebrated with traditional Roman decorum as was appropriate for a divinity who had been domesticated in the very heart of the city and even associated with its foundation legend (as the mother of Romulus and Remus)" (Wiseman 1985:201; see Livy 29.14; Dionysius of Halicarnassus, *Antiquitates Romanae* 19.1, 19.4).

10. For a review of the contact literature, see Murray 1995a:279–92.

11. Livy (37.9.9, 38.18.9–10) and Polybius (21.6.7, 37.4–7). Roscoe (1996a:224) interpreted begging as a "niche" after "the economic viability of the temples they once staffed declined." It would seem to me that recognition by the Roman state must have increased the number of temples and, therefore, the total number of their staff.

Through the end of Republican times, official Roman worship of Cybele did not include the *galli* or their patron Attis, although "excavation of Cybele's temple on the Palatine revealed that right from the beginning in the early second century B.C., her worshippers were dedicating votive statuettes of Attis, unmistakable in his Phrygian cap and effeminately plump physique" (Wiseman 1985:203). (Within the pro-natalist imperatives that they felt) the popularity of Attis and the presence of *galli* necessitated that the Senate prohibit Roman citizens from becoming *galli,* probably at the time the cult was introduced.[12] Dionysius of Halicarnassus reported that no native Roman could even walk in Cybele's processions. The Senate also attempted to control begging priests (Cicero, *De Legibus:* 2.16.40; Lucretius, 2:618–21). More than two centuries after the introduction of the Cybele cult to the Roman state religion, the emperor Claudius officially added rites (celebrated in the month of March) honoring Attis, in which (foreign-born) *galli* were central.[13] It is very likely that these had probably been practiced in private all along, or at least for a very long time (Fasce 1978:95–9).[14] Near the end of the first century A.D., Domitian tried to ban castration (*eviratio*) throughout the empire (Suetonius, *Dom.* 8.3).

Begging, foretelling the future, selling cures, and performing wild possession dances in which they cut themselves and shed quantities of their blood, *galli* were ubiquitous throughout the empire of the first and second centuries. The best-known representation of them is that in Apuleius's fable *Metamorphoses* ("The Golden Ass," 8.27–28), but they were also mentioned by Lucian (or an imitator of Lucan in another version of the same story of the man turned into an ass; *Lucius* §36–41), Ovid, Maritial,[15] Juvenal, Seneca, Livy, Pliny, Plutarch, and others. including many early Christian "church fathers," not least Saint Augustine, who wrote that these men who had (horrifyingly) "removed their manhood with their own hands . . . passed through the streets and alleys

12. This is Roscoe's surmise as well as that of Stevenson (1995:498). Vermaseren (1977:43) suggested that for some time Attis worship was confined to the Cybele temple atop the Palatine Hill. In Phrygia, it seems that Attis was mourned by Cybele worshippers but was not himself worshipped (Schied 1996).

13. Claudius, who relied heavily on a secular eunuch, Posides (Suetonius, *Claudius* 28), was part of a family that was centrally involved in welcoming Cybele (i.e., the meteor) to Rome and had long been among the prime promoters of Cybele veneration (Vermaseren 1977:41, 178).

14. Plutarch, who lived into the second century A.D., regarded Attis as an intruder from foreign superstition, creeping in surreptitiously (*Erotikos* 756).

15. Martial 3.81 has a *gallus* who licks women, not men.

of Carthage, with dripping oily hair and [white-]painted faces [*facie deal-bata*], with soft limbs and a flowing feminine walk, exacting from merchants the means to continue to live shamefully" (*De civitate Dei* 7.26). He claimed that Romans believed that the *galli* (symbolically?) added to the virile power of Rome by sacrificing their virility.[16] Vermaseren summarized ancient reports of extravagantly unmasculine personal appearance as follows:

> On the Day of Blood (*dies sanguinis*) [the gallus] forever discarded his male attire; henceforth he wore a long garment (stola), mostly yellow or multi-coloured, with long sleeves and a belt. On their heads these priests wore a *mitra*, a sort of turban, or a *tiara*, the [Phyrigian] cap with long ear-flaps which could be tied under the chin. The chest was adorned with ornaments, and sometimes they wore ornamented reliefs, pendants, ear-rings, and finger-rings. They also wore their hair long. . . . By preference they had their hair bleached. On the day of mourning for Attis they ran around wildly with disheveled hair, but otherwise they had their hair dressed and waved like women. Sometimes they were heavily made up, their faces resembling white-washed walls. (1977:97)

The *galli* practice most incomprehensible and shocking to Romans was self-castration, though precisely what this involved is far from clear: "procedures called 'castration' in ancient times encompassed everything from vasectomy to complete removal of penis and testicles" (Roscoe 1996a:203). Moreover, it is dubious whether all the priests of the Cybele cult, especially in its central temple in Pessinus, were castrated. As among the modern South Asian *hijra* (Nanda 1990), it appears that not all *galli* underwent any operation on their reproductive equipment, and that some unknown percentage retained (but did not use) fully intact male genitalia under female dress.

The prototypical *gallus*, however, was castrated. In poem 63, Catullus (who lived between 84 and 54 B.C.) prayed to Cybele not to be seized by the sacred frenzy (lines 91–93)[17] after imagining Attis waking up distraught to discover that he has become a *vir sterilis* (line 69). Such regret is what a proper Roman would expect any castrated male to feel, not a report of any who did feel it.

---

16. "[Romani] credita vires adiuvare Romanorum exsecando virilia virorum" (7.26).

17. This is evidence that it was conceivable—for a poet who shows what has been variously interpreted as passivity and masochism toward his mistress Clodia, toward his *puer* Juventius, and in the guise of Sappho in poem 51. See Whigham 1969:42; Wiseman 1985:198–206.

More or less contemporaneously, in *Fasti* (4 m.184) Ovid referred to *galli* as *semimares* ("half men"). Pliny (*Naturalis historia* 11.109) mentioned that *galli* castrated themselves without ill effects (*cintra perniciem amputantibus*). He called them *semiviri* (half-man, 7.15, 7.39).[18] Martial (3.91.2) and Minucius Felix (*Octavius* 22.4) also called them sterile *semivir*. Centuries later, Augustine contended that a castration does not change a man into a woman, although the person does not remain a man.[19] Another Christian writer, Prudentius, also thought that *galli* ceased to be men without becoming women.[20] In *Ad nationes* (1.20.4) Tertullian labeled them a *tertium sexus* ("third sex").[21]

Both *genus* (derived from birth) and *sexus* seem to me biological terms, rather than terms for achieved status (in the recent academic sense of *gender* in English). The data are equivocal on whether non-*galli* regarded *galli* as unsexed (zeroeth sex) or as another (third) sex. The consul Marcus Aemilius Lepidus's decision in 77 B.C. that the Roman *gallus* Genucius could not inherit, because he was neither a man nor a woman (reported approvingly by Valerius Maximus 7.7.5–6) suggests that, jurally, a *gallus* was "null," a nonperson, rather than being a "third" kind of person.[22] The Roman focus on potency and male generativity-based civic functioning on the possession of mature testes. *Testi-* is the root of *testimony* and *testament*. Only those with mature testes could be witnesses in court or make wills (Justinian's *Digest* 28.2.6). In Roman

18. The two other kinds were hermaphrodites and eunuchs.

19. "Hic ita amputatur virilitas, ut nec convertatur in feminam nec vir relinquitar" in *De civitate Dei*, 7.24. Will Roscoe (1996a:213), generally a proponent of identifying "third gender roles," acknowledged that "as the term *semivir*, used synonymously with *cinaedus*, suggests, it may be more accurate to think of *cinaedi* as occupying a subdivision of the male gender role rather than a third gender as such."

20. "[Galli] medium retentat inter alternumgenus mas esse cessat ille, nec fit femina," (*Peristephanon* 10.1071–72).

21. "Habetis et uos tertium genus, etsi non de tertio ritu, attamen de tertio sexu: illus^d aptius de uiro et feminina uiris et feminis iunctum." which, with the help of Louis Crompton, I render as "Indeed, you have a third kind of being, though not a third mode [of behavior] but a third sex, more fittingly mocked by men and women than counted among either of them." All of the ancient literature on the *galli* was written by unsympathetic nonparticipants, as Roscoe (1996a:213) stressed.

22. *Tertium* indubitably means "third," and someone using the label *tertium sexus* must conceive of more than two sexes (or, if sex and gender are not distinguished, more than two sex genders). *Tertium genus* would be better evidence of a conception of "third gender," if it were attested by non-Christians two to four centuries before Tertullian (who was born some time between 155 and 160 A.D.). For eunuchs rather than *galli*, it is: "tertium genus hominum eunochos" (in the Severus Alexander biography of the *Historia Augusta* 23.7; eunuchs are again referred to as a *genus hominum* in 45.5).

law, and I would suggest in Roman society, there was a binary classification of citizen and everyone else. This residual category of inferior— hence penetrable—human beings included females, slaves, prepubescent male children of citizens, and those whose testicles had been removed (*castrati*) or crushed (*thaladiae*).

Also like *hijra*, the *galli* were generally assumed to be prostitutes, sexually receptive to men, that is, they were seen as *mollitia* and called *cinaedi* (derived from the Greek term *kinaidoi*).[23] As the Jews defined themselves by contrast to the polytheism of nearby peoples, the early Christians defined themselves against the Phrygian cult that also celebrated the birth, sacrifice, death, and resurrection of a god, Attis.[24] As Roscoe (1996a:206) elaborated, there were syncretisms (especially the cult of the Naasenes) and "long after the pagan temples stood in ruins (the last recorded official observance of the rites of Cybele and Attis in Rome occurred in 394), Christian fathers found it necessary to pass canon laws against the practice of self-castration by fanatical ascetics in those very regions where the galli had once been so prominent, Asia Minor and the Near East."

As Greenberg (1988:98) noted, none of the Hellenistic sources mentioned ritualized homosexuality, that is, homosexual conduct that was sacralized and part of the religion. I know of no reports indicating that providing semen to a *gallus* conferred any spiritual or magical or medical reward to the inseminator or was a religious duty, or that the semen ejaculated into a *gallus* in any sense became a sacred substance carrying benefit or blessing other than release to the ejaculator. Certainly, homosexual conduct (specifically, performing fellatio) was often attributed to

23. *Mollitia* connoted weak and cowardly, not "feminine" in some neutral descriptive sense. Through the medieval *molles* (e.g., in the 1192 chronicle of Richard of Devizes), this became the designation of a gender variant man in seventeenth-century England as a *molly*. (The Oxford English Dictionary derives *molly* from "Mary.")

24. The *hilaria*, a rite celebrating Attis's rebirth, was added in the mid-third century A.D. (Roscoe 1996a:205). In reviewing psychoanalytical interpretations, Roscoe stressed the lack of a Father God: Attis is not emasculated by a paternal competitor, but does it himself. He thus "eliminates the primordial threat which is the source of the father's power over the son" and usurps that power. For Catullus (63.64–67), Attis was avoiding the transition from being a much-courted, receptive *puer delicatus* to becoming an insertor husband. That Attis (and his *galli* emulators) offers his severed penis to the goddess suggests fear of women's sexuality, more specifically of having to penetrate women. He thus can remain woman-like in sexual behavior and can become more woman-like in dress (see Farnell 1896:300–301 on "ecstatic craving to assimilate oneself to the goddess and to charge oneself with her power," i.e., flight to female power rather than just flight away from the demands of male potency).

the *galli,* but this seemed to follow from their gender status rather than from their religious calling.

Another "eastern religion" that also, shockingly, lacked the traditional Roman obsession with male generative power, followed the Cybele cult in both time and space:

> Probably the most celebrated eunuch of antiquity was the ante-Nicene Father Origen [185?–254? A.D.] whose most famous (infamous) action was his youthful self-castration [inspired by a literal interpretation of Matthew 19]. There are those who would deny that Origen ever did such a thing, and yet the evidence of the period overwhelmingly confirms that self-castration was not uncommon for Christians in this period. Christianity was spreading the ancient ascetic principles of the East to Rome and probably played no smaller role in establishing the eunuch throughout the region than did the cult of Cybele. (Stevenson 1995:506)

Origen et al. were not prostitutes—sacred, temple, or any other kind of prostitutes.

Ancient South and Southwest Asia
Anatolia

What we know about the *galli* mendicant priests of the Great Mother is primarily from Roman sources, and is discussed immediately above. Whether or not there is any historical connection between *galli* and South Asian *hijras,* structural similarities between the castrated men in the two cults should be obvious in the discussion below (pp. 306–11; also see Roscoe 1997).

Persia

Eunuchs were present in Assyrian and Babylonian courts and temples. According to Xenophon (*Cyropaedia* 7.60–65), Cyrus the Great, who ruled a vast Persian empire in the sixth century B.C., preferred eunuch military officers because men without wives and incapable of siring sons would be loyal only to him. His successors placed eunuchs in nearly all the chief offices of state administration, and made some generals. One, Bagoas, conquered Egypt. "Not every eunuch was used homosexually, but many were," as Greenberg (1988:123) summarized scattered, sketchy literature.

India

In pre-Islamic South Asia, the techniques of the "arts of love" were extensively elaborated. Section 2.9 of the *Kāma Sūtra* (ca. fifth century A.D.) includes instructions on how to be fellated (*maukhya*) by eunuchs (*tṛīyā prakrti*). A Hindu notion of those neither man (*puṃs*) nor woman (*strī*) was particularly elaborated by several cults.[25] These present the usual problem of inferring whether such persons are defective males, social non-entities, or a "third kind" of person (i.e., zeroeth sex, defective first sex, or third sex, but not socially or jurally a kind of woman). Roscoe (1997:74–75) argued for third **gender**:

> the *Nātya-s'āstra,* a drama manual (200 B.C.E.–200 C.E.), places guidelines for portraying such persons together with those for male and female roles in a chapter on the *prakrti,* literally, the "genders" (chap. 24). Other relevant Sanskrit terms include *tṛīyā prakṛti,* or "third nature" (*Kāmasūtra,* 2.9; *Mahābhārata,* 4.59 [northern variant]; *Ubhayābhisārikā,* v. 21), *strīrūpini/strīpumān,* "woman-man," (*Kāmasūtra,* 2.9; *Mahābhārata,* 5.189.5; *S'ukasaptati*) and *napuṃsaka,* "not male" (*Nātya-s'āstra,* 24.68–69; *Ayurveda;* in Sethi 1970:42).

Zwilling and Sweet (1996:362) treat *napuṃsaka,* "not a male" as the original generic category for a "distinct though stigmatized social group, with institutionalized roles as practitioners of traditionally female occupations: singers, dancers, and, later [than in Vedic times], prostitutes." Although originally incorporating gender ambiguity, it became a category for a third sex "determined at conception by purely biological causes" just like the other two sexes (specifically, by the ratio of father's seed and mother's blood) in *āyurveda* medical theory.[26]

Zwilling (1992:205) characterized *napuṃsaka* as a quality, the lack

25. Vallabhacarya is a particularly flamboyant one devoted to Krsna's mistress, Radha, exalted to the role of heavenly consort. Devotees of Radha's cult "assume the garb of women with all their ordinary manners and affect to be subject even to their monthly sickness" (Bhandarkar 1913:86).

26. "The word *linga,* or sex, was adopted as the technical term for grammatical gender, a move that precipitated much confusion and complexity," especially for trying to distinguish third gender from third sex (Zwilling and Sweet 1996:365). Zwilling and Sweet (1996:375) asserted that except for the Jain one(s), no other Indian system of thought separated biological sex (*dravyalinga*) from psychological gender (or sexuality: *bhāvalinga*). While the two were supposed to be usually congruent, they were not necessarily so, having different causes. Another aspect of conception with consequences is position: if the woman is on top, the child conceived will grow up to be an anally receptive male or a

of maleness. The generic category for those with this quality was *"pan-daka,* a word of obscure origin but that ultimately may be derived from apa + anda + ka, 'without testicles'" (204). In classic Buddhist texts, *pan-daka* were described as being incapable of religious discipline because they have the defiling passions of both sexes and are without the modesty and capacity for shame that might hold the passions in check (205). As were the kinds of effeminate pathics discussed in Hellenistic and Muslim medical treatises (see pp. 257–59), the *pandaka* were represented as being hyperlibidinous.

Generally, in South Asian religious views, sexual desire is a form of attachment, and all attachments are impediments to spiritual transcendence of the cycle of rebirths. Homosexual attachments are not inherently any greater impediment than are heterosexual ones. In that third-sexed persons were thought to be hyperlibidinous with both male and female sexual desires, attaining spiritual liberation was thought to be more difficult, but not absolutely impossible.[27] This theoretical doubling of sexual desires (i.e., for both males and females) was considered a reason to bar ordination in Buddhist and Jain monastic communities: "normative males and females were assumed to be safe from sexual temptation in gender-segregated communities, but the bisexual third-sex person would be at risk himself, and a source of danger to others, among either males or females."[28]

Ritual purity was more severely compromised by heterosexual than by homosexual sex on the part of the upper three (of four phyla of) Hindu castes, judging by the rituals prescribed in sacred law texts, the most famous of which is the third-century A.D. *Code of Manu.* Ritual purity was not expected of the lowest caste or outcastes—or of the gods, who freely cross dressed (see O'Flaherty 1980:88–89). Some of them combined sexes (see many hermaphrodite representations), or alternated them. For instance, Shiva, who is worshipped by pouring milk on a stone phallus called a *lingam,* impregnated Vishnu with a son (Harihara or Ayappa), while Vishnu was appearing as a woman. There is a view

---

lesbian, according to the Sanskrit medical treatise *Sushruta* (3.2.45; Sweet and Zwilling 1993:597).

27. For Jain theory, see Zwilling and Sweet (1996:368–70, 372); in their "survey of the canonical literature we did not encounter any reference to actual bisexual practices of third-sex persons" (373).

28. Over time, the ban was relaxed (Zwilling and Sweet 1996:378); on the Buddhist bar, see Zwilling 1992:209. Proscriptions were primarily for monks, with some for nuns; "the question of sexual ethics for laypeople is one that was little addressed by Indian Buddhist thinkers" (Zwilling 1992:210).

that only Vishnu is entirely male, so that all other creatures—and especially those worshipping Vishnu as incarnated as Krishna—are female in relation to him.[29] How widespread or salient this interpretation is cannot be determined from literature on the congeries of beliefs and practices termed "Hinduism."[30]

Eunuchs staffed important posts in Indian courts as early as the fourth century B.C. (Kautilya, *Arthas'āstra* 1.12, 20; see Saletore 1974: 43–47, 195–99). Early Indian law books proscribe "eunuchs" from inheriting, while specifying that they be maintained by the king.[31] By the time of the Mughals, an elaborate organization of eunuchs existed in most courts (*Fo-Sho-Hing-Tsan-King*, 1.5.388; Saletore 1974:47, 196– 209; Sharma 1984:383–84). Some had affairs with their masters; many were made eunuchs for sexual purposes. Their role in Indian life continued well into the nineteenth century.

The *Nārada Smṛti*, an Indian law book from the fourth or fifth century A.D., defines fourteen categories of "impotent men," including those "naturally impotent," men who have been castrated, those cursed by a supernatural, those afflicted by jealousy, those who spill their seed, and those who are shy (12.11–19; see Sweet and Zwilling 1993:592–94). I see these not as "genders" or "sexes" (or as "homosexuals") but as kinds of non-procreative men, some of whom are potent with males and some of whom receive male potency in one or another of their own orifices. The most famous counterfeit eunuch is the legendary archer Arjuna in the fourth book of the *Mahābhārata* (ca. 0 ±200), who disguises himself as a heavily bangled eunuch named Brihannala and lives in the harem of Virata, king of Yudhistira, for a year.

Contemporary South Asia
*Hijra*s

In northern South Asia (what is now northern India, Pakistan, and Bangladesh) itinerant groups of castrated and/or cross-dressed men dancing and demanding money at weddings and celebrations of male births were noticed and written about by alien travelers, colonists, and anthropologists (see Hall 1997: 431–37, 453n. 2). American anthropologist

29. And there is one tradition in which even Krishna splits himself into a male and a female in order to copulate with his female half, Naradapañcaratra-Samhita (reported with palpable horror by Bhandarkar 1913:86).

30. On its plurality, see Walker 1968.

31. Roscoe (1997) cited *Gautama-dharmasūtra* (300–100 B.C.), 28.43; *Arthas'āstra* (324– 300 B.C.), 3.5; *Vasistha-dharmasūtra* (300–100 B.C.), 17.52–53, 19.35; *Manusmrti*, 9.201.

Morris Opler criticized the India-born Scottish psychiatrist Morris Carstairs (1967 [1957]:59–60) for representing *hijras* (in the *maharajate* of Mewar in north India, where Carstairs grew up and where he did fieldwork in 1950 to 1952) as transvestite prostitutes, "believed always to be passive homosexuals" (Carstairs 1956:130). On the basis of one 1949 interview with three *hijras* in Allahabad (a north Indian city in southern Uttar Pradesh), Opler (1959, 1960) insisted that *hijras* were ritual specialists, devotees of the Mother Goddess, Bahucharta Mata, and that they did not prostitute themselves.[32] Their castration allowed them to confer their blessings on newborn sons and newly wed couples, and they had neither economic or erotic motivation to have sex with men, but were only dancers, according to Opler. Obviously, some persons labeled *hijra* are both prostitutes **and** celebrants of rites of passage, although no one has yet endeavored to measure either the relative time spent or the relative income derived from the two kinds of performance. If there were longitudinal data, I would hypothesize that reliance on sex is increasing, and that for most *hijras* the income derived from prostitution exceeds that earned at weddings and birth celebrations.[33] Based on fieldwork with *hijras*, American anthropologist Serena Nanda concluded that

> there is absolutely no question that at least some *hijras*—perhaps even the majority—are homosexual prostitutes. . . . That *hijras*, at least in modern historical times, engage in widespread homosexual activity, undermines their respect in society but does not negate their ritual function.
>
> *Hijras* are well aware that they have only a tenuous hold on legitimacy in Indian society and that this hold is compromised by even covertly engaging in sexual relations and practicing prostitution. The idea of *hijras* as "wives" (of ordinary men) and

32. Opler denied any moralistic motivation in arguing against Carstairs, writing to me in a 1982 letter: "I do not find that I generalized from the testimony given to me by the Hijras I interviewed. They told me that they did not act as male prostitutes and were probably telling the truth, for they lived and worked in a region where the demand for their traditional ceremonial services was great. I reported this for what it was worth and did not pursue the topic, since the interview was based on a chance encounter and was unconnected with the village study I had gone to India to make." Naqvi and Mujtaba (1997) provide a case study of a contemporary *hijra* in Pakistan, Farzana, who "says her devotion to God is indicated by her sexual abstinence and by the way she earns her living: 'I have a special relationship with God because I make my living by uttering his name. All I do is give God's blessings to people: may God give you a son, may God give you a long life.'"

33. Roscoe (1991b:125) made a similar surmise. Hall (1997:430) estimated that there are 1.2 million *hijras* now living in India.

prostitutes obviously runs counter to their claims to be ascetics
or other-worldly religious mendicants, that is, people who have
renounced sexual activity. (1990:10–11; also see 52–54)

One *hijra* prostitute, Kamladevi, bluntly told her: "Those who say they
have no sexual interest are all telling lies. Those who say they have
less interest—that they like only to sing and dance—they are the aged
people. When they were young, sex was their main desire. Now they say,
'Oh, I think only of God and religion,' but that's all nonsense. When you
enter the 'dragon' of this life, you get the bad habits first; then when you
become old you become less desirous of this sexual interest and think
more of religion. It is only from getting older" (57; see also Allahbadia
and Shah 1992:48).[34]

Although castration is a socially sanctioned and defining feature
of the role, South Asians, including *hijra*s, call some uncastrated cross-
dressing men *hijra*s. That is, some males classify themselves and/or are
classified by others as *hijra*s without this purportedly defining feature.[35]
Not all ever get around to arranging the transformative operation—although pressure increases on such deviants within *hijra* communities
and in interactions in which legitimacy to confer blessings of the Mother
Goddess are challenged by customers and skeptical bystanders. In addition to avoiding the embarrassment of being regarded as inauthentic—
and even as fraudulent—another encouragement is that those who can
display the scars of castration make more money (Hall 1995:124). In
that this "defining" feature is variable, it is obvious that (natal/biological)
males are *hijra*s first (i.e., regard themselves as *hijra*s and are regarded as
*hijra*s by others), and only later ponder the irreversible role commitment
that castration inscribed directly on the body.

The *hijra* views collected by Nanda (1990) are that *hijra*s are born
*hijra*s. Older *hijra*s identified some of them when celebrating their births.
Some felt they were *hijra*s and went to join their "own kind." Not a few
were impelled by the labeling of non-*hijra*s, but this was conceived by
them as recognition (not creation) of their nature. At least in South
Asian folklore and in some foreigner observers' claims, some children

34. Only near the end and in passing in Hall's discussion of *hijra*s' gender (449) does
she mention "servicing men sexually in private." Despite her thorough knowledge of the
Hindi and English literature on *hijra*s, in which it is often reported and sometimes debated,
she never mentions "prostitution" at all.

35. Moreover, while uncastrated *hijra*s generally maintain "that they never have sex
with each other, nor do they penetrate . . . [in] one-on-one discussion in a *besharam*
(shameless) environment, some have revealed the opposite" (Ś. Khan 1997b:4).

are kidnapped or sold to *hijras* (i.e., they are manufactured rather than innately *hijra*). Lawrence Cohen found class differences in non-*hijra* explanations in Varanasi, a city of about a million in the northern Indian state of Uttar Pradesh:

> Pramod, from a poor petty-bourgeois family, once said to me that as a rule *hijras* are born third[-sexed], discovered by other *hijras* when they come to see newborn babies and examine their genitals. Middle class men and women I knew from Varanasi often said *hijras* were never born that way nor did they elect an operation, but were kidnapped and sold into a sexual slave trade, for which purpose they were castrated and penectomized. Men across class also said *hijras* were impotent men, literally nonmen, and that their thirdness was secondary to their inability to please a wife. (1995:283–84)

While some *hijras* no doubt devote themselves entirely to their sacred callings and abstain from sex, not a few of those who told their stories to Nanda mentioned that they did not desire sex with women. For instance, Lalitha told Nanda "We are all men, born as men, but when we look at a woman, we don't have any desire for them. When we see men, we like them, we feel shy, we feel some excitement" (1990:16; also see Sinha 1967). Some come to like sexual receptivity that they first experienced as coercion. That is they "get spoiled." [36] Others find it relatively easy, relatively lucrative work. Some find "husbands. Allahbadia and Shah (1992:48) noted that "to satisfy this [homosexual] need they go and stay with other men in the neighborhoods who are living alone or whose wives are sick or away from home. They do all the household work and agree to receptive anal intercourse, from which they get sexual gratification." Some *hijras* try to avoid sex altogether, especially as age decreases their marketability.[37] As for other eunuchs in other times and places, there is a general presumption that *hijras* are available sexual receptacles, even if some are uninterested in any kind of sex.

36. Kamladevi in Nanda (1990:16). An unnamed one is quoted similarly by Vyas and Shingala (1987:45). Having interviewed thirty-five Bombay *hijras*, Allahbadia and Shah (1992) contended that coercion is the general route with children kidnapped or sold by indigent parents (most of those they interviewed originated in southeastern India in Tamil Nandu, i.e., far from Mumbai/Bombay). Nanda (1990:10) referred to three turn-of-the-century reports of *hijras* kidnapping children (also see Hall 1997:434). Many *hijras* told Shivananda Khan of "an early involvement in anal penetration in their villages" (1997b:4).

37. Moreover, at least in Bangladesh, *hijras'* fees for sex are less than those of female or male prostitutes, and these fees decrease with age, according to S. Khan (1997a:5).

Badruddin Khan, a native of Karachi, the capital of Pakistan, has insisted to me that *hijras* (whom he defines as "men who dress as women, including transvestites, castrati, and true hermaphrodites") are a kind of man (not a third sex or third gender),[38] socially regarded as inadequate men because of their failure—or refusal—to procreate. As he explained the generalized Pakistani view, men who are sterile or impotent or exclusively homosexual also belong to this class (sometimes glossed as "impotents," e.g., by Sinha 1967). Absence of procreativity, not any erectile incapacity or desire for male sexual partners, is what is most noticed in South Asian societies where the family is close to being everything and is at least the meaning as well as the source of life, and producing children is a prerequisite of full adulthood (see B. Khan 1997a, 1997b; S. Khan 1998:3). According to Hall (1997:444), *hijra* nonprocreativity is viewed (by their natal families) as possibly contagious, Thus, *hijras* should be cut off from the families they could have but have refused to increase.

Although the ideological rationale for *hijra* communities is shared devotion to the Mother Goddess, gurus function as pimps or bordello keepers without any religious legitimation.[39] So far as I know, no one has claimed that *hijras* are engaged in "sacred prostitution"). Like totally secular equivalents, "the community of gurus and prostitutes provides their working space, a steady source of customers, a minimum assurance of physical security in case customers get rowdy, and someone to pay off the police so that they are not arrested" (Nanda 1990: 53–54). Besides sacred and secular work, *hijra* households provide economic security for the aged and for any who become disablingly ill, and social support for those cut off from their natal families. As Nanda (1990:48) noted, in

38. Nanda (1990:xviii) and Hall (1995:63) reported "free variation" of male, female, and neuter pronouns when among themselves, though Hall (1995:84) called attention to the use of (former) males names during disputes between *hijras*, and for commands (84, 88). She suggested that feminine forms build and signal intimacy/solidarity, masculine forms power and distance. She wrote of *hijras* being "outside and therefore inferior to the female/male dichotomy" (218), i.e., as a zeroeth rather than a third gender. Like Wikan, Nanda was reluctant to let go of John Money's universal biologically determined entity, the *transsexual* (Nanda's book includes a preface by him).

39. Oedipal resentment of gurus is not missing, either. For instance, Murmatz, an uncastrated Baluchi *hijra* dancer in Pakistan, told Naqvi and Mujtaba, "I did not get myself castrated despite constant pressure from other hijras. You see, these gurus get their protégés castrated for their own personal interests. Once the chela is castrated, he is bound to the guru for life and that means he has to give his guru the lion's share of his income. I am like other males, and I have sexual desires like them, for male sexual partners" (1997:263).

South Asia, "being independent of the group means not freedom, but so-cial suicide."

Other Cross-Dressed Prostitutes in Pakistan and India

Zenanas or *jankhas* (men who sometimes dress like women and dance like *hijra*s, but who do not get castrated) have been represented by social scientists as incomplete or preoperative *hijra*s (L. Cohen 1995: 285, 276). *Hijra*s say that *zenanas* are in it just for the *dhanda* (business). But, as Naqvi and Mujtaba explained,

> the zenanas themselves do not always claim that they are hijras. Says Sunny, who is avowedly a zenana, "I am not a hijra. Only my *ruh* [soul] is that of a woman. I started realizing I was differ-ent from other people at the age of 16. It was as if flames were rising in my heart. My father used to get angry with me. 'Why do you walk like this and where do you go?' he used to ask me. He once put me in chains. Then I fell in love with a man, but he is now a *pardesi* (a lover who has gone away, perhaps to foreign lands)."
>
> Sunny markets his wares in Karachi's Empress Market, hang-ing out with other zenanas in cafés and other public places. He lives with his family and does tailoring at home, but makes ex-tra cash by prostituting himself—without the knowledge of his parents. Sunny says that a lot of men prefer hijras to women. "They like the hijra gestures, which are very different from those of normal women." (1997: 265)

Males seeking males for sex, if they have an automobile or motorbike, drive around north Indian and Pakistani cities or, if not, visit certain restaurants, cinemas, hotel lobbies, video-game shops, parks, or railroad stations. Many of those stalking paying customers prefer to "conduct business" in the backseats of clients' cars or to go to hotel rooms rather than to run the risk of being assaulted or robbed by someone taking them to their home (if they have a home with any privacy for sexual li-aisons). Turning tricks in cars and hotels also allows boys to get back and to connect with another customer sooner.

A large number of the full-time male prostitutes are runaways. How-ever, there are also many part-time prostitutes—especially schoolboys and those working in hotels and garages—who prostitute themselves on the side for extra money, clothes, and gifts, or for other jobs (especially the promises of television or cinema roles). Most range in age from fifteen to twenty-five. Theirs is a short career in which the product's market value generally declines rapidly.

In Pakistan, the ethnic origins of male prostitutes and their clients varies. Their ranks include natives of all the four provinces, along with refugees from Afghanistan and Iran. Most have had little or no education. Average earnings are in the range of five thousand to seven thousand rupees a month (fifty rupees are equivalent to one U.S. dollar), although those whose clients are foreign tourists, sailors, and marines earn considerably more. The lowest stratum of prostitutes is composed of those from poor families who rent their bodies to other low-income men. Some lower-class boys also function as "wives" of poor men who cannot afford to get married.

Assaulting boys and then photographing them in the nude is a common way of trapping boys "into the life" of prostitution. Many were sexually abused at an early stage in their lives. Mujtaba (1997) estimated that every ninth or tenth boy in school or at local *madrassahs* or even at work is sexually molested. The boy never reports this to his parents out of fear that they will blame him rather than the perpetrator.[40]

Some families turn a blind eye to their son's profession because they are dependent on income from his trade. This is especially the case if the son has migrated to a city and is supporting the family by sending them monthly money orders. Generally, families of male prostitutes are blissfully ignorant of the son's profession, because the boys take great care to avoid discovery. Indeed, acquiescing to the demands of someone who threatens to expose something discrediting (not always involvement in sex) about them is a recurrent motif in the accounts of their careers. Mujtaba provided an example in which a group of policemen terrorized a youth into providing them with both sex and income from sex he had with others:

> Once Farrukh was apprehended by a group of drunken policeman late at night. They beat him until he told them his name, address, and profession. "Then they took me to their quarters and gang-raped me. Following that they demanded that I 'work' for them or they would throw me behind bars and tell my father."
>
> It was this fear of his father that turned Farrukh into a full-time prostitute. . . . On average he makes five hundred to six hundred rupees for three to four hours work an evening. Out of this, two hundred rupees go to the police as *bhatta* [a bribe]. Sometimes, he says, he works with the police to blackmail un-

40. As in other Islamic societies (see Murray 1997b:18), anyone who is known to have been penetrated has greater difficulty in warding off others who want to use him sexually.

suspecting clients. Routinely, the policemen also present him as a "favor" to their homosexual seniors. Police officials also often smuggle boys into various jails across the country to service select inmates. Another boy explains that it is difficult to be independent because "pimps and the hotel owners harass us a great deal and the police are with them, so we don't dare mess with them."

Indeed, a lot of boys are frequently picked up by policemen who use them without payment. In Karachi and Hyderabad many pimps and male prostitutes act as informers for the police and the CIA. Extortion and blackmail by plainclothes police (or those pretending to be police) occur in virtually every area where male prostitution exists. (1997:269)

Similar police expropriation of the bodies of sex workers has been reported from all over the subcontinent (e.g., *Ki Pukaar,* April 1996:17).

In Dhaka, Bangladesh, S. Khan (1996:19) interviewed rickshaw drivers and "tea shop/restaurant boys" who occasionally provided sexual services for money, and described a park in which twenty to thirty male prostitutes per day work. Ranging in age from sixteen to forty, "these boys are self-defined as *kothi* [effeminate]." He found that most have other jobs and that some are married and have children. "All the boys in this group have used contraceptive pills to enlarge their breasts. They stated that their clients like the larger breasts, which they squeeze while having sex." What their wives think of this, Khan did not inquire. He did establish that the younger the *kothi,* the higher the price; that the price for sex in the park was lower than that for going outside it to have sex (middle-class clients preferring and being able to afford to take the *kothi* elsewhere); that sex mostly took the form of anal penetration of the *kothi;* and that, as for *hijras,* "there was a guru system operating, where all the boys belonged to the social group within the park. The group maintains price levels and provides advice and support."

A Naz Foundation study of one Delhi massage parlor found that the eight masseurs earned about five thousand rupees a month, while the owner earned twenty thousand. There was a premium on youth (though the age range was only from sixteen from twenty-five). Vinod, the owner, estimated that 98 percent of the customers were seeking sex. The masseurs were trained in how to perform fellatio. Some of them reported anally penetrating some customers. All denied being penetrated. Those interviewed had had sex with females, do not consider themselves "gay," enjoy sex with males, and do not tell their family about the source of their income (*Ki Pukar,* Jan. 1998, 22–23).

The Indian lesbian activist and founder of Sakhi resentfully contrasted the lack of surviving religious traditions for females:

> The *hinjra* tradition of men who have given up their "masculinity" and thereby assumed a "feminine gender" still has a large following as well as their goddess temples. However, the earlier lesbian tradition linked to similar goddess traditions are virtually unknown. The temples that exist from these traditions have been taken over by men, for example the Tara-Tarini temple traditions in Orissa. . . . Whereas cultural categories for men allow for a certain fluidity, women are confined within the "lakshman rekha". Stepping out of these boundaries results in either being labeled a *dayin* (witch) in most rural traditions, or being labeled "Western" in the urban context.(Thadani:1996:114–15)

Northeastern Siberia's Transformed Shamans
Chukchi

Vladimir Bogoraz (1904)[41] described at some length the transvestite, homosexual male shaman of the North Siberian Chukchi.[42] He noted that "family shamans" were very common among the Chukchi: "almost every third or fourth person" (413). As in other societies around the world with shamanism or spirit possession,[43] the role was not sought and, often, was resisted: "The shamanistic call manifests itself in various ways. Sometimes it is an inner voice which bids the person enter into intercourse with the 'spirits.' If the person is dilatory in obeying, the calling spirit soon appears in some outward, visible shape, and communicates the call in a more explicit way. . . . Young people, as a rule, are exceedingly reluctant to obey the call, especially if it involves the adoption of some characteristic device in clothing or in the mode of life" (418). Individual resistance was countered by parental hopes for higher status:

> The parents of young persons "doomed to inspiration" (*ene nitvu ll nyo*) act differently. . . . especially in families rich in children,

41. In his youth, before he completed coursework at the University of St. Petersburg, Vladimir G. Bogoraz (1865–1936) was exiled to Siberia for political activity. His scientific study of the environment (human and physical) in northeastern Siberia earned recognition from the St. Petersburg Academy of Science, and he was invited to join the American Museum of Natural History's famed Jesup Expedition, which surveyed and collated information about the peoples on both sides of the North Pacific.

42. The name is from *cawcu*, the self-designation of the reindeer breeders, according to Jakobson et al. (1957:219). Their self-designation was (is?) "Luorawetlan" (genuine man).

43. The distinction is one of agency, with shamans harnessing the power of spirits, spirits taking over the bodies of their chosen human mediums.

with large herds, and with several tents of their own. Such a family is not inclined to feel anxious about a possible loss of one of its members. On the contrary, they are desirous of having a shaman of their own, a special solicitor before the 'spirits,' and a caretaker in all extraordinary casualties of life.

For men, the preparatory stage of shamanistic inspiration is in most cases very painful, and extends over a long time. The call comes in an abrupt and obscure manner, leaving the young novice in much uncertainty regarding it. He feels "bashful" and frightened; he doubts his own disposition and strength, as has been the case of all seers from Moses down. (420)

As in other traditions, the Chukchi shamans denied any learning:

Various tricks performed by the Chukchee shamans, including ventriloquism, have to be learned in the preparatory stage. However, I could obtain no detailed information on this point, since the shamans, of course, asserted that the tricks were done by "spirits," and denied having any hand whatever in proceedings of such a character. . . . Most of the shamans I knew claimed to have had no teachers, but to have acquired their art by their own individual efforts. I am not aware of a single instance of the transfer of shamanistic power in the whole domain of Chukchee folklore. (425)

Bogoraz adduced a common temperament among those chosen by the spirits:

Nervous and highly excitable temperaments are most susceptible to the shamanistic call. The shamans among the Chukchee with whom I conversed were as a rule extremely excitable, almost hysterical, and not a few of them were half crazy.

The Chukchee are well aware of the extreme nervousness of their shamans, and express it by the word *ninI rkIlqin* ("He is bashful"). By this word they mean to convey the idea that the shaman is highly sensitive even to the slightest change of the psychic atmosphere surrounding him during his exercises. For instance, the Chukchee shaman is diffident in acting before strangers, especially shortly after his initiation. A shaman of great power will refuse to show his skill when among strangers, and will yield only after much solicitation; even then, as a rule, he will not show all of his power. He is shy of strange people, of a house to which he is unaccustomed, of "alien" drums and charms. . . . The least doubt or sneer makes him break off the performance and retire. The shamanistic "spirits" are likewise described as "fleeting" (nIrInAqen). (415–17)

Stages of Transformation

After providing considerable detail about shamanistic performances (including a number involving the display of the shaman's genitals to the moon), Bogoraz considered the transvestitic aspects of Chukchi shamans:

> A separate branch of Chukchee shamanism, dealing with the perversions of sexual sense . . . refers to that shamanistic transformation of men and women in which they undergo a change of sex in part, or even completely. This is called "soft man being" (*yIrka'ǯ-la' ul-va'rgin*); "soft man" (*yIrka'ǯ-la' ul*) meaning a man transformed into a being of a softer sex. A man who has changed his sex is also called "similar to a woman" (*ñe'uchica*), and a woman in similar condition, "similar to a man" (*qa'cIkIchēca*). Transformation is gathered only from hearsay [i.e., Bogoraz did not observe any]. Transformation takes place by the command of the *ke'let*, usually at the critical age of early youth when shamanistic inspiration first manifests itself. It is, however, much dreaded by the youthful adepts; and in most of those cases in which I spoke of the young shamans preferring death to obedience to the call of the "spirits," there was connected with the call a reference to change of sex. There are, however, various degrees of transformation of this kind.
>
> In the first stage, the person subjected to it [im]personates the woman only in the manner of braiding and arranging the hair of the head. This usage is widespread among the Chukchee, and is adopted not only by shamans at the command of the "spirits," but also by sick persons at the bidding of shamans. In the latter case the aim is to change the appearance of the patient so as to make him unrecognizable by the "spirits."
>
> The second stage is marked by the adoption of female dress, which is also practiced either for shamanistic or for medico-magical purposes. . . . Adoption of the dress, although the most conspicuous feature of the transformation, does not confer the extraordinary power which is considered to be the rightful appurtenance of the change.
>
> The third stage of transformation is more complete. A young man who is undergoing it leaves off all pursuits and manners of his sex, and takes up those of a woman. He throws away the rifle and the lance, the lasso of the reindeer herdsmen, and the harpoon of the seal-hunter, and takes to the needle and the skin-scraper. He learns the use of these quickly, because the "spirits" are helping him all the time. Even his pronunciation changes

from the male to the female mode. At the same time his body alters, if not in its outward appearance, at least in its faculties and forces. He loses masculine strength, fleetness of foot in the race, endurance in wrestling, and acquires instead the helplessness of a woman. Even his physical character changes. The transformed person loses his brute courage and fighting spirit, and becomes shy of strangers, even fond of small-talk and of nursing small children. Generally speaking, he becomes a woman with the appearance of a man.

That is, is at least socially, the transformed male shaman becomes a member of "the second sex." [44] In an earlier report Bogoraz wrote:

The invert assumes the clothing of the opposite sex, its pronunciation, all its pursuits and habits, and adopts them with astonishing facility and ease. . . . According to information supplied by the Chukchee, some effeminates after a while change physically and acquire female organs, but those womanish-men whom I saw, notwithstanding their female garb and marriage, were really tall and strong men.

They did not take woman's names, but, although there are distinct stocks of Chukchi men's names and of women's names, some males who were not transformed males bore women's names. (1900:28–29)

Husbands

"Becomes a woman" included having a husband:

The most important of the transformations is, however, the change of sex. The "soft man" begins to feel like a woman. He seeks to win the good graces of men, and succeeds easily with the aid of the "spirits." Thus, he has all the young men he could wish for, striving to obtain his favor. From these he chooses his lover, and after a time takes a husband. The marriage is performed with the usual rites, and I must say that it forms a quite solid union, which often lasts till the death of one of the parties. The couple live much in the same way as do other people. The man tends his herds and goes hunting and fishing, while the "wife" takes care of the house, performing all domestic pursuits and work. They cohabit in a perverse way, *modo Socratis* [i.e., anal intercourse], in which the transformed wife always plays the passive rôle. In this, again, some of the "soft men" are said to lose altogether the man's desire and in the end to even acquire the

---

44. I think that by "appearance of a man" Bogoraz meant size and hirsuteness. Female dress was already adopted in the second stage.

organs of a woman; while others are said to have mistresses of
their own in secret and to produce children by them.

In his earlier account, (Bogoraz 1900:29) also wrote that "the male-to-
female transformed shaman (*jbIpkà-láyl*) "marries and lives with his
spouse in the Socratic mode, occupying at the same time a passive role."

Later, Svendrup (1937) claimed homosexual desire was the motivation for gender transformation. In describing what appeared to be a tall
woman of forty to fifty years of age whose need to shave her whiskers
originally mystified him, Svendrup (1937:125) recounted that Naeaanpakjin lived as a man until the age of twenty-five, and then "decided he
wanted to wear women's clothing and live like a woman, and has taken
a new name. . . . The man was homosexual and had changed his name
and way of life because he 'needed men.' My friends named three other
men who dressed like women." Presumably "needed men" was a native
explanation. Svendrup made no mention of a supernatural call in this instance, but noted, "Naeaanpakjin played his part as a woman perfectly,
worked in his tent, cooked, sewed, and talked with the switching pronunciation and the high-pitched voice of the women" (1937:126; HRAF
translation). According to Bogoraz, the human husband is not the household's only one:

> Each "soft man" is supposed to have a special protector among
> the "spirits," who for the most part is said to play the part of a
> supernatural husband (ke'le-uwä'que) of the transformed one.
> This husband is supposed to be the real head of the family and
> to communicate his orders by means of his transformed wife.
> The human husband, of course, has to execute these orders
> faithfully under fear of prompt punishment. Thus, in a house-
> hold like that, the voice of the wife is decidedly preponderant.
> The husband often takes the name of his wife as an addition to
> his own name, e.g., Tēlu'wgē-Ya'tirgin (Ya'turgin, husband of
> Tilu'wgi).
>
> The ke'lE-husband is very sensitive to even the slightest
> mockery of his transformed wife, because he knows that the
> "soft man" feels exceedingly "bashful," and also because he is
> doubtless conscious that the position of the latter is ridiculed. . . .[45]
>
> Speaking further of the marriage relation with supernatural
> beings, some shamans of untransformed sex are said also to have
> ke'lE-wives, who take part in the everyday life of their
> house. . . . "Soft men," of course, are supposed to excel in all

45. Bogoraz (1900:30) noted, "All his shaman power and the fear inspired by it, does
not save him from ridicule, particularly women's."

branches of shamanism, including the ventriloquistic art, not-withstanding the fact that they are supposed to be women.[46] Be-cause of their supernatural protectors, they are dreaded even by untransformed shamans, who avoid having any contests with them, especially with the younger ones, because they are ex-ceedingly "bashful" and readily stand back before the preten-sions of other people; but afterward the supernatural husband retaliates for the slight.

Although not the "boss" in his household and although his "wife" was physically more imposing than he was, the husband of a soft man Bogoraz knew best was not lacking in masculinity:

> Of all the transformed shamans whom I have chanced to know, the most remarkable was Tilu'wgi. I met him at a small trade gathering among the camps of Reindeer people on the Wolver-ine River. He and a party of traders came from the Chukchee Peninsula. He was of Maritime origin, but his family had some reindeer, and spent most of their time tending the herd. Tilu'wgi was young, and looked about thirty-five years of age. He was tall and well developed. His large rough hands especially exhibited no trace of womanhood.
>
> I stayed for two days in his tent and slept in his small inner room, which was hardly large enough to accommodate four sleepers. Thus, I had a chance to observe quite closely the de-tails of his physique, which, of course, were all masculine. He refused obstinately, however, to permit himself to be fully in-spected. His husband, Ya'tirgin, tempted by the offered price, tried to persuade him, but after some useless attempts, was at last silenced by one scowling look from his "wife." He felt sorry, however, that I had been baffled in gratifying my curiosity, and therefore offered me, to use his own words, his eyes in place of my own.
>
> He described the physique of Tilu'wgi as wholly masculine, and well developed besides. He confessed that he was sorry for it, but he hoped that in time, with the aid of his ke'let, Tilu'wgi would be able to equal the real "soft men" of old and to change the organs of his sex altogether, which would be much more convenient than the present state. Notwithstanding all this, and even the brownish down which covered his upper lip, Tilu'wgi's face, encircled with braids of thick hair arranged after the man-ner of Chukchee women, looked very different from masculine faces. It was something like a female tragic mask fitted to a body

---

46. "Female shamans do not possess ventriloquism" (Bogoraz 1900:28).

of a giantess of a race different from our own. All the ways of this strange creature were decidedly feminine. He was so "bashful" that whenever I asked a question of somewhat indiscreet character, you could see a blush spread over his face, and he would cover his eyes with his sleeve, like a young beauty of sixteen. I heard him gossip with the female neighbors in a most feminine way, and even saw him hug small children with evident envy for the joys of motherhood; but this even the ke'lE-husband could not place within the limitation of transformation.

The human husband of Tilu'wgi was an undersized fellow, shorter than his "wife" by at least half a head. He was nevertheless healthy and strong, a good wrestler and runner, and altogether a normal, well-balanced person. He was a cousin of Tilu'wgi, as generally the transformed shamans prefer to choose a husband from among their nearest relatives.

The division of labor between the two followed, of course, the usual rules. In the evening Ya'tirgin would sit idly within the inner room, while Tilu'wgi busied himself outside with the hearth and the supper. Ya'tirgin received the best pieces of meat, and the transformed "wife," according to custom, had to be content with scraps and bones. In the more serious affairs of life, the voice of the "wife" was, however, dominant.

I heard also from their neighbors a curious story, that one time, when Ya'tirgm was angry at something and wanted to chastise his giant wife, the latter suddenly gave him so powerful a kick that it sent him head foremost from their common sleeping room. This proves that the femininity of Tilu'wgi was more apparent than real[?].

The transformation in Tilu'wgi began in his very early youth, after a protracted illness from which he freed himself by the song and the drum. He gave a shamanistic séance in my presence, which had no peculiar features, except that the ke'lE-husband often appeared and talked to the public, extolling the shaman. In the very beginning, Tilu'wgi called him and asked him to mend the drum, which, as he pretended, had not the proper ring. We hear the ke'lE-husband blow with great force over the cover of the drum, after which its sound at once improved. (For description of other individuals, see Murray 1992a: 304–05.)

Later Misinterpretations

The Jesup Expedition volumes being rare, and earlier travelers' accounts of Siberia, Alaska, and the islands in between being rarer still,

Bogoraz's observations are not readily available, and misrepresentations of them cannot easily be checked. Probably the most influential of these is the synthesis of shamanism literature by Charles Ducey. Ducey (1976: 184) cited Bogoraz for a number of observations that Bogoraz did not make. For instance, Ducey claimed that "the transformation is demanded by the spirits at puberty," although Bogoraz does not specify whether the young shamans were pubescent or pre-pubescent, and noted some calls of spirits to adults. Similarly unwarranted is Ducey's claim that "the most striking behavioral characteristic of the future shamans in his childhood is his schizoid behavior, the invariant indicator of later shamanizing powers" (184). Bogoraz did not have the longitudinal/developmental data on which to stake such a claim, and did not make it. He did not even elicit recollections by others of the development or characteristics of transformed shamans before they received their call. Bogoraz's general-ization about "nervous and excitable" temperament was based on those he observed, not on tracking those who were going to receive a call. And, rather than warrant for Ducey's (1976:184–85) claim of the early loss of parents (specifically, through starvation) as the other notable feature in the shaman's childhood, Bogoraz (quoted above) wrote of relatively affluent families wanting to have a shaman of their own. Relative (oral) deprivation as an etiological factor in shamanism may be deduced from Freudian principles, but is not substantiated by what Bogoraz or other turn-of-the-century ethnographers wrote. The same is true of the al-leged "hysterical pseudohypersexuality" (Ducey 1976:186). Instead of the shaman exhibiting "compulsive sexuality" or "erotomania," Bogoraz (and other observers, e.g., Sternberg 1925) wrote of others vying to **marry** the transformed shaman, specifically, "He has all the young men he could wish for, striving to obtain his favor. From these he chooses his lover, and after a time takes a husband."

That transformed shamans had sexual relations with ordinary males is clear. Although there were no instances for Bogoraz to "inspect" and verify, in Chukchi theory a shaman might change sex. There is not a glimmer of a conception of hermaphroditism (third sex). Bogoraz wrote both that the Chukchi viewed some (natally male) shamans as women (socially) and as "like women" (while referring to the natally female one only as "transformed woman"). Bogoraz provided no indication of there being a Chukchi trichotomy of men/women/transformed shamans. The role was (normatively cross) gendered, and one might interpret what Bogoraz recorded about stages of what I would term gender crossing as four gender states (untransformed plus three stages of transformation) of shamans, though these do not seem to have been marked with particular terms,[47] and they seem to me to be part of a process of crossing from one gender to the other rather than *shaman* contrasting with the *male/female* dichotomy.

Sexual receptivity was a component of the role. However, in the native view, it followed upon gender transformation, and when gender transformation occurred, it was a subsidiary part of the shaman's vocation. In the native view, a desire to have sex with persons of the same sex or to dress and act like a person of the other sex could not "motivate" one to become a shaman, because one did not choose the role. Rather, one was chosen by the spirits (and eventually was able to master them). Lacking information about the early life of transformed shamans, even atheistic analysts can only extrapolate suspicions about the depth psychology of such lives. Instead of doing that, I want to note that husbands of transformed shamans did not differ discernibly from other Chukchi men, and that the benefits they received were from association with those having spiritual power and concomitant income (in kind) as healers. The husbands did not gain spiritual power by penetrating the transformed shamans, and there is no record of sexual intercourse being part of any shamanistic professional activity (nor was it the idiom of spirit-human contact).

Although the Chukchi were the only group in which transformed shamans were still observable at the end of the nineteenth century, the role had existed earlier among neighboring peoples, including the Koryak,[48] the Kamchadal, and the Asiatic Eskimo.

Koryak Memories

Another political exile who did major ethnographic work with the Jesup Expedition in Northeastern Siberia, Vladimir Iokalson (Waldemar Jochelson in earlier romanization; he lived from 1855 to 1937), noted that there had been a religious component to the lapsed Koryak role:

> Traditions are preserved of shamans who change their sex in obedience to the commands of spirits. I do not know of a single case of this so-called "transformation" at the present time [1901]. . . . Among the Koryak they [men clothed in woman's attire, who are believed to be transformed physically into women]

47. It is also not clear whether the distinctions were made by Chukchi or by Bogoraz.
48. The term derives from "qorak," reindeer driver; "Nyml'an" (inhabitant) was the self-designation according to Jakobson et al. (1957:220). Their territory is the northern part of the Kamchatka Peninsula.

were called quav'u or qeve'u. In his chapter on the Koryak, Krasheninnikoff makes mention of the ke'yev, i.e., men occupying the position of concubines, and he compares them with the Kamchadal koe'kcuc, as he calls them, i.e., men transformed into women. "Every koe'kcuc," says Krasheninnikoff, "is regarded as a magicians and interpreter of dreams;" but, judging from his confused description, it may be inferred that the most important feature of the institution of the koe'kcuc lay, not in their shamanistic power, but in their position with regard to the satisfaction of the unnatural inclinations of the Kamchadal. The koe'kcuc wore women's clothes, they did women's work, and were in the position of wives or concubines. . . . The Koryak told me of the same with reference to their qava'u. (1905:51–53)

Iokalson collected a number of tales involving changing sex. I only include one short one here that describes a woman functioning as a man as well as a man removing his penis:

Big Raven said, "Let me transform myself into a woman." He cut off his penis and made a needle-case of it; from his testicles he fashioned a thimble; and from the scrotum a work-bag. He went to a Chukchee camp and lived there for some time, refusing, however, all the young people who offered to take him for a wife.

Then Mití [a White Whale woman of considerable independence] ran short of food. She dressed herself like a man and tied a knife to her hip. From her stone maul she made a penis. She came to the Chukchee camp, driving a reindeer team, and remained there to serve for Big-Raven's marriage price. She proved to be so nimble and active that very soon she was given the bride.

They lay down together. "Now how shall we act?" Mití asked Big-Raven.

He answered, "I do not know." After awhile his penis and testicles returned to their proper place, and he was transformed into his former state. Then he could play the husband and said to Mití, "Let us do as we did before" (tale 127; see Murray 1992a:315–21 for the texts of four other ones about males giving birth and/or changing anatomies).

Iokalson (1905:755) had his own (sexual) explanation for individual predispositions for transsexualism as well as one for the ready cultural niche:

Like the present Chukchee irkala'ul, Koryak "transformed men" contracted marriage with men, or, when there was another real wife, would be kept as concubines, and lived with the so-called husband in improper intimacy. This, of course, cannot be treated as a normal institution of marriage. Such cases were few in number. Bogoras states that among three thousand Kolyman Chukchee he registered five cases of men who were believed to be transformed into women; but of these, only two were "married" to other men. I think abnormal sexual relations have developed under the influence of the ideas concerning shamanistic power, which the "metamorphosed" men obtain from the spirits at whose bidding and with whose help the change of sex is accomplished. These beliefs have found fertile soil in individuals of abnormal physical and psychical development. With the decadence of shamanism among the Koryak, and the Russianization of the Kamchadal, these practices have disappeared in both tribes. (1905:755)

Apparently, none of the Jesup ethnographers asked about homosexuality without cross dressing and curing, either in the disrupted cultures they could observe or in the "memory culture" of aboriginal life before Cossack "pacification" of the far reaches of Siberia (see Murray 1992a: 325n. 4).

There were no transformed individuals for Iokalson to query, even had he wished to explore the psychodynamics of sexual transformation among the Koryak. However, the tales he collected provide some basis for interpreting motivation. In them, men do not change their sex to perform cures. Indeed, the one shamanistic soul flight following upon beating the shaman's drum (in tale 116) does not involve a cross-dressing shaman. Moreover, the White-Whale women change into men and seek women as sex partners without any shamanistic rationale (in tales 116, 117, and 127). River-Man (in tale 113) does not seek or attain shamanistic powers, and Illá temporarily turns into a woman for pragmatic reasons that have nothing to do with shamanism. While a woman, he seems to want to play the insertor role in sex with River-Man, even though he is at the time a woman. Similarly, in the tale included above (127), Big-Raven does not take up shamanism after he turns his male sexual organs into implements of women's handicraft, and eventually grows back what he cut off (in tale 127). The tale does not explain why he decided to transform himself into a woman nor why he decided to switch back and be Mití's husband rather than her wife after she (as a man) married him (as a female).[49]

---

49. Neither of the men who bear children (in tales 85 and 129) seems to have been changed into women thereby.

Czaplicka's Comparative Perspective

In a broader perspective on *Aboriginal Siberia,* Marie Antoinette Cza-plicka (1914:253–54),[50] who argued that shamans are a "third class," stressed that there was also transvestitism and homosexuality without shamanism and shamanism without homosexuality (so that shaman-hood is not the only means for expressing such desires), and firmly re-jected predilection for sexual receptivity as an explanation for undertak-ing the role:

> The question of the change of sex, especially as it concerns the most powerful shamans, cannot be explained on a purely physi-cal basis. Several perversions occur among these people, as they do in all primitive and even in more civilized societies; but it does not follow that every pathological individual is the subject of magical worship. On the contrary, when reading the detailed description of the transformed shamans in Bogoras and Jochel-son, we see that in nearly every case these shamans are at first normal people and only later, by inspiration of spirits, have to change their sex. Some of them have secretly, along with an official husband of the same sex, normal sexual relations with a person of the other sex, and we may even assume that some of them actually became sexless, although in certain cases the out-ward show required by religious considerations may cover ab-normal passions. . . . Sexually, he [the shaman] may be sexless, or ascetic, or have inclinations of homosexualistic character, but he may also be quite normal. (253–54)

A Mid-Twentieth-Century Echo

Recalling Bogoraz's account of the Russian agent Gondatti's attempts to suppress shamanism, Murphy (1964:75) reported:

> Nevertheless, the tradition of transvestism and homosexuality either separately or as part of shamanizing has not been entirely extinguished on St. Lawrence Island.[51] The St. Lawrence term for "soft man" or "womanly man" is *anasik,* and the counterpart for women is *uktasik.* In 1940, one informant recalled a "trans-formed" male visitor from Siberia who believed himself to be pregnant. . . . In the village population between 1940 and 1955,

50. She was another exile (who died in 1921). Murray 1992a(329–39) excerpts her ethnology of Siberian transformed shamans.

51. St. Lawrence Island lies between mainland Alaska and Siberia, south of the Bering Strait.

one man was said to be anasik and another "partly anasik," but neither one shamanized. It thus seems evident that, by mid-century, this aspect of the shaman's role had been suppressed, however effective it may once have been in underscoring the exceptional nature of those who became shamans.

Thus, a special efficacy in sexual transformation remained a part of North Pacific belief systems beyond the time of "transformed shamans."

Araucanian *Machi*

A number of observers (e.g., Métraux 1946:324; Steward 1946:723; Bedford 1995) were struck by the similarities between the tambourine-centered curing ceremonies of cross-dressing male shamans in the far north Pacific and in southwestern South America. The territory south of Santiago in Chile, extending into Argentina, of the Mapuche, (called Araucanian in the anthropological literature) is not even contiguous to other South American groups sharing the trait of spirit possession (Bourguignon 1968).

Seventeenth- through nineteenth-century accounts of *machi*, effeminate transvestitic shamans living with the young men of southern tribes recounted by Métraux (1942; 1967:181–84; echoed by J. Cooper 1946: 750) portray eloquent, delicately constituted nonwarriors in a warfare-focused culture undertaking a culturally validated role with special powers. Male Araucanian shamans were individuals "more than a little aberrant." Among the predisposing or explanatory features noted were epilepsy, nervous/hysterical/emotional/feminine temperaments, St. Vitus Dance, and blindness, as well as the native's own explanation: imperative calls to serve by a spirit and lengthy apprenticeship by already recognized shamans.

Over the course of the first half of the twentieth century, male homosexuality allegedly remained common among the Araucanians,[52] but fieldwork done around midcentury found most *machis* to be women. Titiev wrote, explaining Araucanians' historical views with his own understanding of gender nonconformity,

> Many years ago the office was generally held by men and it is practically certain that they were abnormal, at least with respect to sexual conduct. Some of them may have been true hermaphrodites, the rest were berdaches or transvestites, and widespread

52. Hilger 1957 (68, 128, 249); all three references appear to rely on assurances of one non-Araucanian informant.

indulgence in sodomy and pederasty were common. There then followed a period when the post of *machi* might be filled by a man or a woman, and at this stage sexual irregularity is less frequently charged, particularly in regard to female practitioners. At present, male *machis* are rare, and some sexual irregularity is still associated with them. Certainly, they wear feminine clothes while performing their duties, and it is not unlikely they are homosexuals. . . . The novice goes to live with her tutor for a period of a year or more, during which they work and sleep together. Whether or not they actually enjoy homosexual relations is uncertain. (1951:115–7)

The existing accounts are inconclusive about whether all male *machis* were effeminate and/or homosexual, but provide no claims or evidence that sexual relations with *machis* had any special spiritual rewards.

The first extended Spanish account of the Araucanians, by their "happy captive" Francisco Núñez de Piñeda y Bascuñán (1974 [1663]: 159; 1977 [1663]:58, 83), included descriptions of passive homosexual curers (*hueye*) who cross dressed (wearing a blanket instead of breeches), wore their hair long and loose (like Araucanian women), and whose profession was highly respected by both men and women.

The Irish Jesuit Thomas Falkner wrote:

The wizards are of both sexes. The male wizards are obliged (as it were) to leave their sex, and to dress themselves in female apparel, and are not permitted to marry, though the female ones or witches may. They are generally chosen for this office when they are children, and a preference is always shewn to those, who at that early time of life discover an effeminate disposition. They are cloathed very early in female attire, and presented with the drum and rattles belonging to the profession they are to follow.

They who are seized with fits of the falling sickness, or the chorea Sancti Viti, are immediately selected for this employment, as chosen by the demons themselves; whom they suppose to possess them, and to cause all those convultions and distortions common in epileptic paroxysms. (1774:117)

A lack of rapport with the "native view" is patent in "demons whom they suppose to possess them," and it seems unlikely that Falkner inquired about whether Araucanians regarded female gender appearance as necessary or formative, but at least in his view it was an invariable part of the "wizard" role.

Louis Faron (1964:154) provided an explanation for a decreasing function for male *machi,* specifically, that the only distinctively male function of *machi* was forecasting the outcome of military actions. The final pacification of the Araucanians in the late nineteenth century obliterated the import of this part of the role. It is not completely clear in early reports (reviewed by Bedford 1995) that there was one role played by both those born male and those born female or two roles, for example, "jugglers" and "medicine men" of both sexes in contrast to female "witches" and male "soothsayers."

After noting that "there has never been a *machi* who was considered fully masculine" Faron (1964:152) suggested that the husbands of *machi* are also not particularly masculine: "It seems that *machi* take the initiative in arranging marriage for themselves, marrying their choice of subservient males, selecting one who is not a member of a traditional wife-receiving group, in a ceremony that does not involve the custom of brideprice and the sets of rights and obligations surrounding the traditional linkage of two patrilineal descent groups. With regard to patterns of inheritance, marriage, and residence, then, *machi* seem to operate outside the traditional structure of Mapuche social relationships" (1964:155). Faron's is one of the few accounts by anthropologists of any culture in which the husband of the gender-unconventional man is regarded as less than fully masculine, whether or not this is the Araucanians' own view.

Transformed Shamans in Borneo, the Philippines, and Mainland Southeast Asian

Borneo

There are scattered reports of cross dressing (natally) male shamans with husbands from Southeast Asia, Indonesia, and Mindanao (Yengoyan 1983:136, 139). From Borneo, H. Roth (1896) included several reports of Iban transformed shamans. The first, quoted from Hugh Brooke Low (1849–87),[53] is the most explicit about sex and gender aspects of the role, although it drips with disgust (and is rather chaotically organized and internally contradictory about the status of the *manang bali* and the motivations of their husbands):

> There are two descriptions of *manangs,* the regular and the irregular. The regular *(manang ngagi antiu)* are those who have

---

53. The son of the governor of Labuan, he was educated in England, and then worked for eighteen years for the Raja of Sarawak (otherwise known as Charles Brooke).

been called to that vocation by dreams, and to whom the spirits have revealed themselves. The irregular (*manang ngaga diri*) are self-created and without a familiar spirit.

The regular are male and female *manang laki* and *manang indu,* and also *manang bali,* or unsexed males. When a person conceives a call from the spirit he bids adieu for awhile to his relatives, abandons his former occupation, and attaches himself to some thorough-paced *manang,* who, for a consideration, will take him in hand and instruct him until he is fully qualified to practice on his own account. It is not enough, however, for him to simply say that he feels himself called; he must prove to his friends that he is able to commune with the spirits, and in proof of this he will occasionally abstain from food and indulge in trances from which he will awaken with all the tokens of one possessed by a devil, foaming at the mouth and talking incoherently. . . .

The *manang bali* is a most extraordinary character, and one difficult to describe: he is a male in female costume, which he will tell you he has adopted in obedience to a supernatural command, conveyed three separate times in dreams. Had he disregarded the summons, he would have paid for it with his life. Before he can be permitted to assume female attire he is sexually disabled.[54] He will then prepare a feast and invite the people. He will give them *tuak* to drink, and he will sacrifice a pig or two to avert evil consequences to the tribe by reason of the outrage upon nature.[55] . . . Thenceforth he is treated in every respect like a woman and occupies himself with feminine pursuits. His chief aim in life is to copy female manners and habits so accurately as to be indistinguishable from other women, and the more nearly he succeeds in this, the more highly he is thought of, and if he can induce any foolish young fellow to visit him at night and sleep with him, his joy is extreme; he sends him away at daybreak with a handsome present, and then, openly before the women, boasts of his conquest, as he is pleased to call it. He takes good care that his husband finds out. The husband makes quite a fuss about it, and pays the young fellow's fine with pleasure. As episodes of this kind tend to show how successfully he has imitated the character of a woman, he is highly gratified and rises, accordingly, in the estimation of a tribe as a perfect

54. Given "unsexed" above, when Low first mentioned the *manang bali,* this would seem to mean castrated, though castration is not reported by other observers *of manang bali.*
55. One may doubt that this is the native explanatory model.

specimen.[56] As his services are in great request and he is well
paid for his troubles, he soon grows rich, and when he is able to
afford it, he takes to himself a husband in order to render his assumed character more complete. But as long as he is poor, he
cannot even dream of marriage, as nothing but the prospect of
inheriting his wealth would ever induce a man to become his
husband, and thus incur the ridicule of his whole tribe. The position as husband is by no means an enviable one: the wife
proves a very jealous one, and punishes every little infidelity
with a fine. The women view him, the husband, with open contempt and the men with secret dislike. His only pleasure must be
in seeing his quasi wife accumulate wealth and wishing her a
speedy demise, so that he may inherit the property.[57] . . .

It is difficult to say at what age precisely a person may become
a *manang bali.* One thing, however, is certain, he is not brought
up to it as a profession, but becomes one from pure choice or by
sudden inclination at a mature age. He is usually childless, but it
sometimes happens that he has children, in which case he is
obliged to give them their portions and to start afresh, unen-
cumbered in his new career, so that when he marries, if he be so
minded, he can adopt the children of other people, which he frequently, nay, invariably, does, unless it so happen that his husband is a widower with a family of his own, in which case that
family now becomes his.[58]

The *manang bali* is always a person of great consequence, and
manangs, not unfrequently, become the chief of the village. He
derives his popularity not merely from the variety and diversity
of his cures, but also largely from his character as a peacemaker,
in which he excels. All little differences are brought to him, and
he invariably manages to satisfy both parties and to restore good
feeling. Then again, his wealth is often at the service of his fol-

56. To the contrary, this "shameless" advertising of adultery is not feminine, familiar
as it is from transvestitic homoseual roles in various cultures.

57. Presumably, access to continually accumulating wealth, not just the prospects of
inheritance, would be considered even by someone as entirely focused on material advantage as Brooke Low in his vision of the husband of the *manang bali.* Vicarious participation
in the prestige of the *manang bali* might also enhance the attractiveness of the role, not to
mention a sexual outlet for someone too poor to marry a woman. Gomes (1911:180)
viewed the husband of an upper Krian River *manang bali* as "a lazy good-for-nothing who
lived on the earnings of the *manang bali.*" "Living off" the earnings of a partner in a transvestitic homosexual role is also familiar from diverse societies.

58. Note that the husband in this passage is no longer too young and poor to have married anyone else. Gomes (1911:180) wrote that the *manang bali* was usually old and childless, and was never young.

lowers, and if they are in difficulty or distress, he is ever ready to help. (H. Roth 1896, 1:266, 270–71)

According to the Venerable Archdeacon J. Perham, "the peculiar attribute of the *manang* is the possession of mysterious powers rather than special knowledge" (H. Roth 1896, 1:271), but this is contradicted in Low's report quoted above and also in Perham's own [1887] description of fourteen rites and of three levels of *manang* initiation (reproduced in H. Roth 1896, 1:280–81 and in Murray 1992a:289–90). Perham did not mention castration or transvestism of *manangs* of the third grade, (or, indeed, anything about their everyday life, when not involved in curing) but did comment on the association of Iban curing and femininity:

> Women as well as men may become *manangs*. In former time, I believe, all *manangs* on their initiation assumed female attire for the rest of their lives; but it is rarely adopted now, at least on the coast districts; and I have only met one such. If you ask the reason of this strange custom, the only answer forthcoming is, that the spirits or deities who first taught Dyaks the knowledge of the powers of manangism gave them an injunction to assume the woman's garb. It will be observed that most of the beings mentioned or invoked by *manangs* are addressed as *Ini*, "Grandmother," which perhaps implies that all the special deities of the *manang* world are supposed to be of the female sex, and, to be consistent with this belief, it might have been deemed necessary for the *manang* to assume the outward figure and the dress of his goddess. . . .
>
> The Shaman priest on particular occasions worked himself into an ecstasy; the *manang* runs round and round, and pretends to fall in a faint, at which time his greatest power is exercised. . . . But in these days, in practice, the *manang* answers to the idea of the Doctor, rather than to that of the Priest; for his presence is not necessarily required for any purposes except that of treating the sick. (from H. Roth 1896, 1:282–83)

In contrast to gender-crossing homosexuality in neighboring islands, the early reports of Iban *manang bali* did not allude to doing "women's work." Haddon and Stout (1936:42) specifically stated that they "wear women's dress and behave in all ways like women, except that they avoid . . . taking any part in the domestic labor."

Van der Kroef (1954:260) noted that "the nature of transvestism among the Ngadju [of southern Borneo {Kalimantan}] as well as among the Iban Dayans [Dayaks,] often appears not to have the slightest sacred connotations and the homosexuality of the *basir* is often practiced quite independently of religious meaning." A century earlier, Hupe (1846: 145–46) and Schwaner (1853:186) also had difficulty deciding whether *basir* were priests by day and prostitutes by night, or whether sodomizing them had religious and/or curative meanings for Dayaks. Perelaer (1870:35) added some detail about their appearance: "The clothes of the *basir* are in all respects similar to those of the *balian,* with the exception that he wears no headcloth. The *basir* dresses like a woman in private life also, and parts his hair in the middle of the forehead, just like a woman." Needham (1973:11) asserted that a Ngaju man who has thus assumed femininity is thought to be more efficacious in the supernatural sphere than a woman is, although this contention does not seem to derive from the work he translated. I can see no basis for distinguishing relative efficacy insofar as each symbolizes totality (i.e., constitutes a "gender fusing" type, outside sex-gender dichotomies).

Among the Iban of central Borneo, effeminate shamans are conceived of as women, not as a third sex, according to Sutlive (20 Feb. 1990 letter). Sutlive's analysis (1992 [1976]) oscillates between a Devereux-like view that the Iban *manang* role was "an alternate route to normality" for those too cowardly to function as warriors, and the recognition that the high status of the *manang* is indicated by parents' eagerness to employ a master-shaman (*manang bali'*) whose name and status are female, to train any son who tells them of dreaming about magic quartz crystals and hosting initiation feasts (*Bebangun*). The reports of Iban transformed shamans date from the nineteenth century, so resolving the issue is impossible. "Iban shamans described in modern ethnographic accounts are apparently sexually, mentally and physically normal . . . indicat[ing] that while Iban shamanism may have been an alternate route to normality during periods when the main road to achievement was the warpath, it has now become one among many avenues to power and influence" (Winzeler 1993:xxiv).

Among the Baluy Kayan, where a (nontrancing) priest role has split from a (trancing) shaman one, Rousseau (1993:141) heard of a transvestite priest active before World War II who "was already adult by the time he took on a female social identity. He wore women's clothes, had long hair like a woman, had a husband (and was apparently a jealous man, fearing that his husband would sleep with other women) and he did women's work. However, he was not tattooed on arms and legs as women normally are. He was deemed to have great supernatural power, and was paid accordingly." This was the only transvestite Kayan priest of whom Rousseau heard. He noted that "most villages had at least one berdache, and these men took on a female identity without becoming priests" (141), and added that "most Kayan men interpreted the assumption of a female identity as a trick in order to shirk men's work. Some transvestites were homosexuals, others attempted to have heterosexual (extra-marital) relations; few of them were married [to a man] like Lake'" (148n. 14). There are a number of other Borneo people in which male "priestess" roles have faded (reviewed in Murray 1992a: 259–61). Such salvage of their memories as has been published does not claim religious warrant of payoff for the sexual receptivity of such "priestesses," nor does it instantiate (homo)sexual conduct as part of any rite.

At least as recently as the 1930s, southern Sulawesi had

> male priests, referred to as *bisu*, who practice a limited form of transvestism during the rituals [notably at planting-time when they went into trance and were possessed] and act homosexually in everyday life.[59] In the previous century, the *bisu* were probably more numerous; then they often resided at courts where they took care of the sacred royal ornaments. Since then, and also as a result of the increasing Islamization of the southern Sulawesi area, the number of *bisu* has declined greatly, although in not a few regional communities they still perform their function. . . .
>
> Makassarese society, long familiar with homosexuals called *kawe*, provided something of an institutional legitimation of their conduct through the *bisu* office, even permitting them to attain considerable social prestige as *bisus*. The Makassarese allow those young boys who at an early age show no liking for the ways of their sex to dress and act as girls. These male "women" are not permitted to have normal sexual relations with a woman on pain of expulsion from the group of women. This too seems to imply an "either-or" pattern of role playing. To satisfy his sexual needs, the male *kawe* must therefore turn to male partners and his homosexuality—characteristic of the *bisu*—is thus socially encouraged and apparently not especially frowned upon. With the decline of the *bisu*, the *kawe* have remained, seeking to

59. "During the ornament rituals the *bisu* is not entirely dressed as a woman, but half as a woman and half as a man. The *bisu* on that occasion wears the sarong and typical jacket of women, with a wealth of female adornments, but at the same time he wears the kris and head cloth of the male" (van der Kroef 1954:262). Especially since dichotomous gender is stressed, this mixing of dress does not warrant characterization as a native "third gender" conception or "transvestite." "Gender mixing" seems apt.

satisfy their needs and plying their profession in markets and busy city quarters. (Van der Kroef 1954:261)

Although seeing sexuality rather than gender variance as defining the role, Chabot (1950:205) asserted that the Makassarese viewed *kawe kawe* as a third gender. On occasion, he also used the Dutch-influenced *seorang het* ("an it person"). He did not contrast *kawe kawe* with *bisu*, but saw the *bisu* role as a traditional niche for homosexually inclined boys: "Individuals who, in earlier times, showed homosexual tendencies and then found a place as *bissu* at the royal courts now populated market-places as male prostitutes" (158). He added that he knew of no men who became *kawe kawe* after puberty. In the Makassarese view, "sexual contact with their female peers is regarded as out of the question" (157). With men, Chabot asserted that mutual masturbation was the usual sexual act (158).

The Philippines

In the Spanish contact literature about the Philipinne Archipelago, there are several accounts of socially valued transvestites. The Jesuit Francisco Combés attributed (projected?) celibacy to men who dressed as women and did women's work in Cebu. In his account, originally published in 1667, he waxed rhapsodic about them (translated in volume 4 of by Blair and Robertson 1900; reproduced in Murray 1992a:185–87). Combés may have mistaken lack of interest in sex with females for lack of interest in sex: he does not seem to have inquired about whether they had sex with males.

In northwestern Luzon (far north of Cebu), another Jesuit, Domingo Pérez, reported cross-dressed Sambal priests in a 1680 manuscript (translated in volume 47 of Blair and Robertson 1900; excerpted in Murray 1992a:187–89). The term for these priests, *bayoc*, seems cognate to the modern Cebuano term for effeminate/transvestite males described by D. Hart (1968) and Whitam (1992). Pérez wrote nothing about the everyday life of the *bayoc*, or about their sexual conduct. Although he considered the *bayoc* presiding over worship of the devil and refused to credit genuine possession, it is clear from his *Relación* that the *bayoc* role was highly esteemed by the Sambal. It is also clear that the *bayoc* was not merely a man passing for a woman. The *bayoc*'s dress mixed male and female characteristics. Pérez's description of selection, recruitment, and initiation to the *bayoc* role (304) is deficient in information about individual motivation and sexual behavior or native views of cross dressing and of spirits choosing to communicate through *bayoc.* The possessing spirits/idols seem male from his description.

Mainland Southeast Asia

In analyzing the motivation of Burmese shamans who are possessed by *nats* (spirits) of the opposite sex, the Freudian anthropologist Melford Spiro stressed gender crossing more than sexuality (his faith in the analytical usefulness of "latent homosexuality" may render this a distinction without a difference).

Coleman, Colgan, and Gooren (1992) outlined their understanding (based on a short trip to Myanmar [Burma]) of a role—labeled *acault* that involves exclusive homosexuality and varying degrees of gender-crossing of those born males who are possessed by a *nat* named Manguedon. Two of their three case studies had male gender identity and appearance. Toto, the full-time transgendered one, "expressed some frustration with the current situation. She found relationships with other men disheartening because her boyfriends seemed to want only sex with her. She would like to be married to a man. In terms of her sexual activity, she usually performed oral sex on her male partners. She would get erections, but disliked that. Her satisfaction came from giving pleasure" (317). The transgendered behavior of one of the two male-identified *acault* "appeared to be restricted to ceremonial activities and status" (318), and he was unwilling to talk about his sexual behavior. Maaye, the other male-identified *acault,* had a "husband" whom he supported (by having sex with other men for money). "Maaye had no desire to have a female body, as he reported that he liked his penis and the good feeling he derived from his genitals" (318). Although there is no sacredness attached to *acaults'* sex with males in this report, Manguedon is believed to be jealous of any contact with terrestrial females they might have. I would count this as religious proscription of sexual contact with females, a syncretism between Burmese animism and Burmese (Theravada) Buddhism.

In northern Thailand, Gehan Wijeyewardene (1986:159) reported ten female spirit mediums for every male one there, and elaborated:

> It is often said by Chiang-mai people that male mediums are either transvestites or homosexuals or both—the [originally central] Thai word [*gatuhy*] may be used in both senses. . . . Some are quite blatant in their adoption of female clothes. . . . More frequently they may adopt female gait and mannerisms, sometimes wear female clothes and adorn themselves with lipstick,

rouge and eye shadow. Men who will be appalled at the suggestion that they are homosexuals will flirt with them in public—
at least in a joking way, and in local communities they fit into a
recognizable public role. Men mediums may not always wear female clothes when they are not performing as mediums. Many
have feminine gait and mannerisms and few of them seem to
have any marital relations with women. Some of them dress and
make themselves up as women when possessed. (58–59)

A report on rural Vietnam in the late 1960s by Heimann and Cao
(1975) is very confusing, since they stated that there was "no socially established homosexual or transsexual role" in one paragraph, and in the
next noted that "in the Vietnamese countryside, isolated from Western
influence, transsexual behavior is openly practiced. 'Hermaphrodite'
men dressed as women are known as 'witch doctors' and have the power
of communicating with evil spirits and curing diseases by complicated
rituals" (91). Unfortunately, the authors did not supply data about these
"witch doctors" (nor did they give the native terms for them).

During a day-long ceremony in present-day Vietnam, Len Dong (a
folk/Taoism/Buddhism syncretism) spirit mediums are possessed by
series of (up to thirty) spirits of both sexes. "The trance is light throughout the ceremonies. . . . Whether female shamans are also sexually
anomalous (as virtually all of the male shamans are) remains to be determined (i.e., anomalous in sex-gender behavior, comportment, and
object-choice, not in genitalia). There are some French sources that report that the female *ba dong* (males are *ong dong*) are disproportionately
divorced or otherwise anomalous in terms of marriage-kinship, but they
are vague about any sexual dimension." (Frank Proschan 12 June 1998
E-mail). The homosexuality of the males who are possessed is not assigned religious meaning (see Proschan 1998).

Spiritual Vocations in Western Africa

Among his people, the Dagara of southern Burkina Faso, Malidoma
Somé explained,

The Earth is looked at, from my tribal perspective, as a very, very
delicate machine or consciousness, with high vibrational points,
which certain people must be guardians of in order for the tribe
to keep its continuity with the gods and with the spirits that
dwell there—spirits of this world and spirits of the other world.
Any person who is this link between this world and the other
world experiences a state of vibrational consciousness which is
far higher, and far different, from the one that a normal person

would experience. This is what make a gay person gay. This kind of function is not one that society votes for certain people to fulfill. It is one that people are said to decide on prior to being born. You decide that you will be a gatekeeper before you are born. And it is that decision that provides you with the equipment that you bring into this world. So when you arrive here, you begin to vibrate in a way that Elders can detect as meaning that you are connected with a gateway somewhere. (1993:7)[60]

His 1994 book *Of Water and Spirits* relates some of his own experiences during (a belated) initiation after running away from a French missionary school. Somé wondered about Dagara, "who feel the way that certain people feel in this culture that has led to them being referred to as 'gay.' . . . When I asked one of them, who had taken me to the threshold of the Otherworld [as one of the elders supervising his initiation cohort], whether he feels sexual attraction towards another man, he jumped back and said, 'How do you know that?' He said, 'This is our business as gatekeepers.'" (7)

Somé stated that "the gay person is very well integrated into the community" and that this particular man had a wife and children. Dagara, including Somé, believe that the survival of the cosmos (not just of the earth) depends on such gatekeepers. He also noted that among the Dogon, "a tribe that knows astrology like no other tribe that I have encountered, the great astrologers of the Dogon are gay" and generalized that outside Christendom, "everywhere else in the world gay people are a blessing" (8). While claiming religious justification for homosexual desire (not exclusive of heterosexual functioning), Somé did not claim that any sexual relations with the gatekeepers convey spiritual benefits.

Hausa Roles

Besmer (1983) discussed in detail a possession cult among the (generally Islamic) Hausa that is strikingly similar to New World possession cults among those of West African descent. As in Haitian voudou(n), the metaphor for those possessed by spirits is "horses ridden" by the spirit. Homosexual transvestites in the Hausa *bori* cult are called 'Yan Daudu, son of Daudu. "Daudu is a praise name for any Galadima (a ranked title), but specifically refers to the *bori* spirit Dan Galadima (literally, son of Galadima; the Prince) [who is] said to be 'a handsome young man, popular with women, a spendthrift, and a gambler.' Informants were

60. Permission from Bert Hoff to quote passages from his interview of Malidoma Somé is gratefully acknowledged. *M.E.N. Magazine*, September 1993, 1, 6, 8. © 1993 Bert Hoff.

unable to provide a reason why male homosexuals should be identified with his name" (Besmer 1983:30n. 4). Joseph Greenberg (1941:56) noted that "the group of Hausa spirits known as 'Yan Dawa, 'children of the forest' have their counterpart in the Dahomey *aziza,* the Bambara *kokolo,* and the Yoruba divinity Arnoi." *'Yan daudu* are not possessed by Dan Galadima, and are not possessed by other spirits when he is present. Instead, they make and sell "luxury snacks—i.e., more expensive, more prestigious food such as fried chicken" (Pittin). *'Yan daudu* also operate as intermediaries between (female) prostitutes and prospective clients. Besmer(1983:18) noted: "Women provide the bulk of membership for the cult and are stereotyped as prostitutes," and Pittin (1983:296) reported that "the economic enterprises of the 'Yan Daudu are centered on three related activities: procuring, cooking, and prostitution. Procuring, the mobilisation of women for illicit sexual purposes, clearly demands close ties between the procurer and the women. The 'dan daudu [sing.], in his combination of male and female roles, can and does mediate between men and women in this context." Living among women in the strangers' quarters of Hausa towns provides "a cover for men seeking homosexual services. The 'dan daudu and his sexual partners can carry out their assignations with greater discretion than would be possible if the 'yan daudu lived together, or on their own outside the gidan mata," where visitors would be marked as seeking sex with she-males (Pittin 1983:297).

In patriarchal Hausa society, the *bori* cult provides a niche for various sorts of low-status persons:[61] "Women in general and prostitutes in particular. . . . Jurally-deprived categories of men, including both deviants (homosexuals) and despised or lowly-ranked categories (butchers, night-soil workers, poor farmers, and musicians) constitute the central group of possessed or participating males" plus "an element of psychologically disturbed individuals which cuts across social distinctions" (19).

Besmer's account leaves problematic how Hausa individuals (inside or

---

61. In a 23 February 1995 E-mail, Rudolf Gaudio cautioned against inferring theological or official or institutional approval of homosexuality from a concentration of gender- or sex-variant priests in cults. The seemingly disproportionate number of Roman Catholic priests who are homosexually inclined is not officially approved or based on any Catholic theology or doctrines valorizing homosexuality, even though (at least in Latin America, and, I think, in Mediterranean Europe as well), not particularly masculine boys and/or those not showing signs of being sexually interested in females are channeled to the priesthood, so that there is a social view of the priesthood as a niche. "Niches" are not necessarily approved of, and the positing of one should not be taken as claiming any religious significance for it.

outside the *bori* cult) come to be defined by themselves or by others as homosexual or transvestite.[62] He stressed the augmentation of status, albeit in an alternative status hierarchy (122–23).

Although the *bori* cult provides a niche in which there is an alternative to the larger society's prestige hierarchy, the cult itself remains marginal. As Besmer noted: "Status ambiguity is not completely eliminated through involvement in the *bori* cult. While an initiated individual achieves a specific, formal status within the cult, since possession is institutionalized, it is not possible for him to escape the general social assessment of his behavior as deviant" (21). There are, however, at least indications of rejection of the stigma of the cult and its adepts (18); Besmer did not attempt to discover the degree to which adepts accept the disvaluation of their "kinds of people" in the dominant Islamic Hausa culture.

From Bayero University (in Kano, Nigeria), Kleis and Abdullahi (1983; building on Abdullahi's interviews of 140 '*yan daudu*) presented a functionalist analysis of a wholly secular '*dan daudu* role. In their view, prostitutes provide a "safety valve" in a Hausa society in which female seclusion has been increasing since the early nineteenth century. Unlike the Omani *khanith* described by Wikan (1977; see pp. 275–80 above), who are prostitutes, the '*dan daudu* procures females for males, recruiting runaway women and "socializing them in the seductive arts" and, on a routine basis, "soliciting suitors, arranging contacts, extolling and advertising her charms, and managing relations with the authorities" for these female prostitutes, who live and work literally outside the walled city core (*birni*). The '*dan daudu* is paid for his services both by customers and prostitutes, and these commissions "constitutes the bulk of his daily income" (45). Kleis and Abdullahi argued that the economic rewards are "sufficient to account for recruitment without assuming a personality predisposition" (52) to dress and behave like a woman. In explaining why they undertook the '*dan daudu* role, 56 percent attributed their decision to economic reasons. Only 7 percent explained being a '*dan daudu* as due to "nature"; another 22 percent cited the influence of friends and associates (53n. 10). Kleis and Abdullahi considered the role as an economic niche for poor emigrants (not all of whom are Hausa) from the countryside, not especially a refuge for males seeking sex with males. They noted that "many 'yan daudu are assumed also to be homosexuals, although this does not seem to be the major feature of their social status,

---

62. Moses Meyer (1993 notes) asserted that the "'Yan Daudu are not the same as homosexuals. There is a distinct homosexual identity in Nigeria that is different from the 'Yan Daudu. They overlap socially because both communities practice same-sex sex."

which hinges more on their self-identification as females" (44). They suggest that "a male with masculine gender identity and pronounced heterosexual interests would be less suitable as a broker because he might well find it difficult to separate his personal and professional involvements with the prostitute and would risk becoming a rival of her customers" (46). They did not consider that a "homosexual" '*dan daudu* might become a rival for female prostitutes' customers, and do not appear to have inquired about who are the sexual partners of '*yan daudu*.

They noted that there is no Hausa or Sohari role for women acting like men, and stressed that both Omani *khanith* and the Hausa '*dan daudu* are conceived as kinds of males. Indeed, "they occupy these positions precisely because they are anatomical males." That is, '*dan daudu* is a role some males take—and sometimes abandon. Like the *khanith*, the '*dan daudu* "can temporarily, alternately, or permanently switch back and take up conventional male roles—a course definitely unavailable to anatomical females" (49).

Like Kleis and Abdullahi, Gaudio discounted the connection between possession cults and '*dan daudu* in Hausa society. He focused more than they did on sexual relations involving (secular) '*yan daudu* and other Hausa men. Talking to members of what he calls "Kano's gay male community" about a 1994 Muslim Brotherhood–affiliated Hausa newspaper article, Gaudio observed "challenges to the newspaper's characterization of homosexual marriages as a Western practice alien to Hausa Muslim culture. Few of the self-described Hausa homosexuals I met were even aware of Western gay life." His "conversations with Hausa gay men suggest that they perceive homosexuality and homosexual marriage as practices that are indigenous to Hausa Muslim culture [even] as they are marginal within it" (1996 African Studies Association meeting abstract).

Gaudio (1996:123) argued that *gay* is appropriate in that these Hausa men "are conscious of themselves as men who have sex with men and who consider themselves to be socially distinct from men who do not have this kind of sex." One term for those who do not is *mahaho*, "blind man" (127).[63] Those Hausa men whom Gaudio called "gay" "refer to themselves as *masu barka* 'those who do the business,' often abbreviated to *masu yi*, 'those who do (it)'" (135n. 7), and do not see homosexuality as

---

63. There also terms for the male patrons of '*yan daudu: fararenbula* ("civilians"), *miji* ("husband"), *saurayi* ("boyfriend"), and '*yanaras*, which has no other or literal meaning (127, 128, 136n. 13). The masculine partner is expected to be sexually insertive and to regularly provide presents (money, clothes, travel) as to a female sexual partner (129).

incompatible with heterosexuality, marriage or parenthood, which constitute strong normative values in Muslim Hausa society: at some point in their lives most of the men I am calling 'gay'—including those who identify as womanlike—marry women and have children, even as they maintain their covert identity as men who have sex with men. . . . Most Hausa people do not see marriage as a choice but rather as a moral and social obligation [to sire children]. . . . My Hausa acquaintances did not see a necessary connection between marriage and heterosexual desire. (125–26)

While they seem to regard their homosexual desires as real and as intrinsic to their nature, they also view inseminating women as obligatory, and ultimately more important (in contrast to *wasa*, "play" (129).[64] They most certainly do not have any interest in having their (in the Muslim view, God-given) genitals excised: "I never heard any *'yan daudu* discuss transsexualism as an option they would like to have available to them" and that even the most effeminate *'dan daudu* is understood by all Hausas to be male," Gaudio wrote (136n. 19).

Although there is no indication of any sacred benefit from sexually mounting *bori* initiates, some Hausa (and other Nigerians) believe that secular benefits are magically transmitted in homosexual intercourse. Male prostitutes interviewed in Kano and Lagos by Tade Akin Aina, a sociologist at the University of Lagos

still believe that there are magical and witchcraft effects associated with male homosexual intercourse. They also believe that if

64. In addition to the gendered idiom for the homosexuality of effeminate *'yan daudu* and their patrons, there is another for men who are not notably effeminate in self-presentation and who have sex with younger men. The older, wealthier man is called *k'wazo* (a masculine noun, in other contexts meaning "hard-working"); the younger man who is sexually penetrated and receives presents as female sexual partners do is called *baja*, a feminine noun meaning "merchandise" (130). Feminine-identified males sometimes have sex with each other, calling it *kifi*: "lesbianism" (132), a term also extended to sex between two masculine-identified males, who may *ti canji* "do an exchange." As Gaudio noted, labeling non-role-bound sex between males as "'lesbian' and therefore 'feminine,'" reveals the normative strength of the idea that a valid sexual encounter involving a 'real' man must entail a distinct power asymmetry." Moreover, "many gay Hausa men—including *'yan daudu*—deride or condemn 'lesbian' sexual relations between *'yan daudu* as absurd or immoral" (132), although sex between two masculine-identified men is not condemned (133). Apparently, real sex requires at least one masculine person, but need not include a feminine one. Thus, while there are age-stratified and non-role-defined homosexual relations, the Hausa dominant (conceptual and social) organization of male-male sex is one of gender differentiation.

the dominant partner is a businessman, such associations confer spiritual benefits to his business. This, they state, affects the price they place on their services. Also it is felt that homosexuality conveys some unique advantages on its practitioners; for instance, they feel that homosexuals tend to be rich and successful men. . . . [They] feel that they are at risk of becoming impotent (the "eunuch effect") or permanently incapable of conventional heterosexual relations once any of their clients exploit the relationship for ritual or witchcraft purposes. (1991:88) [65]

Common but Incidental Male Homosexuality in Afro-Brazilian Possession Religions

Writing about the caboclo possession religion(s) [66] of Bahia during the late 1930s, Ruth Landes (1940:393) asserted that the majority of male Afro-Brazilian possession religion leaders and followers "are passive homosexuals of note." Roger Bastide (1961:309) asserted that instances of "passive pederasty" were "very common" in certain *terreiros* (temples) in Bahia. Seth and Ruth Leacock (1972:104) reported that in Belém there was "a widespread belief, both within and without the Batuque religion, that men who wear ritual costumes and dance in public ceremonies are indeed homosexuals." [67] Peter Fry, who studied Afro-Brazilian possession in Belém during the early 1970s, wrote:

No one went so far as to say that all those who danced in the *terreiros* were *bichas* [effeminate homosexuals], but, in two observed instances, accusations of being a *bicha* were made solely on the basis of cult participation. One *pai de santo* [priest] who defined himself as a *bicha* denied that all cult members were

65. The direction of benefit is the opposite to that among the Pangwe, discussed on p. 197. In both West African instances, the intercourse and its purported benefits are secular, specifically increase in fortune.

66. The usual generic noun, "cult," seems to me loaded with specifically Christian animus, so I eschew its use except in quotations of others. For analyses of other aspects of Afro-Brazilian religions (and of their African roots) see Bastide 1961; Carneiro 1954; and Simpson 1978.

67. Ribeiro (1970:129) and the Leacocks (1972) hinted at some female homosexuality in the *terreiro*, as well. The instance described by Landes (1947:47) seems to show less tolerance for female homosexuality than for male. Totonia, who had inherited an Oxum chapel from her aunt "was the mother by her aunt's dying command, so she went into the temple to train further. Not long after, while still in retreat, she was discovered in a relationship with another priestess. The women were disturbed, for they considered this an abuse of the sacredness of the temple and of her office; but they couldn't or wouldn't discharge her, so they appointed their senior priestess to be acting mother" (Landes 1947:47).

bichas on the grounds that 'her man,' also a medium, was not a *bicha*. . . . Whether or not the proportion is as high as the 80 percent estimate made by the treasurer of the Federation of Afro-Brazilian cults of Para, cannot be known, but as one young b*icha* who was not a cult member argued, 'o povo aumenta mas não inventa' (public opinion exaggerates but does not invent). (1995:206)

All of these reports refer to northern and northeastern Brazil, where the most recent West African slaves were concentrated, not to the more southern metropolises Rio de Janeiro or São Paulo.

Each *terreiro* traditionally has been led by a *mãe de santo* (mother of the god) who tries with varying degrees of success to maintain control over subordinate mediums (*filhos de santo;* children of the god). Devotees meet more or less regularly for *seasoes,* or *trabalhos* or *festas,* during which the mediums are possessed by spirits (usually, by the same one as possessed them on previous occasions). Except for the most "traditional" Candomblé *terreiros* of Bahia, the possessed medium not only dances, but also speaks with clients, providing advice and ritual protection. The ritual normally ends with the departure of the spirits.

Landes argued that traditional (i.e., non-caboclo) Afro-Brazilian *terreiros* of Bahia were female turf: "Tradition says baldly that only women are suited by their sex to nurse the deities, and that the service of men is blasphemous and unsexing," she wrote (1940:388; also see 1947:37). She suggested that men only began to emerge as *pais de santo* between the world wars, when the "new cults . . . immensely relaxed the restrictions surrounding 'mothers,'" so that the rigorous initiation procedures gave way to the upsurge of new leaders who had not passed through the lengthy and costly rites (1940:392). She wrote that she "never saw a caboclo ceremonial that did not include one or more 'sons'" (392), and presented the following breakdown of the sex of leaders in the traditional (Nagō) and caboclo temples from a partial enumeration by Carneiro:

Table 2. Breakdown of Sex of Leaders in Temples

| | *Mães* (mothers) | *Pais* (fathers) | |
	%	%	N
Nagō	87.0	13.0	23
Caboclo	22.7	77.3	44

Source: Landes 1940:393.

In addition to a dramatically different sex ratio in the newer forms,[68] evidence that the pattern was new was that the caboclo *pais de santo* to be found in the caboclo were all under forty-five years of age (at the time of her 1938–39 fieldwork), many being in their early twenties. The *pais de santo* were young and unmasculine: according to Landes, *pais de santo* were recruited from the "passive homosexuals of note [who] were vagrants and casuals of the streets."[69] The relaxation of the strict taboos in the non-Nago *terreiros* and especially the fact that the bars were let down to men, did not, however, obliterate the fundamental tenet that femininity alone could nurse the gods. All men considered normal in Bahia were, therefore, still debarred. By being possessed and participating in caboclo, such "feminine" males rose considerably in status. They forged "a new and respected status for themselves" (386) and were "supported and adored by those normal men of whom they were before the butt and object of derision" (393). She described them as "handsome in a boyish way" and noted that all she had seen were mulattos.

She affirmed that in Bahia there was a clear distinction between active and passive homosexuals, and that while "condemnation of passive homosexuals puts them into the outcaste group, their [*activo*] partners "pass unremarked and are very often men of importance" (386–87). Passive homosexuals "solicit on the street in obscene whispers and make themselves conspicuous by mincing with sickening exaggeration, overdoing the falsetto tones, and using women's turns of phrase. All their energies are focused upon arranging the sexual act in which they take the female role" (387).

Landes knew some ten *pais de santo* among whom she distinguished different types. "The famous 'fathers' like Bernardino and Procopio worry about masking the cruder signs of homosexuality—though they never abandon its practice—and devote themselves to their mystical duties, like their women colleagues" (395). Those like Bernardino, the head of an Angola temple, "break their street ties completely and cultivate cult followers who are normal men dazzled by the mystery that surrounds a cult head" and do what they can to "conceal their homosexuality" (398).

68. These are more dramatically different than in other studies elsewhere in Brazil, e.g., D. Pierson (1942:277) reported that five of twelve Nagō-Gēge leaders were male, in contrast to five of six Congo-Angola ones. Ribeiro (1969:11) noted that in Recife, as in Bahia, most members are female, but found the sex balance more equal among leaders, with male leaders predominating in the "orthodox" possession religions (54 percent of the leaders being male) in contrast to 69 percent of the leaders of syncretic ones being male.

69. D. Pierson (1942:299) reported that sixteen male affiliates were hucksters, stevedores, day laborers, a porter, a tinsmith, a painter, a baker, a tailor, and a typesetter.

Mães de santo "respect him because his work is good. He is a big powerful man who dances wonderfully, but in the style of the women. . . . 'You should see him dance. He rivals the best of the women, although he's a big man. He dances in the woman's way, sensuous and aloof, and he's so competent in his work that the mothers have almost forgotten his original sex'" (1947:38, 204).

Others, like João, "retain the old ties along with the new" (1940: 398): Landes described João as "quite unashamed, half-mincing in the streets, writing love letters to the men of his heart, wearing fancy blouses whose colors and cut set off his fine shoulders and skin—and straightening his hair" (1940:396). She continued:

> People know he is a homosexual because he straightens his long thick hair, and *that* is blasphemous: "What! How can one let a hot iron touch the head where a saint resides!" the women cry.[70] . . . I looked at the young father with interest, because he was notorious for his love affairs with other men and for failing to command discipline from the daughters of his caboclo temple. . . .
> "It's not altogether his fault," [Brazilian anthropologist] Edison [Carneiro] answered Manoel. "He is about twenty-four, and he inherited the post about nine or ten years ago. Naturally he wasn't prepared." (1947:38, 238)

Landes also constructed a "bisexual" type of others such as Vava, who, like João, allowed his *terreiro* to be used for amorous encounters, thus "attaining for himself access to the men who visited there originally for heterosexual motives. At the same time he is happily married to an attractive white girl, having been married several times in his twenty-five years" (397). In fact, João also later married (Landes 1 Apr. 1989 letter to author), whether or not he "abandoned the practices" of homosexuality.

Landes (1940) offered distinct but not incompatible explanations for what she considered the new situation of male priestesses. The first explanation is that "passive homosexuals" enter the *terreiros* in order to act out female roles: "Passive homosexual fantasies are realizable under the protection of the cult, as men dance with women in the roles of women, wearing skirts and acting as mediums. . . . They care to be women, and constantly surround themselves with women priests" (1940:394, emphasis in original). Rather than fantasies of being sexually penetrated,

---

70. Similarly, Matory (1988) was chided for touching the head of a *santero*: "You wouldn't go and touch a married woman's privates, would you?" That is, the god who possessed the *santero* owned his head.

this sounds like transsexual desire (more than a quarter of a century before the words *transsexual* was coined in English). She also suggested
conscious planning to acquire higher status as religious leaders to com-
pensate for their despised homosexual status—or their elsewhere despised effeminacy. (Like many Brazilians, she did not make a distinction
between sexual receptivity and effeminacy.)

Her close Brazilian associate Edison Carneiro (1940:272–73) con-
curred that "formerly the candomblé was a woman's business. . . . The
ascendancy of women dates from the introduction of the candomblé
in Brazil by the establishment of the Nagō house of Engenho Velhno
around 1830. . . . [and] 'fathers' try to assimilate the ideal type of the
'mother,' assuming feminine attitudes, giving themselves up to homosexuality, where they take the passive rôle" (272–73).

Reviewing Landes's 1947 book *City of Women,* the leading American
Africanist anthropologist Melville Herskovits (1947) challenged her thesis that the candomblé priestly role was inherently or even predominantly a female reserve. He contended that there were fewer male cult
chiefs for economic reasons, arguing that in Brazil, as in Africa, "it is easier to support a women in the cult house than to withdraw a man from
productive labor for months on end" (1947:125; reiterated 1955:232).
Moreover, he chided, "Miss Landes overstresses the homosexuality of
male priests—there are many 'orthodox' as well as caboclo priests who
have no tendency towards inversion" (125). Less than consistently, except in animus for Landes, Herskovits went on to repeat Arthur Ramos's
(1942:187) denial that the priestly role was necessarily female, observing that "the best-known cult leaders of the black cult in Bahia, as in
other parts of Brazil, are, as it happens, men, as was evident in the two
Afro-Brazilian congresses and in the register of African sects of Bahia."
Ramos also categorically rejected claims about male homosexuality he
misattributed to Landes: "I know myself a few homosexuals *pais de santo,*
just as there are a few blacks, mulattos and Indians who are also homosexuals without this having anything to do with defining characteristics
of the cult. . . . The presence of homosexuals in the Candomblés has neither religious nor ritual significance, but implies only individual sexual
deviance" (Ramos 1942:188, 192).

Landes nowhere claimed "religious or ritual significance" for homosexuality within caboclo, that all *pais de santo* were homosexual, or that
all Bahian homosexuals were *pais de santo* or even devotees of Afro-
Brazilian religions. She certainly never claimed to have observed "ritual
homosexuality," as Ramos (1942:189, 191) misrepresented her as hav-

ing done. She argued that homosexuality preceded entrance into the priesthood, not that males coupled with other males out of religious ambition, or any resocialization to homosexuality after joining a temple and/or being possessed.

Wafer's vivid (1991) experiential ethnography does not mention the words "homosexual" or "homosexuality," though it is obvious that the temple into which he was initiated took his homosexuality and that of others (not least his Brazilian male sexual partner and research assistant) for granted. Endeavoring to show what initiation into the group of believers was like, and to avoid imposing an alien sense of homosexuality being problematic and in need of explanation, he did not raise the kinds of questions about social functions and individual etiology that have preoccupied other social scientists who have written about homosexuality and Afro-Brazilian religions.

When asked, devotees deny that there is any explanation for the correlation between homosexuality and participation in their religion. That is, in their view, homosexuality is of no religious significance: "'A vida no centro não tem nada a ver com a vida particular' (The ritual life is in no way connected to one's private life) is a central doctrine. The spirits are believed to interfere with the lives of their hosts only when their hosts fail to fulfill their obligations to them; strictly secular affairs are of no concern to the spirits."[71] A *pai de santo* told Fry, "I am a bicha; everyone knows that I am a bicha and I have never denied that I am a bicha. At the same time, I am a pai de santo and was initiated (*feito*) in Bahia. When I have a ritual (*festa*) these things are left aside" (1987:76; 1995a:206).

Some Brazilians (especially, one supposes, nonbelievers) suggest that bichas are common in Afro-Brazilian religious rites because of the opportunity provided there to "hunt" (*caçar*) men.[72] Some Belémites told Fry that "by dancing in the cults, bichas, who were generally held to like to show themselves off, had sanction for dressing up in fine clothes, and competing with other bichas, and thereby attracting the 'men' present," but he undercut the plausibility of this, noting that, "although festas do attract large publics, some of whom are on the lookout for possible sexual adventures, these are usually arranged by non-participants, rather

71. Leacock and Leacock 1972 (75, 106). In 1996 Randy Matory told me that those he asked in Brazil told him the same thing.

72. Finding male sexual partners is also the reason *travestis* gave Kulick (1998a) for modifying their bodies and dressing as (super-sexy) women. They expressed revulsion at being (surgically) turned into women, and, indeed, revulsion at natural female genitalia.

than by cult members, who have little chance to interact with persons outside the terreiro" (1987:77; 1995:207).[73] Moreover, "although males were frequently possessed by female spirits, they were also possessed by male ones," and one told him, "There is no need for me to mix my private life with my work, for the simple reason that I am much more of a coquette than any of the caboclos I receive" (1987:78; 1995:208). Ribeiro (1969) also noted little or no correlation between the sex of patron spirits and the sexuality of their adepts. And Matory (1988) argued that insofar as female gods penetrate their worshippers, they are structurally male, filling receptacles with spirit. One *mãe de santo* adamantly maintained to Fry, "The sexuality of the *santos* under no hypothesis interferes with the physical integrity of their sons (filhos)" (1987:80n. 10; 1995a:209n. 9).

In sum, none of the native explanations contains even a tinge of belief in "ritualized homosexuality," that is, that homosexuality is intrinsic to their religion or that the spirits especially bless men who fuck religious functionaries. In Fry's extensive inquiries about homosexuality and candomblé religion, no one suggested that the spirits preferred *bichas* as mediums (1987:80; 1995:208). Except in constructing straw-man arguments to contest, I do not think that anyone has claimed that all or even most *bichas* in Brazil are candomblé functionaries, only that *bichas* are more common in these ranks than in the society in general. Even those who acknowledge the disproportion treat homosexuality as having **religious** significance.

Native North America

In his splendid synthesis of historical records of the Native North American type of person until very recently called "berdache,"[74] Roscoe

73. To believe that spirits possess people is not to believe that every claim to possession is authentic, so skepticism about the genuineness of particular person's possession is not the same as doubting that there are spirits that possess people (see Hong and Murray 1997).

74. The term derives from Old Persian and Arabic *bardag*, which meant "slave" (male or female with no connotations of gender, or of sexual service). Via French, "berdache" was applied—from the late-seventeenth century on—to effeminate, nonprocreative males. Some contemporary First Nations people wishing to connect with historical roles and a few anthropologists ignorant of the etymology have claimed that "berdache" is a "Western term meaning 'catamite'" and attempted to retroject their own (ultra-Western!) term "two spirits" on the historical record. I continue to use "berdache" as an etic term in preference to contemporary ones such as "gay," "homosexual," "transsexual," "transgendered." and "two-spirited," and to be very skeptical that contemporary "gay Indians" are playing the same role(s) with the same cultural valuations as were precontact berdaches. Good emic

(1998) lists documentation for 157 peoples ("tribes") with male gender-mixing or -crossing roles. He also lists 50 with female gender-mixing or -crossing roles, sometimes with distinct terms, sometimes with a generic term used for females and males. Cross dressing was the most visible aspect of the role, especially for outsiders, but Roscoe's comparative analysis shows that "mixed-gender work was the most common defining trait of alternative gender identity from the native perspective. Despite the shorthand description of berdaches as "doing the work of the opposite sex," they often engaged in a combination of men's and women's activities, along with pursuits unique to their status. Among the various activities that were regarded as "women's work" among a particular people, the male berdache often specialized in some, rather than undertaking all. The same was the case for female berdaches and "men's work." There were also berdache specialties (i.e., tasks that did not involve doing the work of the sex other than the berdache's natal one). Preparing corpses for burial was a particularly common instance (especially in California). There were also other special responsibilities in other rites of passage. Childhood (i.e., prepubertal) interest in a kind of work often indicated that a child would not take the path of his or her natal sex. Prototypically (among Plains peoples), the test involved a child picking up a bow (the synecdoche of the male warrior) or a burden strap (the synecdoche of female labor). As for "shamans" and spirit mediums elsewhere in the world, this call was not always welcome. Fletcher (1884:281) wrote of a young Plains tribesman who committed suicide rather than answer the call to become a berdache.

We do not know enough about the subjectivity of First Nations people before or after contact and conquest to know whether they distinguished gender, gendered divisions of labor, and sexuality, and, if so, which of these was primary in the self-definition of those called berdache by outside observers. Sex with persons of the same natal sex is less often a **documented** aspect of the role than occupational specialization is.[75]

---

analysis, including Roscoe's (1991a, 1998) close analysis of several individuals, uses a particular language's terms. But emic analysis is not the only kind, and even it loses some of the richness of contextual differences in how emic categories are deployed and the complexity of individual meaning.

75. Great caution should be taken in assuming that absence of reports about the sexual partners of those in berdache roles is valid evidence of absence of berdache sexual partners. In particular, one should not take percentage of "tribes" with reports of same-sex sex as percentage of "tribes" with same-sex sex, as Lang (1998:256) did. Ideally, to establish that there is a role, rather than the conduct of one individual, there should be either a role term or multiple examples. E.g., does mention of a Mrs. Chavez of Isleta, who dressed as a

What was the most salient aspect either for the berdache or for non-berdaches in particular First Nations is not clear. It is clear that the roles were not only sexual roles, and perhaps not always roles with a sexual component. As Roscoe noted, "There are few accounts of berdache sexuality.[76] . . . However, when the sexual preferences of berdache have been reported a definite pattern emerges. Males and female berdaches were sexually active with members of their own sex and this behavior was part of the cultural expectations for their role. . . . A few berdaches may not have been sexually active at all, although institutionalized celibacy was a foreign concept in native cultures (1998:9–10)." As among the other kind of "Indians" (i.e., in South Asia), nonprocreativity seems to be the defining feature of berdache sexuality (for natally male and natally female berdaches).

Roscoe's (1991a, 1998) biographies of individual berdaches show that some berdache were highly respected individuals within their society. Especially the Zuni We'wha and the Navajo Hastíín Klah acted as liaisons to the encroaching white society, as the Zapotek *muxes* in contemporary southern Mexico are.[77] The view advanced by Alfred Kroeber (1940), the dean of Native California studies, and his student George Devereux (1937 et seq.) who wrote extensively about the Mojave of southeastern California, is that the role as a niche for timid, weak male failures does

---

man, was "an independent traveler and trader and member of the War society" (Parsons 1939:38) instantiate an Isleta warrior woman role, or just that there was once one Isleta woman who was accepted into a war society? In the section in Parson's Isleta monograph on anomalous kinds of persons, she wrote about several nineteenth-century male berdache (*lunide*) but did not mention female berdache (1932:245–47).

76. And the ones that do exist are mostly very brief and often opaque. Take, for instance, Cornelius Osgood's of the Alaskan Ingalik, which Lang (1998:193) coded as establishing that natally male Ingalik berdaches had male and female sexual partners. What Osgood (1958:216) wrote on the page Lang cited about "male impersonators" and "female impersonators" was that "there is no indication that transvestites are normally sexual inverts. On the contrary, it must be presumed on the available evidence that these individuals are rather asexual and sometimes narcissistic, rather than being homosexual, heterosexual or bisexual. On the other hand, quite possibly, these variations of behavior may sometimes occur." I would interpret this as either a circumlocution around "I don't know what they do sexually" or as "neither sex with men nor sex with women is an expected— and certainly not a criterial—aspect of the role." In the following two pages Osgood told of a "man pretender" infuriated by a cousin trying to arrange a wife for her. Not wanting a wife is not evidence of not wanting sex, but neither is it evidence for Ingalik female berdache–female sexual relations.

77. Chiñas (1995:300) attributed this to *muxe* obtaining more education than other isthmus Zapoteks and to their having fewer responsibilities for supporting and raising children.

not fit the honored accomplishments of berdaches who negotiated for their people and on occasion took arms.[78] There were valued economic and ceremonial "niches" with positive standards for achievement, not just a collection of failed men and failed women (or abjected captives!). Navajo *nadle* ("weaver" or "transformed") were especially notable for their wealth and power. In this society, with matrilineal inheritance, the *nadle*'s legal status is that of a woman, Walter Hill (1935:275) reported. He also wrote:

> The outlook of Navaho society toward the nadle is very favorable. They are believed to have been given charge of the wealth in the beginning and to control it to the present date. . . . All the older Navaho have a genuine respect for the nadle and only in rare instances do the younger ones scoff at them. They were never made fun of and their abnormalities were never mentioned to them or by themselves. This respect verges almost on reverence in many cases. . . . One states, "They know everything. They can do both the work of a man and a woman. I think when all the nadle are gone, that it will be the end of the Navaho." Another says, "If there were no nadle, the country would change. They are responsible for all the wealth in the country. If there were no more left, the horses, sheep, and Navaho would all go. They are leader just like President Roosevelt." (274)

Even "their promiscuity is respected. . . . Two informants stated that the nadle commonly paid the other person to perform the act. The only limit to these relations is that the clan incest tabu must be observed" (276). One told Hill of having had sexual relations with more than a hundred men (278).

Whether they were anti-procreative or nonprocreative, those enacting berdache roles (filling the berdache niche) did not produce children.[79] Their sexual partners (including those treated as husbands of male berdache and wives of female ones) were mostly of their natal sex and conventional in gender.

78. E.g., the Crow *boté* with the very martial name Finds Them and Kills Them (see Roscoe 1998:23–38).

79. Some had produced children before receiving a vision (or other recognitions of a call). The Mojave simulated childbirth as well as menstruation, which I interpret as a kind of joining "the second sex"—a transsexual reading, but whether it is that of Mojaves or of the Freud-intoxicated analyst is difficult to determine (as Herdt:1991:494] and Roscoe:1997:67–26 have noted). There is no report from any other tribe remotely similar to the fake pregnancies of the *alyha,* not even among linguistically related neighboring tribes.

Sacred warrant existed in many "tribes," some creation stories include hermaphrodites along with men and women, and some berdache roles involved particular ceremonial responsibilities. While it is clear that legitimate social roles existed with recurrent supernatural sanctions for the existence of the role and/or for particular occupants taking a position in the religio-social-economic structure, I would hesitate to generalize from this literature that the berdache roles were "sacred roles," or even that most berdaches were "technicians of the sacred." [80] And I see no evidence from any of the First Nations that having sex with a berdache was a religious duty or one that produced religious benefits. [81] The economic benefit of marriage to a hardworking, proficient craftsperson is obvious, as is the aphrodisiac aura of the powerful in all societies; not that we can conclude that such benefit was the most important basis for the non-berdache's relationship with the berdache. As with the other gender-crossing/-mixing healers (etc.) considered in this section, being sexually penetrated was not part of ceremonies, [82] but homosexual behavior without gender markings in occupation and dress does not appear to have made either males or females into berdache or any other distinct type or role in North American aboriginal societies. Without taking a position on

80. Most did more prosaic work. Lang (1998:256) coded berdaches being "sacred persons" as a component of the berdache role in about 15 percent of recorded instances (of cultures) and as healers in about 20 percent. Since most of the accounts of berdache did not involve systematic inquiry about whether this or that was a component, these are probably underestimates. The visions of Plains persons were regarded as sacred. I have not heard of any that involved sex with berdaches. In the Pueblo societies, visions were neither sought nor welcome. "Although some Pueblo berdaches were religious specialists, and their supernatural counterparts were portrayed in ceremonies, if they were considered 'holy,' it was not because of their berdache status as such, but because of their religious training, which required the mastery of complex oral literature and ceremonial procedures" (Roscoe 1997:6–21). Roscoe (1997:6) discussed evidence for incipient priesthoods in sedentary horticultural societies around the time of European conquest(s).

81. The passing mention by Erikson (1963:153) that some Sioux (Lakota) berdaches "are said to be married to other men, some to have been visited by warriors before war parties" might suggest bringing luck in war parties, avoidance of sexual contact with women rather than avoidance of sex on the eve of battle, or some expected continuities between "topping" males sexually at night and in other ways the next day in battle. Marriage to a Mojave *alyha* reputedly brought good luck in gambling. Although the etic distinction between "magic" and "religion" is not unproblematic, these seem prototypically "magical" (like the help contemporary *dang-gis* in Taiwan provide in choosing lottery numbers). The "medicine"/"religion" boundary is murkier, even where monotheistic religions dominate.

82. Roscoe (10 July 1997 personal communication) cautioned, "The active/passive distinction is not formally articulated in most native cultures, although it is always implied. But the cultures weren't organized around it."

whether there were two, three, four, or multiple genders in the cos-mologies of these people, the roles called (mostly by outside observers) "berdache" indubitably were **gendered**.[83]

Conclusion
Local models of motivation

Generally, the indigenous view of causation for males taking on trans-vestite religious and/or healer roles is involuntary. Gods and spirits choose the occupants of these roles rather than an individual's desire. People no-ticed that many of those possessed by spirits also sought sex with males at times other than during rituals. They did not understand observed correlation between medico-religious vocations and homosexuality as causal in the way some alien observers posit. That is, homosexual desire of technicians of the sacred is common, even expected, but is not a basis for or even a necessary part of such spiritual vocations. Rather than seek-ing a niche for their gender or sexual abnormalities, the recurrent native view is that those who became transvestite-possessed healers and shamans resist the call of the spirits. Such vocations inspired awe. Heal-ers received rewards from clients, but these rewards did not seem so great that many males were eager to undertake such roles to reap them. Homosexual desire follows, but does not cause someone to undertake one of these roles.[84] Being sexually penetrated does not have religious meaning. Even what might seem from outside a faith to be analogous penetrations (by spirits and men) are not seen by those inside the faith as being related. The spirits are not believed to penetrate anally those

83. "A gendered division of labor is a means of accomplishing production by assigning tasks not to bodies but to types of persons" (Roscoe 1998:130). Hairdresser is a gendered role in South and North American societies, but not a gender. Most hairdressers are female, and the masculinity of male hairdressers is suspect (though the homosexual ones are pre-sumed to have male genitalia, and some male hairdressers are known to sexually penetrate women). Elsewhere (Murray 1994a, 1996:163–64; even before the prominence of Den-nis Rodman's gender bending) I argued that "NBA basketball player" is as much or as little a "gender" as is Native American berdache. My criterion (which is not exclusively for lex-ical items) for establishing that some social role is a "gender" is that it contrast with mas-culine and feminine on the same level. If a society has men's dress and women's dress and a distinct third kind of dress (rather than a mixture of men's and women's, or men wear-ing women's, or women wearing men's), or men's space, women's space, and a separate space for a third (, fourth, etc.) kind of adults, I would find "third gender" credible. (I have never questioned that there are views of a "third sex," only of "third gender.")

84. Some of these roles were regarded as hyperlibidinous. The *galli* were, shamans not, with African and Afro-Brazilian intermediate. Similarly, some berdache were, while others seem to have been uninterested in sex.

Figure 9. Dance of the *berdache*.

they "mount," but, rather, to seize the heads of their mediums. *Hijra*s may rent their orifices. Many *hijra*s may be sexually available for hire. But it is not their sexual behavior that makes them special in South Asian societies. It is not their sexual behavior that underlies the power of their blessings and curses. Nor is it their dress. It is their initiation into the *hijra* role, particularly the sacrifice of their genitals.

The old meaning of *effeminate* in English is "preferring the company of females to that of males." Contempt for unmasculinity did not preclude suspicions that effeminate males sought to have sex with females, that they were not just gossiping and comparing coutures and coiffures. Some conventionally masculine men in the societies discussed in this chapter (including ancient Rome, contemporary South Asia, West Africa, and Brazil) suspect/ed that some men simulate femininity as a cover for seducing women. Even castrated males were not always above suspicion.

Dress

Some roles have requisite garb, but, again, in native explanatory models it is not desire to cross dress, but rather the call of the spirits, that impels men to these roles. The garb is often different from both that which is gender specific in a society, whether this includes mixing what is usually male with what is usually female, and from things that are distinctive. The same is true for coiffures.

Prestige and Marriage Marketability

The prestige of these medico-spiritual roles in the tribal societies that have or had them is high, and the incumbents of the roles often acquired relative abundance of material goods, making them "good prospects" for husbands. The ideology of doing women's work better than women also made them seem "good prospects." Even for the less elevated status of prostitute, since time immemorial, there have been men eager to live off the earnings of both male and female prostitutes.[85]

Having a healer in the family is widely seen as an advantage, and one who can call down aid from the spirit world is even more of one. The husbands of Siberian transformed shamans reaped benefits but seem to have lived in some fear of their wives' power. The accounts across time and space of sacralized transvestite roles do not attest that marrying or having sex with someone in one of these special occupational roles confers any particular blessing on the husband (or other inseminators) of such a person or that their sexual partners receive spiritual benefits as well as material ones. Would that we knew what meaning either the receptacles or those penetrating them believed that sexual receptivity had!

There are no systematic data from anywhere on the question of how husbands' masculinity is conceived by other men in any of these societies. That of transformed shamans seem somewhat dubious in the ethnographic record. However, it is difficult to gauge whether it appears this way as a result of the contempt of alien observers, or whether it reflects local consensus.

---

85. For contemporary examples see Kulick 1998a; Prieur 1998.

Part Three

EGALITARIAN HOMOSEXUALITIES

Even "modern" homosexuality involving persons with gay or lesbian identities does not involve invariant and perfectly balanced sexual reciprocity. Reported sexual reciprocity is a possible criterion for egalitarian homosexuality in "premodern" societies. A more significant one is at least approximately equal social status between partners, particularly, similarity in age, prestige, gender presentation, and accesses to resources. Descriptions of these relationships are generally lacking in detail, but there are at least indications of egalitarian same-sex sexual patterns before forensic psychiatric discourse allegedly constructed "the modern homosexual" and "the modern lesbian" (both of which were transgendered types rather than partners in egalitarian relationships, anyway) and beyond even the most exaggerated fantasies of psychiatry's influence.

 This part begins with fleeting glances at indications of both female and male same-sex relations lacking significant status differences between partners in ethnographic reports and in classic Greek, Roman, Islamic, and Chinese literature. In that there is a vast literature on lesbian and gay life of recent decades in North America (far in excess even of that which I discussed in *American Gay*), I have not felt the need to include detail about it here. After discussing what "the modern homosexual" is, and a few aspects of "modernity," I turn to the diffusion of the word "gay," mixed with the tendency for local traditional conceptions of homosexuality to seep into the word borrowed to challenge precisely such conceptions, bring together behavioral data from Mexico and Peru that indicates behavior less constrained by the cultural dichotomization of masculine and feminine roles than culturalists have supposed, and discuss some indications of gay conception and incipient social organization from within the Abode of Islam.

 This section revisits many of the locales of earlier (in this book) representations of age- and gender-structured homosexualities. This should reinforce the message of the book's introduction that more than one type of homosexuality may occur in one time and place.

8
Premodern

Egalitarian Female Homosexuality in "Tribal" Societies

There are a number of scattered reports of relationships of sexual mutuality between women in "traditional"/"tribal" societies, especially Oceanic
ones. First, three stray references from Africa:

Southeastern Africa

Homosexuality among speakers of Khoisan languages, reportedly,

> is fairly common among both men and women, and especially
> among young married women. There exists among the Naman
> a practice whereby two individuals, either of the same or of op-
> posite sex, will enter into a specially intimate bond of association,
> *soregus,* with each other. This is initiated by one of the parties
> drinking from a bowl of water (or nowadays often coffee), and
> then handing the rest of the liquid to the other to drink. . . . As
> a rule the relationship thus entered upon primarily implies deep
> friendship and mutual assistance, especially in economic mat-
> ters. But, according to Falk, it is also used as a means of estab-
> lishing a homosexual relationship, especially by boys, who jeal-
> ously watch over each other. The customary form of homosexual
> practice is mutual masturbation, among both men and women;
> pedication (coitus in anum) between men, and the use of an
> artificial penis between women, are also found, but more rarely.
> (Schapera 1930:242–43; see Falk 1925)

West African Glimmers

According to Eva Meyerowitz's fieldwork in the Gold Coast (now
Ghana) during the 1940s, "lesbian affairs were virtually universal among
unmarried Akan women, sometimes continuing after marriage. Whenever possible, the women purchased extra-large beds to accommodate
group sex sessions involving perhaps half-a-dozen women." Perhaps
as a result of discussion about the relative status of the partners with
Meyerowitz, David Greenberg (1989:66) considered this an instance of
egalitarian homosexuality. The quoted statement has seemed very dubious to several West Africans and Africanists with whom I have spoken.

The major pre–World War II American Africanist anthropologist Melville Herskovits wrote that "homosexuality is found among women as   359

well as men; by some it is claimed that it exists among women to a greater extent" (1938:289). Male suspicion of what women are up to among themselves, on the one hand, and women's formation of emotionally intense relationships as shelters from men, on the other, are common patterns in West African cultures.

Melanesian Societies

The female-female sexual play Bernard Deacon (1934:171) mentioned—clearly recognized as a definite type of sexual desire, that women engage in because it gives them pleasure (170)—may have been egalitarian rather than necessarily linked to initiation (i.e., age stratified).

Recently, Wulf Schiefenhövel (1990:410) discussed adult sexual relationships between women among the Eipo in the eastern highlands of Irian Jaya:

> Eipo friends of the author quite openly told him about some adult females of the village community who were alleged to engage in mutual sexual stimulation (*kwat mamun;* vagina close together) apparently by rubbing the vulva against some parts of the partner's body. The essence of the explanation was, "They are horny and that's why they are doing that." No reproachful or otherwise discriminative attitude could be detected with regard to these adult females, whose names were known to everyone. Rather, one spoke of them with definite humorous amusement and with some form of respect for the strength of their sexual desire.

Along with an anomalous Highland report of Gadsup girls "associat[ing] intimately with one another, caressing and petting the breasts and genitals of the other; in this homosexual play they assume the position of intercourse with one lying on the other" (DuToit 1975:220), there are what Herdt (1984:75) considered questionable allusions by Baumann (1955:228) and Harrison (1937:362, 410), passing mention in Barker's (1975:150) dissertation and in Godelier (1982:82), and little else. However, one should be wary of this lack of data about lesbian behavior, as Herdt (1984:75) cautioned, because most Melanesianists have been males studying males. For instance, Ian Hogbin (1970) noted that Wogeo women have a ceremonial life apart from men, but had information only from Wogeo men about what women do. Raymond Kelly did not explore Etero female ideology about growing girls, and left readers to wonder if there is any female ideology and any female-female sexual contact on the 291 days of the year that heterosexual contact is unsafe, or whether he did not (or, as a man, could not) inquire about female behavior and beliefs.

Aboriginal Australian Societies

Géza Róheim reported that "homosexuality also plays a conspicuous part in the life of a young girl" among Central Australian Aranda women, stressing that, as for men, appropriate homosexual partners follow the same incest/kinship logic of heterosexual relations in aboriginal Australian societies:

> The *iminta* is a little stick round at the end with string so as to imitate the *para kapita* (glans penis). Two women use it, usually cross cousins (*ilchila*), for the cross cousin is the proper person for all kinds of sexual intimacy. All the *wonka* girls (virgins) do this, old Yirramba says, when they *mbkarilama* (get excited). One of them plays the part of the male, and introduces the artificial penis into the vagina of her friend. Before doing this they show their vagina to each other. They may also use *yalla* roots instead of the *iminta*. Morica describes the mutual onanism of two women. She calls it *kityili-kityili*—tickling the clitoris with the finger. After having excited each other for some time like this, one of them will lie on top of the other like a man, and they rub the two *chelia* together. While they do this tickling of the clitoris, one of them will say to the other, "a man will come with a big penis and cohabit with you." (1933:238; also see Kaberry 1939:257)

Róheim (1974:183–84) also stressed mutuality ("when two girls become excited, they often manipulate each other's genitals"), and, in passing, also mentioned a pair of cross cousins from Tauru (Ferguson Island) who "ran away into the inland and lived there, mutually doing cunnilingus to each other."

Polynesian Societies

In Tahiti, "transient homosexual contacts between women are said to be frequent. These are said to involve mutual mouth-genital contact or mutual masturbation. These contacts are not considered particularly abnormal or signs of altered sexuality. They involve women who also engage in ordinary heterosexual behavior" (R. Levy 1968:141). That is, there is lesbian behavior, but "no evidence for a full homosexual role corresponding to the *mahu* . . . [The term] *Mahu* is considered by many to be misused for describing female homosexuals" (141). The term *raerae* [a male switch-hitting role; see p. xx] is sometimes used, also *vahine pa'I'a* which means "woman rubbing together genitals without penetration" (140). Earlier, the French colonial physician Jacobus X (1893:388) blamed contact with the whites for "the introduction of two vices unknown to the ancient Tahitians: masturbation and female Sapphism, whose existence I have positively recognized among a certain number of the prostitutes of Papeete" (1893:388; my translation); by "sapphism" he meant friction with a clitoris.[1]

Seventeen of twenty-five Samoan girls queried by Mead (1928:85) related homosexual experiences, which Mead asserted were treated casually (90), but this fieldwork, and in particular the placid attitude toward sexuality attributed by Mead to the Samoans, and her uncritical acceptance of self-reported data on sexual behavior, have been severely criticized by Freeman (1983, 1998), who (just as uncritically) accepts late-twentieth-century hyper-Christian reports of ideal norms from elderly women.

On Hawai'i, Handy and Pukui (1978:73) noted the term *wahine-h'oo-wahine* ("female husband" or "female's wife"), paralleling *kane-ho'o-kane* ("male wife" or "male's husband") and mentioned two women, Kuku and Kama, who were devoted friends and called each other *aikane* (or *kane*, for short), a relationship that can exist between two females, or between two males, but not between a male and a female (on male *aikane* at the time of first European contacts, see pp. 97–99 above).

A Micronesian Society

On the Micronesian atoll of Ulithi, mutual masturbation by women was reported by William Lessa:

> Young girls sometimes practice mutual masturbation, and they too [like boys there], if discovered, are scolded and possibly beaten by their parents, as well as rebuked and ridiculed by the other members of the community. Girls carry on the act less frequently than they used to. Women of mature age sometimes indulge in mutual masturbation, though since this is a matter of great secrecy its frequency is hard to determine. The practice is the result of lack of attention from males and is resorted to as a substitute for normal sexual congress. (1950:182)

One might wonder how he knew of either behavior or causality.

---

1. Frank Proschan, who called my attention to these passages, noted that in "explaining" pederasty in Indochina, Dr. X exculpated the French, claiming that when they arrived, the "vice [sodomy/fellatio] was innate, and the Europeans found it flourishing, and some, very few, let us hope, have taken advantage of it" (1893:60).

Egalitarian Male-Male Sexual Relationships in "Tribal" Societies

As in the previous section, this one begins with representations of "traditional" African societies before focusing on Oceanic and Amazonian ones. There is a bit more observation and considerably more assertion about male-male sexual relations than about female-female ones in the contact and anthropological literatures, but, it is similarly alien observers' conceptions rather than what any of "the natives" said about what they did and how they felt about their same-sex sexual relations.

Nykakyusa Age Grades

Monica Wilson's 1951 book *Good Company* (based on fieldwork done during the mid-1930s) of Bantu-speaking Nykakyusa (on both sides of the Tanzania/Zimbabwe border in eastern Africa) is a classic account of extreme age grading. The inhabitants of each village contained only one age cohort (spanning five to eight years) of males.[2]

For unmarried male contemporaries to dwell together for a while in temporary villages or in men's houses (especially during initiation) was traditional in sub-Saharan Africa.

> The peculiarity of the Nyakyusa consists in the fact that contemporaries live together permanently through life, not merely as bachelors. . . . The Nyakyusa themselves associate living in age-villages with decency in sex life—the separation of the sex activities of successive generations, and the avoidance of incest. . . . The emphasis on the separation of parents and children is matched by the value laid on good fellowship (*ukwangala*) between contemporaries. . . . The value of good fellowship with equals is constantly talked about by the Nyakyusa, and it is dinned into boys from childhood that enjoyment and morality alike consist in eating and drinking, in talking and learning, in the company of contemporaries. (M. Wilson 1963 [1951]:159, 162–63)

Nykakyusa derided heterosociality and feared sharing of food and beer between fathers and sons. An "exceptionally reliable informant" told Wilson that a man "never dreams of making love to another man" and

---

2. Wives come from multiple villages, and most women are inherited at least once. Because men inherit wives older than themselves and continue to marry younger brides, the women in a village vary more in age and do not form an age set.

that "not many cases of grown men having intercourse together come to light, but only of boys together or of a man and a boy." He elaborated:

> When a boy sleeps with his friend they sleep together; it is nor forbidden. Everyone thinks it all right. Sometimes when boys sleep together each may have an emission on the other (*bitundanila*). . . . If they are great friends there is no wrong done. . . . Boys sometimes agree to dance together (*ukukina*) and work their evil together and that also is no wrong.[3] . . . Boys do this when they are out herding; then they begin to dance together and to have intercourse together. . . . To force a fellow this is witchcraft (*bo bulosi*); he is not a woman. But when they have agreed and dance together, then even if people find them, they say it is adolescence (*lukulilo*), all children are like that. And they say that sleeping together and dancing is also adolescence. (196)

He reported that interfemoral intercourse is "what boys mostly do," and also reported anal and oral sex. He was aware of and disapproving of "some, during intercourse, work[ing] in the mouth of their friend, and hav[ing] an orgasm. . . . That of the mouth people do very rarely when they dance together" (196).

Reciprocated sex between adolescent friends seems to have been most common, although some age stratification also occurred: "When out herding, some of the older boys do evil [see note 3] with the young ones, the older persuade the little one to lie down with them and to do what is forbidden with them between the legs. Sometimes two older boys who are friends do it together, one gets on top of his fellow, then he gets off and the other one mounts" (196–97). Two other informants agreed that homosexuality occurred frequently in boys' villages: "A boy has intercourse with his fellow, but a grown man? No, never, we've never heard of it. They always want women; only when a man cannot get a women he does this, only in youth. A few men do not marry but they are half-wits who have no kind of intercourse at all" (197).

A Sometimes Lifelong "Adolescent Phase" in Dahomey

According to Melville Herskovits (1938:289), the Fon, the predominant people in Dahomey (now Benin), considered homosexuality an adolescent phase: "[When] the games between boys and girls are stopped, the boys no longer have the opportunity for companionship with the girls, and the sex drive finds satisfaction in close friendship between boys in the same group. . . . A boy may take the other 'as a woman' this being

3. If it is not wrong, one has to wonder what was translated as "working evil together"!

called *gaglgo,* homosexuality. Sometimes an affair of this sort persists during the entire life of the pair." The last statement shows the insufficiency of either the native model or of Herskovits' understanding of it. As the need to carefully conceal homosexual relationships that continue beyond adolescence demonstrates, the Fon model of a transient "stage" is prescriptive rather than descriptive.

Melanesia

William Davenport (1965, 1977) provided a rare account of reciprocal satisfaction among peers alongside the common Melanesian patterns of pederasty and believing that heterosexual coitus is harmful to a young man until his beard is fully grown. In the Nabakaenga District of Graciosa Bay, Santa Cruz Island (east of the Solomon Islands, i.e., farther from New Guinea), Davenport (1965:200) wrote, "it is considered a kind of duty to obligingly accede to the demands of an older man," but, also, "with young men of the same age, homosexual interaction often occurs between persons who are merely good friends, sometimes even brothers. One partner assumes the passive role when the other requests it, and, subsequently, the favor is returned. Men who behave thus are not regarded as homosexual" (199). This lack of self-identity excludes the case from the type "gay," despite the unusual reciprocity and the sexual relations.[4] In the same culture, there are also nonritualized age-structured same-sex relations.[5] According to Davenport, Santa Cruz Islanders did not regard the two homosexual patterns as dissonant or trouble themselves with historical explanations of conduct that they did not consider problematic, and in which all engaged on occasion: "At some time during his life, very nearly every male engages in extensive homosexual activities. . . . [It] usually begins with foreplay, which consists of mutual or unilateral masturbation, and ends with anal intercourse culminating in orgasm" (199).

Recognizing the difficulty of the question, especially in the current *zeitgeist* in anthropology, I asked Professor Davenport if he was certain

4. Indeed, Davenport reported no term for egalitarian homosexuality among Santa Cruz Islanders, discounting the occurrence of love or emotional bonds growing out of Santa Cruz male homosexual liaisons (W. Davenport 1965:199–200).

5. Married adult men may continue to anally penetrate boys (W. Davenport 1977: 155): they neither "graduate" out of pederasty (as among the Sambia studied by Herdt 1981 et seq.), nor have a continued role in masculinizing boys by inseminating them (as among the Marind-anim described by Van Baal 1964), and the childhood sex segregation of societies with "ritualized homosexuality" masculinizing boys out of their primary socialization in a world of women is absent in this instance (W. Davenport 1965:169–70).

that the egalitarian pattern was indigenous. He noted that on his last visit
to the Nabakaenga Region in the early 1980s "it was difficult to get any
more data, because of the enormity of the changes that had taken place
there. All but one of my elder informants had died; men's houses were
not operating at all as they had been, the church was more fully accepted
than ever before, and both primary and secondary mission schools were
firmly established" (21 Apr. 1990 letter). Reflecting on the contact history, he wrote

> I do not rule out egalitarian homosexuality having some kind of
> origins in European influences. One of the reasons why I would
> accept the possibility of European influences has to do with ho-
> mosexual behavior among fellow recruits in the labor lines on
> distant plantations, and, for Santa Cruz Island men, at the tim-
> ber operations on Vanikoro Island. Two long-time recruiters,
> both Europeans, more than once remarked to me that the Santa
> Cruz "boys" were notable for their pairing off into couples. One
> of the field bosses, also a European, at Vanikoro told me the
> same, and I was present on several occasions where there was
> open joking about it, and certainly no denials of such pairing.
> So, it could be that for Santa Cruz men, such partnerships did
> commence in the recruiting situation and was brought back to
> the island and incorporated into men's house behavior. Recruit-
> ment to plantations meant a great deal of culture contact, be-
> cause labor on the big plantations was drawn from many dif-
> ferent societies in the Solomon Islands, and in the early days
> recruits from the Santa Cruz Islands were taken (legally) even to
> the New Hebrides. (Vanuatu)

Not only did sexually segregated labor camps exert an influence, but Europeans interested in homosexuality also lived in the Santa Cruz Islands.
One of Davenport's informants recalled having had sexual relations with
a European missionary years before.[6] Some Europeans made concerted

---

6. Davenport wrote me that "he is still fondly remembered on Santa Cruz Island by his
Santa Cruz name, Mebuano (Man who Catches Sharks.) He was involved in homosexual
relations, both egalitarian and with young boys. He was found out by the Mission, relieved
of his post, and publicly shamed before his fellow missionaries. While waiting to be shipped
back to England, he committed suicide" (21 Apr. 1990 letter). In a 1 May 1990 letter, Davenport wrote that he saw "no reason to protect him or the old Melanesian Mission (now
Church) anymore. There's no good reason to hide anything now." In a letter of 14 May
1990, he added that there was no Santa Cruz identification of young men with sharks.
Noosing sharks was one of the most prestigious craft specialties of Santa Cruz Islanders, so
that "Mebuano" was a highly complimentary name, and one with no homosexual reso-

attempts to extirpate "native homosexuality," so a consciousness of a pattern of "homosexuality" as problematic clearly owed something to European influence. The traditional view rendered egalitarian homosexuality as "more comparable to masturbation, indeed including mutual masturbation, not put in the same category as heterosexual relations (which, I agree, seem never to be free of some restrictions imposed by the concept of incest, however that may be defined)."

While agreeing that the egalitarian homosexuality he described was unusual, Davenport reminded me that

> Graciosa Bay culture has some other unique features: the concubine pattern, the brideprice/naming/adoption complex, the geometrically-graded currency, and the *tepuki* canoe are four other culture complexes that are also unique. Every human culture is apt to have some unique features and complexes. Innovation is always taking place and cultures are constantly undergoing change and reformulation. I certainly wish that I knew the histories of each and every unique feature or configuration in Santa Cruz Islands culture, but I don't and I regard the achievement of such an ideal ethnographic situation as impossible to obtain. . . . The fact that some aspects of Santa Cruz culture are different from others, and perhaps even unique, is just a fact that at the present state of the discipline cannot be fully explained. (21 Apr. 1990 letter)

Herdt (1984:42, 271) skeptically listed claims made in unpublished ethnography by T. N. Barker for sanctioned homosexual relations between brothers among the Ai'i, DuToit's (1975) assertion of homosexual activity that is neither age-graded nor role-bound among the Akuna of the Eastern Highlands, and Mead's (1930:126) men of relations between unmarried young males on the Manus Island.[7] These cultures are all outside the swath of highland New Guinea cultures with ritualized boy-inseminating initiation rites. This fact makes evaluating the plausibility of claims more difficult.

---

nances. I am very grateful to Professor Davenport for granting his permission to quote what he wrote me to aid in interpreting his classic Nabakaenga publication.

7. "We do find a form of homosexual play. This is referred to as *itueranenu*, meaning simply 'play'. . . . In this homosexual play among boys, one will assume the active and another the passive role, while the first places his penis in the anus of the other. This seems to be relatively common among boys as they become increasingly segregated from their female age-mates, and informants explain that it usually continues until the sixteenth or seventeenth year of life. Among the girls there is something similar [to male homosexual

Knauft (1986:268) discussed a pair of young Highland (Gebusi) men in their mid-twenties maintaining an "unsanctioned," apparently exclusive and sexually reciprocal relationship beyond the age at which they should have married women. In that society in which age-graded homosexuality is not part of initiation ritual, homosexuality is a common topic for joking among men who in their youth participated in it, while avoiding incestuous unions (Knauft 1985:32–33, 264–67, 298–99).

Schneebaum (1984:47) claimed that in Western New Guinea among the Asmat, "All children are allowed to play with each other sexually. It's considered normal. As the boys get older, they continue the sexual relationship with their *mbai,* as the male friend is called. . . . This is a lifelong relationship . . . between men of the same age group." Given the fantasies from childhood about "the Wild Man of Borneo" Schneebaum (1979) discussed, and the earlier mistaken reading of his South American fantasies as empirical reportage, even as ethnography (Schneebaum 1980; see Murray 1987), extreme skepticism is called for in evaluating Schneebaum's latest claims to having found the land where his dreams of sexual utopia come true.

Australia and Micronesia

Róheim 1974 (243; also see 1945:94–95) included a story about two failed aboriginal Australian hunters who, after boasting to each other about the grandeur of their penises, engaged in mutual masturbation and then took turns at anal intercourse. This is actually the only explicit mention of what men did sexually with each other in the folklore (native oral literature) that he discussed.[8]

On the Micronesia atoll of Ulithi after World War II, Lessa (1950:182) noted that "boys sometimes indulge in mutual masturbation, though Christianity has decreased the frequency of the practice. The act is performed as secretly as possible, usually, in the woods, for if the parents of the boys come to know about it they either scold or beat them. If other members of the community hear what has happened, they rebuke and ridicule the boys."

---

play] in which two girls associate intimately with one another caressing and petting the breasts and genitals of the other. In this homosexual play they assume the position of intercourse with one lying on the other. In neither case, it seems, is orgasm reached" (DuToit 1975:220).

   8. Róheim (1974:183–84) also mentioned sexual reciprocity between Aranda women. On contemporary aboriginal gay and lesbian identity see Gays and Lesbians Aboriginal Alliance (1994).

Polynesia

Raymond Firth (1936:494–95) alluded to mutual masturbation as well as anal intercourse among adolescents on the Polynesian island of Tikopia in the late 1920s. Acknowledging that he "collected few data on this subject," he could nonetheless write, "it can certainly be said that it plays no great part in the native sexual life."

Mead (1928:136) also made passing mention of groups of Samoan boys engaged in "casual homosexual practices," including group masturbation. Although she did not mention homosexual conduct in regards to a young man who had been caught in *moetolo* ("sleep-crawling" rape of girls), in describing the plight—"once caught, once branded, no girl will ever pay attention to them again"—the following seems to imply such conduct: "Often partially satisfactory solutions are relationships with men.[9] There was one such pair in the village, a notorious *moetolo*, and a serious-minded youth who wished to keep his heart free for political intrigue" (95). She also wrote, "There were several pairs of boys in the village who had been circumcised together and were still inseparable companions, often sleeping together in the house of one of them. Casual homosexual practices occurred in such relationships" (70), but she did not specify which practices. Homosexuality remains unstigmatizing so long as there is no gender deviance in Samoa, according to Shore (1981:210). According to Besnier (1994:304, 560n. 4), by the early 1990s, Samoans "who understand themselves as having a gay identity in the Western sense of the term and position themselves in society differently from *fa'afāfine*" had emerged, even including gay political activism both in Western Samoa and among Samoan immigrants to New Zealand.

Robert Morris has asserted that consistent differences of class, status, age, or gender do not exist in the sexualized same-sex friendship *aikane* relationship in traditional Hawaiian kingdoms (see p. 99). This also appears to have been true of the traditional Maori *'Takatapui:* "an intimate companion of the same sex" (N. Miller 1992:302).

In the Tahitian capital city of Papeete, in addition to the *māhū* role, a non-gender-defined role, the *raerae*, had emerged by the mid-1960s (i.e., before possible diffusion of American gay liberation):

---

9. It is unclear whose judgment "partially satisfactory" is. In contrast to this "solution" of a lack of access to heterosexual activity, Mead (1928:148) mentioned one twenty-year-old male she and the village recognized as a "real pervert."

For most people in Piri [the village where Levy did fieldwork], it is known as a slang equivalent for *māhū,* but some people in Papeete use it to differentiate nontraditional types of homosexuality from the more traditional *māhū. Raerae* refer to inverted overt physical sexual behavior of either males or females. Thus, a man who lives a female role in the village and who does not engage in sexual activity would be a *māhū* but not a *raerae,* whereas somebody who does not perform a female's village role and who dresses and acts like a man, but who indulges in exclusive or preferred sexual behavior with other men would be *raerae* but not *māhū.* (R. Levy 1973:140)

Robert Levy observed a semantic shift in process. Similarly, in contemporary Latin America the loanword *gay* is taken into the traditional stigmatized, gender-demarcated semantic space (so that *gay* is synonymous with *pasivo*) by some, while for others it marks a new conception (Murray and Arboleda 1987, 1995; Murray 1995c). As in Latin America, reorganization has occurred rapidly. MacFarlane (1983:12) claimed that there had been an increase of *raerae* prostitutes since the early 1950s and a diffusion of the new role from Papeete to villages. One of Levy's (1973:137) *māhū* informants opined that anal intercourse (in which he sometimes engaged) was a recent, "not-Tahitian" (specifically French) activity, and contrasted it with traditional fellatio. Raleigh Watts, who treated *māhū* as a third gender, noted that some Tahitians use *raerae* and *māhū* interchangeably. Trying to make sense of one Tahitian's explanation that "men with swishy hips were called *raerae,* but transvestites were called *māhū,*" Watts interpreted "swishy hips" to mean "masculine men who are basically in masculine roles but are slightly affected in feminine ways, while still remaining definitely within the masculine gender category. This is similar to the gender status held by many American gay men. . . . The other category would refer to males who are not in the male gender category, who might also have swishy hips, but for whom that is not the distinguishing characteristic, given that they are in a gender category entirely of their own" (1987:40–41). My conjecture is that the allusion to hips links to anal sex, contrasting with *mahū* fellators.

When R. Levy did his study in Tahiti (from 1962 to 1964) and even at the time of the Danielssons' article (1978), the *māhū* role was one of a limited number of cultural forms that still persisted in Tahitian communities. When elderly *māhū* die, new ones may no longer emerge to take their place. Instead, they are replaced by *raerae.* This initially urban "modern gay" patterning preceded the gay liberation discourse in America (and France).

"Sentimental Effusions" of Genital Contact in Amazonia

In Northwest Amazonia, as in Melanesia, initiation, more than marriage,[10] is the central passage from the asexual world of childhood to the sexual world of adulthood, and from a particular family to being a member of society. According to Stephen Hugh-Jones (1979:110),

> From an outsider's point of view, one of the most noticeable manifestations of this is the incidence of joking sexual play among initiated but unmarried men. . . . Missionaries working in the Pira-parana are frequently shocked by the apparent homosexual behavior of Indian men. However, the Barasana distinguish between this playful sexual activity and serious male homosexuality. This play, rather than coming from a frustration of 'normal' desire, is itself seen as being normal behavior between 'brothers-in-law' and expressed their close, affectionate, and supportive relationship.

He claimed that "such play does not entail sexual satisfaction," without explaining how he had concluded this. Claude Lévi-Strauss, who had reported "reciprocal sexual services" by classificatory "brothers-in law" among the Nambikwara in 1943 (407; also see 1948a:95–96, 1948c: 366) suggested (in a personal communication cited by Hugh-Jones) that "it appears to provide unmarried men with an outlet for sentimental effusions." Lévi-Strauss (1974 [1955]:313) also remarked, "It remains an open question whether the partners achieve complete satisfaction or restrict themselves to sentimental demonstrations, accompanied by caresses, similar to the demonstrations and caresses characteristic of conjugal relationships." Reading this "clarification," I wonder whether it was Lévi-Strauss who defined homosexuality out of the possibility of "complete satisfaction" and also how "conjugal relationships" could exclude ejaculations! Although maintaining that "the brother is acting as a temporary substitute" for his sister, he admitted that "on reaching adulthood, the brothers-in-law continue to express their feelings quite openly" (314).

10. Christine Hugh-Jones (1979:160) did not consider marriage a significant event in the typical life cycle, because,

> marriage was described as an event in another domain—that of kinship and inter-group relations. Although there is a sense in which marriage is obviously a life-cycle event, it is not ritualized like birth, menstruation, Yurpary rites and death. The physiological possibility of a new generation has already been ritually recognized in initiation.

In most of these tribes, as among many African ones, chiefs monopolized women.

Stephen Hugh-Jones (1979:110) reported, "A young man will often lie in a hammock with his 'brother-in-law,' nuzzling him, fondling his penis, and talking quietly, often about sexual exploits with women." Christine Hugh-Jones (1979:160) similarly noted, "Boys approaching initiation are sometimes involved in homosexual teasing which takes place in hammocks in public: this play is most common between initiated but unmarried youths from separate exogamous groups."

One is left wondering if fondled penises on occasion produce effusions more tangible than "sentimental," as they do elsewhere in the world, especially among young men who, having little sexual experience and few approved sexual outlets, are "given over to personal display" and to talking about real or fantasized sexual exploits. Similarly, one wonders how Altaschuler (1964:231) could have been so sure that the young Cayapa boys he saw wrapped around each other on the floor or sharing hammocks confined themselves to "homoeroticism" in contrast to "homosexuality."[11]

Among the Yanomamo, "Some of the teen-age males have homosexual affairs with each other. [There, too,] the females of their own age are usually married" (Chagnon 1977:76). In his dissertation, Chagnon wrote of "most unmarried young men having homosexual relations with each other but no stigma attached to this behavior. In fact, most of these bachelors joked about it and simulated copulation with each other in public" (1967:62–63; note the contrast between "some" and "most"). Alves da Silva (1977:181) attested public mutual masturbation by Tucano boys, although officially, homosexuality only occurs in the initiation rites for pubescent boys (380).

A more extended description of widespread homosexual play and of fairly enduring but "open" relationships in northwestern Amazonia was provided by Sorenson (1984:184–88). He wrote, "Young men sit around enticingly sedate and formal in all their finery, or form troupes of panpipe-playing dancers." Occasional sex is regarded as expectable behavior among friends: "One is marked as nonfriendly—enemy—if he does not join, especially in the youth age group (roughly 15–35). . . . Homosexual activity is limited neither to within an age group nor to unmarried men" (185). Moreover, intervillage homosexuality is encour-

11. His credibility is further reduced by the argument based on Bieber that the "innovation" of homosexual intercourse could not exist, because homosexual behavior is based on feelings of inadequacy, and those who feel inadequate cannot innovate. Pierre Clastres's (1974, 1977) similar trivialization of Guayakí homosexuality to "erotic play" is ably shredded by Goldberg (1991:52–54, 1992:189–93).

aged, and some "best friends" relationships develop. That the "best friend" is more likely later to marry a sister of his "best friend" is implied in what Sorenson wrote, a seeming analogy to Australian and Melanesian patterns of partner preferences.

Most of the instances discussed in this chapter involve boys having sex with other boys,[12] though some of these sexual relations persist— and in more than a few (also see pp. 25–27) one marries the sister of his male intimate and thereby continues a bond between families.

Heroic Male Couples in Ancient Greek Literature

As dominant as were relatively short-term age-stratified relations in ancient Greece, the mythic heroes—Akhilles and Patroklus, Herakles and Iolaus, Theseus and Perithous, Orestes and Pylades—had lifelong relations of mutuality rather than *erastes/eromenos* asymmetry. And, as Roberto Calasso stressed, Apollo was represented as violating even the taboo of accepting payment from a lover (Admetus)—

> like a *pórnos,* a merest prostitute, unprotected by any rights, a stranger in his own city, despised first and foremost by his own lovers. It was the first example of bonheur dans l'esclavage. That it should have been Apollo who submitted to it made the adventure all the more astounding.
>
> Apollo, lover par excellence, took his love to an extreme where no human after him could follow. Not only did he confound the roles of lover and beloved, as would Orestes and Pylades, Achilles and Patroclus, but he went so far as to become a prostitute of his beloved, and hence one of those things "considered the worst of all perverts," in whose defense no one in Greece ever ventured to speak so much as a word. And, as servant to his beloved, he attempted to roll back the borders of death, something not even Zeus himself had dared interfere with, not even for his own son, Sarpedon. (1955:516)

In the *Odyssey* (3.399–403) King Nestor welcomes Telemachus to Pylos and has him sleep by his unmarried son Peisistratos. Peisistratos accompanies Telemachus to Sparta, where they sleep together again. In both cases, they are contrasted to married couples. "Peisistratos cannot be a typical *eromenos:* Though quite young, he is 'a leader of warriors' and

---

12. Also in almost all of the African instances of reciprocal male relationships (from Bafia, Bambara, Duala, Herero, Iteso, Naman, Pangwe, Wawihé, Yaka—and Nykakyusa) discussed in Murray and Roscoe 1998.

old enough to participate in sacrifice (456). . . . Like Achilles and Patroclus, Telemachus and Peisistratos are almost the same age" (Sergent
1986:311n. 29). As in the more famous instance in the *Iliad,* those assimilating Homeric male couples to later age-stratified models have difficulty deciding who is the *eromenos,* who the *erastes.* Buffière (1980:373–
74) sees Telemachus as the *erastes;* Oka (1965) sees Peisistratos as the
erastes.

Aristophanes's speech in Plato's *Symposium* about love reuniting pri-
mal unity does not distinguish between insertor and insertee. (I presume
the two halves must be the same age.) A fragment surviving from a late-
fifth-century comedy by Theopompus has young men (*meirakion,* presumably in their twenties, older than *ephebes*) giving themselves to their
coevals.

Two of the twenty-two surviving idylls written by Theokritos (ca.
310–250 B.C.) express a hope for a mutuality (return) of love, "so that
like Achilles and his friend may we be to each other" (29.34), and in the
most famous instance:

> O that the Loves might breathe alike on us both,
> That we two might become a legend for all men hereafter!
> Divine were they among those who lived in earlier time,
> The one the inspirer . . . the other the mirror . . .
> And under an equal yoke did they love one another.
> Then were there golden men, when the beloved reflected the
>   love of the lover.
> (12.10–16, trans. T. Sargent 1982:47)

There is still an inspirer/inspired, lover/beloved distinction in this. Moreover, such love is represented as being something exceptional, something to be commemorated in later days. Nonetheless, it is conceived and
sought by the poet.[13]

In the late-second-century A.D. *Erotikos* of pseudo-Lucan, Callicratidas, the Athenian advocate of boy-love contends that "When the honourable love inbred in us from childhood matures to the manly age that
is now capable of reason, the object of our longstanding affection gives
love in return and it's difficult to detect which is the lover [*erastes*] of

---

13. Whether the poet is speaking for himself or as a character is, as usual, open to
question. Many of the other idylls have characters. I fail to see why the supposed "normal"
love for a girl expressed by a character Simichidas should be taken as more autobiographical than the poems of desire for males and longing for male love that are written in the first
and second person and not attributed to any named characters.

which, since the image of the lover's tenderness has been reflected from the loved one as though from a mirror. . . . We have been glad to receive it and we tend its shrine with a pure heart" (§48, trans. M. D. Macleod).[14] Callicratidas points to Orestes and Pylades as examples in §47. Akhilles and Patroklos may have reached such an age, but there is no evidence in Homer that their love was ever other than mutual.[15]

Ancient Greece and Rome
Greece

The Thesmophoria, a late-autumn festival devoted to Demeter, excluded men and involved married women gathering together away from families for three days and nights. Allegedly, "facsimiles of male genitals" were thrown to the pigs, and "at some time during these proceedings, the women indulged in an exchange of obscenities (*aischrologia*), literally the 'speaking of shameful things,'" but perhaps sexual congress (Keuls 1993:353). While there are no observations or memories written by participants (men who spied on the festival were supposed to be castrated), the Thesmophoria made husbands uneasy (Burkert 1985:105, 242–46), though female independence and the valuing of females were probably more threatening than any sexual conduct that may have occurred among women. Like other strictly finite inversions of the usual gender order, it is possible to see the temporary freedom of women in the Thesmophoria as a means of releasing resentment (a cultural safety valve) and as maintaining the fundamental single-sexedness of politics (albeit temporarily switching the sex) rather than as any resistance against the patriarchal control during the rest of the year (the other exception being the Skira, see p. 224).

The somewhat better-known Dionysian rites of the Maenads ("raving

14. It is the lack of reciprocal desire that for Cleitophon in Achilles Tatius's (late Hellenistic era) novel *Leucippe and Cleitophon* (2.37.6–10) makes male-male inferior to male-female sexual relations (of which he claims to be largely ignorant). Ovid had made the same comparison in Latin (*Ars Amatoria* 2.683–84). Generally, potential longevity of the relationship was an argument for the love of women in contrast to the evanescence of boyhood. As Halperin (1992:251) rightly stressed, both parties in such disputes were extremist in having such marked preferences for one particular sexual object in contrast with the general laissez-faire "take and enjoy whichever is available" norm in which one kind of desire did not preclude another.

15. Classical reading two and a half millennia ago of the time of the Trojan War may already have been anachronistic, retrojecting their age's usual roles. Similarly, Theomnestus's doubts that there can be *philia* without *hēdonē* (pleasure) at the close of the dialogue cannot simply be generalized to earlier times.

women") similarly excluded males, and similarly provoked male concerns about what "hysterical" women were doing without them.[16] Possibly the women were content to dance together where no man was (Euripides, *Bacchae* 876–77), so that the Maenads were homosocial and homoaffective rather than genitally homosexual. Like the mythical Amazons, imagined by men to live beyond the edge of civilization,[17] and the mythical Lemnian women who murdered the men on their island (Herodotus 6.138; Apollonius Rhodius 1), the Maenads appeared as more sororial than matriarchal to Dowling (1989:104), who speculated that "perhaps the presence of the dismembered god—the god without a phallus—served as an invitation to explore pleasures for which no substitute phallus is needed," and noted that "the women participants were not unmarried virgins, but wives, matrons," so that it was not a puberty rite and certainly not a defloration rite. She imagined it as "an initiation of women by women into women's own sexuality."

Imperial Rome

Cantarella (1992:165) read the effusiveness of Fortunata and Scintilla at Trimalchio's banquet in the *Satyricon* (67) as "suspect," and argued that "although the reference to homosexuality in their relationship is not explicit, it shows through the words of Petronius, who describes them as 'they stand over there, all stuck together.'" Their presence and public drunkenness are certainly unseemly for Roman wives (Fortunata is Trimalchio's), but being falling-down drunk together does not seem to me sufficient warrant for reading sexual intimacy, let alone an ongoing sexual relationship.

Ancient Rome
Males

Roman homosexuality was stratified by both age and gender. From very early on, the sexually receptive younger partner in Roman pederasty was used for pleasure, rather than groomed to become a warrior, and having enjoyed being penetrated as a youth was contemptuously brought up in political conflicts even about emperors. Nevertheless, sexual reciprocity was at least thought to occur. Catullus's poem 57 about

16. If it was not better known, it was least more discussed: Keuls (1993:357) noted that "less is known and more has been written about the ritualistic madness known as Maenadism than about any other aspect of Greek cult life."

17. Generally in the vague "Scythia," north of the River Tanais. See Herodotus (4.113–16).

the *cinaedi* Mamurra and Caesar scoffs at them competing in the women's market (line 9). Calling them twins (6) and describing them as being "erudite in the skills of one divan" ("uno in lecticulo erudituli ambo") in the previous line have been read as alluding to a sexual relationship between them in which they alternated roles (Lilja 1982:57n. 30; 13). In the second oration against Cataline (after Cataline had left the city of Rome), Cicero seems to accuse him of being not only a seducer of youths (including the specifically named Tongilius when the latter was still in the *toga pratexta*, worn by boys up to the age of sixteen [2.4]), but of being sexually versatile. In reference to youths he seduced, Cicero says, "qui alios ipse amabat turpissime, aliorum amori flagitiosissime serviebat, allis fructum libidinum . . . " (2.8), that is, "he made shameful love to some, and served the amorous desires of others," which might mean he made arrangements for them or that he personally satisfied them. As for his followers—who were, according to Cicero, soft and delicate youths ("pueri tam lepidi ac delicati"), though all would soon die in the battle of Pistoia—without a single one fleeing or surrendering to a numerically far superior army—they had learned to love and to be loved ("amare et amari . . . didicerunt") (2.23).

The elder Seneca listed *muto impudici* (mutual unchastity) in a list of improprieties, derided (effeminate) youth for "assaulting one another's chastity while neglecting to defend their own"[18] and for outraging each other's honor (committing *stuprum*) to satisfy their lusts.[19] Caligula was said to have engaged in reciprocal sex with Marcus Lepidus and the dancer Mnester; Suetonius categorized this as committing mutual *stuprum*.[20] Behavior that is labeled is not unthinkable, though behaviors labeled *stuprum* and *impudicum* were far from being praised.

The trio of major characters in the *Satyricon* "describe themselves and each other as *fratres* as if they were equals, equivalents of each other, although it seems that, normally Giton fulfills the role of *puer* for both Encolpius and Ascyltos. All three will take on whatever role is most expedient, heterosexual or homosexual . . . [and] both Encolpius and Ascyltos accuse each other of having been pathics and/or prostitutes (9.6, 9.10, 81.4–5)" (Richlin 1983:190–91). Moreover, both Ascyltos and Encolpius appear to have taken the insertive role with men, as well as with women (92.10, 109.3), and even the young Giton engages in heterosexual intercourse, although he does not initiate it (in §§25 and

18. "expugnatores alienae pudicitiae, neglegentes suae" (*Controversiae* 1.9).

19. Males "qui suam alienamque libidinem exercent mutuo sturpri" (*Epistulae* 99.13).

20. "Commercio mutui stupri" (*Caligula* 36).

26 he is seduced by a mistress of Encolpius) and is nowhere the insertive partner in sex with another male.

Art historian John Clarke (1998:86) recently claimed that the the Warren cup artist "strove to make the two [males, one who is lowering himself onto the erect penis of the other on side A] as equal as possible in age, size, and activity." I would grant size. Activity is patently one way, and though beards were out of fashion in the early empire, the bearded/ nonbearded distinction was at least familiar from the Greek art that poured into the center of the Roman Empire. Clarke's suggestion that "a scarcity of evidence in ancient texts for socially established homosexual relationships between freeborn men of the same age may simply mean that being a *cinaedus* (like being a woman in ancient Rome) was incompatible with the act of writing" (84) is possible, but strikes me as special pleading.

Muslim Non-Role-Demarcated Male Homosexual Relations

Throughout the Abode of Islam, same-sex sex mostly continues to be structured by age, class, and/or gender differences, although there are some cosmopolitan men today who seek more egalitarian relations. Such conduct is not entirely new. If what is supposedly al-Tīfāshī's thirteenth-century compilation (trans. Lacey 1988) is authentic, role versatility was recognized long ago, for example, "Others prefer teenage boys, whom they can fuck and be fucked by" (180), and "Young boys can perform equally well on top or on the bottom, whereas women are limited to the role for which nature destined them: they're good for only one thing" (74; also see 77, 180–81, 210, 224 for examples). Even if not genuinely thirteenth century, this is unquestionably an Arabic manuscript.

Rowson (1991b:66) quoted al-Raghib: "If you're empty-handed and out of cash, it seems to me the best course is to buy a fuck with a fuck." Some ostensible *lūtī* were suspected of seeking to penetrate rather than to be penetrated (Rowson 1991b:64 quoted two examples in verse). Wanting to undertake both roles appears not to have been conceived. Upon their reunion in Konya, the legendarily blunt dervish Shamsüddin Tabríz (d. 1248) and the poet Jalāl al-Din al-Rūmī (1207–73) "embraced each other and fell at each other's feet, so that one did not know who was lover and who was beloved" (quoted by Schimmel 1975:313).[21]

---

21. It was "in the experience of this consuming love [that] Rūmī became a poet" (Schimmel 1975:314)—a poet considered by many of the faithful to be heretical and obscene, though even what some consider obscene metamorphoses into mystical allegories. The Rūmī-Shams couple provide the best-known Persian expressions of skepticism about

Lover and beloved are generally fused in Rūmī's poetry (much of which he published in his dead partner's name). For instance,

> What am I to do
> If love throws its arms around me?
> I too put my arms around it
> And take it to my heart.
> (translated by Halman 1983:36)

Similarly, 'Obeyd-e Zakani's (parodic) hero Rostam engages in reciprocal sex with Human, his usual antagonist and rival. Also, in one of 'Obeyd's stories, at least one of the "blessed" old men must have been sexually receptive if the two had sex at the top of a minaret.

Even without any name in general use for the phenomenon, twentieth-century representations of Arab egalitarian homosexuality include the relations between T. E. Lawrence's escorts and between Ridwan and Hilmi in Naguib Mahfouz's (1992 [1957]) novel *Sugar Street*.[22] Schmitt (1992:19) attested some loanwords from European languages used in contemporary North Africa for sexually versatile men: *dublifas* (double faced) in Cairo, *crêpe* and *disque* (done on both sides, played on both sides) in Algiers.

Representations of Female Sexual Reciprocity in China

Chapter 38 of *Qingbei leichao*, an early-twentieth-century novel by Xu Ke, features a group of Shanghai prostitutes who find sex with males repugnant. Their preference for tribadism with each other leads to them being called *mojingdang* ("Mirror-Polishing Gang"—alluding to the friction of polishing smooth surfaces).[23] In addition to tribadism, less delicately called "grinding bean curd" (*mo dou-fu*), and, as discussed above on p. 239, sometimes viewed as a way of getting two females ready for male penetration, some Chinese females used double-headed dildoes with

---

the spiritual guise for the worship of beauty: Shams in asking, "Why look at the reflection [of the moon in a bowl of water], when you can look at the thing itself [in the sky]?", and Rūmī exclaiming, upon being told that Awhadu'd-Din sought the company of the beautiful with purity of purpose, "Would rather that his desires had been carnal, and that he had outgrown them!" (E. Browne 1920:140). Rūmī also said, "The road is far from lust to love" (translated by Halman 1983:26). It is tempting to read autobiographical reference into both of these statements—and indeed into most of his oeuvre, since a personal God and Love and Shams are so regularly and inextricably wrapped together.

22. The two young men often sleep together (Mahfouz 1992:55–56). Ridwan and the couple's patron, Abdal-Rahim Pasha, both state their lack of sexual interest in women (119, 284;.59, 279). There is no explicit sex, heterosexual or homosexual, in the novel.

23. Xiao (1984:275–76) provides a summary.

Figure 10. Cairo men.

each other, or engaged in cunnilingus. Even penetration by a foot stunted by binding was reported.[24]

A 1983 study of fifteen Hong Kong lesbians also found rubbing to be the preferred sexual technique. "The next favorite was mutual masturbation. No subject reported employing cunnilingus, and only one reported using a false penis" (Lieh-Mak et al. 1983:27). Nine had had their first homosexual experience by age nineteen and another four by age twenty-four.

24. Levy (1966:143) culled a reference to a woman who penetrated seven or eight women a night with her foot, which does not seem very plausible to me, though Hinsch (1990:175) cited it without expressing any doubts.

9

Modern Egalitarian Homosexualities

The "Modern Homosexual"

Once upon a time, I provoked Barry Adam into providing a wonderfully crisp characterization of the "modern gay" type of homosexuality. The distinctive features of this mode are (1) a group consciousness of comprising a distinct kind, (2) a separate subculture based on the possibility of same-sex relations that (a) are egalitarian (not gender-role bound or involving the submission of the young) and (b) have the chance to be exclusive (not bisexual) for both partners (Adam 1979; elaborated in Adam 1987:6). Like gender-structured and age-structured relations of same-sex sexuality, this is an ideal type —"ideal" in the normative sense of "aspiration" as well as in the sense of abstraction from empirical cases that do not fully match it. It seems impossible sufficiently to stress "possibility" in it.

Consciousness of Kind and Its Products

Consciousness of shared experiences, aspirations, and interests makes group action possible—not only political action but residential clustering, along with the services, organizations, and businesses catering to a kind of person. A shared sense of oppression is probably more important to the persistence of consciousness of kind and to solidarity than are items of lifestyle, even if the latter become symbols of it. Consciousness of kind is achieved over time; it is not innate or automatic. Its development depends upon experiences (and the feelings about and cognition of those experiences) and sympathetic identification with others of a kind (including martyrs and survivors peopling what is constructed as "tradition" or "history"). This is true of ethnic consciousness or class consciousness as much as of gay consciousness.

Some individuals fight the expectation that they ought to be part of any such "we," while others eagerly seek a sense of commonalty. Social stigmas inhibit identification. Sometimes, however, a critical mass develops to challenge a stigma—either by asserting "We are not like that" or by proclaiming "The ways we are different are fine, or even valuable." Stigmas then become badges of honor. They may also become stimuli to collective action challenging discrimination and affirming the value of the group's formerly stigmatized characteristics. (See Kitsuse 1980, building on Goffman 1963.)

Advocates and adversaries both foster collective identification, which is a necessary (but not sufficient) prerequisite to collective action.[1] Even those who have the feeling of being part of a group may still not join in collective action, which is rarely—if ever—characteristic of any population. Homosexual behavior does not necessarily lead to either a lesbigay identity or to associating with gay men and women. Even gay identity and gay sociation do not necessarily lead to gay collective action, even ad hoc action. One could substitute "ethnic derivation" and "ethnic" for "homosexual behavior" and "gay" in these false inferences without loss of validity. Sporadic action by a self-selected vanguard is more common for class-based or ethnic-based groups, as well as for lesbians or gays.

Subculture

Over the course of the 1970s, gay men in Australian, Western European, and North American cities developed a fairly complete set of basic social services beyond bars and bathhouses. These included bookstores, churches and organizations within churches, travel agencies and other specialized businesses, periodicals, musical groups, sports leagues, historical societies, mental-health and substance-abuse programs, charities, and so forth, as well as local, national, and international political organizations. Indeed, in San Francisco and other cities, "Gay Yellow Pages" feature myriad other gay businesses and services, just as the "Hispanic Yellow Pages" and the "Chinese Yellow Pages" contain listings of those seeking business from those minorities. As I argued in Murray (1979a:170), urban North American gay communities were, even then, more institutionally complete than were ethnic communities.[2] More important, such gay communities were in the process of adding rather than abandoning distinctive institutions. That is, urban gay communities not

---

1. Masters (1962:55–64) included a case study of a "free rider" early in the "homosexual revolution." Characteristics of those persons who undertake high risk and/or high expenditure (of time and energy) participation in social movements when many are getting the benefits (free rides) has been the central concern of the sociology of social movements (see Snow et al. 1980; McAdam 1982; McAdam et al. 1996).

2. In contrast to ethnic communities in the same place studied by Breton (1964). Not all gay-targeted businesses are gay owned. San Francisco neighborhoods, particularly the Castro, have resisted attempts by chains to open outlets that displace independently owned businesses.

only were more institutionally complete than ethnic communities, but were moving in the opposite direction: toward de-assimilation into specifically lesbigay institutions in contrast to assimilation away from ethnic institutions. Institutional elaboration is what I called the process in a 1979 article.[3]

Not everyone is equally adept at maneuvering within or equally committed to any culture's norms: intracultural variability is ubiquitous. Even nuclear families contain diversity without anyone denying that *families* exist (Suttles 1972:35; see C. Hart 1954). After the initial sociological work on the florescence of gay institutions was published in the late 1970s (in addition to Murray 1979, see Harry and Devall 1978, Lee 1979, M. Levine 1979, Humphreys and Miller 1980), the initial response to the ravages of AIDS was community based, though gay activists were largely pushed aside when money became available to credentialed "professionals." Criticism of "instrumental" sexual relations in "meat market" conditions and recognition of "fast-lane burnout"[4] before AIDS could be used by social conservatives like William F. Buckley, Pat Buchanan, and (more recently) Gabriel Rotello as warnings that multipartner sex violates the ordinances of God and nature.

In recent years, both gay conservatives and young self-styled "queers" have decried being "defined" by (homo)sexuality.[5] There are still many gay institutions, some lesbigay ones, and a few lesbian ones, though the high casualty toll of AIDS and fantasies that if we just settle down

3. The term has been picked up and used widely, generally without attribution. On the substantial growth in numbers of gay organizations between 1972 (when cities with populations of less than 300,000, other than college towns, generally had no gay organizations) and 1985 (when almost every city with a population greater than 200,000, even in the South, had one or more) (Wesier 1986:288–89). Studies of lesbian and gay communities outside the American capitals of San Francisco and New York have been published with increasing frequency: see Harry and Devall 1978, Krieger 1983, Whittier forthcoming, Beemyn 1997, Howard 1998, Montini 1998, and there is Fellows' 1997 collection of life histories of gay men who grew up on Midwestern U.S. farms.

4. Adam (1978b), Harry and Devall (1978a), Altman (1982). The major fictionalizations of clone self-hatred, Andrew Holleran's *Dancer From the Dance* (1978) and *The Beauty of Men* (1996), and of gay-clone hatred, Larry Kramer's (1978) *Faggots,* might also be advanced as evidence. However, it seems to me that both authors were smoldering with disgust at their own all-consuming lusts and at those who did not love them before they experienced the gay-clone world of the 1970s. Cf. Brodsky 1993; and Mains 1984 on senses of the sacredness of sites of multipartner gay sex.

5. The latter claim to value "transgressivity" and to resist "assimilation." Their "in your face" tactics are abandoned once they get jobs, so that it becomes hard to distinguish neoclosetry from the old-fashioned "I don't want to be defined as homosexual" sort.

and marry no one will hate us have curbed further elaboration of gay institutions.

Egalitarian Relations

"Traditional" homosexual relations in urban North America, as elsewhere, were exogamous. Straight-identified "trade" inserted their penises in "queers" while saving any love for females (Reiss 1961). Males could have sex more often with males than with females and still consider themselves "normal"/"heterosexual" (Chauncey 1994, Humphreys 1970). Role dichotomization was maintained even in ongoing relationships and in social networks focused on partying (Leznoff 1954). Friendships between "queers" tended to taboo "incest" between "sisters."[6] The major shift between "traditional" and "modern" homosexuality was from gender and identity exogamy to gender and identity endogamy, that is, gay men forming relationships with gay men and lesbians with lesbians rather than with "straight" partners. Valuing both partners in a relationship and shared identity as gay or as lesbian are the criteria—**not** exactly calibrated sameness in gender self-presentation or perfectly balanced reciprocity in sex.

The "modern" gay or lesbian may be gender variants, but does not have to be to fit into gay and lesbian circles or to find sexual partners. Moreover, it is widely recognized that some masculine-appearing and acting men and women are bottoms ("butch in the streets, femme in the sheets").

Erasure of Gender within Gay and Lesbian Couplings?

Despite the greater visibility and seeming viability of butch/femme role dichotomization among lesbians than among gay males, the ideology of egalitarianism has been stronger among lesbians, especially lesbian feminists. For a time (the late 1970s) such role enactment was vociferously condemned, though since then the right to play at, play with, and even commit to such roles has been asserted by women (see Nestle 1987, Faderman 1992, Weston 1997). Among males in the hypermasculine gay culture of the late 1970s, sexual receptivity was unlinked from unmasculinity: being able to "take it like a man" meant taking pain to some, multiple penetrations to others, but the important

---

6. The "What would two queens do together? Rub pussies?" query pops up in other places with primarily gender-stratified homosexuality, e.g., among Hausa *'yan daudu* (Gaudio 1998) and Brazilian transvestite male prostitutes (Kulick 1998b). Butch dykes didn't get it on with other butch dykes either, but I do not know what (if any) metaphors they used.

point is that what a clone wanted sexually[7] was not mapped onto gender roles. Top:bottom could be and usually was butch:butch in general appearance and demeanor. (Also see Humphreys 1971, Humphries 1985, and Bech 1997:134 on the modern gay refiguration of masculinity.)

Even for lesbians, role play at home is often (but not invariably) less dichotomized. Divisions of domestic labor are more complex than is dichotomization into butch and femme tasks, though the "partner" with less economic resources tends to have greater domestic responsibilities, and this is feminizing, Carrington (1999) found that both partners (in both lesbian and gay couples) tend to overestimate the degree of sharing and to stress less-stigmatized interests and careers of the more domestic partner.

The "modern" view is that desire for same-sex partners need not involve abandoning the gender of the sex into which one is born. The popular view of gender deviance as intrinsic to homosexuality shapes how those seeking partners without knowing much about lesbigay worlds go about attracting the attention of prospective partners. The need to be visible to prospective partners, more than any sense of being "a woman trapped in a man's body" may account for the flamboyantly unmasculine dress of homosexual prostitute roles such as the Omani *khanith* and the South Asian *hijra*.[8] Similarly, a butch phase may have made a woman's sexual interest in other women visible, rather than indicating any deep-seated need to be man-like. As Marisa recalled in Moraga (1984:13–14), "I never wanted to be a man, I only wanted a woman to want me that bad." Thongthiraj (1994) described a somewhat analogous contemporary Thai situation in which the appearance of the butch *tam* (from tomboy) woman cues femme *dees* (from ladies), who make the approaches.

Gagnon and Simon (1973 [1967]:147–49) and alluded to the tendency of novices to American gay male scenes to go through a transient stage of enacting effeminacy in the process of coming out, before they begin to distinguish societal expectations of effeminacy from actual gay cultural expectations.[9] Gagnon and Simon (1973 [1967]:198) and

7. Given the extent of vertical sex, "what he did in bed" would be misleading.

8. Wikan 1977, 1982:172–73; Nanda 1990. On the primacy of homosexual desire in the incumbents of these roles see Murray 1997a:250 and Roscoe 1991b:121, respectively.

9. Neophytes tend to rigidly (ritualistically) play their preconceptions of a role (Goffman 1961:130, 152). Persons who decide they are gay or lesbian without having directly observed gay or lesbian people are more likely be guided by societal stereotypes ("the homosexual role" of McIntosh 1968) than those who have been exposed to openly gay or lesbian role models.

Kennedy and Davis (1993:203) noted an analogous ultra-butch phase for lesbians coming out in pre-liberation times. Chauncey (1994:102) documented a decline in this necessity in New York City in the early years of the twentieth century, and Joel Brodsky suggested that trans-gendered romanticizers and others have overestimated the "pre-liberation" importance of female drag: "Pre-transition era gay life was hardly dominated by the drag clubs described by [Esther] Newton. At least by the mid-1960s the audiences in these were already straight. By then, one could find men without dressing up as Marilyn Monroe. . . . Gay (and lesbian) fashion trends have lots to do with who you want to go to bed with and who you imagine would want to go to bed with you if you project a certain image, not who you want to be."[10] Wanting to attract a man is not the same as wanting to be a woman, or even to live as one. Some of the decline of drag during the clone era can be attributed to the greater visibility of other ways of being gay. Homosexuality was delinked from the necessity of gender nonconformity. It is certainly the case that some lesbians and some gay men were contemptuous of gender nonconformity before Stonewall; they did not want to associate with or be associated with it and rejected those who persisted in doing so. It is also the case that gender nonconformity did not disappear during the 1970s. Indeed, more recently, it has become chic in some ("queer") circles. The transformation ended the **necessity,** not the existence of gender-nonconforming homosexuals.

Sexual Versatility

The other recurrent confusion about the egalitarianism of "modern homosexuality" is an out-of-this-world requirement for perfect versatility. While it is not as top/bottom role-dichotomized as Gutiérrez (1997) claimed, there clearly are preferences. Not everyone wants to take turns ("You do me then I'll do you") or 69. There are some tops and bottoms even in post-modern North American cities. Some of these regard tops as masculine and superior and bottoms as feminine and inferior, despite egalitarian lesbigay ideology and the readily observable "contradictions" between visible gender and preference for role in sex (i.e., effeminate males preferring to penetrate and ultrabutch men seeking to be penetrated). The gay transvaluation of "it is more blessed to give than to receive" a penis is not "we must do both and balance the frequency of giving and receiving" but "get what you want; wanting one or the other

10. 30 Sept. 1993 comments on a draft of what became Murray 1996.

does not make you better or worse than someone wanting the other." I think that this is more than laissez-faire suspension of judgment. It is respecting what others want to do with their bodies as we hope they will respect what we want to do with ours—a golden rule that is the positive basis for solidarity among sexual minorities.

Within gay or lesbian communities or networks, one unlearns the requirements of the "queer" or "dyke" role (at least as conceived in the dominant society) and learns what others involved in homosexual scenarios really expect. This generally differs substantially from what individuals with little or no experience of openly lesbigay people (or of lesbigay media) imagine will be expected of them.[11] In North America, many of those who find their way to urban gay communities discover that gender variance is not requisite, and, indeed, is stigmatized by many within the communities.[12] In recent years, an exaggeration of the socially appropriate gender has also occurred, for example, "lipstick lesbians" and gay male "clones."

The traditional phase of cross-gender role exaggeration may be attenuated for those growing up with homosexual desires who can see positive representations of lesbians or gay men who do not appear or act cross gendered. Still, the trend in the United States toward greater tolerance for homosexuality should not be overemphasized. Even the young who find their way to the combination therapy group and gay/lesbian finishing school of Horizons (in Chicago, described by Herdt and Boxer 1993) begin with some of the devastating old patterns of believing "I'm the only one who feels like this." Sears (1991) and Zeeland (1996) attested that some members of the same generation are still acting out "if I'm gay/lesbian I have to be gender-deviant," and "'faggot' remains the most humiliating insult a male teenager can give another" (Alonzo 1983:20; also see Louganis 1995:75.) Escalating levels of violence involved in "fag-bashing" also indicate something less than sexual

---

11. I do not mean to imply that societal stereotypes are never eroticized, or otherwise unconsciously maintained. See Brodsky 1993, Brian Miller 1978, 1987:185, Klein 1989, Nestle 1987, Kennedy and Davis 1993, Murray 1996a:81–89. For an example of the realization that lesbians and gay women were not all "obvious," see Lorde (1982:160–62). I am not convinced that what Paul Monette (1992:1) called "imprisonment [in] the self-delusion of uniqueness" has ended. More representations are available, but "I can't be like that" remains a reaction to some of the most pervasive ones. In particular, the equations of homosexuality with effeminacy or with isolation remain robust even in European and American metropolises.

12. Noted early on by Gagnon and Simon 1973 [1967]:147–49, 152.

or gender pluralism among the young of the post-feminist, post-gay-liberation era.[13]

Exclusivity

Like perfect versatility, exclusive homosexuality is not a criterion for "modern" "gay" homosexuality. The aspiration of gay liberation was that one should be able to live one's sex life as one chose, not to prescribe what others should do, not to substitute compulsory versatile homosexuality for compulsory heterosexuality in the appropriate "sex role." There were many liberation theorists (e.g., Altman 1971, building on Marcuse 1955) who foresaw untrammeled polymorphous perversity and hoped for the end of the category "homosexual" (and "heterosexual," though that seemed a lesser concern to those not wanting to be labeled "homosexual"). Anyone who looked around can (and could) find males who don't consider themselves gay (homosexual, etc.) who have sex with males, females who don't consider themselves lesbian (gay, homosexual, etc.) who have sex with females, females who consider themselves lesbian who have never had sex with a female, males who consider themselves gay who have never had sex with a male, males who identify as gay who are in sexual relationships with females, females who identify as lesbian who are in sexual relationships with males, self-identified bisexuals who have sexual relationships with only one sex, and so on. Sexual identification and behavior are correlated, but imperfectly, and it is far from clear which explains and predicts which. Many sociologists expect repeated behavior to crystallize into a social identity (when and where one is available), and psychologists tend to expect behavior to flow from a unitary self. I would argue that there are (and have been) pragmatic accommodations in appearances to the expectation that one is either homosexual or heterosexual by some who have emotional and/or sexual relationships with partners of both sexes, just as there have been accommodations in appearances of heterosexuality by some of those who are and want to be exclusively homosexual. Both my impression and Whisman's (1996) data on differences between male models that homosexuality is determined and female models that it is chosen fit with gay male's firmer sense of a stable sexual orientation in contrast to the frequent lability of lesbians'. While there are persons of both sexes who emerge from producing and raising children saying that they were always homosexual in orientation, desire, and fantasy, my

13. Harry 1982b, Nardi and Bolton 1991, Herek and Berrill 1992.

observation has been that there are minisculely few males who are for a time openly gay and who then become exclusively heterosexual even in behavior,[14] let alone in desire and fantasy. In contrast, many females who have identified themselves as lesbian "go straight."[15]

The basis for the abstraction of a modern homosexuality is the **possibility** of not **having** to produce children without withdrawing from the quotidian world into a celibate niche, and the **possibility** of sustained egalitarian relationships between same-sex partners. Obviously, there are many lesbians and gay men who want to raise and even to produce children, and there are many who accommodate to or even eroticize domination/subordination within their relationships. What is distinctively modern is that there are other choices and possibilities.[16]

An Aside on Modernity

Perhaps the primary basis of modern socioeconomic relations is that the individual sells his or her labor as an individual, not as a member of a particular family or neighborhood. Ascribed statuses became less im-

14. My impression is that the "ex-gays" who present themselves as exemplary may have been involved in recurrent sex with males, but were not openly gay. "Relapses" to homosexual sex are common among those pronounced "cured," and a cessation of fantasizing about male sexual patterns is not even claimed.

15. I have not dared to ask those I know what they think about while having sex with their current spouses, though I have elicited retrospections. I do not want to get into speculating about whether males fixating on a "type" (a particular appearance) more frequently than females is a luxury based on generally having more options. Insofar as females are exchanged by males, rather than mutual choice, males have enjoyed greater mobility away from the hearth, male infidelity has been more accepted than female infidelity, and human females' preferences have had little importance in determining who their inseminators have been. Against this cozy sociobiological functionalism is the quantitative difference in the relative number of partners males and females have, which could just as easily accommodate an argument that it is functional for females to fixate (albeit only after marriage) on one partner and for promiscuous males to be indiscriminate. Paralleling heterosexual patterns, greater serial monogamy for lesbians contrasts with more sex on the side in cases of gay male relationships that may endure longer than the lesbian ones. There is also a higher percentage of single gay men than of single lesbians. On lesbians' greater degree of concern with drawing boundaries, contrast what Rust (1993) reported from studying women with the men quoted by Murray (1996a:199–202).

16. Even if there are some who are more than ready to prescribe their choices as the only right way to be. This is an era in which "the personal" is not just "political" but is often policed, notably by feminists (such as Andrea Dworkin) eager to sanction not only what men do around women, but what women do around men, and to interpret most of what men do around men as harming women in some direct or indirect way. The innate moral superiority of females makes it unnecessary to extend censorious surveillance to what women do with women.

portant determinants of life chances as young men not only could but more or less had to seek to make their way to cities or foreign colonies.[17] Modern humans are increasingly able to escape from constraints of religious congregation, local community, and extended family. Given the lack of dependence—and indeed reliability—of such traditional bases of assistance in finding jobs ("making a living") and in providing support in the case of disability ("social insurance"), individuals are not only free to but generally **must** forge multiple ties and build up a primary group that is not primarily based on shared blood and marriage ties. Shared sexual orientation is one of the possible bases, though not an inevitable or necessary one.

Both the impersonality of "modern" societies and the fixedness of "traditional" ones have been exaggerated in all "modernization" schemata (including avowedly "postmodernist" ones). There was internal disorder and intracultural variance in tribal societies, witchcraft being one particularly recurrent instance of such phenomena. (See Kluckhohn 1967; Basso 1969; Selby 1974; Hart 1954; and, generically, Sapir 1938). And there is considerable conformity in the modern and postmodern societies of discretionary consumption, brand names, and unavoidable mass media. The extent to which premodern and/or non-Western persons lack a sense of self has also been exaggerated in the Durkheimian contrast of stable "tradition" and a "modern" flux of individuals.[18] (There is considerable challenge to assumptions that a sense of individuation (having a self) distinct from ascribed social roles is genuinely new.[19] The conception of having a "sexuality" is more convincingly new, though, as we have seen, conceptions of recurrent—and even of exclusive—preferences for same-sex sexual partners have existed in other times and places. Such patterns were recognized not only by men cruising specific urban spaces to find partners for sex (and, in some instances, more enduring partnership), but also by state functionaries since the Renaissance.[20] Although a

17. This is not to say that every young male sought his own living among strangers. Clearly, there was chain migration and ongoing attempts by earlier immigrants to provide help to family members or former neighbors, just as members of elites have helped each other.

18. E.g., Simon 1994, 1996; Simon and Gagnon 1986; the *locus classicus*, Mauss 1978 [1938], and Bech's (1992:140) assertion that "The Ideologies of self-analysis are ever expanding, leaving practically no one without some idea that they have an inner self and sexuality."

19. On Asian and West Pacific ground, see Elvin 1985, Spiro 1993, Hong and Murray 1997.

20. Rey, Rocke, and Ruggiero on Paris, Florence, and Venice, respectively. David Greenberg (27 Nov. 1998 comments) wrote that "Greek and Roman antiquity also knew

"village queer" as an outlet for surplus libido existed in rural areas of the West (fulfilling one of the functions of *māhūs* and berdache, though often without the visible effeminacy incumbent on those roles in Polynesia and Native North America), the "modern homosexual" is "of the city, not merely in the city," as Bech (1997:262) phrased it. Diversification of gay types and niches cannot occur without numbers, and the aggregation of those with gay interests only occurs in cities (even if a group then migrates together to a communal rural setting).

In large cities, at least since early in the twentieth century, there were small-scale entrepreneurs seeking to profit from those seeking same-sex sexual partners and safe spaces for socializing with like-minded others (Chauncey 1994). Simulteneously, moral entrepreneurs of vice commission, police forces, and (after Prohibition) state liquor-control boards zealously obstructed assemblies of "perverts," thereby making long-term investment risky. Unpredictable raids of bathhouses and bars kept them from being safe spaces. Indeed, the chances of being busted in a raid on a bar seem to have been higher than those of being busted while having sex in a mostly deserted night-time park, in that escape outside in the dark was easier and the men were less spatially concentrated for police roundups. Dangers of other forms of violence were a countervailing threat to homosexual connections outside commercial establishments. Even now, when state disruption of gay commercial spaces does not include rounding up customers and carting them off to jail—that is, when commercial establishments are legal and patronizing them is not going to get one arrested and named in the paper as a "pervert"—there are still males who prefer to connect outside the domain of cover charges or room charges. Motivations vary. Those I have heard expressed include resisting capitalist relations (the selling of access to each other), a preference for the outdoors (sex as a part of "nature") and the excitement of "outlaw" sex in "public" ("transgressivity").

Just as modernity has led to a florescence of identity politics rather than to the complete atomization of all "bonds," and to a revitalization of "fundamentalist" religious fervors,[21] rather than to secularization, the

---

the existence of distinctive [homo]sexual proclivities," and, as mentioned above on pp. 144–52, 158–60, 255–63, these were decried by some.

21. In some sense the "bonds" of ethnicity and religion that were once more or less automatic are chosen by modern men and women, but there have been many initiatives to impose such definitions as a "Christian America" that is "one nation under [the Christian] God" or a Catholic-only Croatia on polities, so that little practical choice is available to people in increasingly polarized struggles for the soul of particular places. Rather than the boundless choices of identification available to those living in an allegedly postmodern

targeting of gay (and, to some extent, lesbigay) markets has not produced a homogeneous mass of consuming atoms. It seems to me (as it did to Harry and Devall 1978) that growth has led to diversification rather than to homogenization. "Globalization" of the economy has stimulated "tribalization" in many places. The best example from modern lesbigay Europe and North America of such tribalization is the "leather community." The targetable "gay market" to which multinational corporations now advertise products in sanitized glossy magazines (e.g., *Out* and *The Advocate*) is one of a series of "market niches" in the larger society, even while the penetration of advertising to more specialized publications (such as black gay magazines) to some degree finances increasing consciousness of being a more particular kind able to imagine a particular community.[22]

New Bottles: Stigma Transformation and Relexification of Gendered Homosexuality in the International Diffusion of *Gay* and *Lesbian*

In most contemporary societies, the word *gay* is known and used by some as a label for "modern," egalitarian homosexuality, challenging traditional stigmatization of a gender-variant partner in homosexual relations. Nevertheless, outside Anglophone North America, the new container *gay* recurrently has been filled with old negative connotations of sexual receptivity.

I will not again review the drift of *gay* in English before the 1960s (see Murray 1995c: 298–301). The proclamation that "gay is good"[23] became a rallying cry against a background of attempted structural changes and empowerment to bring about "the Great Society" in the United States during the 1960s. It was used in contemptuous contrast with "the homosexual is sick and deserving of compassion" approach that gay liberationists believed the homophile movement preferred. The liberationist generation claimed *gay* for "a consciousness of our own wholeness and worth as human beings and our responsibility to educate people and confront prejudice wherever it exists" (Hood 1973:21). During the early 1970s, *gay* became the preferred positive self-designation in the United States. As Scott Tucker (1982:60) wrote, "many of us define ourselves as gay because we associate that term with pride and self-definition, whereas we associate homosexual with oppression and manipulation." As Mark Thompson (1987:xi) later explained, "*Gay* implies a social identity and consciousness actively chosen, while *homosexual* refers to a specific form of sexuality." Or as a self-labeled gay clone put it in the late 1970s, "The *gay community* is a state of mind, not body. It doesn't matter what you do in bed. . . . Anyone who considers himself gay is gay." *Gay* strongly implies sexual preference, if not necessarily sexual activity.[24]

Gay was "free from the usual stigmas," having, in particular, "no odium of the effeminate stereotype about it," as Cory (1963 [1951]:107) long ago wrote. For those adopting it in self-reference, *gay* symbolized an alternative reality to the sick, unmasculine *homosexual, fairy, pansy,* and *queer*.[25] Precisely because it delegitimated the traditional stigma, its use was resisted by North American print media into the 1980s (see Lee 1981; Signorile 1992).[26]

Under the aegis of *gay*—an aggressively stigma-challenging label without the negative connotations of *queer* or *queen*—a shift from what might be considered an exogamous system of sexual exchange in which those identifying themselves or fantasized by their partners as *straight* (*trade*) were sought—to an endogamous system in which both partners

24. *Gay* may not be a subset of *homosexual* in Anglo North America, but (applied to adults) it is close to being one. In three surveys of San Francisco gay men, more than three-quarters of white gay men, half of Latin American and African American gay men, and 38 percent of Asian-Pacific Islander gay men included someone who says he is gay as part of the *gay community* even in the absence of same-sex sexual activity (Murray 1996a:205).

25. According to Chauncey's (1994) magisterial history of New York City, between the world wars, *queer* was deployed to distinguish gender-conventional men from visibly effeminate *fairies*.

26. Given the nineteenth-century usage, the claims of robbing the English language of a lovely, unsexual word are patently spurious, although they continue to be made. Similar objections to "kidnapping" words such as *faggot, fairy,* and *fruit* or *straight* are conspicuously absent (Stone 1981).

identify themselves as *gay* has occurred in Anglo North America and elsewhere.

Latin America

When the word *gay* was unknown in Latin America—which was as recently as the mid-1970s in Mexico City and Rio de Janeiro, and later in less cosmopolitan places—homosexual identification was analogous to the pre-gay pattern in Anglo North America: those whose homosexual behavior was confined to the *activo* (insertor) role did not consider themselves defined or even implicated by such behavior. Neither did their *pasivo* partners. Even those persons who switched roles tended to identify themselves by one role designation or the other and to attempt to constrain any publicity about the other, although there were terms— *moderno* in Peru and *internacional* in Mesoamerica—for such dichotomy-transcending conduct.

In Lima in 1976, the term *gay* was not used, and was known only to a very few Peruvians who had traveled to Europe or North America. By 1980, however, the term was widely known and was preferred above the previously standard term *entendido* (in the know) or *de ambiente* (of the ambiance) by most informants, both self-identified *pasivos* and self-identified *activos*. Although, outside homosexual networks, *gay* was an unfamiliar locution, in October 1980 the popular magazine *Gente* ran a cover story entitled "Los gays Peruanos son libres" (Peruvian Gays are Free). The article itself oscillated between linking *gay* with effeminacy and using it in the stigma-challenging sense common in North America (Arboleda 1986). That it was used at all to refer to a group usually invisible in respectable publications and completely stereotyped in tabloids in Latin America was remarkable, not least because the small organization seeking to overcome heterosexist oppression, Movimiento Homosexual de Lima, had *homosexual* rather than *gay* in its name(Arboleda 1987: 114). By 1982, *gay* had entirely replaced *entendido* as a self-designation, but in some cases the spelling pronunciation (gaI) was used rather than the phonetic realization borrowed from French or English (i.e., ge).[27] Nevis (1985:158) noted that this was also the case in Finnish, yielding *gei*. Another solution is translation. For instance, the Urdu word *khush*

---

27. Wooden (1982) reported the other solution to the problem of borrowing into Spanish a word that is spelled in a way other than the one pronounced, i.e., changing the spelling, in Colombia and Venezuela, although an intermittently produced Colombian newspaper was entitled *Ventana gay* (Gay Window) in Spanish, the spelling *gai* predominates. Thus, *gai* provides another Catalán/Spanish difference (see Adam 1987:143, 138).

(happy) has been taken by South Asians as an affirmative label for individuals and for a Toronto gay South Asian organization.

In Guatemala in 1978, two of five *pasivos* I interviewed offered *gay* as a term for men who chose other men as sexual partners. The three *pasivo* informants who reported having no friends with similar preferences nor any involvement in settings where such persons congregated were not familiar with the term. Both those who identified themselves as *internacional* (and were much traveled) used *gay* and remarked that the term was achieving ever-wider currency in their country. Of the three *activos* from whom I elicited lexical data, one did not know the word, one knew it but did not apply it to himself, and one both knew it and applied it to himself.[28]

Words that are borrowed do not necessarily retain the same meaning they had in the source language. For some Latin Americans during the late 1970s and early 80s, *gay* seemed to be used as a fashionable (new and foreign) term that simply replaced older ones in an unchanged conception of homosexuality. That is, *gay* was a relexification of the pre-existing conceptual order. For others, however, the new word seemed to reflect a new conception of homosexuality, paralleling the stigma transformation involved in replacing *queer* and *homosexual* with *gay* in Anglo North America. Table 3 shows which of these models was held by informants in Lima, Guatemala City, and Mexico City, varying by their (self-reported) role preference.

Those who answered "no" to the ritualized cruising question, "¿Eres activo o pasivo?" rather than choosing one or the other, invariably considered those who are *activo*, as well as those who are *pasivo*, to be *gay*. For more than a third of those who identified themselves as *activo* and more than half of those who identified themselves as *pasivo* and who were familiar with the word, *gay* was a new word for the already existing conception of homosexuality. Interestingly, those who are stigmatized by this conception were less likely than those who seemingly profit in social esteem by it to embrace the wider conception of who is *gay*. A number of explanations might be proffered—including false consciousness, covert prestige among the stigmatized, and cognitive dissonance and/or ambivalence on the part of heavily involved *activos*. For me, it is evidence of *pasivos* shoring up (fantasizing) the hypermasculine reputation of the *activos* who fuck them.[29]

28. See Murray (1980, 1995b) for description of the elicitation procedures and social characteristics of this sample.

29. This interpretation is elaborated in Murray (1987a:195–97, 1995a:55–63).

Table 3. Frequency of Conceptions of *Gay,*
         by Era and Self-Reported Sex Role

	Term *Gay* Unknown %	*Gay* Equivalent to *Pasivo* %	*Gay* Includes *Activo* and *Pasivo* %	N
Reported Role				
Activo	36	23	41	39
Pasivo	43	28	30	40
Moderno/				
Internacional	0	0	100	17
Period				
Late 1970s	50	27	23	30
Early 1980s	24	18	58	66

Source: Murray 1995a:141.
Note: As reported by informants in Lima, Guatemala City, and Mexico City.

   Although Manuel Arboleda and I observed change in process, it bears emphasizing that we attested all three lexical-cognitive models from some men involved in homosexuality in Latin America. Some still used the old word(s). Others had borrowed the word *gay* but used it in the same slot (relexification). For some others, *gay* referred to a "new man" who can enact (*estar*) pasivo behavior without being (*ser*) *un pasivo.* paralleling the "I can get fucked and still be a man" stigma-transformation under the aegis of *gay* in Anglo North America.

   As I have argued repeatedly (e.g., in Murray 1980, 1987a:118–28, 1995a:33–48) lack of social insurance, housing shortages, residence patterns, censorship of materials that can be interpreted by individual policemen or judges as politically subversive or incitements to vice, the absence of religious pluralism with its concomitant traditions (and freedoms) of voluntary associations, and other factors that may have been crucial to the history of gay institutional elaboration in Anglo North America are quite different in Latin America and at the very least influence how "modern homosexuality" enfolds there. Some Mexican liberation organizations eschew the term *gay* because their leadership do not consider Anglo gay culture to be what they aspire to emulate.[30] They are also sensitive about "cultural imperialism" from the north and about the elitism of expensive local replicas of American gay bars and discos.

---

   30. Nonetheless, in Mexico City there is a *Circulo Cultural Gay* and *Guerilla Gay* (along with *Colectivo Sol* and the *Grupo Homosexual de Acción Revolucionaria*); in Tijuana there is a gay paper entitled *Frontera Gay* (Lumsden 1991:67, 78).

Japan

In Japan today, homosexuality is not illegal, although only a very few homosexuals usually publicly identify themselves as such. The institution of the family continues to be highly valued in Japan: marriage and parenthood are generally regarded as an individual's social obligation.[31] So long as those obligations are met, one's sexual activity is not anyone else's legitimate concern. It can be argued that a lack of official concern with sexual behavior (in particular, no sodomy laws), a certain affectlessness in relationships, and the lack of countercultures in Japan have precluded the formation of an adversary gay subculture.

The word *gay* was borrowed into the Japanese language during the 1950s (see Braybrooke 1975:181). Mishima's *Kinjiki* (*Forbidden Colors*), originally serialized between January 1951 and August 1953, describes a *gei pati* ("gay party"), explaining that "*gei* is the American equivalent for homosexual [*nanshoku-ka;* an aficionado of male love]" (1968:155). *Gei* was rendered in Roman script in the original. Use of the loanword became more common in the mid-1950s, and was rendered in Japanese phonetic symbols by 1959, with Miyao (1959:239) noting, "During the Showa period [1926–1988] we have come to use the term 'gay,' but [same-sex] intimate relationships are not much different from those of three hundred years ago."[32] According to Summerhawk et al. (1998:6), "The term 'lez' entered Japanese from English but carries a pornographic, decadent nuance. . . . The first lesbian-feminist center was established in 1985 within JOKI, a cooperative office for feminist groups, and was known as Legumi Studio. *Le-* is the first syllable of the Japanese word for lesbian, *lezubian*. The second part, *gumi,* means union."

Gei in the Japanese of the 1990s does not necessarily mean the same things as *gay* in the United States. Often missing in Japanese usage are the positive sexual identity and activist concepts. "*Gay* conveys a sense of effeminate behavior, even cross-dressing, and is close to the native

---

31. "A person who remains single is at risk of being an outcast. Promotions in companies and status in a particular group are threatened by singles" (Summerhawk et al. 1998:5; also see 78, 85, 153–55, 191–92). The pressure is so great that, as Lunsing (1996) detailed, gay male magazines include advertisements for wives. The majority want something like a traditional marriage (in which males spend few waking hours at home). Kirkup (1962:174) approvingly observed that Japanese "relationships are not based on 'love' but on more tangible things, more enduring things like mutual respect and consideration" (also see 380–81).

32. Gary Leupp (14 Dec. 1990 letter) found and translated this passage, and noted that Miyao used the term very generally and without any connotations of effeminacy.

word *okama*. *Homo* on the other hand, foregrounds the sex of the participants and encompasses more masculine styles as well" (Pflugfelder 17 Nov. 1990 letter). As in Finnish (Nevis 1985:159), *homo* lacks the negative connotations it has in English.[33]

An adversary gay subculture in revolt against the society is inconceivable to those men and women born in Japan with whom I have discussed it. As an Osaka lesbian told American journalist Neil Miller (1992:152), "The policy of our society regarding something it doesn't like or feels uncomfortable with is to ignore it. People don't criticize it or say it's bad. They just pretend it isn't there. Japanese don't think about themselves or examine themselves. They don't ask the question, 'Who am I?' So it is hard to develop a sense of identity." This is starkly illustrated in the film "Okogé" when the not-very-verbal Goh tells his matchmaking brother and mother that he is gay and is not going to marry. After a moment of horrified silence, his family totally ignores that he said anything. The lack of decorum in proclaiming a gay identity is not punished or even criticized. Rather, it is ignored, as if it were a belch. What Kirkup (1962:167) characterized as "the happy Japanese ability not to see what they don't want to see" can be maddeningly annihilating to those, like Goh, wanting to declare their difference and establish an oppositional (or only unconventional) identity. One, whom I will call Tomo, told me,

> In Japan men spend most of their time with men and are not close
> to any woman except the mother, and, maybe, grandmother. I
> mean straight men, not just gay men. As long as we don't rock
> any boats—by which I mean rubbing gay relationships in the face
> of our families or employers, no one cares very much how we get
> off or with whom. Many Westerners think we're indistinguishable
> ants, but there are many opportunities to slip away and have sex,
> and as long as we don't challenge the conventions, we can do what
> we want on the side.
> *SM:* Only on the side?
> *T:* Pretty much. There are some men who openly live with male
> lovers, but this does not seem possible to most men, and there
> are comforts provided by wives, whether or not you're interested

33. While agreeing that *homo* is neutral in the usage of Finnish adults, e.g., in the title of a 1994 book, *Homona ja lesbona euroopassa* (Being a gay man or lesbian in Europe) James Lee Haines (2 Sept. 1996 personal communication) reported that "in the past couple years I've noticed that primary school kids seem to be calling each other *homo* as a sort of all-purpose insult, sort of like *nerd, dweeb,* or *jerkoff.* This is also pretty common in graffiti, though there it might possibly be intended as a sexual insult."

in their vaginas. They may not be that interested in your cock, either, and happy to have you out of their way most of the time.

Such gays bars and clubs as exist are relatively invisible to public scrutiny.[34] Even taking into account recent stirrings, by Western standards, the gay (and, even more so, lesbian) organizations and publications that do exist in Japan are few, comprised of determinedly closeted individuals, and have primarily been social support groups (Bornoff 1991:434). Nonetheless, in 1997 the Japanese lesbigay organization OCCUR won a lawsuit against discrimination, specifically not allowing it to meet at a youth activity center in the Tokyo suburb of Fuchu in 1990 (detailed in Summerhawk et al. 1998:206–11).

The Philippines

In urban Cebu, Hart and Hart (1990:28) discussed a more masculine, gay role, *sward,* distinct from the *bayot* role described in earlier work on rural Cebu by D. Hart (1968) and Whitam (1992 [1980]).[35] Tan (1995a:87) wrote that alongside the traditional lower-class *bakla'* and (mostly straight-identified) call boys like those Whitam wrote about, a gay subculture "has become visible only in the last two decades in Metro Manila. Many [middle- and upper-class men] self-identify as 'gay,' 'homosexual' or 'bisexual,' and in contradistinction to the lower-class *bakla/parlorista.*[36]" He added that "it is the middle-class group that has been actively organizing the country's gay men's organizations" though "the middle-income groups, far more vulnerable to economic dislocation, tend to remain in the closet even as they become active in gay groups. High-income gay men are more willing to come out, but are essentially apolitical and limit their activities to socializing" (87–88).

Tan (1995a:87) noted that in Metro Manila "as of February 1993 at least sixteen gay bars and massage parlors offering male sex workers, as against three exclusively 'gay' and six 'gay-friendly' establishments that do not actively promote male sex workers," existed, and asserted that "outside Metro Manila, there are no gay bars but there are many freelance male sex workers."

---

34. Ken Togo (in Burke 1983:39) asserted that there were three hundred gay bars just in the Shinjuku district of Tokyo. Most are tiny.

35. The origin of the word *sward* is unclear, and the distinction between *sward* and *bayot* may be more one of class than of gender display.

36. From beauty parlor, the prototypical place of employment for flamboyantly effeminate *bakla'*.

Thailand

With economic development; urbanization (especially the rapid growth of Bangkok); increased contact between Thais and non-Thais (especially European, North American, and Japanese gay tourists); increased availability of representations of homogender homosexuality (i.e., masculine men being sexually penetrated) in hardcore magazines and pirated videotapes; and international AIDS discourse; "modern, gay" homosexuality has become increasingly apparent in Thailand. As elsewhere, the borrowed word tends to be fit into the old model it is supposed to transcend, so that in the use of many, *gay* is a relexification of *gà'tuhy*, the traditional term for an effeminate insertee: "A Thai of the lower classes may deny that he's gay, associating it with it getting fucked (as one expects of *gà'tuhy*). He may, in fact, respond "I am a man"— meaning he is the insertor or *gay king*. A *fàràng* [foreign] gay's claim that he's a "gay man" is often met with bewilderment, as the two words together to him are illogical" (Allyn 1991:144; also see Jackson 1989:22).

Publicly masculine, married men may be insertees in homosexual behavior in private. In a mid-1980s survey, Bangkok "offboys" (males who are available to be taken out of the bar to have sex with customers) reported that 50 percent of their customers were kings, 30 percent were queens, and 20 percent were both (Allyn and Collins 1988:chap. 5, 3–4). The (straight-identified) advice columnist "Uncle Go" frequently obliged his correspondents who asked "Am I gay, and if so what kind of gay am I?" with typifications. At least initially, he upheld a traditional model of bisexual *kings* and passive *kweens*, urging the *gay kings* to try to stick to women and not become habituated to homosexuality, while counseling the *gay queens* to accept their fate, to make the best of it, and not to feel that there is anything unnatural in enjoying being penetrated by men. In one response (likely later than most of the others), he counseled a letter-writer who had resisted anal penetration (and whom Go classified as *bisexual*) to relax and be modern: "If your heart was a bit warmer you would probably let someone come in your back gate, too. Because these days the words 'gay queen' don't mean the guy only takes it. The world is evolving, the gay queen can be an active gay king, too" (P. Jackson 1989:160, 1995:168). Go supplemented this acknowledgment that mores were changing by telling Eric Allyn in 1989 that "nowadays gay queens often think they can be a king too" (in P. Jackson 1995:117–18).

An extremely clear divide occurs between Pisan Archaraseranee's 1985 film "Playing Soot Tai" (The last song) and his 1986 sequel "Rak

Toraman" (Tortured love). The first film shows an unhappy female impersonator distraught about losing his lover to a woman. In the final scene, he cuts off his long hair and shoots himself on stage. The second film involves his masculine twin brother seducing the fickle lover in a complicated revenge. As they are first rolling around beside a swimming pool, the avenging brother (who is, incidentally, a mechanic) is asked if he is a *king* or a *kween*. He responds "I am *gay*" and confounds the expectations (presumably those of much of the audience, as well as of his brother's errant "husband") of gender-dichotomizing role separation.

Creatively using the obviously borrowed terms *king* and *kween,* Thais soon elaborated the typology to include *kwings* for those without fixed preference (or at least with a wider repertoire). *King* was not used as the gender complement of *queen* in the English use of *queen* in homosexual discourse. That someone who is neither exclusively a *king* or a *queen* is a *kwing* seems much more conceptually orderly and transparent than someone who is neither *trade* nor *a queen* being *gay.*

Despite an increase in the conception of mutual pleasure in homosexual sex replacing "taking pleasure" from an other, the term *gay* itself has been fit into the traditional model in Thailand, so that *gay* has become a fairly derogatory term, "increasingly used by the public for *gà'- tuhy. . . .* Even the Thai gay magazines have confused gay and transvestite" (Allyn 1991:144).[37] The decorous term there is *māi'bhà dio gan,* literally "the same trees in the same forest," along with the "primarily academic" *rāk'rūam-pēd* for same-sex love (Allyn 1991:145).

Recollections of exciting connections in three Thai gay magazines— indigenously generated material from the late 1980s—show that some Thai men distinguish *gay* from *gà'tuhy* (explicitly in Allyn 1992: 55, 61, 76; implicitly on 66, 79, 6).[38]

37. However, "*gay-ray* is an adjective one might lavish on a full man (*pōo-chai dhem'- dhua)*" (Allyn 1991:278), and some lower-class Thais "apply the term 'gay-boy' to himself or another to mean he likes men" in contrast to *lady-boy* for an effeminate insertee.

38. *Gay* is used in fifteen of thirty-four stories in the collection. Narrators refer to themselves as *gay* on pages 47, 49, 84, 102, and (arguably) 20, 29, 66, and 122. (There is also typification of the narrator by a gay sexual partner on page 96). Narrators on pages 22, 37, 55, 79, and 94 distinguish at least their past selves (before the relationship they are writing about) as aware of but distanced from the category (and another three attestations, on pages 55, 61, 76, neither embrace nor reject the term). The same corpus shows some men distinguishing *gay* from *gà'tuhy,* e.g., "I had sex with some gay guys and a few *gà'tuhy*" on page 55; the recollection that earlier "I didn't know what was 'gay' and couldn't imagine what the 'gay life' was like. I only knew about effeminate men, the so-

Emerging "Modern Lesbian" Homosexualities in Thailand, India, and Japan
Thailand

Neil Miller (1992) reported that Anjaree, a representative of a recently (in 1990) formed lesbian group, addressed the Third Asian Lesbian and Gay Conference in Bangkok (discussed by one of its founders in Suvarnananda 1995). He translated *Anjaree* as "those who have different behavior," allegedly because there is no word for "lesbian" in Thai. There were several (see Allyn 1992:229, quoted on p. 247 above), including *lesbian* (which like *gay* in Thai, has become impolite) and the *tam/dee* distinctions derived from TOMboy and laDY. Thongthiraj (1994:49) added *amphibian* for a woman who is not consistently either butch (*tam*) or femme (*dee*). Rosalind Morris (1994:29) asserted that *tut* (from the film "Tootsie") is synonymous with *tam* and that the latter is used as a generic term for lesbians (i.e., not just those breaking with gender norms) and claimed that the predominance of loanwords for *phuuying thii choop phuuying* ("women who like women") indicates its recency and foreignness:

> Compared to the already slender vocabulary for male homosexuality, there is additional linguistic poverty surrounding lesbianism. . . . In dominant representations, there is a general tendency to deny the transgressive dimensions of lesbianism by construing it as a form of friendship which, despite its supposedly dangerous sexual excesses, does not ultimately threaten a woman's ability to fulfill her role in the heterosexual contract. Unlike gay male sex, which is legitimated by the term *len sawaat* (playing [with] lovers) as a full expression of romantic love, lesbian sex is called *len pheuan* (playing [with] friends) and is often denigrated as the mere pursuit of physical pleasure (*khwaam suk*). So, too, gay male lovers can be accorded the term for heterosexual lovers, specifically *faan*, but female lovers are rarely referred to in this manner. The corollary, of course, is that a woman's sexual relations with other women will never be allowed to inhibit her fulfillment of other social obligations. (30)

As in South Asian culture, homosexual relationships and female sexual agency have not been taken seriously enough for Thai leaders (local or national) to try to extirpate them. Rather than "toleration," a "will not to

---

called *gà'tuhy* on page 61. Murray (1999a) analyzes the occupations and sexual behavior in this corpus.

know" (not just invisibility but determined not looking) seems to me to better portray the lack of overt condemnation and repression.[39]

India

Giti Thadani noted that in India, passionate same-sex friendships "are seen as a sometimes necessary passage to heterosexual marriage," but

> the moment homosociality between women becomes homosexual as well, it transgresses the economy of heterosexuality and the elaborate apparatus of the extended Indian family. It can only be reincorporated when the sexual aspects are veiled. . . . As homosociality is accepted, there is less problem for two lesbian women living together than for a non-married heterosexual couple. But acceptance is given only because the homosocial relationship is presumed to be non-sexual. The moment the sexual aspects of the relationship become visible, the acceptance ceases and the lesbian couple more often than not are excommunicated. Acceptance may be given, but only if one can be subsumed within the family economy, at best as a devoted daughter, sister or eccentric aunt. Tolerance is often a form of exchange which maintains the conspiracy of silence and the non-articulation of an autonomous lesbian identity. Many women have a closet existence, which allows access to heterosexual privilege. (1996:97–98)

Some consciousness of kind has developed, and female writers of letters to the *Bombay Dost* after 1990 (when the first public statement by the Indian lesbian organization Sakhi appeared) "all identified with the word 'lesbian', even though for many English was not their first language. Most of the married women who sent letters did not see themselves as bisexual but as married lesbians. It was as if to say that marriage was a social imposition, whereas the concept of lesbian arose from one's own desire" (116).

Japan

The Yoshiwara pleasure district of Edo (now Tokyo) during Tokugawa times included a section for lesbian prostitution.[40] Leupp (1998:11, 22)

---

39. The Buddhist view that the self is an illusion and that forms are transitory discourages crystallization of a sexual identity or mobilization around a shared identity (though folk Buddhism seems little affected by such doctrines and is very concerned with how the self does in the present world). Native analysts Sittirai et al. (1991:106) maintained that it is "more acceptable to see homosexuality between women rather than between men."

40. H. Levy (1973:10); Childs (1977:42). Japanese women, even commoners, could

Figure 11. A print from *Gugen sansai chie* (Foolish talk) ca. 1810.

included three nineteenth-century illustrations of women using two-headed dildoes with each other,[41] and of advertisements for such implements (23-27). At least one specified the use as being production

also engage male concubines; Japanese women were buyers as well as sellers in the "floating world" of commercial sex from at least the eighteenth century onward (Leupp 1995: 188–89).

41. Leupp (1998:20) saw an age difference in one of these. One is swooning and the other is "cool" and "in control," as he noted, but I do not see this as compelling evidence of an age difference.

Figure 12. Utamaro print.

of mutual pleasure of two women (24). Visual evidence indicates a Tokugawa-era view that women can experience mutual pleasure with other women. "The erotic prints plainly affirm that one woman can bring another to orgasm, if usually via the usage of a dildo" (33).

Leupp concluded that in Tokugawa times, "genuinely egalitarian sexual relationships do not seem to have been part of the male homosexual experience. Female homosexuality, in contrast, may sometimes have entailed a genuine mutuality. . . . [The evidence suggests that] some women involved in lesbian activity shared and exchanged sexual pleasure to a degree that men could not—in either heterosexual or homosexual relationships. Neo-Confucian ideology and the Tokugawa status system militated against such experience. But, conceivably, in early modern Japan, some women may have loved other women as equals and peers, and found in lesbianism a liberating alternative to heterosexual relationships" (36).

The term "lesbian" (*rezubian*), although attested since the early 1900s, was not adopted by Japanese women to name a politicized female identity until the 1970s (J. Robertson 1992b:176). Since then, activities for feminists and lesbians in Japan have increased, albeit very discretely. Lesbians are even less publicly visible than gay men. Bornoff (1991:439) noted that the only exclusively lesbian bar, "Space Dyke[,] sank into oblivion after blossoming only briefly during the first half of the eighties. Developers eyed the building housing it, and, besides, the number of women coming brazenly out of the closet were too few to warrant opening it again elsewhere."

Heterogender homosexuality remains common. Lunsing noted that

> many politically aware lesbians refer to themselves as *rezubian* and some condemn the use of *rezu* because of its association with pornography made for men, which is the main means by which the words *rezu* and to a lesser extent *rezubian* are known in Japan. Other lesbians use the two terms interchangeably, or refer to themselves as *daiku* (dykes), especially in public, because few people know the meaning of the word. Onabe was used by a small group of transvestite lesbians, but is generally considered to be derogatory. (1995:80)

Yoko, a member of Regumi Studio, told Neil Miller (1992:168) "Most Japanese lesbians are isolated and alone. They find a lover and they stay by themselves." However, in the view of another couple, also Regumi Studio members,

> social options for Tokyo lesbians were expanding. All-night dance parties now took place once a month in Shinjuku, with as many as a hundred and fifty women in attendance. "Some women arrive with sleeping bags," Atsuko said. She also noted that feminist gatherings increasingly featured workshops about lesbian sexuality. These workshops always drew the largest crowds. "In a way, the pressure we get is very strong but we have more places to talk about our issues than gay men do," Atsuko said. "Women have a lot of different networks. Men have bars, but we have a lot of gatherings where we can be open about being lesbians." . . .
>
> "Still, not many heterosexual feminists come to the women's dances," Minako said. "They are more used to discussing or reading a book. Many lesbians are the same way. They are just starting to find they can have fun, too. Maybe it is just a question of opportunity. We think we have to create different kinds of activities." (N. Miller 1992:171; also see Cherry 1992)

With increasing female participation in the paid labor force, economic independence—a prerequisite for marriage resistance and living with whom one chooses—is increasing for Japanese women. The influence of Western-style lesbian feminism appears to be increasing in Japan, considerably more than in Thailand, Indonesia, or the Philippines.

What has most commonly been lost in diffusion is the Anglo-American sense of peoplehood. Egalitarian sexual relationships are only a part—and probably not the most important part—of what *gay* means to gay North Americans. The challenge to a choice between being an *activo/king* or a *pasivo/kween* has diffused. The word *gay* has also diffused, but for many people, especially those not involved in emerging, but institutionally incomplete gay communities, *gay* has come to be a politer substitute for terms like *maricón, pasivo,* and *gà'tuhy* by which to refer to those who are penetrated. The label *gay* for some is a symbol of an alternative conception of same-sex relations for those involved in gay organizations or commercial establishments.[42] It may also serve as a symbol of participation in American-style leisure culture. Fascination with American popular culture continues to wax, especially among those identifying themselves as *gay.* The equation of effeminacy with sexual receptivity, and with same-sex desire, sex, and love, is being challenged. Borrowing *gay* is at once a symbol of challenging such a traditional equation and a by-product of the diffusion of a gay organization of same-sex sexuality. Although traditional cultural paradigms tend to ooze into even those words borrowed to signal new/different conceptions, because Anglo North American usage continues to be carried by visitors from North America and by returning visitors to North American gay communities, one cannot be sure whether, in the long run, the new or old meaning of *gay* will prevail in languages other than English.

"Modern" Homosexual Behavior in Mexico and Peru

The considerable actual flux and uncertainty of sexual expression (suggested on p. 274) are ignored "by the culture," or, rather, by Latinos who don't want to know, talk about, or think that masculine appear-

---

42. This seems to be the case in Turkey, where the effeminized insertee has been termed *ibne,* and, more recently, *lubunya,* but where an overtly masculine, urban, young, educated "new sexually conscious stratum of the homosexual population have introduced the word 'gay' with which to identify themselves" (Tapnic 1992:46; cf. Necef 1992). Similarly, in Hungary, translators of Tony Kushner's *Angels in America: A Gay Fantasia* "didn't know how to translate the word 'gay,' because there's no word in Magyar that isn't pejorative: I mean really insulting. So they used the word 'gay' with the specific intention of introducing it into the language" (Kushner, quoted by Hurwitt 1994:D5). The word had been borrowed for self-designation earlier—it was in use when I visited Budapest in 1988—but may not have appeared in written Magyar until the translation of Kushner's play.

ances do not necessarily validate untainted masculine essence. I believe that "wants" are to some extent culturally shaped, and that the will not to know" is at least as much cultural as individual/voluntaristic. Silva (1979) and Chocrón (1972) provided especially powerful representation. Braiterman (1992:10) discussed a method of getting fucked that is relatively safe for the masculine reputation: hire a hyperfeminine prostitute (who is unlikely to be believed if "she" reports the behavior to those whose opinion matters to the client). The "Queen of the Night" in Abreu's (1990 [1988]:82) *Dragons* proclaims that "all young men like to get fucked, some are even queer." I have discussed my own experience of being told by young men whom I have fucked that they never get fucked (Murray 1996b:239). Reinaldo Arenas (1992) similarly recalled many masculine men eager to be fucked by a queen. The insistence on *activo* identity even by someone who has just engaged in *pasivo* behavior is exemplified by the following recollection by Arenas of picking up a muscular adolescent:

> Once inside my home, [he] surprisingly asked me to play the role of the man. . . . I fucked him and he enjoyed it like a convict. Then, still naked, he asked me, "And if anybody catches us here, who is the man?" He meant who fucked whom. I replied, perhaps a little cruelly, "Obviously, I am the man, since I stuck it into you." This enraged the young man, who was a judo expert, and he started to throw me against the low ceiling; thank God, he would catch me in his arms on the way down, but I was getting an awful beating. "Who? Who is the man here?" he repeated. And I, afraid to die on this one, replied, "You, because you are a judo expert." (103; also see 113–14, 152)

Quantitative research on sexual behavior in the age of AIDS has found considerable behavioral departure from the simple *activo/pasivo* norms. In a 1986 sample of 2,400 men tested for HIV-antibodies in Guadalajara, Mexico, 74 percent reported engaging in **both** insertive and receptive anal intercourse (Vázquez et al. 1988; discussed in Carrier 1989:132). Other studies conducted during the late 1980s of men who have sex with men have also found substantial sexual versatility. In a study sponsored by the Mexican Ministry of Health in which "gays of the cabaret" (i.e., those who frequent night spots catering specifically to the gay patron) from eighteen cities were interviewed, 95 percent of 732 "homosexual" men and 77 percent of "bisexual" men reported engaging in receptive anal intercourse, 88 percent and 95 percent reported engaging in insertive anal intercourse; and 89 percent and 72 percent "practiced fellatio" (García et al. 1991:53–54).

The study by Cáceres et al. (1991) of Lima, Peru, is more directly comparable to the pioneering ethnographic studies of Latino male homosexuality in that less than 30 percent of the men in the study were recruited at an HIV-antibody testing site. The sample appears to have been better educated and higher incomed than the national average.[43] Nearly all (97.6 percent) engaged in anal intercourse with men, and 87.9 percent reported participation in fellatio with men. Two-thirds of those who engaged in fellatio and 61.6 percent of those who engaged in anal intercourse were both receptive and insertive. If these men seem *muy moderno,* those seeking HIV-antibody testing in Mexico are even more so.

Probably not coincidentally, they are also more highly educated.[44] This vitiates direct extrapolation of the reported sexual behavior in these studies to the population of men who have sex with men in Mexico. Nonetheless, these data show that there is—at the very least—a segment of men concerned about the dangers of HIV infection who depart markedly from the traditional cultural schema of *activo/pasivo* distinctions. The departure is more pronounced in Mexico City than it is in the second- and third-largest cities (comparing Hernández et al. 1992 with Izazola-Licea et al. 1991) and more in the three largest cities than in Acapulco, Monterey, and Mérida (Izazola-Licea et al. 1992). Hernández et al. (1992:892) take their data as establishing that mixed-role behavior is as prevalent in Mexico City as in U.S. cities, so that "the pattern of sexual behavior that has been reported to be normative in Mexico—homosexuals practicing either exclusively insertive or receptive behavior— may in fact be the practice of a minority of individuals."

Although I believe that there is considerable behavioral departure from the rigid role dichotomization of ideal norms in Mexico (the country and especially the capital city), I think it premature to conclude from samples of those seeking HIV-antibody tests that mixed behavior within same-sex sexual encounters is the statistical norm in Mexico. The

43. Of those in the sample, 21.8 percent had received some post-secondary education, in contrast to 12.4 percent of Peruvian men in the 1981 census (Wilkie et al. 1992:230). Cáceres et al. (1991:309) coded 58.8 percent of the sample as middle class and 21.0 percent as upper, and reported that 34.7 percent had salaries more than three times the minimum wage.

44. Of those surveyed, 59.1 percent had some post-secondary education (Izazola-Licea et al. 1991). Ca. 1980, only 7.9 percent of Mexican men had some post-secondary education (Wilkie et al. 1992:230). One would expect higher concentrations of educated men in cities than the national average, and in the capitals (Lima, as well as Mexico City) in contrast to other cities, but the 70 percent Mexico City figure far exceeds such explanation. It seems more reasonable to suppose that there is a connection between education and seeking HIV-antibody testing.

Table 4. Attributes of Mexican and Peruvian Men Engaging in Sex with Men (percent)

	Mexico City (Hernández)		Mexico City, Tijuana, Guadalajara (Izazola-Licea)	Monterey, Acapulco, Mérida (Izazola-Licea)	Lima (Cáceres)
	Homosexual	Bisexual			
Aged 30+	37.4		10.9		16.1
With some post-secondary education	70.0		59.1		21.8
Married to a woman	5.7		3.3		
Engaging in anal sex with a man	92.5	86.3	80.0	71.0	97.6
Only insertive	5.9	20.6	11.2	12.7	16.5
Only receptive	7.0	4.6	12.5	31.0	26.4
Insertive and receptive	87.8	74.8	76.2	56.3	57.0
Mixed, mostly insertive	25.0	33.8	31.2	15.5	
Mixed, mostly receptive	15.7	4.6	17.5	22.5	
Both, in half or more encounters	47.1	36.2	27.5	18.3	
N	1,759	555	378	328	124

"modern" gay rejection of role dichotomization clearly exists in Mexico. One can safely say that there are "gay" Mexicans, but whether they constitute the majority of those recurrently involved in same-sex sexual relations, even in the capital, remains open to question. The traditional *activo/pasivo* rhetoric persists, especially among male transvestite prostitutes (in Mexico and Brazil, as in the United States) along with recurrent confounding of expectations based on the gendered appearance of sexual partners (see Kulick 1996, 1998a; Prieur 1998:204 passed on a native estimate of 30–40 percent variance).

Table 4 summarizes the findings of the quantitative studies. Hernández et al. (1992) reported sexual behavior of "bisexuals" (behaviorally defined as men who had sexual relations with women in the six months preceding the study and sex with men since 1979) and "homosexuals" (men who had not had sex with women in the preceding six months and had had sex with men since 1979). Izazola-Licea et al. (1991) split their report of homosexual behavior into two sets of Mexican cities. Neither study reported demographic attributes separately for these groupings. The percentages below the line in the middle of table are of those who reported anal sex with men (with those reporting mixed receptive and insertive behavior further broken down to predominant patterns).

Behavioral variance to some limited extent corrodes certainty in the ideal norms of a world divided between masculine *activos* and effeminate *pasivos,* though less than gay Anglos expect. Perhaps variance from roles (queens taking the *activo* role, masculine men taking the *pasivo* role) is not cognized (see Bolton 1991:126, 151–52; Arenas 1993:281; Prieur 1998:138, 189). As Arenas learned, it is better not to press too hard for acknowledgment even of what one knows from direct involvement happened. I have also been told by young Latinos with semen inside their rectums that they are never penetrated, which I take to mean that they are not the kind of person who takes women's roles (elaborated in Murray 1996b).[45] One of the problems with self-reported data about sexual behavior is that some people apparently do not cognize some of what they do. Others consciously dissemble—to researchers, among others (see Bolton 1991, Coxon 1996, Murray 1999b)—and it seems likely that sexual behavior departing from cultural norms is underreported.

---

45. Loyalty to ideal norms is considerable. They are constantly reiterated in many media, especially in primary socialization. The *machismo* complex may not be a *sui generis* reality, but belief in and approval of it at least somewhat channel behavior to conformity— and variation to silence.

Incipient Muslim Gay Organization of Male Homosexuality

Not just mutual, non-role-dichotomized homosexuality, but some "modern gay" homosexuality has been documented recently in a few Muslim societies. According to Crapanzano (1980:34, 48), young Moroccans practice mutual masturbation as well as anal penetration.[46] In recalling adolescent "comparative masturbation," the Algerian writer ʿAli Ghanem (1986:78) mentioned the widely shared belief that this strengthened (i.e., virilized) youths' penises.

In Turkey, a new overtly masculine, urban, young, educated "new sexually conscious stratum of the homosexual population have introduced the word 'gay' with which to identify themselves" (Tapinc 1992: 46; cf. Necef 1992). The incipient Turkish gay movement has participated in more general countercultural politics (Sofer 1992; Tapinc 1992). These urban Turks appear to aspire to "modern" gay homosexuality in a secular, European state.[47]

Gay Emergence in Indonesia (with Dédé Oetomo)[48]

About twenty percent of the 200 million people in Indonesia, (a vast archipelago containing three hundred ethnic groups) live in cities. Most Indonesians, both "traditional" (Nusantara) and urban/modern, are unfamiliar with the concept of a gay identity not based on distinctions of age and gender differences between sex partners. Few distinguish *homosexual* from *waria*, males who behave effeminately (a woman who behaves in a 'masculine' manner, is called a *banci*).

Homosexual behavior that was once accepted was later deemed an example of the moral decadence that caused the defeat of Nusantara armies by 'morally superior' European powers. Modern Indonesian society is heavily influenced by the condemnations of homosexuality in Western and in contemporary Islamicist ("fundamentalist") cultures. Many Indonesians who feel that they are modern and that their society

46. "Moroccans of his [Tuhami's] background do not have oral intercourse," according to Crapanzano (1980:104). "They talk about it a lot; they say the French do it all the time."

47. The vast majority of Turkey's population is Muslim, but the military maintains a civil religion that was initially organized by Ataturk, who is a main object of posthumous cultic veneration. Turkey is a member of the North American Treaty Organization and has sought to become a member of the European Economic Community.

48. This section draws on a number of presentations by Dédé Oetomo that I pulled together for an anthology. The editors decided not to use it. The observations, assertions, and most of the words in this section are Oetomo's.

is rapidly becoming so are apt to claim—and even to believe—that homosexuality no longer exists. In this increasingly homophobic climate, members of Nusantara societies in which institutionalized homosexual behavior is still practiced are reluctant to admit its existence. Still, homosexuals are generally left alone as long as they behave discreetly, and some flamboyant manifestations are accepted and even cherished in traditional theater and dance troupes.

Modern Indonesians, particularly those of the lower class, easily tolerate flamboyant transvestites. However, a pervasive stigma on homosexual behavior exists among the middle class and modern urban Indonesians. As in the West, overt nontransvestitic homosexual behavior is primarily an urban phenomenon. Most Indonesian gays choose to live in large cities where they can remain anonymous and pursue relationships without fear of disgracing their families. Life in metropolitan areas allows Indonesian gays more opportunities to meet other gays who are open about their sexuality.

Most Indonesians who identify themselves as *gay* or *homosexual* belong to the upper and middle classes, while most who identify as *waria* are of the lower classes.[49] In Indonesia, the stereotype persists that gays are to be found in "glamorous" jobs such as fashion design, art performance, and show business, although most Indonesian homosexuals lead a less glamorous life, and are more or less closeted. For Indonesians of all sexual preferences, there is an emphasis on the individual's relationship with his family. As gays get older, there is increasing pressure to relinquish gay contacts, marry, and produce children, even while continuing to have covert homosexual relations. Self-identity does not have anything at all to do with men's sexual behavior with their male partners: some "real" men ask to be the insertee in anal or oral intercourse with gay men or *waria*.

Indonesian lesbians and gay men look for entertainment, sociability, and partners in bars, pubs, and discos as well as in parks. In the big cities, at least on Java, one finds illegal brothels providing male sex workers. Freelance sex workers are also plentiful in gay hangouts. Some lesbians make use of the services of the semi-legal female sex-worker complexes. Still other lesbians and gay men find their partners in ordinary locales, such as homes, schools, workplaces, places of worship, and so forth. Very few Indonesian gays are really open in every context.

Gay rights movements in Western countries have acted as catalysts for the emergence of organizations and publications geared toward In-

49. This parallels lower-class *bakla'* and middle-to-upper-class *gays* in the Philippines.

donesian lesbians and gay men. On 1 March 1982, Lambda Indonesia was founded. Clearly the symbol Lambda was Western, specifically from DÚdÚ Oetomo's time at Cornell University. As soon as Lambda Indonesia announced in leading print media a post-office box number, letters began to flow (sometimes forty letters a week, from people in different places). People desperately wanted to get to know each other—and to learn about the existence of others like themselves. There was a clear distinction between men who were *homo* and *gay* (the term *gay* was starting to be used in Indonesian by then) and those who presented themselves as *waria*. Particularly around 1981, the men in the *homo* communities said that they only liked to sleep with *laki-laki asli* (genuine men). When a *homo* slept with another *homo,* other *homos* considered it "lesbian."

Many homos paid for *laki-laki asli* to have sex with them, whereas "genuine men" usually paid the *waria* for sex. This was a source of tension in Surabaya (where Oetomo lives), but the chairperson of the *waria* organization was willing to sit down and talk it over. Within about two or three years, the two groups were getting along very well, although they continued to be organized separately.

Lambda published a bulletin, *G: gaya hidup ceria* (G: The gay lifestyle) until 1985. Lambda Indonesia continued to exist (with branches in many of Indonesia's cities) until 1987. In Jogjakarta in the beginning of 1985, Persaudaraan Gay Jogjakarta (PGY; Jogjakarta Gay Brotherhood) was established. It published the limited circulation magazine *Jaka* (Young man/bachelor). In November 1987, in the East Javanese town of Pasuruan near Surabaya, the group Kelompok Kerja Lesbian and Gay Nusantara (KKLGN, or the Working Group for Indonesian Lesbians and Gay Men) was born. The group publishes a bimonthly magazine, *Gaya Nusantara,* which includes articles on gay issues, as well as gay fiction and poetry and a classified "pen pal" section. In addition, the group has done some networking with international AIDS service organizations. The scope of the magazine is national and includes the concerns of gays, lesbians, and *waria*. In 1987, PGY changed its name to Indonesian Gay Society (IGS) in an effort to expand to a national membership, but folded in late 1988 because its activists were graduating and pursuing professional careers elsewhere. Some activists of PGY/IGS are currently active again in monthly meetings of the Jogjakarta chapter of KKLGN.

The first newsletter ceased publication in 1984, although *Gaya Nusantara,* which Oetomo and his partner started in 1987, was, in many ways, a continuation of the first newsletter with a different name and with a considerable focus on HIV/AIDS. At first much was censored. For instance, "anal sex" could not be mentioned; it had to be abbreviated to just "sex," which confused people. After about three or four years, the journalists became desensitized, and eventually even the word "lubricant" could be printed in a very respectable Catholic newspaper like *Kompas.*

By 1991–92, more groups started organizing in Indonesia. Up until then, there were only groups in Surabaya and Yogya. The groups organized in different ways. In some places a group of friends who already did things socially together would write to the group and say, "We declare ourselves an organization. We have a P.O. Box number or an address or—in some cases—even a phone number. Please list us in the magazine."

Tolerance in Indonesia is a bit different than in some other places in Asia. In Thailand, for example, there are twenty commercial magazines, but no activist magazine like *Gaya Nusantara.* There is not a single commercial magazine in Indonesia. In the Philippines and Malaysia, gay centers are in the capital cities, and gay-identified men tend to be middle- or upper-middle-class people. There is little or no contact with the working-class gay men, whereas the Indonesian gay organizations' base is more lower-middle class and working class. Almost all *waria* used to be poor and illiterate. Many have increased their income and social status, especially those who run beauty parlors or are entertainment artists or dance teachers: modern dance teachers especially are *waria* these days. Nowadays a *waria* may celebrate "her" birthday with a mock wedding party in the most expensive restaurant in Surabaya, with a mixture of *waria* and gay guests. Some of the gay men would go in drag. The *laki-laki asli* would be there, too (though they would be shy and reserved). Some of the educated younger *waria* are alienated by the uneducated older *warias,* and prefer to be members of the gay network. Recently, it happened that Miss *Waria,* East Java, was a gay man who dressed in drag only for that contest. Tension have been rising between gay men and *waria* in this domain of beauty contests, which used to be monopolized by *waria.*

Increasingly, *homo* men sleep with each other. It has also become acceptable to live together, to form a household around two gay men. In many places in Indonesia, if you want to sleep with someone, you have to be introduced, usually by an older person, who is a long-term member of the community. In almost every Indonesian city, gay men socialize in any available public space—shopping malls, parks, streets.

Within the organizations, people acknowledge and are proud to have a gay identity. *Laki-laki asli* differ in this regard. Some are prostitutes, but then some of the gay men also accept money. On the street "beat" in Surabaya, where about four hundred to five hundred people gather on a Saturday night, there is a kind of territoriality. People know each other, because they've slept with each other. Everyone is friendly to each other. However, the gay-identified men are spatially separated from *laki-laki aslis*, though male prostitutes mingle with both sets. Yet, the sexual acts performed by the different groups are not so different.[50] *Laki-laki asli* sometimes are anally penetrated, but this does not change their self-identification.

As activists reach their late twenties, some get married. Their gay comrades are very supportive, asking, "Could we come to your wedding?" When told "no," they say, "oh, alright—could we give you a wedding gift?" and are told "yes, but please don't come!" The activists tend to be very androgynous. Many of those who have got married still come to gay organizations' meetings. They can still hold offices in the organizations. Sometimes they bring along a baby. The Indonesian state has become obsessed with the happy family—the happy Indonesian family—mummy, daddy and two kids: "ya, dua saja!" ("just two!"—the slogan of Indonesia's family-planning campaign). Gay people's response is: we want family, but our own family. The obsession with the family means that most people who are in our organizations, or even those who just subscribe to or read *Gay Nusantara,* come out to their families. The main interest of readers is finding a partner and forming a relationship.

There is no queer bashing, although there is police extortion. The police might round up about twenty-five people, have sex with them in the police station, and then ask for money. This is not to say that the police are always the penetrators: the police can be penetrated, the army guys can be penetrated; sometimes they beg to be penetrated.

The Indonesian criminal code was revised when the Dutch East Indies was a French colony under Napoleon, so decriminalizing homosexual acts has not been necessary for the emergent gay movement there. Some of the fundamentalist Muslims would like to criminalize them, but they have not been aggressive denouncers of homosexuality.[51]

Lesbi is known by some Javanese, though negative media coverage of debauchery has made respectable women want to distance themselves

50. This is based on Oetomo's interviews and personal experience.
51. If someone gay speaks out openly, Islamic fundamentalists might make harsh comments. But that would be one out of three hundred people in the room. In one instance in Bandung, a man who said Oetomo should be in hell was told to sit down by the other members of the audience. In Southeast Asian culture, it is considered more impolite to make such public attacks than it is for a gay man to speak publicly.

from it, according to Gayatri 1993. In her fieldwork in Jakarta, Alison
Murray (1995) found such lesbian subculture as exists to be highly frag-
mented, with little basis for coalition with gay men. She found some
butch-femme role playing among working-class Jakatra women, as
Wieringa (1996) also did and as E. Blackwood (1995) did in Sumatra.
Oetomo wrote:

> Lesbian couples exist in many parts of Indonesia. There are cer-
> tain hang-outs (pubs, restaurants) frequented by lesbians, but
> such contacts are necessarily limited, given the limitations on
> going out alone or even in groups, especially at night, that
> women face in Indonesian society. There have been reports that
> some lesbians hang out at prostitution complexes and buy sex
> there, and that a small number of female sex workers are pre-
> dominantly homosexual. . . . Since the pressure to get married
> and set up a family is even stronger on women [than on men],
> most lesbians are, have been, or will be married. Some women
> in Bali, Bandung, Surabaya, and Jakarta belong to predominantly
> male local groups connected to the national confederation Gaya
> Nusantara, and the 1996 Gaya Nusantara directory includes
> a lesbian organization, Lembayung Celebes, Ujungpadang, Su-
> lawesi. (1991:125)

AIDS as a Rationale for Some Public
Discussion of Homosexuality

Gay life has a low profile in Malaysia. There is only one gay bar in
Kuala Lumpur, so friendship networks, cruising in parks and shopping
centers, and discreet advertising for "male friends" in mainstream publication are the major ways men interested in sex with men meet. However, as elsewhere in the world (see Altman 1988), some pragmatism
and concern about reducing the costs of AIDS has led to slightly more
open recognition of homosexuality than had occurred earlier and to
some organizing by self-consciously gay men to protect others from HIV
infection. Pink Triangle, founded in 1987 by gay men in the capital city
of Kuala Lumpur to provide AIDS-prevention information to gay men,
registered as an AIDS-prevention and counseling organization, but became known, despite its silence about its members' sexuality, as a "gay
group." The group persuaded the Ministry of Public Health (MPH) to alter a 1988 pamphlet's advice to avoid homosexual sex to "avoid unsafe
sex." Legitimized in part by funds from international agencies and by
cautious support from the MPH, Pink Triangle gained mass media attention for its work, and has been invited to make AIDS-prevention pre-

sentations at factories and schools. Janitex Condoms became the group's first commercial supporter, donating funds and condoms to the group. During the late 1980s, Pink Triangle ran ads in mainstream publications as an "AIDS-information hotline," later changing the wording to "AIDS and sexual identity counseling."

Licensing requirements for any publication that contains "news" has inhibited the formation of a gay press. Pink Triangle did, for a while, publish an in-house newsletter called *Pink News,* but now only issues an AIDS-education flyer called *Pink Page.* (Allyn 1991; also see Osteria and Sullivan 1991).

A diaspora Iranian group publishes the periodical *Homen.* The Naz Foundation, a South Asian diaspora group, works in Dhaka, Bangladesh, as well as in London and Delhi (see S. Khan 1995). What has been reported of its research in Dhaka mostly involves gender-structured homosexuality.

If there is any "modern" female homosexuality in any Islamic society, it has not been studied. Female sexuality of any sort is not a legitimate topic for public discussion. What Baraheni (1977:47–48) wrote could be generalized to other Islamic societies, as well: "Female homosexuality in Iran is hushed up in such a way that no woman, in the whole of Iranian history, has been allowed to speak out for such tendencies. . . . To attest to lesbian desires would be an unforgivable crime." Note his stress on repression of any affirmation or self-representation: not that it does not exist, but that it cannot be spoken of, and, especially, cannot be written about.

10

Conclusions

Whether partners differ from each other in age or gender (the recurrent status differences within homosexual relations) is crosscut by what I would characterize as a variable of valuation of the lower-status partner. Even if being sexually receptive is incidental rather than criterial for effeminized male religious specialists, those sexual receptors have some special positive status somewhere within their societies. An elevated alternative status is lacking for those available for penetration who do not have any spiritual vocation or some other special role. Similarly, there are age-stratified relations in which the expected future status of the boys is to become men every bit as masculine as those to whom they are sexually subordinated, and others in which men don't even purport to care about the future of those they use sexually. In some highland New Guinea instances, those donating semen view themselves as giving some of their vitality to the young, whom they view as being nourished by the semen. Elsewhere, particularly in the circum-Mediterranean cultural complex carried by conquerors of "the New World," men view semen as something that good health requires be expelled regularly.

I do not see a similar continuum for the instances of age-stratified female homosexualities (though I have not forgotten that the documentation is both less frequent and less full than is that for age-stratified male homosexualities). For gender-stratified female homosexuality, the "more butch" one often seizes male prerogatives, not least of which are autonomy and mobility. Females who are "femmes" tend not to have labels, and to be objectified by and subordinated to butch partners. At least in the prototypical case of 1950s North America, the "femmes" often earned a living and supported the "butches," just as some male "femmes" support their idle masculine poseur "husbands." Earning the household's income does not automatically translate into power within the relationship, although it provides at least a basis for greater agency, so that there is a range of valuations of the subordinate across the instances—and within the modern one—of female gender-stratified homosexuality. There are also a few analogs of masculine female "shamans" whose perceived power translates into a status higher than that of ordinary women in the society. And there are natal females taking on male roles, including that of "husband," in Africa, but there is not unequivocal evidence

420

that ravishing females is part of the male roles they enact (see Carrier and Murray 1998).

The existence of "premodern" instances of female and male homosexuality not involving status differences shows that egalitarian homosexuality was not impossible before industrial capitalism. Nonetheless, mobility—both in space and in occupations differing from one's parents'—is a precondition for the urban concentration and multiplication of potentially exclusive and non-role-bound relationships of "modern homosexuality." Industrialization occurred first in tandem with urbanization and capitalism. Some other configuration is imaginable, but this is the one that occurred. Subsequently, there have been places that have industrialized under the auspices of state ownership of the means of production and (at least in the case of Taiwan) outside cities. I have argued that it is not ownership of the means of production that matters, but the availability of social insurance other than family support and of sufficient housing stock (at least some of which families do not control) that make possible the formation of a critical mass of those desiring and/or having same-sex relationships. Again, an evenhanded provision of housing by a central state authority is imaginable, but it has been a market of living spaces that has occurred and is occurring. *Lebensraum* at an individual level, and some modicum of security of income, are highly correlated with the emergence of "modern homosexuality," both male and female.

The ability to earn a living is vital. Clearly, there are "women-identified women" in places where marriage to a man is compulsory, and less exclusive homosexuality among lesbians than among gay men in even those societies in which there is at least formal equality between men and women. If there were substantive equality (at least, equal pay), it is possible that there would be more exclusive, egalitarian lesbians, and I hypothesize a positive correlation between the frequency of "modern lesbians" and an approximation of pay equity (while recognizing the difficulty of measuring the former).

The possibility of living a "modern homosexual" existence is not irresistible —although paranoid upholders of "traditional family values" seem to believe that heterosexuality cannot compete in a "free market" or if the possibility of homosexuality is allowed to be general knowledge. In reality, however, it is not even irresistible to all those desiring same-sex sex (e.g., current "queers" as well as traditional "closet cases"). Youth and gender variance continue to be eroticized by many, even in societies with highly developed modern lesbigay institutions. Just as

aspirations for love between equals existed (and exists) where homosexual relations are primarily structured by age or gender differences,
pederasty and transvestitic homosexuality persist in cities of northern
Europe and North America where there is a visible "modern gay" presence. I suspect that with sufficiently thorough inquiry (or highly in-
trusive surveillance), some instances of all three major types of homosexuality (and probably some "boy tops" and "femme tops" of both
sexes) occur in any relatively spatially concentrated large population.

In short, there is a range of homosexualities in a society, and the
dominant discourse of the predominant sexual ideology ("sexual culture") may occlude but does not preclude different kinds of relationships.
There is always intracultural and intrapsychic variance, but there are also
recurrent social patterns, many of which include role labels. The remainder of the conclusion will attempt to examine correlates between
visible patterns of homosexuality and other customs and structures.

Correlating Organizations of Homosexuality and Other Social Structures

For the societies in which there is sufficient discussion of male homosexuality to code the presence of gender-stratified, age-stratified, or
non-status-stratified (egalitarian) organizations,[1] it is possible to correlate the occurrence of each of these types to other parts of culture and
social structure, as coded in the Human Relations Area Files (HRAF) organized by George Peter Murdock, and to cross-classify the presence of
particular social and cultural structures with types of homosexuality.
Table 5 lists the societies with discernible patterns of organization of homosexuality by type and (natal) sex. Within types, especially gender-
structured, geographical clusterings are listed.

The following analysis shows correlations between organizations of
homosexuality and other social patterns. I recognize that confidence
that anything can be known or compared has shriveled in the face of
postmodernist nihilism, so that current fashion is to write about the
ethnographer's angst away from home (with the people s/he visits occasionally impinging, or to write hyperparticularized "local history"). I am
well aware that this chapter (and, indeed, book) will be castigated for

---

1. I do not deploy "non-status-stratified" as a residual category for places in which
there is not information about organization. There must be positive indications that partners were of the same status (generally, unmarried young males) and/or practiced sexual
reciprocity. "Homosexuality" is an abbreviation for "sexual relationships between persons
of the same natal sex."

Table 5. Societies' Structuring of Male Homosexual Relationships

Gender-Role Stratified

Male

African

Akan, Ambo, Amhara, Baigishu, Bambara, Dahomey, Fanti, Gisu, Hausa, Ila, Iteso, Kongo/Nquiti, Konso, Krongo, Lango, Maale, Meru, Nuer, Nyoro, Ondonga, Otoro, Rwandan, Umbundu, Wolof, Yoruba, Zulu

Native North American

Aleut, Apache (Chiricahua), Blackfeet, Cheyenne, Choctaw, Creek, Crow, Delaware, Flathead, Fox, Gros Ventra, Havasupai, Hopi, Iroquois, Kaska, Micmac, Mojave, Naskapi, Navajo, Ojibwa, Omaha, Paiute (Kaibab), Pawnee, Pima, Sanpoil, Tewa, Timucua, Tlingit, Wintu, Zuni

Other Societies

Babylonian, Imperial Roman, Spanish (Andalusia), Brazilian, Korean, Badjau, Minangkabau, Japanese, Alorese, Pukapukan, Maori, Hawaiian, Samoan, Marquesan, Tahitian, Tongan, Cagaba, Mapuche, Tapirapé, Warrau, Aymara, Siriono, Piaroa, Witoto

Homosexuality Usual in Particular Occupational Roles

Chukchi, Koryak, Javanese, Iban, Toradja, Makassarese, Burmese, Thai, Vietnamese, Korean

Female

Hausa, Dahomey, Tsonga, Minangkabau, Japanese, Imperial Roman, Albanian, Aymara, Apache (Chiricahua), Atsugewi, Blackfeet, Cheyenne, Kaska, Klamath, Kutenai, Paiute (Kaibab), Mojave, Quinault, Wintu

Age-Role Stratified

Male

African

Ambo, Anyin, Bafia, Bangala, Eritrean, Gangella, Ila, Krongo, Mesakin, Mossi, Ndemu, Nkundu, Nyakyusa-Ngonde, Nyoro, Nzema, Ondonga, Pangwe/Pahouian, Rwandan, Tsonga, wives of mine (Mpondo etc.), Zande, Zulu; possibly also Hausa

Other Societies

Japanese, Korean, Southern Chinese, Javanese, Balinese, Aranda. Murngin, Walbiri, Malekulan, Gidjingali, Ajie, Riffian, Tunisian, Siwan, Egyptian, Syrian, Turk, Imperial Roman, Albanian, Persian, Uzbeki, Pathan, Sindhi, Central Tibetan, Tucuna, Tupinamba, Trumai, Ajie, Keraki, Kimam, Marindanim

Female

Apache (Chiricahua), Japanese, Marquesan, Naman, Sotho, Kaguru, Cape Bantu

Egalitarian

Male

African

Bafia, Bambara (among slaves), Bangala, Dagari, Duala, Herero, Iteso, Kru, Naman, Nandi, Nyakyusa-Ngonde, Pangwe/Pahouian, Wawhihé/Viye, Xun, Yaka

Other Societies

Orokaiva, Tiwi, Wogeo, Manu, Santa Cruz Islander, Hawaiian, Lau Fijian, Samoan, Tahitian, Cayapa, Nambikwara, Tucano, Tucuna, Yanomamo

Female

Aranda, Malekulan, Tahitian, Akan, Herero, Naman

considering patterns around the globe and, indeed, for suggesting that there *are* patterns, even statistical patterns in a single time and place. So be it. I would be the first to welcome more detailed ethnography examining homosexuality and how it fits with other aspects of social structure in specific local contexts outside North America and northwestern Europe, and far greater detail of both the subjectivities and the intersubjective meanings of same-sex sexual relationships anywhere. Alas, at present (and in the foreseeable future) there is very little for ethnologists to work with except the record compiled by early European travelers and ethnographers operating under the protection of colonial regimes.

Most purported "social constructionism" consists of idiosyncratic interpretations of a few European or North American texts (mostly printed ones) with, perhaps, a claimed link to "capitalism," "globalization," or "professional dominance." In the absence of influence of forensic medical (particularly psychiatric) texts, the special (discourse) creation of "the homosexual" should not have occurred in "traditional" societies. Creationist orthodoxy provides no claims or hypotheses about the organization of homosexuality in "tribal" societies, because it does not expect there to be any—and allegedly "social" constructionists rarely bother to compare even as many as two societies.

More a guiding hunch than an explicit hypothesis in my own work has been that the acceptance and the elaboration of male and or female homosexual relations is more likely where females have relatively greater economic independence and (therefore, in my Weberian expectation) higher status. Having significant responsibilities in the major production activities is intuitively an avenue to status.[2] Matrilineal inheritance, similarly, might seem to make male roles less highly valued than they are where inheritance is patrilineal,[3] so that we might expect the development of female homosexual roles (however organized) and of male homosexual roles organized by gender to be more common where there is matrilineal inheritance.

A recurrent explanation for homosexual relations is the unavailability of heterosexual relations. HRAF codings of "free love" and of the length of postpartum sex taboos provide indicators of males' "deprivation" from sexual access to females. Those who view homosexuality as "situational" would expect it to be more likely to occur where there are

2. This is attenuated (but not eliminated) if women do not control the resources they produce or help produce.

3. In a sense, males become "sex objects" exchanged by matrilines, as women are in patrilineal societies (on this way of analytical thinking, see Lévi-Strauss 1969; Rubin 1975).

longer postpartum taboos and for it not to occur where there is "free love," that is, a lack of sanctions against heterosexual sex.

Anti-creationist historian John Boswell (1980) asserted a relationship in medieval Europe between urbanization and repression of homosexuality, while quasi-Marxists (e.g., Adam 1987; Greenberg 1988) have related urbanization (at least in a capitalist context) to the development of "modern homosexuality" and to attempts to suppress it.

For distinguishing the social structural correlates of the three basic organizations of homosexuality, there is no theory beyond the quasi-evolutionary progression from age structuring to gender structuring to egalitarian homosexuality (with the last found only in industrial and post-industrial societies).

Correlational claims should not be misinterpreted as causal ones, and the existence of counterinstance does not invalidate a statistical relationship. The associations between sociocultural phenomena that are examined below are tendencies. These are statistical—not exceptionless—relations. While I am devoid of functionalist optimism that everything fits together to produce stable equilibrium, I do think that the co-occurrences are often recursive, that is, rather than A causing B, A bolsters B, which bolsters A. Unfortunately, data to sort out the historical priority of organization(s) of homosexualities to that of other sociocultural features are unavailable for most societies.

Harder to grasp, even for those who are comfortable thinking statistically, is that rather than being a single trichotomized dependent variable, the occurrence of each type is a distinct dependent variable. There are societies in which more than one type has been recorded. This reduces the apparent differentiation (between rows in the tables below) of (other) social structural patterns and types of homosexuality. If I had the certainty to identify a single, dominant organization of homosexuality for each of these societies, differences would be more striking than they are in these tables, and statistical difference of means tests might make some sense.[4]

Inheritance

In aboriginal North America, more than twice as many societies than the North American average (even though that average includes them) with gender-stratified male homosexuality had matrilineal inheritance. In aboriginal Africa, societies with gender-stratified male homosexuality

---

4. The questionable orthogonality of the cases (Galton's problem) would remain an obstacle to inferential statistics.

Table 6. Moveable Property Inheritance Patterns by Reported
          Organization of Homosexuality

	Patrilineal %	Matrilineal %	Either Sex %	N
Gender stratified				
Male African	75	25	0	16
Male North American	14	43	43	14
Male with occupation	40	60	0	10
Male without occupation	54	8	38	13
Total	47	32	21	53
Female	92	8	0	13
Age-stratified				
Male African	85	15	0	13
Male non-African	79	5	16	19
Total	81	9	9	32
Female	100	0	0	5
Not role defined				
Male African	82	9	9	11
Male non-African	67	0	33	3
Total	79	7	14	14
Female	67	33	0	3
Comparison samples				
Africa	73	23	5	102
North America	58	16	26	57
World	69	14	17	361

Source: Murdock (1981:139).

were not significantly more likely to also have matrilineal inheritance. In the rest of the world, societies with gender-stratified male homosexuality involving occupational specialties were four times more likely than the world average to have matrilineal inheritance. Overall, societies with gender-stratified male homosexuality were twice as likely as the world average to have matrilineal inheritance.

Inheritance in societies with age-stratified male or female homosexuality were markedly less matrilateral and less ambilineal (i.e., more patrilateral) than it was in regional and global rates. Inheritance in societies with non-roled-defined homosexuality was no more likely to be patrilateral inheritance than regional and global rates (though it was more likely to be matrilateral in societies with female non-roled-defined homosexuality).

Table 7. Dominant Social Organization of Homosexuality,
by Subsistence Patterns

	Primarily Agriculturalist %	Reliance on Agriculture mean %	Reliance on Domesticated Animal mean %	N
Gender stratified				
Male Africa	90	54	28	21
Male North America	17	22	1	30
Male with occupation	82	52	23	11
Male without occupation	78	42	12	23
Total	60	40	13	85
Total without North America	84	51	20	55
Female North America	0	3	0	12
Female other	100	61	20	9
Age stratified				
Male Africa	94	58	19	16
Male non-Africa	71	50	20	31
Total	86	53	19	47
Female	100	48	24	5
Egalitarian				
Male Africa	88	44	42	9
Male non-Africa	71	44	7	14
Total	83	44	23	23
Female	50	28	22	6

Subsistence Activities

The major difference shown in Table 7 is geographic: between "traditional" Africa and "traditional" Native North America.

Native North America (of salvaged memory) was notably unagriculturalist, especially in comparison to other places with patterns of homosexual relations. As I already noted about sub-Saharan Africa (1998c: 288), there is no apparent difference in primary means of subsistence correlating with the different types of homosexuality, male or female. Both agriculture and animal domestication were somewhat more important in African societies (ca. the colonial era) than in others (particularly herding in African societies, in which egalitarian homosexual relations were recorded), but there is no evidence of more "primitive" means of production associated with any particular form of male homosexuality. Although the number of societies in which egalitarian female homosexual relations were recorded is very small, that half of those for which subsistence codings are available (two Khoisan-speaking southwestern African peoples and one aboriginal Australian one) may be enough to keep this hope for an evolutionary pattern alive among some.

Sexual Division of Labor

Primary female involvement in the main means of making a living is a presumptive indicator of—and basis for—higher female status. Table 8 fails to support a hypothesis that greater female participation in making a living facilitates gendered male or female homosexuality. Compared to Murdock's (1981) world sample, societies with reported gender-stratified or egalitarian female homosexuality are less than half as likely

Table 8. Organization of Homosexuality, by Sexual Division
         of Labor of Major Survival Activity

Organization of Homosexuality	*Sexual Division of Labor*			
	Greater Male Participation %	Greater Female Participation %	Equivalent Participation %	N
Gender stratified				
Male Africa	29	38	33	21
Male North America	10	45	45	29
Male with occupation	36	0	64	9
Male without occupation	22	17	61	23
Total	21	30	49	84
Female	36	14	50	14
Age stratified				
Male Africa	18	53	29	17
Male non-Africa	25	29	46	28
Total	22	38	40	45
Female	33	50	17	6
Egalitarian				
Male Africa	45	27	27	11
Male non-Africa	14	43	43	14
Total	28	36	36	25
Female	67	17	17	6
Comparison samples[a]				
Africa	33	48	19	100
North America	15	48	37	46
World	34	31	35	361

Source: Murdock 1981:141.

[a]For agriculture, not always the predominant means of making a living.

as the world average to be societies in which females' participation in agriculture is greater than males. Although the equation of primary subsistence activity to agriculture is far from exact, herding domesticated animals and hunting tend to be male activities (and gathering foodstuff to be female), so that the comparison would seem biased toward male predominance. The female N's are small, particularly the nongendered ones.

Male predominance in the main means of making a living is especially striking for those societies outside Africa and North America in which nonmasculine males who have sex with males have particular occupational specializations. The reliance on male labor is greater in societies with all three types of male homosexuality in Africa than the pan-African average (the latter being notably low, even though that average includes the African societies in all three "Male Africa" rows). Table 8 seriously challenges the assumption that where women's economic importance is greater (so that nonmasculine males have less far to fall in status) gendered homosexual relations will flourish. Rather, egalitarian homosexuality seems to flourish more where the sexual division of labor is greater (i.e., less egalitarian). The apparent correlation between African egalitarian homosexuality and equivalent participation by both sexes (Murray 1998c:289) does not hold up in global comparisons.

Lack of Male Sexual Access to Females

Although male sexual access to unmarried females is a category for which "missing data" is particularly common in HRAF coding (specifically, Murdock 1967), Table 9 provides some indication that where boys are freest to engage in sex with girls, they also more freely—or, at least, more visibly—have sex with each other. This relationship is strongest in Africa; indeed it is perfect, but it rests on only two cases from there. Control of sexuality—not just of procreativity—is marked in non-African societies with age-stratified male homosexuality and is comparatively more common in societies with gender-stratified homosexuality, except for those with no occupational specialization.

In contrast, African societies with gender-stratified male homosexuality and non-African age-stratified male homosexuality tend to demand virginity from brides. Even if the codings are valid and the lack of information about the true distribution of values of permissiveness is random, data are not available for most societies, (They are missing especially often for those with non-status-stratified homosexuality.)

Another cultural practice that keeps females away from adult-male penetration (and, often, from any direct contact) is a postpartum sexual

Table 9. Organization of Homosexuality, by Permissiveness for Female Premarital Intercourse in a Society

Organization of Homosexuality	*Permissiveness for Female Premarital Intercourse*			
	Virginity Necessary for Brides %	Weakly Negatively Sanctioned %	Free, or Allowed Barring Pregnancy %	*N*
Gender stratified				
Male Africa	50	25	25	8
Male North America	35	29	35	17
Male with occupation	50	40	10	10
Male without occupation	15	46	38	13
Total	35	35	29	48
Female	36	14	50	14
Age stratified				
Male Africa	25	0	75	8
Male non-Africa	61	28	11	18
Total	50	19	31[a]	26
Female	33	50	17	6
Egalitarian				
Male Africa	0	0	100	2
Male non-Africa	22	11	67	9
Total	18	9	73	11
Female	67	17	17	6

[a]Free are Oceanic.

taboo. Such taboos are nearly ubiquitous.[5] Table 10 shows that societies with egalitarian male homosexuality have longer postpartum sex taboos than do societies with age- or gender-stratified male homosexuality.

As usual, the paucity of female cases makes drawing any conclusions difficult. There is at least an indication that egalitarian female homosexuality co-occurs with shorter postpartum taboos against male sexual access to recent mothers.

Taken together, these tenuous data suggest that difference in organization of male homosexuality is not a function of lack of male sexual access to females, as is claimed by the "situational" scarcity explanation for homosexuality. Whereas societies with egalitarian male homosexuality evidence less concern about the virginity of brides, they are more likely to have longer postpartum taboos on sexual contact than do societies with the other organizations of male homosexuality. Whereas the two

5. They are ubiquitous in traditional African societies, where they also tend to be lengthy.

Table 10. Organizations of Homosexualities, by Length of Time of Postpartum Sexual Taboos

Organization of Male Homosexuality	Length of Postpartum Sexual Taboos			
	<180 days %	6–12 months %	1+ years %	N
Gender stratified				
Male Africa	0	22	78	9
Male North America	70	10	20	2
Male prof	80	0	20	5
Male other	58	25	17	12
Total	54	15	30	46
Total non-Africa	68	14	19	37
Female	66	7	26	15
Age stratified				
Male Africa	28	0	71	7
Male non-Africa	75	17	8	12
Total	58	11	32	19
Female	60	0	40	5
Egalitarian				
Male Africa	25	0	75	8
Male non-Africa	0	17	84	6
Total	14	7	78	14
Female	67	33	0	3

potential indicators of "sex positivity" point in the same direction for egalitarian female homosexuality (i.e., away from scarcity of opportunities for sex with males), they point in different directions for egalitarian male homosexuality, specifically, toward less regulation of premarital sex of females and more regulation of married ones. It seems to me that longer postpartum sex taboos and the insistence upon brides' virginity are antinatalist.

Adolescent Male Isolation and Genital Mutilation

The previous two tables having dealt with restrictions on females, the next one considers traumas young males must undergo in some societies.[6] Table 11 cross-tabulates organization of homosexuality by male experiences of (a) circumcision at varying ages and (b) adolescent extrusion from the childhood home. With the exception of the sexually receptive Tapirapé males (Wagley 1977:160) none of the societies with

6. "Genital mutilation" is Murdock's category for what others call "circumcision" or "alteration." (The two African societies he coded as having male transvestitism are the Amhara and Hausa.)

Table 11. Organization of Adolescent Male Segregation from Natal Family, and Lack of Male Genital Mutilation, by Organization of Homosexuality

	No Segregation %	Live/ Sleep Away %	Live Apart with Relatives %	Live Apart with Age Mates %	N	Percentage without Male Genital Mutilation (N)
Gender stratified						
Male Africa	25	31	19	25	16	47 (17)
Male North America	81	12	8	0	26	100 (30)
Male with occupation	100	0	0	0	10	80 (10)
Male without occupation	88	6	0	6	17	79 (19)
Total	72	13	7	7	69	78 (78)
Female	71	24	6	0	17	77 (14)
Age-stratified						
Male Africa	23	31	31	15	13	40 (15)
Male non-Africa	67	10	0	24	21	50 (26)
Total	50	18	12	21	34	46 (41)
Female	60	40	0	0	5	17 (6)
Egalitarian						
Male Africa	43	29	0	29	7	20 (10)
Male non-Africa	50	10	20	20	10	60 (10)
Total	47	18	12	24	17	40 (20)
Female	0	60	20	20	5	40 (5)

gender-stratified homosexuality separated young males to live together (for initiation or any other reason). None of the societies with gender-crossing occupational roles extruded young males from their families.[7] The societies that extruded young males from natal households are Melanesian, Amazonian, and African—the homelands of male initiation rites. (Not all of these involved boy insemination.) Extrusion of boys from the household is not reported for the societies with female gender- or age-stratified homosexuality. I would expect that where boys were thrown together they would be more likely to pair off with each other than to enter a sexual relationship with an elder, and the African data seem to fulfill this expectation (Murray 1998c:293), but on a global scale, there is no substantive difference in boys living together with age mates away from their natal family (or away from their extended family either) between societies with age-stratified in contrast to egalitarian male homosexualities.

Male genital mutilation is considerably more common (nearly twice as common) in societies with gender-stratified (male and female) homosexuality than in societies with either of the other two types. It is also more African, missing altogether in Native North American societies with any reported organization of homosexuality.

Class and Urbanization

The HRAF coding "mean size of local community" has five categories for societies whose aggregations are less than a thousand persons, but shifts to noting the largest aggregation for societies with settlements of a thousand or more persons. Most of the African societies included in Murdock's (1967) survey are in the fifty to one thousand range, whereas those with age-stratified homosexuality have a median "mean size" of five thousand, and most of those with gender-stratified and those with non-stratified homosexuality have aggregates of more than five thousand. Only some with gender-stratified homosexuality have cities of fifty thousand or more.

As can be seen in Table 12, the worldwide pattern is less clear-cut than the African one. Native North America (north of Mexico) lacked cities of fifty thousand or more persons altogether; a number of circum-Mediterranean societies with age-stratified (male and female) homosexuality had urban centers. This leaves societies with egalitarian (male and female) homosexualities: none had urban centers (though more than half of the African ones had at least large towns).

---

7. Young Pawnee and Tlingit slept in relatives' compounds.

Table 12. Urbanization, by Type of Homosexuality

Organization of Male Homosexuality	Percentage of Societies in which Population of Largest Indigenous Settlements is 50,000+ (N)	Median Largest Settlement Size
Gender stratified		
Male Africa	38 (8)	27,500
Male North America	0 (20)	150
Male with occupation	62 (8)	50,000+
Male without occupation	31 (13)	350
Total	25 (49)	
Female	21 (14)	150
Age stratified		
Male Africa	0 (10)	3,500
Male non-Africa	39 (24)	27,500
Total	42 (37)	
Female	25 (4)	2,500
Egalitarian		
Male Africa	0 (7)	27,500
Male non-Africa	0 (9)	250
Total	0 (14)	
Female	0 (4)	700

Another indicator of societal complexity is the crystallization of classes—"complex stratification into social classes correlated in large measure with extensive differentiation of occupational statuses" is the category in Murdock (1967:57). Paralleling the urbanism finding, gender-stratified male homosexuality is the only kind that has been reported in indigenous African class-based societies,[8] whereas non-status-stratified homosexuality is considerably more common in classless societies than in African societies with either of the other two organizations of male homosexuality. Many of the same (mostly Muslim) circum-Mediterranean societies with age-stratified homosexuality and cities are also class based. As with urbanism, this leaves egalitarian as the only type of male homosexuality occurring without social classes. The African class:gendered homosexuality connection holds up globally for female homosexuality.

Relatively egalitarian societies are more likely to have male homosexual relations not structured by differences in age or gender status. Urban societies are notably inegalitarian, so the results in Tables 12 and 13 dovetail.

8. I combined Murdock's "elite stratification" category with his "class" one; he coded Zulu as the former.

Table 13. Dominant Organization of Homosexuality,
and Socioeconomic Stratification

Stratification System	Organization of Homosexuality				
	Wealth Egalitarian %	Hereditary Nobles/Social Distinctions %	Commoners %	Classes %	N
Gender stratified					
Male Africa	11	28	39	22	18
Male North America	77	7	17	0	32
Male with occupation	9	27	9	55	11
Male without occupation	29	19	33	19	21
Total	40	19	25	17	81
Female	39	28	44	11	18
Age stratified					
Male Africa	13	27	53	7	15
Male non-Africa	36	14	7	43	28
Total	28	19	23	30	43
Female	20	20	60	0	5
Egalitarian					
Male Africa	36	45	18	0	11
Male non-Africa	57	21	21	0	14
Total	48	32	20	0	21
Female	17	50	33	0	6
Comparison samples					
Africa	37	13	43	7	107
North America	62	24	12	2	120
World	45	19	22	13	549

Summary

Most of these data do not yield a neat functionalist package in which the dependent variable (an organization of homosexuality) can be tidily attributed to one or more independent variables (other social patterns), although some "if x, not y" findings can be drawn from them. There are also bunchings of features when rates across societies with different organizations of homosexuality and/or with HRAF samples are compared. Because there are comparably fewer attestations of patterned female homosexuality (so that almost all the cells in female rows in the tables within this chapter—and, indeed, in many of the rows—include fewer than five cases, the standard minimum for interpreting differences) and because the syntax of this summary is complex enough without trying to consider both male and female patterns in the same summary sentences, I shall first take up male correlations and will then address female ones.

Male

First, there is geographical patterning. Within Africa, I found that stratification by gender roles is the most commonly reported kind among the historically more northern of the sub-Saharan African peoples, whereas stratification by age roles is slightly more common than by gender roles in West Africa and nearly as common among Bantu-speaking societies in central and southern Africa. Homosexuality that is not stratified by age or gender is more common in the Southeast than in other parts of Africa, but is not the most frequent organization in any of the table's four geohistorical clusters of languages. On a larger scale, there are some noticeable differences in social patternings between Africa and the rest of the world, and, even more, between Native North America and the rest of the world.

Societies with gender-stratified male homosexuality are more likely to have matrilineal inheritance than are societies with the other two types. Native North American societies with gender-stratified male homosexuality were far less patrilineal than were Native North American societies in general. In societies with gender-stratified male homosexuality, the major means of making a living involved greater male than female participation more often than it did for societies with the other two types, and the proportion of female to male participation in these societies exceeded the regional and world averages, undercutting the "boys can be girls where girls have more important economic roles" hypothesis. African societies with gender-stratified male homosexuality were more likely than societies with the other types to have virginity demands for brides, but elsewhere, societies with gender-stratified male homosexuality were less likely than those with age-stratified homosexuality to have such a requirement. Societies with gender-stratified male homosexuality were considerably less likely to extrude young males from the household in which they had grown up, and societies outside Africa did not segregate young bachelors with age mates. In African societies with cities (i.e., settlements of fifty thousand or more) or class stratification, the only ones with recorded patterns of male homosexuality had gender-stratified ones.

In the rest of the world, age-stratified male homosexuality was more common among urban and class-based societies than were the other two types. Age-stratified male homosexuality was not recorded in Native North America. Societies with age-stratified male homosexuality were the most patrilineal in inheritance, and the least ambisexual. Compared to regional and global patterns, these were also more patrilineal in inheritance. Similarly, they were less likely to have equivalent male and female involvement in the primary survival activity than were societies with the other two types or in contrast with African and world patterns. Outside Africa, they were the most likely to insist on female premarital virginity, so that rather than "boys will be girls where it doesn't matter" it is "boys will be used sexually where girls' virginity is especially carefully guarded." Societies with age-stratified male homosexuality are intermediate between the other two types in terms of the length of postpartum sexual taboos and in terms of shipping pubescent males off to live together. This is more common in non-African societies with age-stratified homosexuality than in non-African societies with the other two types, and least common for African societies with patterned male homosexuality.

Non-status-stratified male homosexuality has not been reported from the Eurasian land mass, from the southern shores of the Mediterranean, or from Native North America. None of the societies (which include kingdoms, not just hunter-gatherer bands) in which it has been attested had cities or social classes. They are the least likely to have had matrilineal inheritance (in the direction of greater patrilineal, not ambilineality). They relied less on male participation in the major survival activity than did societies with the other two types, and, outside Africa, less on greater female participation. Bridal virginity requirements and long postpartum sexual taboos were not characteristic. In short, these societies were relatively egalitarian in aspects other than male homosexual relations.

Female

Societies with gender-stratified female homosexuality are more likely to have patrilineal inheritance than are societies in general or societies with egalitarian female homosexuality in particular.[9] Outside Native North America, all the societies with gender-stratified female homosexuality are agriculturalist. Societies with gender-stratified female homosexuality are as likely as societies with gender-stratified male homosexuality to be marked by greater male participation in the major survival

9. The exception is the Minangkabau of Sumatra.

activity, and more likely than societies with age-stratified or egalitarian female homosexuality to be so marked. Most of the societies with gender-stratified female homosexuality are ones that practice male genital mutilation (but not female genital mutilation), though they are mostly not societies that extrude young males from the household in which they grew up.

All the societies with age-stratified female homosexuality are primarily agriculturalist. They are notable for having weak negative sanctions for premarital chastity (only a Polynesian people in this category, the Marquesans, are coded "free love"), and mostly do not practice male genital mutilation (with the same exception). None of the societies with age-stratified female homosexuality are class based or urban. Indeed, they are markedly less urban than societies with age-stratified male homosexuality.

Only half of the societies with non-status-stratified female homosexuality are primarily agriculturalist, in contrast to all the societies with status-stratified female homosexuality outside Native North America. The two southeastern African herding societies are unusual in that males and females have equivalent responsibilities for the animals on which they depend. Additionally, two other societies with non-status-stratified female homosexuality (Akan and Malekula) rely on equivalent responsibility for their primary survival activity, agriculture. Reversing the male pattern, societies with egalitarian female homosexuality are more likely to demand premarital virginity than are societies with other types (and than societies with any of the male types or subtypes; only another Polynesian people in this category, the Tahitians, are coded "free love"). They are also less likely to be coded as "egalitarian" in the HRAF coding of stratification systems than are societies with other patterns of female homosexuality (and societies with male egalitarian homosexuality are three times as likely to be egalitarian). The only instance of an attested pattern of female homosexuality in a society in which young males are extruded from their childhood home to live with age mates has egalitarian female homosexuality (Malekula). None of the traditional societies with egalitarian female homosexuality are class based or urban. (Using a non-Marxist definition of "class," an argument could be made that Tahiti is an exception.)

A Mirror?

That the same basic types of organization of homosexuality exist for female homosexuality as for male homosexuality underlay the explorations of this book as a whole. Males and females in most society differ in permissable mobility and, thereby, in the possibilities for interacting outside family surveillance. I do not know that there is less female-female than male-male genital sexual contact, although I believe there is (here, there, and everywhere). Patterns of ongoing female-female sexuality have been reported less often and in less detail than have male-male patterns. Given the number of female fieldworkers and the number of fieldworkers interested in female sociation (overlapping sets), I do not think this disparity is primarily an observer effect. I believe that it reflects a difference that is out there in the world. There may well be more homoaffectionality among females—here, there, and everywhere—than among males, and I am well aware that a focus on genital contact is variously regarded as masculinist, unliberated, and pre-postist.

Evelyn Blackwood (1985, 1996) and others have castigated those who suggest female-female sexual relations "mirror" what goes on inside male-male, ones—in particular in the expressions of affection. Here, I instead want to look at whether similar social correlates for female and male homosexual roles occur. The tables in this chapter have thus far been laid out so that the rates can easily be compared, so the reader can easily establish her/his own criteria for degree of similarity in scrutinizing Tables 5–13. Table 14 puts the male and the female summaries together to show what I think are similarities of sociocultural patterns that co-occur with each of the three abstract types of homosexuality. (I have

Table 14. (Rough) Parallelism of Rates, by Type,
for Male and Female Homosexuality

Nonsexual pattern	Organization of Homosexuality		
	Gender Stratified	Age Stratified	Unstratified
Dependence on agriculture	+	+	−
Patrilinearity	−	+	+
Matrilinearity	−	+	
Ambilinearity	−		
Sexual division of labor	−	−	−
Virginity requirement	+	−	−
"Free love"	−	−	−
Length of postpartum sexual taboo	+	+	−
Adolescent male extrusion	+	+	−
To congregation of age mates	+	−	−
Presence of cities	+	−	+
Egalitarian	+	+	−

left blank cells where the addition or subtraction of a single case would change the sign.)

Whereas there were African and Native North American exceptions for social patternings correlating with types of male homosexuality, for types of female homosexuality the exceptions are primarily Polynesian. The correlates of gender-stratified female and gender-stratified male homosexualities are quite similar, and the correlates for age-stratified homosexuality are also fairly similar. Such egalitarian-female homosexuality as has been attested occurs in quite different kinds of societies than those in which egalitarian male homosexuality has been attested, specifically, in those which are in other ways less egalitarian.

Who Is Desiring Whom? And Does It Matter?

In *A Clock without Hands,* Carson McCullers famously wrote that in a love relationship there is always one who loves and one who is loved, the lover and the beloved. In that the one who is loved has the power of the lesser interest, the prey has power over the hunter trying to capture him/her. Many lovers want to be loved, not just accepted, and more than a few beloveds want and try to love back. But even when there is mutuality of love, its force is rarely (if ever) exactly equal in both directions.

For age-stratified homosexuality, at least the social script is for the elder to want the body and/or soul of the younger, and for the younger to acquiesce to worthy suitors and to resist unworthy ones. The normative primary direction of desire is from the older and the direction of duty from the younger (whatever the particular sexual acts desired may be). Credibly performing lack of interest (whether the lack is real or feigned) often attracts interest and worldly goods, ranging from presents and payments to long-term support.

For gender-stratified male homosexuality, it is often the penetrated male who eagerly seeks relatively indifferent penetrators. In Mediterranean, Latin American, and Anglo North American societies, some penetratees pay for being "serviced" by "real men," even though males in the same societies pay to penetrate females.[10] For gender-stratified female homosexuality, it seems that it is generally the nonfeminine female who is visible, but there is considerable variety in whether "femmes" find and select "butches" or whether "butches" seduce and take "femmes"—and, in the latter instance, whether the "femmes" are passive or are simulating passivity. Similarly, conventionally masculine males have often been

10. I am using "payment" to include gifts, support, and patronage, as well as money.

passive, paid by, (or, in ongoing relationships, supported by) an unmasculine male eager to be penetrated and willing to provide other kinds of support, not only orifices for phalli to visit.

And for the non-status-defined? Who is the lover and who the beloved was already being asked about Akhilles and Patroklos by (post-Homeric) ancient Greeks. This type includes those with complementary desires that are not carried over to the subordination of one by the other, as well as the reciprocity of alternating roles.[11] In that status, income, sexual drive, and the insertive/receptive balance are rarely (if ever) precisely equal, the subtle power of the lesser interest—both lesser feeling of love and lesser investment of resources other than the self (see Carrington 1999)—can operate. Perhaps it is that the kinds of status (age, class, and gender) that structure relationships are more visible, the division of rights and obligations less clearly structured (and possibly more fluid) without the clearer expectations of dominance, submission, and resistance.

11. I would hope that various examples in this book have already built caution about any equation of agency and activity. Success(ful agency) is getting what one wants, not the contents of the want(s).

Acknowledgments

This work has been wholly unsupported by grants. For my surprising survival and almost-as-surprising ability to persist without a job or any institutional support and in the face of considerable hostility from some smug "queer" employees of U.S. and European universities, I am most grateful to my life partner Keelung Hong, and very grateful to my physician, Lawrence Goldyn, and to my attorney, Sandra Springs, for pulling me back from various brinks.

For comments on drafts of earlier sections and/or for sharing their insights into various sexual cultures, I am grateful to Barry Adam, Nii Ajen, Niyi Akinnaso, Eric Allyn, Dennis Altman, Deborah Peters Amory, Manuel Arboleda, Barry Baker, June Bedford, Dianne Beeson, Evelyn Blackwood, the late Philip Blumstein, Ralph Bolton, Erika Bourguignon, the late Joel Brodsky, the late Roger Brown, Gary Bukovnik, Joseph Carrier, Héctor Carillo, Christopher Carrington, Chen Bou-See, Lawrence Cohen, Reid Condit, the late Steven Corbin, Peter Daniels, John De-Cecco, Dennis Deniega, William Devall, Keith DeVries, Mildred Jeffrey Dickemann, Alan Dishman, the late Cora DuBois, Wayne Dynes, John Elia, Steven Epstein, Stephen Eyre, Manuel Fernández-Alemany, Peter Fry, John Gagnon, Rudolf Gaudio, Kent Gerard, Maurice Godelier, Michael Gorman, Meredith Gould, John Grube, James Lee Haines, Dieter Haller, Joseph Harry, the late William Hawkeswood, the late Joseph Hayes, Gilbert Herdt, Richard Herrell, Ross Higgins, John Hollister, Keelung Hong, the late Laud Humphreys, Dell Hymes, Peter Jackson, Merilee Jenkins, Ole Johnsen, Ginu Kamani, Elizabeth Kennedy, Badruddin Khan, Joseph P-Y Kao, Paul Kay, Kathryn Kendall, Donald Keene, Badruddin Khan, Christiaan Klieger, Michael Kobayashi, Don Kulick, Paul Kutsche, the late Ruth Landes, William Leap, John Alan Lee, Gary Leupp, the late Martin Levine, Paul Lockman, Mary McIntosh, Martin Manalansan IV, Lorand Matory, Stuart Michaels, Brian Miller, Douglas Mitchell, Theresa Montini, Luiz Mott, Peter Nardi, Dédé Oetemo, Morris Opler, Luis Paloma, Richard Parker, the late Kenneth Payne, Luis Diaz-Perdomo, Gregory Pflugfelder, the late Arnold Pilling, Ken Plummer, Wenshen Pong, Mary Porter, Frank Proschan, Ricardo Ramos, Will Roscoe, Gayle Rubin, the late Jesse Sawyer, Paul Gordon Schalow, Beth Schneider, Peter Sieger, William Simon, the late George Eaton Simpson, Bruce Smith, Deborah Spehn, Gerard Sullivan, Michael

Sweet, the late Rosendo Tabtab, Clark Taylor, Pablo Tellez, Walteen Grady Truley, Randolph Trumbach, Amparo Tusón, Theo van der Meer, Jim Wafer, Delores Walters, Frederick Whitam, David Whittier, Saskia Wieringa, Unni Wikan, Andrea Williams, Walter Williams, Deborah Goleman Wolf, Wayne Wooden, and Leonard Zwilling.

For help with languages I do not know, I am grateful for help from Deb Amory, Maynard Chen, Louis Crompton, Wayne Dynes, Kent Gerard, David Greenberg, Keelung Hong, Everard Longland, Will Roscoe, and the late Bradley Rose.

For comments on the book as a whole, I am grateful to Louis Crompton; Douglas Mitchell; and, for especially painstaking (and occasionally pain-giving) comments, David Greenberg. I have had the good fortune to work with University of Chicago Press senior editor Douglas Mitchell on this book and on *American Gay* and am among those who would designate him a national treasure. I am also grateful for the heroic labors on an unwieldy manuscript of Ruth Barzel, Robert Devens, Jenni Fry, and Matthew Howard.

References

Abbreviations

AA   *American Anthropologist*
AAA American Anthropological Association
AE   *American Ethnologist*
AJS   *American Journal of Sociology*
ASB   *Archives of Sexual Behavior*
ASR   *American Sociological Review*
JH   *Journal of Homosexuality*

Abdullahi, Salisu A. 1984. *A Sociological Analysis of the Institution of 'Dan Daudu in Hausa Society.* Ph.D. diss. Bayero University (Kano, Nigeria).
Abreu, Caio Fernando. 1983a. "Sergeant Garcia." In Leyland (1983:267–77).
———. 1983b. "Those two." In Leyland (1983:278–84).
———. 1990. *Dragons.* London: Boulevard, 1990.
AbuKhalil, As'ad. 1993. "A note on the study of homosexuality in the Arab/ Islamic civilization." *The Arab Studies Journal* 1, 2:32–34, 48.
Achmat, Zackie. 1993. "'Apostles of civilised vice': 'Immoral practices' and 'unnatural vice' in South African prisons and compounds, 1890–1920." *Social Dynamics* 19:92–110.
———. 1995. "My childhood as an adult molester: A Salt River moffie." In Gevisser and Cameron (1995:324–41).
Ackerley, Joe R. 1961. "Kobo Daishi." *The Listener* 1692 (31 Aug.): 316–18.
Adam, Barry D. 1978a. *The Survival of Domination.* NY: Elsevier.
———. 1978b. "Capitalism, the family, and gay people." *Sociologists' Gay Caucus Working Paper* 1.
———. 1979. "Reply." *Sociologists Gay Caucus Newsletter* 18:8.
———. 1985. "Structural foundations of the gay world." *Comparative Studies in Society and History* 27:658–70.
———. 1986. "Age, structure and sexuality." *JH* 11:19–33.
———. 1987. *The Rise of a Gay and Lesbian Movement.* Boston: Twayne.
———. 1992. "Sex and caring among men: Impacts of AIDS on gay people." In *Modern Homosexualities,* ed. K. Plummer, 75–83. London: Routledge.
Adam, Barry D., Jan Willem Duyyendak, and André Krouwel. 1998. *The Global Emergence of Gay and Lesbian Politics.* Philadelphia: Temple University Press.
Adams, James Noel. 1982. *The Latin Sexual Vocabulary.* London: Duckworth.
Adelman, Janet. 1985. "Male bonding in Shakespeare's comedies." In Erickson and Kahn (1985:73–103).
Adriani, Nicolaus, and Albert C. Kruyt. 1950. *De Bare's sprekende Toradjas van Midden Celebes.* Amsterdam: Noord-Hollandsche Vitgevers Maatschappij. (HRAF translation)
Aina, Tade Akin. 1991. "Patterns of bisexuality in Sub-Saharan Africa." In

Bisexuality & HIV/AIDS, ed. R. Tielman, M. Carballo, and A. Hendriks, 81–90. Buffalo, NY: Prometheus.

Allahbadia, Gautam N., and Nilesh Shah. 1992. "Begging eunuchs of Bombay." *The Lancet* 339 (4 Jan.):48–49.

Allyn, Eric. 1990. *An Interview with "Uncle" Goh Bhaknam*. Bangkok: Bua Luang.

———. 1991. *Trees in the Same Forest: Thailand's Culture and Gay Subculture*. Bangkok: Bua Long.

———. 1992. *The Dove Coos: Gay Experiences by the Men of Thailand*. Bangkok: Bua Luang.

———. 1993. "The Pink Triangle group." *Society of Lesbian and Gay Anthropologists' Newsletter* 13, 3:53–53. Incorporated in Murray and Roscoe (1997:297–98).

Allyn, Eric, and John P. Collins. 1988. *The Men of Thailand: Noom Thai*. 2nd ed. Bangkok: Bua Long.

Alonso, Andrea M., and Maria T. Koreck. 1988. "Silences: 'Hispanics,' AIDS and sexual practices." *differences* 1:101–24.

Alonzo, D. 1983. "Stories out of school." *Los Angeles Edge* 7, 13:20–21.

Altaschuler, Milton. 1964. "The Cayapa." Ph.D. diss., University of Minnesota.

Altman, Dennis. 1971. *Homosexual: Oppression and Liberation*. NY: Avon.

———. 1982. *The Americanization of the Homosexual, The Homosexualization of America*. NY: St. Martin's.

———. 1988. "Legitimation through disaster: AIDS and the gay movement." In *AIDS: The Burdens of History*, ed. E. Fee and D. Fox, 301–16. Berkeley: University of California Press.

Alves da Silva, Alcionilio Brüzzi. 1977 [1962]. *A civilizacao indigena do Uaupes*. Roma: Piazza Ateneo Salesiano.

Anderson, Benedict R. 1992 [1983]. *Imagined Communities: Reflections on the Origin and Spread of Nationalism*. London: Verso.

———. 1996 [1965]. *Mythology and the Tolerance of the Javanese*. Ithaca, NY: Cornell University Press.

Andrews, Edmund, and Irene D. Andrews. 1944. *A Comparative Dictionary of the Tahitian Language*. Chicago Academy of Sciences Special Publication 6.

Angiolello, Giovan Maria. 1985 [1513]. *Il sultano e il profeta: Memorie di uno schiavo vicentino divenuto tesoriere di Maometto II il Conquistatore*. Milan: Serra e Riva Editori.

Arberry, Arthur J. 1956. *The Mystical Poems of Ibn al-Farid*. Dublin: Emery Walker.

Arboleda G., Manuel A. 1980. "Gay life in Lima." *Gay Sunshine* 42:30.

———. 1986. "Peru: Gay activism takes hold within a complex multi-ethnic society." *The Advocate* 445 (29 April): 29–33.

———. 1987. "Social attitudes and sexual variance in Lima." In Murray (1987:101–17). Rev. version in Murray (1995a:100–110).

———. 1997. "On some of Lancaster's misrepresentations." *AE* 24:931–34.

Arboleda G., Manuel A., and Stephen O. Murray. 1985. "Lexical inferences and Maori homosexuality." *JH* 12:121–29.

Arenas, Reinaldo. 1984. *Arturo, la estrella mas brilliante* In *Old Rosa: A Novel in Two Stories*. NY: Grove, 1989:49–104

————. 1992. *Antes que anochezca.* Barcelona: Tusquets Editores. Trans. as *Before Night Falls,* NY: Viking, 1993.

Ariès, Philippe. 1962. *Centuries of Childhood.* NY: Vintage.

Arnaud, Daniel. 1973. "La prostitution sacrée en Mésopotamia: Un myth historiographique?" *Revue de l'histoire des Religions* 183:115–35.

Asano-Tamanoi, Mariko. 1987. "Shame, family, and state in Catalonia and Japan." In *Honor and Shame and the Unity of the Mediterranean,* ed. D. Gilmore, 104–20. Washington, DC: American Anthropological Association.

Ashworth, A. E., and W. M. Walker. 1972. "Social structure and homosexuality." *British Journal of Sociology* 23:146–58.

Aston, W. G. 1972 [720]. *Nihongi: Chronicles of Japan from Earliest Times to A.D. 697.* Tokyo: Tuttle.

Ayalon, David. 1946. "The plague and its effects upon the Mamlūk army." *Journal of the Royal Asiatic Society* 1946:67–73. Reprinted in Ayalon 1977.

————. 1949. "The Circassians in the Mamlūk Kingdom. *Journal of the American Oriental Society* 69:135–47. Reprinted in Ayalon 1977.

————. 1956. *Gunpowder and Firearms in the Mamlūk Kingdom.* London: Valentine & Mitchell.

————. 1960. Studies in al-Jabartī I: Notes on the transformation of Mamlūk Society in Egypt under the Ottomans. *Journal of Economic and Social History of the Orient* 2:148–74, 3:275–325. Reprinted in Ayalon 1977.

————. 1968. "The Muslim city and the Mamlūk military aristocracy." *Proceedings of the Israel Academy of Sciences and Humanities* 2:311–29. Reprinted in Ayalon 1977.

————. 1975a. "Preliminary remarks on the Mamlūk military institution in Islam." In *War, Technology and Society in the Middle East,* ed. V. J. Parry and M. Yapp, 44–58. Oxford: Oxford University Press.

————. 1975b. "The impact of firearms on the Muslim world." *Princeton Middle East Papers* 20:32–43. Reprinted in Ayalon 1994.

————. 1977. *Studies on the Mamlūks of Egypt.* London: Variorum Reprints.

————. 1979a. "On the eunuchs in Islam." *Jerusalem Studies in Arabic and Islam* 1:67–124. Reprinted in Ayalon 1988a.

————. 1979b. "Halka." *Encyclopedia of Islam* 3:99.

————. 1980 [1950]. "Mamlūkiyat." *Jerusalem Studies in Arabic and Islam* 2:321–49. Reprinted in Ayalon 1988a.

————. 1986. "The Mamlūk novice: On his youthfulness and on his original religion." *Revue des Études islamiques* 56:1–8. Reprinted in Ayalon 1994.

————. 1987a. "The end of the Mamlūk Sultanate." *Studia Islamica* 65:124–48. Reprinted in Ayalon 1994.

————. 1987b. "Mamlūk military aristocracy: A non-hereditary nobility." *Jerusalem Studies in Arabic and Islam* 10:205–10. Reprinted in Ayalon 1994.

————. 1988a. *Outsiders in the Lands of Islam: Mamlūks, Mongols, and Eunuchs.* London: Variorum Reprints.

————. 1988b. "Islam versus Christian Europe: The case of the Holy Land." In *Pillars of Smoke and Fire,* ed. M. Sharon, 247–56. Johannesburg: Southern Book.

————. 1990. "Mamlūk." *Encyclopedia of Islam* 6:314–21. Expanded in Ayalon 1994.

————. 1994. *Islam and the Abode of War: Military Slaves and Islamic Adversaries.* London: Variorum Reprints.

Babinger, Franz C. H. 1978. *Mehmed the Conqueror and His Time.* Princeton, NJ: Princeton University Press.

Bakhtin, Mikhail M. 1986. *Speech Genres & Other Late Essays.* Austin: University of Texas Press.

Baldauf, Ingeborg. 1988. *Die Knabenliebe in Mittelasien: Bacabozlik.* Berlin: Das Arabische Buch, 1988. Partially translated as "Bacabozlik," *Paidika* 2, 2(1990):12–31.

Baldinger, Kurt. 1974. *Dictionnaire Étymologioque de l'Ancien Français.* Québec: Les Presses de l'Université Laval.

Bao, Daniel. 1993. "*Invertidos sexuales, tortileras,* and *maricas machos:* The construction of homosexuality in Buenos Aires, Argentina, 1900–1950." *JH* 24:183–219.

Baraheni, Reza. 1977. *The Crowned Cannibals: Writings on Repression in Iran.* NY: Vintage.

Barber, Noel. 1973. *The Sultans.* NY: Simon and Schuster.

Barker, T. N. 1975. "Some Features of Ai'i Society." Ph.D. diss., Laval University.

Barley, Nigel. 1988. *Not a Hazardous Sport.* NY: Holt.

Barnstone, Willis. 1965. *Sappho.* NY: New York University Press.

Barth, Fredrik. 1983. *Sohar: Culture and Society.* Baltimore: Johns Hopkins University Press.

Basso, Keith H. 1969. *Western Apache Witchcraft.* Tucson: University of Arizona Press.

Bastian, Adolf. 1872 [1860]. *Die Rechtsverhältnisse bei verschiedenen Völkern der Erde.* Berlin: G. Reimer.

Bastide, Roger. 1961. *O Candomblé de Bahia.* São Paulo: Nacional.

Baudier, Michel. 1624. *Histoire générale du serrail, e de la cour du Grand Seigneur, empereur des Turcs.* Paris: C. Cramoisy.

Baumann, Hermann. 1955. *Das doppelte Geschlect: Ethnologische Studien zur Bisexualität in Ritus und Mythos.* Berlin: Dietrich Reimer.

Beaglehole, J. C. 1967. *The Journals of Captain James Cook.* Stanford, CA: Stanford University Press.

Beaulieu, Augustin de. 1705. *Navigantium atque Itinerontium Bibliotheca.* London: Bennet.

Bech, Henning. 1997. *When Men Meet: Homosexuality and Modernity.* Chicago: University of Chicago Press.

————. 1992. "Report from a rotten state: 'Marriage' and 'homosexuality' in 'Denmark.'" In *Modern Homosexualities,* ed. K. Plummer, 134–47. London: Routledge.

Bedford, June. 1995. "The Mapuche female shaman-*Machi.*" Paper presented at the American Indian Workshop. Universidade Fernando Pessoa, Oporto.

Beemyn, Brett. 1997. *Creating Places for Ourselves: Lesbian, Gay, and Bisexual Community Histories.* NY: Routledge.

Beidelman, Thomas O. 1973. "The Kaguru of Central Tanzania." In *Cultural Source Materials for Population Planning in East Africa: Beliefs and Practices.,* ed. A. Molnos, 262–73. Nairobi: East African Publishing House.

Bell, Alan P., and Martin S. Weinberg. 1978. *Homosexualities.* NY: Simon and Schuster.

Bell, Joseph Norment. 1979. *Love Theory in Later Hanbalite Islam.* Albany: State University of New York Press.

Bellah, Robert N. 1996. Review of Ikegama, *The Taming of the Samurai. Contemporary Sociology* 25:110–12.

Berlin, Brent. 1992. *Ethnobiological Classification.* Princeton, NJ: Princeton University Press.

Berlin, Brent, Dennis Breedlove, and Peter H. Raven. 1968. "Covert Categories and Folk Taxonomies". *AA* 70:290–99.

———. 1973. "General Principles of Classification and Nomenclature in Folk Biology." *AA* 75:214–42.

Berlin, Brent, and Paul Kay. 1991 [1969]. *Basic Color Terms: Their Universality and Evolution.* Berkeley: University of California Press.

Bérubé, Allan. 1990. *Coming Out Under Fire: The History of Gay Men and Women in World War Two.* NY: Free Press.

Besmer, Fremont E. 1983. *Horses, Musicians, and Gods: The Hausa Possession Trance.* S. Hadley, MA: Bergin & Garvey.

Besnier, Niko. 1981. *Tuvaluan Lexicon.* Washington, DC: Peace Corps.

———. 1991. "Literacy and the notion of the person on Nukulaelae atoll." *AA* 93:570–87.

———. 1994. "Polynesian gender liminality through time and space." In *Third Sex, Third Gender,* ed. G. Herdt, 285–328. NY: Zone Books.

Bethe, Eric. 1907. "Die dorische Knabenliebe, ihre Ethik, ihre Idee." *Rheinisches Museum* 57:438–75. Reprinted in Dynes and Donaldson 1992:10–47.

Beurdeley, Michel. N.d. *Erotic Art of Japan: The Pillow Book.* Hong Kong: Leon Amiel.

Bhandarkar, R. G. 1913. *Vaisnavism and Minor Religious Systems.* Varnasi: Series Encyclopedia of Indo-Aryan Research.

Biddle, George. 1968 [1920]. *Tahitian Journal.* Minneapolis: University of Minnesota Press. Pages 63–64 reprinted in Roscoe 1995, 111–13.

Bing, Peter, and Rip Cohen. 1991. *Games of Venus: An Anthology of Greek and Roman Erotic Verses from Sappho to Ovid.* NY: Routledge.

Binns, J. W. 1974. "Women or transvestites on the Elizabethan stage: An Oxford controversy?" *Sixteenth Century Journal* 5:95–120.

Birley, Anthony. 1976. *Lives of the Later Caesars.* NY: Penguin Classics.

Blacking, John. 1959. "Fictitious kinship amongst girls of the Venda of the Northern Transvaal." *Man* 59:255–58.

Blackwood, Beatrice. 1935. *Both Sides of the Buka Passage.* Oxford: Clarendon.

Blackwood, Evelyn. 1985. "Breaking the mirror: The construction of lesbianism in anthropological discourse on homosexuality." *JH* 11, 3/4:1–17.

———. 1995. "Falling in love with an-Other lesbian: Reflections on identity in fieldwork." In *Taboo,* ed. D. Kulick and M. Wilson, 51–75. London: Routledge.

———. 1996. "Reading sexuality across cultures: Lesbian studies in anthropology since 1980." Paper presented at the AAA annual meetings in San Francisco.

Blair, Emma H., and James A. Robertson. 1910. *The Philippine Islands, 1443–1803.* 54 vols. Cleveland: Arthur H. Clark.

Blanch, Lesley. 1983. *Pierre Loti: Portrait of an Escapist.* London: Collins.

Bleibtreu-Ehrenberg, Gisela. 1990. "Pederasty among primitives." *JH* 20: 13–30.

Bleys, Rudi C. 1995. *The Geography of Perversion: Male-to-Male Sexual Behavior Outside the West and the Ethnographic Imagination, 1750–1918.* NY: New York University Press.

Bloch, Iwan. 1938 [1901]. *Sexual Life in England, Past and Present.* London: Francis Aldor.

Blount, Thomas. 1670. *Glossographia.* London: T. Newcomb. First ed., 1656.

Blumstein, Philip W., and Pepper Schwartz. 1983. *American Couples.* NY: Morrow.

Boas, Franz. 1905. "The Jesup North Pacific Expedition." *American Museum Journal* 3:72–119.

———. 1937. "Waldemar Bogoras." *AA* 39:314–15.

Boelaars, J. H. 1981. *Head Hunters about Themselves.* The Hague: Martinus Nijhoff.

Bogoraz, Vladimir [Bogoras, Waldemar G]. 1900. *Materials for the Study of Chukchee Language and Folklore Collected in the Kolyma District.* St. Petersburg: Imperial Academy of Science.

———. 1902. "The folklore of Northeastern Asia as compared to that of North-western America." *AA* 4:577–683.

———. 1904. *The Chukchee.* American Museum of Natural History Memoir ll,2.

Bolton, Ralph. 1991. "Mapping terra incognita: Sex research for AIDS prevention—An urgent agenda for the 1990s." In *The Time of AIDS,* ed. G. Herdt and S. Lindenbaum, 124–58. Newbury Park, CA: Sage.

Bornoff, Nicholas. 1991. *Pink Samurai: Love, Marriage and Sex in Contemporary Japan.* Tokyo: Pocket Books.

Boswell, John. 1980. *Christianity, Social Tolerance, and Homosexuality.* Chicago: University of Chicago Press.

———. 1990. "Concepts, experience and sexuality." In *Forms of Desire,* ed. E. Stein, 133–74. NY: Garland.

Bouge, L-J. 1955. "Un aspect du rôle rituel du 'mahu' dans l'ancien Tahiti." *Journal de la Société des Océanistes* 11:147–49.

Bouhdiba, Adelwahib. 1985. *Sexuality in Islam.* Boston: Routledge & Kegan Paul.

Bourguignon, Erika. 1968. "World distribution and patterns of possession states." In *Trance and Possession States,* ed. R. Price, 3–34. Montréal: R. M. Bucke.

Bowie, Theodore. 1970. *Studies in Erotic Art.* NY: Basic Books.

Bradford, Nicholas J. 1983. "Transgenderism and the cult of Yellamma: Heat, sex, and sickness in South Indian ritual." *Journal of Anthropological Research* 39:307–22.

Braiterman, Jared. 1990. "Fighting AIDS in Brazil." *Gay Community News* 17, 39. Quoted from its reprinting in *Coming Out,* ed. S. Likosky, 295–307. NY: Pantheon.

———. 1992. "Beauty in flight: Rio and beyond." *Whorezine* 15:9–11.

Bram, Jean Rhys. 1975. *Ancient Astrology Theory and Practice: Matheseos Libri VIII by Firmicus Maternus.* Park Ridge, NJ: Noyes Classical Studies.

Brandes, Stanley. 1981. "Like wounded stags: Male sexual ideology in an Andalusian town." In *Sexual Meaning*, ed. S. Ortner and H. Whitehead, 216–39. NY: Cambridge University Press.

Brandon, James R. 1975. *Kabuki: Five Classic Plays*. Cambridge, MA: Harvard University Press.

Brantôme, Pierre de Bourdeille. 1965 [ca. 1610]. *The Lives of Gallant Ladies*, London: Panther Book.

Bray, Alan. 1982. *Homosexuality in Renaissance England*. London: Gay Men's Press.

———. 1990. "Homosexuality and the signs of male friendship in Elizabethan England." *History Workshop Journal* 29:1–19.

———. 1993. "Historians and sexualities." *Journal of British Studies* 32:189–94.

Braybrooke, Neville. 1975. *The Ackerley Letters*. NY: Harcourt, Brace, Jovanovich.

Bredbeck, Gregory W. 1991. *Sodomy and Interpretation: Marlowe to Milton*. Ithaca, NY: Cornell University Press.

———. 1992. "Tradition and the individual sodomite: Barnfield, Shakespeare, and subjective desire." *JH* 23, 1:41–68.

Bremmer, Jan. 1979. "The legend of Cybele's arrival in Rome." In *Studies in Hellenistic Religions*, ed. M. J. Vermaseren, 9–22. Leiden: Brill.

———. 1980. "An enigmatic Indo-European rite: Paederasty." *Arethusa* 13:279–98.

Breton, Raymond. 1964. "Institutional completeness of ethnic communities." *AJS* 70:195–205.

Brodsky, Joel I. 1993. "The Mineshaft: A retrospective ethnography." *JH* 24:233–51.

Brooks, Beatrice A. 1941. "Fertility cult functionaries in the Old Testament." *Journal of Biblical Literature* 60:227–53.

Brooten, Bernadette J. 1996. *Love between Women*. Chicago: University of Chicago Press.

Brown, Judith C. 1986. *Immodest Acts: The Life of a Lesbian Nun in Renaissance Italy*. Oxford: Oxford University Press.

Brown, Roger. 1996. *Against My Better Judgment: An Intimate Memoir of an Eminent Gay Psychologist*. Binghamton, NY: Harrington Park.

Brown, Roger, and Albert Gilman. 1960. "The Pronouns of Power and Solidarity." In *Style in Language*, ed. T. Sebeok, 253–76. Cambridge: MIT Press.

Browne, Edward G. 1920, 1956. *A History of Persian Literature: The Tartar Dominion, 1265–1502*. NY: Cambridge University Press.

Browne, W. G. 1806. *Travels in Africa, Egypt and Syria from the Year 1792 to 1798*. London: T. Cadell and W. Davies.

Bruckner, Gene. 1971. *The Society of Renaissance Florence*. NY: Harper & Row.

Bryk, Felix. 1939. *Dark Rapture: The Sex-Life of the African Negro*. NY: Walden.

Buckingham, James Silk. 1827. *Travels in Mesopotamia*. London: Henry Colburn.

Buckley, Sandra. 1991. "'Penguin in bondage': A graphic tale of Japanese comic books." *Cultural Politics* 3:163–83.

Buffière, F. 1980. *Eros adolescent: La pederastie dans le Grèce antique*. Paris: Belles Lettres.

Bullough, Vern L. 1976. *Sexual Variance in Society and History*. NY: Wiley.

Bullough, Vern L., and James Brundage. 1982. *Sexual Practices and the Medieval Church*. Buffalo: Prometheus.

Burg, B. R. 1983. *Sodomy and the Perception of Evil.* NY: New York University Press.

Burke, Christopher. 1983. "Gay life in Japan: Interview with activist Ken Togo." *Advocate* 359 (6 Jan.): 39–41.

Burkert, Walter. 1987. *Ancient Mystery Cults.* Cambridge: Harvard University Press.

Burton, Richard Francis. 1864. *Mission to Gelele, King of Dahome.* London: Tinsley Brothers.

———. 1930 [1886]. *The Sotadic Zone.* NY: Panurge Press.

Buruma, Ian. 1984. *Behind the Mask.* NY: Meridian.

Busbecq, Ogier Ghiselin de. 1968. [1554–62]. *The Turkish Letters.* Translation. Oxford: Clarendon.

Cabezón, José I. 1993. "Homosexuality and Buddhism." In *Homosexuality and World Religions,* ed. A. Swidler, 81–101. Valley Forge, PA: Trinity.

Cáceres P., Carlos. Eduardo Gotuzzo, Stephen Wignall, and Miguel Campos. 1991. "Sexual behavior and frequency of antibodies to HIV-1 in a group of Peruvian male homosexuals." *Bulletin of the Pan-American Health Organization* 25:306–19.

Cady, Joseph. 1992. "'Masculine love,' Renaissance writing, and the 'new invention' of homosexuality. *JH* 23, 1:9–40.

———. 1996. "The 'masculine love' of the 'princes of Sodom' 'practicing the art of Ganymede' at Henry III's court." In *Desire and Discipline: Sex and Sexuality in the Premodern West,* ed. J. Murray and K. Eisenbichler, 123–54. Toronto: University of Toronto Press.

Cahen, Claude. 1970. "Note sur l'esclave musulman et la devshirme ottoman à propos de travaux récents." *Journal of the Economic and Social History of the Orient* 13:211–18.

Calame, Claude. 1977. *Les choeurs de jeunes filles en grèce archaïque.* Rome: Edizioni dell'Ateneo and Bizzarri.

Calasso, Roberto. 1995. "The marriage of Cadmus and Harmony." In *The Penguin Book of International Gay Writing,* ed. M. Mitchell, 498–527. New York: Viking.

Caminha, Adolfo. 1979 [1895]. "Bom-Crioulo." In Leyland (1979:82–96).

Cantarella, Eva. 1992 [1988]. *Bisexuality in the Ancient World.* New Haven, CT: Yale University Press.

Cao Xueqin, and Gao E. 1987. *The Story of the Stone.* 5 vols. Hammondsworth: Penguin.

Carey, Peter, and Vincent Houben. 1987. "Spirited Srikandhis and sly Sumbadras: The social and economic role of women at the Central Javanese courts in the eighteenth and early nineteenth centuries." In *Indonesian Women in Focus,* ed. E. Locher-Scholten and A. Niehof, 12–42. Dordrecht: Foris.

Carneiro, Edison. 1940. "The structure of African cults in Bahia." *Journal of American Folklore* 53:271–78.

———. 1954. *Candomblés da Bahia.* Rio de Janeiro: Andes. First ed., 1948.

Caron, François. 1671. *A True Description of the Mighty Kingdoms of Japan.* London: Robert Boulter.

Carrier, Joseph M. 1972. *Urban Mexican Male Homosexual Encounters,* Ph.D. diss., University of California, Irvine.

———. 1976. "Cultural factors affecting urban Mexican male homosexual behavior." *ASB* 5:103–24.

———. 1989. "Sexual behavior and the spread of AIDS in México." *Medical Anthropology* 10:129–42.

———. 1995. *De los Otros: Mexican Male Homosexual Encounters.* NY: Columbia University Press.

Carrier, Joseph M., and Stephen O. Murray. 1998. "Woman-woman marriage in Africa." Murray and Roscoe 1998:255–66.

Carrière, Jean. 1948. *Théognis de Megare.* Diss. Université de Paris.

Carrington, Christopher. 1999. *No Place Like Home: Relationships and Family Life among Lesbians and Gay Men.* Chicago: University of Chicago Press.

Carstairs, George Morrisson. 1956. "*Hinjra* and *jiryan:* Two derivations of Hindu attitudes to sexuality." *British Journal of Medical Psychology* 29:128–38.

———. 1960. "'Mother India' of the intelligentsia: A reply to Opler's review." *American Anthropologist* 62:504.

———. 1967 [1957]. *The Twice Born: A Study of a Community of High-Caste Hindus.* Bloomington: Indiana University Press.

Cartledge, Paul. 1981a. "The politics of Spartan pederasty." *Proceedings of the Cambridge Philological Society* 27:17–36.

———. 1981b. "Spartan wives." *Classical Quarterly* 75:84–105.

———. 1994. *Lakonia: A Regional History, 1300–362 B.C.* Boston: Routledge & Kegan Paul.

Ceballos Maldonado, José. 1969. *Después de todo.* México: Premiá.

Chabot, Hendrik Theodorus. 1965 (1959). *Kinship, Status and Sex in the South Celebes.* New Haven, CT: Human Relation Area Files.

Chagnon, Napoleon A. 1967. "Yanomamo Warfare, Social Organization and Marriage Alliance." Ph.D. diss., University of Michigan.

———. 1977. *Yanomamo.* NY: Holt, Rinehart and Winston.

Chambers, Mortimer. 1963. *The Fall of Rome.* NY: Holt, Rinehart and Winston.

Chandruang, Kumut. 1940. *My Boyhood in Siam.* NY: John Day.

Chard, Chester S. 1961. "Sternberg's materials on the sexual life of the Gilyak." *Anthropological Papers of the University of Alaska* 10:13–24.

Chauncey, George W. Jr. 1982. "From sexual inversion to homosexuality." *Salmagundi* 58:114–46.

———. 1985. "Christian brotherhood or sexual perversion? Homosexual identities and the construction of sexual boundaries in the World War One era." *Journal of Social History* 19:189–211.

———. 1994. *Gay New York: Gender, Urban Culture and the Making of the Gay Male World, 1890–1940.* NY: Basic Books.

Cherry, Kittredge. 1987. *Womansword.* NY: Kodansha.

———. 1992. "Japanese lesbian life." In Murray (1997a:407–08).

Childs, Maggie. 1977. "Japan's homosexual heritage." *Gai Saber* 1:41–45.

———. 1980. "*Chigo Monogatori:* Love stories or Buddhist sermons?" *Monumenta Nipponica* 35:127–51.

Chiñas, Beverly. N. 1995. "Isthmus Zapotec attitudes toward sex and gender anomalies." In Murray (1995a:293–302).

Chittick, William C. 1983. *The Sufi Path of Love: The Spiritual Teachings of Rumi.* Albany: State University of New York Press.

Chocrón, Isaac. 1972. *Pájaro de mar por tierra.* Caracas: Tiempo Nuevo.

Chojnacki, Stanley. 1972. "Crime, Punishment and the Trecento Venetian State." In *Violence and Civil Disorders in Italian Cities,* ed. L. Martines, 184–228. Berkeley: University of California Press.

Choy Bong-Youn. 1971. *Korea.* Tokyo: C. E. Tuttle.

Christ, Johann Friedrich. 1727. *Historia Legis Scantiniae.* Halle an der Saale: C. Krebs.

Christowe, Stoyan. 1941. *The Lion of Yanina: A narrative based on the life of Ali Pasha, Despot of Epirus.* NY: Modern Age Books.

Churchill, Wainwright. 1967. *Homosexual Behavior among Males.* NY: Hawthorn.

Cieza de Léon, Pedro. 1959 [1553]. *The Incas.* Norman: University of Oklahoma Press.

Clark, Ross. 1979. "Language." In *Prehistory of Polynesia,* ed. J. Jennings, 249–70. Cambridge: Harvard University Press.

Clarke, John R. 1991. "The decor of the House of Jupiter and Ganymede at Ostia Antica: Private residence turned gay hotel?" In *Roman Art in the Private Sphere,* ed. E. Gazda, 89–104. Ann Arbor: University of Michigan Press.

———. 1998. *Looking at Lovemaking: Constructions of Sexuality in Roman Art, 100 B.C.–A.D. 250.* Berkeley: University of California Press.

Clarke, W. N. 1978. "Akhilles and Patroclus in love." *Hermes* 106:381–96.

Clastres, Pierre. 1972. *Chronique des Indiens Guayaki.* Paris: Plon.

———. 1974. *La Société contre l'état.* Paris: Éditions de Minuit.

———. 1977. "The bow and the basket." In *Society against the State,* 83–107. NY: Urizen. Translation of Clastres 1974.

Cohen, David. 1991. *Law, Sexuality, and Society: The Enforcement of Morals in Classical Athens.* NY: Cambridge University Press.

Cohen, Lawrence. 1995. "The pleasures of castration: The postoperative status of hijras, jankhas and academics." In *Sexual Nature, Sexual Culture,* ed. P. Abramson and S. Pinkerton, 276–304. Chicago: University of Chicago Press.

Colcutt, Martin. 1981. *Five Mountains: The Rinzai Zen Monastic Institution in Medieval Japan.* Cambridge, MA: Council on East Asian Studies.

Cole, Fay-Cooper. 1922. *The Tinguian.* Chicago: Field Museum Publication 209.

———. 1945. *The Peoples of Malaysia.* NY: Van Nostrand.

Coleman, Eli, Philip Colgan, and Louis Gooren. 1992. "Male cross-gender behavior in Myanmar (Burma): A description of the acault. *ASB* 21:313–21.

Colin, Jean. 1965. "Juvenal et le mariage mystique de Gracchus." *Atti dell' Accademia delle scienze di Torino* 90:114–216.

Colson, Elizabeth. 1958. *Marriage and the Family Among the Plateau Tonga of Northern Rhodesia.* Manchester: Manchester University Press.

Coon, Carleton S. 1931. *Tribes of the Rif. Harvard African Studies* 9.

Cooper, John M. 1946. "The Araucanians." *Handbook of South American Indians* 2:687–760.

Cooper, Michael. 1965. *They Came to Japan: An Anthology of European Reports on Japan, 1543–1640.* Berkeley: University of California Press.

Cory, Donald Webster [Edward Sagarin]. 1963 [1951]. *The Homosexual in America*. NY: Paperback Library.

Coxon, Anthony P. 1996. *Between the Sheets: Sexual Diaries and Gay Men's Sex in the Era of AIDS*. London: Cassell.

Crapanzano, Vincent. 1973. *The Hamadsha*. Berkeley: University of California Press.

———. 1980. *Tuhami: Portrait of a Moroccan*. Chicago: University of Chicago Press.

Creasy, Edward S. 1877. *History of the Ottoman Turks*. London: Bentley.

Creed, Gerald W. 1984. "Sexual subordination: Institutionalized homosexuality and social control in Melanesia." *Ethnology* 23:157–76.

Crompton, Louis. 1978. "Gay genocide from Leviticus to Hitler." In *The Gay Academic*, ed. L. Crew, 67–91. Palm Springs, CA: ETC.

———. 1980. "The myth of lesbian impunity." *JH* 6, 1/2:11–25.

———. 1985. *Byron and Greek Love: Homophobia in Nineteenth-Century England*. Berkeley: University of California Press.

———. 1994. "The Theban Band." *History Today* 44, 11:23–29.

———. 1996. "France: from Calvin to Louis XIV." Manuscript chapter 11 from *Homosexuality and Civilization*.

Curb, Rosemary, and Nancy Manahan. 1985. *Lesbian Nuns*. Tallahassee, FL: Naiad.

Cureau, Adolphe Louis. 1904. Essai sur la psychologie des races nègres de l'Afrique Tropicale." *Revue générale des sciences pures et appliquées* 15:638–95.

Czaplicka, Marie. 1914. *Aboriginal Siberia*. Oxford: Clarendon.

Dall'Orto, Giovanni. 1983. "Antonio Rocco and the background of his *L'Alcibiade Fanciullo a Scola*." *Among Men/Among Women* 1:224–32.

———. 1988. "'Socratic love' as a disguise for same-sex love in the Italian Renaissance." *JH* 16:33–66.

Damata, Gasparino [Gasparino de Mata e Silva]. 1976. *Os solteirões*. Rio de Janeiro: Pallas.

———. 1983 [1976]. "The volunteer." In Leyland. (1983:151–63).

Daniel, Marc. 1959. "Les amants du soleil levant." *Arcadie* 66:246–51.

———. 1977. "Arab civilization and male love." *Gay Sunshine* 21:1–11, 27.

Daniel, Norman. 1975. *The Arabs and Medieval Europe*. London: Longman.

Danielsson, Bengt. 1956. *Love in the South Seas*. NY: Dell.

Danielsson, Bengt, and Marie T. Danielsson. 1978. "Polynesia's third sex." *Pacific Islands Monthly*, Aug:10–11.

Danly, Robert L. 1990. Review of Schalow 1990. *Journal of Asian Studies* 29:940–41.

Darmesteter, James. 1880. *The Zend-Avesta*. Oxford: Clarendon. Reprinted in three volumes. Westport, CT: Greenwood, 1972.

Davenport, Guy. 1965. *Sappho*. Ann Arbor: University of Michigan Press.

Davenport, William H. 1965. "Sexual patterns and their regulation in a society of the Southwest Pacific." In *Sex and Behavior*, ed. F. Beach, 164–207. NY: Wiley.

———. 1977. "Sex in cross-cultural perspective." In *Human Sexuality*, ed. F. Beach, 155–63. NY: Wiley.

Davey, Richard. 1897. *The Sultan and his Subjects*. London: Chapman and Hall.
Davidson, Michael. 1988 [1970]. *Some Boys*. London: Gay Men's Press.
Deacon, A. Bernard. 1934. *Malekula*. London: Routledge.
Dearing, James W. 1992. "Foreign blood and domestic politics: The issue of AIDS in Japan." In *AIDS: The Making of a Chronic Disease*, ed. E. Fee and D. Fox, 326–44. Berkeley: University of California Press.
De Martino, Gianni. 1983. "An Italian in Morocco." In Sofer and Schmitt (1992:25–32).
D'Emilio, John. 1983. *Sexual Politics, Sexual Communities*. Chicago: University of Chicago Press.
Devereux, George. 1937. "Institutionalized homosexuality of the Mohave." *Human Biology* 9:498–527.
Devi, Shakuntala. 1977. *The World of Homosexuals*. New Delhi: Vikas.
DeVos, George. 1973. *Socialization for Achievement*. Berkeley: University of California Press.
———. 1978. "The Japanese adapt to change." *The Makings of Psychological Anthropology*, ed. G. Spindler, 217–57. Berkeley: University of California Press.
DeVries, Keith. 1990. "Homosexuality and Athenian Democracy." Unpublished manuscript being revised for publication by Oxford University Press.
———. 1993. "The 'frigid eromenoi' and their wooers revisited: a closer look at Greek homosexuality in vase paintings." Paper presented at CLAGS conference, New York City, 2 Dec.
Dickemann, Mildred. 1993. "Reproductive strategies and gender construction: An evolutionary view of homosexuality." *JH* 24:55–71.
———. 1997. "The Balkan sworn-virigin." In Murray and Roscoe (1997: 197–203).
Doi Takeo. 1973. *The Anatomy of Dependence*. Tokyo: Kodansha.
Domingos, Jorge. 1983. "The wedding for the king of spades." In Leyland. (1983:297–313).
Donoso, José. 1966. *El jugar sin límites*. México: Joaquín Mortiz.
Douneau, Frank. 1988. "A Tokyo guide for *gaijins*." *Advocate* (15 March) 32–34.
Dover, Kenneth J. 1966a. "Aristophanes's speech in Palto's *Symposium*." *Journal of Hellenic Studies* 86:41–50.
———. 1966b. "Eros and nomos." *Bulletin of the Institute of Classical Studies* 11:41–50.
———. 1972. *Aristophanic Comedy*. Berkeley: University of California Press.
———. 1975. *Greek Popular Morality in the Time of Plato and Aristotle*. Berkeley: University of California Press.
———. 1978. *Greek Homosexuality*. Cambridge: Harvard University Press.
———. 1988. *The Greeks and Their Legacy*. NY: Basil Blackwell.
Dowling, Christine. 1989. *Myths and Mysteries of Same-Sex Love*. NY: Continuum.
Drabkin, I. E. 1950. *On Acute Diseases and on Chronic Diseases*. Chicago: University of Chicago Press. Translation of *De morbis acutis & chronicis libri*, Caelius Aurelianus's Latin translation and elaboration of the now-lost Greek treatise by Soranus of Ephesus.
Drake, Christopher. 1991. "Mirroring Saikaku." *Monumenta Nipponica* 46: 513–41.

Drake, Jonathan [Parker Rossman]. 1966. "'Le Vice' in Turkey." *International Journal of Greek Love* 1:13–27. Reprinted in *Asian Homosexuality*, ed. W. Dynes and S. Donaldson, 27–41, NY: Garland, 1992.

DuBois, Cora. 1944. *The People of Alor*. Minneapolis: University of Minnesota Press.

Ducey, Charles. 1976. "The life history and creative psychopathology of the shaman." *Psychoanalytic Study of Society* 7:173–230.

Duchesne-Guillemin, Jacques. 1966. *Symbols and Values in Zoroastrianism*. NY: Harper & Row.

Dumézil, Georges. 1969. *Heur et malheur de guerrier*. Paris: Payot.

———. 1986. Preface to Sergent (1986), vii–ix.

Duncan, Robert. 1944. "The homosexual in society." *Politics* 1, 7:209–11. Reprinted in Ekbert Faas, *Young Robert Duncan*, Santa Barbara CA: Black Sparrow, 1983, 319–22.

Dundes, Alan, Jerry W. Leach, and Bora Özkök. 1972. "The strategy of Turkish boys' verbal dueling rhymes." In *Directions in Sociolinguistics: The Ethnography of Communication*, ed. J. Gumperz and D. Hymes, 130–60. NY: Holt, Rinehart, and Winston.

Dunne, Bruce W. 1990. "Homosexuality in the Middle East." *Arab Studies Quarterly* 12, 3:55–82.

DuToit, Brian M. 1975. *Akuna*. Rotterdam: Bakema.

Duvert, Tony. 1976. *Journal d'un innocent*. Paris: Editions de Minuit.

Dyer, Richard. 1993. *The Matter of Images*. London: Routledge.

Dynes, Wayne R. 1976. "Tradition and innovation in medieval art." In *Medieval Studies*, ed. J. Powell, 313–42. Syracuse, NY: Syracuse University Press.

———. 1978. "Orpheus without Eurydice." *Gai Saber* 1, 3/4:267–73.

———. 1981. "Privacy, sexual orientation and self-sovereignty of the individual." *Gay Books Bulletin* 6:20–23.

———. 1985. *Homolexis*. NY: Gay Academic Union (*=Gai Saber Monograph* 4).

———. 1987, 1995. "Portugayese." In Murray (1987:183–91) and Murray (1995a:256–63).

———. 1990a. "Aristocratic Vice." In *Encyclopedia of Homosexuality*, ed. W. Dynes, 74–75. NY: Garland.

———. 1990b. "Wrestling with the social boa constructor." In *Forms of Desire*, ed. E. Stein, 209–38. NY: Garland.

Dynes, Wayne R., and Warren Johansson. 1984. "London's medieval sodomites." *Cabirion* 10:5–7, 34.

Edwardes, Allen. 1959. *The Jewel in the Lotus: A Historical Survey of the Sexual Culture of the East*. NY: Julian.

Edwards, Catherine. 1993. *The Politics of Immorality in Ancient Rome*. NY: Cambridge University Press.

Egerton, Clement. 1939. *The Golden Lotus*. 4 vols. London: Routledge.

Eickelman, Dale F. 1981. *The Middle East: An Anthropological Approach*. Toronto: Prentice-Hall.

Eissler, Kurt R. 1961. *Leonardo da Vinci: Psychoanalytic Notes on the Enigma*. NY: International Universities Press.

Ellis, Alfred B. 1965 [1890]. *The Ewe-Speaking Peoples of the Slave Coast of West Africa*. London: Chapman and Hall.

Elvin, Mark. 1985. Between the earth and heaven: Conceptions of the self in China." In *The Category of the Person,* ed. M. Carrithers, S. Collins, and S. Lukes, 156–89. New York: Cambridge University Press.

Eppink, Andreas. 1977. "Moroccan boys and sex." In Sofer and Schmitt (1992: 33–41).

Epprecht, Mark. 1998a. "'Good God Almighty, what's this!': Homosexual 'crime' in early colonial Zimbabwe." In Murray and Roscoe (1998:197–222).

———. 1998b."The 'unsaying' of indigenous homosexualities in Zimbabwe." *Journal of Southern African Studies* 24:631–51.

Erickson, Peter, and Coppélia Kahn. 1985. *Shakespeare's "Rough Magic": Renaissance Essays in Honor of C. L. Barber.* Newark, NJ: University of Delaware Press.

Erikson, Erik H. 1963. *Childhood and Society.* New York: Norton. First ed., 1950.

Eriksson, Brigitte. 1980. "A lesbian execution in Germany, 1721." *Journal of Homosexuality* 6, 1/2:27–40.

Ernst, Earle. 1974. *The Kabuki Theater.* Honolulu: University of Hawaii Press.

Ernst, Thomas M. 1991. "Onabasulu male homosexuality: Cosmology, affect, and prescribed homosexual activity among the Onabasulu of the Great Papual Plateau." *Oceania* 62:1–11.

Ersine, Noel. 1933. *Dictionary of Underworld Slang.* Upland, IN: A. D. Freese.

Estermann, Carlos. 1976. *The Ethnography of Southwest Angola.* New York: Africana.

Evans-Pritchard, Edward E. 1970. "Sexual inversion among the Azande." *AA* 72:1428–34.

———. 1971. *The Azande.* Oxford: Clarendon Press.

Faderman, Lillian. 1978. "The morbidification of love between women by nineteenth-century sexologists." *JH* 4:73–98.

———. 1981. *Surpassing the Love of Men.* NY: Morrow.

———. 1991. *Odd Girls and Twilight Lovers: A History of Lesbian Life in Twentieth-Century America.* NY: Columbia University Press.

———. 1992. "The return of butch and femme." *Journal of the History of Sexuality* 2:578–96.

Fairbanks, John King, and Edwin O. Reischauer. 1960. *East Asia: The Great Tradition.* Boston: Houghton Mifflin.

Falk, Kurt. 1925. "Homosexualität bei den Eingeborenen in Südwest-Afrika." *Geschlecht und Gesselschaft* 13:209–11. Translated in Murray and Roscoe (1998:187–96.)

Falkner, Thomas. 1774. *A Description of Patagonia and the Adjoining Parts of South America.* London: C. Pugh. Facsimile ed. with notes by Arthur Neumann, Chicago: Armann & Armann, 1935.

Fantham, Elaine. 1991. "*Stuprum:* Public attitudes and penalties for sexual offences in Republican Rome." *Échos du Monde Classique* 35:267–91.

Farnell, Lewis R. 1896. *Cults of the Greek States.* Vol. 1. Oxford: Clarendon.

Faron, Louis C. 1964. *Hawks of the Sun.* Pittsburgh: University of Pittsburgh Press.

Fasce, Silvana. 1978. *Attis e il culto metroaco a Roma.* Genova: Tilgher.

Feinberg, Leslie. 1993. *Stone Butch Blues.* Ithaca, NY: Firebrand.

Feldman, Harry. 1981. "Kapekape: Contexts of malediction in Tonga." *Maledicta* 5:143–50.

Fellows, Will. 1997. *Farm Boys*. Madison: University of Wisconsin Press.

Fernández Alemany, Manuel. 1999. An Ethnography of the Macho/Loca Relationship. Ph.D. diss., University of Southern California.

Feuerstein, G., and S. al-Marzooq. 1978. "Omani *xanith.*" *Man* 13:665–67.

Fiedler, Leslie. 1972. *The Stranger in Shakespeare*. NY: Stein and Day.

Fillmore, Charles J. 1975. "An alternative to checklist theories of meaning." *Proceedings of the Berkeley Linguistic Society* 1:123–31.

Fineanganofa, Longosai. 1978. "I was born to be like this." *Pacific Islands Monthly*, Aug.:12–13.

Finley, Moses I. 1980. *Ancient Slavery and Modern Ideology*. NY: Viking.

Firth, Raymond. 1936. *We, the Tikopia*. London: Allen & Unwin.

Fitzpatrick, William. 1955. *Tokyo After Dark*. NY: Macfadden.

Flaubert, Gustave. 1973. *Correspondence I, 1830–1851*. Paris: Gallimard.

Fletcher, Alice. 1884. "The elk mystery or festival of the Ogallala Sioux." *Reports of the Peabody Museum of American Archaeology and Ethnology* 5, 3:276–88.

Floor, Willem M. 1971. "The *Lutis:* A social phenomenon in Qajar Persia." *Die Weld des Islams* 13:103–21.

Ford, Charles Henri, and Parker Tyler. 1933. *The Young and the Evil*. Paris: Obelisk.

Ford, Clellan S., and Frank A. Beach. 1951. *Patterns of Sexual Behavior*. NY: Harper & Row.

Forker, Charles R. 1990. "Sexuality and eroticism on the Renaissance stage." *South Central Review* 7, 4:1–22.

———. 1996. "'Masculine love,' Renaissance writing and the 'new invention' of homosexuality." *JH* 31, 3:85–93.

Foster, David William. 1991. *Gay and Lesbian Themes in Latin American Literature*. Austin: University of Texas Press.

Foster, Herbert Baldwin. 1906. *Dio's Rome*. Vol. 6. Troy, NY: Pafraets.

Foucault, Michel. 1980. *The History of Sexuality*. NY: Vintage.

———. 1986. *The Use of Pleasure*. NY: Vintage.

Freed, Stanley A., Ruth S. Freed, and Lalia Williamson. 1988. "Capitalist philanthropy and Russian revolutionaries: The Jesup North Pacific Expedition (1897–1902)." *AA* 90:7–24.

Freeman, Derek J. 1983. *Margaret Mead and Samoa*. Cambridge: Harvard University of Press.

———. 1998. *The Fateful Hoaxing of Margaret Mead*. Boulder, CO: Westview.

Freeman, James M. 1979. *Untouchable: An Indian Life History*. Stanford, CA: Stanford University Press.

Friedl, Ernestine. 1994. "Sex the invisible." *AA* 96:833–44.

Friedrich, Paul. 1966. "Structural implications of Russian pronominal usage." In *Sociolinguistics*, ed. W. Bright, 214–49. The Hague: Mouton.

———. 1978. *The Meaning of Aphrodite*. Chicago: University of Chicago Press.

Frommel, Christopher L. 1979. *Michelangelo und Tommaso de' Cavalieri*. Amsterdam: Castrum Peregrini.

Fry, Peter. 1987 [1974]. "Male homosexuality and Afro-Brazilian possession cults." In Murray (1987:55–91) and Murray (1995a:193–220).

Frymer-Kensky, Tyka. 1992. *In the Wake of the Goddesses*. New York: Free Press.

Fusco, Domenico. 1953. *L'Aretino sconosciuto e apocrifo*. Turin: Berruto.

Gagnon, John, and William Simon. 1973. *Sexual Conduct.* Chicago: Aldine.

Gamboa, Victor, and Henry J. Feenstra. 1969. "Deviant stereotypes: Call-girls, male homosexuals and lesbians." *Philippine Sociological Review* 16:136–48.

García G., María de Lourdes, José Valdespino, José Izazola, Manuel Palacios, and Jaime Sepúlveda. 1991. "Bisexuality in Mexico." In *Bisexuality & HIV/AIDS,* ed. R. Tielman, M. Carballo, and A. Hendriks, 41–58. Buffalo, NY: Prometheus.

Gardiner, Kenneth H. J. 1969. *The Early History of Korea.* Honolulu: University of Hawai'i Press.

Gasparro, Giulia S. 1985. *Soteriology and Mystic Aspects in the Cult of Cybele and Attis.* Leiden: E. J. Brill.

Gaudio, Rudolf P. 1996. "Unreal women and the men who love them." *Socialist Review* 121–36.

———. 1998. "Male lesbians and other queer notions in Hausa." In Murray and Roscoe (1998:115–28).

Gay, Judith. 1985. "'Mummies and babies' and friends and lovers in Lesotho." *JH* 11:97–116.

Gayatri, B. J. D. 1993. "Coming out but remaining hidden: A portrait of lesbians in Java." Paper presented at the International Congress of Anthropological and Ethnological Sciences in México, D. F.

Gays and Lesbians Aboriginal Alliance. 1994. "Peopling the empty mirror: The prospects for lesbian and gay aboriginal history." *Gay Perspectives II,* ed. R. Aldrich, 1–62. Sydney: Australian Centre for Gay and Lesbian Research.

Gerard, Kent. 1988. *The Pursuit of Sodomy in Renaissance and Enlightenment Europe.* New York: Harrington Park (*=JH* 16, 1).

Gevisser, Mark. 1995. "A different fight for freedom: A history of South African lesbian and gay organisation from the 1950s to the 1990s." In Gevisser and Cameron (1995:14–86).

Gevisser, Mark, and Edwin Cameron. 1995. *Defiant Desire: Gay and Lesbian Lives in South Africa.* NY: Routledge.

Ghanem, 'Ali. 1986. *The Seven-Headed Serpent.* NY: Harcourt, Brace, Jovanovich.

Giffen, Lois Anita. 1971. *Theory of Profane Love among the Arabs: The Development of the Genre.* NY: New York University Press.

Gifford, Edward W. 1929. *Tongan Society.* Honolulu: Bishop Museum.

Gilmore, David D. 1990a. *Manhood in the Making: Cultural Concepts of Masculinity.* New Haven, CT: Yale University Press.

———. 1990b. "Men and women in Southern Spain: 'Domestic power' revisited." *AA* 92:953–70.

Ginarte, Lucio. 1983 [1960]. "Orgy." In Leyland (1983:15–52).

Glazer, Mark. 1976. "On verbal dueling among Turkish boys." *Journal of American Folklore* 89:88–91.

Gleason, Maud W. 1990. "The semiotics of gender: Physiognomy and self-fashioning in the second century C.E." In *Before Sexualtiy,* ed. D. Halperin, J. Winkler, and F. Zeitlin, 389–415. Princeton, NJ: Princeton University Press.

———. 1995. *Making Men: Sophists and Self-Presentation in Ancient Rome.* Princeton, NJ: Princeton University Press.

Glubb, John B. 1973. *Soldiers of Fortune.* Toronto: Hodder & Stoughton.

Gluckman, Laurie K. 1967. "Lesbianism in the Maori." *Australian & New Zealand Journal of Psychiatry* 1:98–103.

———. 1974. "Transcultural consideration of homosexuality with special reference to the New Zealand Maori." *Australian & New Zealand Journal of Psychiatry* 8:121–25.

Godelier, Maurice. 1982. *La Production des Grands Hommes.* Paris: Fayard.

———. 1986. *The Making of Great Men.* Cambridge: Cambridge University Press.

Goens, Rijklov van. 1956. *De Vijf Bezantschapsreizen van Rijklof van Goens naar het hof van Mataram, 1648–1654.* The Hague: Nijhoff.

Goffman, Erving. 1961. *Encounters.* Indianapolis: Bobbs-Merrill.

———. 1963. *Stigma.* Toronto: Prentice-Hall.

Goldberg, Jonathan. 1991. "Sodomy in the new world: Anthropologies old and new." *Social Text* 29:45–56. Incorporated in Goldberg (1992:179–93).

———. 1992. *Sodometries.* Stanford, CA: Stanford University Press.

Goldstein, Melvyn C. 1964. "A study of the *Ldab ldob.*" *Central Asiatic Journal* 9:123–41.

———. 1989. *A History of Modern Tibet, 1913–1951: The Demise of the Lamaist State.* Berkeley: University of California Press.

Gombrowicz, Witold. 1988 [1953–56]. *Diary, 1953–56.* Evanston, IL: Northwestern University Press.

Gomes, Edwin H. 1911. *Seventeen Years among the Sea Dyaks of Borneo.* London: Seeley.

Gonfroy, Francoise. 1978. "Homosexualité et ideologie escalvagiste chez Ciceron." *Dialogues d'histoire ancienne* 4:219–65.

Goode, William J. 1960. "Role strain." *American Sociological Review* 25:483–96.

Goodenough, Ward H. 1990. "Evolution of the human capacity for beliefs." *AA* 92:597–612.

Goodich, Michael. 1979. *The Unmentionable Vice.* Santa Barbara, CA: Ross-Erikson.

Goody, Jack. 1977. *The Domestication of the Savage Mind.* NY: Cambridge University Press.

Graere, R. P. A. M. 1929. "L'art de guérir chez les Azande." *Congo* 1:361–582.

Grahn, Judy. 1984. *Another Mother Tongue: Gay Words, Gay Worlds.* Boston: Beacon.

Grant, Michael. 1988. *The Rise of the Greeks.* NY: Scribner's.

Grayson, A. Kirk, and Donald B. Redford. 1974. *Papyrus and Tablet.* Toronto: Prentice-Hall.

Greci. 1930. "Benvenuto Cellini nei delitti e nei processi fiorentini, riconstruiti attraverso le leggi del tempo." *Archivio di antropologia criminale* 50:342–85, 509–42.

Green, Peter. 1973. *Ancient Greece: An Illustrated History.* London: Quartet.

Greenberg, David F. 1988. *The Construction of Homosexuality.* Chicago: University of Chicago Press.

———. 1995. "The pleasures of homosexuality." In *Sexual Nature, Sexual Culture,* ed. P. Abramson and S. Pinkerton, 223–56. Chicago: University of Chicago Press.

Greenberg, David F., and Marcia H. Bystryn. 1982. "Christian intolerance of homosexuality." *AJS* 87:515–48.

———. 1984. "Capitalism, bureaucracy and male homosexuality." *Contemporary Crises* 8:33–56.

Greenberg, Joseph H. 1941. "Some aspects of Negro-Mohammedan culture contact among the Hausa." *AA* 43:51–61.

Greenblatt, Stephen. 1988. *Shakespearean Negotiations: The Circulation of Social Energy in Renaissance England.* Oxford: Clarendon.

Griswold, Wendy. 1983. "The Devil's techniques." *American Sociological Review* 48:668–80.

Grube, John. 1986. "Queens and flaming virgins." *Rites* 2, 9:14–17.

———. 1990. "Natives and settlers: An ethnographic note on early interaction of older homosexual men with younger gay liberationists." *JH* 20:119–35.

Grunebaum, Gustave E. von. 1952. "The aesthetic foundation of Arabic Literature." *Comparative Literature* 4:323–40.

Guerra, Francisco. 1971. *The Pre-Columbian Mind.* London: Seminar Press.

Guiraud, Pierre. 1968. *Le jargon de Villon, ou le gay savoir de la coquille.* Paris: Gallimard.

Gundesheimer, Werner. 1972. "Crime and punishment in Ferrara." In *Violence and Civil Disorder in Italian Cities,* ed. L. Martines. Berkeley: University California Press.

Gunson, Niel. 1964. "Great women and friendship contract rites in prechristian Tahiti." *Journal of the Polynesian Society* 73:53–69.

Gunth, Christine. 1987. "The divine boy in Japanese art." *Monumenta Nipponica* 42:1–23.

Gutiérrez, Ramon A. 1997. Response. *Cultural Anthropology* 12:278–80.

Gutmanis, June. 1985. *Kahuna La'au Lap'au.* Honolulu: Island Heritage.

Guttman, Matthew C. 1996. *The Meanings of Macho: Being a Man in Mexico City.* Berkeley: University of California Press.

Hachimonjiya Jisho. 1969. *The Actor's Analects.* NY: Columbia University Press.

Haddad, Merv. 1992 [1973]. "The discreet charms of gay life in Japan." Murray (1992a:371–73).

Haddon, Alfred C., and Laura E. Stout. 1936. *Iban Sea Dyak Fabrics and Their Patterns.* Cambridge: Cambridge University Press.

Hage, Per. 1981. "On male initiation and dual organization in New Guinea." *Man* 16:268–75.

Hahn, Johann Georg von 1853. *Albanesische Studien.* Jena: Mauke.

Hall, Kira. 1995. "Hijra/Hijrin: Language and Gender Identity." Ph.D. diss., University of California, Berkeley.

———. 1997. "'Go suck your husband's sugarcane!': Hijras and the use of sexual insults." In *Queerly Phrased: Language, Gender, and Sexuality,* ed. A. Livia and K. Hall, 430–60. NY: Oxford University Press.

Hall, Lisa Kahaleole Chang, and J. Kehaulani Kauanui. 1994. "Same-sex sexuality in Pacific literature." *Amerasia* 20:75–81.

Hall, Radclyffe. 1928. *The Well of Loneliness.* Garden City, NY: Sun Dial.

Hallett, Judith P. 1989. "Female homoeroticism and the denial of Roman reality in Latin literature." *Yale Journal of Criticism* 3:209–27.

Halman, Talat Sait. 1983. "Love is all: Mevlana's poetry and philosophy." In *Medvlana Celaleddin Rumi and the Whirling Dervishes,* 9–46. Istanbul: Dost.

Halperin, David. 1986. "Plato and erotic reciprocity." *Classical Antiquity* 5:60–80.

———. 1990. *One Hundred Years of Homosexuality.* NY: Routledge.

———. 1991. Review of Schalow (1990a). *Journal of Japanese Studies* 17:398–403.

———. 1992. "Historicizing the sexual body: Sexual preferences and erotic identities in the Pseudo-Lucianic *Erōtes.*" In *Discourses of Sexuality from Aristotle to AIDS,* ed. D. Stanton, 236–61. Ann Arbor: University of Michigan Press.

———. 1996. "Homosexuality." In *The Oxford Classical Dictionary,* 3rd ed. Ed. S. Hornblower and A. Spawforth, 720–23. NY: Oxford University Press.

———. 1998. "Forgetting Foucault." *Representations* 63:93–120.

Hambly, Wilfred D. 1937. *Source Book for African Anthropology.* Chicago: Field Museum.

Handler, Richard. 1984. "On sociocultural discontinuity." *Current Anthropology* 25:55–71.

Handy, E. S. Craighill. 1923. *The Native Culture in the Marquesas. Bishop Museum Bulletin* 9.

Handy, E. S. Craighill, and Mary Kawena Pukui. 1978. *The Polynesian Family System in Ka'u, Hawaii.* Tokyo: Tuttle.

Harbage, Alfred. 1952. *Shakespeare and the Rival Traditions.* NY: Macmillan.

Hardman, Edward T. 1889. "Habits and Customs of the Natives of Kimberly, Western Australia." *Proceedings of the Royal Irish Academy,* 3rd series, 1:70–75.

Hare, Thomas B. 1986. *Zeami's Style: The Noh Plays of Zeami Motokiyo.* Stanford, CA: Stanford University Press.

Harrer, Heinrich. 1996 [1953]. *Seven Years in Tibet.* NY: Putnam.

Harries, Patrick. 1990. "Symbols and sexuality: Culture and identity in the early Witwatersrand mines." *Gender and History* 23:318–36.

———. 1993. "Through the eyes of the beholder: Junod and the notion of primitive." *Social Dynamics* 19:1–10.

Harry, Joseph. 1982a. *Gay Children Grown Up.* NY: Praeger.

———. 1982b. "Derivative deviance: The cases of fag-bashing, blackmail, and shakedown of gay men." *Criminology* 19:546–64.

Harry, Joseph, and William Devall. 1978. *The Social Organization of Gay Males.* NY: Praeger.

Hart, C. W. M. 1954. "The sons of Turimpi." *AA* 54:242–61.

Hart, Donn V. 1968. "Homosexuality and transvestism in the Philippines." *Behavioral Science Notes* 3:211–48. Reprinted in Murray (1992a:193–230.)

Hart, Donn V., and Harriet Hart. 1990. "Visayan Swardspeak: The language of a gay community in the Philippines." *Crossroads* 5:27–49.

Hatem, Mervat. 1986. "The politics of sexuality and gender in segregated patriarchal systems: The case of eighteenth and nineteenth century Egypt." *Feminist Studies* 12:251–74.

Hayes, Joseph J. 1976. "Gayspeak." *Quarterly Journal of Speech* 62:256–66.

———. 1981. "Lesbians, gay men and their 'languages.'" In *Gayspeak,* ed. J. Chesebro, 28–42. NY: Pilgrim.

Hecker Filho, Paulo. 1951. *Inernato*. Rio de Janeiro: Edição Fronteira. Trans. E. A. Lacey as "Boarding school." In Leyland (1983:245–66).

Heimann, Elliott M., and Cao Van Lê. 1975. "Transvestism in Vietnam." *ASB* 4:89–96.

Helms, Richard. 1896. "Anthropology." *Transactions of the Royal Society of South Australia* 16, 3:237–332.

Henderson, Jeffrey. 1991 [1975]. *The Maculate Muse: Obscene Language in Attic Comedy*. New Haven CT: Yale University Press.

Henriksson, Benny. 1995. *Risk Factor Love: Homosexuality, Sexual Interaction and HIV Prevention*. Göteborg, Sweden: Göteborgs Universitet Institutionen för socialt arbete.

Henshaw, Richard A. 1994. *Female and Male: The Cultic Personnel [in] the Bible and the Rest of the Ancient Near East*. Allison Park, PA: Pickwick.

Henthorn, William E. 1971. *A History of Korea*. NY: Free Press.

Herbert, Thomas. 1971 [1626]. *A Relation of Some Yeares Travaile into Afrique, Asia, and the Indies*. NY: Capo.

Herdt, Gilbert H. 1981. *Guardians of the Flute*. NY: Macmillan.

———. 1984. *Ritualized Homosexuality in Melanesia*. Berkeley: University of California Press.

———. 1987a. "Homosexuality." *Encyclopedia of Religion* 6:445–52. NY: Macmillan.

———. 1987b. "Introduction to the paperback edition." In *Guardians of the Flutes*, xiii–xvii. NY: Columbia University Press.

———. 1987c. *The Sambia: Ritual and Gender in New Guinea*. NY: Holt.

———. 1990a. "Developmental discontinuities and sexual orientation across cultures." In *Homosexuality/Heterosexuality: Concepts of Sexual Orientation*, ed. D. McWhirter, S. Sanders, and J. Reinisch, 208–36. NY: Oxford University Press.

———. 1990b. "Representations of homosexuality, I." *Journal of the History of Sexuality* 1:481–504.

———. 1991. "Representations of homosexuality, II." *Journal of the History of Sexuality* 1:603–32.

———. 1992a. Preface to the paperback edition of Herdt (1984), vii–xlii.

———. 1992b [1981]. "Semen depletion and the sense of maleness." In Murray (1992a:33–68).

———. 1994. *Third Sex, Third Gender*. London: Zone.

———. 1997. *Same Sex, Different Cultures*. Boulder, CO: Westview.

———. 1999. *Sambian Sexual Culture*. Chicago: University of Chicago Press.

Herdt, Gilbert H., and Andrew M. Boxer. 1993. *Children of Horizons*. Boston: Beacon.

Herdt, Gilbert H., and F. J. Poole. 1982. "Sexual antagonism." *Social Analysis* 12:3–28.

Herdt, Gilbert H., and Robert J. Stoller. 1990. *Intimate Communications*. NY: Columbia University Press.

Herek, Gregory M., and Kevin Berrill. 1992. *Hate Crimes: Confronting Violence against Lesbians and Gay Men*. London: Sage.

Hernández M., P. Uribe, S. Gortmake. C. Avila, L. E. De Caso, N. Mueller, and J. Sepulveda. 1992. "Sexual behavior and status for human immunodeficiency virus type-1 among homosexual and bisexual males in Mexico City." *American Journal of Epidemiology* 135:883–94.

Herrup, Cynthia. 1996. "The patriarch at home: The trial of the Second Earl of Castlehaven for rape and sodomy." *History Workshop Journal* 41:1–18.

Herskovits, Melville J. 1938. *Dahomey. An Ancient West African Kingdom.* NY: Augustine.

———. 1947. Review of Landes (1947). *AA* 50:23.

———. 1969. *The New World Negro.* NY: Minerva.

Herter, Hans. 1959. "Effeminatus." *Reallexikon fur Antike und Christentum* 4:620–50.

Hervé, Guy, and Theirry Kurest. 1980. *Les enfants de Fez.* Paris: Libres-Hallier.

Hiatt, L. R. 1971. "Secret pseudo-procreation rites among the Australian Aborigines." In *Anthropology in Oceania,* ed. L. Hiatt and C. Jayawardena, 77–88. Sydney: Angus & Robertson.

Hibbett, Howard. 1975. *The Floating World in Japanese Fiction.* Tokyo: Tuttle.

Hidden, Alexander. 1916. *The Ottoman Dynasty.* NY: privately printed.

Hilger, M. Iñez. 1957. *Araucanian Child Life and Its Cultural Background. Smithsonian Miscellaneous Collection* 133.

Hill, W. W. 1935. "The status of the hermaphrodite and transvestite in Navaho culture." *AA* 37:273–79.

Hinewirangi. 1993. "Woman." In *Screaming Moko,* 14. Aotearoa, New Zealand: Taranga Moana.

Hinsch, Bret. 1990. *Passions of the Cut Sleeve: The Male Homosexual Tradition in China.* Berkeley: University of California Press.

Hitchcock, Tim. 1996. "Redefining sex in eighteenth-century England." *History Workshop Journal* 41:73–92.

Hocquenghem, Guy. 1978. *Homosexual Desire.* London: Allison & Busby.

Hodgen, Margaret. 1964. *Early Anthropology in the Sixteenth and Seventeenth Centuries.* Philadelphia: University of Pennsylvania Press.

Hoek, Jan. 1949. "Dajakpriesters: Een bijdrage tot de analyse van der Religie de Dajaks." Ph.D. diss., University of Amsterdam Summarized by van der Kroef 1954.

Hoffman, Richard J. 1980. Review of Dover (1978). *JH* 5:418–21.

Hofstader, Richard. 1956. *The Progressive Era.* NY: Vintage.

Hogbin, Ian. 1946. "Puberty to marriage: A study of the sexual life of the natives of Wogeo, New Guinea." *Oceania* 16:185–208.

———. 1970. *The Island of the Menstruating Men.* Scranton, PA: Chandler.

Holt, Claire. 1939. *Dance Quest in Celebes.* Paris: Archives internationales de la danse.

Holt, P. M. 1961. "The beylicate in Ottoman Egypt during the seventeenth century." *Bulletin of the School of Oriental and African Studies* 24:214–48.

———. 1975. "The position and power of the Mamlūke Sultan." *Bulletin of the School of Oriental and African Studies* 38:237–49.

———. 1990. "Mamlūks."*Encyclopedia of Islam* 6:321–31.

Hong, Keelung, and Stephen O. Murray. 1997. "A Taiwanese Woman Who Became a Spirit Medium: Native and Alien Models of How Taiwanese Identify Spirit Possession." Paper presented at the North American Taiwan Studies Conference in Berkeley, CA.

Hood, Jim. 1973. "History of the word 'gay.'" *Gay Sunshine* 16:21.

Hooker, Evelyn. 1957. "Adjustment of male overt homosexuals." *Journal of Projective Techniques* 21:18–31.

Hopkins, Keith. 1978. *Conquerors and Slaves: Sociological Studies in Roman History I.* NY: Cambridge University Press.

Hourani, Albert. 1991. *A History of the Arab Peoples.* Cambridge, MA: Harvard University Press.

Howard, Jean E. 1988. "Crossdressing, the theatre, and gender struggle in early modern England." *Shakespeare Quarterly* 39:418–40.

Howard, John. 1998. *Carryin' on in the Lesbian and Gay South.* NY: New York University Press.

Howard, Philip. 1977. *New Words for Old.* New York: Oxford University Press.

Hugh-Jones, Christine. 1979. *From the Milk River.* NY: Cambridge University Press.

Hugh-Jones, Stephen. 1979. *The Palm and the Pleiades.* NY: Cambridge University Press.

Hulstaert, Gustave. 1938. *Le mariage des Nkundó.* Brussels: Librairie Falk.

Humphreys, Laud. 1971. "New styles of homosexual manliness." *Transaction* Mar.:38–65.

———. 1975. *Tearoom Trade.* Chicago: Aldine.

———. 1979. "Exodus and identity." In M. Levine (1979:134–47).

Humphreys, Laud, and Brian Miller. 1980. "Identities in the emerging gay culture." In *Homosexual Behavior,* ed. J. Marmor, 142–56. NY: Basic Books.

———. 1981. "Satellite cultures." In *Homosexuality,* ed. J. Marmor, 142–56. NY: Basic Books.

Humphries, Martin. 1985. "Gay machismo." In *The Sexuality of Men,* ed. A. Metcalf and M. Humphries, 70–85. London: Pluto.

Hupe, Conrad. 1846. "Korte Verhandeling over de Godsdienst, zeden, enz. der Dajakkers." *Tijdschrift voor Neêrlands' Indie* 8, 3:127–72, 245–80.

Hurwitt, Robert. 1994. "'Angels' creator touches down: Kushner ventures where playwrights fear to tread." *San Francisco Examiner,* 27 Feb., D1, D5.

Hyde, H. Montgomery. 1970. *The Love that Dared Not Speak Its Name: A Candid History of Homosexuality in Britain.* Boston: Little, Brown.

———. 1976. *The Cleveland Street Scandal.* NY: Coward, McCann, and Geoghegan.

Ibn Hazm. 1953. Ca. 1025. *The Ring of the Dove: A Treatise on the Art and Practice of Arab Love.* London: Luzac.

Ibn Iyās. 1945. *Histoire des mamlouks circassiens.* Cairo: L'Institut français d'archéologie orientale textes et traductions d'auteurs orientaux 6.

Ibn-Sasrā, Muhammad ibn Muhammad. 1963 [ca. 1398]. *A Chronicle of Damascus, 1389–1397.* Berkelely: University of California Press.

Ichiko Teiji. 1955. *Chusei Shosetsu no Kenykyu.* Tokyo: Daigaku Shuppankai.

Ihara Saikaku. 1956 [1686]. *Five Women Who Loved Love.* Tokyo: Tuttle.

———. 1964 [1682]. *The Life of an Amorous Man.* Tokyo: Tuttle.

———. 1972 [1687–1696]. *Comrade Loves of the Samurai.* Tokyo: Tuttle.

———. 1990 [1687]. *The Great Mirror of Male Love.* Stanford, CA: Stanford University Press.

Ikegami, Eiko. 1995. *The Taming of the Samurai: Honorific Individualism and the Making of Modern Japan.* Cambridge: Harvard University Press.

Inalcik, Halil. 1973. *The Ottoman Empire: The Classical Age*. London: Wiedenfeld and Nicolson.

Inawara Yoshinobu, and Kawatake Toshio. 1981. *The Traditional Theater of Japan*. Tokyo: Weatherhill.

Iokalson, Vladimir. 1905. *The Koryak*. *Memoirs of the American Museum of Natural History* 6.

Iryon. 1973 [ca. thirteenth century]. *Samguk Yusa*. Seoul: Yansei University Press.

Isomura, S., and M. Mizogami. 1992. "The low rate of HIV infection in Japanese homosexual and bisexual men: An analysis of HIV seroprevalence and behavioural risk factors." *AIDS* 6:501–03.

Istrati, Panaït. 1926. *Kyra Kyralina*. NY: Knopf.

Iwata Jun'ichi. 1974 [1930–33]. *Honchō nanshoku kō* (Researches on Boy Love in Our Country). Ise: Kogawa shoten. [Parts in Watanabe 1989]

Izazola-Licea, J. A., et al. 1991. "HIV-1 seropositivity and behavioral and sociological risks among homosexual and bisexual men in six Mexican cities." *Journal of AIDS* 1:614–22.

Jackson, Earl Jr. 1989. "Kabuki narratives of male homoerotic desire in Saikaku and Mishima." *Theatre Journal* 41:459–77.

Jackson, Peter A. 1989. *Male Homosexuality in Thailand*. Amsterdam: Global Academic Publishers.

———. 1995. *Dear Uncle Go.: Male Homosexuality in Thailand*. Bangkok: Bua Luang.

Jakobson, Roman, Gerta Hüttl-Worth, and John F. Beebe. 1957. *Paleosiberian Peoples and Languages*. New Haven, CT: HRAF.

Janson, Horst W. 1963. *The Sculpture of Donatello*. Princeton, NJ: Princeton University Press.

Javadi, Hasan. 1988. *Satire in Persian Literature*. Rutherford, NJ: Fairleigh Dickinson University Press.

Jay, Peter. 1981. *The Greek Anthology*. Baltimore: Penguin Classics.

Jennings, Jesse P. 1979. *Prehistory of Polynesia*. Cambridge: Harvard University Press.

Jordan, Mark D. 1997. *The Invention of Sodomy in Christian Theology*. Chicago: University of Chicago Press.

Junod, Henry. 1927. *Life of a South African Tribe*. London: MacMillan.

Kaberry, Phyllis M. 1939. *Aboriginal Women*. London: Routledge.

Kahn, Coppélia. 1985. *Man's Estate: Masculine Identity in Shakespeare*. Berkeley: University of California Press.

Kamau. 1998. "'A feeling within me': A twenty-five-year-old Kikuyu." In Murray and Roscoe (1998:41–62).

Kame'eleihiwa, Lilikalā. 1992. *Native Lands and Foreign Desires*. Honolulu: Bishop Museum.

Katō Shūichi. 1979. *A History of Japanese Literature: The First Thousand Years*. Tokyo: Macmillan.

Kawaguchi, Ekai. 1909. *Three Years in Tibet*. Madras, India: Theosophist Office.

Kay, Paul. 1978. "Tahitian words for 'class' and 'race.'" *Publications de la Société des Océanistes* 39:81–91.

Kay, Paul, and Chad K. McDaniel. 1978. "The linguistic significance of basic color terms." *Language* 54:610–46.

Kazantzakis, Nikos. 1953. *The Greek Passion.* NY: Simon & Schuster.

Keene, Donald. 1961. *Major Plays of Chikamatsu.* NY: Columbia University Press.

———. 1988. *The Pleasures of Japanese Literature.* NY: Columbia University Press.

Keener, Will. 1978. "Fakaleiti in Tonga." *Pacific Islands Monthly,* Oct.:8–9.

Kelly, Raymond. 1976. "Witchcraft and sexual relations." in P. Brown and G. Burchinder, *Man and Woman in the New Guinea Highlands,* 36–53. Washington, DC: AAA.

———. 1977. *Etero Social Structure.* Ann Arbor: University of Michigan Press.

Kendall, Laura. 1985. *Shamans, Housewives and Other Restless Spirits.* Honolulu: University of Hawai'i Press.

Kennedy, Elizabeth Lapovsky, and Madeline D. Davis. 1993. *Boots of Leather, Slippers of Gold: The History of a Lesbian Community.* NY: Routledge.

Keuls, Eva C. 1993. *The Reign of the Phallus: Sexual Politics in Ancient Athens.* Berkeley: University of California Press.

Khan, Badruddin. 1997a. *Sex, Longing, and Not Belonging: A Gay Muslim Journey.* Bangkok: Bua Luang.

———. 1997b. "Not-so-gay life in Karachi. In Murray and Roscoe (1997: 275–96).

Khan, Shivananda. 1995. "The Naz Project and the Islamic viewpoint on AIDS?" *Chi Pukaar: The Newsletter of the Naz Project* 9:3, 20. Reprinted in Murray and Roscoe (1997: 299–300).

———. 1996. *Dhaka Report 2.* London: Naz Foundation.

———. 1997a. *Observations on Male to Male Sexual Behavior in Bangladesh.* London: Naz Foundation.

———. 1997b. "Sexual workshops in Bangladesh and India for males who have sex with males." *Ki Pukaar: The Newsletter of the Naz Foundation* 17 (Apr.):3–5, 23.

———. 1998. "There are no homosexuals in India—There are married men and men who will get married." *Ki Pukaar: The Newsletter of the Naz Foundation* 18 (Jan.): 3, 5.

Khowaiter, Abdul-Aziz. 1978. *Barbars I.* London: Green Mountain.

Kidd, Dudley. 1904. *The Essential Kaffir.* London: Adam and Charles Black.

Kidson, M. A., and I. H. Jones. 1968. "Psychiatric disturbances among Aborigines of the Australian Western Desert." *Archives of General Psychiatry* 19:413.

Kim Pusik. 1989 [1145]. *Samguk Sagi.* Seoul: Kwangsin Ch'ulp'ansa.

Kim Young Ja. 1981. "The Korean *Namsadang.*" *Drama Review* 25:9–16.

King, Katherine Callen. 1991. *Akhilles: Paradigms of the War Hero from Homer to the Middle Ages.* Berkeley: University of California Press.

Kinsey, Alfred C., Wardell B. Pomeroy, and Clyde E. Martin. 1948. *Sexual Behavior in the Human Male.* Philadelphia: Saunders.

Kirkup, James. 1962. *These Horned Islands: A Journal of Japan.* London: Collins.

Kitsuse, John I. 1980. "Coming out all over: Deviants and the politics of social problems." *Social Problems* 28:1–13.

Klaatsch, H. 1908. *Some Notes on Scientific Travel amongst the Black Populations of Tropical Australia.* In *Report of the Eleventh Meeting of the Australian Association for the Advance of Science* (Adelaide), 577–92.

Klein, Alan M. 1989. "Managing deviance: Hustling, homophobia, and the bodybuilding subculture." *Deviant Behavior* 10:11–27.

Kleinman, Arthur. 1980. *Patients and Healers in the Context of Culture*. Berkeley: University of California Press.

Kleis, Gerald W., and Salisu A. Abdullahi. 1983. "Masculine power and gender ambiguity in urban Hausa society." *African Urban Studies* 16:39–53.

Kluckhohn, Clyde. 1943. Review of *Sun Chief*, by Leo Simmons. *AA* 45:267–70.

———. 1967 [1944]. *Navaho Witchcraft*. Boston: Beacon.

Klunzinger, C. B. 1878. *Upper Egypt*. NY: Scribner & Armstrong.

Knauft, Bruce M. 1985. *Good Company and Violence: Sorcery and Social Action in a Lowland New Guinea Society*. Berkeley: University of California Press.

———. 1986. "Text and social practice: Narrative 'longing' and bisexuality among the Gebusi of New Guinea." *Ethos* 14:252–81.

———. 1987. "Homosexuality in Melanesia." *Journal of Psychoanalytic Anthropology* 10:155–91.

———. 1990. "The question of ritualised homosexuality among the Kiwai of South New Guinea." *Journal of Pacific History* 25:188–210.

Knowles, Dom David. 1959. *The Religious Orders in England*. Vol. 3. Cambridge University Press.

Knox, Bernard. 1979. "The Socratic method." *New York Review of Books*, 25 Jan.:5–8.

Koehler, Ludwig, and Walter Baumgartner. 1995. *The Hebrew and Aramaic Lexicon of the Old Testament*. Leiden: E. J. Brill.

Kramer, Larry. 1979. *Faggots*. NY: Warner Books.

Krauss, F. R. 1911. "Erotisch-skatologisches Glossar der Albanesen." *Anthropophyteia* 8:35–39.

Krauz, Luis. 1990. "Filhos do terceiro sexo." *Leia* 136 (Feb.) 15–19.

Krieger, Susan. 1983. *The Mirror Dance*. Philadelphia: Temple University Press.

Krige, Eileen Jensen, and Jacob Daniel Krige. 1943. *The Realm of the Rain Queen: A Study of the Pattern of Lovedu Society*. Oxford: Oxford University Press.

Kroeber, Alfred L. 1940. "Psychosis or social sanction?" *Character and Culture* 8:204–15.

———. 1947. "Culture groupings in Asia." *Southwestern Journal of Anthropology* 3:322–30.

Kroll, Wilhelm. 1921. "Kinaidos." *Paulys Realencyclopädie der Classischen Altertumswissenschaft*. Vol. 21, pt. I., 459–62. Munich: Alfred Druckenmüller im Artermis.

Kronhausen, Phyllis, and Eberhard Kronhausen. 1987. *The Complete Book of Erotic Art*. NY: Bell.

Kulick, Don. 1996. "Public scandal as 'resistance' among Brazilian transgendered prostitutes." *Anthropology Today* 12, 6:3–7.

———. 1998a. *Travesti*. Chicago: University of Chicago Press.

———. 1998b. "Female trouble: The unsettling place of lesbians in the self-images of Brazilian *travesti* prostitutes." *Sexualities* 1:299–312.

Kumar, Ann. 1980. "Javanese court society and politics in the late eighteenth century: The record of a lady soldier." *Indonesia* 29:1–46.

Kutsche, Paul. 1983. "Situational homosexuality in Costa Rica." *Anthropological Research Group on Homosexuality Newsletter* 4, 4:8–13.

———. 1995. "Two truths about Costa Rica." In Murray 1995a:111–37.

Kutsche, Paul, and J. Bryan Page. 1991. "Male sexual identity in Costa Rica." *Latin American Anthropological Review* 3:7–14.

Labalme, Patricia H. 1984. "Sodomy and Venetian justice in the Renaissance." *Legal History Review* 52:217–54.

Labov, William. 1972. *Sociolinguistic Patterns*. Philadelphia: University of Pennsylvania Press.

Lacey, E. A. 1979. "Latin America." *Gay Sunshine* 40:22–31.

———. 1983. Introduction to Leyland (1983), 7–13.

———. 1988. *The Delight of Hearts: Or What You Will Not Find in Any Book*. San Francisco: Gay Sunshine.

La Fontaine, Jean S. 1959. *The Gisu of Uganda*. London: International African Institute.

Lakoff, George, and Mark Johnson. 1980. *Metaphors We Live By*. Chicago: University of Chicago Press.

Lambert, Wilfried G. 1992. "Prostitution." *Xenia* 32:127–57.

Lancaster, Roger N. 1992. *Life is Hard: Machismo, Danger, and the Intimacy of Power in Nicaragua*. Berkeley: University of California Press.

Landes, Ruth. 1940. "A cult matriarchate and male homosexuality." *Journal of Abnormal and Social Psychology* 35:386–97.

———. 1947. *The City of Women*. NY: Macmillan.

———. 1970. "A woman anthropologist in Brazil." In *Women in the Field*, ed. P. Golde, 119–42. Chicago: Aldine.

Lane, Edward. 1908. *Manners and Customs of the Modern Egyptians*. NY: Dutton.

Lane, Erskine. 1978. *Game-Texts: A Guatemalan Journal*. San Francisco: Gay Sunshine.

Lane-Poole, Stanley. 1898. *Cairo*. London: J. S. Virtue.

Lang, Sabine. 1998. *Men As Women, Women As Men: Changing Gender in Native American Cultures*. Austin: University of Texas Press.

Langham, Ian. 1976. "The Maturing of Social Anthropology at Cambridge." Ph.D. diss., Princeton University.

Langton, Edward. 1977. *A Study of the Character of Satan Through the Ages*. London: Skeffington.

Layard, John. 1959. "Homoeroticism in primitive society as a function of the self." *Journal of Analytical Psychology* 4:101–15.

Lea, Henry Charles. 1907. *A History of the Inquisition of Spain*. Vol. 4. NY: Macmillan.

Leacock, Seth, and Ruth Leacock. 1972. *Spirits of the Deep*. NY: Doublesday.

Lebra, Takie Sugiyama. 1976. *Japanese Patterns of Behavior*. Honolulu: University of Hawai'i Press.

Ledyard, John. 1963. *Journals*. Corvallis: Oregon State University Press.

Lee, John Alan. 1979. "The gay connection." *Urban Life* 8:175–98.

———. 1981. "Resistance of the media to the word 'gay' meaning 'homosexual.'" In *Communication Studies in Canadian Society*, ed. Liora Salter, 3–19. Toronto: Butterworth.

Lee, Peter H. 1959. *Studies in the Saenaennorae: Old Korean Poetry. Serie Orientale Roma* 22.

———. 1969. *Lives of Eminent Korean Monks*. Cambridge: Harvard University Press.

Legman, Gershon. 1941. "The language of homosexuality: An American glossary." In *Sex Variants*, ed. G. W. Henry, 1147–78. NY: P. B. Hoeber.

Leiter, Samuel L. 1979. *Kabuki Encyclopedia*. London: Greenwood.

Lenneberg, Eric H. 1953. "Cognition in ethnolinguistics." *Language* 29:463–71.

Lessa, William. 1950. *Ulithi: A Micronesian Atoll*. Los Angeles: University of California.

Leupp, Gary P. 1995. *Male Colors: The Construction of Homosexuality in Tokugawa Japan*. Berkeley: University of California Press.

———. 1998. "'The floating world is wide . . . ': some suggested approaches to researching female homosexuality in Tokugawa Japan (1603–1868). *Thamyris* 5:1–40.

Levenson, Lew. 1934. *Butterfly Man*. NY: Macaulay.

Lévi-Strauss, Claude. 1943. "Social uses of kinship terms among Brazilian Indians." *AA* 45:395–401.

———. 1948a. "La vie familiale et sociale des Indiens Nambikwara." *Journal de la Société des Americanistes de Paris* 37:75–96.

———. 1948b. "Tribes of Upper Xingu." *Handbook of South American Indians* 3:321–48.

———. 1948c. "The Nambicuara." *Handbook of South American Indians* 3:361–70.

———. 1969 [1949]. *The Elementary Structures of Kinship*. Boston: Beacon.

———. 1974 [1955]. *Tristes Tropiques*. NY: Atheneum.

———. 1984. "The birth of historical societies." Hitchcock Lecture delivered at the University of California, Berkeley. 24 Sept.

Levin, Richard A. 1985. *Love and Society in Shakespearean Comedy*. Newark, NJ: University of Delaware Press.

Levine, Laura. 1986. "Men in women's clothes: Anti-theatricality and effeminization from 1579 to 1642." *Criticism* 28:121–43.

Levine, Martin P. 1979. *Gay Men*. NY: Harper & Row.

Levy, Howard S. 1966. *Chinese Footbinding*. NY: W. Rawls.

———. 1971. *Sex, Love and the Japanese*. Washington, DC: Warm-Soft Village.

———. 1973. *Japanese Sex Jokes*. Taipei: Orient Culture Service.

———. 1974. *Chinese Sex Jokes in Traditional Times*. Taipei: Orient Culture Service.

Levy, Robert I. 1971. "The community functions of Tahitian male transvestites." *Anthropological Quarterly* 44:12–21.

———. 1973. *Tahitians: Mind and Experience in the Society Islands*. Chicago: University of Chicago Press.

Lewis, Archibald R. 1974. *Knights and Samurai: Feudalism in Northern France and Japan*. London: Temple Smith.

Lewis, Bernard. 1971. *Race and Color in Islam*. NY: Harper & Row.

Lewis, Ioan. M. 1966. "Spirit possession and deprivation cults." *Man* 1:307–29.

Leyland, Winston. 1978. *Gay Sunshine Interviews*. San Francisco: Gay Sunshine.

———. 1979. *Now the Volcano: An Anthology of Latin American Gay Literature*. San Francisco: Gay Sunshine.

———. 1983. *My Deep Dark Pain Is Love: A Collection of Latin American Fiction*. San Francisco: Gay Sunshine.

Leznoff, Maurice. 1954. *The Homosexual in Urban Society*. M.A. thesis, McGill University.

Li Yu. 1970. *Quanji* [Complete Works]. Taipei: Cheng-wen chu-pan-she.

——. 1990. *Silent Operas.* Hong Kong: Research Centre for Translation, Chinese University of Hong Kong.

Lieh-Mak, F., K. M. O'Hoy, and S. L. Luk. 1983. "Lesbianism in the Chinese of Hong Kong." *ASB* 12:21–30.

Lilja, Saara. 1982. *Homosexuality in Republican and Augustan Rome. Societas Scientiarum Fennica Commentationes Humanarum Litterarum* 74.

Lings, Martin. 1971. *A Sufi Saint of the Twentieth Century: Shaikh Ahmad al-Alawi.* London: Allen & Unwin.

Linnekin, Jocelyn S. 1983. "Defining tradition: Variations on the Hawaiian identity." *AE* 10:241–52.

Linton, Ralph. 1939. "Marquesan culture." In *The Individual and His Society,* ed. A. Kardiner, 197–250. NY: Columbia University Press.

Lock, Margaret. 1992. "The fragile Japanese family: Narratives about individualism and the postmodern state." In *Paths to Asian Medical Knowledge,* ed. C. Leslie and A. Young, 98–125. Berkeley: University of California Press.

Lombard, Maurice. 1975. *The Golden Age of Islam.* Amsterdam: North Holland.

London, Jack. 1907. *The Road.* NY: Macmillan.

Long, Jacqueline. 1996. *Claudian's* In Eutropium *Or How, When and Why to Slander a Eunuch.* Chapel Hill: University of North Carolina Press.

Long, Scott, and John Borneman. 1990. "Power, objectivity, and the other: The creation of sexual species in modernist disourses." *Dialectical Anthropology* 15:285–331.

Lorde, Audre. 1982. *Zami: A New Spelling of My Name.* Trumansburg, NY: Crossing Press.

Louganis, Greg. 1995. *Breaking the Surface.* NY: Random House.

Lovejoy, Arthur O., and George Boas. 1935. *Primitivism and Related Ideas in Antiquity.* Baltimore: Johns Hopkins University Press.

Low, Hugh B. 1848. *Sarawak.* London: Bentley.

Lowe, Frederic. 1972. *Daily Life in Japan at the Time of the Samurai.* London: Ruskin.

Lu Hsun [Xun]. 1976. *A Brief History of Chinese Fiction.* Beijing: Foreign Language Press.

Lumsden, Ian. 1991. *Homosexuality, Society and State in México.* Toronto: Canadian Gay Archives.

Lunsing, Wim. 1996. "Japanese gay magazines and marriage advertisements." In *Gays and Lesbians in Asia and the Pacific,* ed. G. Sullivan and L. Leong, 71–88. NY: Haworth.

Luzio, Alessandro. 1888. *Pietro Aretino.* Turin: Loescher.

Lybyer, Albert H. 1913. *The Government of the Ottoman Empire in the Time of Suleiman the Magnificent.* Cambridge: Harvard University Press.

Lynton, Harriet Ronken, and Mohini Rajan. 1974. *The Days of the Beloved.* Berkeley: University of California Press.

Lyons, Phyllis I. 1985. *The Saga of Dazai Osamu.* Stanford, CA: Stanford University Press.

McAdam, Doug. 1982. *Political Process and the Development of Black Insurgency, 1930–1970.* Chicago: University of Chicago Press.

McAdam, Doug, John D. McCarthy, and Mayner N. Zald. 1996. *Comparative Perspectives on Social Movements.* NY: Cambridge University Press.

McCullough, Helen Craig. 1966. *Yoshitsune: A Fifteenth-Century Japanese Chronicle.* Stanford, CA: Stanford University Press.

MacFarlane, Deborah F. 1983. "Trans-sexual prostitution in Polynesia." *Pacific Islands Monthly,* Feb.:11–12.

———. 1984. "Trans-sexual prostitution in New Zealand: Predominance of persons of Maori extraction." *ASB* 13:301–9.

McIntosh, Mary. 1968. "The homosexual role." *Social Problems* 16:182–92.

Mackerras, Colin P. 1972. *The Rise of the Peking Opera, 1770–1870.* NY: Oxford University Press.

McMahon, Keith. 1988. *Causality and Containment in Seventeenth-Century Chinese Fiction.* Leiden: Brill (= *Monographies du T'oung Pao* 15).

MacMullen, Ramsey. 1982. "Roman attitudes to Greek love." *Historia* 31:484–502.

Mageo, Jeannette Marie. 1992. "Male transvestism and cultural change in Samoa." *AE* 19:443–59.

Mahfouz, Naguib [Najib]. 1992 [1957]. *Sugar Street.* NY: Doubleday.

Mains, Geoff. 1984. *Urban Aboriginsals.* San Francisco: Gay Sunshine Press.

Makowski, John F. 1989. "Nisus and Euryalus: A Platonic relationship." *Classical Journal* 85:1–15.

Makrīzī, Ahmad ibn 'Ali. 1980 [ca. 1400]. *A History of the Ayyubid Sultans of Egypt.* Boston: Twayne.

Manalansan, Martin F. IV. 1991. "Neo-colonial desire." *Society of Lesbian and Gay Anthropologists Newsletter* 13:37–40.

Mandeville, Bernard. 1724. *A Modest Defence of Public Stews; or, An Essay upon Whoring, as It is Now Practis'd in These Kingdoms . . .* London: A. Moore.

Mannheim, Karl. 1936. *Ideology and Utopia.* New York: Harcourt, Brace, & World.

Mao, Nathan K., and Liu Tsun-yan. 1977. *Li Yu.* Boston: Twayne.

Marchant Lazcano, Jorge. 1983. "Killing the Lady of the Camellias." In Leyland (1983:122–26).

Marcus, Eric. 1992. *Making History: The Struggle for Gay and Lesbian Equal Rights.* NY: Harper Collins.

Marcuse, Herbert. 1955. *Eros and Civilization.* Boston: Beacon.

Mark, Mary Ellen. 1981. *Falkland Road: Prostitutes of Bombay.* NY: Knopf.

Marrou, Henri. 1982 [1948]. *A History of Education in Antiquity.* Madison: University of Wisconsin Press.

Marsot, Afat Lutfi al-Sayyid. 1979. *Society and the Sexes in Medieval Islam.* Malibu: Undena.

———. 1984. *Egypt in the Reign of Muhammed Ali.* NY: Cambridge University Press.

Martin, JoAnn. 1990. "Motherhood and power: The production of a women's culture of politics in a Mexican community." *AE* 17:470–90.

Martin, Richard. 1963. *Jou Pu Tuan.* NY: Grove.

Mass, Lawrence D. 1990. *Homosexuality as Behavior and Identity.* NY: Haworth.

Masters, R. E. L. 1962. *The Homosexual Revolution: A challenging exposé of the social and political directions of a minority group.* NY: Julian.

Mathews, R. H. 1900a. "Tribes of Western Australia." *Proceedings of the American Philosophical Society* 9:123–25.

———. 1900b. "Phallic rites and initiation ceremonies of the South Australian aborigines." *Proceedings of the American Philosophical Society* 9:622–38.

Matory, J. Lorand. 1986. *Vessels of Power: The Dialectical Symbolism of Power in Yoruba Religion and Polity.* M.A. diss., University of Chicago.

———. 1988. "Homens montados: Homossexualidade e simbolismo da possessão nas religiões Afro-Brailerias." In *Escravidão e Invenção da Liberdade: Estudos sobre o Negro no Brasil,* ed. J. Reis, 215–31. São Paulo: Brasiliense.

———. 1994. *Sex and the Empire That Is No More: Gender and the Politics of Metaphor in Oyo Yoruba Religion.* Minneapolis: University of Minnesota Press.

Matthes, B. F. 1872. "Over de Bissoes of Heidensche Priesters en Presteressen de Boeginezen." *Verhandelingen der Koninklijke Akademie van Wetenschapen* 7:1–50.

Maurier, Daphne du. 1975. *Golden Lads: Sir Francis Bacon, Anthony Bacon, and Their Friends.* Garden City, NY: Doubleday.

Mauss, Marcel. 1979 [1938]. "A category of the human mind: The notion of person, the notion of self." In *The Category of the Person,* ed. Michael Carrithers, Steven Collins, and Steven Lukes, 1–25. New York: Cambridge University Press.

Mauzalaoui, M. A. 1979. "Tragic ends of lovers: Medieval Islam and the Latin West." *Comparative Criticism* 1:37–52.

Maxwell, Gavin. 1983. *The Lords of the Atlas.* London: Century.

Mayer, Leo Ary. 1952. *Mamlūk Costume.* Geneva: A. Kundig.

———. 1956. *Islamic Architects and Their Works.* Geneva: A. Kundig.

Mazzarino, Santo. 1966. *The End of the Ancient World.* NY: Knopf.

Mead, Margaret. 1928. *Coming of Age in Samoa.* NY: Morrow.

———. 1930. *Growing Up in New Guinea.* NY: Morrow.

———. 1935. *Sex and Temperament.* NY: Morrow.

———. 1949. *Male and Female.* NY: Morrow.

———. 1961. "Cultural determinants of sexual behavior." In *Sex and Internal Secretions,* ed. W. C. Young, 1433–79. Baltimore: Williams and Wilkins.

Meeker, Richard [Forman Brown]. 1990 [1933]. *Better Angel.* Boston: Alyson.

Meigs, Anna. 1976. "Male pregnancy and the reduction of sexual opposition in a New Guinea Highlands society." *Ethnology* 25:393–407.

Ménage, V. L. 1960. "Devshirme." *Encyclopedia of Islam* 2:210–13.

———. 1966. "Some notes on the Devshirme." *Bulletin of the School of Oriental and African Studies* 29:64–78.

Mesnil, Jacques. 1938. *Botticelli.* Paris: A. Michel.

Métraux, Alfred. 1940. *Ethnology of Easter Island.* Honolulu: Bishop Museum (=Bulletin 160).

———. 1942. "Le shamanisme araucan." *Revista del Instituto de Antropologia Universidad Nacional de Tucuman* 2:309–62.

———. 1946. "Ethnography of the Chaco." *Handbook of South American Indians* 1:137–370.

———. 1967. *Religions et magies indiennes d'Amérique du Sud.* Paris: Gallimard.

Métraux, Alfred, and Herbert Baldus. 1946. "The Guayakí." *Handbook of South American Indians* 1:435–44.

Mez, Adam. 1937. *The Renaissance of Islam*. Patna: Jubilee.

Middleton, Thomas. 1599. "Ingling Pyander." In *Micro-cynicon: Sixe Snarling Satyres*. London. C4v–C5r. London: Humphrey Moseley.

Miller, Barnette. 1941. *The Palace School of Muhammad the Conqueror*. Cambridge: Harvard University Press.

Miller, Brian. 1978. "Adult sexual resocialization." *Alternative Lifestyles* 1:207–34.

———. 1987. "Counseling gay husbands and fathers."In *Gay and Lesbian Parents*, ed. F. Bozett, 175–87. NY: Praeger.

Miller, Neil. 1992. *Out in the World*. NY: Random House.

Mishima Yukio. 1966. *Death in Midsummer and Other Stories*. NY: New Directions.

———. 1968 [1951–53]. *Forbidden Colours*. Middlesex: Penguin.

Mishina Shoei. 1943. *Shiragi Karo no Knkyu*. Tokyo.

Miyao Shigeo. 1959. *Sei fuzoku* [Sexual manners]. Vol. 3. Tokyo: Yuzanka-ku.

Miyoshi, Masao. 1974. *Accomplices of Silence: The Modern Japanese Novel*. Berkeley: University of California Press.

Monette, Paul. 1992. *Becoming a Man*. NY: Harcourt Brace Jovanovich.

Montaigne, Michel. 1948. *Journey to Italy in the Years 1580 and 1581*. Stanford, CA: Stanford University Press.

Monteagudo, Jesse G. 1991. "Miami, Florida." In *Hometowns*, ed. J. Preston, 11–20. NY: Dutton.

Monter, E. William. 1990. *Frontiers of Heresy: The Spanish Inquisition from the Basque Lands to Sicily*. NY: Cambridge University Press.

Montero, Oscar. 1993. "Before the parade passes by: Latino queers and national identity." *Radical America* 24, 4:15–26.

Montini, Theresa. 1998. "Moving from the singular to the plural: Comparing gay communities in San Francisco and Honolulu." *Research in Community Sociology* 8:275–84.

Moodie, T. Dunbar, Vivienne Ndatshe, and British [Mpande Wa] Sibuyi. 1988. "Migrancy and male sexuality in the South African Gold Mines." *Journal of Southern African Studies* 14:228–56. Rev. in M. Duberman et al., *Hidden from History: Reclaiming the Gay and Lesbian Past*. NY: New American Library, 1989, 411–25.

Moraga, Cherríe. 1984. *Giving Up the Ghost*. Los Angeles: West End.

Morris, Donald R. 1965. *The Washing of the Spears: A History of the Rise of the Zulu Nation under Shaka and Its Fall in the Zulu War of 1879*. NY: Simon and Schuster.

Morris, Ivan. 1985 [1964]. *The World of the Shining Prince: Court Life in Ancient Japan*. NY: Penguin.

Morris, Robert J. 1990. "*Aikāne:* accounts of Hawaiian same-sex love and friendship in the Cook voyage journals." *JH* 19:21–54.

———. 1992. "Same-sex friendship in Hawaiian lore: Constructing a canon." In Murray (1992a:71–102).

———. 1995. Review of Kame'eleihiwa (1992). *Journal of Homosexuality* 29, 1:124–35.

Morris, Rosalind C. 1994. "Three sexes and four sexualities: Redressing the discourses on gender and sexuality in contemporary Thailand." *Positions* 2: 15–43.

Mott, Luiz. 1995. "The gay rights movement and human rights in Brazil." In Murray (1995a:221–30).

Mott, Luiz, and Aroldo Assunção. 1989. "Love's labors lost: Five letters from a seventeenth-century Portuguese sodomite." *JH* 16:91–101.

Mowat, Farley. 1970. *The Siberians.* Boston: Little, Brown.

Mueller, Martha B. 1977. "Women and Men in Rural Lesotho: The Periphery of the Periphery." Ph.D. diss., Brandeis University.

Mujtaba, Hasan. 1997. "The other side of midnight: Male prostitution in Karachi." In Murray and Roscoe (1997: 267–74).

Mumcu, Halil. 1963. *Osmanli Devletinde Siyaseten Katl.* Ankara: Ajans-Türk Matbaasi.

Munt, Sally R. 1998. *Butch/Femme: Inside Lesbian Gender.* NY: Cassell.

Murdock, George Peter. 1967. *Ethnographic Atlas.* Pittsburgh: University of Pittsburgh Press.

———. 1981. *Atlas of World Cultures.* Pittsburgh: University of Pittsburgh Press.

Murgatroyd, P. 1977. "Tibullus and the *puer delicatus.*" *Acta Classica* 20:105–19.

Murphy, Jane M. 1964. "Psychotherapeutic aspects of shamanism on St. Lawrence Island, Alaska." In *Magic, Faith and Healing,* ed. A. Kiev. NY: Free Press.

Murray, Alison. 1995. "Class and status issues in Indonesia's emerging lesbian subcultures." Paper presented at the Emerging Lesbian and Gay Communities conference at the University of Sydney, 29 Sept.

Murray, Stephen O. 1979a. "The institutional elaboration of a quasi-ethnic community." *International Review of Modern Sociology* 9:165–77.

———. 1979b. "The art of gay insults." *Anthropological Linguistics* 21:211–23.

———. 1980. "Lexical and institutional elaboration: The 'species homosexual' in Guatemala." *Anthropological Linguistics* 22:177–85.

———. 1981. "Socially structuring prototype semantics." *Forum Linguisticum* 8:95–102.

———. 1982. *Cultural Diversity and Homosexualities.* San Francisco: Obregón.

———. 1983. "Fuzzy sets and abominations." *Man* 19:396–99.

———. 1984. *Social Theory, Homosexual Realities.* NY: Gay Academic Union.

———. 1985. "Remembering Michel Foucault." *Sociologists' Gay Caucus Newsletter* 43:9–12.

———. 1986. "Edward Sapir in 'the Chicago School of sociology.'" In *New Perspectives in Language, Culture, and Personality: Proceedings of the Sapir Centenary Conference,* ed. K. Koerner et al., 241–91. Amsterdam: John Benjamins.

———. 1987a. *Male Homosexuality in Central and South America.* NY: Gay Academic Union.

———. 1987b. "Snowing canonical texts." *AA* 89:443–44.

———. 1988. "Homosexual acts and selves in early modern Europe." *JH* 16:457–77.

———. 1991a. "'Homosexual occupations' in Mesoamerica?" *JH* 21:57–64. Rev. in Murray (1995a:71–79).

———. 1991b. "Sleeping with natives as a source of data." *Publications of the Society of Lesbian and Gay Anthropologists Newsletter* 13:49–51.

————. 1991c. "Social constructionism and ancient Greek homosexuality." *Society of Lesbian and Gay Anthropologists Newsletter* 16:19–26.

————. 1992a. *Oceanic Homosexualities*. NY: Garland.

————. 1992b. "Components of *gay community* in San Francisco." In *The Culture of Gay Men*, ed. G. H. Herdt, 107–46. Boston: Beacon.

————. 1992c. "The 'underdevelopment' of modern/gay homosexuality in Latin America and Thailand." In *Modern Homosexualities*, ed. K. Plummer, 29–38. London: Routledge.

————. 1994a. "Subordinating native cosmologies to the Empire of gender." *Current Anthropology* 35:59–61.

————. 1994b. *Theory Groups in the Study of Language in North America*. Amsterdam: John Benjamins.

————. 1995a. *Latin American Male Homosexualities*. Albuquerque: University of New Mexico Press.

————. 1995b. "Some Southwest Asian and North African terms for homosexual roles." *ASB* 24:623–29.

————. 1995c. "Stigma transformation and relexification in the international diffusion of *gay*." In *Beyond the Lavender Lexicon*, ed. W. Leap, 215–40. NY: Gordon & Breach.

————. 1996a. *American Gay*. Chicago: University of Chicago Press.

————. 1996b. "Male homosexuality in Guatemala." In *Out in the Field: Reflections of Lesbian and Gay Anthropologists*, ed. E. Lewin and W. Leap, 236–60. Urbana: University of Illinois Press.

————. 1996c. "Historical truths and partisan misrepresentations." *Anthropological Linguistics* 38:355–60.

————. 1997a. "The Sohari *khanith*." In Murray and Roscoe (1997:244–55).

————. 1997b. "The will not to know: Accommodations to homosexuality in Islamic societies." In Murray and Roscoe (1997:14–53).

————. 1997c. "Explaining away same-sex sexuality when it obtrudes on anthropologists' attention." *Anthropology Today* 13, 3:2–5.

————. 1997d. "Corporealizing medieval Persian and Turkish Tropes." In Murray and Roscoe (1997:132–41).

————. 1997e. "Male homosexuality in Ottoman Albania." In Murray and Roscoe (1997:187–96).

————. 1998a. "Self size and observable sex." In *Public Sex, Gay Space*, ed. W. Leap, 167–96. NY: Columbia University Press.

————. 1998b. "Subjectivities of some dark(-haired) objects of desire." *Journal of Homosexuality* 35, 1:114–33.

————. 1998c. "Organizations of homosexuality and other social structures in sub-Saharan Africa." In Murray and Roscoe (1998:283–98).

————. 1999a. "Increasingly gay self-representations of male-male sexual experiences in Thailand." *Journal of Gay and Lesbian Social Services* 9: 81–96.

————. 1999b. "Widely plausible deniability of what is 'sex.'" *Sexualities* 2:254–57.

Murray, Stephen O., and Manuel A. Arboleda G. 1987, 1995. "Stigma transformation and relexification in the diffusion of 'gay' in Latin America." In Murray (1987:129–38) and Murray (1995a:138–44).

Murray, Stephen O., and Wayne R. Dynes. 1987, 1995. "Hispanic homosexuals:

a Spanish lexicon." In Murray (1987:170–82) and Murray (1995a: 180–92).

Murray, Stephen O., and Kent Gerard. 1983. "Renaissance sodomite subcultures?" *Onder Vrouwen, Onder Mannen* 1:182–96.

Murray, Stephen O., and Badruddin Khan. 1997. "Keeping male-male sexual relations invisible in Pakistan." In *Sociolegal Control of Homosexuality: A Multi-Nation Comparison*, ed. R. Green and D. West, 119–26. NY: Plenum.

Murray, Stephen O., and Will Roscoe. 1997. *Islamic Homosexualities*. NY: New York University Press.

———. 1998. *Boy Wives and Female Husbands: Studies of African Homosexualities*. NY: St. Martin's.

Nachman, Steven R. 1984. "Lies My Informants Told Me." *J. Anthropological Research* 40:536–55.

Näcke, Paul. 1965 [1907]. "Über Homosexualität in Albanien." *Jahrbuch für sexuellle Zwischenstufen* 9:325–37. Trans. Warren Johansson. *International Journal of Greek Love* 1:39–47.

Nadel, Siegfried F. 1947. *The Nuba*. Oxford: Oxford University Press.

Naim, C. M. 1979. "The theme of homosexual (pederastic) love in pre-modern Urdu poetry." In *Studies in Urdu Gazal and Prose Fiction*, ed. U. Memon, 120–42. Madison: University of Wisconsin Press.

Nakano Eizō. 1988. *Kōshoku bungei hon jiten*. Tokyo: Yūzankaku.

Nanda, Serena. 1990. *Neither Man Nor Woman: The Hijras of India*. Belmont, CA: Wadsworth.

Naqvi, Nauman, and Hasan Mujtaba. 1997. "Two Baluchi Buggas, a Sindhi Zenana, and the Status of Hijras in Contemporary Pakistan." In Murray and Roscoe (1997: 262–66).

Nardi, Peter M., and Ralph Bolton. 1991. "Gay-bashing: Violence and aggression against gay men and lesbians." In *Targets of Violence and Aggression*, ed. R. Bolton, 349–400. Amsterdam: Elsevier North Holland.

Ndatshe, Vivienne. 1993 [1982]. "Two Miners." In *The Invisible Ghetto*, ed. M. Krouse. 45–51. Johanesburg: COSAW.

Necef, Mehmet U. 1985. "Turkey on the brink of modernity." In J. Sofer and A. Schmitt, 71–75 (1992:71–75).

Needham, Rodney. 1973. *Right and Left: Essays on Dual Classification*. Chicago: University of Chicago Press.

Nestle, Joan. 1987. *A Restricted Country*. Ithaca, NY: Firebrand.

———. 1992. *The Persistent Desire: A Femme-Butch Reader*. Boston: Alyson.

Neuringer, O. 1989. "On the question of homosexuality in actors." *ASB* 18:523–29.

Nevis, Joel A. 1985. "*Gai, gei, homo,* and *homoseksuali* in Finnish." *Maledicta* 8:158–60.

Nicholl, Charles. 1995. *The Reckoning: The Murder of Christopher Marlowe*. Chicago: University of Chicago Press.

Nisbet, Robert A. 1970 [1964]. "Kinship and political power in first-century Rome." In *Tradition and Revolt*, 203–24. NY: Vintange.

Noda Yosiyuka. 1976. *Introduction to Japanese Law*. Tokyo: University of Tokyo Press.

Noel, Joseph. 1940. *Footloose in Arcadia*. NY: Carrick & Evans.

Noma Koshin. 1976 [1643]. "Shin'yūki" [The record of heartfelt friends]. In *Kinsei Shikidō Ron*. Vol. 60 of *Nihon Shisō Taikei*, 7–25. Tokyo: Iwanami Shoten.

Noordam, Dirk J. 1983. "Homosocial relations in Leiden. 1533–1811." *Among Men/Among Women* 1:218–23.

Nootenboom, C. 1948. "Aantekeningen over de Cultuur der Boeginezan en Makassaren." *Indonesië* 2:245–55.

Norton, Rictor. 1992. *Mother Clap's Molly House*. London: Gay Men's Press.

Novy, Marianne. 1984. *Love's Argument: Gender Relations in Shakespeare*. Chapel Hill: University of North Carolina Press.

Núñez de Piñeda y Bascuñán, Francisco. 1974 [1663]. *Cautivero Feliz, y Razón de las Guerras Dilatadas del Reino de Chille*. Santiago: Zig-Zag Trans. William Atkinson as *The Happy Captive*, London: Folio Society, 1977.

'Obeyd-e Zakani, Nezam al-Din. 1985 [ca. mid-fourteenth century]. *The Ethics of the Aristocrats and Other Satirical Works*. Trans. and ed. Hasan Javadi. Piedmont, CA: Jahan Books.

Odulok, Taeki. 1934. *Snow People*. London: Methuen.

Oetomo, Dédé. 1991. "Patterns of bisexuality in Indonesia." In *Bisexuality & HIV/AIDS: A Global Perspective*. ed. R. Tielman, M. Carballo, and A. Hendriks, 119–26. Buffalo, NY: Prometheus.

O'Flaherty, Wendy D. 1980. *Women, Androgynes, and Other Mythical Beasts*. Chicago: University of Chicago Press.

Ohlmarks, Ake. 1939. *Studien zum Problem des Schamanismus*. Lund: Gleerup.

Oka, M. 1965. "Telemachus in the *Odyssey*." *Journal of Classical Studies* 13:33–50.

Oliver, Douglas L. 1974. *Ancient Tahitian Society*. Honolulu: University of Hawai'i Press.

———. 1981. *Two Tahitian Villages*. Honolulu: Institute for Polynesian Studies.

———. 1989. *Oceania*. Honolulu: University of Hawai'i Press.

Opler, Morris E. 1959. Review of Carstairs (1957). *AA* 61:140–42.

———. 1960."The hijara of India and Indian national character." *AA* 62: 505–11.

Orgel, Stephen. 1989. "'Nobody's perfect': Or why did the English stage take boys for women?" *South Atlantic Quarterly* 88:7–29. Special issue also issued as *Displacing Homophobia*. Durham, NC: Duke University Press, 1989.

Osborne, Francis. 1656. *Political Reflections upon the Government of the Turks*. . . . London: Printed by J. G. for Richard Royston, and sold by Thomas Robinson. (pp. 219–90)

Osgood, Cornelius. 1958. "Ingalik social structure." *Yale University Publications in Anthropology* 53: 1–289.

Osteria Trinidad, and Gerard Sullivan. 1991. "The impact of religion and cultural values on AIDS education programs in Malaysia and the Philippines." *AIDS Education and Prevention* 3:133–46.

Ovalle, Alonso de. 1646. *Historica relacion del Reyno de Chile*. Rome: F. Caualli.

Page, Denys Lionel. 1951. *Alcman, The Partheneion*. Oxford: Clarendon. Reprint., Salem, NH: Ayer Co, 1985.

Palmer, J. A. B. 1953. "The origins of the Janissaries." *Bulletin of the John Rylands Library* 35:448–81.

Palmer, Richard. 1979. "Physicians and surgeons in sixteenth century Venice." *Medical History* 23: 451–60.

Papoulia, Basilike D. 1963. *Ursprung und Wesen der 'Knabenlese' in osmanischen Reich.* Munich: Oldenbourg.

Parker, Peter. 1989. *Ackerley.* NY: Farar, Straus, Giroux.

Parker, Richard G. 1987. "Acquired Immune Deficiency in Urban Brazil." *Medical Anthropology Quarterly* 1:155–75.

———. 1991. *Bodies, Pleasures, and Passions: Sexual Culture in Contemporary Brazil.* Boston: Beacon.

———. 1999. *Beneath the Equator: Cultures of Desire, Male Homosexuality, and Emerging Gay Communities in Brazil.* NY: Routledge.

Parry, V. J. 1976. *A History of the Ottoman Empire to 1730.* NY: Cambridge University Press.

Parsons, Elsie Clews. 1932. "Isleta, New Mexico." *Bureau of American Ethnology Annual Reports* 47:193–466.

———. 1939. *Pueblo Indian Religion.* Chicago: University of Chicago Press.

Partner, Nancy F. 1996. "Did mystics have sex?" In *Desire and Discipline: Sex and Sexuality in the Premodern West,* ed. J. Murray and K. Eisenbichler, 296–311. Toronto: University of Toronto Press.

Patterson, Orlando. 1982. *Slavery and Social Death.* Cambridge: Harvard University Press.

Patzer, Harald. 1982. *Die griechische Knabenbliebe.* Wiesbaden: Franz Steiner.

Pausacker, Helen. 1991. "Srikandhi and Sumbadra: Stereotyped role models or complex personalities?" In *The Art and Culture of South-East Asia,* ed. L. Chandra, 271–97. Delhi: Aditya Prakashan.

Pavan, Elizabeth. 1980. "Police des moeurs, société et politique à Venise à la fin du Moyen Age." *Revue historique* 264: 241–88.

Payer, Pierre J. 1982. Introduction to Peter Damian, *Book of Gomorrah* [1048], 1–23. Waterloo, Ontario: Wilfred Laurier University Press.

———. 1985. "Foucault on penance and the shaping of sexuality." *Sciences Religeuses* 14: 313–20.

———. 1991. "Sex and confession in the thirteenth century." In *Sex in the Middle Ages,* ed. J. Salisbury, 126–42. NY: Garland.

Paz, Octavio. 1962. *The Labyrinth of Solitude: Life and Thought in Mexico.* NY: Grove.

Peacock, James L. 1968. *Rites of Modernization: Symbolic Aspects of Indonesian Proletarian Drama.* Chicago: University of Chicago Press.

———. 1972. "Symbolic reversal and social history: Transvestites and clowns of Java." In *The Reversible World: Symbolic Inversion in Art and Society,* ed. B. Babcock, 209–24. Ithaca, NY: Cornell University Press.

Pedretti, Carlo. 1973. *Leonardo da Vinci.* Berkeley: University of California Press.

Pellat, Charles. 1977. "Liwāt." *Encyclopedia of Islam,* 3:776–79. Leiden: Brill.

Penteado, Darcy. 1979. "Snow White revisited." In Leyland (1979:237–45).

———. 1983. "Part-time hustler." In Leyland (1983:241–44).

Pequigney, Joseph. 1985. *Such is My Love: A Study of Shakespeare's Sonnets.* Chicago: University of Chicago Press.

Percy, William Armstrong III. 1996. *Pederasty and Pedagogy in Archaic Greece.* Urbana: University of Illinois Press.

Perelaer, Michael T. H. 1870. *Ethnographische Beschrivjing der Dajaks.* Zalt-Bommel: Noma.

Perry, Mary E. 1980. *Crime and Society in Early Modern Seville.* Hanover, NH: University Press of New England.

———. 1988. "The 'nefarious sin' in early modern Seville." *Journal of Homosexuality* 16:67–89.

Petros, Prince [of Greece and Denmark]. 1963. *A Study in Polyandry.* The Hague: Mouton.

Pettiway, Leon E. 1996. *"Honey, Honey, Miss Thang": Being Black, Gay, and on the Streets.* Philadelphia: Temple University Press.

Pflugfelder, Gregory M. 1990. "'Sisters' and 'same-sex love': Schoolgirl intimacy in early twentieth-century Japan." Paper presented at the Lesbian, Bisexual, and Gay Studies Conference at Harvard University.

Phillips, Herbert P. 1987. *Modern Thai Literature with an Ethnographic Interpretation.* Honolulu: University of Hawai'i Press.

Pierson, Donald. 1942. *Negroes in Brazil.* Chicago: University of Chicago Press.

Pierson, Robin. 1978. "Polynesia's third sex." *Pacific Islands Monthly,* Aug.:11–12.

Pilling, Arnold R. 1992. "Homosexuality among the Tiwi of North Australia." In Murray (1992a:25–32).

Piloti, Emmanuel. 1958 [1420]. *Sur le passage en Terre Sainte.* Paris: Béatrice-Nauwelaerts.

Pimpley, P. N., and S. K. Sharma. 1985. "Hijaras: A study of an atypical role." *Avadh Journal of Social Sciences* 2:381–89.

Pinkerton, John. 1811. *A General Collection of the Best and Most Interesting Voyages and Travels in All Parts of the World.* Vol. 7. London: Longman.

Pipes, Daniel. 1978. "From Mawla to Mamlūk: The Origins of Islamic Military Slavery." Ph.D. diss., Harvard University.

Pittin, Christin. 1983. "Houses of women: A focus on alternative life-styles in Katsina City." In *Female and Male in West Africa,* ed. C. Oppong, 291–302. London: Allen & Unwin.

Plomer, William. 1936. *Ali, the Lion.* London: Jonathan Cape.

Poasa, Kris. 1992. "The Samoan fa'afafine: One case study and discussion of transsexualism." *Journal of Psychology and Human Sexuality* 5, 3:39–51.

Poliak, Abraham N. 1939. *Feudalism in Egypt, Syria, Palestine and Lebanon,1250–1900.* London: Royal Asiatic Society. Reprinted, Philadelphia: Porcupine, 1977.

Ponse, Barbara. 1978. *Identity in the Lesbian World.* Westport, CT: Greenwood.

Porter, Joseph Ashby. 1988. *Shakespeare's Mercutio.* Chapel Hill: University of North Carolina Press.

———. 1989. "Marlowe, Shakespeare, and the canonization of heterosexuality." *South Atlantic Quarterly* 88:127–48. Special issue also issued as *Displacing Homophobia.* Durham, NC: Duke University Press, 1989.

Porter, Mary A. 1996. "Talking at the margins: Kenyan discourses on homosexuality." In *Beyond the Lavender Lexicon,* ed. W. Leap, 133–54. NY: Gordon and Breach.

Postel, Guillaume. 1560. *De la république des Turc.* Poitiers: E. de Marnef.

Poucqueville, François. 1813 [1805]. *Travels in Morea, Albania, and Other Parts of the Ottoman Empire.* London: Henry Colburn.

Prescott, Henry W. 1920. "Inorganic rôles in Roman comedy." *Classical Philology.* 15:245–81.

Prieur, Annick. 1998. *Mema's House, Mexico City.* Chicago: University of Chicago Press.

Proschan, Frank. 1995. "Hypersexuality and Social Disease." Paper presented at the AAA annual meetings in Washington, DC.

———. 1998. "Filial piety and non-procreative male-to-male sex among Vietnamese." Paper presented at the AAA annual meetings in Philadelphia.

Prynne, William. 1633. *Histrio-Mastix: The Players Scourge, or, Actors Tragaedie.* London: Michael Sparke.

Puig, Manuel. 1976. *El beso de la mujer arana.* Barcelona: Seix Barral. Trans. Thomas Colchie as *The Kiss of the Spider Woman,* New York Knopf, 1979.

———. 1983. "Classical Farrah." In Leyland (1983:75–76).

Pukui, Mary Kawena, E. W. Haertig, and Catherine Lee. 1972. *Nana I Ke Kumu* (Look to the Source). 2 vols. Honolulu: Hui Hanai.

Purcell, Brabazon H. 1893. "Rites and customs of Australian aborigines." *Zeitschrift für Ethnologie* 25:286–89.

Quinn, Kenneth. 1972. *Catullus: An Interpretation.* London: Batsford.

Rackin, Phyllis. 1987. "Androgyny, mimesis, and the marriage of the boy heroine on the English Renassiance stage." *PMLA* 102:29–41.

Rainolds, John. 1599. *Th' Overthrow of Stage-Playes.* Middleburgh: Richard Schilders.

Ramos, Arthur. 1942. *Aculturação Negra no Brasil.* Rio de Janeiro: Biblioteca Brasileira.

Rappaport, Roy A. 1979. *Ecology, Meaning and Religion.* Richmond, CA: North Atlantic Books.

Ravenscroft, A. G. B. 1892. "Some habits and customs of the Chingalee." *Transactions of the Royal Society of South Australia* 15:121–22.

Rawson, Philip. 1968. *Erotic Art of the East.* NY: Putnam's.

Read, Kenneth E. 1952. "The Nama Cult of the Central Highlands, New Guinea." *Oceania* 23:1–25.

———. 1992 [1979]. "Looking back at the Gahuku." In Murray (1992a:69–70).

Rechy, John. 1961. *City of Night.* NY: Grove.

Reiss, Albert J. 1961. "The social integration of 'queers' and 'peers.'" *Social Problems* 9:102–20.

Repp, R. C. 1968. "Some further notes on the *devshirme.*" *Bulletin of the School of Oriental and African Studies* 31:137–19.

Rey, Michel. 1982. "Police et sodomie à Paris au XVIIIᵉ siècle." *Revue d'histoire moderne et contemporaire* 29:113–24.

———. 1985. "Parisian homosexuals create a lifestyle, 1700–1750." *Eighteenth Century Life* 9:179–91.

Ribeiro, René. 1969. "Personality and the psychosexual adjustment of Afro-Brazilian cult members." *Journal de la Société des Americanistes* 58:109–20.

———. 1970."Psicopatologia e pesquisa antropologica." *Universitas* 6:123–34.

Ribondi, Alexandre. 1983. "The blue crime." In Leyland (1983:331–42).

Ricaut, Paul. 1971 [1668]. *The History of the Present State of the Ottoman Empire.* NY: Arno.

Rich, Adrienne. 1980. "Compulsory heterosexuality and lesbian existence." *Signs* 5:631–61.

Richardson, T. Wade. 1984. "Homosexuality in the *Satyricon*." *Classica et Mediaevalia* 25:105–27.

Richlin, Amy. 1981. "The meaning of *irrumare* in Catullus and Martial." *Classical Philology* 76:40–46.

———. 1983. *The Garden of Priapus: Sexuality and Aggression in Roman Humor.* New Haven, CT: Yale University Press.

———. 1993. "Not before homosexuality: The materiality of the *cinædus* and the Roman law against love between men." *Journal of the History of Sexuality* 3:523–73.

Ricklefs, Merle Calvin. 1974. *Jogjakarta under Sultan Mangkubumi, 1749–1792: A History of the Division of Java.* NY: Oxford University Press.

Rind, Bruce, Philip Tromovitch, and Robert Bauserman. 1998. "A meta-analytic examination of assumed properties of child sexual abuse using college samples." *Psychological Bulletin* 124:22–53.

Ritter, Hellmut. 1955. *Das Meer der Seele.* Leiden: Brill.

Robertson, Carol E. 1989. "The māhū of Hawai'i." *Feminist Studies* 15:312–28.

Robertson, Jennifer. 1992a. "The politics of androgyny in Japan: sexuality and subversion in the theater and beyond." *AE*19:419–42. (Repr. in Robertson 1998:47–88).

———. 1992b. "Doing and undoing 'female' and 'male' in Japan: The Takarazuka Revue." In *Japanese Social Organization,* ed. T. Lebra, 165–93. Honolulu: University of Hawai'i Press.

———. 1998. *Takarazuka: Sexual Politics and Popular Culture in Modern Japan.* Berkeley: University of California Press.

Rocke, Michael. 1988. "San Bernardino and Tuscan sodomy." *JH* 16:17–32.

———. 1996. *Forbidden Friendships: Homosexuality and Male Culture in Renaissance Florence.* NY: Oxford University Press.

Rodgers, Bruce. 1972. *The Queens' Vernacular: A Gay Lexicon.* San Francisco: Straight Arrow.

Róheim, Géza. 1926. *Social Anthropology.* NY: Boni & Liveright.

———. 1932. "Psychoanalysis of primitive cultural types." *International Journal of Psychoanalysis* 13:1–254.

———. 1933. "Women and their life in Central Australia." *Journal of the Royal Anthropological Institute* 62:207–65.

———. 1950. *Psychoanalysis and Anthropology.* NY: International University of Press.

———. 1974. *Children of the Desert.* NY: Basic Books.

Roscoe, Will. 1988. "Making history: the challenge of gay and lesbian studies." *JH* 15:1–40.

———. 1991a. *The Zuni Man-Woman.* Albuquerque: University of New Mexico Press.

———. 1991b. Review of *Neither Man Nor Woman: The Hijras of India,* by Serena Nanda. *JH* 21, 3:117–25.

———. 1995. "Was We'wha a homosexual?" *GLQ* 2:193-235.

———. 1996a. "Priests of the goddess." *History of Religions* 35:295–330.

——. 1996b. *Queer Spirits*. Boston: Beacon.

——. 1997. "Precursors of Islamic male homosexualities." In Murray and Roscoe (1997:55–86).

——. 1998. *Changing Ones*. NY: St. Martin's.

Rosenzweig, Julie M., and Wendy C. Lebow. 1992. "Femme on the streets, butch in the sheets: Lesbian sex-roles, dyadic adjustment, and sexual satisfaction." *JH* 23, 3:1–20.

Roth, Henry Ling. 1896. *Natives of Sarawak and British North Borneo*. London: Truslove & Hanson.

Roth, Norman. 1991. "Fawn of my delights: Boy-love in Hebrew and Arabic Verse. In *Sex in the Middle Ages*, 157–72. NY: Garland.

Roth, W. E. 1906. "Notes on government, morals and crime." *North Queensland Ethnography Bulletin* 8:1–12.

Rougemont, Denis de. 1955. *Love in the Western World*. NY: Pantheon.

Rousseau, George S. 1985. "The pursuit of homosexuality in the eighteenth century: 'Utterly confused category' and/or rich repository?" *Eighteenth Century Life* 9:132–68.

Rousseau, Jérôme. 1993. "From shamans to priests: Towards the professionalization of religious specialists among the Kayan." In Winzeler (1993:131–50).

Rowson, Evert K. 1991a. "The effeminates of early Medina." *Journal of the American Oriental Society* 111:671–93.

——. 1991b. "The categorization of gender and sexual irregularity in medieval Arab vice lists." In *Body Guards*, ed. J. Epstein and K. Straub, 50–79. NY: Routledge.

Ruan Fangfu and Tsai Yungmei. 1987. "Male homosexuality in traditional Chinese literature." *JH* 14, 3–4:21–33.

Rubin, Gayle. 1975. "The traffic in women." In *Toward an Anthropology of Women*, ed. R. Reiter, 157–210. NY: Monthly Review Press.

——. 1984. "Thinking sex." In *Pleasure and Danger: Exploring Female Sexuality*. ed. C. Vance, 300–309. NY: Routledge.

Ruggiero, Guido. 1974. "Sexual criminality in early Renaissance Venice, 1338–1358." *Journal of Social History* 8: 18–37.

——. 1978a. "Law and punishment in early Renaissance Venice." *Journal of Criminal Law & Criminology* 69:156–66.

——. 1978b. "Co-operation of physicians and the state in the control of violence in Renaissance Venice." *Journal of the History of Medicine* 33:156–66.

——. 1985. *The Boundaries of Eros: Sex Crime and Sexuality in Renaissance Venice*. NY: Oxford University Press.

Rust, Paula C. 1993. "Neutralizing the political threat of the marginal woman: Lesbians' beliefs about bisexual women." *Journal of Sex Research* 30:214–28.

Rutt, Richard. 1961. "The flower boys of Silla: Notes on the sources." *Transactions of the Asiatic Society of Japan* 38:1–66.

——. 1964. *Korean Works and Days: Notes from the Diary of a Country Priest*. Rutland, VT: C. E. Tuttle Co.

Sabbah, Fatna A. 1984. *Woman in the Muslim Unconscious*. NY: Pergammon.

Saletore, R. N. 1974. *Sex Life under Indian Rulers*. Delhi: Hind Pocket.

Salmond, Anne. 1991. *Two Worlds: First Meetings Between Maori and Europeans*. Auckland: Viking.

Sanders, Stephanie A., and June M. Reinisch. 1999. "Would you say you 'had sex' if . . . ?" *Journal of the American Medical Association* 281:275–77.

Sankar, Andrea. 1985. "Sisters and brothers, lovers and enemies: Marriage resistance in southern Kwangtung." *JH* 11:69–81.

Sapir, Edward. 1938. "Why cultural anthropology needs the psychiatrist." *Psychiatry* 1:7–12.

Sargent, G. W. 1959. *The Japanese Family Storehouse, or the Millionaire's Gospel Modernized.* NY: Cambridge University Press.

Sargent, Thelma. 1982. *The Idylls of Theocritus: A Verse Translation.* New York: Norton.

Sarotte, Georges-Michel. 1978. *Like a Brother, Like a Lover.* Garden City, NY: Doubleday.

Sasama Yoshiko. 1989. *Kōshoku engo jiten.* Tokyo: Yūzankaku.

Saslow, James M. 1986. *Ganymede in the Renaissance: Homosexuality in Art and Society.* New Haven, CT: Yale University Press.

———. 1989. "Homosexuality in the Renaissance: Behavior, identity, and artistic expression." In *Hidden from History,* ed. M. Duberman, M. Vicinus, and G. Chauncey, 90–105. NY: New American Library.

Schalow, Paul G. 1981. "Saikaku on 'manly love.'" *Stone Lion Review* [Harvard] 7:3–7.

———. 1987. "'Woman-hater' as homosexual: Literary evidence from seventeenth-century Japan." In *Homosexuality, Which Homosexuality? Proceedings, Literature and Arts,* 1:41–53. Amsterdam: Free University.

———. 1989a. "Male love in early modern Japan: A literary depiction of 'youth.'" In *Hidden From History,* ed. M. Duberman, M. Vicinius, and G. Chauncey, 118–28. NY: New American Library.

———. 1989b. "Literature and legitimacy: Uses of irony and humor in seventeenth–century Japanese depictions of male love." *Literary Studies East and West* 2:53–60.

———. 1990a. Introduction to *The Great Mirror of Male Love.* Stanford, CA: Stanford University Press.

———. 1990b. "Spiritual dimensions of male beauty in Japanese Buddhism." Paper presented at the American Academy of Religion annual meetings in New Orleans.

———. 1992. "Kūkai and the tradition of male love in Japanese Buddhism." In *Buddhism, Sexuality, and Gender,* ed. José Cabezón, 215–30. Albany: State University of New York Press.

———. 1993. "The invention of a literary tradition of male love: Kitamura Kigin's *Iwatsutuji.*" *Monumenta Nipponica* 48:231–61.

———. 1996. "Today's tales of yesterday." In *Partings at Dawn: An Anthology of Japanese Gay Literature,* ed. D. Miller, 55–66. San Francisco: Gay Sunshine.

Schapera, Isaac. 1930. *The Khoisan Peoples of South Africa.* London: Routledge.

———. 1938. A *Handbook of Tswana Law and Custom.* NY: Oxford University Press.

Schärer, Hans. 1946. *Die Gottesidee der Ngadju Dajak in Süd-Borneo.* Leiden: Brill. Trans. Rodney Needham as *Ngaju Religion: The Conception of God among a South Borneo People.* The Hague: Martinus Nijhoff, 1963.

Schied, John. 1996. "Attis." In the *Oxford Classical Dictionary,* ed. S. Hornblower and A. Spawforth, 213. NY: Oxford University Press.

Schiefenhövel, Wulf. 1990. "Ritualized adult-male/adolescent-male sexual behavior in Melanesia." In *Pedophilia: Biosocial Dimensions*, ed. J. R. Feierman, 394–421. Berlin: Springer-Verlag.

Schieffelin, Edward L. 1976. *The Sorrow of the Lonely and the Burning of the Dancers*. NY: St. Martin's.

Schifter Sikora, Jacobo. 1990. *La formación de una contracultura: Homosexualismo y sida en Costa Rica*. San José, Costa Rica: Guayacán.

Schifter Sikora, Jacobo, and Johnny Madrigal Pana. 1992. *Hombres que Aman Hombres*. San José: Ediciones Ilep-SIDA.

Schimmel, Annemarie. 1975. *Mystical Dimensions of Islam*. Chapel Hill: University of North Carolina Press.

———. 1982. *As Through a Veil: Mystical Poetry in Islam*. NY: Columbia University Press.

Schmidt, E. A. 1947. "Kunstler und Knabenliebe." *Euphorion* 68:437–46.

Schmitt, Arno. 1985. "Some reflections on male-male sexuality in Muslim society." In *Klein Schriften zu zwischmannlicker sexualität und Erotik in der muslimischen Gesellschaft*, ed G. de Martino and A. Schmitt, 54–58. Berlin: privately printed.

———. 1992a. "Different approaches to male-male sexuality/eroticism from Morocco to Uzbekistan." In Sofer and Schmitt(1992:1–24).

———. 1992b. "Sexual meetings of East and West: Western tourism and Muslim immigrant communities." In Sofer and Schmitt(1992:125–29).

Schneebaum, Tobias. 1979. *Wild Man*. NY: Viking.

———. 1980. "Realities loved and unloved." In *The Don Juan Papers*, ed. R. de Mille, 91–93. Santa Barbara, CA: Ross-Erikson.

———. 1984. Interview (by Steve Abbott). *The Advocate* 396: 44–50.

———. 1987. *Where the Spirits Dwell*. NY: St. Martin's.

Schodt, Frederick. 1983. *Manga! Manga! The World of Japanese Comics*. Tokyo: Kodansha.

Schoeffel, Penelope. 1979. "Daughters of Sina: A Study of Gender, Status, and Power in Western Samoa." Ph.D. diss., Australian National University.

Schrijvers, P. H. 1985. *Eine medizinische Erklärung der männlichen Homoseuxalität der Antike: Caelius Aurelianus De Morbis chronicis IV 9*. Amsterdam: B. R. Grüner.

Schurhammer, Georg. 1921. "Kōbō Daishi, nach den gedruckten und ungedruckten Missionberichten des 16 and 17 Jarhundertrs." *Zeitschrift für Missionswissenschaft Münster* 12:89–97.

———. 1922. "Die Yamabushis." *Zeitschrift für Missionswissenschaft Münster* 13:206–28.

Schuyler, Eugene. 1876. *Turkistan: Notes of a Journey in Russian Turkistan, Kokand, Bukhara and Kuldja* NY: Scribner, Armstrong.

Schwaner, C. A. L. M. 1853. *Borneo*. Amsterdam: P. N. van Kampen.

Scott, A. C. 1955. *The Kabuki Theatre of Japan*. London: Allen & Unwin.

Sears, James T. 1991. *Growing Up Gay in the South*. Binghamton, NY: Haworth.

Selby, Henry A. Jr. 1974. *Zapotec Deviance*. Austin: University of Texas Press.

Senelick, Laurence. 1990. "Mollies or men of mode? Sodomy and the eighteenth-century London stage." *Journal of the History of Sexuality* 1:33–67.

Sergent, Bernard. 1986. *Homosexuality in Greek Myth*. Boston: Beacon.

Serpenti, Laurent M. 1965. *Cultivators in the Swamps*. Assen: Van Gorcum.

––––––. 1984. "The ritual meaning of homosexuality and pedophilia among the Kimam-Papuans of South Irian Jaya." In Herdt (1984:318–36).

Sesser, Stan. 1994. "Hidden death." *The New Yorker* 14 Nov: 62–90.

Shah, A. M. 1961. "A note on the hijadas of Gujerat." *AA* 61: 1325–30.

Shapiro, H. A. 1981. "Courtship scenes in Attic vase-painting." *American Journal of Archaeology* 85:133–43.

Sharma, Satish K. 1984. "Eunuchs: past and present." *The Eastern Anthropologist* 37:381–89.

Shen, Fu. 1960 [ca. 1800]. *Chapters from a Floating Life*. NY: Oxford University Press.

Shephard, Robert. 1996. "Sexual rumours in English politics: The cases of Elizabeth I and James I." In *Desire and Discipline: Sex and Sexuality in the Premodern West*, ed. J. Murray and K. Eisenbichler, 101–22. Toronto: University of Toronto Press.

Shepherd, Gill. 1978a. "Transsexualism in Oman?" *Man* 13: 133–34.

––––––. 1978b. "Oman *xanith*." *Man* 13:663–65.

––––––. 1987. "Rank, gender and homosexuality: Mombasa as a key to understanding sexual options." In *The Cultural Construction of Sexuality*, ed. P. Caplan, 240–70. London: Tavistock.

Shively, Donald H. 1968. "Bakufu vs. kabuki." In *Studies in the Institutional History of Early Modern Japan*, ed. J. Hall and M. Jansen, 231–61. Princeton: Princeton University Press.

––––––. 1970. "Tokugawa Tsunayoshi." In *Personality in Japanese History*, ed. A. Craig and D. Shively, 85–126. Berkeley: University of California Press.

––––––. 1978. "The social environment of Tokugawa kabuki." In Studies in Kabuki, ed. J. Brandon et al., 1–61. Honolulu, University of Hawaii Press.

Shore, Bradd. 1981. "Sexuality and gender in Samoa." In *Sexual Meaning*, ed S. Ortner and H. Whitehead, 192–215. Cambridge: Cambridge University Press.

Showerman, Grant. 1900. "Was Attis at Rome under the Republic?" *Transactions and Proceedings of the American Philological Association* 31:46–59.

Shweder, Richard A. 1991. *Thinking Through Culture*. Cambridge, MA: Harvard University Press.

Sibuyi, Mpande wa. 1993. "*Tinoncana etimayinini:* The wives of the mine." In *The Invisible Ghetto: Lesbian and Gay Writing from South Africa*, ed. M. Krouse, 52–64. Johannesburg: Cosaw.

Signorile, Michelangelo. 1992. "Out at the *New York Times*." *The Advocate* 603 (18 May):38–42.

Silva, Aguinaldo. 1979. "Greek love." In Leyland (1979:190–218).

Simon, William. 1994. "Deviance as history: The future of perversion." *ASB* 23:1–20.

Simon, William, and John Gagnon. 1986. "Sexual scripts." *ASB* 15:97–120.

Simpson, George Eaton. 1978. *Black Religions in the New World*. NY: Columbia University Press.

Singer, Kurt. 1973. *Mirror, Sword and Jewel: A Study of Japanese Characteristics*. NY: Braziler.

Sinha, A. P. 1967. "Procreation among the eunuchs." *Eastern Anthropologist* 20:168–76.

Sittirai, Wiresit, Tim Brown, and Sirapone Virulrak. 1991. "Patterns of bisexuality in Thailand." In *Bisexuality and HIV/AIDS,* ed. R. Tielman, M. Carballo, and A. Hendriks, 97–117. Buffalo: Prometheus.

Smedley, Agnes. 1943. *Battle Hymn of China.* NY: Alfred Knopf.

Smith, Arthur Henderson. 1899. *Village Life in China: A Study in Sociology.* NY: F. H. Revell.

Smith, Bruce R. 1991. *Homosexual Desire in Shakespeare's England: A Cultural Poetics.* Chicago: University of Chicago Press.

———. 1992. "Making a difference: male/male 'desire' in tragedy, comedy, and tragi-comedy." In *Erotic Politics: Desire on the Renaissance Stage,* ed. S. Zimmerman, 127–49. NY: Routledge.

———. 1995. "Rape, rap, rupture, rapture: R-rated futures on the global market. *Textual Practice* 9:421–44.

Smith, M. G. 1962. *Kinship and Community in Carriacou.* New Haven, CT.: Yale University Press.

Smith, Robert J. 1983. *Japanese Society.* NY: Cambridge University Press.

Snow, David A., Louis A. Zurcher Jr., and Sheldon Ekland-Olson. 1980. "Social networks and social movements: A microstructural approach to differential recruitment." *ASR* 45:787–801.

Snow, Edward. 1985. "Language and sexual difference in Romeo and Juliet." In Erickson and Kahn (1985:168–92).

Sofer, Jehoeda. 1992a. "Sodomy in the law of Muslim states." In Sofer and Schmitt (1992:131–49).

———. 1992b. "The dawn of a gay movement in Turkey." In Sofer and Schmitt(1992:77–81).

———. 1992c. "Testimonies from the Holy Land: Israeli and Palestinian men talk about their sexual encounters." In Sofer and Schmitt(1992:105–19).

Sofer, Jehoeda, and Arno Schmitt. 1992. *Sexuality and Eroticism Among Males in Moslem Societies.* Binghamton, NY: Harrington Park.

Somé, Malidoma Patrice. 1993. "Gays as spiritual gate keepers." *White Crane Newsletter* 4, 9:1, 6, 8.

———. 1994. *Of Water and the Spirit: Ritual, Magic, and Initiation in the Life of an African Shaman.* NY: Putnam.

Sorenson, Arthur P. 1984. "Linguistic exogamy and personal choice in the Northwest Amazon." *Illinois Studies in Anthropology* 14:180–93.

Spanneut, Michel. 1957. *Les stoicisme des pères de l'église.* Paris: Éditions du Seuil.

Spencer, Baldwin, and F. J. Gillen. 1927. *The Arunta.* London: Macmillan.

Spiro, Melford E. 1967. *Burmese Supernaturalism.* Toronto: Prentice-Hall.

———. 1993. "Is the Western conception of the self 'peculiar' within the context of world cultures?" *Ethos* 21:107–53.

Spix, Johann Baptist von, and Karl F. P. von Martius. 1824. *Travels in Brazil . . . 1817–1820.* London: H. E. Lloyd.

Stallybrass, Peter. 1992. "Transvestism and the 'body beneath': Speculating on the boy actor." In *Erotic Politics: Desire on the Renaissance Stage,* ed. S. Zimmerman, 64–83. NY: Routledge.

Stamford, John D. 1982. *Spartacus International Gay Guide.* Amsterdam: Spartacus.

Statler, Oliver. 1961. *The Japanese Inn.* NY: Random House.

Stein, Arlene. 1997. *Sex and Sensibilities: Stories of a Lesbian Generation.* Berkeley: University of California Press.

Stephens, Henry Morse. 1906. *Sodoma.* Boston: Bates and Guild.

S[h]ternberg, Leo. 1925. "Divine election in primitive religion." *Compte rendu de la XXIᵉ session, Congrès international des Américanistes,* 2, 472–512.

Stevens, John. 1990. *Lust for Enlightenment: Buddhism and Sex.* Boston: Shambhala.

Stevenson, Walter. 1995. "The rise of eunuchs in Greco-Roman antiquity." *Journal of the History of Sexuality* 5:495–511.

Steward, Julian H. 1946. "South American cultures." *Handbook of South American Indians* 5:669–723.

Stokes, Henry S. 1974. *The Life and Death of Yukio Mishima.* NY: Farrar, Straus Giroux.

Stone, Charles. 1981. "The semantics of gay." *The Advocate* 325 (3 Sept.):20–22.

Storey, John. 1992. "Taking on Tokyo: A Japanese publisher makes a mint and a movement." *Advocate* 614 (20 Oct.):53.

Strehlow, Carl. 1913. *Das sociale Leben der Aranda-und Loritja-Stämme.* Frankfurt: Baer.

Strobel, Margaret. 1979. *Muslim Women in Mombasa, 1890–1975.* New Haven: Yale University Press.

Stubbes, Philip. 1583. *Anatomie of Abuses.* London: R. Iones. Reprinted, New York, Johnson Reprint, 1972.

Suggs, Robert C. 1966. *Marquesan Sexual Behavior.* NY: Harcourt, Brace, & World.

———. 1971. "Sex and personality in the Marquesas." In *Human Sexual Behavior,* ed. D. Marshall and R. Suggs, 163–76. NY: Basic Books.

Sullivan, J. P. 1979. "Martial's sexual attitudes." *Philology* 123: 288–302.

Summerhawk, Barbara, Cheiron McMahill, and Darren McDonald. 1998. *Queer Japan: Personal Stories of Japanese Lesbians, Gays, Bisexuals and Transsexuals.* Norwich, VT: New Victoria.

Surieu, Robert. 1967. *Sarve Naz: An Essay on Love and the Representation of Erotic Themes in Ancient Iran.* Geneva: Nagel.

Sutlive, Vinson H. Jr. 1992 [1976]. "The Iban manang." In Murray (1992a:273–84).

Suttles, Gerald. 1972. *The Social Construction of Communities.* Chicago: University of Chicago Press.

Suvarnananda, Anjana [Tang]. 1995. "Lesbians in Thailand: Implications for a political movement." Paper presented at the Emerging Lesbian and Gay Communities conference at the University of Sydney, 29 Sept.

Svendrup, Harald U. 1937. *Hos tundra folket.* Oslo: Gyldendal Norvsk Forlag.

Sweet, Michael J., and Arnold Zwilling. 1993. "The first medicalization: The taxonomy and etiology of queerness in classical Indian medicine." *Journal of the History of Sexuality* 3:590–607.

Tafoya, Terry. 1992. "The two-spirited." In *Positively Gay,* ed. B. Berzon, 253–59. Berkeley, CA: Celestial Arts.

Takahashi Mutsuo. 1975. *Poems of a Penisist.* Chicago: Chicago Review Press.

Takahashi Ryuzo. 1935. "The system of official Zen monasteries in the Rinzei Zen school." *Kokushigaku* 23:9–43 (in Japanese).

Talbert, Richard J. A. 1988. *Plutarch on Sparta.* London: Penguin.

Tan, Michael L. 1995a. "From *bakla* to gay: Shifting gender identities and sexual behaviors in the Philippines." In *Conceiving Sexuality,* ed. R. Parker and J. Gagnon, 85–96. NY: Routledge.

———. 1995b. "Tita Aida and emerging communities of gay men: Two case studies from Metro Manila, the Philippines." *Journal of Gay and Lesbian Social Services* 3, 3:31–48.

———. 1995c. "Survival through pluralism: The gay and lesbian movement in the Philippines." Paper presented at the Emerging Lesbian and Gay Communities conference at the University of Sydney, 29 Sept.

Tapnic, Huseyin. 1992. "Masculinity, feminity, and Turkish male homosexuality." In *Modern Homosexualities,* ed. K. Plummer, 39–49. London: Routledge.

Tarán, Sonya Lida. 1985. "Eisi triches: An erotic motif in the *Greek Anthology.*" *Journal of Hellenic Studies* 105:90–107.

Tauxier, Louis. 1912. *Les Noirs du Soudan: Pays Mossi et Gouronni.* Paris: Émile LaRose.

Taylor, Clark L. 1978. "El Ambiente: Homosexual Social Life in Mexico City." Ph.D. diss., University of California, Berkeley.

———. 1995. "Legends, syncretisms and continuing echoes of homosexuality from pre-Columbian and colonial México." In Murray (1995a:80–99).

Taylor, William B. 1987. "The Virgin of Guadalupe in New Spain: An inquiry into the social history of Marian devotion." *AE* 14:9–33.

Tazelaar, C. M. 1967. "Some notes on the Spartan stages of youth." *Mnemosyne,* 4th ser., 20:127–53.

Te Awekotuku, Ngahuia. 1991. "Dykes and queers: facts, fairytales and fictions. In *Mana Wahine Maori: Selected Writings on Maori Women's Art, Culture and Politics,* 36–41. Auckland: New Women's Press.

Temple, R. C. 1907–1936. *The Travels of Peter Mundy, 1608–1667.* 5 vols. Cambridge: Hakluyt Society.

Tessman, Gunther. 1904. *Die Pangwe.* Berlin: E. Wasmuth.

Thadani, Giti. 1996. *Sakhivani: Lesbian Desire in Ancient and Modern India.* London: Cassell.

Thesiger, Wilfred. 1964. *The Marsh Arabs.* London: Longmans.

Thomas, Keith. 1994. "As you like it." *New York Review of Books,* 22 Sept.:9–12.

Thompson, Mark. 1987. *Gay Spirit.* NY: St. Martin's.

Thomsen, Ole. 1992. *Ritual and Desire: Catullus 61 and 62.* Aarhus, Denmark: Aarhus University Press.

Thongthiraj, Took Took. 1994. "Toward a struggle against invisibility: Love between women in Thailand." *Amerasia* 20:45–58.

Thornton, Russell, and Peter M. Nardi. 1975. "Dynamics of role acquisition." *AJS* 80:870–84.

Tierno Galván, Enrique. 1961. "Los toros, acontecimiento nacional." In *Desde el Espectáculo a la Trivilización,* 53–77. Madrid: Taurus.

Tindall, Ralph H. 1978. "The male adolescent involved with a pederast becomes an adult." *JH* 3:373–82.

Titiev, Mischa. 1951. *Araucanian Culture in Transition.* Ann Arbor: University of Michigan Press.

Tonomura, Hitomi. 1994. "Black hair and red trousers: Gendering the flesh in medieval Japan." *American Historical Review* 99:129–54.

Topley, Marjorie. 1975. "Marriage resistance in rural Kwangtung." In *Women in Chinese Society,* ed. M. Wolf, 67–88. Stanford, CA: Stanford University Press.

Tracy, Valeria A. 1976. "Roman dandies and transvestites." *Echos du Monde Classique* 20:60–63.

Traub, Valerie. 1992. "The (in)significance of 'lesbian' desire in early modern England." In *Erotic Politics: Desire on the Renaissance Stage,* ed. S. Zimmerman, 150–69. NY: Routledge.

Trix, Frances. 1993. *Spiritual Discourse: Learning with an Islamic Master* [the Nektashi murshid Baba Rexheb]. Philadelphia: University of Pennsylvania Press.

Trumbach, Randolph. 1977. "London's sodomites." *Journal of Social History* 11: 1–33.

———. 1978. *The Rise of the Egalitarian Family: Aristocratic Kinship and Domestic Relations in Eighteenth-Century England.* NY: Academic.

———. 1985. "Sodomitical subcultures, sodomitical roles, and the gender revolution of the eighteenth century." *Eighteenth Century Life* 9:109–21.

———. 1988a. "Sodomitical assaults, gender role, and sexual development in eighteenth-century London." *JH* 16:407–29).

———. 1988b. Review of Ruggiero (1985). *JH* 16:506–10.

Tucker, Scott. 1982. "The power of naming." *Christopher Street* 58:50–63.

Turnbull, John. 1813. *A Voyage Round the World.* London: Maxwell.

Turner, C. F., L. Ku, S. Rogers, L. Lindberg, J. Pleck, and F. Sonenstein. 1998. "Adolescent sexual behavior, drug use, and violence." *Science* 280:867–73.

Turner, Ralph H. 1978. "The role and the person." *AJS* 84:1–23.

Tytheridge, A. C. 1922. "Beobachtungen über Homosexualität in Japan." *Jahrbuch für sexuelle Zwischenstufen* 22:23–36.

Urbanowicz, Charles F. 1977. "Tourism in troubled times." In *Hosts and Guests: The Anthropology of Tourism,* ed. V. Smith, 83–92. Philadelphia: University of Pennsylvania Press.

Vacha, Keith. 1985. *Quiet Fire: Memoirs of Older Gay Men.* Trumansburg, NY: Crossing.

Valaam Monastery. 1978 [1894]. *The Russian Orthodox Religious Mission in America, 1794–1837.* Fairbanks: Limestone.

Van Baal, J. 1966. *Dema.* The Hague: Nijoff.

———. 1984. "The dialectics of sex in Marind-Anim culture." In *Ritualized Homosexuality in Melanesia,* ed. G. Herdt, 128–66. Berkeley: University of California Press.

Vance, Brenda, and Vicki Green. 1984 "Lesbian identities." *Psychology of Women Quarterly* 8:293–307.

Van der Kroef, Justus M. 1954. "Transvestism and the religious hermaphrodite in Indonesia." *University of Manila Journal of East Asiatic Studies* 3:257–65.

Van Gulik, Robert H. 1961. *Sexual Life in Ancient China.* Leiden: E. J. Brill.

van Onselen, Charles. 1976. *Chibaro: African Mine Labor in Southern Rhodesia, 1900–1933.* London: Pluto.

———. 1982. *Studies in the Social and Economic History of the Witwatersrand, 1886–1914*. Vol. 2. *New Nineveh*. Johannesburg: Ravan.

———. 1984. *The Small Matter of a Horse: The Life of "Nongoloza" Mathebula, 1867–1948*. Johannesburg: Ravan.

Varley, H. Paul. 1970. *The Samurai*. London: Weidenfield & Nicolson.

———. 1973. *Japanese Culture*. New York: Praeger.

Vázquez Valls, Eduardo, et al. 1988. "Prevalence of antibody to HIV in a group of homosexual men in Guadalajara." Presented at the International Conference on AIDS in Stockholm.

Vermaseren, Maarten J. 1977. *Cybele and Attis: The Myth and the Cult*. London: Thames and Hudson.

Verstraete, Beert. 1975. "Ovid on homosexuality." *Classical News and Views* 19:79–83.

———. 1980. "Slavery and the social dynamics of male homosexual relations in ancient Rome." *JH* 5:227–36.

Veyne, Paul. 1985 [1978]. "Homosexuality in ancient Rome." In *Western Sexuality*, ed. Philippe Ariès and André Béjin, 26–35. Oxford: Basil Blackwell.

Vincentdon-Dumoulin, Jean, and C. Desgraz. 1843. *Iles Marquises ou Nouka-Hiva*. Paris: A. Bertrand.

Vitiello, Giovanni. 1992. "The dragon's whim: Ming and Qing homoerotic tales from *The Cut Sleeve*." *T'oung Pao* 78:341–72.

———. 1994. "Exemplary Sodomites: Male Homosexuality in Late Ming Fiction." Ph.D. diss., University of California, Berkeley.

Volney, Constantin-Francois. 1787. *Travels through Syria and Egypt, in the years 1783, 1784, and 1785*. London: G. G. J. and J. Robinson.

Vryonis, Speros Jr. 1956. "Isidore Glabas and the Turkish *devshirme*." *Speculum* 31:433–43.

———. 1964. Review of Papoulia (1963). *Balkan Studies* 5:145–53.

———. 1971. *The Decline of Medieval Hellenism in Asia Minor and the Process of Islamization from the Eleventh through the Fifteenth Centuries*. Berkeley: University of California Press.

Vyas, M. D., and Yogesh Shingala. 1987. *The Life of the Eunuchs*. New Delhi: Anmol.

Wafer, Jim. 1991. *The Taste of Blood: Spirit Possession in Brazilian Candomblé*. Philadelphia: University of Pennsylvania Press.

———. 1996. "Out of the closet and into print: Sexual identity in the textual field." In *Out in the Field*, ed. E. Lewin and W. Leap, 261–73. Urbana: University of Illinois Press.

———. 1997. "Vision and passion: The symbolism of male love in Islamic mystical literature." In Murray and Roscoe (1997:107–31).

Wagley, Charles. 1977. *Welcome of Tears*. NY: Oxford University Press.

Wakeman, Frederic Jr., 1985. *The Great Enterprise: The Manchu Reconstruction of Imperial Order in Seventeenth-Century China*. 2 vols. Berkeley: University of California Press.

Waley, Arthur. 1970. *Yuan Mei*. Stanford, CA: Stanford University Press.

Walker, Benjamin. 1968. *The Hindu World*. London: Allen & Unwin.

Walker, Pamela. 1986. "More mysticism than lust: Were there Renaissance lesbians?" *Rites* 2 (April):10.

Wallace, Anthony F. C. 1952a. "Individual differences and cultural uniformities." *ASR* 17:747–50.

———. 1952b. *The Modal Personality Structure of the Tuscarora Indians. Bureau of American Ethnology Bulletin* 150.

Walters, Delores M. 1991. "Cast among the outcastes: Interpreting sexual orientation, racial, and gender identity in Yemen." *Society of Lesbian and Gay Anthropologists Newsletter* 13:43–45.

Ward, Edward. 1709 [1703]. *Secret History of London Clubs.* London: NPL.

Ward, Martha C. 1989. *Nest in the Wind: Adventures in Anthropology on a Tropical Island.* Prospect Heights, IL: Waveland.

Warren, Carol A. B. 1974. *Identity and Community in the Gay World.* NY: Wiley.

Watanabe Tsuneo. 1980. "Man, modernity and the homosexual taboo." *Research Reports of Kochi University* 29:121–47 (in Japanese).

———. 1989. *The Love of the Samurai.* London: Gay Men's Press.

Watts, Raleigh. 1987. "Gender Variance among Male Polynesians." M. A. thesis, University of Washington.

———. 1992. "The Polynesian *mahu.*" In Murray (1992a:171–84).

Weinberg, Thomas S. 1978. "On 'doing' and 'being' gay." *JH* 4:143–56.

Weiser, Jay. 1986. "Gay identity." In *Gay Life,* ed. E. Rofes, 283–93. Garden City, NY: Doubleday.

Weiss, Jerome. 1977. "Folk Psychology of the Javanese of Ponorgo." Ph.D. diss., Yale University.

Wendel, Charles. 1974. "The denizens of Paradise." *Humaniora Islamica* 2:29–59.

Werner, Dennis. 1979. "A cross-cultural perspective on theory and research on male homosexuality." *JH* 4:345–62.

Wescott, Glenway. 1990. *Continual Lessons: The Journals of Glenway Wescott.* NY: Farrar Straus Giroux.

West, Donald J., and Buz Villiers. 1993. *Male Prostitution.* Binghamton, NY: Harrington Park.

Westermarck, Edward. 1906. *The Origin and Development of Moral Ideas.* London: Macmillan.

Weston, Kath. 1991. *Families We Choose: Gays, Lesbians, and Kinship.* NY: Columbia University Press.

———. 1997. *Render Me, Gender Me.* NY: Columbia University Press.

Westphall-Hellbusch, Sigrid. 1997 [1956]. "Institutionalized gender-crossing in southern Iraq." In Murray and Roscoe (1998:233–43).

Wheeler, Richard P. 1985. "'. . . And my loud crying still': *The Sonnets, The Merchant of Venice,* and *Othello.*" In Erickson and Kahn (1985:193–209).

Whigham, Peter. 1969. *The Poems of Catullus.* Berkeley: University of California Press.

Whisman, Vera. 1996. *Queer by Choice: Lesbians, Gay Men, and the Politics of Identity.* NY: Routledge.

Whitaker, Ian. 1981. "'A sack for carrying things': The traditional role of women in northern Albanian society." *Anthropological Quarterly* 54:146–56.

Whitam, Frederick L. 1992. "Bayot and callboy: Heterosexual:homosexual relations in the Philippines." In Murray (1992a:231–48).

White, Geoffrey M., and John Kirkpatrick, eds. 1985. *Person, Self, and Experience: Exploring Pacific Ethnopsychologies.* Berkeley: University of California Press.

Whittier, David Knapp. Forthcoming. *Outside the Gay Ghetto: The Social Organization of Male Homosexualities in a Southern Town.* University of Wisconsin Press.

Widengren, Gro. 1969. *Der Feudalismus in alten Iran: Männerbund, Gefolgswesen, Feudalismis in der iranischen Gesselschaft im Hinblick aufdie ineogermanischen Verhältnisse.* Koln: Westdeutscher Verlag.

Wieringa, Saskia. 1987. *Ue Toegenegen Dora D., Riesbrieven.* Amsterdam: Furie.

———. 1996. "Desiring bodies or defiant cultures: Butch-femme lesbians in Jakarta and Lima." Paper presented at the AAA annual meetings in San Francisco.

Wiet, Gaston. 1964. *Cairo: City of Art and Commerce.* Norman: University of Oklahoma Press.

———. 1966. *The Mosques of Cairo.* Paris: Hachette.

Wijeyewardene, Gehan. 1986. *Place and Emotion in Northern Thai Ritual Behaviour.* Bangkok: Pandora.

Wikan, Unni. 1977. "Man becomes woman: Transsexualism in Oman as a key to gender roles." *Man* 12:304–19.

———. 1978a. "The Omani *xanith:* A third gender role?" *Man* 13:473–75.

———. 1978b. "The Omani *xanith.*" *Man* 13:667–71.

———. 1982. *Behind the Veil in Arabia: Women in Oman.* Baltimore: Johns Hopkins University Press.

———. 1984. "Shame and honour: A contestable pair." *Man* 19:635–52.

Wikander, Stig. 1938. *Der arische Männerbund.* Lund: H. Olson.

Wilbur, Clarence Martin. 1943. *Slavery in China during the Former Han Dynasty, 206 B.C.–A.D. 25.* Chicago: Field Museum of Natural History (Anthropological series vol. 34).

Wilken, G. A. 1893. *Handleiding voor de Vergelij Kende Volkenukunde van Nederlandsch-Indies.* Leiden: Brill. Translated as *Manual for the Comparative Ethnology of the Netherlands East Indies,* New Haven, CT: HRAF, 1961.

Wilkie, J. W., B. E. Lorey, and E. Ochoa. 1988. *Statistical Abstract of Latin America.* Vol. 26. Los Angeles: UCLA Latin America Center.

———. 1992. *Statistical Abstract of Latin America.* Vol. 27. Los Angeles: UCLA Latin America Center.

Wilkinson, John C. 1987. *The Imamate Tradition in Oman.* NY: Cambridge University Press.

Wilkinson, L. P. 1978. "From the point of view of antiquity, 4: Homosexuality." *Encounter* 51:20–31.

Willetts, R. F. 1962. *Cretan Cults and Festivals.* London: Routledge.

Williams, Craig A. 1994. "The concept of *stuprum* and the social regulation of sexuality in ancient Rome." Paper presented at the American Historical Association meetings in San Francisco.

———. 1995. "Greek love at Rome." *Classical Quarterly* 45:517–39.

Williams, Walter L. 1985. "Sex and shamanism: The making of a Hawaiian *mahu.*" *The Advocate* 417(2 Apr.): 48–49.

———. 1990. "Homosexuality as a means of promoting village unity in Ponorogo, East Java." Paper presented at the AAA annual meetings in New Orleans.

Wilson, James. 1799. *A Missionary Voyage to the Southern Pacific Ocean.* London: Chapman.

Wilson, Monica. 1963 [1951]. *Good Company: A Study of the Nyakyusa Age Villages.* Boston: Beacon Press.

Wilson, William Scott. 1979. *Hagakure: The Book of the Samurai.* Tokyo: Kodansha.

Winkler, John J. 1990. *The Constraints of Desire. The Anthropology of Sex and Gender in Ancient Greece.* NY: Routledge.

Winter, J. W. 1902. "Beknopte bescrijving van get Hof van Soerakarta in 1824." *Bijdragen tot de Taal-, Land- en Volkenkunde* 54:15–172.

Winzeler, Robert L. 1993. *The Seen and the Unseen: Shamanism, Mediumship and Possession in Borneo.* Williamsburg, VA: Borneo Research Council.

Wiseman, Timothy Peter. 1985. *Catullus and His World.* NY: Cambridge University Press.

Wittkower, Rudolf, and Margaret Wittkower. 1963. *Born Under Saturn: The Character and Conduct of Artists.* London: Weidenfeld and Nicolson.

Wolf, Deborah Goleman. 1983. *Growing Older Gay and Lesbian.* MS.

Wolf, Eric. 1990. "Facing Power." *AA* 92:585–96.

Wood, William Alfred Rae. 1935. *Land of Smiles.* Bangkok: Krungdebarnagar.

Wooden, Wayne S. 1982. "Cultural antecedents and the development of a gay community: The case of Venezuela." Paper presented at the American Sociological Association meetings, San Francisco.

Woods, Gregory. 1992. "Body, costume, and desire in Christopher Marlowe." *JH* 23, 1:69–84.

Wuthnow, Robert. 1985. "State structures and ideology." *American Sociological Review* 50: 799–821.

Wright, Arthur F. 1959. *Buddhism in Chinese History.* Stanford, CA: Stanford University Press.

X, Dr. Jacobus. 1893. *L'amour aux colonies: Singularités physiologiques et passionnelles, observées durant trente années de séjour dans les colonies françaises.* Paris: Liseux.

Xiao Mingxiong. 1984, 1997. *History of Homosexuality in China.* Hong Kong: Samshasha (in Chinese).

Yamamoto Jōchō. 1979 [1716]. *Hagakure: The Book of the Samurai.* Tokyo: Kodansha.

Yengoyan, Aram. 1983. "Transvestitism and the ideology of gender: Southeast Asia and beyond." In *Feminist Re-Visions,* ed. V. Patraka and L. Tilly, 135–48. Ann Arbor: University of Michigan Women's Studies Program.

Young, Allen. 1973. "Gay gringo in Brazil." In *The Gay Liberation Book,* ed. Len Richmond and Gary Noguera, 60–67. San Francisco: Ramparts.

Yourcenar, Marguerite. 1980. *Mishima.* NY: Farrar Straus Giroux.

Zaehner, R. C. 1961. *The Dawn and Twilight of Zoroastrianism.* London: Weidenfeld and Nicolson.

Zapata, Luis. 1979. *Los aventuras, descenturas y sueños de Adonis García.* México: Grijalbo. Trans. as *Adonis García.* San Francisco: Gay Sunshine, 1981.

———. 1983. "My deep dark pain is love." In Leyland (1983:89–97).

Zeeland, Steven. 1996. *The Masculine Marine.* NY: Haworth.

Zolbrod, Leon. 1977. *Tales of Moonlight and Rain.* Tokyo: Tuttle.

Zwilling, Arnold. 1992. "Homosexuality as seen in Indian Buddhist texts." In

Buddhism, Sexuality, and Gender, ed. J. Cabezón, 203–14. Albany: State University of New York Press.

Zwilling, Arnold, and Michael J. Sweet. 1996. "'Like a city ablaze': The third sex and the creation of sexuality in Jain religious literature." *Journal of the History of Sexuality* 6:359–84.

Index

497

Wallace, Anthony, 7
waria, 413–16
Warren Cup, 378
warrior society, 23, 34, 38, 77–78, 91,
    161–63, 244
wasagaji, 249–50
Watts, Raleigh, 29n, 370
Weber, Max, 17–18, 424
Whitam, Frederick, 267n
Wikan, Unni, 138, 139, 275–80, 310n
will not to know, 235, 269, 271, 274–75,
    278, 312, 399–400, 409–19
Winkler, John, 10, 104, 106, 214, 229–
    32, 234, 235–36, 255, 256, 257
"women's work," done by natal males,
    93–95, 109n, 111, 162, 163, 165–68,
    184, 213, 214, 218, 261, 280–81,
    284, 287, 316–17, 323, 329–31, 334,
    349, 351, 355, 386
women warriors, 206n, 224, 230, 250–
    53, 350n, 376. *See also* Amazons

Xenophon, 37–38, 40, 41n, 101, 303
xiaochang, 185n, 186

'Yan Daudus, 337–42
Yanomamos, 372
yenicheri, 53, 57, 58, 59
Yichungxingzhi, 240
yin/yang, 181, 183, 187n, 239, 240
Yorubas, 345n
Yoshimitsu, 171–72

zamel, 136, 195–96
Zande, 91, 161–63
Zapoteks, 350
Zeami, 171–72
zenanas, 311
zeroeth gender, 301, 304, 309, 310n, 333
Zoroaster, 131–32
Zulus, 163–64, 165, 211, 434n
Zunis, 350